EU Environmental Law

EU Environmental Law

Professor Dr Ludwig Krämer

Former Judge at Landgericht in Kiel, LL.D.
Former Head of the Unit for Governance in DG Environment of the European
Commission

SWEET & MAXWELL

 THOMSON REUTERS

First Edition	1992
Eighth Edition (hb)	2015
Eighth Edition (pb)	2016

Published in 2016 by Thomson Reuters (Professional) UK Limited trading as Sweet & Maxwell, Friars House, 160 Blackfriars Road, London, SE1 8EZ (Registered in England & Wales, Company No 1679046.
Registered Office and address for service: 2nd floor, 1 Mark Square, Leonard Street, London EC2A 4EG)

For further information on our products and services, visit *www.sweetandmaxwell.co.uk*

EU material in this publication is acknowledged as © European Union, 1998–2015. Only EU legislation published in the electronic version of the Official Journal of the European Union is deemed authentic.

Typeset by Letterpart Limited, Caterham on the Hill, Surrey, CR3 5XL.

Printed and bound in Great Britain by CPI Group (UK) Ltd, Croydon, CR0 4YY.

No natural forests were destroyed to make this product; only farmed timber was used and re-planted.

A CIP catalogue record of this book is available for the British Library.

ISBN: 978-041-4056046

Preface to the Eighth Edition

This eighth edition updates the description of the evolution of EU environmental law until May 2015. The evolution over the last four years was marked by the neo-liberal approach which the Barroso-Commission and even more so the Juncker-Commission took with regard to the EU: what is good for business is good for Europe and for its environment. Such an approach sacrifices one of the sectors of EU policy which is most popular among the citizens of the EU, to economic considerations. There is little concern that the Lisbon Treaties have another concept of the environment in the overall establishment and functioning of the EU, as it is laid down in Articles 3 and 21 TEU, and 11 and 191 TFEU, as it is reflected in citizens rights and transparency of EU activities, in openness, democracy and participation. The EU did not come closer to the Lisbon Treaties' concept of a European Union, but rather went further away from it, promoting secrecy, technocratic approaches and – under the cover of "better regulation" – deregulation. Why then should a citizen, who cares for the environment, participate in European elections? The continuously decreasing number of citizens who vote in such elections and the increasing number of anti-EU movements in numerous Member States witness this evolution.

The commonplace that the environment has no voice and cannot protest against its slow, but progressive degradation remains true, but finds almost no attention at EU level. A good illustration of this are the discussions on free trade agreements with Canada and the United States. As the responsible member of the EU Commission stated, they aim at creating a transatlantic internal market. However, this is intended to be an internal market without the environment: within the EU, the free circulation of goods and services must not prevail over environmental concerns, as proven by Articles 36, 114 (4) and (5), 193 TFEU, the Cassis-de-Dijon doctrine of the Court of Justice, furthermore the requirement to aim at a high level of environmental protection and to integrate environmental requirements into the establishment and implementation of trade as well as other EU policies. Apparently, nothing of these balancing factors is foreseen in the trade agreements which pursue the negative integration of markets, but not (also) at the protection of environmental, consumer and social standards. And the EU negotiator, the European Commission knows best what is the general Union interest: it avoids public discussions, keeps negotiations confidential and has no interest in a democratic, public discussion, such as on REACH and US standards for chemicals, on GMO approaches, standards in fracking, or precautionary approaches in legislation.

It is worthwhile remembering, what the Heads of States and Governments had to say in this regard:

PREFACE TO THE EIGHTH EDITION

"Economic expansion is not an end in itself. Its first aim should be to enable disparities or living conditions to be reduced. It must take place with the participation of all the social partners. It should result in an improvement in the quality of life as well as in standards of living. As befits the genius of Europe, particular attention will be given to intangible values and to protecting the environment, so that progress may really be put at the service of mankind".

This statement dates from the very first European Summit which took place from 19 to 21 October 1972 in Paris. However, some inconvenient truths remain true even after a long time, and neo-liberal thinking must not ignore that there are things in the life of a society which money can't buy.

At times, one has the impression that EU environmental policy is reduced to the promotion of a low carbon economy, though all problems which were mentioned in the Preface of 2011 – climate change, loss of biodiversity, omnipresence of chemicals, resource management, fight against poverty and the full application of existing environmental standards – continue to exist.

More than ever, we need a public discussion on the kind of society and of the kind of environment, we want to live in. Next to the environmental challenges mentioned, new issues such as demography, migration, or assistance to the third world—in one way or the other all linked to the planet's environment—cannot find a response from individual countries, but require common EU answers. It is sad that the EU is not engaging in an open, transparent discussion on Europe's common future, and it is hoped that the present book contributes to facilitate such a discussion on the protection of the European environment, by law and by citizens.

Ludwig Krämer
July 2015

Preface to the Seventh Edition

This book on European Union environmental law is the result of almost 40 years of occupation with this topic. Indeed, in the early 1970s, as a young judge at the Landgericht Kiel (Germany), I was delegated to the European Commission in Bruxelles and worked, since its very beginnings, in the newly established environment protection service which became later the Directorate General for the environment. Thus, I had the privilege to live the evolution of European environmental law from the first hour, and as my delegation to the Commission continued until 2004, I was able to participate in the elaboration and the monitoring of this law for decades. As I had started, for personal reasons, also an academic career, I lectured on EU environmental law since 1985 in some twenty European universities and in six languages. After 2004, I continued lecturing, while acting at the same time as a private consultant. I tried to insert this experience as judge, European official, lecturer and private consultant into the different chapters of this book.

It is obvious that European environmental law has evolved, these last 40 years, in a spectacular manner. In numerous Member States of the Union, it is the first source of national environmental law which is almost at 100 per cent derived for EU environmental law. In the other Member States, it exercised a very strong influence on national environmental law and continues to do so: there is no section of the environment where EU law did not considerably influence the elaboration and application of national environmental law.

While thus the balance of these 40 years is largely positive, the perspectives for European environmental law do not incite optimism: EU environmental law slowly moves towards a cumulation of good intentions—a high level of protection, the polluter and not the taxpayer shall pay for pollution, a sustainable development the integration of environmental requirements into other policies, the utilisation of the best technique, etc.—which are later on forgotten or bypassed when concrete rules are elaborated and in particular, when rules are to be applied and enforced. In the conflict of environmental interests and economic interests, in 999 out of 1,000 cases, the environment loses. The main reason for this is that the environment has no voice, does not vote and has no important social group behind it—such as agricultural law the farmers, fisheries law the fishermen, competition law the competitors or transport law the transporters (or the transported). To this has to be added that in all Member States of the EU and also at European level, the protection of the environment has been laid into the hands of the administration: it is the administration which grants permits, plans and realises large and less large infrastructure projects, monitors, controls and examines pollution, the use of resources and which solves conflicts of interests.

However, the administration is neither the owner of the environment nor necessarily its best defendant. And in times of economic or financial crisis, the administrations are looking for solutions, even at the price of environmental protection.

Four problems appear to put at risk European environmental law: the first is the obvious lack of political will of the institutions, in particular of the Commission, to keep the promise, often given and lastly repeated in the Lisbon Treaties, to ensure a high level of environmental protection in Europe and therefore conceive, elaborate and apply effective provisions in order to ensure this protection. European environmental law is more and more reduced at general terms which are hardly applicable and the application of which is hardly controlled, neither by the European Commission nor by the European Parliament nor by the national, regional or local administrations in the Member States.

The second problem which goes hand in hand with the first one is the effective application of European environmental law. The Commission which practically has a monopoly in the monitoring of this application, limits itself more and more to oversee the legal transposition of the European provisions into national law, but does not really look at the effective application of these provisions in concrete, specific situations. The Commission argues that the Member States shall ensure the implementation of EU environmental law, though it knows quite well—it had publicly stated that itself in 2001—the European (environmental) law is treated at national level as a foreign law: you cannot always avoid having to deal with foreigners, but it is better to try to avoid them.

Nothing undermines the credibility of a State more that laws which are not applied. The Commission did not develop structures or mechanisms to improve the control of environmental law application, for example by transferring tasks to the European Environmental Agency, or granting to civil society representatives the right of standing in order to defend EU environmental law, or be it the setting up of a European inspection service. This passivity contributes so largely to the fact that EU environmental law is no longer altogether taken seriously. One may dare the comparison with the ten commandments: of high moral value, almost never openly disputed, used in Sunday speeches or in the introduction to solemn treaties, but of limited practical application.

This lack of practical application is clearly demonstrated by the fact that the state of the environment within the European Union diverges very considerably from one Member State to the other, even when the European provisions apply everywhere. This difference is explained by the more or less determined national policy to protect the environment. The EU institutions decreasing integrative capacity finds it reflection—and this is the third problem—at global level. Confronted with worldwide problems—climate change, the loss of biodiversity, the omnipresence of chemical substances, the use of natural resources and the fight against poverty—the European Union is not able to present itself as a union. It does not offer a model for the third world how to reconcile economic growth and protection of the environment. Whether it is a system of fair trade, fisheries agreements which care for the environment, a climate change agreement with the Cotonou countries of Africa, the Caraibes and the Pacific, provisions on corporate social and environmental responsibility of European undertakings, agreements with other regions in the world of the "Aarhus Convention type"—the foreign environmental policy of the European Union lacks concrete initiatives. The EU wants to play at the same level as the USA and China, and forgets that it has a specific vocation.

The last problem, again linked to the previous one, concerns the fight against poverty. The European Union is the only region in the world which had fixed itself the objectives of economic growth and sustainable development which ensures the protection of the environment. However, it has still not elaborated and put into practice a policy of sustainable development towards the third world, systematically supported by the development of policies in the areas of water, waste, soil protection, nature conservation, etc. The EU development policy continues to be marked by some mercantilistic spirit. And there are few signs that the EU would re-orient itself—despite the fact that scientists think that there might be some 200 to 250 million environmental refugees by 2050. An environmental policy towards and with the third world is thus more necessary than ever.

Environmental law is the attempt to protect the environment with the means of the law. "Between the strong and the weak, it is the law which makes free and it is freedom which oppresses". In modern society, it is the environment which is, without doubt, the weak part. Environmental law can play its part in the efforts for protection—if it were taken seriously by its authors and by its addressees. I hope that this book will contribute to a better knowledge of law and to a better protection of the environment, in Europe and elsewhere.

Legislation and jurisprudence were taken into consideration until end of March 2011; later texts were only partly considered.

Ludwig Krämer
July, 2011

TABLE OF CONTENTS

CONTENTS

CONTENTS

CONTENTS

CONTENTS

CONTENTS

CONTENTS

ALPHABETICAL TABLE OF CASES

ALPHABETICAL TABLE OF CASES

NUMERICAL TABLE OF CASES

TABLE OF DECISIONS

xliii

TABLE OF DIRECTIVES

xlix

1

TABLE OF REGULATIONS

TABLE OF REGULATIONS

TABLE OF INTERNATIONAL CONVENTIONS AND TREATIES

TABLE OF EUROPEAN CONVENTIONS AND TREATIES

CHAPTER 1

Objectives, Principles and Conditions

1. THE ENVIRONMENT IN EU LAW

The Lisbon Treaty on European Union (TEU) which entered into effect on 1 **1–01**
December 2009,[1] fixes in art.3(3) TEU as one of the objectives of the European
Union "a high level of protection and improvement of the quality of the
environment". In the same paragraph, sustainable development is fixed as one of
the aims of the Union, and both the protection of the environment and the
sustainable development are also mentioned in Recital 9 of the Treaty on
European Union. The objectives of art.3(3) TEU are completed by the specific
environmental objectives in art.191 of the Treaty on the Functioning of the Union
(TFEU) which are a high level of protection, a prudent use of natural resources, a
contribution to human health and the promotion of environmental protection at
international level.

Neither of these provisions, though, define "environment"; nor do the other
provisions of the Treaties contain any definition. It follows from arts 191(1) and
192(2) TFEU that the environment includes human beings, natural resources,
land use, town and country planning, waste and water. These categories include
practically all areas of the environment, in particular fauna and flora which are
part of the natural resources, and climate. The inclusion of issues concerning
town and country planning underlines that the environment is not limited to
natural elements, but also includes the man-made environment.

Article 177(2) TFEU provides for the setting up of a Cohesion Fund which
shall provide a financial contribution to transport infrastructure projects of the
trans-European networks and to the environment. Regulation 1300/2013 on the
Cohesion Fund argues that the promotion of sustainable transport and the
removal of bottlenecks in key network infrastructures constitute environmental
measures,[2] including "rail, river and sea transport, intermodal transport systems
and their interoperability, the management of road, sea and air traffic"[3] as well as
clean urban transport and public transport. Such an interpretation of the notion
"environment" is too large: indeed, the management of traffic and, for example,
the organisation on the transport of containers or of petrol by sea has not much to
do with the environment.

When the section "environment" was first included in the EC Treaty in 1987, **1–02**
there was already extensive secondary European legislation adopted on the basis

---

[1] [2008] OJ C115/1.
[2] Regulation 1300/2013 on the Cohesion Fund [2013] OJ L 347/281, art.4.
[3] Regulation 1300/2013, Recital 4.

of three environment action programmes and this was generally perceived as legislation on the environment. This secondary legislation covered water and air, noise and chemicals, nature conservation, waste and some measures of a general character. Furthermore, in June 1990, shortly before the commencement of the negotiations on the Maastricht Treaty on European Union, the Community Heads of State and Government adopted a "Declaration on the Environment",[4] where they proclaimed a right to a healthy and clean environment, which included, in particular:

> "... the quality of air, rivers, lakes, coastal and marine waters, the quality of food and drinking water, protection against noise, protection against contamination of soil, soil erosion and desertification, preservation of habitats, flora and fauna, landscape and other elements of the natural heritage, the amenity and quality of residential areas."

It must be assumed that by using the concept "environment" in this legal, political, economic and ecological context, the authors of the Treaties have given to the term the emphasis which it had at that time in EU law. The term "environment" is thus all-embracing and includes economic, social and aesthetic aspects, the preservation of natural and archaeological heritage, and the man-made as well as the natural environment.

"Environment" in art.3 TEU and 4, 191–193 TFEU is different from the "working environment" used in arts 114 and 153 TFEU, which obviously concerns the conditions at the workplace, such as air pollution, noise, risk of accidents, etc. The specific conditions of the workplace justify a different treatment of "environment" and "working environment", although in the early 1970s, EU environmental policy did not make this distinction[5] and some directives do not really differentiate between worker protection and environmental protection.[6] Working environment provisions come, therefore, under art.153 or, as the case may be, under art.114 TFEU.

1–03 Doubts were sometimes raised as to whether "environment" also includes animal welfare. However, wild animals are part of the natural environment, thus protection measures for wild animals—not only as a threatened species, but as living creatures—are environmental measures. The Amsterdam Treaty on European Union added a protocol to the EC Treaty, according to which the Union's policies on agriculture, transport, the internal market and research had to pay "full regard to the welfare of animals".[7] The TFEU took this up and inserted a new art.13 which declared that "since animals are sentient beings", full regard had to be paid to the welfare requirements of animals. It is obvious, though, that this provision refers to domestic, not wild, animals and therefore does not contradict the interpretation given here.

The uncertainty of how to classify (wild) animal welfare became obvious when the Commission made a proposal for a directive on the protection of zoo animals. In view of the subsidiarity debate, the Commission repealed this

---

[4] European Council Resolution of 15 June 1990 (1990) *Bulletin of the European Communities*, para.1.36.
[5] See 1st Environment Action Programme [1973] OJ C112/1, p.43.
[6] See Dir.2012/18 on the prevention of industrial accidents [2012] OJ L197/1.
[7] [1997] OJ C340/110.

proposal and replaced it with a proposal for a recommendation. However, the Council rearranged the text so as to be a text that was mainly concerned with protecting animals as endangered species and adopted, on that basis, a directive in 1999.[8]

Geographically, the environment mentioned in the Treaty is not limited to the European Union's environment, as is clear from the mention of "measures at international level and regional or worldwide environmental problems" in art.191(1) TFEU. Consequently, the European Union can—and did—take measures to protect the environment outside the territory covered by the Treaties, such as measures to protect the ozone layer, combat climate change, protect endangered species in the Third World or ban the export of waste to non-industrialised countries.

The question of whether the Union should deal with matters of a purely local **1–04** nature is something to be answered under the general principle of subsidiarity. In the past, the Commission has sometimes rejected requests to take initiatives on a specific environmental problem, arguing that such matters could be better solved at local or regional level; such questions concerned, for instance, noise from nightclubs and discothèques, bicycle facilities in urban areas or noise in the vicinity of airports. However, it may well be that, for example, in order to ensure equal competition conditions within the European Union and protect, at the same time, the environment, some day the ambient noise level in the neighbourhood of airports will become the subject of an EU regulation, as the Commission had already announced in 1992.[9]

Furthermore, it may well be argued that the quality of the (local) bathing waters, of drinking water or of urban waste water treatment, are questions of purely local nature and should, therefore, not be regulated at EU level. The EU legislature has, in all three cases, decided that there should be EU-wide minimum standards, and no Member State ever invoked the subsidiarity principle in this regard. My own opinion is that there is a large margin of discretion of the EU legislature as to whether a specific problem should be dealt with at EU level or not. I consider all three pieces of EU legislation compatible with the subsidiarity principle.

When, in 2006, the Commission made a proposal for a directive on the assessment and management of floods, some Member States suggested that this proposal was limited to river basins which affected more than one Member State. However, this suggestion was rejected, probably because coastal floods were also included and because the management of such floods, including any financial assistance from the European Union, would not be made easier; the directive which was adopted covered all types of floods.[10]

More generally, there is no EU environment distinguishable from any **1–05** individual, local, regional or national environment. Therefore, the EU measures need not be and are not restricted to transfrontier environmental problems. Quite rightly, art.5(3) TEU abandoned the notion of a "transfrontier" dimension of a measure which was contained in art.5 EC Treaty, and only refers to the "scale" of the measure as one criterion among others for assessing the application of the

---

[8] See Dir.1999/22 [1999] OJ L94/24; see for more details para.5–39, below.

[9] COM(92) 494 of 2 December 1992.

[10] See Dir.2007/60 on the assessment and management of flood risks [2007] OJ L288/7.

subsidiarity principle. As mentioned above, the definition of "environment" is, as regards its content and its geographical extension, very wide and includes human beings, fauna and flora, soil, water, air, climate, landscape, material assets, and natural heritage.[11] Environmental law is the totality of the legal measures which try to prevent, protect and improve parts or all of the environment.

2. GENESIS AND DEVELOPMENT OF EU ENVIRONMENTAL LAW

1–06   The original EC Treaty of 1957 did not contain any provision on the environment, environmental policy or environmental law. Subsequent to the discussions of the late 1960s, where the Club of Rome described the limits to growth, the European Commission announced in 1970 the necessity of establishing a Community action programme on the environment. In 1971 it submitted a first communication on Community environmental policy,[12] where it suggested the establishment of EU measures for the protection of the environment recurring, if necessary, to the possibilities for action outlined in art.308 EC (now art.352 TFEU). This Communication was soon followed by a proposal for an environment action programme.[13]

In 1972, the United Kingdom, Denmark and Ireland joined the European Union. In the autumn of that year, the Heads of State and Government met for the first time, agreed on the necessity to take action on the environment and asked for an EU environment action programme.[14] Since this programme was already before the Council, discussions advanced relatively quickly. France in particular considered, however, that EU action should not be based on the EC Treaty provisions, but should instead take place in the form of intergovernmental cooperation, as the EC Treaty did not contain an explicit competence provision. For this reason, the finally adopted programme was agreed in the form of a joint "declaration" by the Community and by the representatives of Member States meeting in Council.[15] In the same way, the agreement to inform the Commission of national environmental measures which could have a direct effect on the functioning of the internal market was made in the form of a non-binding gentleman's agreement[16]; this policy continued throughout 1973 and 1974.[17]

---

[11] Enumeration from Dir.2011/92 on the assessment of the effects of certain public and private projects on the environment [2012] OJ L26/1, art.3.

[12] Commission, First communication on a Community policy for the environment, SEC(71) 2616 of 22 July 1971.

[13] [1972] OJ C52/1.

[14] Commission Sixth General Report (1972), p.8.

[15] [1973] OJ C112/1.

[16] [1973] OJ C9/1.

[17] See Agreement of 20 July 1974 to complete the 1973 agreement [1974] OJ C86/1; Resolution of 3 March 1974 on energy and the environment [1975] OJ C168/2; Recommendation 75/436 of 3 March 1975 on cost allocation and action by public authorities on environmental matters [1975] OJ L194/1; Resolution of 24 June 1975 on a second group of air pollutants which are to be studied [1975] OJ C168/4; Resolution of 15 July 1975 on adapting Community measures to technical progress [1975] OJ C168/5; Decision of 8 December 1975 setting up a common procedure for an inventory of information sources on the environment [1976] OJ L31/8.

The first legally binding instruments on environmental issues were adopted in 1975, based on art.94 EC and/or art.308 EC (now arts 115 and 352 TFEU). The choice of measures was determined both by the environment action programme and by the necessity of selecting areas which did not come under the responsibility of the internal market or agricultural services of the Commission. This was the case in particular for measures in the area of water and waste.[18]

The EC Treaty was amended in 1987 to complete, by the end of 1992, the internal market.[19] Majority voting for internal market measures was introduced by inserting a new art.95 (now art.114) into the Treaty. And for the first time, a section was introduced for environmental measures (arts 174–176, now arts 191–193 TFEU). However, such measures had to be adopted unanimously. This led to considerable discussions on the legal basis for environmental measures, which the Commission and the European Parliament often wished to base on the actual art.114, while the Council and Member States preferred the present art.192.

1–07

When the Maastricht Treaty on European Union amended the EC Treaty in 1993 it introduced majority decisions in environmental matters (art.192), though some matters remained subjected to unanimous decisions.[20]

The Amsterdam Treaty,[21] which entered into effect on 1 May 1999, introduced the co-decision procedure for environmental matters (art.192(1)) and aligned this provision thus further to that of art.114, though the unanimity clause for some areas (art.192(2)) was not deleted. The Treaty of Nice, which came into effect on 1 February 2003, did not significantly change the provisions of arts 191–193. Also, the Lisbon Treaty on European Union did not bring changes to these provisions, except that the fight against climate change was inserted into art.191 TFEU as one of the objectives of EU environmental policy.

3. SOURCES OF EU ENVIRONMENTAL LAW

The broad definition of objectives of EU environmental policy, as laid down in art.3 TEU and 191(1) TFEU, hardly leaves any area of environmental policy, as it is perceived in any one of the 28 Member States, outside EU competence. Measures to realise the objectives of the Union's environmental policy may be based on any relevant article of the FEU Treaty, although arts 191 and 192 remain the most relevant provisions for EU environmental action. Thus, measures which concern agricultural aspects of environmental protection will normally be based on art.43 TFEU; an example was Directive 91/414 on the authorisation and marketing of plant protection products.[22] Measures on environmental aspects of transport may be based on art.91 TFEU; an example is Directive 99/62 on the

1–08

---

[18] See, in chronological order, Dec.75/437 of 3 March 1975 to adhere to the Paris Convention on marine protection from land-based sources [1975] OJ L194/5; Dir.75/439 of 16 June 1975 on waste oils [1975] OJ L194/23; Dir.75/440 of 16 June 1975 on surface water [1975] OJ L194/26; Dir.75/442 of 16 June 1975 on waste [1975] OJ L194/23; Dir.76/160 of 8 December 1975 on bathing water [1976] OJ L31/1.
[19] Single European Act [1987] OJ L169/1.
[20] [1992] OJ C191/1.
[21] [1997] OJ C340/1.
[22] [1991] OJ L230/51.

charging of heavy goods vehicles for the use of certain infrastructures.[23] The choice of the correct legal basis is important because the elaboration of the proposal, the participation of other Union institutions, the intensity of this participation (see arts 293–294 TFEU) and the residual rights for Member States are different from one provision to another.

The rules of arts 191 and 192 TFEU are not directly applicable: while, for instance, art.34 TFEU states that "quantitative restrictions on imports and all measures having equivalent effect shall ... be prohibited between Member States", no similar formulation can be found in arts 191 or 192 TFEU, stating that pollution is prohibited or that the polluter shall pay for pollution. Therefore, arts 191 and 192 need to be operationalised and made precise by secondary legislation in order to become applicable for administrative bodies and courts or used for or against polluters.

The most relevant other provisions, on which EU environmental measures can be based, are art.114 TFEU for measures aimed at the establishment and the functioning of the internal market; art.43 TFEU for agricultural and fisheries measures; art.91 TFEU for measures concerning transport; art.207 TFEU for commercial measures; and art.182 TFEU on research and development. Environmental measures in the energy sector were in the past frequently based on art.192 TFEU, as there was no specific chapter on energy policy in the EC Treaty; an example is Directive 2001/77 on the promotion of electricity produced from renewable energy sources in the internal electricity market.[24] Otherwise, art.352 TFEU was used. The Lisbon Treaty introduced a new provision, art.194 TFEU. This provision is now being used for energy-related environmental measures.[25]

1–09 The choice of the correct legal basis for an environmental matter will be discussed further at paras 2–72 et seq., below and the rights of Member States at paras 3–37 et seq., below.

International conventions, to which the European Union has adhered, are part of EU law, see art.216(2) TFEU. They rank below the primary law of the FEU Treaty, but above secondary legislation and thus prevail over conflicting environmental directives or regulations.[26] However, the Court of Justice only allows a provision of an international environmental convention to be relied on in court, when it is of direct effect.[27] When this is not the case, national courts are requested to do their best in order to give full effect to such a provision in national law (*effet utile*).[28] For itself, the Court has not yet accepted that it is under an obligation to apply the *effet utile* doctrine in such cases.

---

[23] [1999] OJ L187/42.

[24] [2001] OJ L283/33.

[25] See, e.g. Dir.2012/27 on energy efficiency [2012] OJ L315/1.

[26] See Court of Justice, *IATA and ELFAA* (C-344/04) [2006] E.C.R. I-403 at [35]: "Article 300(7) EC [now art.216(2) of the TFEU] provides that 'agreements concluded under the conditions set out in this Article shall be binding on the institutions of the Community and on Member States'. In accordance with the court's case-law, those agreements prevail over provisions of secondary Community legislation".

[27] Court of Justice, *Council and European Parliament v Milieudefensie and Stichting Stop Luchtverontreiniging Utrecht*, (joined cases C-401/12P and C-402/12P), ECLI:EU:C:2015:4; *Council and Commission v Stichting Natuur en Milieu and Pesticide Action Network Europe* (joined cases C-404/12P and C-405/12P) ECLI:EU:C:2015:5.

[28] Court of Justice, *Lesoochranárske zoskupenie* (C-240/09) [2011] E.C.R. I-1255 at [50]: "it is for the national court, in order to ensure effective judicial protection in the fields covered by EU

The European Union has adhered to a considerable number of international environmental conventions and to numerous protocols, drawn up in pursuance of these conventions. All these conventions are so-called "mixed" conventions: the competence for the subject-matter regulated by the conventions was partly in the hands of the European Union and partly in the hands of Member States. Where exactly the line is drawn between the Union's responsibility and Member States' responsibility inevitably varies from one convention to the other.

As decisions which are based on art.192 TFEU and transpose environmental **1–10** conventions into EU law have as a consequence that Member States may, under art.193 TFEU, introduce more stringent provisions in that area at national level, such decisions can never establish an exclusive EU competence for the subject-matter regulated by the convention.[29]

In practice, an international environmental convention only plays a significant role in EU law where the Union has adopted a directive or a regulation in order to transpose the content of the convention into EU law. Where there is only a Council decision to adhere to a convention, but no transposing secondary legislation, the Commission omits to enforce the content of the convention against Member States. Member States are left at their discretion to also ratify the convention and to apply it. This practice is well established, although it clearly contradicts art.17 TEU, which assigns the task to the Commission to ensure that *all* EU law is applied within the European Union.[30] Indeed, the European Union, by adhering to an international convention, commits itself with regard to the other contracting parties to comply with the convention's requirements throughout the territory of the European Union, independently from the question, whether the EU Member State in question has made, through its own ratification, a commitment that pertains to its national territory.

The European Union has adopted an important number of pieces of environmental legislation in the form of regulations, directives and non-binding recommendations. Their exact number depends on the classification of measures. Thus, for example, since at least the mid-1980s standards for air emissions or noise levels from cars have been set and strengthened in order to better protect the environment; nevertheless, they were based on arts 115 or 114 TFEU, because the two basic directives on air and noise emissions from cars had been adopted, in the 1970s, as part of an EU programme for the elimination of technical barriers to trade in the internal market. The reason for recurrence to art.114 TFEU is the existence of art.193 TFEU: the car industry, EU institutions and probably also Member States have an interest in establishing uniform standards for cars and avoiding different national standards which create barriers to the free circulation of cars.

The different instruments will be further discussed at paras 2–29 et seq., **1–11** below. Environment action programmes are, since the end of 1993, regulated by art.192(3) TFEU; they are now adopted in the form of a legally binding

---

environmental law, to interpret its national law in a way which, to the fullest extent possible, is consistent with the objectives laid down in Article 9(3) of the Aarhus Convention"; see in the same way *Boxus a.o.* (joined cases C-128/09 to C-131/09, C-134/09 and C-135/09) [2011] E.C.R. I-9711.

[29] See para.3–43, below, for concrete cases where the question of exclusive competence became relevant at EU level.

[30] Article 17 of the TEU: "the Commission shall … ensure the application of the Treaties and of the measures adopted by the institutions pursuant to them".

decision.[31] This constitutes a significant difference to the five environment action programmes which had been adopted between 1973 and 1993. These had been elaborated by the Commission and sent to the other EU institutions. The Council, together with governments from Member States, had normally approved their concept and the approach in the form of a unanimously adopted (political) resolution, but had carefully avoided any statement that it adopted the programme as such.[32]

In future, the content of an EU environment action programme which was adopted under art.192(3) TFEU will constitute a source of law. Thus where, for example, the 6th Environment Action Programme[33] requested in art.7(1) that "chemicals that are dangerous should be substituted by safer chemicals or safer alternative technologies not entailing the use of chemicals with the aim of reducing risks to man and the environment", this clearly constitutes the recognition of the substitution principle in EU environmental law, which may influence the interpretation of arts 34, 36, 114, 192 or 193 TFEU.[34] Also, the interpretation of the subsidiarity principle will be influenced by decisions under art.192(3): where a decision under this provision explicitly provides for an EC measure on a specific item, it will normally not be possible to object to such an EU measure by invoking the subsidiarity principle—though much depends, of course, on the exact content of the measure.

4.   OBJECTIVES OF ENVIRONMENTAL POLICY

(a)   General remarks

1–12   Article 3 TEU[35] fixes the general environmental objectives of the European Union, which are completed by the specific objectives fixed in art.191[36]; it is common understanding that the tasks of art.3(3) TEU are not an exhaustive enumeration.

The different objectives of the Treaties are not in a hierarchical order. The European Union has to try to attain all its objectives. Should different objectives

---

[31] See Dec.1600/2002 laying down the 6th Community Environment Action Programme [2002] OJ L242/1.

[32] See, e.g. Resolution of the Council and the Representatives of the Governments of the Member States, meeting within the Council of 1 February 1993 [1993] OJ C138/1: "... approve the general approach and strategy of the programme towards sustainability presented by the Commission ..."; Against the binding nature of the 5th Environment Action Programme: Court of Justice, *Rovigo v Commission* (C-142/95P) [1996] E.C.R. I-6669, n.32.

[33] See Dec.1600/2002 laying down the 6th Community Environment Action Programme [2002] OJ L242/1.

[34] On the substitution principle, see also Court of Justice, *Kemikalieinspektionen* (C-473/98) [2000] E.C.R. I-5681.

[35] Treaty on European Union [2008] OJ C115/1, art.3(3): "The Union shall work for the sustainable development of Europe, based on ... a high level of protection and improvement of the quality of the environment."

[36] TFEU art.191(1): "Union policy on the environment shall contribute to pursuit of the following objectives: preserving, protecting and improving the quality of the environment; protecting human health; prudent and rational utilisation of natural resources; promoting measures at international level to deal with regional or worldwide environmental problems, and in particular combating climate change."

conflict in a specific case, then the EU institutions must try to find a compromise (see art.7 TFEU). Conflicts—for instance between the establishment of an internal market for goods and the need to protect the environment via the precautionary principle—are frequent. Article 11 TFEU,[37] which was introduced by the Treaty of Amsterdam, does not lead to a different interpretation. Indeed, any such hierarchy would have needed clearer expression in the Treaty.

The different environmental objectives do not lead to concrete requirements for legislative action. It is not possible, for instance, to deduce from the requirement of a prudent use of natural resources the right to limit land use, e.g. for agricultural purposes. Nor are the objectives, in practice, enforceable. The possibility of an action under art.265 TFEU against the European Union, the Council or the Commission for not pursuing the environmental objectives, is theoretical, since EU institutions have a very large discretion for taking—or not taking—action.

EU action shall *contribute* to achieving the different objectives, as is stated in art.191 TFEU. Next to EU measures there are also national, regional, local or international measures which exist to help reach the objectives. The responsibility and competence of the European Union in environmental matters is thus shared with Member States, but is not exclusive. In specific cases the environment action programmes specify which action is to be undertaken in order to approach or even reach one or several objectives of the EU Treaties; nevertheless, the individual measures still need to be adopted by a formal EC instrument (see art.288 TFEU), for which the relevant decision-making procedure under the different Treaty provisions must be followed.

1–13

(b)   Sustainable development

The Amsterdam Treaty 1999 introduced the concept of sustainable development into EU law: the Preamble to the TEU, art.3 of that Treaty, as well as art.11 TFEU mention this objective[38] without defining it. Already, art.2 in the version of the Maastricht Treaty, had fixed as one of the Community objectives "sustainable growth", also without defining it. Both notions go back to a report which an ad hoc "World Commission on Environment and Development" chaired by Gro Brundtland (Norway) had made in 1987 to the United Nations and which was entitled *Our Common Future*. In that report, the need for economic development was emphasised which should, however, be "sustainable". Sustainable development was described as a "development which meets the needs of the present without compromising the ability of future generations to meet their own needs".

1–14

However, even after 30 years of discussions, the precise meaning of the notion is unclear. "It cannot usefully be defined. It seems clear, though, that a policy of economic growth which disregards environmental considerations will not meet

---

[37] TFEU art.11: "Environmental protection requirements must be integrated into the definition and implementation of the Union policies and activities, in particular with a view to promoting sustainable development." An almost identical text had been inserted, in 1987, into an earlier version of the present art.191(2.3) of the TFEU.

[38] Article 9 of the Recitals of the TEU mentions that sustainable development is a "principle".

the criterion of sustainable development".[39] This, though, was exactly what the Lisbon European Council did in 2000 when it fixed as an objective for the European Union to become, within 10 years, "the most competitive and dynamic knowledge-based economy in the world, capable of sustainable economic growth with more and better jobs and greater social cohesion". In 2001, the Göteborg European Council tried to repair this (deliberate) omission, by adding the environmental aspects to the Lisbon declaration.[40]

In 2005, the Commission declared that sustainability of the EU policy required actions with regard to climate change, clean energy, public health, social exclusion, demography and migration, management of natural resources, global poverty and challenges to development.[41] This was followed by a declaration on guiding principles for sustainable development which the Council approved; these were environmental protection, social equity and cohesion, economic prosperity and the assuming of international responsibility.[42] And in June 2006, the European Council adopted a declaration on a strategy for sustainable development where it fixed seven objectives of sustainable development: climate change and clean technologies, sustainable transport, sustainable consumption and production, conservation and management of natural resources, public health, social inclusion, demography and migration, global poverty and the challenges of sustainable development. The European Council also fixed ten leading principles and seven main challenges which should be addressed. For each challenge, it fixed a number of actions to be taken by the EU institutions, though it carefully avoided giving them any legally binding form.[43]

1–15   In the political practice since 2006, most of the European Union's policy and legislation followed the principle of "business as usual". It is true, though, that the fight against climate change became, for the Union's internal policy, one priority. With regard to the other strategic objectives, it appears that the Union

---

[39] P. Birnie and A. Boyle, *International Law and the Environment*, 2nd edn (Oxford, 2002), p.45; on sustainable development, see also M. Lee *EU Environmental Law* (Oxford and Portland 2005), pp.25 et seq.

[40] See Presidency Conclusions, Göteborg European Council (2001) 15 and 16 June, nos 19 and 20: "Sustainable development—to meet the needs of the present generation without compromising those of future generations—is a fundamental objective under the Treaties. That requires dealing with economic, social and environmental policies in a mutually reinforcing way. The European Council agrees a strategy for sustainable development which completes the Union's political commitment to economic and social renewal, adds a third, environmental dimension to the Lisbon strategy and establishes a new approach to policy making."

[41] Commission, COM(2005) 37. See, also Dec.1600/2002 on the 6th Environment Action Programme [2002] OJ L242/1 Recitals 6 and 7: "A prudent use of natural resources and the protection of the global eco-system together with economic prosperity balanced social development are a condition for sustainable development. The Programme aims at a high level of protection of the environment and human health and at a general improvement in the environment and quality of life, indicates priorities for the environment dimension of the sustainable development strategy and should be taken into account when bringing forward actions under the strategy."

[42] Commission COM(2005) 218.

[43] Council, document 10917 of 26 June 2006.

institutions do not pay more than lip-service to the objective of reverting to the unsustainable tendencies identified by the Commission and to put the strategy of 2006 into reality.[44]

In secondary legislation, "sustainable development" was only rarely defined; as can be seen such a definition is not really meaningful:

> "Sustainable development means the improvement of the standard of living and welfare of the relevant populations within the limits of the capacity of the ecosystems by maintaining natural assets and their biological diversity for the benefit of present and future generations."[45]

Taken literally, nobody could comply with such requirements.

The basic difficulty remains of knowing which economic development is sustainable. It might well be argued that the use of nuclear energy, which includes the generation of radioactive waste for which no safe disposal technology exists as yet and which will continue to be hazardous for thousands of years, most certainly affects future generations and is therefore not sustainable. Another example is the gradual, progressive contamination of groundwater, which often shows its effects only decades later, when the groundwater is used. Further examples are the disappearance of fauna and flora species, urbanisation and the construction of motorways. At the end of 2003, the Council approved, by way of Council conclusions and thus in a non-binding form, a list of 14 headline indicators to assess sustainable development, among them three "environmental" indicators, namely greenhouse gas emissions, energy intensity of economy and the volume of transport.[46] Reliable EU-wide data on the last two indicators do not yet exist and it might well be argued that these indicators do not mean anything, e.g. for biodiversity loss, groundwater pollution or noise levels.

Eurostat, the Commission's Statistical Office, publishes every two years a report of the European Union's sustainable development strategy, which gives a large number of statistical data on economic, social and environmental issues.[47] These data are arranged in chapters on socioeconomic development, sustainable consumption and production, social inclusion, demographic changes, public health, climate change and energy, sustainable transport, natural resources, global partnership and good governance. However, data on these issues and trends which may be deduced from them, do not necessarily allow any conclusion on the state of the environment and its development towards sustainability.

1–16

In view of this contradictory and confusing use of the word "sustainability", it is not surprising that the Union practice shows an inflationary use of the expression "sustainable" which is linked to very different activities—sustainable transport, sustainable tourism, sustainable use of energy or water, sustainable regional development, sustainable business, sustainable future, sustainable

---

[44] See Eurostat, *Sustainable Development in the EU. 2009 Monitoring Report on the EU Sustainable Development Strategy*, Luxembourg 2009; *2011 Monitoring Report*, Luxembourg 2011; *2013 Monitoring Report of the European Union's Sustainable Development Strategy*, Luxembourg 2013.

[45] Definition from art.2 of Reg.2493/2000 [2000] OJ L288/1; see also earlier Reg.3062/95 [1995] OJ L327/9, art.2(4).

[46] Council, Conclusions of 8 December 2003 on structural indicators, document 15875/03.

[47] See Eurostat (fn.44, above).

production and consumption—in order to give them a green colour[48]; contents are put into the notion of "sustainability", which are later derived from it, and the notion is increasingly used as a substitute for "positive, favourable development", thereby losing all its environmental content. Generally, it seems impossible to determine precisely if and when future generations will be able or unable to meet their own needs. For example, the construction of the Via Appia some 2,500 years ago has affected the location of towns and villages; in the same way, any town siting and road construction today will affect future generations' rights to determine their own needs, i.e. their own town siting or road construction. The different provisions in the Treaty on sustainable development and their practical application thus give more of a guideline to policy action than any meaningful legal concept.

(c) High level of protection

1–17   The objective to reach a high level of environmental protection is now enshrined in art.3(3) EU Treaty[49] and is repeated in similar terms in art.191(2.1) TFEU.[50] A similar provision is to be found in art.114(3) TFEU.[51] Neither article specifies what is a high level of protection: certainly, it is not the highest level one could think of.[52] A high level can probably best be determined by looking at environmental standards which Member States that normally have a high standard of environmental protection (Denmark, the Netherlands, Sweden, Finland, Austria, Germany) have set; the practice of other industrial states with a recognised strong environmental policy, such as Switzerland or Norway, may also be considered. Policy declarations, resolutions and targets can be an important indicator, especially in areas where no standards have yet been set at national or international level, or where scientific uncertainty is great. As art.3 TEU expressly declares the improvement of the quality of the environment to be one of the objectives of Union policy, any measure aiming at a high level must therefore aim at improving the existing situation.

The specific reference to a high level of protection no longer permits the adoption of measures which only provide for the lowest common denominator of environmental protection and lets individual Member States, which are in favour

---

[48] The 6th Environment Action Programme, Dec.1600/2002 (fn.27, above) used the word, in its different forms (sustain, sustainable, sustainability), not less than 64 times; the 7th Environment Action Programme, Dec.1386/2013 [2013] OJ L354/171 uses it 115 times.

[49] [2008] OJ C115/1.

[50] TFEU art.191(2.1): "Union policy on the environment shall aim at a high level of protection taking into account the diversity of situations in the various regions of the Community."

[51] TFEU art.95(3): "(The Commission, in its proposals concerning environmental protection) will take as a base a high level of protection taking account in particular of any new development based on scientific facts. Within their respective powers, the European Parliament and the Council will also seek to achieve this objective."

[52] See also Court of Justice, *Germany v Parliament and Council* (C-233/94) [1997] E.C.R. I-2405 at [48] for a case of consumer protection where under art.153 of the EC (now art.169 of the TFEU) a high level of protection is required: "Admittedly, there must be a high level of consumer protection …; however, no provision of the Treaty obliges the Community legislature to adopt the highest level of protection which can be found in a particular Member State. The reduction in the level of protection which may thereby result in certain cases through the application of … the Directive does not call into question the general result which the Directive seeks to achieve, namely a considerable improvement in the protection of … [consumers] within the Community."

of more stringent measures, adopt such measures by virtue of art.193 TFEU at national level. Indeed, the high level is to be achieved by the Union as a whole, not by national measures. Article 191 TFEU clarifies that the interests of regions which are environmentally lagging behind shall be duly taken into account, allowing them to catch up; this again pleads for a high level, not the highest level of protection.

A high level of environmental protection cannot be enforced in court. This follows from the fact that art.3 TEU and art.191 TFEU refer to the environmental policy as a whole, not to the individual measure adopted under that policy; also, the policy has to "aim at" a high level and can thus always argue that it is on its way towards this attainment. *Epiney* who is of the opinion that the provision is legally binding and can be enforced, practically reaches the same conclusion by emphasising the wide discretion which the EC institutions have in interpreting the notion.[53]

In contrast to art.3 TEU and art.191 TFEU, art.114 TFEU requests Commission proposals to be made at a high level of environmental protection; thus, it refers to individual measures, not to the policy in general. Where a Commission proposal is not based on a high level of environmental protection, the European Parliament has a right of action against the Commission[54] under art.263 TFEU. This follows from the procedural provisions of arts 293 and 294 TFEU. Indeed, where the Commission has made a "high level" proposal (case A), the Council can reach a common position and adopt a proposal that lowers the protection, only by unanimity (art.293 TFEU); however, where the Commission has made a "low level" proposal (case B), the Council can reach a common position and finally adopt the proposal by a qualified majority, at a lower level (provided it conforms to the low level proposal from the Commission) since it does not amend the Commission's proposal. The Council's common position may only be challenged by an absolute majority of the European Parliament. Where the European Parliament's majority opinion is concurrent with the Commission's opinion, the Council must decide unanimously (case A); where this majority opinion does not concur with the Commission's opinion, the Council may decide by majority (case B).[55]

1–18

These considerations are of theoretical character. The European Parliament has, until now, never attempted such a case against the Commission; without doubt, this practice is also due to the difficulties of determining what is in reality a "high level". In all situations—under arts 114 and 192 TFEU—that have occurred up until now, the practice of the Commission and the Council indicates that both institutions use the formula of a high level in its reversed order: whatever is proposed or adopted is considered to be a high level of environmental protection.

The "sanction" for not proposing or adopting measures on a high level of environmental protection is art.193 TFEU for measures under art.192 and art.114(4)–(9) TFEU: in both cases, Member States may, under certain

---

[53] A. Epiney, *Umweltrecht der Europäischen Union*, 3rd edn (Baden-Baden, 2013), pp.142 et seq.

[54] The Parliament has no such right against the Council, since art.114(3) of the TFEU expressly provides that the Council shall only "seek to achieve" a high level of protection.

[55] Jans-Vedder, *European Environmental Law*, 3rd edn (Groningen, 2008), is of the opinion that a Commission proposal is not an "act", in the sense of art.263 of the TFEU, and thus cannot be tackled in court.

conditions, maintain or introduce more stringent national measures. In theory, one might argue that the lower the level of protection the Union measure is, the greater becomes the pressure from Member States with a high level of protection to opt out of the Union environmental measure and take or maintain national measures. In practice, though, economic operators rather push for lowering the high level also in Member States with more stringent measures than the European Union, arguing that otherwise they would be at a competitive disadvantage.

(d)   The specific objectives of art.191(1) TFEU

1–19   The four specific objectives mentioned under art.191(1) are rather detailed in their description; but these details do not, in fact, add too much to the objective to protect the environment. They clarify that the Union protection measures are not limited to the Union's territory, which, in practice, these measures never were. Measures to protect human health[56] can, as the case may be, pursue an environmental, internal market, agricultural, consumer protection or public health objective and thus be based on other Treaty provisions than arts 191–193. In the context of its examination of national legislative measures (under art.114(4–8) TFEU) the Commission does not accept that a national measure is based on health considerations, as that provision only allows considerations to protect the environment; this practice contradicts the provision of art.191 TFEU, according to which environmental measures also aim at the protection of human health.[57]

"Natural resources" is a vague term: it probably covers the management of all resources which are found in the environment, fauna and flora, timber, minerals, air, water, soil, oil, natural gas and chemicals. Measures to prevent degradation or impairment of these resources, such as accident prevention and the safe disposal of waste, are included in the term "prudent and rational use". Identifying the objective, eventually the main objective, of a measure is important, because the objective is one of the determining factors of the legal base for the measure; and the decision-making procedure, the content of the measure and Member States' residual rights and obligations vary according to the legal base applicable.

5.   PRINCIPLES OF ENVIRONMENTAL ACTION

(a)   General remarks

1–20   Part one of the TFEU, arts 1–17, is entitled "Principles". It fixes the basics of the TFEU, objectives, institutional and procedural rules and a number of other provisions of a general character. As regards the environment, art.5 TEU on

---

[56] The difference between "health of humans" (art.36 of the TFEU), "human health" (art.191, but also art.169) and "public health" (title of art.168 of the TFEU) has lost its legal precision; see also Court of Justice, *Biologische Produkten* (C-272/ 80) [1981] E.C.R. 3277, where the Court refers to art.30 of the EC (now art.36 of the TFEU) as protecting "public health". See, furthermore, Court of Justice, *Standley* (C-293/97) [1999] E.C.R. I-2603, where the Court considered Dir.91/676 on the protection of water from nitrates pollution to be a directive which protects "public health".
[57] See Ch.3, below.

subsidiarity[58] and art.11 TFEU on integration[59] are of relevance. To these general principles, art.191(2.2) TFEU adds some specific environmental principles.[60]

It is doubtful whether all these different provisions have the same legal character. As regards the principles of art.191(2.2) TFEU, they constitute, in my opinion, general guidelines for the Union's environmental policy, but not binding rules of law which apply to each individual Union measure. They *allow* the taking of specific measures in favour of the environment, but do not *oblige* the EU institutions to take such measures. Therefore, they could only be enforced by the European Court in very extreme cases where a systematic disregard of the principles in the policy is demonstrated.

This reasoning is contested. Some authors see the principles of art.191(2.2) TFEU as binding rules of law, which have to be respected in each individual measure.[61] The wide discretion of Union institutions, however, for taking measures could only lead to the illegality of a measure in exceptional cases because the principles had been disregarded. As can be seen, the practical results are not really very different.

The discussion on principles in environmental law and policy is, to a large extent, a spill-over from discussions which take place under the auspices of public international law. In that context, principles may play an important role in contributing to the shaping of international environmental law. However, it should not be forgotten that the essential part of public international environmental law is soft law, which is not really binding on the states. In contrast to that, EU law is binding and capable of fixing provisions that have binding force on Member States and on private persons. In the same way as, for example, the United Nations' Declaration on Human Rights remains of high value for the international community, but is of secondary importance in Europe, where the Council of Europe's Convention on Human Rights established binding, enforceable human rights, the environmental principles in the TFEU are less important for EU environmental law, which has developed a large number of binding provisions that materialise these principles for the actual, concrete situations.

1–21

The Court of Justice has in one case interpreted EU law in the light of one of the principles of art.191(2.2) TFEU.[62] In that judgment, the Court had to decide whether a regional ban for waste imports was compatible with the EU provisions on the free circulation of goods, although such waste imports from other Member States were treated differently from imports of waste from other regions of that state. The Court found no discrimination in this case.[63]

---

[58] TEU art.5(3): "Under the principle of subsidiarity, in areas which do not fall within its exclusive competence, the Union shall act only if and in so far as the objectives of the proposed action cannot be sufficiently achieved by the Member States, either at central level or at regional and local level, but can rather, by reason of the scale or effects of the proposed action, be better achieved at Union level."

[59] TFEU art.11 (fn.37, above).

[60] TFEU art.191(2.2): "[Union policy] ... shall be based on the precautionary principle and on the principles that preventive action should be taken, that environmental damage should as a priority be rectified at source and that the polluter should pay."

[61] See the different contributions in R. Macrory (ed.), *Principles of European Environmental Law* (Groningen, 2004).

[62] *Commission v Belgium* (C-2/90) [1992] E.C.R. I-4431.

[63] *Commission v Belgium* (C-2/90) [1992] E.C.R. I-4431 at [34]: "... in order to determine whether the obstacle in question is discriminatory, the particular type of waste must be taken into account. The

1–22   In other cases, the Court frequently recurred to the formula that provisions of EU law could not be interpreted in such a way "as to give rise to results which are incompatible with the general principles of Community law and in particular with fundamental rights".[64] The question is whether also the environmental principles of art.191(2) TFEU are such principles which EU legislation may not infringe. In my opinion, this is not the case. Rather, they constitute guiding principles for political or legislative decisions and are often used—as a sort of leitmotif—to explain or justify a decision which was taken. But they cannot really be used to declare an EU measure void with the argument that it contradicts one of these principles.

The judgment in the above-mentioned case C-2/90 was given under the 1987 version of the present art.191 TFEU, which referred to Community action rather than to Community policy. Under that provision it could be argued that the principles of art.191 TFEU referred to individual measures. By contrast, the present wording of that article considers the EU policy as a whole; it does not require that each individual EU measure take into account all the principles of art.191(2.2) TFEU. Requesting that the principles of art.191 apply to each individual EU measure would mean that numerous measures would contradict, for instance, the polluter-pays principle, since they do not contain any provision about it.[65]

Even where the principles of art.191 TFEU are seen as general guidelines for EU policy only, they have some indirect legal significance. They place an obligation on the Union to base its policy on these principles and to plan policy and measures accordingly. Moreover, observance of these principles can play an important part in deciding, case by case, whether the objectives of art.191(1) TFEU cannot be sufficiently achieved by the Member States and are therefore capable of being better achieved by the Union (subsidiarity, art.5 TEU). Where, for instance, the Union takes a measure on environmental liability, it could invoke the prevention and the polluter-pays principle to justify the EU action against subsidiarity arguments; this example shows at the same time the limited usefulness of the principles, since Member States which oppose the measure could argue that the subsidiarity principle would not allow action to be taken at EU level.

---

principle that environmental damage should as a priority be rectified at source—a principle laid down by Art.174(2) E.C. for action by the Community relating to the environment—means that it is for each region, commune or other local entity to take appropriate measures to receive, process and dispose of its own waste...". See also *R. v Minister of Agriculture* (C-157/96) [1998] E.C.R. I-2211 and *United Kingdom v Commission* (C-180/96) [1998] E.C.R. I-2265, where the Court interpreted the prevention principle.

[64] Court of Justice, *Dow Chemical* (joined cases 97/87, 98/87 and 99/87) [1989] E.C.R. I-3165 at [9].
[65] The judgment in *Commission v Belgium* (C-2/90) [1992] E.C.R. I-4431 seems to have been influenced by some policy considerations which might explain some inconsistencies: the principle of art.191(2.2) of the TFEU was applied to a national measure, although the article refers to EU policy; the Court did not examine whether the Belgian measure was proportional; the Court transformed the principle into a rule of law; it also justified its finding by reference to the Basel Convention on the shipment of hazardous waste, although the Union was, at the time of the judgment, not a member of that Convention, etc.

The principles could also be used to justify the chosen legal basis—art.192 TFEU or another provision—for a specific measure and its content[66] and to interpret secondary EU legislation.

(b) Subsidiarity

The subsidiarity principle,[67] which is now laid down in art.5 TEU, was first inserted into the EC Treaty in 1987, but in a different version and limited to environmental matters.[68] The Maastricht Treaty 1993 repealed that provision and inserted a new art.3b—the present art.5 TEU—into the Treaty. The Amsterdam Treaty 1997 added to this, as an annex to the EC Treaty, a "Protocol on the application of the principles of subsidiarity and proportionality",[69] where, in 13 detailed points, rules were laid down on subsidiarity and proportionality. The Lisbon Treaty slightly reworded the principle, placed it at art.5(3) TEU and also took over the Protocol. The style of this Protocol gives the impression that it was drafted less from the perspective of a European Union, but rather with the aim of containing as far as possible the threat of European integration which was perceived as reducing the amount of power that regional or national administration had up until then. Article 5 TEU and its Protocol were probably inspired by the old art.130r(4) EC and a preceding draft from the European Parliament on a general Treaty on European Union.[70] It establishes a general rule for all Union activity, including the environment.

1-23

It is not a rule of competence but a principle which concerns the exercise of that competence, and predetermines the activity of the European Union[71]; as such, it has legal force. When taking action, EU institutions will have to demonstrate for each individual measure that the conditions of art.5 TEU and its Protocol are actually complied with. They benefit, however, from a large amount of discretion on the question of what content a measure would have. In practice, recitals of environmental regulations or directives often contain a clause, that the legislative act in question respects the principle of subsidiarity.

The discussion on subsidiarity is ongoing at EU level, in particular since the signature of the Maastricht Treaty, concentrating on the deregulation and simplification of legislation and of the possibility of the national parliaments and the Committee of the Regions to apply to the Court of Justice, when they consider that an EU measure does not comply with the principle of subsidiarity. Political approaches were started in 1992, in the name of subsidiarity, to review

---

[66] See, for the integration principle of art.11 of the TFEU, *European Parliament v Council* (C-62/88) [1990] E.C.R. I-1527: "[the integration requirement which] reflects the principle whereby all Community measures must satisfy the requirements of environmental protection, implies that a Community measure cannot be part of Community action on environmental matters merely because it takes account of these requirements."

[67] See, for this principle in general (without specific reference to the environment), Commission COM(93) 545 of 29 November 1993; COM(94) 533 of 25 November 1994; SEC(95) 580 of 24 November 1995; SEC(96) 2 of 14 June 1996, SEC(96) 7 of 27 November 1996.

[68] EC Treaty art.130r(4) (1987 version): "The Community shall take action relating to the environment to the extent to which the objectives referred to in paragraph 1 can be attained better at Community level than at the level of the individual Member States."

[69] [1997] OJ C340/105.

[70] [1984] OJ C77/33 arts 55 and 59.

[71] See also Commission SEC(92) 1990 of 27 October 1992.

existing environmental directives, where Member States felt obliged to undertake financial investments to clean the environment: this discussion has been particularly intense in the water sector. In contrast to that, there is hardly ever a discussion on subsidiarity when questions of EU funding for economically weaker regions are in question, where measures are considered which improve the competitivity of EU economic operators or where financial assistance for small- and medium-sized enterprises is discussed.

1–24 For the environment, much depends on the interpretation given to the requirement that the objective of environmental protection cannot be sufficiently achieved by Member States and can thus be *better* achieved at Community level. Probably the best illustration of the practical difficulties is the discussion in the Economic and Social Committee on the proposal for Directive 96/61 on integrated prevention and pollution control.[72] The Committee discussed the pros and cons of fixing Community-wide emission limit values for industrial installations and concluded:

> "the subsidiarity principle, properly understood, is not inconsistent with the establishment of limit values at European level. The high level of protection in the Community called for in the EC Treaty can only be achieved if European limit values are set."

A minority view of the Committee (eight members) stated in contrast to that[73]:

> "the subsidiarity principle, properly understood, is consistent with the establishment of limit values at Member State level. The high level of protection in the Community called for in the EU Treaty can only be achieved if Member State limit values are set and implemented."

It is not easy to establish general rules to show when environmental policy objectives can be better attained at EU level. Member States with an active environmental policy of their own may well think that measures at the level of individual Member States are a better solution. At present, there is a wide gulf between the individual Member States' national environmental policies and regulations. Member States such as Denmark, the Netherlands, Sweden, Austria and Germany are far more convinced of the need for environmental protection measures than, for instance, Greece, Spain, Portugal or Italy—though the governmental approach to environmental issues also depends on the political party which is in power. In some Member States—Ireland, Greece, Portugal, Spain or the Member States which acceded since 2004—environmental legislation often consists of not much more than the transposition of measures which had previously been adopted at EU level. Consequently, action at EU level is often a means of ensuring that environmental measures are taken in *all* Member States. If, instead, it were left to the Member States to take action, it could not be ensured that all and not only some Member States would adopt provisions on that specific environmental problem. Even if they did, concepts, contents and timing would rarely coincide. Where Member States take action at

---

[72] For this Directive, see para.4–40, below.
[73] [1995] OJ C195/54 and App.II.

different times, there is once again a danger for the Union as a whole of imbalances, distortions of competition and of trade patterns, the creation of new barriers to trade, etc.

Furthermore, river and sea water, air pollution, protection of fauna and flora species, climate issues, ozone layer protection, acidification, eutrophication and the management of products which have finished their useful lifetime (waste) cannot seriously be tackled at national level alone. In such cases the efforts of one Member State would easily be frustrated by the passivity of another Member State. This would also have an effect on the location of industrial undertakings, employment and quality of life, for example. Therefore, the objectives of art.191(1) TFEU can normally be attained faster and more effectively by and within the entire European Union, i.e. for the EU ecosystem as a whole. This is the reason why EU legislative activities practically covers all areas of environmental protection.

1–25

It must also be borne in mind that some Member States find it difficult, if not impossible, to conceive and implement measures to provide effective protection for the environment in general, and for fauna and flora in particular, since environmental protection measures are perceived as slowing down economic development. The negative effects of environmental impairment normally become more visible and therefore also politically more relevant when economic development is sufficiently advanced. Poverty is the biggest environmental pollutant; in Western Europe there is an element of economic divide between the north and the south, to which new EU Member States of Central and Eastern Europe have to be added. In these countries, environmental awareness and readiness to act are distinctly less prevalent, due to differences in the public discussion of environmental matters, traditions (e.g. hunting, bull fighting, fox hunting), education, public and media sensitivity, administrative determination, law enforcement, political priorities, etc. EU discussions on where environmental protection can be better achieved may not leave these considerations aside, although this often happens in Germany or the United Kingdom.

Precisely what "better" means in art.5 TEU is not at all clear; it could mean quicker, more effective, cheaper, more efficient, closer to the citizen (i.e. not too centralised), more democratic, more uniform, more consistent with measures in other parts of the industrialised world, or the global or the European Union, without these concepts being more precise.[74] It will, therefore, have to be decided on a case-by-case basis, considering all the facts, whether or not it is better to take measures at EU level, in order to attain the Union's environmental objectives. The aim must be to protect and improve the quality of the environment in the whole European Union. Due consideration must be given to the differences in the Member States' environmental legislation, the differing awareness of environmental issues, the environmental infrastructure in Member States, the risk that national protection measures might be differently timed or formulated, the danger of relocating industrial undertakings to countries with lower standards, the possible deflection of trade and the potential changes in the competitive position within the European Union and of the European Union towards non-EU

---

[74] The European Parliament is of the opinion that the notions in art.5 are deliberately vague in order to increase the legislative discretion of Union institutions, Resolution of 20 April 1994 (1994) OJ C128/190 n.5.

countries. The main concern is to improve the quality of the environment, to reach a high level of protection and to ensure sustainable development over the broadest possible area. Article 5 mentions the scale or effects of the proposed action as examples where objectives can be better achieved at Union level.

1–26   If one tries to apply all these theoretical issues to the debate as to whether there should be EU legislation on, for example, environmental liability, the following aspects would also have to be considered: there is legislation on liability in all Member States, but this differs as to questions of liability for negligence or strict liability, burden of proof, protected assets and damages; there are differences as to the application of these provisions to damage to the environment itself; environmental damage is differently defined; *locus standi* varies; the number of cases decided by the courts varies considerably; costs for economic operators are likely to increase, e.g. due to insurance premiums; the environmental problem is not one of accidental pollution, but the progressive accumulation of pollutants in the environment; many an impairment is caused by a multitude of polluters, not by a single one; where an economic operator respects existing legislation, he should not be liable for environmental impairment, and so on. At the end of such a list of considerations, the conclusion cannot be other than that the question of whether there should be EU legislation on liability for damage to the environment or not and what content such legislation should have, is a political one, not a legal one of subsidiarity.[75]

Another good example is the discussion on binding EU energy efficiency targets: Member States oppose such binding targets, arguing that under the principle of subsidiarity, questions on energy efficiency are of their competence. Others argue that in order to ensure efficient measures in all 28 Member States which contribute to the fight against climate change, EU action is necessary. The outcome of this discussion was finally determined by political, not legal considerations.[76]

1–27   There are many other examples of the ambiguous nature of the subsidiarity principle: why should, under subsidiarity auspices, the Union be competent to ban the import of furs from third countries which do not prohibit leg-hold traps[77] but not be competent to stop bullfighting, foxhunting or cockfighting? Why should there be common measures on smog in urban zones,[78] but not on the quality of bathing water in public swimming pools?

It is submitted that at the end of almost any discussion on a specific topic, the lawyer is placed in a position behind the policy-maker, who has to weigh political, economic, social, cultural, legal and environmental aspects as best he can: his decision usually remains a political decision.

---

[75] See Dir.2004/35 on environmental liability with regard to the prevention and remedying of environmental damage (2004) OJ L143/56.

[76] In 2009, EU-wide binding measures were rejected by the Council. In 2012, the European Parliament and the Council adopted Dir.2012/27 on energy efficiency [2012] OJ L315/1.

[77] See Reg.3254/91 (1991) OJ L308/1.

[78] See Dir.2008/50 (2008) OJ L152/1.

(c) Integration

The present art.11 TFEU[79] had antecedents in the environmental chapter of the EC Treaty: the 1987 version of art.174 contained a clause on integration,[80] which was formulated in such a way that it could, using the Court of Justice's doctrine of direct effect, be applied directly. The clause was considered both too precise and too vague and was therefore replaced by a phrase that was similar to the one used now in art.11 TFEU.[81] As it was felt that some other Union policies did not sufficiently integrate environmental considerations into their policies and measures, the discussion prior to the Amsterdam Treaty on European Union focused on the request to incorporate into the chapters on agriculture, transport, competition and so on, a reference to environmental considerations. This was objected to by the sectors concerned as being too precise and thus led to the removal and slight reformulation of the provision to the present art.11 TFEU.[82]

1–28

The provision states that environmental considerations must be fully taken into account in the elaboration and implementation of other Union policies. It is based on the concept that environmental requirements and, subsequently, environmental policy cannot be seen as an isolated green policy which groups specific actions on the protection of water, air, soil, fauna and flora. Rather, the environment is affected by other policies such as on transport, energy and agriculture, for example. Article 11 TFEU therefore calls for a permanent, continuous "greening" of all Union policies. As mentioned above, though, art.11 TFEU does not allow priority to be given to environmental requirements over other requirements; rather, the different objectives of the Treaties rank at the same level and the policy must endeavour to achieve all of them; this is also the meaning of art.7 TFEU.

"Union policies and activities" referred to are the different policies listed in arts 3 and 4 TFEU. They include all activities of the Union under the FEU Treaty. Policies under the EURATOM Treaty are not included, as the EURATOM Treaty, essentially a Treaty to promote the use of nuclear energy, is not mentioned in art.11 TFEU. In my opinion the Union has spent, from the beginning, too much EU money on nuclear energy compared with expenses for renewable energy; art.11 TFEU would allow a reversal of this policy, if the political will existed to promote renewable energies. Again, this is a question of policy, not of law: there is no legal obligation to invest increased sums into the promotion of renewable energies.

"Environmental protection requirements" are first of all the different objectives laid down in arts 3 TEU and 191(1) TFEU. Thus, the objectives of ensuring a sustainable development, of preserving, protecting and improving the quality of the environment shall also have to be considered within the framework of other policies. The principles laid down in art.191(2.2) TFEU also form part of

1–29

---

[79] See fn.37, above.

[80] EC (1987 version) art.130r(2.2): "Environmental protection requirements shall be a component of the Community's other policies."

[81] EC (1993 version) art.130r(2.3): "Environmental protection requirements must be integrated into the definition and implementation of other Community policies."

[82] See also arts 167 (culture), 168 (public health) and 169(2) (consumer protection) of the TFEU, which also contain a requirement of integration; however, these policies are not mentioned in art.11 of the TFEU.

environmental protection requirements. Indeed, it does not make sense to apply the precautionary principle, under the environmental policy, and take action without the last scientific evidence of a substance's harmfulness, and then take the opposite approach in the context of the internal market policy. The Court of Justice reached the same conclusion when applying the principle of preventive action of art.191(2) TFEU to the BSE ("mad cow disease") case, which had no relationship whatsoever with environmental protection issues.[83]

In the same way, it would be contradictory to provide for preventive measures in environmental policy, but not to do so in other policies, thus limiting EU action to remedial measures which try to repair the environmental damage. Indeed, the greatest damage to the environment is caused by transport, agriculture, energy, industrial development and other policies, not by measures taken within the framework of environmental policy.

The whole debate on how to classify a specific Union measure is rather futile: whether the protection of waters from nitrates of an agricultural source is a measure of agricultural or environmental policy should not have any influence on the principles which are to be taken into consideration. The same applies to a ban on asbestos fibres, the use of phthalates, pollution-abatement measures for cars, fuels or industrial installations. It seems rather old-fashioned to classify a specific measure as belonging to a specific policy: art.11 TFEU contributes to progressively overcoming this artificiality. Therefore, its interpretation is wide: wherever a measure is taken under the FEU Treaty, full consideration must be given to protecting the environment. This wide interpretation should not let us forget that environmental requirements should be taken into consideration at the formulation and implementation of policies, not of individual measures: it is true, however, that a specific policy is made operational by individual measures. It is therefore doubtful whether each individual measure in the internal market, agriculture or transport policy must take into consideration the environmental requirements which appears too far-reaching. In any case, EU institutions have a very broad discretion in putting the principle of art.11 TFEU into practice. Since art.11, in contrast to its 1987 version, no longer states a fact but rather propounds the necessity of procedure for EU policy, its application in practice will depend almost entirely on the political will of EU institutions to make this provision operational. Again, only in extreme cases could it be argued that EU policies do not take into account environmental protection requirements in their definition and implementation. Normally, the wide discretion which is available under art.11 TFEU would not make such an action successful.

1–30   To give some examples: to what extent transport policy promotes a European network of high-speed trains is a question, for or against which a number of environmental and other arguments can be raised. The promotion of biomass for

---

[83] *R v Minister of Agriculture* (C-157/96) [1998] E.C.R. I-2211 at [63]–[64]; *United Kingdom v Commission* (C-180/96) [1998] E.C.R. I-2265 at [99]–[100]: "Where there is uncertainty as to the existence or extent of risks to human health, the institutions may take protective measures without having to wait until the reality and seriousness of those risks become fully apparent. That approach is borne out by art.130 r(1) of the EC Treaty, according to which Community policy on the environment is to pursue the objective, inter alia, of protecting human health. Article 130r(2) provides that that policy is to be based in particular on the principles that preventive action should be taken and that environmental protection requirements must be integrated into the definition and implementation of other Community policies."

fuel by agricultural policy would save fossil fuels, but would at the same time promote monocultures, large-scale use of pesticides and reduce biodiversity. Other examples are provisions to ban aeroplane flights at night, the decommissioning of used platforms at sea, development of an electrical windpark in or next to a natural habitat, the requirement for an environment impact assessment in all cases where a project is co-financed with EU funds, and so on. The question to what extent such measures are to be taken is in all these cases of a political, not a legal nature. The integration requirement of art.11 TFEU does not provide for a useful solution to these problems.

Until now, the Court of Justice never discussed the question, whether an EU Act would have to be annulled, because it did not take into consideration environmental requirements. Some legal writers are of the opinion that such a legal Act would, as a matter of law, have to be annulled. An example is Regulation 1954/2003[84] which gave the EU fishing fleet access to the waters around the Azores, without even discussing the impact on the very vulnerable local ecosystems. The Azores brought a case to the General Court[85]; however, their application was considered inadmissible, and the appeal was rejected.[86] In my opinion, the complete lack of even considering the environmental impact of the Regulation constitutes a breach of art.11 TFEU and could lead to the annulment of the Regulation.

(d)   Precautionary principle

The precautionary principle was inserted into art.174(2) EC in 1993, while the prevention principle had already been present in the Treaty since 1987. Origin and content of the precautionary principle are unclear. Since no definition exists in the Treaties, the principle is open to broad interpretation. The Convention on the protection of the marine environment in the North-East Atlantic (OSPAR), to which the European Union adhered,[87] describes the precautionary principle as a principle:

1–31

> "by virtue of which preventive measures are taken when there are reasonable grounds for concern that substances or energy introduced directly or indirectly into the environment may bring about damage to human health, harm living resources, … even where there is no conclusive evidence of a causal relationship between the inputs and effects."

The principle was mentioned in the Declaration of the United Nations Conference in Rio de Janeiro in 1992[88] and increasingly it is understood to

---

[84] Regulation 1954/2003 [2003] OJ L289/1.

[85] General Court, *Azores v Council* (T-37/04) [2008] E.C.R. II-103.

[86] Court of Justice, *Azores v Council* (C-444/08P), ECLI:EU:C:2010:819.

[87] Decision 98/249 [1998] OJ L104/1.

[88] Rio de Janeiro Declaration on Environment and Development, 16 June 1992, Principle 15: "In order to protect the environment, the precautionary approach shall be widely applied by States according to their capabilities. Where there are threats of serious or irreversible damages, lack of full scientific certainty shall not be used as a reason for postponing cost-effective measures to prevent environmental degradation." The reference to "approach" rather than to "principle" was due to US objections to the use of the word "principle".

allow[89] the taking of measures also in cases where scientific uncertainty exists as to the cause and extent of environmental impairment. In its reviewed strategy on sustainable development of 2006—mentioned in para.1.14, above—the European Council defined the precautionary principle as follows, clearly going beyond the Rio Declaration: "In case of scientific uncertainty, use the appropriate assessment procedures and preventive measures in order to avoid damage to human health and the environment".

An example for the application of the precautionary principle is the taking of measures to ban or restrict the circulation of substances or products such as asbestos, cadmium and phthalates: under Regulation 793/93,[90] economic operators asked that for each of these products a risk assessment be made to find out whether the environmental and human risk justifies restrictions. Applying the precautionary principle would mean that EU measures can be taken without waiting for full evidence by such a risk assessment, which all too often takes several years to be elaborated, is inconclusive or is interpreted differently as to the results. Another example is climate change: the European Union adhered to the United Nations' Convention on Climate Change which undertakes to combat global warming, while the latest scientific evidence of man-made global warming—at least in the eyes of some—is still lacking.

1–32 Sometimes it is argued that the adoption of the precautionary principle requires a scientific assessment of risks.[91] This argument seems to stem more from political efforts to reduce the field of application of this principle as far as possible; indeed, art.191(2) TFEU does not contain any such condition and the above-mentioned examples show the political character of these arguments: if for precautionary measures a scientific risk assessment is necessary, it would be necessary for any measure. However, such a requirement could only be introduced by way of legislation.[92]

Similar considerations apply to other requests to limiting the application of the precautionary principle to cases where there is the possibility of an extreme, irreversible hazard, where there is a need to adopt measures urgently or to limit it to provisional measures only. None of these conditions are found in art.191(2) TFEU, which demonstrates the political rather than legal character of these arguments.

The Court of Justice applied the precautionary principle in the above-mentioned cases C-157/96 and C-180/96,[93] though the English version referred to the prevention principle only, whereas the German and other languages mentioned the precautionary *and* prevention principles. Of course, the Court did

---

[89] I would not go so far as to argue that in certain cases, the precautionary principle *obliges* public authorities to act, though theoretically such a possibility might exist. No practical case is known, where a court had judged that such an obligation existed.

[90] See in detail paras 6–25 et seq, below.

[91] See, e.g. Dir.1999/39 on baby food [1999] OJ L124/8, Recital 4: "Whereas, taking into account the Community's international obligations, in cases where the relevant scientific evidence is insufficient, the precautionary principle allows the Community to provisionally adopt measures on the basis of available pertinent information, pending an additional assessment of risk and a review of the measure within a reasonable period of time."

[92] See also Court of Justice, *Afton Chemical* (C-343/09; ECLI:EU:C:2010:419) where neither the Commission nor the Court considered a risk assessment to be necessary before the decision on the restriction of use of a chemical substance was taken.

[93] See fn.83, above.

not request that the Commission, before pronouncing an export ban for British beef, should have made a risk assessment. The General Court considered it a "general principle of Community law".[94]

In 2000 the Commission adopted a Communication on the precautionary principle where it stated[95]:

> "whether or not to invoke the precautionary principle is a decision exercised where scientific information is insufficient, inconclusive, or uncertain and where there are indications that the possible effects on the environment, or human, animal or plant health may be potentially dangerous and inconsistent with the chosen level of protection."

(e) Prevention principle

It is unclear to what extent the prevention principle has content independent from the precautionary principle, although the history of the principles' insertion into the EC Treaty suggests there is one. There seems to be no EU action which would be possible under the precautionary principle, but not under the prevention principle—and vice versa. Since both principles are, in practice, almost always used together and there is no definition for either of them in the TFEU, the added legal value of one to the other is not visible; therefore, they should be used synonymously.[96]

1–33

The precautionary/prevention principle is of overriding importance in every serious environmental policy, since it allows action to be taken at an early stage. Measures are no longer primarily meant to repair damage or impairment after it has occurred: instead, measures are to be taken earlier, to prevent impairment or damage occurring. This also makes economic sense since it is normally far more costly to clean up or remedy impairment after it has occurred—if any remedy is possible at all. Article 191(2) TFEU does not specify which form the preventive action should take: it is probably "better" to produce goods without cadmium, but once cadmium-containing products are on the market—batteries, crates, window frames, etc—should they be recycled, burnt with or without energy recovery, or landfilled? No answer can be found in the prevention/precautionary principle.

---

[94] General Court, *Artegodan a.o. v Commission* (joined cases T-74/00, T-76/00 and others) [2002] E.C.R. II-4945, n.184: "the precautionary principle can be defined as a general principle of Community law requiring the competent authorities to take appropriate measures to prevent specific potential risks to public health, safety and the environment, by giving precedence to the requirements related to the protection of those interests over economic interests. Since the Community institutions are responsible, in all their spheres of activity, for the protection of public health, safety and the environment, the precautionary principle can be regarded as an autonomous principle stemming from the abovementioned Treaty provisions. It is settled case-law that, in the field of public health, the precautionary principle implies that where there is uncertainty as to the existence or the extent of risks to human health, the institutions may take precautionary measures without having to wait until the reality and seriousness of those risks become fully apparent."

[95] Commission, Communication on the precautionary principle COM(2000) 1.

[96] See also cases C-157/96 and C-180/96 (fn.83, above) where the Court based its reasoning that in order to combat the BSE disease, full evidence of the extent and seriousness of a risk was not required in order to take action on the prevention principle, not on the precautionary principle.

(f)   Rectification of damage at source

1-34   The principle that environmental damage[97] should, as a priority, be rectified at source was inserted into the Treaty in 1987. It represents wishful thinking rather than reality. Indeed, to rectify environmental damage from cars—air pollution, land use, noise, traffic congestion, waste generation, etc—at source would mean that cars would have to be abolished or at the very least absolute priority be given to public transport, the price of fuel be increased in order to reduce the use of cars, restrictions on the making of cars—maximum fuel consumption, maximum speed and so on—be imposed or other measures taken. This would have implications on production, employment and investments for which no country in the world seems to be prepared. The present technology of catalytic converters for cars is clearly an end-of-the-pipe technology, but it is not seriously challenged. Similar examples could easily be given for measures regarding climate change, waste generation, forest decline, acidification or marine pollution.

It is not clear what "rectified" means. Certainly, as in all other cases, EU institutions have a large discretion as to what measures they wish to take, and the time-span and content of these measures. Since environmental damage (impairment) often cannot really be completely rectified, it must be up to the legislature to decide how the damage, once it has occurred, can be minimised, how the environment can be restored—at the same or at a different place—and further damage be prevented.

As mentioned above at para.1–21, above, the Court of Justice has justified a regional import ban for waste amongst other arguments with this principle, which leads, in the Court's opinion, to the necessity of disposing of waste as close to the place of waste generation as possible. In a similar case, the Court of Justice declared a German provision which required that the disposal of waste take place in Germany to be compatible with the Treaty since it:

> "reflects the pursuit of an objective which is in conformity with the principle laid down in Article 130r(2) of the Treaty that environmental damage should, as a principle, be rectified at source."[98]

1-35   As stated, the judgment in the first case seems more motivated by considerations about the division of responsibilities between the European Union and Member States. It seems impossible to deduce a legal rule that "waste shall be disposed at the closest possible place" from the principle that is discussed here. Legal literature discusses whether the principle of rectifying damage at source does not lead the European Union to be required, in future, to adopt, as a priority, emission limit values rather than adopt or favour quality standards.[99]

---

[97] About half of the linguistic versions of the Treaty use the word "damage", the other half "impairment".

[98] *Commission v Germany* (C-422/92) [1995] E.C.R. I-1097; the judgment referred to a time when EU secondary law did not yet contain a provision which dealt with the export or import of wastes for disposal. The judgment therefore dealt only with primary law. The relevant EU provisions were introduced in 1993.

[99] H. Sevenster, *Milieubeleid en Gemeenschapsrecht* (Deventer, 1992), p.111; Jans-Vedder, *European Environmental Law*, 4th edn (Groningen, 2012), p.48.

EU practice, though, certainly prefers quality standards for air and water pollution.[100] This tendency has been more pronounced since 1991–1992, when the EU debate on deregulation, subsidiarity and flexibility started.

Using the same reasoning as in the two waste judgments mentioned above, the Court of Justice could, in theory, state that the principle of rectification at source requires EU legislation to be based mainly on emission standards. Also, the Court could come to the conclusion that the catalytic converter approach, which EU law had adopted to minimise car emissions, was not compatible with this principle and that cars and fuels had to be developed which generate fewer pollutants. These examples demonstrate how far the reasoning could go if the principles of art.191(2) TFEU are turned into legal rules—even leaving aside the point that at best they only constitute legal rules for EU, not for national or regional, provisions.

The conclusion is that this principle well *allows* that EU provisions are established which deal with import or export bans on waste, but it does not *require* the elaboration of such provisions. The principle allows EU emission limit values to be preferred over quality standards, but it does not require that such an approach be taken: a ban on waste exports to developing countries[101] may be supported by this principle, but the principle does not impose such a ban to be pronounced. No Member State could bring the Council before the European Court, if the Council were adopting other measures; and it may be added that no Member State would have been entitled, in the absence of a Council measure on the export ban, to pronounce such an export ban unilaterally.

(g) Polluter-pays principle

This principle was introduced into the Treaty in 1987, though it has existed at EU level since 1973.[102] Its linguistic versions are quite different: while the English version states "the polluter should pay", there are several versions which affirm "the polluter pays" and the German text talks of the principle of causation. As all versions are of equal value and the principle, as any other notion of EU law, must be interpreted autonomously by virtue of EU law and without recourse to national interpretations,[103] its content is difficult to determine: who is a polluter? A person who contaminates the environment or a person who exceeds existing limit values? Is a car driver a polluter, the car manufacturer or the producer or importer of the fuel? Furthermore, who is to pay (or should pay) for emissions or the damage that was caused? What about damage in another Member State or in a third country? Should car manufacturers or drivers also pay for the construction of roads? How much should be paid? Is an investment in cleaner technologies also a payment?

The questions demonstrate that the polluter-pays principle is first of all an economic principle and has to be understood as expressing the concept that the cost of environmental impairment, damage and clean-up should not be borne via taxes by society, but that the person who caused the pollution should bear those

1–36

1–37

---

[100] See paras 7–01 and 8–01, below.

[101] Example given by P. Pagh, *E.U.-Miljoeret*, 2nd edn (Copenhagen, 1996), p.81.

[102] See Rec.75/436 (fn.17, above).

[103] See *Kraaijeveld* (C-72/95) [1996] E.C.R. I-5403.

costs. Its transfer to the EU Treaties has led to all sorts of anomalies which have not much to do with law. First, hardly any Union text contains provisions on who shall pay for what or any other provision which puts the polluter-pays principle into practice: if the principle were legally binding and enforceable, this would be a systematic omission that could hardly be tolerated; however, no one has as yet invoked that principle and claimed damages.

Secondly, if the polluter and not the taxpayer had to pay for pollution, subventions and state aids would not be in line with this principle and would have to be deleted. However, EU measures have from the very beginning accepted that undertakings and other economic operators may receive state aid and have set up general rules for such aid.[104] The same applies to EU environmental aid, which is given to Member States under the Structural Funds, the Cohesion Fund, LIFE+ and other budgetary titles. If the polluter-pays principle were a legally binding principle, the Cohesion Fund would certainly be partly incompatible with it since it also finances clean-up measures. However, no legal writer has ever claimed any enforcement of the polluter-pays principle with regard to state aids.

1–38   In reality, in all Member States and at EU level the clean-up of the environment is seen as a task for public authorities which exists independently from the question of whether a polluter can be identified and asked to pay for pollution. Such an identification is practically impossible in cases of groundwater or coastal water pollution, forest decline, soil erosion, desertification, climate change, smog in urban areas and numerous pollution from past activities. Public authorities are thus the only ones to ensure a clean-up or to take other remedial or preventive measures to stop continued contamination.

A rather sad illustration on the application of the polluter-pays principles is found in Directive 2004/35 on environmental liability.[105] The Commission proposal had suggested that in the case, where the polluter of environmental damage could not be identified or was unable to pay, the Member States should be obliged to restore the impaired environment. The final version of the Directive, invoking the polluter-pays principle, provides that in such cases no obligation exists to restore the environment. Thus, it is to be expected that, in such cases, the environment is normally not restored, and the high number of contaminated sites within the EU demonstrates that this is part of a deliberate policy.

The Court of Justice referred to the polluter-pays principle in particular in cases on waste law, where provisions in EU directives declared the principle to be applicable. The Court used the principle to concretise the responsibility of persons beyond the wording of the legislation, though its findings appear reasonable.[106] In case C-534/13, the Court rejected the possibility of relying on the polluter-pays-principle of art.191 TFEU in order to take measures at national level against the owner of land that had been contaminated by a previous owner.[107] The Court declared that art.191(2) TFEU only laid down the general environmental objectives for EU policy. Without secondary legislation which put

---

[104] See Rec.75/436 (fn.17, above).

[105] See Dir.2004/35 (fn.75, above).

[106] Court of Justice, *Van de Walle a.o.* (C-1/03) [2004] E.C.R. I-7613; *Commune de Mesquer* (C-188/07) [2008] E.C.R I-4501; *Futura* (C-254/08) [2009] E.C.R. I-6995; *Pontina Ambiente* (C-172/08) [2010] E.C.R. I-1175.

[107] Court of Justice, *Fipa Group* (C-534/13) ECLI:EU:C:2015:140.

the principles into concrete application, the polluter-pays-principle could neither be relied on by individuals nor by national public authorities. This judgment confirms the understanding which was defended in paras 1–20 to 1–21, above.

On the whole, the polluter-pays principle *allows* EU institutions to adopt measures which charge persons who cause environmental pollution to bear the cost of pollution; however, this possibility would also be available to EU institutions without the principle being inserted in art.191(1) TFEU: in its 2006 strategy for sustainable development, mentioned in para.1–14, above, the European Council interpreted the polluter-pays principle as follows: 1–39

> "Prices shall reflect the true societal costs of consumption and production and polluters should pay for the damage which they caused to human health and the environment."

This, indeed, is far away from a legally binding principle.

6. CONDITIONS FOR ACTION

(a) General remarks

Article 191(3) TFEU lists a number of conditions which EU environmental policy should take into account. This obligation refers to the policy as a whole, not to each individual measure adopted at EU level. The provision addresses all EU institutions and bodies. The words "taken into account" indicate that the paragraph does not contain preconditions for EU actions, which is further clarified by the fact that no details are given as to which condition is to be attained, which level of regional development requires action (or derogations) nor what data would be needed for action. No other sector of EU policy has such conditions laid down in the Treaty. 1–40

In EU practice, the four conditions only play a subordinate role. They are rarely mentioned in the recitals of legal texts; references to them are slightly more frequent in explanatory memorandums for legislative proposals. Their legal impact is hardly measurable except for the cost-benefit condition, which is used by economic operators to object to measures that would internalise the environmental costs or make the polluter pay.

(b) Available scientific data

This criterion states the obvious: it only requires that account be taken of the available data. The European Union need not even order its own studies before shaping its policy or take individual measures, but may simply draw on the available data. Nor is there any need to give scientific evidence that a specific measure would be effective, which is not really possible in any case. In particular, the precautionary/prevention principle allows action without definite scientific proof being available. This principle would lose much of its force if unequivocal data had to be produced before any measure could be taken. In order to improve information on the environment, a European Environment Agency was set up in 1–41

Copenhagen[108] which has been operational since the end of 1993. The Agency has the task to collect, process and distribute data on the environment in order to improve knowledge of scientific and technical data.

It also has the task of publishing a report, at regular intervals, on the state of the EU environment.[109]

(c) Regional conditions

1–42   The provision that the environmental conditions in the various regions of the Union be taken into account is a reminder that the environment within the European Union is by no means uniform, but that geographical, climatic, soil, water and other conditions vary greatly from one area to another. The provision does not require the taking into account of divergence: for this reason some EU legislation contains specific derogations whilst other legislation does not. Where derogations are given, they are never directly applied to a specific region (though sometimes to small islands, mountainous areas or outermost regions) but instead to a specific Member State,[110] which well reflects the small direct influence that regions have in the decision-making procedure. Instead of giving a direct derogation for a Member State, EU legislation may provide for indirect derogations, e.g. for less sensitive or mountainous areas or small islands;[111] another form is to formulate a derogation which in practice only applies to one Member State, in general terms, without naming that state.[112]

(d) Potential benefits and charges

1–43   This condition reads "advantages and charges of action or lack of action" in most EU languages but not in English, because it was thought, in 1987 when the provision was inserted, that "costs and benefits" were equivalent to "advantages and charges". This is obviously not the case, at least not in the political debate, where discussion on the advantages and disadvantages of EU environmental measures has been reduced, de facto, to the economic costs and benefits of an EU

---

[108] Regulation 1210/90 on the establishment of the European Environment Agency and the European Environment Information and Observation Network [1990] OJ L120/1.

[109] To date, the Union has published nine reports on the state of the environment: State of the environment, First Report (Brussels, Luxembourg, 1977); State of the environment, Second Report (Brussels and Luxembourg, 1979); The state of the environment in the EEC (Luxembourg, 1986); The state of the environment in the European Community, COM(92) 23, Vol.III of 3 April 1992; European Environment Agency: Environment in the European Union (Copenhagen, 1995); European Environment Agency: Environment in the European Union at the turn of the century (Luxembourg, 1999); European Environment Agency: The European Environment. State and outlook 2005 (Copenhagen, 2005); European Environment Agency: The European Environment. State and outlook 2010 (Copenhagen, 2010); The European Environment: State and Outlook 2015 (Copenhagen 2015).

[110] Examples: Dir.88/609 on large combustion plants (1988) OJ L336/1 where Spain, Portugal and Greece obtained special derogations; see also para.8–29, below; Dir.94/62 on packaging and packaging waste [1994] OJ L365/10 where Greece, Portugal and Ireland obtained derogations; on this Directive, see also para.10–46, below.

[111] See, e.g. Dir.1999/31 on landfills (1999) OJ L182/1 which provides in art.3(4) for derogations for small islands and isolated settlements.

[112] See, e.g. Dir.2008/98 on waste (2008) OJ L312/3, which contains in art.16(1) a derogation for Czech waste incinerators, and in art.21(3) a derogation for the handling of waste oils in Italy—without naming these two states.

measure for economic operators. Also since economists have, up until now, not yet developed a standardised method of how to calculate in monetary terms the environmental benefits of a measure, this debate is all too often reduced to the question of how much the envisaged measure will cost trade and industry. This development has been particularly evident in EU activity since the early 1990s and more specifically in the measures to combat air pollution in the transport sector, where the Commission justified a number of derogations with nothing more than the argument that they were not "cost-effective". The advantages-charges factor suggests that the full range of short-, medium- and long-term measures be considered in an attempt to assess the effect of taking action or failing to do so. This consideration is not to be limited to economic aspects, but has to include social, employment, ecological, human and other aspects. At the end of this appraisal, if doubts still persist as to whether the measures will be sufficiently effective, the precautionary or prevention principle comes into play, together with the express mandate of art.191(1) TFEU that the European Union not only preserve but also improve the quality of the environment.

The provision gives no details of the ways and means of taking account of the potential charges and advantages. In this respect, the political resolutions adopted by the Council and the decisions on the EU environment action programmes under art.192(3) TFEU become of importance: where the Union institutions approved or adopted a programme or a number of actions of environmental measures, this will normally be sufficient proof that according to the best knowledge of the EU institutions the advantages of a specific measure outweigh the disadvantages.

(e) Economic and social development

The condition on the economic and social development of the Union as a whole **1–44** and the balanced development of its regions is meant to reflect the less-developed Member States' concern that environmental protection provisions should not be imposed at the expense of economic growth. This criterion is so broadly drafted that it covers practically all economic and social development. Every EU-wide rule inevitably implies a degree of standardisation and harmonisation and cannot, therefore, take account of every individual region. Similarly, the same scientific and technical data which demonstrate a need for action may not be available in every region; however, this cannot be a decisive factor in differentiating. The European Union also has the task of ensuring environmental improvement in all parts of the Union, although it is obvious that any specific measure will bring greater advantages for some regions than for others.

The Union institutions must weigh up all these factors and produce an overall assessment. At the end of the day it is up to the Council and the European Parliament to decide to what extent regional differences should lead to specific wording in the final texts adopted at EU level.

EU practice has never taken into consideration the situation of specific regions, but, as already mentioned, has from time to time given derogations to specific Member States—which, until 2004, mainly coincided with the so-called "Cohesion Fund-countries" (Greece, Spain, Portugal, Ireland) that were lagging behind economically. In the area of air pollution, a directive was adopted in 2001 on "national emission ceilings", which fixed a certain level of premitted pollution emissions per Member State.[113] As can be seen, this concept has little to do with regional differences (which could be very great between Lombardy and Calabria, Catalunya and Estremadura, Essex and Northern Ireland, Hamburg and Thüringen, etc) but more to do with a certain renationalisation of environmental policy.

---

[113] See Dir.2001/81 [2001] OJ L309/22.

CHAPTER 2

Actors, Instruments, Decision-making Procedures

1. ACTORS

EU environmental policy is conceived and elaborated by the EU institutions, with of course, considerable input from national governments and other national actors. The EU institutions contribute in differing degrees to the making of EU environmental policy; art.288 TFEU provides for the legal instruments to carry out the Union tasks in the making of EU environmental law. Hereafter, the different actors will be described, followed by the instruments for the making of environmental law and the decision-making procedure.

2–01

(a) The European Commission

The Commission has in particular the following tasks (see also art.17 TEU):

2–02

- make proposals for new environmental legislation;
- ensure that the provisions of the EU Treaties and the measures taken by the institutions pursuant thereto are applied;
- formulate opinions and recommendations; take decisions and "participate in the shaping of measures" where the Treaty so provides.

(i) Administrative structures

The Commission consists of 28 commissioners—one for each Member State—appointed for five years by the Council.[1] The provision of Article 17(5) TEU, according to which the number of Commissioners should be reduced as of 2014, did not become operational, as the European Council guaranteed Ireland a post, in order to influence an Irish referendum; as all the other states then requested the same treatment, the reduction was abandoned. The President of the Commission is appointed by the Council acting in its composition of Heads of State and Government and with approval of the European Parliament.[2]

2–03

---

[1] See art.17(5) TEU: "as from 1 November 2014, the Commission shall consist of a number of members, including its President and the High Representative of the Union for Foreign Affairs and Security policy, corresponding to two-thirds of the number of Member States, unless the European Council, acting unanimously, decides to alter this number".
[2] For details see art.17(7) TEU.

The Commission autonomously divides the general work among its members. Each ordinary member of the Commission has a private office which consists of six members who assist him in his task.

The administrative services of the Commission consist of Directorate-Generals for the different areas (e.g. transport, agriculture and information); at present there are some 30 Directorate-Generals, some of which, as for instance the Legal Service, are known as "Services". A General Secretariat organises the daily administration of the Commission and the Directorates-General. A member of the Commission may be responsible for several Directorates-General; conversely, one general directorate may, for different parts of its activity, be under the responsibility of several commissioners. Overall, there is a staff of some 32,000 officials, among whom are a number of national officials on secondment with the Commission for up to three years and persons employed on a contractual basis. The Commission works in all the official languages—at present 23 (art.55 TEU)—though in daily practice English and French dominate.

2–04 Environmental matters are mainly, but not exclusively, the responsibility of the Directorate-General for Environment (DG ENV) which, between 2014 and 2019, is placed under the responsibility of the Maltese member of the Commission, Mr Karmenu Vella. After the establishment of a new Directorate-General for climate change issues, the Directorate-General for the environment comprises about 450 officials, to which a number of persons on secondment and under contract (overall some 50) have to be added; about half of these officials have a university education. The Commission's staff policy tries to ensure that officials change their jobs every three to five years. This policy, introduced under UK influence, favours technocratic behaviour, not expert knowledge. Combined with strong incitements for striving for promotion—annual assessment, increased payment, power and prestige—this leads to officials' attitudes as " his master's voice" rather than to conceive policies, strategies, programmes and legislation which effectively protect the environment; this influence of staff policy is particularly strong for senior officials.

The 2014 budget—the overall EU budget was €135 billion—provided for environmental expenses of about €407 million, compared for example with €58 billion for agricultural policy and €33 billion for regional policy.[3] About €121 million are earmarked for biodiversity loss, some €35 million as a financial contribution to the European Environment Agency. Other activities which had appeared in earlier budgets, were transferred to other sectors; this concerns, for example, forest management, civil protection and natural disasters, marine pollution, and awareness-raising measures. However, the €407 million only cover the expenses coming under the management of Directorate-General ENV; they do not include expenses, for example, on alternative energies—it is interesting to see that the budget for energy (Chapter 32) does not provide for support for alternative energies, but €154 million for nuclear energy—clean transport, agricultural measures, research, etc. For climate measures, the budget (Chapter 34) provides for a sum of €121.5 million. In 1992, the Commission estimated the total EU expenses for the environment at €600 million per year; no new overall

---

[3] [2014] OJ L51/1. The Commission's environmental expenditures are listed p.II/357 for the environment and on p.II/1159 for climate action.

estimation has been made since, though this figure might now be higher; all depends on what is considered to be an "environmental" measure.

The structure and working methods of the Commission continue to be considerably affected by the original aim of the EC Treaty to organise a common agricultural policy, to open up national markets and to realise the four fundamental freedoms of the EU Treaties, free movement of goods, services, capital and labour. Environmental policy, which started in the early 1970s without an express legal basis in the Treaty, was considered an illegitimate child, and this perception only gradually began to disappear when, in 1987, the Single European Act "legitimised" it by inserting an environmental chapter into the Treaty; the economic crisis, which began in 2008, seems to put the environment again into a marginal position within the EU policies, in direct opposition of the demands of European citizens.

The Commission's environmental activity, orientated towards achieving the objectives laid down in arts 3 and 191(1) TFEU, may be structured for the purpose of presentation into activities initiating new measures, activities of management and monitoring activities. Legal questions of monitoring activities will be discussed in detail in Chapter 12. **2–05**

(ii) Commission initiatives

Under the FEU Treaty the Commission has the exclusive right to initiate new environmental legal measures at EU level. As in the early 1970s, when the European Union started an environmental policy, no explicit legal basis for environmental matters existed in the EC Treaty, it was considered opportune to lay down the objectives, principles and priorities of EU action in environmental action programmes. These different environmental action programmes consti- tuted, at least in the past,[4] a frame for initiatives, but never put limits on such actions. Indeed, numerous proposals for directives or regulations which were made had never been previously announced by an environmental action programme, and initiatives which the action programmes announced were not necessarily presented by the Commission.[5] The action programmes are completed by annual working programmes which the Commission publishes every year: the published version, however, only contains the most important new activities. Furthermore, each member of the Commission may have for his area of responsibility, a work programme which directs the work of the administrative services. **2–06**

Next to these general programmes, the Commission submits from time to time action programmes for specific sectors, such as groundwater and biodiversity, for example, for which the environmental Directorate-General is, as for the general environmental action programme, the file-leading department. Under the 6th

---

[4] Since 1993, art.192(3) TFEU provides that general environmental action programmes are adopted in the form of a decision by the European Parliament and the Council jointly. See Dec.1600/2002 laying down the 6th Environment Action Programme [2002] OJ L242/1.

[5] A recent example of a legislative proposal which was not announced in the 6th Environment Action Programme is the proposal for a directive on the assessment and management of floods, [2006] OJ C67/38, which later became Dir.2007/60 [2007] OJ L288/27. An example of legislation which was announced, but never proposed until now, is a directive on construction and demolition waste, 6th Environment Action Programme [2002] OJ L242/1, art.8(2)(IV).

Environment Action Programme, the European Union decided to develop thematic strategies for soil protection, urban environment and the marine environment, the use of pesticides, the use of natural resources, the recycling of waste and air pollution[6] which constitute, de facto, sectoral action programmes. These thematic strategies were to be submitted to the European Parliament and the Council and were, where appropriate, adopted under art.251 EC.[7] This provision aimed at avoiding a circumvention of art.192(3) TFEU which gives the European Parliament a co-decision right for environmental action programmes. The 7th General Environment Action Programme does not provide for any action programme for a specific sector.[8]

More general communications which the Commission submits are presented as Green Papers, White Papers, strategy papers or else are given another name, without any specific difference between these communications; normally, they do not provide for specific legislative measures. Examples of recent times concern communications on adapting to climate change,[9] on the halting the loss of biodiversity beyond 2010,[10] on a roadmap for a low-carbon economy in 2050[11] and on a roadmap to a resource-efficient Europe.[12]

2–07   As requested by art.11 TFEU, precursors of which have appeared in similar Treaty provisions since 1987, other initiatives in other areas such as agriculture, industrial or regional policy or transport shall take into consideration the environmental requirements. Initiatives—programmatic initiatives or individual measures—are prepared by the Directorate-General responsible, with generally close participation from the environmental and other interested Directorate-Generals.

The Commission decides on all drafts as a college (i.e. all Commissioners decide on the drafts). This also leads to situations where the Commission does not dare to take majority decisions—better: make proposals based on the majority of its members—for fear of appearing not united in the public opinion. Examples are initiatives on climate change (increasing the EU commitment to a 30 per cent reduction of greenhouse gas emissions until 2020) or a clear position of the safety of nuclear installations within the European Union, following the Japanese nuclear incident of March 2011. This clearly appears as lack of leadership in the eyes of the public.

In view of the shortage of staff in all its departments and the often considerable length of these (agriculture, industry, foreign trade and competition) drafts, it remains only theoretical that a proposal, which has been developed for several months or even years by the file-leading department, can still be significantly amended by other departments. The general approach, the structure and most of the detailed provisions are de facto carried in the form proposed by the file-leading department and are only in exceptional cases put into question at the political level of the Commission. The shortage of staff thus makes it

---

[6] 6th Environment Action Programme [2002] OJ L242/1.
[7] 6th Environment Action Programme [2002] OJ L242/1, art.4.
[8] Decision 1386/2013 on a General Union Action Programme to 2020 "Living well, within the limits of our planet" [2013] OJ L354/171 (7th Environment Action Programme).
[9] Commission, COM(2009) 147.
[10] Commission, COM(2011) 244.
[11] Commission, COM(2011) 112.
[12] Commission, COM(2011) 571.

extremely difficult to integrate environmental requirements into other policies on an everyday basis. Indeed, identifying the specific environmental interest in the numerous discussions and preparatory meetings for decisions inside the Commission requires time, human and financial resources and efforts, which the present Directorate-General for the environment does not have at its disposal.

In order to improve the integration of environmental requirements within its own administration, the Commission adopted internal rules in 1993,[13] which were revised in 1997 and 2002[14] and provide that all Commission proposals shall be checked for their economic, social and environmental impact; where such impact is likely, a detailed impact assessment is to be made on all three aspects, including consultations with stakeholders. No agreed method for making such assessments exists and time pressure, political requirements or ambitions, lobby influence and similar aspects limit their usefulness. The economic and social value of the environment is not easily accessible to econometric determination— what is the economic value of a butterfly species, a woodlouse or a mosquito? In practice, therefore, these Commission impact assessments are not very credible and are often used to impede or restrict environmental initiatives which are considered detrimental to economic interests.[15]

2–08

Suggestions to take initiatives for new legislative measures come from all sources. The Council and the European Parliament may, via resolutions, ask for this or that new proposal and the Council may, during the debate over or adoption of a Commission proposal, request another measure to be proposed or an existing proposal to be amended. The Commissioner responsible for the environment may wish a given new proposal to be developed or the environmental Directorate-General may take the initiative. From outside the EU institutions, the initiative for action might be suggested by Member States or it might stem from international activities such as existing or new environmental conventions, or be proposed by lobby groups, researchers, environmental organisations or have other origins. In all cases, however, the college of the Commission will have to formally decide on a text which is submitted to it by its administration before there can be any question of a Commission initiative.

The Juncker Commission (2014–2019) introduced a sort of hierarchy within the Commission. Any legislative proposal which a member of the Commission wishes to present to the college of Commissioners, must first be approved by one of the Commission's vice-presidents and, subsequently by Vice-President Timmermans. As the Juncker Commission announced that its priorities for the years to come were "jobs, growth and investment", new initiatives in the area of the environment are not likely.

Connected to these legislative initiatives is the possibility of the Commission initiating new orientations for environmental policy. Examples of the past concern soil management (2006), marine environment protection (2002), an integrated product policy (2001) or the management of resources (2006). To what extent such political initiatives are, subsequently, followed by policy re-orientations or concrete actions by the Council and/or the Member States is

2–09

---

[13] Written Question E-649/97 (Díez de Rivera) [1997] OJ C367/33.
[14] Commission, Impact Assessment, COM(2002) 276 of 5 June 2002; see also para.4–36, below.
[15] See for more details L. Krämer, "Impact Assessments and Environmental Costs in EU Legislation" [2014] *Journal for European Environmental Planning and Law* 201.

different from one topic to the other. Generally, political statements by the Commission, the Council or the European Parliament have little or no effect, unless they are, later on, followed by binding legislative proposals and their adoption. This is explained by the fact that the European Union is not a state and political interests and priorities in Member States are often too divergent to accept an integrated, joint environment policy.

(iii)   Administrative activities

2–10   The Commission's task to initiate new policies, strategies and individual measures is perceived by the Commission itself as its most important task: management activities clearly rank lower. One of the reasons for this is the express provision in art.192(4) TFEU, according to which it is the Member States which shall, as a rule, implement the measures decided at EU level. Since most of the Union's environmental legislation is adopted in the form of directives which are addressed to Member States, it is up to the Member States to transpose these directives into national law and to ensure that these provisions are complied with. However, as an autonomous, proper obligation, the Commission has the task of ensuring that EU environmental directives and regulations are properly applied.[16]

Besides this, the Commission has a number of tasks attributed to it by the different environmental directives or regulations, which concern the administering of the "Union acquis". These tasks include:

The collection of national legislation which was adopted in pursuance of the EU provisions.   Since European environmental legislation dates back to the mid-1970s and Member States' legislation is variously amended, renewed, replaced, and often adopted at a regional level, sometimes even referring to non-environmental, more general legislation, the precise knowledge about the state of environmental legislation within the European Union is at times difficult to obtain.[17] The Commission regularly mandates so-called implementation studies which examine the transposition of environmental directives by Member States. However, it refuses to disclose these studies.[18]

2–11   **The collection and comparison of national reports on the transposition and implementation of directives and the publication of European implementation reports.**   Most of European environmental directives and regulations provide for Member States to report regularly on the implementation measures adopted; the Commission is required to establish regular European reports. In view of considerable deficiencies in the national reporting and, subsequently, the Commission's reports, a directive was adopted in 1991 to streamline and improve

---

[16] See paras 12–12 et seq., below.

[17] The Commission publishes on its website the titles of national legislation which was notified as implementation measure, but not the text of the national laws. For example, Member States sent to the Commission, as national implementation measures of Dir.92/43 on natural habitats and wild fauna and flora [1992] OJ L206/7, not less than 928 pieces of national legislation.

[18] See on this General Court, *ClientEarth v Commission*(T-111/11) ECLI:EU:T:2013:482. On appeal, the Court of Justice decided, that such studies could be retained, when the Commission had started proceedings under Article 258 TFEU against a Member State, C-612/13P *ClientEarth v. Commission*, ECLI:EU:C:2015:486.

the reporting.[19] However, this Directive has not brought about the desired improvements. The national and the Commission reports normally continue to be published late or even not at all, their content is frequently incomplete and does not comply with scientific or serious administrative standards. Judgments by the Court of Justice which blamed Member States for not submitting reports[20] had no visible effect.

The collection and comparison of national clean-up or other plans for specific sectors or plants.   Several directives, for instance on air quality, or nitrate concentrations in water, provide for clean-up programmes for regions which are contaminated, where pollutant levels are exceeded or for industrial plants to adapt to new legal requirements. Other directives, such as on the protection of birds, on water or on waste management, provide for management plans.

Member States are regularly obliged to send such plans or programmes to the Commission, which shall align and occasionally also compare them in order to obtain greater coherence. The number of directives asking for planning measures is in continuous increase since the early 1990s, although planning experience in conjunction with EU environmental law matters is anything but a success story. Indeed, the Commission occasionally attacks Member States in court for not having drawn up or submitted plans or programmes. However, the Commission hardly ever evaluates the national plans, compares them, tries to promote planning according to similar criteria or gives an overall assessment of the planning instruments and in particular on their monitoring, implementation and enforcement. In this way, plans give the wrong impression that they improve the protection of the environment, whereas this is often not the case.[21]

Exchange of experience concerning problems with the application of environmental measures.   These comprise environmental directives which regularly ask Member States to plan improvements and clean-up, to promote or impose cleaner technologies and reduce pollutant emissions; examples are directives on the prevention of industrial accidents,[22] on permits for industrial installations[23] or for environmental impact assessment.[24] Discussions during meetings take place on these questions as well as on how provisions in a directive are transposed into administrative practice, and furthermore, on cooperation in

2–12

---

[19] Directive 91/692 standardising and rationalising reports on the implementation of certain directives relating to the environment [1991] OJ L377/48.

[20] See, e.g. Court of Justice, *Commission v Italy* (C-248/02) judgment of 16 September 2004; *Commission v Ireland* (C-406/03) judgment of 26 October 2004; *Commission v France* (C-191/04) judgment of 16 June 2005; *Commission v Luxembourg* (C-61/07) [2007] E.C.R. I-108; *Commission v Italy* (C-85/07) [2007] E.C.R I-194.

[21] For more details, see L. Krämer, *Casebook on EU Environmental Law* (Oxford, 2002), pp.177 and 367. More recent examples, *ClientEarth v Secretary of State for the Environment, Food and Rural Affairs* (C-404/13) ECLI:EU:C:2013:805; *Commission v Italy* (C-323/13) ECLI:EU:C:2013:2290; *Commission v Spain* (C-403/11) ECLI:EU:C:2012:612.

[22] Directive 2012/18 on the control of major-accident hazards involving dangerous substances [2012] OJ L197/1.

[23] Directive 2010/75 on industrial emissions [2010] OJ L334/17.

[24] Directive 2011/92 on the assessment of the effects of certain public and private projects on the environment [2012] OJ L26/1.

frontier regions or with administrations of another Member State. Often such exchanges between Member States' administrations are necessary or useful. They also allow a transfer of environmental know-how from one administration to the other.

Information on new scientific and technical developments. EU directives also age over time and might have to be adapted due to scientific and technical developments. Most of this exchange normally takes place in the different committees for adapting directives to scientific and technical progress.

Elaboration of implementation measures. Directives may require that the Commission deal with forms and formulae, establish lists, registers, collect data, take individual decisions on national derogating measures or other technical measures to ensure a smooth application of the legislation. On its own initiative, the Commission may find it necessary to issue guidance or interpretation documents, convey its understanding of specific legislative provisions and inform about its policy following judgments of the Court of Justice.

2–13   **Administration of funds.** The amount of EU funding for environmental measures including in sectors such as energy, transport or research, has considerably increased over the years. These amounts are monitored according to specific regulations which lay out the legal basis for expenditure.[25] The Commission has to collect the national programmes or projects, assess them, select the most appropriate applications and decide on the European Union's financial participation, assisted in this on a regular basis by a committee made up of representatives from Member States.

Exchange of data. Almost all EU decisions require that the Commission collect data on the state of the environment, such as data on air or water pollution and soil contamination. The Commission organises the networks, the cooperation required between different parties and the related practical questions. These tasks are progressively being transferred to the European Environment Agency or the European Union's Statistical Office which need, however, assistance from the Commission, certainly in the beginning, combined, if necessary, with formal, binding decisions.

Participation in international discussions. Where environmental issues are discussed at international level, the Commission, beyond participation in the elaboration of conventions, etc, coordinates and aligns the position of the Member States and tries to ensure that internationally the Union speaks with one voice.[26]

2–14   **Information of the wider public.** The Commission is not an administrative body that can remain distanced from discussions about the organisation of Europe and its environment. It has to inform about the state of the environment, its policy

---

[25] See, e.g. Reg.1293/2013 (LIFE) [2013] OJ L347/185; Reg.1300/2013 establishing a Cohesion Fund [2013] OJ L347/281.
[26] See for more details art.216 TFEU.

and its individual measures and try to persuade, publicly, in committees or in bilateral meetings, policy makers, interest groups, environmental organisations, the media and the public of its proposals and the Union's decisions. For this purpose, press releases are made, speeches delivered, articles written, interviews granted, conferences, workshops or encounters organised, and information is placed on the website. In so doing the Commission is fulfilling the objective which is outlined in art.17 TEU: to promote the general interest of the Community in environmental issues.

(iv)   The Environment Agency and other "satellites"

During the last decades a number of bodies have been set up to assist the   **2–15**
Commission in its work. The most relevant of these are:

- The European Environment Agency, which was created in 1990,[27] but only became operational in 1993 due to Member States' disagreement on its seat which was finally fixed in Copenhagen. The Agency has the task of collecting, processing and distributing information about the EU environment and publishing at regular intervals a report on the state of the environment. Its advice function is not limited to the Commission, but also extends to the other institutions and to Member States. It is headed by an executive director, who is appointed by the management board; this board is composed of Member States' representatives, two Commission representatives and two scientific experts appointed by the European Parliament. Non-EU states, which are members of the Agency, are also represented. The Agency has an annual budget of about €40 million and a staff of about 120 persons, to which a network of about 2,000 persons in member countries have to be added.

  When the Agency was created there was much debate between the European Parliament and the Council over whether it should also have the function to enforce application of EU environmental law. The compromise reached provided that this question should be decided at a later stage. The amendment of the Agency's statute, adopted in 1999, does not contain anything on law enforcement[28]; as the European Parliament has no historic memory, it forgot its former request; at present, this question is no longer discussed. The Agency has to publish, every five years, a report on the state of the environment in the European Union; this delay was shortened to four years by the Regulation 1367/2006 which transposed the Aarhus Convention into EU law.[29] Until now, the Agency ignored this amendment.

- In 1993, a European Consultative Forum on the environment and sustainable development, was set up by the Commission,[30] consisting of 32 members from business, local and regional authorities, environmental and consumer organisations, trade unions and general environmental experts.

---

[27] Regulation 1210/90 on the establishment of the European Environment Agency and the European Environment Information and Observation Network [1990] OJ L120/1.

[28] Regulation 933/1999 amending Reg.1210/90 [1999] OJ L117/1.

[29] Regulation 1367/2006 [2006] OJ L264/13, art.4(4).

[30] Decision 93/701 [1993] OJ L328/53; amended by Dec.97/150 [1997] OJ L58/48.

The Forum was consulted by the Commission on any problem of European Union environmental policy. The impact of the opinions given by the Forum was rather limited, due mainly to its heterogeneous composition. In 2001, it was closed, because the Commission wanted to establish "a sustainable round table which will report directly to the Commission's President"; this body was set up, but does not deploy any visible activity on environmental matters any more.[31] Whether it continues to exist, is unknown.

- IMPEL. The 5th Environment Action Programme 1992 announced the creation of an implementation network with the primary task of promoting the "exchange of information and experiences and the development of common approaches at practical level, under the supervision of the Commission".[32] This network was set up under the name European Network for the Implementation and Enforcement of Environmental Law (IMPEL) by Member States. The driving force was the intention to avert requests for an EU environmental enforcement body on the one hand, and to give in particular to German Länder the possibility of influencing the making of EU environmental legislation on the other. IMPEL was an informal body and acted as an inter-governmental, not an integrated, EU cooperation network. It tried to improve implementation of EU legislation and influence new Commission initiatives. In 2008, IMPEL transformed itself into an international association of environmental authorities, in order to obtain EU financing more easily. Overall, its impact is limited.

- The Environmental Policy Review Group—also an informal body. Its setting-up was announced by the 5th Action Programme.[33] It groups the Director-Generals from national central environmental administrations who meet with high officials from the Directorate-General Environment of the Commission to discuss the conception and shaping of the Commission's environmental strategies and initiatives. The Group has no secretariat of its own and its deliberations and conclusions are not made public, contrary to any transparency rules of the Commission.

The EU has no advisory body on strategic environmental questions, such as on climate change, environment in agglomerations, resource management, mobility, or the eradication of poverty.

(b) The European Parliament

2–16   The European Parliament has played a prominent role in initiating and strengthening environmental issues at EU level since the early 1970s. Its proposals and suggestions for institutional and administrative structures, for new initiatives or proposals were very often taken up by the Commission, although sometimes after some delay. One of the reasons for this is that the European Parliament also decides—along with the Council—on the Commission's budget and thus has a subtle means of pressure at its disposal.

---

[31] Decision 2001/704 [2001] OJ L258/20.
[32] 5th Environment Action Programme [1993] OJ C138/5, Ch.9.
[33] 5th Environment Action Programme [1993] OJ C138/5, Ch.9.

Parliament's opinions on proposals for directives or regulations, obviously considerably influenced by the very active Parliamentary Committee on Environment, Public Health and Food Safety, may be summarised as follows:

- On general environmental questions or on horizontal legislation, Parliament constantly urges the Commission and the Council to do more and provide for even better environmental protection than the Commission had proposed. There seems to be few Commission environmental proposals where Parliament was of the opinion that they were too ambitious, too far-reaching or too protective. Parliament generally opposed soft law, environmental agreements or recommendations, environmental deregulation and other forms or attempts to reduce environmental protection.
- Proposals of a more technical nature are only exceptionally challenged as to the approach chosen by the Commission. The amendments suggested concern the need for more and stricter environmental protection. Parliament not only looked for more progressive and efficient environmental legislation, but also pleaded for greater transparency in environmental matters, better access to information and greater participation of environmental organisations in the decision-making process.
- Parliament gradually managed to introduce environmental requirements into its opinions on proposals for legislative acts in agricultural and regional matters, the internal market or other policies and in this it was more advanced than the Commission or the Council. This aspect is, however, influenced by the majority groups in Parliament: where these groups are conservative, environmental-minded opinions are more difficult to obtain.

Parliament's influence on the development of environmental legislation has been constantly increased over the years. Article 225(2) TFEU, introduced in the EC Treaty in 1993, gave Parliament the right to require, with the majority of its component members, that the Commission submit a proposal for a directive or regulation. The Lisbon Treaties, introducing the requirement that the Commission has to explain its position, when it does not follow such a request, clarified that the Commission's monopoly of proposing legislation is not affected by art.225. Parliament very rarely recurs to art.225.

Article 192(3) TFEU provides that general environmental action programmes   **2–17**
be adopted by a joint decision of the Council and the European Parliament. Since a decision is "binding in its entirety",[34] the 7th Environment Action Programme and future programmes will be binding. During the review of the 5th and the discussions of the 6th Action Programmes, the European Parliament's objective therefore was to have concrete provisions laid down; it was the European Parliament that insisted on having the thematic strategies under the 6th Programme adopted in the form of legally binding decisions, to have them submitted by the Commission by 2005 and to have an annual progress report on them. With regard to the 7th Environmental Action Programme, Parliament did not really insist in more concrete announcements.[35]

---

[34] Article 288 TFEU.
[35] See Dec.1386/2013 [2013] OJ L354/171.

The problem with Parliament's policy is that it has no historical memory. It occurs quite often that a conflict with the Council is postponed for some years; and when the matter is discussed anew, the Parliament—normally newly composed after elections—does not defend its previous position any more. For example, the Commission did not submit annual progress reports on the environmental thematic strategies, contrary to formal commitments—and the Parliament did not insist on this.

In the past, a considerable part of the Union's legislative activity—in 2004, 2,625 measures were adopted in this way, numerous of them legislative measures—which was subject to the "comitology" procedure (adaptation of existing provisions due to technical or scientific progress) of art.202 EC, was not accessible to the European Parliament, since the procedures for the some 250 different committees (2004), established by the Council,[36] did not provide for its participation. Attempts in the 1990s to enable access of the European Parliament to the different technical committees did not prove successful and though the 1999 review of the procedure brought some improvement,[37] the overall situation remained unsatisfactory for the European Parliament.

2–18   Article 290 TFEU now tries to simplify and clarify the procedure. A delegated act must now be titled as such and may enter into force only if no objection has been expressed by the European Parliament (and the Council). It remains to be seen to what extent this new provision will in practice lead to greater Parliamentary influence on delegated or implementing decisions—these are regulated in art.291 TFEU—by the Commission.

The European Parliament does not attend meetings of the Council or of its working parties. Overall, its influence on the Council is, in the context of a specific legislative environmental act, limited mainly for two reasons: on the one hand, the Parliament had, until the coming into effect of the Amsterdam Treaty in May 1999, a mainly cooperative role and its resolutions were not binding for the Council. As since May 1999, the co-decision procedure of art.294 TFEU applies in almost all cases, the legislative influence of Parliament is progressively increasing, though it must be said that the detailed knowledge of the Parliament of a specific file is less good as that of the Council. On the other hand, the Council frequently discusses a proposal from the Commission before the European Parliament has given its opinion. These discussions rather often lead to a political consensus in Council; then only the opinion of Parliament is waited for before the Council formally adopts its common position. Since there is a tacit agreement in Council not to change a common position if at all possible, Parliament's opinions may only change Council's positions in exceptional cases or for less important aspects. This Council practice, which is not limited to the environmental sector, at the very least contradicts the spirit of the EU Treaties which is based on the idea that the opinions of Parliament, the Economic and Social Committee and the Committee of the Regions are available, when the Council discussions begin—not when they are ended.

In the conciliation procedure of art.294 which is, in environmental matters, quite frequently used, the Council's position regularly prevails over that of the Parliament. The reasons for this are in particular:

---

[36] Decision 87/373 [1987] OJ L197/33.
[37] Decision 1999/468 [1999] OJ L184/23.

1. the Council secretariat plus the number of environmental attachés from each Member State have greater facilities to liaise with each other and with the different capitals to form an opinion on a specific compromise text;
2. while the Member States have officials at their disposal who are experts of the specific file for years and know all details of the previous Council discussions, the European Parliament and its secretariat do not dispose of the same amount of expertise, as the rapporteur, his assistant(s) and almost all the other deputies normally were in contact with the subject-matter only during the two readings of the Commission proposal in Parliament;
3. Parliament's capacity to organise the necessary European know-how at short-term is smaller than that of the Council.

Generally, these reasons reflect the dominant role which public administration plays in all Member States in the legislative standard-setting for the environment.   2–19

(c) The Economic and Social Committee; Committee of the Regions

The European Economic and Social Committee (arts 301 et seq. TFEU) is   2–20
thought to represent the different non-governmental interests within the European Union, although representatives of the environment are not expressly mentioned in art.302(2) TFEU. At present (2010–2015), only three of the 353 members of this Committee indicated that they came from an environmental organisation. The Committee of the Regions (arts 305 et seq. TFEU) is composed of regional and local authorities. The Committee of the Regions may apply to the Court of justice, where it is of the opinion that an environmental measure interferes with its prerogatives (art.263(3) TFEU) or is against the principle of subsidiarity.[38]
Article 13(4) TEU provides that the Economic and Social Committee and the Committee of the Regions both advise the Council, the European Parliament and the Commission. In reality this advisory function is exercised by both Committees only after the Commission has submitted a proposal or made a communication. Nor does the Commission consult these Committees. The opinions of both Committees in environmental matters have not yet reached the point of having any significant influence on the content of EU directives or regulations.

(d) The Council

The Council, while formally one institution, meets under relatively specific   2–21
configurations (e.g. Agricultural Council, Transport Council, Social Affairs Council). In environmental matters, the Council normally meets three times under each presidency—which changes every six months—twice formally in Brussels and once informally at a place which is determined by each presidency. At the informal meetings issues of environmental policy or environmental strategy are discussed, without any decisions being made. The ministers responsible for environmental matters have Council meetings in Brussels or in

---

[38] Protocol No.2 on the application of the principle of subsidiarity and proportionality, [2008] OJ C115, p.206, art.8(2).

Luxembourg, on agenda issues drawn up by the presidency. The Council meetings are not public except where the Council decides otherwise; however, up until now such public meetings, introduced after 1993, have been exceptional and have not been dealing with essential matters. Nor does the Council organise public hearings. Position papers from lobby groups or other organisations are only rarely distributed within the Council or among Member States. Contacts with media or with representatives of vested interests are not organised by the Council, though there is a press release issued after each Council meeting: at best, meetings with the media are organised by individual Member States immediately before or after a Council meeting. Normally, however, such contact takes place at the capital of each Member State; the public is thus informed about a Member State's viewpoint in the Council or during the preparatory meetings by this Member State itself.

There is no possibility of compelling the Council to debate a proposal for a legislative act presented by the Commission. The Council, therefore, can, by not discussing a Commission proposal, let this proposal become obsolete. An example is the Commission proposal for a directive on access to justice in environmental matters.[39] The Council did not discuss the proposal, the official reasons are not known; probably, Member States are of the opinion that this matter does not come under EC competence. Also, a Commission proposal for a directive to protect the soil[40] was only very briefly discussed by the Council; again, reasons of subsidiarity were invoked, though it is known that the United Kingdom, Germany, Netherlands and France opposed the proposal.

Institutional cooperation between the Council and the Commission generally occurs as regards the organisation of work in Council working groups, since here the Commission has to explain and defend its proposals for legislation. This cooperation is, however, limited to organisational questions; if, when, and how often Commission proposals are discussed in Council and within the different Council working groups, is decided by each Council Presidency at its discretion. The Council working groups are normally composed of the environmental attachés of each Member State's Permanent Representation with the Union, as well as of a Commission official; officials from Member States—normally from the environmental department—participate at the discretion of each Member State, mainly in cases where expert advice is needed. The meetings are presided over by an official of the Member State who holds the presidency.

2–22 Institutional cooperation between the Council and other institutions, in particular the European Parliament, practically does not exist in environmental matters, though the increasing number of co-decision procedures has progressively led, during recent years, to more organisational contacts between the two institutions, in particular in view of avoiding a second reading of the Commission's proposal or even a conciliation procedure.[41]

In recent years, the Council, the European Parliament and the Commission meet more and more frequently in the so-called "Trilogue-meetings". These

---

[39] Commission, COM(2003) 624; in 2014, the Commission repealed this proposal; see also para.4–17, below.

[40] Commission, COM(2006) 232; in 2014, this proposal was repealed by the Commission.

[41] See also, as one rare example, the *modus vivendi* between the European Parliament, Council and Commission concerning the implementation measures for acts adopted in accordance with the procedure laid down in art.251 EC [1995] OJ C293/1.

meetings have the objective of avoiding a first or a second reading of a Commission legislative proposal in Parliament, or avoiding a conciliation procedure. The meetings are not public and very little information is made available on the content of the discussions. They contradict the principle of open, transparent discussions on legislation, and, more concretely, the provisions of art. 294 TFEU—which is not at the disposal of the EU institutions.

(e) The European Courts (Court of Justice and General Court)

No detailed description needs to be given of the role of the European Courts in ensuring that "the law is observed" in the interpretation and application of the environmental Treaty provisions and secondary legislation (art.19 TEU). The Courts have frequently tried to interpret existing legislation in a way which is favourable to the environment and to formalise the concept of environmental law which has often been rather general and vague; generally, the Court of Justice is more open to environmental concerns than the General Court. Of course, there have been judgments which have been influenced by political considerations.[42] However, it is usual, also within the EU Member States, that judgments from a supreme court will also include policy considerations and are not given in a policy free environment.

2–23

The division of work between the Court of Justice and the General Court is decided by the Treaty (art.256 TFEU). At present, the General Court decides in particular on all applications from individual persons (art.263(4) TFEU), and in competition matters.

For a number of reasons the Commission does not automatically bring cases concerning a breach of EU law before the Court of Justice. The Court has repeatedly stated that the Commission has, under art.258 TFEU, a discretion as to whether it wishes to bring an action or not.[43] This may well be, but in any case the clear wording of art.258 indicates that the Commission has no such discretion on the question over whether it begins infringement procedures or not against a Member State. Since, however, the Court of Justice has furthermore stated that the Commission cannot be obliged to begin procedures under that article,[44] the Commission's attitude of not beginning procedures under art.258, and thus not bringing them before the Court of Justice either, remains unchallenged. In my opinion, the Court has, by this jurisdiction, created an area where public power is exercised without being controlled by the judiciary, which is to be regretted.

In matters of standing of individuals and NGOs in environmental matters (art.263 TFEU), the Court adopts an extremely restrictive interpretation of art.263; it only grants access when a person or NGO is directly and individually concerned by an EU measure; as the protection of the environment is a general, not an individual interest, this had the consequence that no environmental NGO

2–24

---

[42] This seems to be the case, for instance, with *Commission v France* (C-252/85) [1988] E.C.R. 2243 on traditional hunting; *Commission v Denmark* (C-302/86) [1988] E.C.R. 4607 on a deposit and return system for bottles; *Commission v Belgium* (C-2/90) [1992] E.C.R. I-4431 on import bans for waste; *Commission v Council* (C-155/91) [1993] E.C.R. I-939 on the legal basis for waste legislation.
[43] *Commission v United Kingdom* (416/85) [1988] E.C.R. 3127; *Commission v Denmark* (C-234/91) [1993] E.C.R. I-6273.
[44] *Star Fruit Co v Commission* (C-247/87) [1989] E.C.R. 291; *Emrich v Commission* (C-371/89) [1990] E.C.R. I-1555.

ever had access to the ECJ. Article 9(3) of the Aarhus Convention, which was ratified by the EU, did not make the Court change its position: while it stated that the national judge shall do everything which is possible in order to make art.9 of the Convention have its full effect,[45] it refuses to assume the same obligation for itself.[46]

One essential difference between the judgments given by the Court of Justice and judgments given by a national supreme court is that the Court of Justice's judgment is given in an area in which different legal cultures exist. Thus, for example, a judgment which states that one Member State has breached EU law because it has not submitted clean-up plans, not reported on the implementation of a specific directive or not ensured that the quality of drinking water complies with the requirements of the Union's law, is normally not accepted by the administration of all other Member States as obliging them to make sure that the same omission does not occur under their responsibility; and the national courts do often not either take the Court jurisdiction into account in their daily judgments. In fact, Member States do not really pay too much attention to an environmental judgment that was given against another Member State, at least where this would involve obligations for them. Implementation, application, monitoring and enforcement of EU environmental legislation is thus very different in the different legal cultures.

(f) Non-institutional actors

(i) Professional organisations

2–25   The representation of vested interests at Union level is probably even greater than in most capitals of Member States, though the integration of European organisations is normally considerably looser than that of the national member organisations. The number of representatives in Brussels is estimated at 15,000. Economic operators and their professional organisations discovered the common market, globalisation effects and the advantages of economies of scale a long time ago and are also well aware that European Union trade needs EU legal provisions. Their influence on the shaping of European environmental law is considerable, although only with difficulty is it capable of being demonstrated. This influence is not so much exercised by legal papers which argue this or that rule, but rather by influencing the strategic thinking inside the Commission administration. I estimate that even with Directorate-General ENV, out of the 100 contacts or interlocutors which the Directorate-General has outside the national administrations, more than 90 represent vested interests. Such exchange of views is bound to have some long-term repercussions. The influence of vested interest groups appears to have increased in recent years, due to the economic crisis in Europe and the stronger orientation of the EU policy towards economic growth.

---

[45] Court of Justice, *Lesoochranárske zoskupenie* (C-240/09) [2011] E.C.R I-1255.
[46] Court of Justice, *Council and European Parliament v Milieudefensie a.o* (C-401/12P) ECLI:EU:C:2012. See also Ch.1, fn.28, above.

A number of years ago, the European Parliament and the Commission set up a Transparency Register, where lobby-groups are registered.[47] Registration is voluntary. Registered persons or groups are requested to give some information on their finances and their activity and respect a code of conduct for lobbyists.[48] In 2015, 7,649 organisations were registered.

Examples where vested interests seem to have significantly influenced the EU policy of environmental law are, in my opinion: the abandoning of integrated emission limit values for industries or sectors of industries[49]; the abandoning, as a rule, of setting emission values from point sources at European level[50]; the omission to establish provisions for environmental taxes and charges at European level; the 15-year delay in fixing limit values for CO_2 emissions from cars[51]; the omission to formalise, in some binding form, the polluter-pays principle; active participation in industrial standardisation; the omission to heavily promote alternative energies and the strong financial support for a nuclear energy policy; the omission to fix air quality standards for heavy metals.

(ii)   Environmental organisations

European environmental organisations suffer from a chronic shortage in manpower and financial resources which seriously affects their organisational structures. There is no overall European umbrella organisation which contains all environmental associations. In the mid-1990s, environmental organisations formed a loose cooperation group, Green 10, to pool their forces. Members are: BirdLife International (European Office); Bankwatch Network; Climate Action Network Europe; European Environmental Bureau; European Federation for Transport and Environment; European Public Health Alliance; Friends of the Earth Europe; Greenpeace Europe; International Friends of Nature and World Wildlife Fund (WWF) European Policy Office.

2–26

The "Green 10" organisations frequently divide work priorities among themselves, according to their political preferences. With the exception of Greenpeace they all obtain financial support from the Commission, which is made possible under Regulation 1293/2013.[52] A specific financial amount for the support is not fixed. The attributions to environmental organisations are decided yearly, on the basis of work programmes. It cannot be excluded that the financial support from the Commission also influences the organisation's actions and positions.

One might wonder whether it is not time for environmental organisations to pool their limited personal and financial resources and form an EU Institute for environmental organisations or a similar body. Their current diversity is also an

---

[47] At present Agreement between the European Parliament and the European Commission on the transparency register for organisations and self-employed individuals engaged in EU policy-making and policy implementation [2014] OJ L277/11.

[48] [2014] OJ L277/11, annex III.

[49] See paras 4–46 et seq., below.

[50] See paras 4–40 et seq., below.

[51] See paras 8–15 et seq., below.

[52] Regulation 1293/2013 [2013] OJ L347/185. The financial support through LIFE replaced an earlier decision which had provided for specific support of environmental organisations, Dec.466/2002 [2002] OJ L75/1.

obstacle to the professionalisation. For example, an association such as the European Environmental Bureau, the umbrella environmental organisation of some 140 national organisations, has a permanent staff of some ten people in Brussels, but is thought to cover all facets of EU environmental policy and law. Other organisations are even smaller. The organisations mainly work to influence the opinions of the European Parliament and the public. Overall, the contribution of environmental organisations to EU environmental law is limited. Their best ally is public opinion, and where they do manage to highlight an issue in the public awareness and find access to the media, they may considerably influence EU environmental policy and the content of some measures. Also, in the cases of catastrophies, such as the mad cow disease, accidents—the *Prestige* tanker accident 2002 or the *Aznalcollar* (Spain) accident 1998—or scandals such as the *Brent Spar* platform incident 1995, contaminated food, PVC in toys or others, their ability to influence public opinion definitely influences the EU legislature.

(iii) Individuals

2–27 The environmental provisions of the EU Treaties do not mention individual persons and, as mentioned, are not set out in such a way that they could be, under the Court of Justice's doctrine of direct effect, interpreted so that individual persons could invoke them in disputes with administrations or courts. The European Court made a major effort in increasing the position of individual persons, by declaring, in a landmark decision of 1990, that environmental measures which also aimed at the protection of human health, were to be interpreted in a way that would allow individuals to invoke these rights before the courts.[53] But neither the Commission nor environmental organisations or individual persons have ever pushed this line of thinking further, e.g. by making proposals for introducing a right of action for individuals or their associations against environmental impairment (Commission), or by trying, via an established number of test cases in court, to explore the content and the limits of environmental rights for individuals (environmental organisations) or by trying to bring into action a "right to a clean environment" which is so often referred to by politicians.[54]

EU institutions, and in particular the Commission, start from the premise that the protection of the environment is the task of the public administration—as if the (European Union) administration were the owner of the environment; since the EU administration knows best what is desirable to preserve, protect or improve the quality of the environment, an individual person is, under this concept, rather perceived as a nuisance. This basic concept is the reason why access to environmental information at European level is so much less organised than access to environmental information at national level,[55] why there are no systematic hearings organised for the preparation of environmental legislation in

---

[53] *Commission v Germany* (C-361/88) [1991] E.C.R. I-2567; *Janecek* (C-237/07) [2008] E.C.R. I-6221.

[54] See paras 4–01 et seq., below.

[55] See, on the one hand, Dir.90/313 [1990] OJ L158/56 and Dir.2003/4 [2003] OJ L41/26, on the other hand Reg.1049/2001 on access to documents held by EC institutions [2001] OJ L145/43.

order to overcome the structural imbalance between professional and environmental organisations and why environmental organisations and individuals are simply not given the possibility to contribute to the enforcement of EU environmental provisions. The European Union does not wish to see the basic difference between an environmental action by a professional organisation and by an environmental organisation: an environmental organisation tries to promote the general interest to protect the environment, whereas a professional organisation usually has in mind specific, vested interests, not the general interest.

The Lisbon Treaties introduced, in 2009, a right of citizens' initiative:[56] 1 million citizens which come from at least seven different Member States, may invite the Commission to submit a legislative proposal to the other institutions. By the end of 2014, some 50 such initiatives were started. About 40 per cent of them were held inadmissible by the Commission, because their subject-matter did not come under EU competence. Only three initiatives obtained more than 1 million signatures, but did not cause the Commission to initiate legislation. In view of the bureaucratic system which was put in place and the numerous financial, linguistic and administrative barriers which were erected,[57] the efficiency of the whole system is questionable.

It is the European Commission's omission that it does not try to mobilise private individuals who wish to ensure a better protection of the environment, by making people participate in environmental law-making and implementing. The EU citizenship, introduced by arts 20 et seq. TFEU, is lacking a concrete follow-up in the environmental sector, where individual persons remain receivers of EU environmental law and policy, rather than being given the status of instigators and participants.[58]

    2–28

2. INSTRUMENTS

(a) Legal and political instruments

(i) General remarks

The following presentation of instruments is limited to the FEU Treaty; the terminology of the EURATOM Treaty corresponds to it—except, of course, the numbers of the articles. The CECA Treaty expired in July 2002 and no longer exists.

    2–29

In environmental matters, a number of instruments were developed which are not detailed in the central provision of art.288 TFEU. The main reason for this evolution is the absence of an express chapter in the EC Treaty on environmental policy prior to 1987.

Regulations and directives can only be adopted by the European Parliament and the Council jointly, by the Council alone or by the Commission. The

---

[56] See art.11(4) TEU.
[57] See Reg.211/2011 on the citizens' initiative [2011] OJ L65/1.
[58] As regards participation in decision-making, see paras 4–09 et seq., below.

Commission has the monopoly of initiating legislative measures in all such cases: environmental regulations and directives may only be adopted on proposal by the Commission.

2–30   The possibility to have directives and regulations adopted jointly by the European Parliament and the Council has only existed since 1993. As regards the environment, arts 192(1) for environmental measures, 114 for measures which have significance for the internal market and 192(3) TFEU, for the adoption of environmental action programmes, provide for this joint adoption. In a number of cases the Council alone adopts environment-related regulations and directives, in particular under arts 192(2), 43(3), 113 and 207(3) TFEU. A qualified majority by the Council requires the agreement of 55 per cent of the Member States which represent at least 15 Member States and comprise at least 65 per cent of the population of the Union.[59] It is important to underline that the Council can only amend a Commission proposal unanimously (art.293 TFEU).

The Commission can adopt regulations or directives only where it has expressly been authorised to do so by the Treaty or by secondary EU law (arts 290 and 291 TFEU). The delegation to adopt acts (art.290 TFEU) is specific to each legislative act. The Commission may act according to the delegation, without being assisted by a committee—though existing committees set up under earlier legislative acts are maintained. However, the Parliament and the Council may object to a specific measure with the argument that it is *ultra vires*; in that case, the measure does not enter into effect.[60]

Where implementation powers are given to the Commission (art.291 TFEU), the Commission is assisted by a committee, composed of representatives of Member States and chaired by the Commission. The Commission shall submit a draft implementing act to the Committee. Where the Committee gives a negative opinion, the Commission shall not adopt the measure; where the Committee gives a positive opinion, the Commission shall adopt the measure; and where the Committee gives no opinion, the Commission may adopt the measure.[61]

2–31   Regulations, directives and decisions must "state the reasons on which they are based" (art.296 TFEU). This is the aim of the recitals which precede the different texts and give, in condensed form, the objectives of the legislative act and why the different provisions were adopted in this or that form. The Court of Justice uses the recitals for the interpretation of the provisions; the Court's interpretation is not too severe as regards their content, though it sometimes happens that legal acts are voided because of a lack of reasoning.[62]

Regulations, directives and decisions are published in the *Official Journal of the European Community*, with the exception of those directives and decisions which are addressed to individual Member States or individual persons (art.297

---

[59] See arts 16(4) TEU, 238 TFEU and Protocol 36 to the Treaties on transitional provisions, [2008] OJ C115/322.

[60] See for details art.290 TFEU. As regards the difference between delegated measures and implementation measures, see Court of Justice, *Commission v European Parliament and Council* (C-427/12) ECLI:EU:C:2014:170; *European Parliament v Commission* (C-65/13) ECLI:EU:C:2014:2289.

[61] See for details Reg.182/2011 laying down the rules and general principles concerning mechanisms for control by Member States of the Commission's exercise of implementation powers [2011] OJ L55/13.

[62] See, e.g. *France v Commission* (C-41/93) [1994] E.C.R. I-1829; *WWF v Commission* (T-105/95) [1997] E.C.R. II-313; *Commission v EP and Council* (C-378/00) [2003] E.C.R. I-937.

TFEU). Since 1 July 2013, only the electronic version of the *Official Journal* shall be authentic and shall produce legal effects.[63]

(ii) Regulations

In environmental matters, the Union mainly acts in the form of directives: regulations are exceptional. They are normally adopted when uniform provisions are sought, since regulations are of general application and shall be binding in their entirety and directly applicable to all Member States (art.288 TFEU). A first group is composed of regulations which set up a specific administrative structure, such as the European Environmental Agency,[64] the financial instrument LIFE,[65] or the Cohesion Fund.[66] Furthermore, there are measures which create committees, uniform procedures or structures; examples are the provision on organic agriculture,[67] the procedures for attributing an eco-label[68] and the eco-audit scheme.[69]

2–32

A second group is formed by regulations which transpose obligations of international environmental conventions into EU law. They mainly serve to organise international trade, concerning products, waste, fauna and flora species. Examples are the Regulation on ozone-depleting substances,[70] the shipment of waste[71] and the trade in endangered species.[72] Also, the regulations on an import ban of whale products,[73] on the ban of leg-hold traps and the import of certain furs[74] and the import or export of chemicals[75] belong to this category.

Regulations do not exist in the water, air and noise sector and there are only a few in the area of nature protection, waste and chemicals. However, these last two sectors show a slowly increasing need for uniform provisions. The reasons for this might lie in the necessity of having uniform provisions before the international state or trade community, but also in the wish to avoid, within an internal market which is still developing, different provisions that could lead to competitive distortions and changes in commercial relationships.

---

[63] Regulation 216/2013 on the electronic publication of the *Official Journal of the European Union* [2013] OJ L69/1.

[64] Regulation 1210/90 [1999] OJ L117/1.

[65] Regulation 1293/2013 [2013] OJ L347/185.

[66] Regulation 1300/2013 [2013] OJ L347/281.

[67] Regulation 834/2007 on organic production and labelling of organic products [2007] OJ L189/1.

[68] Regulation 66/2010 on the EU eco-label [2010] OJ L27/1.

[69] Regulation 1221/2009 allowing voluntary participation by organisations in a Community eco-management and audit scheme [2009] OJ L342/1.

[70] Regulation 1005/2009 on substances that deplete the ozone layer [2009] OJ L286/1.

[71] Regulation 1013/2006 on shipments of waste [2006] OJ L190/1.

[72] Regulation 338/97 on the protection of species of wild fauna and flora by regulating trade therein [1997] OJ L61/1.

[73] Regulation 348/81 on common rules for imports of whales or other cetacean products [1981] OJ L39/1.

[74] Regulation 3254/91 prohibiting the use of leghold traps in the Community and the introduction into the Community of pelts and manufactured goods of certain wild animal species originating in countries which catch them by means of leghold traps or trapping methods which do not meet international humane trapping standards [1991] OJ L308/1.

[75] Regulation 649/2012 concerning the export and import of dangerous chemicals [2012] OJ L201/60.

2–33   Although regulations are directly applicable in all Member States, not all provisions of environmental regulations have this direct effect. Several regulatory provisions require an action by Member States, such as the licensing and supervision of environmental auditors,[76] the authorisation of imports, the establishment of documents or certificates,[77] the designation of competent authorities, the supervision of plants, activities or transports, the establishment of reports and the transmission of information to the Commission or to other Member States. In these cases, regulations seem to have more the content of a directive. Furthermore, not all provisions of a regulation are of a directly applicable nature: thus, a provision such as "Member States may apply the system provided for in Titles II and VIII within their jurisdiction"[78] is of purely facultative character.

No environmental regulation outlines details of sanctions which apply in case of non-respect of the regulation. For instance, the Regulation on the shipment of waste provides that Member States[79]:

> "shall lay down the rules on penalties applicable for infringement of the provisions of this Regulation and shall take all measures necessary to ensure that they are implemented. The penalties provided for must be effective, proportionate and dissuasive;"

the REACH-Regulation on the on chemicals asks Member States to[80]:

> "lay down the provisions on penalties for infringement of the provisions of this Regulation and ... take all measures necessary to ensure that they are implemented. The penalties provided for must be effective, proportionate and dissuasive."

Whether the sanction is criminal, administrative or civil, is left to the discretion of Member States. The jurisprudence of the Court of Justice requires that national sanctions are proportional, dissuasive and a deterrent and correspond to sanctions which are pronounced in similar cases under national law.[81]

(iii)   Directives

2–34   Directives[82] are the most frequently used instrument in EU environmental policy. The degree of detail provided for in a directive is less determined by the concept of a "directive" than by the need to attain the different objectives pursued. Thus, directives on harmonising motor vehicles rules quite often contain 50–80 pages of detailed rules, which outline all the details of the composition of products, test

---

[76] Regulation 1221/2009 [2009] OJ L342/1.
[77] Regulation 338/97 [1997] OJ L61/1, art.8.
[78] Regulation 1013/2006 [2006] OJ L190/1, art.33(3).
[79] Regulation 1013/2006 [2006] OJ L190/1, art.50(1).
[80] Regulation 1907/2006 on the registration, evaluation, authorisation and restriction of chemicals (REACH) [2006] OJ L396/1.
[81] Court of Justice, *Commission v Greece* (C-68/88) [1989] E.C.R. 2965.
[82] Article 288 TFEU: "A directive shall be binding, as to the result to be achieved, upon each Member State to which it is addressed, but shall leave to the national authorities the choice of form and methods."

methods and so on.[83] Such detailed directives are frequent for products, but exist also in the agricultural sector. In contrast, environmental directives tend to be of a general nature. In particular, the debate over the last 25 years on subsidiarity and deregulation and the general loss of integration capacity of the European Union has led to environmental directives which limit themselves to outline general rules, framework provisions and basic requirements. Provisions on measuring methods and frequency, emission limit values, quantitative restrictions and other similar provisions are only laid down in exceptional cases. Whether this restriction is really capable of contributing to a high level of environmental protection, is doubtful; such general provisions do not increase the added value of EU environmental law provisions and, furthermore, perpetuate differences in the level of protection among Member States. They allow the EU provisions to be applied if the political will to do so exists, but also allow full application of such rules to be avoided if such a political will does not exist.

Directives address Member States and normally oblige them to act in a certain way. Private persons, undertakings or associations cannot be obligated by a directive; however, they can acquire rights from a directive in those cases where a provision in a directive is sufficiently concrete, precise and unconditional and where the Member State has not transposed that directive completely or correctly into national law (direct-effect doctrine).[84]

Member States have to transpose the provisions of a directive into national law. It is up to each Member State to decide whether this is done by an Act of Parliament or a regulation, whether the transposition measure is one piece of legislation or whether several regional or even local provisions are adopted. It is only relevant that the directive's provisions are transposed for the whole territory of the Member State. The transposing measure may be incorporated in one legal act; more frequently, however, the transposition is ensured by a number of legal measures, in particular in Member States with a decentralised or federal structure.

Where the definition of a provision is relevant, such transposition also needs **2–35** to include the definition in order to establish a common language.[85] For the rest, at the very least those provisions need to be transposed which are capable of creating rights or obligations for private persons. In contrast, provisions which exclusively address the administration (for instance, requiring it to send reports to the Commission or to designate competent authorities) need not be transposed.

The provisions of the directive which have been transposed into national law must actually be applied. This follows from the very nature of a directive, which obliges Member States to achieve a certain result. It is not enough to take all practical steps to reach the directive's objectives; indeed, the directive indicates to Member States how to achieve a certain result, but does not leave it at their discretion as to whether they achieve the result or not. It was for this reason that the United Kingdom was not heard before the Court of Justice with its argument

---

[83] Directive 97/24 on three-wheel cars has a length of 454 pages in the Official Journal [1997] OJ L226/1. Such a length would not be imaginable for a directive on the environment.

[84] See further at para.12–21, below.

[85] See, e.g. Court of Justice, *Commission v Ireland* (C-354/99) [2001] E.C.R. I-7657, where Ireland was found in breach of EC law, because it had not transposed a specific definition; *Commission v Belgium* (C-120/09), ECLI:EU:C:2009:802.

that it had taken all reasonable steps to ensure clean drinking water: the Court requested that the requirements of the drinking water Directive be complied with.[86]

Amendments of directives follow the general rules. Normally, they are adopted by the same institutions which adopted the original directive; however, as pointed out, the Commission may be authorised, under art.290 TFEU, to amend a directive, in particular to adapt it as a result of technical or scientific progress. Furthermore, the legal basis of a directive is determined by its objective and its content, not by the legal basis of a previous directive; thus, where an environmental directive, based on art.192 TFEU, is amended by a directive which has a trade-related objective, art.207 TFEU may become the appropriate legal basis for the amending measure, and the institution which adopts the amendment may be different.[87]

2–36   Legally, differentiations such as "umbrella directive", "daughter directive", etc, are not relevant. Such concepts only signal that the specific directive is placed in a close context with a more general directive; however, the specific directive is to be interpreted by itself, including, of course, possible references to other directives.

Directives do not become obsolete with time. Since they are legal acts, they need to be repealed expressly: in EU practice this normally takes place with the adoption of a new directive. No environmental directive has as yet been repealed without the adoption of new provisions, though the Commission's announcement to simplify its legislation might in future lead to more repeals. The agreement of the Council and the European Parliament will be necessary.

(iv)   Decisions

2–37   Decisions[88] are rather numerous in EU environmental policy. The most frequent types of decisions are: decisions to establish a committee or another body[89]; to grant financial assistance for environmental projects under the Cohesion Fund or the financial instrument LIFE; in the context of competition policy on agreements (art.101 TFEU); abuse of dominant positions (art.102 TFEU) or on state aid (arts 107 and 108 TFEU); on details of putting into operation specific directives or regulations[90] or establishing criteria for the attribution of an eco-label for specific product groups[91]; on the adherence of the European Union to international (environmental) conventions; on environmental action programmes according to art.192(3); and on art.114(4) and (5) TFEU on more stringent national environmental measures.

---

[86] *Commission v United Kingdom* (C-337/89) [1992] E.C.R. 6103; see also *Commission v United Kingdom* (C-404/13) ECLI:EU:C:2014:2382.

[87] See, e.g. Reg.1420/1999 [1999] OJ L166/6 which concerned the shipment of non-hazardous waste and was based on art.133 EC, though the original Regulation 259/93 on the shipments of waste was based on art.175 EC.

[88] Article 288 TFEU: "A decision shall be binding in its entirety. A decision which specifies those to whom it is addressed, shall be binding only on them."

[89] See, e.g. Dec.76/431 setting up a committee on waste management [1976] OJ L115/73.

[90] See, e.g. Dec.2000/532 establishing a list of wastes [2000] OJ L226/3.

[91] Under Reg.66/2010 [2010] OJ L27/1; see, e.g. Dec.93/430 on ecological criteria for dishwashers [1993] OJ L38; Dec.98/488 on ecological criteria for soil improvers [1998] OJ L219/39; Dec.99/205 on ecological criteria for personal computers [1999] OJ L70/46.

(v) Recommendations

Commission or Council recommendations have no binding force (art.288 TFEU).   **2–38**
They play a limited role in EU environmental policy. Indeed, experience has
shown that neither economic operators nor Member States are inclined to respect
recommendations, and the example of international organisations—OECD,
Council of Europe, United Nations—which largely work with recommendations,
demonstrate the very limited effective influence of non-binding environmental
measures.

The Council made environmental recommendations on cost allocation,[92] on
the cost of pollution control to industry,[93] the reuse of waste paper and the use of
recycled paper[94] and coastal zone management.[95] The Commission in particular
made recommendations on birds,[96] on environmental agreements[97] and the use of
CFCs in industry.[98] Where an environmental agreement is made at EU level, the
Commission furthermore issues a recommendation taking up the content of the
agreement.[99]

None of these recommendations had, as far as can be seen, any significant
influence on European or national environmental policy or law.

(vi) Communications

Communications not expressly provided for in the EU Treaty are not legally   **2–39**
binding. They are sent from the Commission to the other institutions, in particular
the Council or the Parliament, and expose the Commission's position on a
particular problem, indicate orientations and discuss options which the
Commission considers possible. As the European Union tries to avoid the
adoption of environmental legislation, the number of communications on
environmental matters has increased during the last years.

Communications appear under different headings, as strategies, Green or
White Papers, reports or communications. Legally, there is no difference.
Communications may be accompanied by a draft for a Council resolution, a
directive or a regulation.

(vii) Action programmes

EU environmental action programmes have been developed since the early   **2–40**
1970s, mainly in reaction to the fact that the EC Treaty did not provide for an
express legal basis for environmental measures. When such specific provisions
were introduced in 1987, the practice of action programmes was maintained.
Action programmes were, legally, communications by the Commission to other
EU institutions, which set out for a period of four to five years, the objectives,

---

[92] Recommendation 75/436 [1975] OJ L194/1.
[93] Recommendation 79/3 [1979] OJ L5/28.
[94] Recommendation 81/972 [1981] OJ L355/56.
[95] Recommendation 2002/413 [2002] OJ L148/24.
[96] Recommendation 75/66 [1975] OJ L21/24.
[97] Recommendation 96/733 [1996] OJ L33/59.
[98] Recommendation 89/349 [1989] OJ L89/56; 90/437 and 90/438 [1990] OJ L227/26 and 30 (CFC).
[99] Recommendation 1999/125 [1999] OJ L40/49.

principles and priorities of EU action which the Commission envisaged. The Court of Justice confirmed that the environmental action programmes did not contain legally binding or enforceable provisions.[100] Action programmes were followed by (political) resolutions by the Parliament and the Council. Between 1973 and mid-1998, five environment action programmes were agreed at EU level.[101] Their main effect was essentially political. They achieved a large consensus among Member States on objectives and priorities of EU environmental policy, and since the majority of Member States did not have a national environmental policy, the measures agreed and adopted at EU level often influenced environmental policy within Member States. Since the end of 1993, environment action programmes have to be adopted by way of a joint decision by the European Parliament and the Council (art.192(3) TFEU) which is, of course, binding.

Action programmes under art.192(3) TFEU must at least outline priority objectives for EU action, provide for measures to achieve these objectives and contain a time period within which the measures are taken. The right for initiative for such a programme rests with the Commission, and no other institution can oblige it to submit a programme.[102]

EU action programmes may oblige the Commission to make proposals for specific measures, with the consequence, in the case of failure to do so, of an action—by the Council and also by the European Parliament—under art.265 TFEU. It is true that the Commission normally has the monopoly for legal initiatives and cannot be compelled to make a proposal. However, primary and secondary law contain a number of exceptions to this rule[103] and there is no provision in EU law which would oppose such an exception. In contrast, it does not seem possible to oblige, by virtue of a programme, the Council or even the Member States to adopt specific measures: in such a case, an all too concrete content—such as, for instance, that the use of certain substances or products will be banned from a specific date onwards—would contradict the form of an action programme; such measures would require a directive or a regulation and would be adopted in respect of the procedures foreseen for those instruments.

2–41   The provision of art.192(3) TFEU creates new possibilities for the European Parliament to influence the legislative programme of the European Union and to see proposals for legislative measures presented. Parliament's interest must therefore be to have environment action programmes as concrete as possible, whereas the interests of the Commission and the Council must be to keep the programme as general and loosely drafted as possible. This difference of interest was very notable in the Commission's proposal for a review of the 5th Action Programme and Parliament's position on it.[104] The final Decision on this review

---

[100]   *Rovigo* (C-142/95P) [1996] E.C.R. I-6669.

[101]   1st Environment Action Programme 1973–1976 [1973] OJ C112/1; 2nd Environment Action Programme 1977–1982 [1977] OJ C139/1; 3rd Environment Action Programme 1982–1986 [1983] OJ C46/1; 4th Environment Action Programme 1987–1992 [1987] OJ C328/1; 5th Environment Action Programme 1993–2000 [1993] OJ C138/5.

[102]   Argument taken from Court of Justice, *Commission v Belgium* (C-347/97) [1999] E.C.R. I-309.

[103]   See, e.g. art.241 TFEU; an example in secondary law was art.1(5) of Dir.91/689 on hazardous waste [1991] OJ L377/20 which requests the Commission to make a proposal on hazardous household waste; Dir.91/689 has now been repealed.

[104]   Commission [1996] OJ C140/5; European Parliament [1996] OJ C362/112.

contained objectives and principles, but not actions.[105] This approach was repeated in the 7th Action Programme (2014–2020) which does not contain one single concrete action.[106]

(viii)   Resolutions

The Treaty does not contain any provision on resolutions. These are political statements adopted by the Council, with or without a proposal from the Commission. Following a consensus in the Council which is not laid down in writing, Council (environmental) resolutions are agreed upon unanimously; it is true that no vote is taken, but the Council redrafts the text until a consensus of all Member States is reached.

2–42

Resolutions often constitute the Council's reaction on a Commission communication concerning an environmental issue. However, the Council is not obliged to react to such communications. Where it adopts a resolution, this gives political or legal orientation to the Commission, the Parliament and private actors without being legally binding for the Council. Also, the European Parliament adopts environmental resolutions as a reaction to a Commission communication or on its own initiative. These resolutions are adopted by majority vote. Again, they are of political, not of legal nature.

(ix)   Environmental agreements

Environmental agreements were defined by the Commission as agreements, by which stakeholders undertake to achieve pollution abatement, as defined in environmental law, or environmental objectives set out in art.191 TFEU.[107]

2–43

Such agreements are not mentioned in art.288 TFEU. Since the European Union may only act within the limits of powers conferred upon it (art.5 TEU), agreements are not capable of regulating substantive parts of Community environmental policy, as this is reserved to the instruments listed in art.288 TFEU. The European Parliament opposed the recourse to environmental agreements which it understood as some form of commitment that was binding for the Commission or the European Union.[108] It invoked in particular that such agreements simply did not conform to the Parliamentary principle. As the European Parliament, the Economic and Social Committee and the Committee of the Regions have institutional rights and guarantees to take part in the EU decision-making procedures, environmental agreements, which set these rights

---

[105] Decision 2179/98 on the review of the 5th Environment Action Programme [1998] OJ L275/1.
[106] 7th Environment Action Programme (fn.8, above).
[107] Commission: Environmental Agreements at Community level, COM(2002) 412 of 17 July 2002. Another definition is given in art.3(12) of Dir.94/62 on packaging and packaging waste [1994] OJ L365/10: "'Voluntary agreements' shall mean the formal agreement concluded between the competent public authorities of the Member State and the economic sectors concerned, which has to be open to all partners who wish to meet the conditions of the agreement with a view to working towards the objectives of this Directive". Directive 2004/12 ([2004] OJ L47/26) now inserted a new art.3bis, according to which the Directive's recycling targets also could be attained by voluntary agreements. As regards the most prominent "agreement" at EU level, that on the reduction of CO_2 from cars, see also paras 8–17 et seq.
[108] EP, Resolutions of 17 July 1997, [1997] OJ C 286/254; 26 October 2000, [2000] OJ C197/433; 18 January 2001 [2001] OJ C262/236.

aside, are legally not permissible. For this reason the Commission declared in two communications that it could only make non-binding environmental agreements at EU level and even included this approach in the very definition of "agreement".[109] And in 2002, the Commission stated that "environmental agreements are not negotiated with the Commission".[110]

Even these basic concerns being left aside, procedures for the making of such agreements—who should negotiate in the name of the European Union?—and the follow-up—how and by whom the agreement would be monitored, enforced, sanctioned, applied to free-riders, such as importers and third country producers?—are not clear; nor are they answered by the Commission's communications.[111] Since Member States would have to monitor and enforce agreements, their participation in the negotiation procedure appears inevitable. However, it is then not clear where the advantage is with regard to a directive which is negotiated and decided in Council and the European Parliament.

2–44   The core of the problem is the attempt to obtain a commitment from the legislature—at EU level mainly from the Commission which has the right of initiating legislation—not to adopt binding legislation. In law, the legislature cannot bind itself in this way. Also, problems under competition policy—arts 101 and 102 TFEU—are not really solved. Agreements among competitors may come under art.101, even where public authorities participate in such agreements. As regards measures which have an impact on imports, international trade provisions may also be applicable.

Looking into the experience with environmental agreements in Member States, it seems that EU environmental agreements may contribute to the protection of the environment in those cases where legally binding measures are also effective; however, in those parts of the European Union where environmental directives are almost or not at all effective, environmental agreements are not likely to have a greater effect.

EU legal policy tries to circumvent these obstacles: in the case of an environmental agreement on CO_2 emissions from cars, negotiations took place in the mid and the end of the 1990s between the Commission and economic operators on what might by an acceptable offer from the car industry; Council and Parliament were informed of the state of negotiations, but did not participate. At the end of these negotiations a statement and a recommendation were issued by the Commission, in the sense that there was no need for binding measures at EU level, since there was a voluntary commitment by the car industry.[112] It should be noted, though, that the agreement was not made with the car manufacturers themselves, but with their industrial associations. Thus, when the Rover company later left the association, it was no longer bound by the agreement.

---

[109] Commission, Communication on Environmental Agreements, COM(96) 561; see also Commission: Environmental Agreements at Community level, COM(2002) 412 of 17 July 2002 and Council Resolution of 7 October 1997 [1997] OJ C321/6.

[110] Commission: Environmental Agreements at Community level, COM(2002) 412 of 17 July 2002, p.4.

[111] Commission: Environmental Agreements at Community level, COM(2002) 412 of 17 July 2002; Council Resolution of 7 October 1997 [1997] OJ C321/6; EP, Resolutions of 17 July 1997, [1997] OJ C 286/254; 26 October 2000, [2000] OJ C197/433; 18 January 2001 [2001] OJ C262/236.

[112] See also para.8–15, below.

A second way consists of negotiations between the Commission and one or more professional organisations on an improvement in environmental performance. At the end of these negotiations, the European professional organisations make a unilateral commitment to the Commission. The Commission adopts a recommendation based on art.288 TFEU, which recommends that those environmental commitments be followed, which the professional organisation had agreed to accept. An example of this model which does not contain any form of "agreement" (i.e. some form of a contract) is the use of detergents, where the Commission made a recommendation in 1998.[113]

2–45

Underlying both types of environmental "agreements" is the Commission's commitment not to make proposals for a directive or a regulation. The above-mentioned statement by the Commission that "the Commission can never, by 'acknowledging' such an engagement, forgo its right of initiative"[114] is legally quite correct. However, politically, an acknowledgment by the Commission is perceived by the economic actors as a commitment not to initiate legislation, and this is, of course, intended.

The main difference to environmental agreements as they are negotiated and concluded, for example, in the Netherlands is that on the one hand the Dutch authorities fix themselves—by way of legislation/regulation or Government decision—the result to be reached, whereas at EU level the result of an agreement to be reached is bargained between the vested interest groups and the Commission. On the other hand, the obligation to publicly lay account at regular intervals on progress is normally much stricter and much more closely monitored by the Dutch public authorities.

As regards environmental agreements at national level, Member States are free to act as they consider appropriate. To what extent Member States might feel bound by any agreement that was produced at EU level and abstain from introducing legislation, is a political decision. On general aspects of the implementation of EU environmental legislation through national environmental agreements, the Commission made a communication and a recommendation in 1996.[115] By end of 2010, only four waste directives[116] contained a clause that allowed Member States to implement some of the Directives' provisions by environmental agreements, for which a number of conditions were laid down. The future will show whether the statement in the 6th Environment Action Programme[117] that "legislation remains central to meeting the environmental challenges and full and correct implementation of the existing legislation is a priority" will have the effect of mitigating the pressure for deregulation through environmental agreements.

2–46

---

[113] Recommendation 98/480 [1998] OJ L215/73; see also Recs 89/349 [1989] OJ L89/56; 90/437 and 90/438 [1990] OJ L227/26 and 30 (CFC) which followed the same pattern, but became obsolete because of the evolution in the sector of ozone-depleting substances.

[114] Commission, [1996] OJ C140/5, p.4.

[115] Commission, Communication on Environmental Agreements, COM(96) 561; Rec.96/733 [1996] OJ L33/59.

[116] Directive 2000/53 on end-of-life vehicles [2000] OJ L269/34, art.10(3); Dir.2012/19 on waste electrical and electronic equipment (WEEE) [2012] OJ L197/38, art.24(3); Dir.94/62 on packaging and packaging waste [1994] OJ L365/10; Dir.2006/66 on batteries [2006] OJ L266/9.

[117] Decision 1600/2002 [2002] OJ L242/1, Recital 12.

(x)   Tripartite contracts and agreements

2–47   At the end of 2002, the Commission proposed the use of tripartite contracts and agreements at EC level.[118] Tripartite contracts were defined as contracts between the European Union, a Member State and regional or local authorities "in direct application of binding secondary Community law (regulations, directives or decisions)", tripartite agreements were such contracts "outside a binding Community framework". In the case of tripartite contracts, an enabling clause in the legislative instrument is necessary, as is a clause in the contract that the Member State alone is responsible for the implementation of EC legislation.

In the environmental sector, tripartite agreements seem in particularly useful in the area of local environmental issues such as coastal zone management, urban environment issues or questions of waste management, where legislation does not really reach. To what extent regions or local authorities will seize the opportunity to enter into direct contractual relationship with the EU level, remains to be seen and might also depend on the availability of financial means. Until the end of 2014, this instrument has never been used.

(b)   Instruments to influence the behaviour of undertakings and individual persons

2–48   EU law contains a number of provisions which aim at influencing the behaviour of undertakings or individual persons towards a better environment. Since the great majority of EU environmental law is made in the form of directives, these provisions do not directly address these private persons; they normally address instead Member States and ask them to "transmit" these messages via their national provisions, to the addressees. The most important instruments that exist under EU environmental law are the following.

(i)   Obligation of notification

2–49   In a number of cases, private persons are obliged to notify the authorities of a Member State of a certain activity or practice. Thus, persons who intend to put new chemical substances on the EU market have to notify public authorities of their intention and submit certain documents referring to the tests of that substance: they may put the substance on the market only 60 days after that notification.[119] Where a chemical, whose use in the European Union is prohibited or restricted, is to be exported into a third country for the first time, this intention must be notified 30 days before the export takes place; the intention behind this provision is to inform the third country ("prior informed consent" principle).[120] A notification obligation also exists for the contained use of genetically modified

---

[118] Commission: A framework for target-based tripartite contracts and agreements between the Community, the states and regional and local authorities, COM(2002) 709 of 11 December 2002.

[119] Regulation 1907/2006 [2006] OJ L396/1; see further at para.6–26, below.

[120] Regulation 649/2012 [2012] OJ L201/60; see also para.6–56, below.

micro-organisms[121] and the deliberate release of genetically modified organisms[122]; sometimes in these two instances, however, the notification is followed by an express authorisation. Also, the production, processing and import of organic agricultural products must be notified.[123]

As regards installations, notification is required for any industrial activity during which certain chemicals are used or produced; notification has to inform the authorities of the substances used, the plant and possible risks of accidents.[124] Furthermore, malfunctions or breakdowns of the functioning of installations sometimes requires notification.[125]

All these obligations for information or notification are intended to inform the authorities responsible in due time, in order to allow them to take appropriate, and if necessary preventive, action.

(ii)   Authorisation

Authorisation is organised in very different ways in Member States. It is thus usual that EU legislature limits itself to requiring that certain activities have an environmental authorisation[126] (sometimes the word "permit" is used,[127] without there being any legal difference) and to setting out conditions for this authorisation.   **2–50**

First, a number of new installations need an authorisation for operating. Directive 2010/75[128] has to some extent harmonised the permits and the conditions thereof; however, this Directive only applies to some bigger installations. The authorisation for discharges into water under Directives 76/464 on water discharges,[129] 2001/80 on large combustion plants,[130] 1999/13 on plants using organic solvents,[131] 78/176 on installations producing titanium dioxide,[132] and 2000/76 on waste incinerators[133] were progressively integrated into the provisions of Directives 2010/75 which became a framework directive. In the waste sector, all installations which recover, collect, treat or dispose of waste, need an authorisation.[134]

---

[121] Directive 2009/41 on the contained use of genetically modified micro-organisms [2009] OJ L175/75.

[122] Directive 2001/18 on the deliberate release into the environment of genetically modified organisms [2001] OJ L106/1, arts 6 et seq.

[123] Regulation 834/2007 [2007] OJ L189/1.

[124] Directive 2012/18 [2012] OJ L197/1.

[125] See, e.g. Dir.2010/75 on industrial emissions [2010] OJ L334/17, arts 8(2) and 37(2); Dir.2010/75 is a recast of Dir.2008/1 on integrated pollution prevention control [2008] OJ L24/8.

[126] See, e.g. Dir.2010/75 [2010] OJ L334/17; Dir.76/464 on the discharge of pollutants into water [1976] OJ L129/23; this Directive was repealed as of 2013; Dir.2006/118 on the protection of groundwater against pollution and deterioration [2006] OJ L372/19.

[127] See for instance Dir.2010/75 [2010] OJ L334/17; Dir.2008/98 on waste [2008] OJ L312/3.

[128] Directive 2010/75 [2010] OJ L334/17.

[129] Directive 76/464 [1976] OJ L129/23.

[130] Directive 2001/80 on the limitation of emissions of certain pollutants into the air from large combustion plants [2001] OJ L309/1.

[131] Directive 1999/13 on the limitation of emissions of volatile organic compounds due to the use of organic solvents in certain activities and installations [1999] OJ L85/1.

[132] Directive 78/176 on waste from the titanium dioxide industry [1978] OJ L54/19.

[133] Directive 2000/76 on the incineration of waste [2000] OJ L332/91.

[134] Directive 2008/98 [2008] OJ L312/3.

Authorisations are also needed to impair the environment. Besides the discharge from installations which are mentioned above, the artificial enrichment of groundwater may be mentioned,[135] or the discharge of waste-water from urban waste-water treatment plants[136]; the discharge of sewage sludge into surface waters has been forbidden since 1998.[137] Product-related authorisations concern the placing on the market of pesticides,[138] biocides[139] and the release of genetically modified organisms into the environment.[140] The import and export of ozone-depleting substances[141] and of endangered species of fauna and flora[142] also fall into this category.

2–51   There is no general rule on the conditions which accompany the authorisation. Early directives established very detailed conditions[143] which were, however, not really controlled. Directive 2010/75 also provides for detailed conditions, such as emission limit values or equivalent parameters, the best available techniques, measurement frequency and methodology, suitable requirements for controlling emissions and measures for other than normal operating conditions. However, the condition requirements are vaguely formulated and leave large discretion to Member States.

In contrast to earlier directives, Directive 2010/75 does not provide for limited authorisation; it only requires that the authorisation be regularly reconsidered (art.21).

The procedural requirements for authorisations are few and far between. Directive 2010/75 requires a written application with a number of minimal indications and a non-technical summary of the documentation (art.12). The application has, for an appropriate length of time, to be made available to the public to enable it to comment. An environmental impact assessment is only required for certain specific projects and, since 2004, for spatial planning and programmes.[144] These Directives provide that the public must be given "the opportunity to express an opinion" on the project, which means that the affected person has a right to be consulted.

2–52   Directive 2010/75 furthermore provides that authorisation be made available to the public; most other directives concur with this requirement. No details are set out, and the requirement for checking on whether the conditions for authorisation continue to be complied with or not has been reduced in recent

---

[135] Directive 2006/118 [2006] OJ L372/19.

[136] Directive 91/271 on urban waste water [1991] OJ L135/40, arts 12 and 14.

[137] Directive 91/271 [1991] OJ L135/40, art.14.

[138] Regulation 1107/2009 concerning the placing of plant protection products on the market [2009] OJ L309/1.

[139] Directive 98/8 concerning the placing of biocidal products on the market [1998] OJ L123/1.

[140] Directive 2001/18 [2001] OJ L106/1.

[141] Regulation 1005/2009 on substances that deplete the ozone layer [2009] OJ L286/1.

[142] Regulation 38/97 on trade in endangered species [1997] OJ L61/1.

[143] See, e.g. Dir.80/68 on the protection of groundwater against pollution caused by certain dangerous substances [1980] OJ L20/43 which required methods of discharge, essential precautions, monitoring arrangements and monitoring groundwater to be detailed.

[144] Directive 2011/92 on the assessment of the effects of certain public and private projects on the environment [2012] OJ L26/1; Dir.2001/42 on the assessment of the effects of certain plans and programmes on the environment [2001] OJ L197/30.

directives. Directive 2003/35 now introduces a right of the public concerned to participate in the authorisation of certain projects, plans and programmes.[145]

While Directive 76/464 and its subsequent different daughter directives outlined detail control requirements, Directive 75/440 on the quality of surface water[146] was even completed by a specific "control" directive[147] and the directives on air quality standards also contained detailed measurement and control provisions.[148] All water and air provisions in this regard are now substituted by more general provisions in the water and air quality framework directives[149] which do not go into such details. Directive 2010/75 introduced monitoring requirements for the installations (arts 14 and 16) and the obligation for the authorities to periodically inspect the installations covered by that Directive.

(iii) Interdiction and obligation to act

EU environmentally relevant interdictions have been pronounced essentially in the product-related legislation. The most important provision was Directive 76/769[150] which was continuously amended to include further restrictions, but has now been replaced by the new regulation REACH on chemicals.[151] Besides that, every measure which fixes emission limit values implicitly contains the interdiction on exceeding these values. Other interdictions and restrictions are found in numerous directives, such as the ban on certain heavy metals or other substances in products, on the discharge of sewage sludge into water[152] or on the non-authorised disposal of waste.[153] Most of these interdictions allow that the interdiction is disregarded in extraordinary circumstances. Occasionally, EU law itself authorises Member States to establish a ban. General authorisation in this regard is found in arts 114(4) and 193 TFEU.

2–53

Further elements exist in secondary law under the so-called safeguard clause: these clauses give the possibility of temporarily prohibiting a product even though it complies with EU requirements. Such a ban provokes an EU control procedure which ends either with an EU-wide prohibition or an invitation to the acting Member State to repeal its ban. Specific authorisations for Member States to issue bans exist for using sewage sludge where certain concentrations of heavy

---

[145] Directive 2003/35 providing for public participation in respect of the drawing up of certain plans and programmes relating to the environment [2003] OJ L56/17.

[146] Directive 75/440 concerning the quality required of surface water intended for the abstraction of drinking water in the Member States [1975] OJ L194/26. This Directive was in the meantime repealed.

[147] Directive 79/869 concerning the methods of measurement and frequencies of sampling and analysis of surface water intended for the abstraction of drinking waters in the Member States [1979] OJ L271/ 44. This Directive was in the meantime repealed.

[148] Directive 80/779 (SO_2 in the air) [1980] OJ L229/30; 82/884 (lead in the air) [1982] OJ L378/15, 85/203 (NO_x in the air) [1985] OJ L87/1. These Directives were in the meantime replaced.

[149] Directive 2000/60 establishing a framework for Community action in the field of water policy [2000] OJ L327/1; Dir.2008/50 on ambient air quality and cleaner air for Europe [2008] OJ L152/1.

[150] Directive 76/769 relating to restrictions on the marketing and use of certain dangerous substances and preparations [1976] OJ L262/201. This Directive was in the meantime integrated into Reg.1907/2006 [2006] OJ L396/1.

[151] Regulation 1907/2006 [2006] OJ L396/1.

[152] Directive 91/271 [1991] OJ L135/40.

[153] Directive 2008/98 [2008] OJ L312/3.

metals are exceeded[154] and for importing/exporting hazardous waste for disposal purposes.[155] EU environmental law only rarely provides for general national derogations of a ban. An example is the possibility of hunting certain birds in specified Member States.[156] Considerably more often it happens that a Member State may grant a derogation of a ban on a case-by-case basis.

Obligations to act are also rather few and far between. They concern, for instance, obligations to keep registers, to measure emissions, to hand over waste to an authorised undertaker, to discharge air emissions via a chimney, etc. Never are sanctions provided: these are left to national legislation.

2–54   Directive 2010/75 sets out "general principles" for the operator of installations that come under that Directive,[157] which probably have a placebo effect because they are hardly enforceable and may be interpreted in many different ways. Also, Directive 2012/18 obliges the operator of a plant to take "all necessary measures" to prevent accidents.

Recent waste legislation started to introduce take-back obligations for cars and electrical/electronic equipment.[158] National take-back schemes are allowed under EU law and sometimes required by EU legislation.[159] Deposit and return systems are likewise possible at national level, but have not yet been imposed by EU legislation. Obligations to ensure financial security only exist for the shipment of hazardous waste to another state.[160] No insurance obligation exists against environmental impairment; the Directive on environmental liability left the question whether there should be compulsory insurance for damage to the environment to the national legislation.[161]

There is no obligation for an undertaking to mandate a person to look into environmental issues. Directive 82/501 contained the obligation for an undertaking coming under that Directive to designate a specific person in charge of security and to implement the accident prevention and evacuation plans.[162] However, Directive 96/82 which replaced Directive 82/501, deleted this provision altogether.

2–55   EU environmental law does not expressly require the taking of the supply of water, electricity or fuel from a specific place, or to deliver waste or waste water to a specific place or installation. However, such an obligation implicitly

---

[154] Directive 86/278 on the use of sewage sludge in agriculture [1986] OJ L181/6, arts 5 and 7.

[155] Regulation 1013/2006 [2006] OJ L190/1.

[156] Directive 2009/147 on the conservation of wild birds [2010] OJ L20/7, art.7(3) and annex II(2).

[157] Directive 2010/75 [2010] OJ L334/17, art.11: For instance: "no significant pollution is caused"; "energy is used efficiently"; "the necessary measures are taken to prevent accidents and limit their consequences" and so on.

[158] Directive 2000/53 [2000] OJ L269/34; Dir.2012/19 [2012] OJ L197/38 where the obligation is limited to waste from electrical and electronic equipment (WEEE) other than WEEE from private households. For such waste from private households, Member States only have to set up return systems, art.5(2).

[159] Directive 2006/66 on batteries and accumulators [2006] OJ L266/1; Dir.94/62 [1994] OJ L365/10, art.7; Dir.96/59 on the disposal of PCB/PCT [1996] OJ L243/31, art.6, furthermore the directives mentioned in fn.158, above.

[160] Regulation 1013/2006 [2006] OJ L190/1.

[161] Directive 2004/35 on environmental liability with regard to the prevention and remedying of environmental damage [2005] OJ L143/56, art.14.

[162] Directive 82/501 on accident prevention [1982] OJ L230/5; see also *Commission v Netherlands* (C-190/90) [1992] E.C.R. I-3265.

underlies the Directive on urban waste water.[163] Member States are free to make provisions for such an obligation, however not for waste which may be recovered. Obligations for remedial action, following an action that impaired the environment, were established by Directive 2004/35 on environmental liability.[164] An indirect obligation flows from art.13 of Directive 2008/98 on waste [165] which ensures that waste disposal does not impair the environment; this provision requires the elimination of illegally disposed waste and the restoration of the impaired environment.[166] Regulation 1013/2006 obliges Member States to take back waste which has been illegally shipped to another Member State.[167]

Liability obligations only exist, up to now, for damage caused by defective products[168]; this Directive also applies to damage caused by waste, although this is contested.[169] Directive 2005/35 on environmental liability does not contain any financial responsibility of a polluter to compensate a victim, but is limited to environmental restoration obligations under public law.

(iv) Information, appeals, warnings

EU environmental law and policy contain numerous addresses and appeals to citizens to behave in a way which is environmentally more beneficial. A good example is the Council resolution on the 5th Environment Action Programme, where the Council declared that "many current forms of activity and development are not environmentally sustainable" and that "the achievement of sustainable development calls for significant changes in current patterns of development, production, consumption and behaviour"; this implied "a sharing of responsibility at global, Community, regional, local and even personal level".[170] It is impossible to measure the impact of such appeals.

2–56

Since 1992, the European Union has tried to re-educate consumers' and users' behaviour towards environmentally "better" products, by establishing an EU eco-label.[171] Since industry associations are not really in favour of a system that classifies some products to be better than others, the work advances very slowly, all the more as the system also has to compete with differing national systems; thus, its effects have been up until now very limited.[172] The EU eco-audit scheme[173] has had more success, though it also has to compete with an international ISO-standard which is less ambitious.[174]

The European Union has never issued warnings against environmentally dangerous products. A recommendation to be careful with toys for small children

---

[163] Directive 91/271 [1991] OJ L135/40.
[164] Directive 2004/35 [2005] OJ L143/56.
[165] Directive 2008/98 [2008] OJ L312/3.
[166] Court of Justice, *Commission v Italy* (C-365/97) [1999] E.C.R. I-2773; on this issue see L. Krämer, *Casebook on EU Environmental Law* (Oxford, 2002), pp.341 and 391. See now Court of Justice, *Commission v Italy* (C-196/13) ECLI:EU:C:2014:2403.
[167] Regulation 1013/2006 [2006] OJ L190/1.
[168] Directive 85/374 on product liability [1985] OJ L210/29.
[169] See also para.4–57, below.
[170] [1993] OJ C138/1.
[171] Regulation 66/2010 [2010] OJ L27/1.
[172] See for more details paras 6–47 et seq., below.
[173] Regulation 1221/2009 [2009] OJ L342/1.
[174] See for more details paras 4–52 et seq., below.

that contain PVC with certain phthalates,[175] was obviously aimed more at protecting health than the environment. Under Directive 2008/50,[176] Member States are obliged to warn the population of each individual Member State where certain levels of ozone concentration are exceeded, a way to replace remedial action by warnings.

2–57   Generally, the effect of EU appeals and information is not significantly greater than that of corresponding national measures. It is correct that EU institutions have, at least in part, greater credit with the population in environmental matters; however, this is balanced by a greater distance towards the ordinary citizen.

(v) Financial assistance

2–58   Up until now, no EU provision has provided for financial advantages of environmentally "better" products. Member States oppose such rules, since environmental protection is of different importance in the different Member States, and they are afraid of competitive disadvantages. Thus, a Commission proposal to introduce a price differentiation between leaded and unleaded petrol and thereby accelerate the introduction of catalytic converters and lead-free petrol[177] was rejected: such differentiation was subsequently introduced at national level. In the same way, the attempt failed to introduce general financial advantages for the introduction of cars with catalytic converters; the final compromise only allowed such encouragement for a limited period of time. Attempts in this direction seem to have been largely abandoned since then, though the idea of "getting the prices right" continues to be mentioned. Attempts to introduce a reduced VAT tax for products which carry an EU eco-label were discussed, but finally not proposed by the Commission.

(vi) Subventions

2–59   National subventions (state aids) are in principle prohibited (art.107 TFEU), but are in practice widespread in all Member States. The total amount of state aids in 2013 was €62.7 billion,[178] the amount of environmental aid—environmental protection and energy saving, as well as heritage conservation—€15 billion. Since 1974 the Commission has fixed an EU framework for environmental aids, which was last reviewed in 2008.[179] The Commission also published Guidelines on greenhouse gas emission trading[180] and on environmental protection and energy.[181] As these Guidelines partially overlap each other, it is difficult to make a general assessment. They fix the framework, within which the Commission

---

[175] Recommendation 98/485 [1998] OJ L217/35.

[176] Directive 2008/50 on ambient air quality and cleaner air for Europe [2008] OJ L152/1.

[177] [1984] OJ C178/5.

[178] Commission, *ec.europa.eu/competition/state-aid/scoreboard/non-crisis-en.html* [Accessed 30 September 2015]; to this has to be added the amount which was given in view of the financial crisis in the European Union and which was, for the years 2008–2013 €661.42 billion.

[179] Commission, Community guidelines on state aid for environmental protection [2008] OJ C82/1. The validity of the Guidelines ended on 31 December 2014.

[180] Commission, Guidelines on certain state aid measures in the context of the greenhouse gas emission allowance trading scheme post 2012 [2012] OJ C154/4.

[181] Commission, Guidelines on state aid for environmental protection and energy 2014–2020 [2014] OJ C200/1.

normally considers environmental state aid compatible with the EU Treaties. Financial encouragements to consumers to acquire environmentally "better" products do not fall into this scheme as long as the aid does not advantage individual undertakings.[182]

EU subventions are particularly granted under the Structural Funds and the Cohesion Fund.[183] The Structural Funds aim at balancing the situation of economically disadvantaged regions, including rural areas (art.174 TFEU). The Member States entitled to receive funds establish programmes which are approved by the Commission; the individual projects which come under these agreed programmes are then realised under the responsibility of the Member State. The priorities and the taking of environmental measures are largely left to the discretion of each Member State.

The Cohesion Fund co-finances individual projects in the environmental and transport sector in those Member States where the gross national product lies below 90 per cent of the EU average. For the period 2014–2020, it benefits Bulgaria, Croatia, Cyprus, the Czech Republic, Estonia, Greece, Hungary, Latvia, Lithuania, Malta, Poland, Portugal, Romania, Slovakia and Slovenia. The regional policy system, applicable since 2007, integrated the Cohesion Fund into the general Regional Fund System which means that the sums which are made available are no longer ear-marked for specific projects. Regional funds may thus also co-finance projects which contribute to the implementation of obligations under EU environmental law, such as the construction of sewers, waste-water treatment plants, waste disposal or recovery installations or nature protection projects which is hardly completely compatible with the polluter -pays principle as laid down in arts 191 and 192(5) TFEU. There are several other EU aid programmes, in particular in the sectors of energy, research or agriculture.

As mentioned, there have been up until now no fiscal advantages granted by EU measures. Likewise, there are as yet no EU rules on environmental charges.

2–60

(vii) Tradable certificates; bubbles

Environmental certificates are used as tokens, which, against payment, are issued by the public authorities and give the right to input into the environment the quantity of pollutants indicated by the token. These certificates are tradable.

2–61

In 2003, The European Union adopted a Directive on tradable emission permits for greenhouse gases.[184] This Directive was brought under the auspices of the Kyoto Protocol to the United Nation Convention on Climate Change[185] which required, internationally, the introduction of tradable certificates by 2008. The EU system has been operational since the beginning of 2005. Undertakings which come under the Directive—some 20,000 installations which emit about 45 per

---

[182] Commission, Community guidelines on state aid for environmental protection [2008] OJ C82/1.

[183] Regulation 1303/2013 laying down general provisions on the European Structural Funds [2013] OJ L347/320; Reg.1300/2013 establishing a Cohesion Fund [2013] OJ L347/281.

[184] Directive 2003/87 establishing a scheme for greenhouse gas emission allowances trading within the Community [2003] OJ L275/32; for more details see para.9–10, below.

[185] See Dec.2002/358 concerning the approval, on behalf of the Community, of the Kyoto Protocol to the United Nations Framework Convention on Climate Change and the joint fulfilment of commitments thereunder [2002] OJ L130/1.

cent of all CO_2 emissions[186]—obtain an allowance for emitting CO_2 gases. Where they invest in cleaner technologies which reduce emissions, they may sell those allowances which they do not need any more. If, conversely, they need more allowances, they can buy them from other undertakings.

Under Regulation 1005/2009 producers of ozone-depleting substances have the possibility, granted by the Commission, of marketing specific quantities of ozone-depleting substances or to use the quantities themselves. Such rights may be transferred to other EU producers of the same substance; the Commission is to be informed of any such transaction.[187] The essential difference to certificates is the fact that this provision deals with a product for which limitations already exist and that the general objective of all these provisions is to progressively reduce and finally completely end the production of such substances.

2–62   The bubble concept requires, within a specific geographical area, that total pollution quantities are taken into account. Within this total quantity, the different emittors may emit differing quantities of pollutants. EU law provided for a bubble concept in Directive 2001/80 on emissions from large combustion plants,[188] where total quantities for sulphur dioxides (SO_2), nitrogen oxides (NOx) and dust emissions have been set for each Member State. These total quantities were to be reduced in two or three stages. It was left to Member States to distribute nationally the total quantities for emissions. In the meantime, this Directive was integrated into Directive 2010/75.[189]

Furthermore, Directive 2001/81 on national emission ceilings asked Member States to reduce, by 2010, air emissions of SO_2, NOx, volatile organic compounds and ammonia by a certain percentage.[190] How Member States achieve this reduction target was left to them. As with the Directive on large combustion plants, the main problem with this Directive is the monitoring of its application. It will hardly be possible for any national or EU body to monitor the application of the targets, or for the Commission to take any action under art.258 TFEU. Indeed, the compilation of data to prove the non-respect of the obligations is much too complicated in the hands of the Member State in question. Therefore, the same remarks as para.2–30, above, apply: where a Member State has the political will to comply with the requirements of Directive 2001/81, it has at its disposal a sufficiently flexible instrument to do so. However, where this political will is absent, almost no enforcement means are available.

A form of bubble concept was incorporated into the Agreement on the transit of the Alps between Austria and the European Union.[191] Lorries which crossed the Alps via Austria were charged with "eco-points"; the number of points varied according to the lorry's pollution emissions. Member States obtained a total number of carriages which they had to attribute to the individual lorries. The total

---

[186] An attempt to include airplanes taking off or landing in the European Union failed due to resistance from many non-EU countries.

[187] Regulation 1005/2009 [2009] OJ L286/1, arts 3(10) and 4(5).

[188] Directive 2001/80 [2001] OJ L309/1.

[189] Directive 2010/75 [2010] OJ L334/17.

[190] Directive 2001/81 on national emission ceilings for certain air pollutants [2001] OJ L309/22.

[191] Agreement between the European Economic Community and the Republic of Austria on the transit of goods by road and rail [1992] OJ L373/6; Reg.3637/92 on a system of distribution of rights of transit (eco-points) for heavy goods vehicles with a laden weight of over 7.5 tonnes registered in a Member State transiting through Austria [1992] OJ L373/1.

number of eco-points was to be reduced by 60 per cent during the 12-year period of the Convention. This agreement became incorporated in the Austrian Accession Treaty when Austria joined the European Union in 1995, but ended in 2003.[192]

(viii) Targets

Beginning with the 5th Environment Action Programme 1993, the EU environmental policy worked more and more with "targets". Targets (in French *objectifs*), are normally numeric objectives to be reached within a specific time-span, for example a 20 per cent reduction of greenhouse gas emissions until 2020. They may be binding[193] or non-binding[194] and may be addressed by Member States or by the European Union. Targets set by the European Council[195] are always non-binding targets, as the European Council does not exercise legislative functions (art.15(1)TEU). Targets are frequent in the EU climate change policy.   **2–63**

    EU targets are, in practice, not enforced. To this contributes without doubt that the measuring results for such targets are only known with a delay of several months or even years and that evidence is not easy to establish, though the main reason is political: the Commission does not wish to take Member States to court with regard to their climate change policy. Thus, for example, when Spain increased its greenhouse gas emissions by more than 50 per cent until 2008, though it was allowed, under Decision 2002/358,[196] to increase it only by 15 per cent, the Commission turned a blind eye to this situation. Targets set for EU institutions could, at best, be enforced by a Member State, but Member States are not keen to do so. The conclusion is that even binding targets set by the European Union are essentially of political, not legal importance.

---

[192] Agreement between the European Economic Community and the Republic of Austria on the transit of goods by road and rail [1992] OJ L373/6; Reg.3637/92 on a system of distribution of rights of transit (eco-points) for heavy goods vehicles with a laden weight of over 7.5 tonnes registered in a Member State transiting through Austria [1992] OJ L373/1.

[193] See, e.g. Dir.2009/28 on renewable energies [2009] OJ L140/16, arts 1 and 3(4): "This Directive . . . sets mandatory national targets. Each Member State shall ensure that the share of energy from renewable sources in all forms of transport in 2020 is at least 10% of the final consumption of energy in transport in that Member State."

[194] See, e.g. Dir.2012/27 on energy efficiency [2012] OJ L315/1, art.3(1): "Each Member State shall set an indicative national energy efficiency target."

[195] See, e.g. European Council Conclusions of 23–24 October 2014, Doc. EUCO 169/14: "(The European Council) endorsed a binding EU target of an at least 40% domestic reduction in greenhouse gas emissions by 2030 compared to 1990."

[196] Decision 2002/358 [2002] OJ L130/1.

3. DECISION-MAKING PROCEDURE

(a) Elaboration of a legislative measure

(i) Commission proposal

2–64   The Commission has, as mentioned, the monopoly on taking initiatives for environmental legal action, although there is a political obligation to take such initiatives under art.225(2) and art.192(3) TFEU.[197] It is at the Commission's discretion to decide what form, objective and content its proposal for a legislative act shall take and what preparatory work is undertaken. Normally, a comparative assessment of national legislation is made as well as one or several studies on the scientific, technical, economic and environmental aspects of a subject and estimations about the impact of the planned measures undertaken. Draft proposals are prepared by the technical units inside the Directorate-General responsible, not by a central "drafting unit".

Consultations with Member States at an administrative level generally start with a first draft of a directive, which is frequently accompanied by background documents which explain the approach chosen, indicate the options and raise other matters that might be of interest. Practice varies as to whether at this stage of the drafting a consensus is sought with other departments inside the Commission before a draft is sent to a wider audience.

Such discussions hardly ever take the form of bilateral discussions with Member States (which would take place in the different capitals rather than in Brussels): they are limited to particularly "important" Member States and they are mainly made to consult on the approach to be taken or the strategy to be adopted. Multilateral discussions on draft proposals for environmental directives between the Commission's administration and Member States' officials always take place. These meetings are convened in Brussels on invitation by the Commission administration which chairs them. Officials from interested Commission departments participate. The invitation to these meetings is addressed to the Permanent Representation of Member States with the European Union and asks them to designate experts to attend the meeting. The experts need not come from environmental administration or even administration at all.

2–65   As environmental law is often technical and has a limited number of national rules to take into consideration, only one or two of such multilateral meetings of experts are usually needed to reach a consensus. In areas where more general problems are touched upon, discussions inside the Commission and with Member States' experts may take a long time. Thus, while the Commission services drafted 23 texts for a proposal on environmental impact assessment[198] before the text could become an official proposal for a directive and be sent to the Council, the Directive on liquid beverage containers[199] had almost as many drafts.

Parallel to those meetings with governmental experts, discussions with organisations from trade and industry and environmental organisations take place. No systematic consultation is organised, although the Commission services

---

[197] See para.2–17, above.
[198] Directive 85/337 [1985] OJ L175/40; for more details see paras 4–30 et seq., below.
[199] Directive 85/339 [1985] OJ L176/18; see also paras 10–46 et seq., below.

prefer consultation with European organisations over national bodies or even individual companies. The sheer number of professional organisations guarantees them a greater chance of consultation, compared to environmental organisations which are under-represented at EU level and lack resources, know-how and expertise in successful lobbying. Internet consultation became, in recent years, more and more frequent; it is almost exclusively done in English. The European Ombudsman considered that consultations which do not take place in all official EU languages, constitute a case of maladministration from the side of the Commission; however, the Commission refused to change its practice.[200]

Since the beginning of 2003, the Commission has established an impact assessment process. For new legislative proposals, an impact assessment is made, which researches the economic, social and environmental implications of the future proposal, including the examination of alternatives, of a zero alternative (not legislating), etc.[201] The impact assessment paper is made available to the public in the form of a Commission working document after the formal adoption of the legislative proposal by the Commission.

At the end of the consultation and impact assessment process, a draft text emerges which the Directorate-General responsible takes back into the Commission in order to start the formal adoption phase. The draft, together with an explanatory memorandum,[202] is sent to all interested Directorates-General and in all cases to the Legal Service with the request for approval. There will be different positions (which of course are also influenced by outside lobbying) with an attempt to reach a compromise text. The revised text then goes into the approval procedure of the Commission itself. At cabinet level, attempts are made to find, if necessary, a political compromise on outstanding questions.

2–66

If the cabinets succeed, the 28 Commissioners normally approve the draft by way of written procedure. Where they do not succeed or where the text is of political importance, the draft is discussed orally: a simple majority of Commissioners is necessary to have a draft adopted as a formal Commission proposal. It may happen that a text is not capable of being approved by the Commission, though this is rather unusual in environmental matters.

The official Commission proposal for a directive or a regulation is published as a COM document, and only in exceptional cases in the *Official Journal of the European Communities*, Part C. The explanatory memorandum, which is not an integral part of the proposal, is made available to the public in the form of an official COM document; in order to avoid lengthy translations, numerous details are put into an SEC (Secretariat) or SWD (Staff Working Document) document which is normally also publicly available. The text of the proposed Act is drafted

---

[200] European Ombudsman, Annual Report 2013 (Strabourg 2014), p.33.

[201] Commission, Communication on Impact Assessment COM(2002) 276.

[202] Internal Commission rules have largely standardised the content of the explanatory memorandum, though each text is adapted to the specific subject matter; as an example, the proposal for a directive on end-of-life vehicles, COM(97) 358 of 9 July 1997, might be quoted which contains the following headings: 1. Introduction; 2. Problems addressed in this proposal; 3. The fifth environmental action programme; 4. Environmental objectives; 5. Internal market and economic objectives; 6. Economic assessment; 7. Situation in Member States; 8. Developments at international level; 9. Subsidiarity and proportionality; 10. Legislative and administrative simplification; 11. Imports from third countries; 12. Consistency with other Community policies; 13. Consultation with stakeholders; 14. Legal basis; 15. Data/scientific bases; 16. Content Article by Article; 17. Impact of the proposal on business with special reference to small and medium-sized enterprises.

in all official languages, while the explanatory memorandum is usually only produced in English, French and German.

(ii) European Parliament, ECOSOC and Committee of the Regions

2–67   The Commission's proposal is transmitted to the European Parliament and the Council, which passes the text on to the Economic and Social Committee and the Committee of the Regions. The Parliament adopts a legislative resolution with textual amendments, the Committees give opinions on the text. These comments are prepared within committees, under the responsibility of a rapporteur for the proposal, who is selected from the committee's members. Commission officials attend committee meetings, answer questions and explain reasons for the options taken. Their position is marked by the necessity to "defend", if possible, the Commission's proposal.

There is no standard practice for how the rapporteurs assemble the necessary know-how to prepare their report and the draft opinion. Both are mostly prepared by means of informal contacts with persons or groups which are politically or professionally close to the rapporteur's political party or group; formal written consultation with groups or public hearings in the Parliament are exceptional and almost never take place in the other two bodies.

In Parliament, the Environmental Committee votes on the draft opinion and all amendments which were presented by members of the Committee. Other committees also deal with the proposal, according to their responsibilities. Thus, for example, the Commission's proposal for a directive on environmental liability was discussed in the Committee on Legal Affairs and Internal Market as the leading committee, the Environmental Committee, the Industry Committee, the Economic Affairs Committee and the Petitions Committee. All these committees may request amendments of the proposed text. Then the text which has been adapted by the leading committee, goes to Parliament's plenary, where again amendments to the draft opinion may be tabled. The opinion is voted upon and is, after adoption, published in the *Official Journal*. The Committees' reports are published on the internet.

2–68   Since 1979, when the European Parliament became elected by general elections, there has been agreement between the Commission and the Parliament that the Commission would take on board amendments suggested by the Parliament wherever possible. Obviously, such a vague clause which raises difficulties in practice, does not satisfy Parliament, which is of the opinion that, as it is an elected body, all amendments to proposals should be accepted by the Commission. It sometimes uses procedural means (delays or refusals to vote, extensive discussions between the rapporteur and the Commission's services or the president of the Environmental Committee and the Commissioner for environmental issues) in order to compel the Commission to accept its amendments. The procedure in the Economic and Social Committee and the Committee of the Regions is similar; also their adopted opinions which generally do not contain precise drafting proposals, are published in the *Official Journal*.

(iii)   Council procedure

At Council level the Commission's proposal is first examined by a working   **2–69**
group, which normally takes up its work without having the opinion of the other
institutions. The frequency of meetings depends on whether the presidency
wishes to get ahead with the proposal[203]; whereas some proposals are
immediately taken up, others might wait for years or not be discussed at all. The
working party starts with a general discussion and then passes through each
individual article. After having revised the proposal and listed all objections to its
different provisions in detail, the working group's chair sends the text to the
Committee of Permanent Representatives (COREPER). He may also do so when
he wishes to receive political instruction on questions which the working group
feels unable to solve. The report sent to COREPER contains the new text
proposal, accompanied by remarks, reservations, suggested compromise solutions or declarations by Member States.

COREPER meets once a week and deals with practically all questions of EU
policy. In environmental matters, COREPER tries to concentrate discussions on
Commission proposals in one or two meetings which take place in preparation of
Council meetings on environmental matters. After discussion of the environmental proposal as it emerged from the working group, the text is either sent back to
the working group with further instructions or—where an agreement by the
Council seems possible—it is sent to the Environmental Council for decision or
for political guidance on basic issues. COREPER prepares the Council agenda,
though the final decision on it is made by the presidency of the Council.

The Council may only take a decision where the opinions of the other
institutions, in particular that of the European Parliament, have been given; and in
all cases the Council must decide unanimously where it amends a Commission
proposal (art.293 TFEU), though the Commission, wanting its proposal to be
adopted, hardly ever refuses to agree to amendments in environmental matters.
The Council's decision in environmental matters consists of the adoption of the
Commission's proposal, where the Parliament has only a consultative function—
mainly arts 192(2) in environmental matters and 43 TFEU in agricultural-
environmental matters—or where Parliament has either not proposed
amendments or the Council adopts all amendments proposed by the European
Parliament.[204] In other environmental cases, the Council establishes its
"position".[205]

Subsequently, the Council's position is submitted to the European Parliament   **2–70**
for a second reading. If Parliament agrees to that position or does not decide, the
Council's position is formally adopted as the legislative act; if Parliament rejects
the Council's position with an absolute majority, the proposal is rejected. If the
Council agrees to all amendments which Parliament has proposed in the second
reading, the legal act is so adopted. In practice, as mentioned in para.2–18, above,

---

[203] As an example, Dir.96/59 on PCB/PCT [1996] OJ L243/31 may be quoted, which took eight years
between the Commission's proposal and the adoption by the Council; in contrast, the proposal for
Dir.96/61 on integrated prevention and pollution control, which now, after several amendments, has
become Dir.2010/75 [2010] OJ L334/17 was adopted within two years.

[204] Article 294 no.4 TFEU.

[205] Article 294 TFEU uses the term "position". Before the entry into force of the Lisbon Treaty, this
Council position was called "common position", and this terminology continues to be frequently used.

the Parliament only very exceptionally succeeds in substantially changing the Council's position. In recent years, more and more informal agreements were made between the Parliament and the Council to even avoid a second reading and to have the legislative act adopted in the first reading. The negotiations leading to such agreements are largely influenced by policy and political party considerations; they are not public and open the door to all sorts of bargaining.

Where after the second reading divergences continue to exist, a Conciliation Committee is convened which consists of 28 members of the Council and the same number of members from Parliament; the Commission participates, but is not a member as such. Also, the Commission is no longer to defend its own proposal, but has the obligation to try to find a compromise between the European Parliament and the Council. Where a compromise is reached, that compromise becomes the adopted legal act. Where no compromise is reached, the proposal is considered rejected. Details of this co-decision procedure, which is the normal procedure in environmental matters since 1999, are laid down in art.294 TFEU.

The co-decision procedure is complicated and can hardly be called a legislative procedure in which citizens have much input. It is marked by the effort to place more influence on the legislative procedure to the European Parliament, the only elected EU institution, without significantly reducing the decision-making power of Member States who meet in Council.

2–71   In order to shorten the legislative procedure, the Council, the European Parliament and the Commission meet more and more frequently in so-called "Trilogue" meetings. In such cases, normally only the Parliament's rapporteur and the shadow rapporteurs of the other political parties represent the Parliament;[206] the discussions during the Trilogue meetings are not public. Where such meetings take place before Parliament has given its opinion on a Commission proposal, the plenary of the Parliament never discusses this proposal, but only the compromise text which emerges from the Trilogue meeting. This procedure is not in compliance with art.294 TFEU.

The procedure of art.294 TFEU is the normal procedure for decisions in environmental matters, as follows from art.192(1) TFEU. However, since art.11 TFEU requires that environmental requirements are taken into consideration when measures in other policy sectors are adopted, measures which aim at protecting or improving the environment need not necessarily be based on art.192(1) TFEU. Rather, art.192(2), art.191(4) for international environmental matters, art.43 for agricultural matters, art.90 on transport, art.113 on taxation, art.114 on the internal market, art.207 on commercial matters or art.188 TFEU on research may also be applicable.

(b)   The choice of the legal basis

(i)   General principles

2–72   The choice of a legal basis of a legislative act is of importance, as the decision-making procedure and in particular the European Parliament's right to participate in the making of the decision is different under different Treaty

---

[206] Rule 70 of the Rules of Procedure of the European Parliament.

provisions. Furthermore, the rights of Member States to adopt legislation at national level after the adoption of the EU Act vary.

The Council favours art.192 TFEU in environmental matters, but does not hesitate, according to circumstances, to choose a double legal basis[207] or to take another legal basis than art.192, in particular arts 114, 90 or 43 TFEU. Sometimes, such a decision also seems to be influenced by political considerations.

The Court of Justice stated at several occasions that the choice of the legal basis for an EU measure is not left to the discretion of the EU institutions, but has to be based on objective criteria, in particular the stated objective and the content of the measure.[208] Furthermore, the Court is of the opinion that where a measure pursues two objectives at the same time, which have exactly the same weight in a given context, preference has to be given to the legal basis that ensures greater participation of the European Parliament.

A situation that two policy objectives have exactly the same weight, seems to be very exceptional. The relevant decision in this regard[209] was taken at a time when the European Parliament had greater participation rights under art.114 TFEU (co-decision rights according to art.294 TFEU) than under art.192 TFEU (at that time cooperation procedure under art.252 EC). These differences no longer exist. It seems impossible to base a legislative environmental act on both arts 192 and 114 TFEU, as the residual powers of Member States under arts 193 and 114(4–9) TFEU are very different and a double legal basis would create considerable legal uncertainty. Consequently, and quite rightly, neither the Commission nor the Council ever tried to base a legislative act on arts 192 and 114 jointly.[210]

2–73

However, in case C-178/03 the Court stated that Regulation 304/2003 on the export and import of dangerous chemicals had to be based on the double legal basis of arts 133 and 175 (now arts 207 and 192 TFEU).[211] It considered, without further discussion, that the co-decision procedure of art.251 EC Treaty (now art.294 TFEU) should apply, though this procedure was foreseen in art.175, but not in art.133 EC Treaty. The Court did not discuss the question of Member States' residual rights; this is problematic, as art.192 TFEU is followed by art.193

---

[207] See, e.g. Dec.94/800 on adhering to the Uruguay agreements (WTO provisions) [1994] OJ L336/1, which was based on (old) arts 43, 54, 57, 66, 75, 84, 99, 100, 100a, 113, 235 EC Treaty; Dec.98/487 on an agreement with the United States on humane trapping methods for animals [1998] OJ L219/24, which was based on (old) arts 113 and 100a EC Treaty. For a recent example see Court of Justice, *Commission v Council* (C-377/12) ECLI:EU:C:2014:1903, where the Council added to a trade agreement with the Philippines arts 79, 91, 100 and 191(4) TFEU to the legal bases 207 and 209 TFEU that had been proposed by the Commission. The Court agreed with the Commission that the additions were not allowed.

[208] *Commission v Council* (C-155/91) [1993] E.C.R. I-939; *European Parliament v Council* (C-187/93) [1994] E.C.R. I-2857; *European Parliament v Council* (C-164/97; 165/97) [1999] E.C.R. I-1139.

[209] Court of Justice, *Commission v Council* (C-300/89) [1991] E.C.R. I-2867.

[210] See as an example on the one hand Dir.2000/53 on end-of-life vehicles [2000] OJ L269/34 which also contained a ban of certain substances in cars; this Directive was based on art.175 EC; on the other hand Dir.2012/19 [2012] OJ L197/38 and Dir.2002/95 [2003] OJ L37/19 which limited the use of certain substances in electrical and electronic equipment. While Dir.2012/19 was based on art.192 TFEU, Dir.2002/95 was based on the present art.114 TFEU.

[211] Court of Justice, *Commission v Council* (C-178/03) [2006] E.C.R. I-107.

TFEU which gives Member States the right to maintain or introduce more stringent environment legislation, whereas art.207 TFEU is not accompanied by a corresponding provision.

Therefore, may a Member State, based on art.193 TFEU, ban the export of a chemical, the export of which was not banned by the Union? It will be interesting to see how this dilemma is finally solved. I plead for an application of art.193 TFEU in such a case, as this would strengthen environmental legislation. The solution which would better correspond to the structure of the Treaty, though, would have been to have opted for art.207 TFEU as the only legal basis: indeed, Regulation 304/2003 which is now replaced by Regulation 649/2012,[212] is a product-related measure and it makes more sense to use, for such product-related provisions, arts 114 (internal market) and 207 (international trade) TFEU.[213]

2–74   Another option was chosen by Regulation 842/2006 on certain fluorinated greenhouse gases[214]: the Regulation was based on the EC Treaty "and in particular, Article 175(1) thereof and Article 95 thereof in relation to Articles 7, 8 and 9 of this Regulation". Thus, within one and the same legislative act, different legal provisions apply. This might help to a certain extent; however, provisions are also to be interpreted in their systematic content (contextual interpretation), which may require subtle ponderations, whether a Member State may deviate from the act's provision or not. It appears doubtful whether this differentiation will increase legal certainty.

Where two or more objectives of an environmental measure have a different emphasis, the Court applies the theory of the "centre of gravity": it looks at the legislative measure as a whole as well as at its different provisions. Where the measure primarily aimed at the protection of the environment, art.192 TFEU applies; where the main emphasis was placed on ensuring the free movement of goods, art.114 TFEU is the appropriate legal basis, even in cases where the measure also aims, secondly, at the protection of the environment.[215] Similar reasoning is applied when other Treaty provisions such as arts 43 or 207 are considered against art.192 TFEU.

The Court summarised its jurisprudence as follows[216]:

> "it is necessary, in order to determine the appropriate legal basis, to consider whether the measures in question relate principally to a particular field of actions, having only incidental effects on other policies, or whether both aspects are equally essential. If the first hypothesis is correct, recourse to a single legal basis is sufficient …; if the second is correct, it is insufficient and the institution is required to adopt the measure on the basis of both the provisions from which its competence derives … However, no such dual basis is possible, where the procedures laid down for each legal basis are incompatible with each other…"

---

[212] Regulation 649/2012 [2012] OJ L201/60.

[213] See also Court of Justice, *Kemikalieinspektionen* (C-288/08) E.C.R. I-11031, where the Court decided that a national export ban of mercury exports was not compatible with EU secondary law. In my opinion, the Court wrongly interpreted EU law against the interests of the environment, see for more details Krämer, comment on case C-288/08, *JEEPL* 2010, p.214.

[214] Regulation 842/2006 on certain fluorinated greenhouse gases [2006] OJ L161/1.

[215] *European Parliament v Council* (C-164/97; 165/97) [1999] E.C.R. I-1139 at [14].

[216] *European Parliament v Council* (C-164/97; 165/97) [1999] E.C.R. I-1139 at [14].

This theory seems to give good results in most cases. However, its concept raises a number of problems. Whether the objective of a directive or a regulation is the protection of the environment or the achievement of the internal market and the free flow of goods, is not at all clear. It is worth mentioning in this regard that the basic Directive on emission standards for cars was adopted as part of the EU programme to eliminate technical barriers to trade, i.e. with the objective of establishing a common market for cars.[217] The fact that a Member State presses for more stringent environmental standards for cars does not detract from the fact that the EU provision is primarily designed to maintain the free circulation of goods and to lay down stringent environmental standards to prevent a disturbance of the internal market. However, it may equally be the objective of an EU provision to take on board the motives of the environmentally conscious Member State and improve the quality of the environment. These reasons for an EU provision may be supplemented by others, such as protection of consumers, protection of the national or European motor industry, the attempt to restrict imports from third countries, or economic, transport or commercial policy reasons.

The introduction of EU car emission standards, which required the introduction of catalytic converters, was motivated by increased air pollution. This was the reason stated in the Directives, which were partly an amendment of Directive 70/220 and partly independent directives[218]; mention was also made of internal market considerations—however, this was in a very accessory way.

Directive 91/173 on restrictions of the use of pentachlorophenol (PCP),[219] based on the present art.114 TFEU, was constructed in a similar way: the Commission was notified by Germany of restrictions on the use of PCP. On its proposal, the Council adopted Directive 91/173 which severely restricted the use of PCP in the European Union, stating in the Directive that the main objective was to reduce the environmental and human health risk of PCP. Directive 2006/66 limits the content of dangerous substances in batteries and accumulators.[220] Its primary objective, as it appears in the preamble and the text of the Directive, is the reduction of dangerous substances in the environment; it was based on the present art.192 TFEU, with the exception of arts 4, 6 and 21 which were based on the present art.114 TFEU. The Directive concerning the reduction of lead in petrol and sulphur in diesel[221] was based on the present art.114 TFEU, the Directive on the reduction of sulphur in diesel alone on the present art.192 TFEU.[222] The restriction and ban of ozone-depleting substances is based on art.192 TFEU,[223] though the Regulation expressly stated that its main objective was the need to reduce the environmental and human health risks.

---

[217] Directive 70/220 [1970] OJ L76/1. In contrast, Reg.443/2009 on emission standards for CO_2 from cars [2009] OJ L140/1 was based on the present art.192 TFEU. The reason for this was probably that the standards were set for the whole car fleet of a producer, not for each individual car.

[218] Directive 88/6 [1988] OJ L36/1; Dir.88/436 [1988] OJ L214/1; Dir. 89/458 [1989] OJ L226/1; Dir.91/441 [1991] OJ L242/1; Dir.93/59 [1993] OJ L186/21; Dir.94/12 [1994] OJ L100/42.

[219] Directive 91/173 [1991] OJ L85/34.

[220] Directive 2006/66 [2006] OJ L266/1.

[221] Directive 98/70 [1998] OJ L350/58.

[222] Directive 1999/32 [1999] OJ L121/13.

[223] Regulation 1005/2009 [2009] OJ L286/1.

2–76   If one were taking the theory of the "centre of gravity" seriously, all these directives would have had to be based on art.192 TFEU alone, since their primary objective, as indicated in their recitals and as it appears from their objective and content, was the protection of the environment. In particular, where a substance or a product is banned or its use restricted, it is almost never the case that the primary objective will be the functioning of the internal market.

The theory of the centre of gravity of a specific measure is not as clear as it might appear. A good example is case C-300/89,[224] relating to Directive 89/428 on the harmonisation of programmes for the reduction of waste from the titanium dioxide industry,[225] where both the Council and the Commission agents based their arguments before the Court of Justice on the primary objective of Directive 89/428. However, while the Commission agent (attorney) saw the primary objective of the Directive as the creation of equal competitive conditions for the titanium dioxide industry and thus wanted to have the present art.114 established as the correct legal basis, the Council agent saw as its primary objective the protection of the environment and pleaded for the present art.192 as the appropriate legal basis. The Court, in that specific case, did not concur with that theory at all and decided, for other reasons, in favour of art.114. Also in case C-178/03, the Commission, Council and Parliament disagreed on the centre of gravity of Regulation 304/2003; in that case, the Court decided that the double legal basis of arts 133 and 175 was the correct basis.[226]

The conclusion from all this is that the wording of the Preamble and the articles of a legal Act cannot be decisive on their own, particularly as it is an EU institution, namely the Council, in fact, which determines the wording of a legislative act, in cases of a common decision together with the European Parliament. Recitals are normally adopted without much discussion. However, the Council is also obliged to respect the provisions of the Treaty; it cannot turn away from it just by arranging the wording of a legislative measure.

2–77   The relevant criterion must therefore be, whether—independent from the wording of the measure—uniformity is necessary to achieve the Treaty's objective. Indeed, as follows from art.26 TFEU, the European Union has the objective of achieving the free movement of goods and services as quickly as possible. This objective requires uniform rules. For this reason, EU instruments laying down common product standards must come under art.114 TFEU. This provision also applies when the measure contains common provisions of a restrictive nature, such as bans, restrictions on use, or maximum concentration levels, for example. If such measures were based on art.192 TFEU, the effect arising from art.193 TFEU would be that the European Union's objective of achieving free circulation of goods or, more generally, of completing the internal market, would never be attained. The legal basis of a measure which affects the environment *and* the circulation of goods should therefore be chosen with a view to permitting achievement of both objectives, namely completion of the internal market (art.26 TFEU) and improvement of the quality of the environment (art.192 TFEU). The better provision for both these objectives is art.114 and, for international measures, art.207 TFEU. Since art.11 TFEU requires that

---

[224] Court of Justice, *Commission v Council* (C-300/89) [1991] E.C.R. I-2867.

[225] Directive 89/428 [1989] OJ L201/56.

[226] Court of Justice, *Commission v Council* (C-178/03) [2006] E.C.R. I-107.

environmental requirements must be integrated into other EU policies, the choice of this legal basis is not really a risk for the environment.

The Council seems, at present, to apply art.192 as a basis for harmonisation of product-related measures, in cases where it does not wish to proceed to total harmonisation under art.114. This approach neglects art.26 TFEU, which expressly requires measures that lead to the achievement of the internal market. Article 26 TFEU is so clear and unambiguous that there is no room for having product-related measures adopted under art.192 TFEU. Article 26 TFEU and, more generally, the whole Treaty is also binding on the Council. It should also be noted that art.114 TFEU also allows the adoption of legislative acts which allow Member States to adopt or maintain more stringent protection measures; a recent example is Directive 2010/63.[227]

In conclusion, therefore, all product-related measures must, under the present FEU Treaty, be based on art.114 TFEU, with the exception, though of art.43, which is *lex specialis* to art.114, as appears from art.38(2) TFEU.[228] For international product-related measures, art.207 TFEU would be the appropriate legal basis.

(ii) Nature protection

Nature conservation measures are a specific problem. Fauna and flora species are not products under the TFEU, as is obvious from art.36 TFEU: if they were to be treated as products, their being mentioned in art.36, which constitutes an exception to art.34 TFEU, would not be justified. It also appears from art.114(4) TFEU that measures for the protection of the health and life of animals and plants are different from product-related measures: under certain conditions, Member States may take such measures, while they are not allowed to do so in order to protect products.

2–78

The Council has therefore quite rightly based nature protection measures on art.192(1),[229] including provisions on trade in endangered species. Exceptions are Regulation 3254/91 on the ban of leg-hold traps and the import of certain furs from specified non-EU countries, which the Council based on the present arts 192(1) and 207 TFEU, jointly,[230] and Reg.1007/2009 which introduced a ban on trade in seal products and was based on the present art.114 TFEU.[231]

Measures on biotechnology also belong to nature conservation measures. Genetically modified organisms as well as genetically modified micro-organisms remain organisms, thus living entities. The fact of basing the deliberate release of genetically modified organisms on art.114[232] only indicates that the borderline between life and non-life has been lost. I would not find it shocking to have different provisions on biotechnology from one Member State to the other, as the ethical and environmental opinions about this technology differ so widely within the European Union. The situation is not fundamentally different from that of

---

[227] Directive 2010/63 on the protection of animals used for scientific purposes [2010] OJ L276/63.

[228] Article 38(2) TFEU: "Save as otherwise provided in Articles 39 to 44, the rules laid down for the establishment and functioning of the internal market shall apply to agricultural products."

[229] Prior to 1987, the Council had used art.308 EC Treaty as the legal basis.

[230] Regulation 3254/91 [1991] OJ L308/1; see also paras 5–38 et seq., below.

[231] Regulation 1007/2009 on trade in seal products [2009] OJ L286/36.

[232] Directive 2001/18 [2001] OJ L106/1.

nuclear technology, waste incineration or the landing and take-off—the "free circulation"—of the *Concorde* airplane, where each Member State decides whether or not to have this technology on its territory. In 2010, the Commission proposed to allow Member States to prohibit or restrict the cultivation of genetically modified organisms in their territory for reasons other than the protection of health or the environment.[233] The proposal, which was based on art.114 TFEU, was finally adopted in 2015.

(iii) Waste

2–79   Another specific problem is the legal basis for waste measures. Wastes are physical objects and as such are capable of being traded between Member States. International legislation has, in the last 30 years, differentiated between waste which is destined for recovery and waste which is destined for final disposal. The reason for this is that a buyer might have an interest in acquiring waste which has an economic value; by contrast, the owner of waste which is destined for disposal would normally be willing to pay for such a disposal, in order to get rid of the waste.

The Court of Justice decided that waste comes under art.34 TFEU, whether it was recoverable or not.[234] The Court justified this decision by pointing out that waste was the subject of commercial transactions and that it was in practice impossible to differentiate between recoverable and non-recoverable waste. The Court added, however, that "waste has a special characteristic. The accumulation of waste, even before it becomes a health hazard, constitutes a threat to the environment because of the limited capacity of each region or locality for receiving it".

Although waste is a product, the Court held, in another judgment, that Directive 91/156[235] on waste was rightly based on art.175 EC (now art.192 TFEU).[236] In this judgment, the Court recurred to the theory of the "centre of gravity", to the primary objective of the legislative act: it saw the Directive as aiming primarily at the protection of the environment and only dealing in an ancillary way with aspects of the internal market. This choice of legal basis was further confirmed in case C-187/93,[237] where the Court again recurred to the theory of "centre of gravity" and held that Regulation 259/93 on the shipment of waste[238] was correctly based on the present art.192 TFEU.

2–80   The Council based directives on titanium dioxide waste[239] and on packaging and packaging waste[240] on art.95 EC (now 114 TFEU). This approach seems to suggest that the Council considers arts 192 and 114 as being equally capable of being used for product-related waste standards and that it chooses the legal basis

---

[233] Directive 2015/412 on the cultivation of genetically modified organisms [2015] OJ L68/1.

[234] *Commission v Belgium* (C-2/90) [1992] E.C.R. I-4431: "waste, whether recyclable or not, should be regarded as a product the movement of which must not in principle, pursuant to Article 30 EEC, be impeded".

[235] Directive 91/156 on waste [1991] OJ L78/32.

[236] *Commission v Council* (C-155/91) [1993] E.C.R. I-939.

[237] *European Parliament v Council* (C-187/93) [1994] E.C.R. I-2857.

[238] Regulation 259/93 [1993] OJ L30/1; this Regulation is now replaced by Reg.1013/2006 [2006] OJ L190/1.

[239] Directive 89/428 [1989] OJ L201/56.

[240] Directive 94/62 on packaging and packaging waste [1994] OJ 365/10.

according to the relative emphasis on free circulation or the protection of the environment as it is expressed in each directive. As mentioned, the Treaty provisions are not at the disposal of the Council and the obligation to complete the internal market as quickly as possible excludes having recurrence to art.192 or 114 at the Council's discretion.

A closer look at Directive 94/62 illustrates the problem. The Directive is based on the present art.114. Of the first 12 recitals, 10 deal with environmental objectives and two with environmental and internal market issues; not one recital deals exclusively with internal market issues. Article 1 indicates the objective of the Directive, stating as the first objective the protection of the environment.[241] Articles 9 and 10 provide for essential requirements which packaging has to comply with. Article 18 stipulates that packaging which satisfies the Directive's provisions shall not be impeded from circulating within the European Union.

It is difficult to see how the main aim of this Directive, according to its objective and content, could be the achievement of the internal market rather than the protection of the environment. All the Court's criteria plead for art.192 TFEU as the legal basis.

Advocate-General Tesauro, in his Opinion on case C-155/91,[242] held that waste directives concerning specific items of waste or waste from specific industrial sectors (such as batteries, packaging waste or waste from the titanium dioxide industry) are to be based on art.114 TFEU, since in such cases the competitive element of an act at EU level is dominant. In contrast, waste measures which tackle the problem of waste generally were to be based on art.192 TFEU, since their primary objective was environmental protection.

2–81

It is not quite clear whether the Court of Justice, in case C-155/91, implicitly adhered to that concept. It has the disadvantage that the impact of a "general" directive or regulation on a specific sector of industry might be as great as the impact of a "specific" directive: the borderline between general acts and specific acts is not at all clear, particularly if one remembers that, for instance, "general" Directive 2008/98 is accompanied by Decision 2000/532 which contains a detailed list of wastes which come under that Directive[243]; and that "general" Regulation 1013/2006 on the shipment of waste contains a long list of waste, the shipment of which undergoes different control procedures or the export of which to third countries is banned.[244]

In conclusion, there is not yet a clear, convincing way to classify waste-related measures under either art.192 or art.114 TFEU. The Council favours art.192, because of the existence of art.193, and because that provision leads to less

---

[241] Article 1 of Dir.94/62: "1. This Directive aims to harmonise national measures concerning the management of packaging and packaging waste in order, on the one hand, to prevent and impact thereof on the environment of all Member States as well as of third countries or to reduce such impact, thus providing a high level of environmental protection, and, on the other hand, to ensure the functioning of the internal market and to avoid obstacles to trade and distortion and restriction of competition within the Community.

2. To this end this Directive lays down measures aimed, as a first priority, at preventing the production of packaging waste and, as additional fundamental principles, at reusing packaging, at recycling and other forms of recovering packaging waste and, hence, at reducing the final disposal of such waste."

[242] *Commission v Council* (C-155/91) [1993] E.C.R. I-939, Advocate Tesauro's Opinion at [10].

[243] Decision 2000/532 [2000] OJ L226/3.

[244] Regulation 259/93 [1993] OJ L30/1; see also para.10–35, below.

uniform EU legislation, leaving national administrations more leeway. The Court of Justice generally accepts this approach. It is to be expected that in future most waste legislation will be based on art.192, also because the European Parliament no longer has more participation rights under art.114 than under art.192 and is thus unlikely to push for the application of art.114.

(iv)   Other environmental measures

2–82   Environmental-related energy measures were, prior to the entry into force of the Lisbon Treaties, based on art.192 TFEU. With the introduction of art.194 TFEU, measures on renewable energies or energy saving are based on art.194.[245] As art.194 does not provide that Member States are allowed to adopt stricter environmental measures, a provision corresponding to art.193 TFEU is inserted in the individual directive or regulation.[246]

Industrial installations and other production-related standards and environmental production standards concern air emissions or water discharges from installations, conditions for landfill sites and accident-prevention measures in industrial plants.

Installations do not circulate freely within the European Union, but the products produced in them do. Environmental standards for plants may have an impact on costs and affect the competitive position of a manufacturer. This is therefore relevant for the establishment and functioning of the internal market which also includes competition that is free from distortion (art.114(4)TFEU).[247] The risk of distortion of competition increases as environmental standards become more stringent, unless uniform provisions prevail throughout the Union. If the objectives "completion of the internal market" and "improvement of the quality of the environment" are to be attained simultaneously throughout the Union, provisions relating to production standards or to plants must be based on art.114 TFEU.

2–83   The Council instead bases all production-related directives on art.192 TFEU and the Commission now follows the same line in its proposals. Underlying this decision is the concept that production standards within the European Union should, in principle, not be harmonised, a decision which was taken implicitly, when Directive 84/360 was substituted by Directive 96/61,[248] and Directive 76/464 repealed by Directive 2000/60.[249] The consequence is that the air or water emission standards from one steel work to the other, from one cement kiln to the other or from one power plant to the other vary within the European Union.

The present practice seems doubtful. Different environmental standards for the production of goods will lead to different competitive situations, the more cost-intensive such standards are, the greater the competitive distortion becomes. It might be acceptable to have differences between one Member State and another of 1 or 2 per cent in the production costs, when the differences are due to different

---

[245] See, e.g. Dir.2010/31 on the energy performance of buildings [2010] OJ L153/13; Dir.2012/27 [2012] OJ L315/1.

[246] Directive 2010/31 [2010] OJ L153/13, art.1(3); Dir.2012/27 [2012] OJ L315/1, art.1(2).

[247] Court of Justice, *Commission v Council* (C-300/89) [1991] E.C.R. I-2867.

[248] Directive 96/61 (1996) OJ L257/26; this Directive was since replaced by Dir.2008/1 [2008] OJ L24/8 and then by Dir.2010/75 [2010] OJ L334/17.

[249] Directive 2000/60 [2000] OJ L327/1.

environmental standards. However, where such differences reach 5, 10 or more per cent of the production costs[250] these differences must be eliminated through the adoption of uniform standards, thus by measures based on art.114. In other words, the dividing line between arts 114 and 192 TFEU is not fixed once and for all: it is flexible, and the more stringent the environmental standards are—always bearing in mind the requirement of a high level of environmental protection—the more it is necessary to base the measure on art.114.

Basing production-related environmental measures on art.192 also bears the political risk that Member States who place low priority on environmental issues will inevitably try to ensure that standards fixed at EU level are low, arguing that Member States with a developed environmental policy could always, under art.193, adopt more stringent protective measures. But a tendency towards lower EU environmental standards is bound to increase discrepancies within the Union and will thus be, from an environmental point of view, counterproductive. Indeed, even environmentally conscious Member States will be reluctant to adopt stricter measures as this would lead to a competitive disadvantage of installations on their territory.[251] Finally, it should be mentioned that the debates at EU level on environmental standards such as air emissions or water discharges or even on quality standards, never centre on the issue of how much pollution of the pollutant the environment can tolerate; the discussion instead focuses on the question of what standards can reasonably be imposed on the polluting industries or other polluters. This demonstrates that it is the competitive aspect—which comes under art.114 TFEU—which is in question, not the protection of the environment—which comes under art.192.

The Council's practice is in the meantime well established. The use of art.192 **2–84** is in Member States' and the affected industries interest, though not necessarily in the interest of competition and of the environment. However, as the environment has no voice, it cannot be expected that the present practice will change.

The Council's practice as to the choice of the legal basis might be summarised as follows:

1. Measures of a general nature are based on art.192. Examples: access to information, environmental impact assessment, eco-audit, measures related to installations, environmental liability.
2. Nature conservation measures are all based on art.192. Exceptions: ban on leg-hold trap and fur trade: arts 192 and 207 TFEU; ban on trade in seal products: art.114.
3. Products: measures are based on art.114. Exceptions: authorisation for pesticides: art.43; ozone-depleting substances, contained use of genetically modified micro-organisms: art.192.
4. Water measures are all based on art.192.
5. Air pollution measures are based on art.192. Exceptions: emissions from cars and motorcycles, composition of petrol and gas: art.114; emissions from airplanes: art.90.

---

[250] In Court of Justice, *Commission v Council* (C-300/89) [1991] E.C.R. I-2867 these differences reached 20 per cent of the production costs.

[251] Such a trend is already visible at the discussion on the introduction of a CO_2 tax at national level.

6.   Product-related noise measures are based on art.114. Exception: noise from airplanes: art.90. Measures on measuring noise levels are based on art.192.
7.   Energy measures to fight climate change are based on art.194.
8.   Waste measures are based on art.192. Exception: packaging and packaging waste, waste programmes from titanium dioxide industry: art.114.

(c)   The different legal bases

(i)   Measures under art.192(1) TFEU

2–85   Legal decisions—regulations, directives, decisions or recommendations—under art.192(1) are taken by the Council and Parliament jointly, according to the procedure of art.294 TFEU. The consultation of the Economic and Social Committee and of the Committee of the Regions is mandatory. When deciding, the Council and Parliament must be in possession of a proposal by the Commission.

Article 192(1) is completed by art.192(5) TFEU which was introduced in 1993. This provision has its origin in the idea, particularly stressed by the less wealthy Member States, that if the protection of the environment were in the general interest of the Union, then the Union should pay for such measures. The provision stipulates that the Council may, together with the legislative measure which it adopts, decide on either a temporary derogation for a specific Member State or a financial support from the European Union for that state. The following conditions must be fulfilled:

1.   The EU measure must be adopted by virtue of art.192(1) TFEU. This condition prevents a single Member State from vetoing the adoption of a Union measure until the state has obtained a temporary derogation or a financial assistance.
2.   There must be a request from a Member State that costs are disproportionate. This condition leads to an examination of the request by the Council, i.e. by all other Member States, and the Commission; thus, trivial requests will more easily be detected.
3.   The costs must be deemed to be inappropriate for the public authorities. It is thus not the cost of the measure itself which will be examined, but rather the cost impact on public authorities; where these authorities have the possibility of charging private undertakings, where in particular they can make the polluter pay, art.192(5) TFEU is not applicable.

The Council decision, which needs a qualified majority, may consist of temporary derogations or financial support from the Cohesion Fund. The possibility of granting a temporary derogation to some Member States existed well before the Maastricht Treaty and was used in a number of cases. This provision demonstrates that non-compliance with environmental provisions brings an economic advantage to the non-complying Member State.

2–86   The financial support from the Cohesion Fund, which, under art.192(5), is not limited to the Member States which are normally beneficiary of the Cohesion

Fund,[252] is not further specified. It may consist of a lump sum or in regular payments over a longer period, or the financing of an investment programme.

Paragraph 5 is introduced by the words "without prejudice to the principle that the polluter should pay". In view of this wording, it could well be argued that non-compliance with EU environmental legislation is a breach of the polluter pays principle.

Until the end of 2014, art.192(5) had not been applied even once by the Council.

(ii) Decisions on programmes, art.192(3) TFEU

Article 192(3) TFEU provides for co-decision majority procedures and also for the adoption of "general action programmes setting out priority objectives to be attained". The initiative for art.192(3) lies with the Commission, which cannot legally be obliged to submit a proposal for a decision on an action programme.[253] An action programme may be limited to a specific sector of environmental policy; it need not cover the whole range of activities.[254]   **2–87**

(iii) Decisions under art.192(2) TFEU

Article 192(2) provides for the adoption of some measures by unanimous decisions. The provision is an exception to art.192(1) and has therefore to be interpreted narrowly. The European Parliament, the Economic and Social Committee and the Committee of the Regions are only to be consulted; the Parliament has no right of deciding together with the Council.   **2–88**

Fiscal provisions. Provisions of a fiscal nature normally come under art.113 TFEU, which expressly provides for unanimous decisions. Article 113 provides for harmonisation of fiscal legislation to the extent that it is necessary for the establishment and functioning of the internal market. Article 192(2) TFEU clarifies that fiscal measures are also permitted in order to achieve the objectives of environmental protection that are mentioned in art.191(1) TFEU. Fiscal measures touch the core of national sovereignty. It is therefore understandable that Member States who did not accept majority decisions under art.113 TFEU were not ready to accept such majority decisions for eco-taxes.

Since the provision only mentions the fiscal character of a measure, acts which provide for environmental charges, environmental fees or an environmental fund for covering damage of the environment do not come under art.192(2) TFEU.[255] For a measure to come under art.192(2), the fiscal content must be the primary objective of the EU measure. Environmental provisions on taxes which form an additional part of another set of rules that are not primarily of a fiscal nature, may be the subject of majority decisions.[256]

---

[252] At present, until 2020, Greece, Portugal, Estonia, Latvia, Lithuania, Poland, Czech Republic, Hungary, Slovakia, Slovenia, Cyprus, Malta, Romania, Bulgaria and Croatia.

[253] See also para.2–06, above.

[254] See, e.g. the proposal for a groundwater action programme [1996] OJ C355/178.

[255] P. Pagh, *EU miljoeret*, 2nd edn (Copenhagen, 1996), p.120; A. Epiney, *Umweltrecht in der Europäischen Union*, 3rd edn (Baden-Baden Köln, 2013), p.101.

[256] See, e.g. the tax provisions in the different directives on car emissions, paras 4–61 et seq., below.

2–89   **Town and country planning and land use.**   The underlying concept of this provision is that Member States should themselves decide how they want to organise their territory. Therefore, measures for town and country planning and land use also have to be adopted unanimously. The provision in particular leaves infrastructural planning decisions to the autonomous decision of each Member State, since it gives to each state, via the unanimity requirement, a veto against EU planning decisions which affect its territory. It is consistent with this understanding that the provision of the EU Treaty, which deals with planning measures for infrastructures, also follows this approach: art.172(2) TFEU concerns the planning of trans-European networks for transport, telecommunications and energy infrastructure; it provides for the elaboration of EU (non-binding) guidelines for such networks, which may be adopted only with the approval of the Member State concerned.

Measures on environmental impact assessment for plans and programmes[257] do not concern town and country planning as such, but the way in which this planning is to be organised; such measures therefore come under art.192(1).

The quantitative management of water resources or affecting, directly or indirectly, the availability of those resources.   This provision was reformulated by the Treaty of Nice; the previous version of the Treaty only talked of "management of water resources". In case C-96/98, the Court of Justice had, against the wording of the Treaty in all but the Dutch and the French language, clarified that this older version only applied to the quantitative but not the qualitative management of water resources.[258] The Court based its interpretation on the objective of the provision, arguing that a measure concerning the quality of water would not affect the availability of the water resource.

2–90   **Land use, with the exception of waste management.**   This provision was also reformulated by the Treaty of Nice. The earlier version had, as a supplementary exclusion, "measures of general nature". It is questionable whether this amendment changed the sense of the provision.

The objective of the exclusion is again to ensure that Member States keep responsibility, if, where and in which dimensions they want to build, e.g. a new airport, a railway line, a port or another infrastructure project. This means in practical terms that, for instance, Directive 91/271 on urban waste water, which requests Member States to build waste-water treatment plants,[259] was rightly not adopted under art.192(2) but under art.192(1) TFEU: indeed, each Member State remains free to decide how many installations are to be built and where they are to be placed.

Whether Directives 2009/147[260] and 92/43[261] principally deal with "land use", is doubtful. Indeed, both Directives aim at the protection of species of fauna and flora and provide for a number of measures in this regard. Directive 2009/147

---

[257] Directive 2001/42 [2001] OJ L197/30.
[258] Court of Justice, *Spain v Council* (C-36/98) [2001] E.C.R. I-779.
[259] Directive 91/271 [1991] OJ L135/40.
[260] Directive 2009/147 on the conservation of wild birds [2010] OJ L20/7; this Directive replaced Dir.79/409 on wild living birds [1979] OJ L103/1. Article 175(1) (now art.192(1) TFEU) remained the legal basis.
[261] Directive 92/43 on the protection of natural habitats and wild fauna and flora [1992] OJ L206/7.

asks Member States to designate a sufficient number of birds' habitats in order to allow, for all those habitats together, to form a "coherent whole", thus a European network of habitats. The individual decision on which habitat is to be designated is up to the Member States. Directive 92/43 requests Member states to establish lists of habitats which might form part of an EU-wide list of habitats. Again, the original choice is thus made by Member states and specific provisions ensure that final, EU-wide designations of a habitat only occur with the agreement of a Member State in question. Furthermore, land use and changes of land use in designated habitats are not prohibited though restrictive assessment criteria apply.

It follows from all this that habitat protection measures in both Directives do not prohibit the land use in designated areas, and that the provisions for the balancing of interests in specific areas allow for a proportionate consideration of diverging interests. As the objective of both Directives is not the regulation of land or of habitats, but of fauna and flora protection, for which comprehensive provisions are made, the centre of gravity of both Directives is not land use, but nature and biodiversity protection. Therefore, art.192(1), not 192(2) TFEU would apply. **2–91**

Energy matters. Unanimous decisions are finally required for "measures significantly affecting a Member State's choice between different energy sources and the general structure of its energy supply". Measures which come under this provision are, for instance, measures which lead to the abandoning, for environmental reasons, of nuclear energy or of lignite or coal that has too high a sulphur content. Conversely, however, an EU measure not to allow the import of petrol from third countries and to rely primarily on nuclear energy throughout EU territory would need unanimity in Council.

In contrast, the decision to adhere to the United Nations Convention on Climate Change[262] was rightly based on art.192(1), not on 192(2), TFEU. Indeed, the Convention neither imposes specific measures which affect energy supply nor does it ask Member States to change their choice of energy sources. Finally, it does not impose the introduction of fiscal measures either, such as the introduction of an energy tax. What measures are taken at EU level in order to comply with the requirements of the Convention need thus to be decided by another measure, but this has not been prejudged by the decision to adhere to the Convention.

When the European Union prepared the adherence to the Kyoto Protocol, a number of Member States were of the opinion that the Council decision would have to be based on art.192(2), as the commitment to reduce greenhouse gas emissions until 2012 by 8 per cent with regard to 1990, significantly affected their energy policy. Only when the Environmental Commissioner threatened to submit this question to the Court of Justice, was the resistance abandoned and art.192(1) as the legal basis accepted. As the reduction of 8 per cent does not prescribe how it is to be achieved, there can be hardly any doubt that art.192(1) was the correct legal basis for the Council decision.[263] **2–92**

While in all these cases of art.192(2) the Council decides unanimously, it may decide to take majority decisions in the future in this area. The provision is of a

---

[262] Decision 94/69 [1994] OJ L33/11.
[263] Decision 2002/358 [2002] OJ L130/1.

rather theoretical nature; indeed, it has existed in a different form[264] since 1987, but has not played any significant role: there has not been one single sector in which the Council has introduced majority decisions.

(iv)   Decisions on international co-operation (art.191(4) TFEU)

2–93   Article 191(4) TFEU gives express competence to the European Union to conclude international environmental agreements (conventions), which are then binding on the institutions of the European Union and on Member States (art.216(2) TFEU). Details are laid down in art.218 TFEU.

Agreements were, prior to the Lisbon Treaty, negotiated by the Commission. Article 218(3) TFEU now provides that the Council appoints a "negotiator" which may also be, if it is not the Commission, the Member State that holds the Presidency of the Council. The Council may give, on the proposal of the Commission, but without the participation of the European Parliament, a negotiating mandate which is not published. During the negotiation period, the Commission continuously consults with a special Council committee composed of Member States' representatives. In practice, Member States also participate in the negotiation of agreements at international level, since such agreements also come into the competence of Member States; in fact, during these negotiations, the influence of Member States, at least some of them, is often greater than that of the Commission.

The question whether decisions to adhere to an international environmental convention, agreement or protocol is to be based on art.191(4), 192(1) or even on art.207 TFEU was, for some time, answered differently by the Commission and the Council. While the Commission, following in this a Court judgment in case C-268/94,[265] based its proposals on art.191(4), the Council adopted the proposals on the basis of art.192(1).[266] A clarification in this controversy was brought by the Opinion 2/00 of the Court,[267] where the question at issue was on which basis the Council decision to adhere to the Protocol of Cartagena[268] should be based. The Commission was of the opinion that arts 207 and 191(4) TFEU constituted the appropriate legal basis, whereas the Council and Member States were in favour of art.192(1) TFEU. The Court examined which the predominant purpose of the Protocol was and concluded that this was an environmental purpose. It excluded the application of art.191(4) TFEU, as the Protocol did not merely establish "arrangements for co-operation in environmental matters", but laid down precise substantive rules; this, it stated, required the Council decision to be based on art.192(1) TFEU. In case C-377/12, the Court held that an agreement with the Philippines on partnership and cooperation was to be based on arts 207

---

[264] Between 1987 and 1993, all environmental measures under art.192 TFEU had to be adopted unanimously.
[265] Court of Justice, *Portugal v Council* (C-268/94) [1996] E.C.R. I-6177; this case concerned the legal basis of art.181 EC which had the same wording as art.174(4) EC (the present art.191(4) TFEU).
[266] Decision 2002/628 [2002] OJ L201/48.
[267] Court of Justice, Opinion 2/00 [2001] E.C.R. I-9713.
[268] Protocol on biosafety, specifically focusing on transboundary movement, of any living modified organism resulting from modern biotechnology that may have adverse effects on the conservation and sustainable use of biological diversity, setting out for consideration, in particular, appropriate procedures for advanced informed agreement [2002] OJ L201/50.

and 209 TFEU alone, as transport, migration and environmental matters were only marginally touched in the agreement.[269]

As practically all international environmental agreements and the accessory protocols go beyond the fixing of arrangements for environmental co-operation, art.191(4) TFEU may thus only be used in rather exceptional circumstances. Following the Opinion of the Court in case 2/00 the Commission abandoned its idea to use, as a rule, art.191(4) as a basis for decisions to adhere to international conventions.

2–94

(v)   Decisions based on other Treaty provisions

As mentioned, EU acts affecting the environment may be based on Treaty provisions other than arts 191 and 192 TFEU. This applies to those environmental provisions where the "centre of gravity"[270] lies in policy areas other than environmental policy. The most relevant provisions are as follows.

2–95

Decisions in the agricultural sector (art.43 TFEU).   Article 43 provides that the Council, in working out and implementing the common agricultural policy, adopts legislation by a qualified majority. Numerous measures in agricultural policy affect air and soil, water, fauna, flora and the landscape. Examples include the use of fertilisers and pesticides, drainage and irrigation measures, land use, discharge of substances, animal waste, the production and marketing of agricultural products. The objective of the rules adopted by virtue of art.43 is the establishment of a common agricultural policy among Member States, which includes the production of uniform products and unified production and marketing conditions.

Since 1988 it has been accepted that measures under art.43 may also protect human health.[271] Also in 1988, the Court of Justice had to decide on the relationship between art.192 and art.43 and concluded that art.43 also included measures to protect the environment. The case concerned the ban on drift-nets for fishing which the Council had established by Regulation 345/92.[272] Some fishermen contested the legality of that ban, arguing, amongst other things, that the regulations should also have been based on art.192, which required, at that time, unanimous decisions. The Court held that the Regulation's principal objective was the protection of living marine resources and that this was an objective of the common fishery policy; thus, the appropriate legal basis was art.43. According to the Court, the application of art.192 was not necessary because environmental requirements had to be integrated into other policies anyway.[273]

All legislation on agricultural pesticides is now to be based on art.43 since that provision prevails, as mentioned at para.2–76, above, on art.114. This is accepted

2–96

---

[269] *Commission v Council* (C-377/12) ECLI:EU:C:2014:1903.
[270] See para.2–70, above.
[271] The landmark decision was *United Kingdom v Council* (68/86) [1988] E.C.R. 855.
[272] Regulation 345/92 [1992] OJ L42/15.
[273] Court of Justice, *Mondiet v Islais* (C-405/92) [1993] E.C.R. I-6133.

for the placing on the market of such pesticides,[274] but there is room for doubt as regards the ban of pesticides. Indeed, Directive 79/117, which first provided for the ban on some pesticides, was based on art.94 EC (now art.115 TFEU). However, this legislation was adopted prior to the above-mentioned Court decision in case 68/86. Today, that legal basis would be replaced by art.43, exactly because there is the new Treaty provision that environmental requirements must be integrated into other policies and measures under such policies. The Court's reasoning in case C-405/92 thus also applies in the case of banning pesticides.

Legal debate has taken place over which legal basis should apply to measures that protect forests against fire or against air pollution. The Council originally adopted such measures on the basis of arts 37 and 308 EC Treaty,[275] as in 1986, there were no environmental provisions in the Treaty. Amendments of 1989 were based on arts 37 and 175 EC Treaty.[276] In 1997, the Council adopted further amendments, basing them exclusively on art.37 EC Treaty.[277] The European Parliament attacked both Regulations 307/97 and 308/97 before the Court of Justice, arguing among other things that the Council had wished to exclude the cooperation of the European Parliament in the elaboration of these Regulations, which had become mandatory since 1993 under art.175(1) EC Treaty. The Court considered art.175 as the appropriate legal basis as it was of the opinion that the protection of forests against fire and atmospheric pollution was primarily an environmental measure and did not establish rules on the production and marketing of agricultural products.[278] This reasoning is all the more convincing, if one considers that the Commission co-financed reforestation projects after fire damage under the Cohesion Fund—which may co-finance environmental, but not agricultural projects.

The question whether environmental measures, which are adopted under art.43 TFEU, allow Member States, under art.193 TFEU to take more stringent measures, will be discussed at paras 3–61 et seq., below.

2–97   **Decisions in the transport sector (Article 90).**   The common transport policy, arts 90–100 TFEU, tries to set common conditions for transport within the European Union and beyond: such conditions may have a very considerable impact on the environment.

Both arts 91 and 100 TFEU now provide, as a rule, for majority decisions by virtue of art.294 TFEU. For that reason, the most relevant question is whether art.193 can be applied to measures adopted under art.90; again, this question will be discussed below at paras 3–61 et seq.

---

[274] Directive 91/414 [1991] OJ L230/51; in 2009, this Directive was repealed and replaced by Reg.1107/2009 [2009] OJ L309/1, which was based on the present arts 43(2), 114 and 169(4.b) TFEU.

[275] Regulation 3528/86 [1986] OJ L326/2.

[276] Regulation 1613/89 [1989] OJ L165/8.

[277] Regulation 307/97 [1997] OJ L51/9.

[278] *European Parliament v Council* (C-164/97; 165/97) [1999] E.C.R. I-1139.

Decisions regarding the internal market.   Article 114 outlines the fulfilment of the objectives set out in art.26 TFEU,[279] i.e. the progressive establishment of the internal market. Its wording clarifies that it can also be the legal basis for measures aimed at the protection of the environment. Indeed, finding the demarcation line between arts 114 and 192 TFEU was one of the biggest legal problems of the past. The Amsterdam Treaty has brought the two provisions much closer to one another, so that only some differences continue to exist concerning the procedures and consequences of maintaining or introducing more stringent national environmental measures than those agreed at EU level.

The Treaty itself does not contain criteria for making a clear distinction between arts 114 and 192. Article 114 wishes to achieve the internal market. Articles 191–193 aim at the protection of the environment at a high level; the provisions do not contain anything explicit that could be described as the "free movement of goods". On the contrary, art.191 explicitly states that different measures are both possible and necessary to protect the environment at a high level. **2–98**

As art.114 is concerned with goods and services, provisions which affect trade in such goods and services should, as mentioned above, be allocated primarily to art.114. Provisions which contribute to the attainment of one of the objectives specified in art.191 should primarily be assigned to art.192. As a consequence of the arguments on the choice of the legal basis given above, at paras 2–70 et seq. the Council should have based the Regulation on ozone-depleting substances[280] and the Regulation on export and import of certain dangerous chemicals[281] on the present art.114, since they both deal with product standards.

Decisions on commercial matters (Article 207 TFEU).   Framework Decisions in the area of commercial policy are taken by the European Parliament and the Council by a qualified majority (art.207(2) TFEU). The Council alone decides, with qualified majority, on the negotiation and conclusion of trade agreements with third countries or international organisations (art.207(4) TFEU); the European Parliament does not participate. The provisions on commercial policy establish exclusive Community competence, which means that there is no longer a Member States' commercial policy. In the past, however, the importance of art.133 EC Treaty (the present art.207 TFEU) for environmental issues was diminished as a result of differences about its meaning. Whereas the Commission considered art.133 EC relevant for all commercial provisions and international agreements, the Council applied art.133 EC only in those cases where the measure in question did not pursue any other than a commercial objective. Thus, where a trade-related measure also aimed at the protection of the environment, art.133 was, according to the Council, not relevant; other provisions applied instead, in particular art.175. In practice, therefore, art.207 TFEU is not applied to environmental matters, at least not without art.192 TFEU being added.

---

[279] Article 26(2) TFEU: "The internal market shall comprise an area without internal frontiers in which the free movement of goods, persons, services and capital is ensured in accordance with the provisions of the Treaties."

[280] Regulation 1005/2009 [2009] OJ L286/1.

[281] Regulation 2455/92 [1992] OJ L251/13. This Regulation is now replaced by Reg.649/2012 [2012] OJ L201/60.

2–99 The respective interpretations have been influenced by the fact that art.133 EC (now art.207 TFEU) gives exclusive competence to the European Union (see art.3(1e) TFEU), whereas, under arts 191–193 TFEU, the competence is shared between the European Union and Member States.

In recent times, the Court of Justice was content to apply its theory of "centre of gravity" to the present art.207 TFEU; this had for a long time not been the case. Thus, in case C-281/01,[282] the Court decided that art.207 was the appropriate legal basis for the decision to conclude an agreement between the United States and the EC on the coordination of energy efficient labelling requirements for office equipment. The Council had based its decision on the present art.192.[283] The Court held that the "predominant" objective of the Agreement was to facilitate trade and therefore commercial policy promotion. In contrast, the Court decided that a decision to ratify the Cartagena Protocol on trade in genetically modified products would have to be based on the present art.192,[284] as environmental considerations were predominant in this Protocol. The Commission had argued in favour of the application of the present art.207.

In view of these decisions, it is not likely that the Council practice will change quickly, all the more as the Court had decided, as mentioned in para.2–72, above, that under certain conditions the present arts 207 and 192 TFEU could be the double legal basis, without discussing Member States' residual rights. Further Court judgments will be necessary to solve this outstanding issue.

2–100 **Decisions on research matters.** Article 188 TFEU provides that the European Parliament and the Council decide on research measures, such as the establishment of joint undertakings or any other structure for the execution of EU research, technological development, demonstration programmes and on measures for the implementation of multi-annual research programmes. Multi-annual research framework programmes are adopted under art.182 TFEU.

Thus, decisions on research and development programmes in the area of the environment are taken on the basis of art.182. Article 192 does not apply since art.179(3) TFEU has solved this potential conflict by stipulating:

> "All Union activities under the Treaties in the area of research and technological development, including demonstration projects, shall be decided on and implemented in accordance with the provisions of this Title."

(vi)   Decisions under the provisions on enhanced co-operation

2–101 The Amsterdam Treaty had introduced a new form of decision-making, the so-called "enhanced cooperation" procedure. This procedure, which was amended by the Treaty of Nice and the Lisbon Treaty, is laid down both in art.20 TEU and arts 326–334 TFEU. It is not limited to environmental matters.

The underlying rationale of the procedure is that some Member States might wish to advance more rapidly than the European Union as a whole. Nothing currently prevents them from concluding a bilateral or multilateral international convention, which would then be governed by public international law and not

---

[282] Court of Justice, *Commission v Council* (C-281/01) [2002] E.C.R. I-11221.

[283] Decision 2001/469 [2001] OJ L172/1.

[284] Court of Justice, Opinion 2/00 [2001] E.C.R. I-9713.

constitute EU law—although, of course, such obligations would have to respect the Member States' obligations under the Treaty on European Union.

The flexibility provisions now offer a new possibility to those Member States that want to proceed more quickly: they may, under certain conditions[285] laid down in art.20 TEU, make use of the institutions, procedures and mechanisms laid down by the Treaties.

For any such enhanced cooperation, the Member States in question need an express authorisation from the Council. The Council may only act on a proposal from the Commission which has its own discretionary power to decide whether it wishes to submit a proposal to the Council or not.[286] The Council shall decide on the authorisation to cooperate by unanimity of those Member States which want to cooperate, after consultation with the European Parliament. **2–102**

As regards the measure adopted under the enhanced cooperation procedure, all the relevant provisions of the Treaty apply. The question once so controversial under art.293 EC (now repealed)—whether the conventions adopted under that provision were part of EU law or were measures of public international law—is answered in the case of the flexibility procedure: they are EU law. Indeed, the Commission, which must make a proposal for an enhanced cooperation measure, has only the competence to propose measures that are mentioned in art.288 TFEU, i.e. a regulation, directive or a decision. As regards the enhanced cooperation procedure, the decision-making in Council, the consultation of or the co-decision with the European Parliament, and the transposition of the measure into national law, its monitoring by the Commission under art. 258 TFEU and the possible judicial control under art.19 TEU—all follow EU law provisions. This leaves no room for the application of provisions of public international law. Article 20(4) TEU provides, though, that only the Member States which participate in the enhanced cooperation are bound by the measures adopted under that procedure, and that accession countries are not obliged to take them over, when they accede to the Union.

In order to illustrate the impact of the flexibility provisions on the environment, the fictitious example of a directive on environmental standards for swimming pools may be given. Under art.20(2) TEU, at least nine Member States could request the Commission to submit a proposal for such a directive. The Commission could then ask the Council to authorise the use of the "institutions, procedures and mechanisms of the Treaty". The Council would normally decide on this proposal by a qualified majority of the Member States which participate in the enhanced cooperation (art.330 TFEU).

The procedure of substance has to be distinguished from the authorisation procedure. The Commission would make a proposal for a directive on water quality in swimming pools, following the institutional procedures of art.192(1). The Directive would be adopted by a qualified majority of those Member States that participate in the cooperation. If, later, another Member State would like to be party to the EU enhanced cooperation procedure, the provisions of art.331 TFEU shall apply; the Council shall finally decide whether the conditions for such a participation are fulfilled. **2–103**

---

[285] See art.329(1) TFEU: "In the event of the Commission not submitting a proposal, it shall inform the Member States concerned of the reasons for not doing so."
[286] Article 329 TFEU.

Nothing would prevent the Commission, during its discussions in Council on a proposal which was intended to cover all Member States, from submitting to the Council a proposal for authorising the enhanced cooperation procedure. Indeed, despite the somewhat unclear wording of art.329 TFEU,[287] the start of the procedure does not depend on the initiative of a majority of Member States. It is up to the Commission to ensure that the flexibility procedure does not put the coherence of the Union at risk.

Articles 326, et seq. TFEU do not provide for the elaboration of a proposal by Member States. Indeed, the reference to the Treaty provisions also has the consequence that the Council may only act upon a proposal from the Commission, as is also foreseen in art.192(1). In particular, art.293(1) TFEU provides that the Council may only unanimously amend a proposal from the Commission.

2–104   This provision would be set aside if the Council could also decide upon a proposal from Member States.

In conclusion, cooperating Member States have the choice to recur either to forms of public international law, or to establish, within the EU framework, EU law.

Since 1999, not one single case occurred where a Member State, in environmental matters, asked for or suggested the application of the enhanced cooperation procedure. The chances that this situation will change in the future are small, though the enlargement of the European Union might make general decision-making more difficult. Candidates for enhanced cooperation are in particular provisions in the area of climate change. Politically, it is feared that a "Europe at different speed" would rather contribute to the disintegration of the European Union as a whole.

---

[287] Article 329 TFEU: "Member States which wish to establish enhanced cooperation between themselves ... shall address a request to the Commission ... The Commission may submit a proposal to the Council to that effect."

CHAPTER 3

Union Powers and Member State Powers

1. GENERAL ASPECTS ON THE DIVISION OF COMPETENCE IN ENVIRONMENTAL MATTERS

The objective of EU environmental policy and law is the preservation, protection **3–01** and, over all, the improvement of the quality of the environment within the European Union. This objective, however, is also that of Member States' environmental policy and law. The protection and preservation of the environment is a fundamental part of the general interest of the European Union[1] and of Member States. Because it is in the general interest, the environment, like the non-commercial assets listed in art.36 TFEU, cannot be left unprotected: as long as the Union fails to take action on a given environmental issue, the Member States retain their powers to adopt provisions to protect and preserve the environment, provided, of course, that these measures are compatible with the general rules laid down in the EU Treaties. When the European Union takes action, this by no means removes Member States' powers to take environmental measures, although such powers then no longer apply to the particular subject governed by EU legislation, in so far as this has been regulated.

Since the protection of the environment is in the general interest of the European Union, the Union is "competent",[2] i.e. responsible for taking legal provisions in order to protect it. In doing so, the European Union has, of course, to take into consideration the principles which the Treaties provide for such action, in particular the subsidiarity principle.[3] Where an EU environmental legal rule conflicts with a national legal rule, EU law prevails, according to the established case law of the Court of Justice.[4] The reason for this is obvious: if the national legal rule prevailed, the EU legal provision would apply only in those Member States which had not taken legal measures. Then, the EU legal rule would not be a rule which applied throughout the Union, but only in those parts

---

[1] See already *Procureur de la République v Assoc. de Défense de Brûleurs de Huiles Usagées* (C-240/83) [1985] E.C.R. 531 at [13]: "environmental protection ... is one of the Community's essential objectives".
[2] The notion of "competence" is used in art.191(4) TFEU and, more generally, in arts 3 and 4 TFEU.
[3] EU Treaty art.4(a): "competences not conferred upon the Union remain with the Member States". Article5(3): "... in areas which do not fall within its exclusive competence, the Union shall act only if and in so far as the objectives of the proposed action cannot be sufficiently achieved by the Member States, either at central level or regional and local level but can rather, by reason of the scale or effects of the proposed action, be better achieved at Union level". Article 5(2): "Under the principle of conferral, the Union shall act only within the limits of the competence conferred upon it".
[4] *Costa v ENEL* (6/64) [1964] E.C.R. 1265; *Simmenthal* (106/77) [1978] E.C.R. 629; *Factortame* (C-213/89) [1990] E.C.R. I-2466; *Nimz* (C-184/89) [1991] E.C.R. I-297.

of it where no national measures had been taken. Also, the EU measure could at any moment be reduced in its application by a subsequent national measure, which would create quite considerable legal uncertainty. Such legal uncertainty would also be created by differences over the question of whether or not the national measure really is applicable in a specific case or not. As the national law would mainly be interpreted by national courts, inevitable discrepancies would follow.

It is therefore now uncontested that, in the case of conflict, EU (environmental) law prevails over national law. From this it follows that EU environmental law cannot be amended by subsequent national law. In other words, the rule *lex posterior derogat legem anteriorem* (the later legal provision prevails over the earlier provision) does not apply to the relationship between EU law and national law.

3–02   Both the European Union and Member States are thus responsible, "competent" or empowered to take action on environmental issues. In view of the almost unlimited scope of the term "environment" in the EU Treaties, this holds true for all environmental issues. The Treaties assign no particular area of environmental legislation exclusively to the European Union or exclusively to Member States. As can be seen from art.193 TFEU, this similarly applies to subjects already covered by EU legislation. Consequently, the inter-relationship between the European Union's and the Member States' competence is flexible, dynamic and complementary.

It follows from the above-mentioned art.5 TEU that EU environmental action is dependent on certain circumstances which have to be fulfilled. EU institutions decide themselves whether this is the case. In the case of dispute, the matter has to be decided by the EU Court of Justice, which has to ensure, under art.19 TEU that the provisions of the Treaty are respected.[5] The logical consequence of art.5 TEU is that in cases where the European Union has not taken action to protect, preserve or improve the quality of the environment, Member States are free to do so. Their competence to deal with environmental issues is unlimited. They can do whatever they wish in whatever form they wish to ensure environmental protection. Limitations to this right to protect—or not to protect—the environment stem from:

- Member States' own national rules such as, for instance, rules on local government and rules for regional responsibility in environmental matters;
- rules of international law, such as existing international Conventions or other written or unwritten rules of international law;
- rules of EU law.

The first two limitations are not dealt with in this book, which deals with EU law. As regards the third limitation, the EU Treaties themselves contain a number of provisions that limit the Member States' possibilities of action. These different limitations will be discussed below.

---

[5] Article 19 TEU: "It [The Court of Justice of the European Union] shall ensure that in the interpretation and application of the Treaties the law is observed."

2. MEMBER STATES' MEASURES IN THE ABSENCE OF EU MEASURES

(a) National environmental measures that affect imports: arts 34 and 36 TFEU

Article 34 TFEU provides that all "quantitative restrictions on imports and all measures having equivalent effect shall be prohibited between Member States"; art.35 TFEU mirrors this provision by stating that "quantitative restrictions on exports, and all measures having equivalent effect, shall be prohibited between Member States".

3–03

From these provisions, art.36 TFEU makes an exception; this provision reads as follows:

> "The provisions of Articles 34 and 35 shall not preclude prohibitions on imports, exports ... justified on grounds of ... the protection of health and life of humans, animals or plants; ... Such prohibitions or restrictions shall not, however, constitute a means of arbitrary discrimination or a disguised restriction on trade between Member States."

Article 36 TFEU thus does allow certain trade restrictions. The Court of Justice has declared, on a number of occasions, that art.36 is an exception to the principle of art.34 and must therefore be narrowly interpreted.[6] In particular, according to the established case law of the Court of Justice, the grounds for restricting trade by virtue of art.36 constitute an exhaustive list and may not be extended.

The protection of the environment is not listed in art.36 TFEU as a possible justification for restrictions to the free circulation of goods of art.34. Therefore, only such national environmental measures that aim at the "protection of health and life of humans, animals and plants" could be justified by art.36. Such measures concern, for instance, provisions on banning or restricting the use of substances or products which are dangerous to health; measures to limit the presence of pollutants in drinking water or in the air; measures to regulate the marketing of pesticides or biocides.

However, there are numerous environmental measures which cannot be considered to protect the health and life of humans, animals or plants. Such measures include environmental label schemes, eco-management systems, environmental taxes and charges, measures to prevent the generation of waste, environmental impact assessment measures, deposit-and-return schemes, liability or information and education. For other measures, it is doubtful whether they can really be considered to protect health and life; such measures are, for instance, provisions to reduce the noise level of cars, the designation of fauna or flora habitats, emission limit values of installations, licensing procedures or measures to protect the ozone layer or to combat global warming.

3–04

The criterion that defines whether or not a measure aims at the protection of health or life is the relationship of the measure to health effects, i.e. its

---

[6] *Marimex* (29/72) [1982] E.C.R. 1309; *Commission v Ireland* (113/80) [1981] E.C.R. 1625; *Commission v Greece* (C-205/89) [1991] E.C.R. I-1361.

"proximity" to health effects. Thus, the Court of Justice decided that the shipment of recoverable waste oils did not pose a threat to the life and health of humans that could justify the application of art.36.[7]

Another example is the restriction on the use of CFCs and other ozone-depleting substances in order to protect the ozone layer. Damage to the ozone layer may increase skin cancer for humans and may have other health effects on humans, animals and plants. However, this possibility is remote and indirect. Therefore, national measures to restrict the use of ozone-depleting substances cannot really be justified on the basis of art.36 TFEU. Likewise, in 2014, the Court of Justice decided that the reduction of greenhouse gas emissions and the fight against climate change is an environmental problem, not a problem of human health.[8]

3-05   Fortunately, however, this problem of subsuming environmental measures under art.36 TFEU has lost its relevance. Indeed, the Court of Justice in 1979 adopted a landmark decision on art.34.[9] The Court declared that in the absence of EU legislation, a national restriction on the free circulation of goods from other Member States had to be accepted to the extent that it was necessary to satisfy mandatory requirements such as the necessity for fiscal controls, fair trading practices and consumer protection, and added that there might be other mandatory requirements. The Court added further that the national measure taken in order to satisfy such a mandatory requirement had to be non-discriminatory and proportional:

> "in the absence of common rules relating to the marketing of the products in question obstacles to free movement within the Community resulting from disparities between the national laws must be accepted in so far as such rules, applicable to domestic and imported products without distinction, may be recognised as being necessary in order to satisfy mandatory requirements recognised by Community law. Such rules must also be proportionate to the aim in view. If a Member State has a choice between various measures for achieving the same aim, it should choose the means which least restricts the free movement of goods."[10]

In 1988, the Court recognised that the protection of the environment was such a mandatory requirement which could justify restrictions on the free circulation of goods.[11] In this case the Commission had attacked a Danish national measure, which introduced a deposit-and-return system for drink containers. The Commission considered that the system could not be justified by art.36 TFEU and that it was incompatible with art.34. It was followed in its assessment by the Advocate-General, but not by the Court of Justice.

As regards the application of art.36, there was practically no dispute: it was not really possible to consider a deposit-and-return system to protect the health or life of humans; art.36 was therefore not discussed by the Court. Instead, the Court held that Denmark was entitled to introduce a deposit-and-return system, since such a system was aimed at the protection of the environment, which was an objective of general Union interest. Denmark, according to the Court, was

---

[7] *Dusseldorp* (C-203/96) [1998] E.C.R. I-4075 at [47].
[8] Court of Justice, *Essent* (joined cases C-204/12 to C-208/12), ECLI:EU:C:2014:2192.
[9] *Rewe v Bundesmonopolverwaltung* ("*Cassis de Dijon*") (120/78) [1979] E.C.R. 649.
[10] Wording from *Commission v Denmark* (302/86) [1988] E.C.R. 4607.
[11] Wording from *Commission v Denmark* (302/86) [1988] E.C.R. 4607.

entitled to set up an efficient system of waste prevention and such a system required the introduction of a deposit-and-return scheme even though the practical circumstances might make it more difficult for non-Danish producers and traders to comply with the system.

The recognition of the protection of the environment as a mandatory requirement under art.34 was confirmed in later Court judgments[12] without the Court sharply distinguishing between justification under arts 36 (health grounds) and 34 (grounds to satisfy a mandatory requirement).[13] Thus, while national environmental measures may restrict the free circulation of goods on either of these grounds, the limits to such national measures follow from the Treaty provisions and from the limits drawn by the very detailed and sophisticated case law of the Court.

Necessity. The first problem is whether a Member State may adopt any trade-restricting measure which seems appropriate to protect the environment or whether it may only adopt some measures, which are "necessary" or, in the Court's words, proportionate. The Court itself has contributed to this debate by not accepting, in case 302/86, a Danish measure which obliged economic operators to use only authorised standardised containers. The Court stated[14]:

3–06

> "It is undoubtedly true that the existing system for returning approved containers ensures a maximum rate of reuse and therefore a very considerable degree of protection of the environment. Nevertheless, the system for returning non-approved containers is capable of protecting the environment."

This seems to indicate that the Court is of the opinion that a "very considerable degree" of environmental protection is not necessary—not proportionate—and therefore not allowed, only a "reasonable" degree of environmental protection—whatever that may be—is permitted. In other words, it is not a Member State which decides on the necessary degree of the environmental protection, but EU law (as interpreted by the Court) which determines what is necessary (or proportionate). This proportionality is measured against the interest in free circulation of goods, as there is no other factor to consider.

The underlying principle of this approach is that EU law provides for the free circulation of goods which is of paramount importance. Restrictions on the free circulation of goods are allowed only where they are necessary (proportionate); in other words, measures to protect the environment are possible where their importance is greater than that of free circulation of goods. This leads to the

---

[12] *Commission v Belgium* (C-2/90) [1992] E.C.R. I-4431; *Commission v Germany* (C-131/93) [1994] E.C.R. I-3303; *Essent* (joined cases C-204/12 to C-208/12), ECLI:EU:C:2014:2192.
[13] See, for example, *Essent* (joined cases C-204/12 to C-208/12), ECLI:EU:C:2014:2192 at [91] and [92]: "the use of renewable energy sources for the production of energy . . . is useful for the protection of the environment inasmuch as it contributes to the reduction in greenhouse gas emissions which are among the main causes of climate change that the EU and its Member States have pledged to combat . . . such an increase [in the use of renewable energy sources] is also designed to protect the health and life of humans, animals and plants, which are among the public interest grounds listed in Article 30 EC [now art.36 TFEU]". In the same sense already *PreussenElektra* (C-379/98) [2001] E.C.R. I-2099 at [75].
[14] *Denmark* (302/86) [1988] E.C.R. 4607 at [20] and [21].

conclusion that the free circulation of goods, in the event of any conflict with environmental (national) measures, will normally prevail, unless it can be proven that environmental interests are more relevant.

3–07 This conclusion, however, is not compatible with the division of competence for the protection of the environment. The protection of the environment is of general Union interest. It is expressly mentioned in the Recital 9 and art.3(3) TEU. Nothing indicates that it is less important than other objectives, in particular the free circulation of goods. On the contrary, the rule of art.11 TFEU according to which environmental protection requirements must be integrated into the definition and implementation of all other policies is rather unique in the Treaties; nowhere in the Treaties is the same said of the free circulation of goods. Furthermore, Commission proposals in the area of the internal market must be based on a high level of environmental protection and the European Parliament and the Council must try to achieve such a high level (art.114(3) TFEU). This is the only provision in the FEU Treaty which contains quality requirements for individual measures that are proposed by the Commission. Finally, art.114(4)–(8) and art.193 TFEU allow Member States, once an EU measure has been taken, to maintain or to introduce more protective environmental measures at national level. Article 114(5)–(8) applies only to environmental measures, not to all non-economic assets of art.36, as is the case with art.114(4) TFEU.

All these provisions clearly show the importance that the Treaties attach to the protection of the environment. In view of this importance, which has been growing continuously and achieved recognition in the different Treaty amendments of 1987, 1993, 1999 and 2003, it cannot be considered that only a reasonable degree of environmental protection is allowed to restrict the free circulation of goods. Rather, it is the Member States which decide on the amount of environmental protection which they wish to ensure.

There are two other arguments which plead against a limitation for environmental measures to "reasonable" measures. First, art.114(5)–(8) TFEU, which was newly introduced by the Amsterdam Treaty 1997, outlined provisions for the Member States to introduce new environmental measures at national level once an EU harmonisation measure under art.114(1) had been adopted. These measures are not limited to reasonable measures, as will be discussed below; rather, the criteria for the national measures are whether the measure constitutes an arbitrary discrimination, a disguised distortion of trade or whether they hamper the functioning of the internal market. It is not consistent to ask for only reasonable measures under arts 34–36 where no EU measure exists, and not to ask for only reasonable measures under art.114.

3–08 Secondly, the only instance which could decide what is proportionate is the Court of Justice—and in the pre-litigation stage, the European Commission. But what criteria could be used, if there is no EU legislation? The EU Treaties give no clarification of what is reasonable or not.

To give a specific example: in the early 1990s Denmark limited the noise level from electrical windmills that are used for energy production; the standards are the stricter, the closer the windmill is installed to residential areas. France protested against this measure, arguing that the sale and export of French windmills to Denmark would be hampered by the Danish measure. It seems obvious that nobody outside Denmark can really decide whether a noise level of

50 decibels is reasonable for the Danish environment and Danish citizens and whether a noise level of 40 decibels is unreasonable. The environmental conditions are specific in each case. No element in the Treaty allows the establishing of EU criteria for such an assessment. As there is no EU legislation on windmills or on acceptable noise levels for citizens, EU law cannot decide what is reasonable or not in Denmark.

Similar reasons argue in favour of the permitted noise levels for pleasure boats, which Sweden introduced in the early 1990s. In view of the thousands of lakes—independently from the endless miles of shoreline—with numerous small islands in Sweden, it would not be possible to allow the marketing of pleasure boats but prohibit their use in all or in parts of Sweden if they exceed a certain noise level. Also, the level of permitted noise cannot, in the absence of EU provisions, be determined by a manufacturer or authorising body from another Member State—or by the European Union. The Swedish problem was "solved" by an EU directive of 1994 which fixed common noise levels for new boats, but allowed Member States to adopt provisions concerning navigation on certain waters for the protection of the environment.[15]

Another example is a restriction on the use of Karlstad airport which Sweden **3–09** had banned for some noisy airplanes, although Directive 92/14[16] provided that these airplanes were allowed to be used until 2002. It is clear that not every airplane which circulates within the European Union may use any airport that exists. Indeed, Member States implicitly regulate access to airports, for example by regulating the number and length of the runways, the size of the airports, or landing and take-off times. Where the neighbourhood is residential or is an ecologically valuable habitat, this may lead to the conclusion that specific airplanes may not use specific airports. The most obvious example is the supersonic airplane, *Concorde*, which was not allowed to land at most EU airports. In the same way as it is possible to prohibit the use of certain roads for trucks—or indeed for cars generally—without impeding the free circulation of cars, it is possible to prohibit the use of certain airports for certain airplanes. It is not clear who else other than the Swedish authorities could determine whether the local environmental conditions at Karlstad make it necessary or not to restrict the landing or take-off of noisy airplanes. Directive 92/14 is not relevant, since airplanes which conform to that Directive are allowed to use Swedish airports, except, perhaps, Karlstad airport.

The Commission based its decision against the Swedish restrictions at Karlstad airport not on art.34 TFEU, but on secondary EU legislation, Regulation 2408/92 and Directive 92/14,[17] and decided that these provisions gave any air transport carrier a right to access to any EU airport[18]; Sweden accepted this

---

[15] Directive 94/25 relating to recreational craft, [1994] OJ L164/25; see for the interpretation of this directive, Court of Justice, *Mikkelsson and Roos* (C-142/05) [2009] E.C.R I-4273; *Sandström* (C-433/05) [2010] E.C.R. I-2885. In these cases, the Court assessed the national restriction measures as regards the use of recreational craft against the proportionality principle. It left the final decision, whether this principle had been respected, to the national courts, though it tried to limit those courts, by extensively interpreting the proportionality principle.

[16] Directive 92/14 on the limitation of the operation of airplanes covered by Pt II, Ch.2, Vol.1 of annex 16 to the Convention on International Civil Aviation, 2nd edn [1992] OJ L76/21.

[17] Regulation 2408/92 [1992] OJ L240/8; Dir.92/14 (fn.14, above).

[18] Commission, Dec.98/523 [1998] OJ L233/25.

decision. If that secondary EU legislation indeed went so far—I question this—the above-mentioned considerations, which start from the assumption that there is no EU legislation regulating this issue, are obsolete.

For restrictions in the free circulation of goods which affect human health and therefore come under art.36 TFEU, the Court of Justice has already come to the same decision. In case C-125/88,[19] it was faced with a Dutch measure concerning the use of a pesticide "Improsol"; the question was whether such a national measure did not unduly restrict the free circulation of that pesticide which was used in other Member States. The Court found that pesticides constituted "significant risks to the health of humans and animals and to the environment" and then continued:

> "It is therefore for the Member States, pursuant to Article 36 of the Treaty and in the absence of full harmonization in this matter, to decide at what level they wish to set the protection of the life and health of humans."

This judgment has been confirmed by several other judgments on pesticides and Member States' measures to restrict their use.

3–10   It is not really imaginable that the Member States themselves set the degree of protection which they wish to ensure for measures to protect the environment which concern the health and life of humans, animals and plants (art.36 TFEU*)*, but that for measures to protect the environment which concern other environmental values and thus come under art.34 TFEU, the Member States are limited to proportionate measures.

The conclusion is that the freedom to set national environmental standards does not allow protectionist measures to be taken or measures to be taken which are not really necessary to protect the local, regional or national environment. These issues will be discussed below. It still remains, however, that there are no specific, autonomous criteria for assessing whether national environmental measures are necessary (proportionate) or not. It is up to Member States to establish the degree of environmental protection at local, regional or national level which they consider appropriate. In this, however, Member States must take into consideration the state of science at international and EU level, such as the statements of the World Health Organisation or the EU scientific committees; the greater the scientific certainty about the risk of a substance, the more reduced is the discretion of the Member State. The attempts by the Court of Justice to limit this discretion by an extensive use of the proportionality principle are to be considered with caution. Indeed, the national legislature also has a large amount of discretion as to the measures which are to be taken in order to protect the environment and humans. The Court of Justice only can control any obvious contravention of this discretion.

3–11   **Non-economic grounds.**   The discretion of Member States is limited by the provisions of the Treaties. When establishing its jurisdiction on the mandatory requirements which justified, under art.34 TFEU, a restriction on the free circulation of goods, the Court of Justice stated that such measures were not allowed to be discriminatory or disproportionate and had to be applied to both

---

[19]   *H. Nijman* (C-125/88) [1989] E.C.R. I-3533.

national and imported products. As can be seen, the two criteria of non-discrimination and proportionality are taken from art.36(2) TFEU,[20] but apply both to measures which are examined under art.36, and to measures assessed, under the *Cassis de Dijon* jurisdiction, under art.34.

To these limits has to be added the proviso that art.36 TFEU itself only refers to non-economic criteria, as can be concluded from art.114(10)[21]; this limitation also applies under art.34 TFEU, as the Court of Justice has clarified: "aims of a purely economic nature cannot justify barriers to the fundamental principle of the free movement of goods". With this argument, the Court of Justice rejected an argument by the Dutch Government that restrictions to the shipment of waste were necessary to enable a Dutch waste recovery installation to operate in a profitable manner with sufficient material at its disposal and to ensure it a sufficient supply of recoverable waste.[22]

Discriminating measures. A discrimination or, as art.36(2) puts it, an arbitrary discrimination exists when goods from other Member States are subject to conditions which are, directly or indirectly, stricter than those on domestic goods. Since the Court of Justice also takes into consideration indirect discrimination, practically every national environmental measure will have to be weighed in the balance as to whether it factually leads to a different treatment of domestic or imported goods or not.   **3–12**

In case 302/86[23] the Commission had tackled the Danish deposit-and-return system by arguing that the mandatory use of reusable containers for drinks and beers indirectly discriminated against imported goods: reusable containers—mainly glass bottles—were considerably heavier in weight than containers made of plastic or other material. Therefore, the costs of transporting them to Denmark and, in their empty state, back to the country of origin, were higher than necessary and created indirect discrimination. If a foreign producer or trader wanted to avoid transport, it had to set up a deposit-and-return system of its own in Denmark which would be costly.

The Court did not discuss questions of discrimination. Since it rejected the Commission's application, it must be presumed that it did not consider the increased transport costs or the difficulties involved in the setting-up of a deposit-and-return system to be sufficiently relevant as to constitute indirect discrimination. In cases C-309/02 and C-463/01 which concerned German legislation on packaging, the question, whether the German mandatory deposit system constituted a discrimination, was not discussed either.[24]

In case C-2/90,[25] the Wallonian Government's import ban on waste from other Member States was tackled by the Commission, which argued that waste from other Member States was not more harmful than waste generated in Wallonia. The Court rejected that argument. It held that waste, while coming under art.34 TFEU, had special characteristics. As there was an obligation to dispose of waste   **3–13**

---

[20] See para.3–06, above.

[21] See art.114(4), (5) and (10) TFEU.

[22] Court of Justice, *Dusseldorp* (C-203/96) [1998] E.C.R. I–4075 at [44].

[23] *Denmark* (302/86) [1988] E.C.R. 4607.

[24] Court of Justice, *Commission v Germany* (C-463/01) [2004] E.C.R. I-11705; *Radlberg* (C-309/02) [2004] E.C.R. I-11763.

[25] *Belgium* (C-2/90) [1992] E.C.R. I-4431.

as close as possible to the place where it was produced in order to transport waste as little as possible, which followed from art.191(2) TFEU,[26] the different treatment between Wallonian waste and imported waste did not constitute, in the opinion of the Court, an arbitrary discrimination.[27]

Another case, which was finally not decided by the Court, as Denmark repealed its national legislation, was the Danish ban on metal cans, introduced in the early 1980s. The Commission had considered that this measure was taken in order to protect the (Danish) environment, and had therefore not attacked this ban before the Court of Justice; the attempts of the United Kingdom, as a third-party intervenor, to have this ban discussed in case 302/86 failed for procedural reasons, since a third-party intervenor may not enlarge the object of litigation before the Court beyond the limits which the main applicant has established by its application.[28]

If it is correct that a Member State, in the absence of EU provisions, itself establishes the necessary degree of protection of the environment which it wishes to achieve at national level, then it is in principle up to the Danish authorities to decide whether they wish to have metal cans in their environment. Such metal cans made from aluminium or steel take more natural resources to produce than glass or cardboard containers, are not reusable, constitute litter in the environment when they are thrown away and reduce the efficiency of reuse systems, which a Member State may have set up.

3–14   Compared with the Danish general ban, however, there was the Irish draft regulation of 1988, which aimed at prohibiting metal cans, however, only for beer.[29] In this case, many of the environmental arguments in favour of such a ban are not really valid, since they would apply, in the same way, to metal cans for soft drinks. The Commission was therefore of the opinion that environmental reasons could not have caused the Irish Government to consider a ban on metal cans for beer, but that this ban constituted an attempt to reduce the import of British beer. Confronted with this argument, Ireland withdrew its draft regulation.

In Denmark, the ban of metal cans was limited to beer and some soft drinks. Other soft drinks, such as iced tea, were allowed to be marketed in metal cans; also, of course, metal cans are used in Denmark for fruit and vegetable preserves and other food products. While fruit and vegetable containers might not really be comparable to drink containers, this is certainly the case with, for example, iced tea or chocolate drinks. It is thus very much a question of weighing up the different aspects of the Danish ban in order to come to a decision whether or not it is discriminating. Also, it should be pointed out that, in 1994, an EU Directive on packaging and packaging waste was adopted, which provides for the free circulation of packaging containers that comply with the requirements of this Directive.[30] Any decision on the Danish ban would therefore take into consideration that Directive and no longer an article of the TFEU. In view of this

---

[26] See para.1–34, above.

[27] See for a critical comment, L. Krämer, *European Environmental Law Casebook* (London, 1993), p.77.

[28] *Denmark* (302/86) [1988] E.C.R. 4607.

[29] See L. Krämer, *E.C. Treaty and Environmental Law* (London, 1998), para.4.58.

[30] Directive 94/62 on packaging and packaging waste [1994] OJ L365/10; see also para.10–46, below.

new legislation, in 1999 the Commission appealed to the Court of Justice and Denmark repealed its ban before a judgment was given.

In 1993, the Netherlands set up a national Covenant on Tropical Hardwoods, which provided that, after 1995, only timber from sustainably managed forests was to be traded or processed in the Netherlands. The Covenant, an environmental agreement, was signed by the Dutch Government, the timber trade and timber processing industry, trade unions and environmental organisations. It was intended to introduce a Dutch approval mark in order to distinguish sustainably produced timber from other timber. Since the Covenant was actively supported and signed by the Dutch Government, it must be considered a national public measure[31] and therefore be assessed under art.34 TFEU.

The discrimination problem lies in the fact that the Covenant referred to timber imports from tropical timber only; other hardwood-producing countries, such as Canada and Russia (Siberia), were not covered. It is not really clear why such differentiation was made; environmental reasons require the same treatment in both cases. The Dutch Covenant, therefore, seems to be discriminatory. It must be mentioned, though, that it never became effective, because no agreement could be found on what constituted "sustainable forest management". **3–15**

Some German Länder had adopted, in the 1980s, smog regulations which provided for restrictions on the use of private cars in the case of smog. Cars equipped with catalytic converters could, during the first stage of smog alert, circulate whereas cars without a catalytic converter could not. The Commission stated that this measure discriminated against car producers from other Member States, since the EU provisions valid at that time had considered the emissions from cars to be equivalent, whether or not the cars were equipped with catalytic converters. According to the Commission, foreign manufacturers were more severely affected by the German measures than German producers.

In the 1980s, there was no EU legislation on smog and, therefore, Member States were free to decide on measures in the case of an extraordinary situation such as smog. Since cars with catalytic converters emit fewer pollutants than cars without such converters, and since all manufacturers were producing, at the time of the German measure, cars with catalytic converters, no discrimination can be seen in the smog regulations, which, in each case, were measures to deal with a temporary situation. When the Commission changed its policy in 1987 and began working towards EU emission limit values which required catalytic converter equipment, it ended the case against Germany.

In case C-379/98, the Court examined whether a German measure to support the production of electricity from renewable sources of energy, but to limit the financial support to persons in Germany, was compatible with the present art.34 TFEU. The Court did not discuss the question of discrimination of persons in other Member States, but held the German measure to be compatible with art.34.[32] **3–16**

These examples might show, in an assessment upon whether a Member State's measure constitutes an arbitrary discrimination of products, how much depends on the specific circumstances of the case. This is confirmed by the jurisdiction of

---

[31] Private measures would have to be assessed as to their compatibility with the TFEU, against arts 101 and 102 TFEU.
[32] Court of Justice, *PreussenElektra* [2001] E.C.R. I-2099.

the Court which appears to differentiate between measures that are discriminating and measures that constitute an arbitrary discrimination. Thus, in several cases, the Court accepted national discriminating environmental legislation which it considered to be environmentally oriented, without discussing, in the majority of these cases, much of their discriminating character. This could mean that national measures which pursue a legitimate environmental objective, may also be justified under arts 34 and 36 TFEU, where they discriminate against products from other Member States.[33] A detailed case-by-case analysis of each specific case is therefore necessary.

3–17   **Disproportionate measures.**   The second requirement set up by the Court of Justice is the proportionality requirement: where it must be examined whether there are other measures available which restrict the free circulation of goods less severely than the measure which was taken. In practice, the proportionality principle is often merged with the necessity requirement, discussed above: when a national measure is not necessary, it is disproportionate.

The proportionality requirement became relevant in case C-131/93 where Germany had prohibited the import of live crayfish in order to protect the health and life of the indigenous crayfish species.[34] The Court did not contest Germany's right to take such measures; however, it argued that Germany could have taken other, less restrictive, steps such as health controls for crayfish imports from other Member States, or licensing requirements for putting live crayfish into German waters. The Court also came to this conclusion because Germany had been rather generous in granting derogations from the import ban and shown that a licence system, together with strict conditions, did ensure a sufficient protection.

In case 302/86[35] the Court considered the Danish measure on only allowing approved drink containers to be part of the Danish deposit-and-return system to be incompatible with art.34 TFEU; a Danish measure to allow some derogations for importers of small quantities was considered disproportionate. The Court did not explain what other, less restrictive, measures Denmark could have taken; its judgment is instead confined to the statement that "a very considerable degree of protection of the environment" was not really necessary to protect the environment. This seems to have the hallmark of a political statement.

3–18   In case C-2/90,[36] the Court did not discuss at all whether or not the Belgian measure to ban waste imports was disproportionate: as Belgium had argued that the measure was taken in order to react to a suddenly increased import of waste and as the judgment was given nine years after the taking of the measure, there would well have been reasons to discuss the proportionality requirement.

In its Decision 98/523,[37] the Commission considered the limitation of access to Karlstad airport to less noisy airplanes disproportionate, except as regards a night curfew between 22.00 and 07.00 hours. The Commission argued, amongst other things, that the airport was situated in a sparsely populated area away from

---

[33] See in this regard, F. Jacobs, "The Role of the European Court of Justice in the Protection of the Environment" in *Journal of Environmental Law* (2006), 185.

[34] *Commission v Germany* (C-131/93) [1994] E.C.R. I-3303.

[35] *Denmark* (302/86) [1988] E.C.R. 4607.

[36] *Belgium* (C-2/90) [1992] E.C.R. I-4431.

[37] Commission, Dec.98/523 [1998] OJ L233/25.

the city centre and that it accounted for a rather low traffic volume. The Commission requested that the Swedish authorities demonstrate the need to take the noise-restriction measures.

In case C-320/03[38] the Court had to decide on regional Austrian legislation which prohibited, for environmental reasons, the transport of certain non-perishable goods on the Brenner Autobahn. The Court did not discuss the question of discrimination. It held that the Austrian measure was disproportionate, because Austria had introduced it at extremely short delay and had not provided for possibilities to transport the goods otherwise.

There is a lot of discussion on questions of the burden of proof or the burden of evidence. However, this rule of procedure simply means that in a dispute attempts must be made from the Commission, other parties, private bodies and Member States to clarify the facts as far as possible. The more substantiated the arguments from one side are, the more detailed those from the other side have to be. Only at the end of this process, where factual aspects remain open, can there be a question of who is to have the charge that a factual aspect has not been clarified.

3–19

It has already been pointed out that environmental protection reasons are, under the EU Treaties, not subordinated to considerations of free circulation of goods. In an assessment under art.34 TFEU, whether the consideration of free circulation of goods or the protection of the environment prevail, Member States have an amount of discretion as to the degree at which level they wish to fix the protection of the environment. It is difficult to understand why a night curfew should comply with the principle of necessity and proportionality but a limitation on access to the airports to less noisy airplanes does not. This issue cannot be solved by shifting the burden of proof.

Also, how difficult the proportionality principle is to apply in practice may be demonstrated by the question of product bans. Member States have pronounced a considerable number of bans of products; besides those mentioned on metal cans (Denmark) or pesticides (Netherlands), one could mention the restriction on phosphates in detergents (Italy–1988), or the Austrian ban of polybromated biphenyls (PBB), non-biodegradable plastic bags (some local authorities in Italy), lead capsules for alcoholic beverages (Germany, Netherlands), waste shredding machines (Germany) or ammunition containing lead (Denmark, the Netherlands) and PVC.

The argument that a ban is not allowed where other means are available which restrict the free circulation of goods less must not be overused. Indeed, as has already been mentioned, the Court of Justice had expressly recognised the right of Member States to ban pesticides which had not been the subject of EU secondary legislation.[39] It would theoretically always be possible to argue that a strict licensing system together with control and surveillance mechanisms would reach more or less the same result, but would be less restrictive than a total ban. The Court's jurisdiction to allow the complete ban of pesticides by Member States means in practice that the Court grants them a considerable amount of discretion to decide on what measures they consider appropriate. Following the same line of reasoning, the Court accepted that the fixing of noise emission limit

3–20

[38] *Commission v Austria* (C-320/03) [2005] E.C.R. I-9871.
[39] *Nijman* (C-125/88) [1989] E.C.R. I-3533.

values for airplanes was the most effective and most appropriate means of combating noise emissions from airplanes; indeed, investments in construction around airports are normally very cost-intensive. Establishing noise emission limit values was therefore not disproportionate.[40]

This reasoning also applies to the German ban on waste shredding machines, which the Commission accepted. Waste shredding machines cut biological waste into small pieces, which are then disposed of together with ordinary waste water. German law provides that waste must first of all be recovered; this conforms to the EU waste hierarchy which is laid down in Directive 2008/98.[41] Disposing of waste by shredding it and discharging it into the sewer system contradicts this principle. Furthermore, the pipes for waste water would become blocked with the mud, filtering would become more difficult and costly, waste water treatment stations would incur increased costs, and so on. It would therefore certainly be possible to prohibit waste disposal together with waste water without banning the shredding machines. In order to find out whether the marketing of waste shredding machines might be prohibited as well, the import of such machines into Germany would have to be considered and the possibility of controlling the ban on using these machines and of disposing of the waste via the waste water flow. Since such a ban could probably never be effectively controlled, a ban on marketing shredding machines appears not to be disproportionate.

Italy, the United Kingdom, Denmark and Sweden took measures, in 1996–1997, to prohibit the marketing of self-chilling cans. These are metal cans for drinks which contain hydrofluorocarbons (HFCs), a cooling gas, which is spread between the wall of the can and the drink, in such a way that the can functions as a mobile mini-refrigerator, chilling the content of the can.

3–21   HFC is a greenhouse gas, used as a substitute to CFC; it is considered, in global warming terms, to have a global warming potential of 11,700 (CO_2 has a global warming potential of 1).[42] In the mid-1990s, and not yet regulated by international agreements or EU legislation, it was identified under the Kyoto Protocol (1998) as one of the greenhouse gases. Its extensive use would undermine efforts in other sectors to reduce CO_2 emissions and thus combat climate change. Therefore, national bans on HFC or on products and equipment that contain HFC are justified under art.34 TFEU.

As regards the Italian ban of phosphates in detergents, it is not clear what less restrictive measure could reduce the eutrophication of rivers, lakes and coastal waters. The same applies to the Danish and Dutch ban on ammunition containing lead which aims at reducing the presence of lead in the environment. If Denmark and the Netherlands consider that there is too much lead in the environment, and that ducks and birds might eat that ammunition, then a ban appears appropriate since equally effective measures, which restrict the free flow of goods less, are not available. The Commission has not taken any legal action against these three Member States. Similar considerations apparently also influenced the Commission in the case of the ban of non-biodegradable plastic bags, which was also accepted.[43] In the case of lead capsules for alcoholic beverages, the European

---

[40] *Aher-Waggon* (C-389/96) [1998] E.C.R. I-4473.

[41] Directive 2008/98 on waste [2008] OJ L312/3, art.4.

[42] See para.9–05, below.

[43] An Italian judge had asked the Court of Justice whether such a ban was compatible with EU law, but omitted to ask for its compatibility with art.34 TFEU. The Court therefore only assessed its

Union thought it appropriate to adopt EU regulations in order to provide for a complete EU-wide phasing-out of such capsules.[44]

In 1999, the Netherlands issued draft legislation which considerably restricted the use of chlorinated paraffins. This measure was a follow-up of a decision taken within the framework of the Paris Convention of 1995,[45] aiming at progressively reducing paraffin in order to prevent marine pollution. The Commission did not object to this restriction on the free circulation of goods.

A similar case is the Austrian ban on PBB. PBB is suspected to cause serious health or environmental problems; however, the definitive scientific evidence on the risk of PBB has not yet been produced. The Commission considered that the OECD had recommended, at international level, that the marketing and use of PBBs be stopped and decided to accept the Austrian ban. This example shows that in the case of conflict between the free circulation of goods (art.34 TFEU) and environmental protection, the precautionary principle of art.191(2) TFEU may apply and lead to preference being given to measures which aim at environmental protection.

3–22

As mentioned in paras 1–32 et seq., above, there are attempts, in particular from economic operators, to also limit the application of the precautionary principle as regards national measures and to require, for its application, that there is a possibility of severe and irreversible hazard, a need to adopt measures urgently and that national legislation is of a provisional nature only. These attempts to reduce the application of the precautionary principle are legally unjustified, as they try to interpret into this principle aspects which it does not contain. The Austrian PBB ban demonstrates well that Member States' discretion under the precautionary and the proportionality principles is wider.

The precautionary principle may also be relevant in cases which concern national measures to restrict or ban the use of PVC. PVC is a plastic product which is mainly used in construction materials, packaging, cars, toys and office equipment. When incinerated, however, it generates dioxins and furans; its recycling as well as its disposal is particularly difficult. The question is whether Member States may, in view of the complications of waste incineration and disposal, restrict the use of PVC products or of certain substances (phthalates or heavy metals) in PVC. In application of the precautionary principle and in the absence of EU measures, it is well within the discretion of Member States to restrict or prohibit the use of PVC; it is not clear what less restrictive measure would be available.[46]

In another case, Greece prohibited the import of diesel cars for private use, arguing that the heavy air pollution in Athens and Thessaloniki required such a measure. It seems obvious that a total import ban on private diesel cars in order to combat air pollution in two regions is disproportionate. At the request of the Commission, Greece amended its legislation and prohibited the use of diesel cars in Athens and Thessaloniki. Such a measure may be proportional, if the air pollution in these two regions is primarily due to the use of diesel cars. However,

3–23

---

compatibility with Dir.75/442—now replaced by Dir.2008/98 on waste [2008] OJ L312/3 and found no problem with this Directive, *Enichem v Cinisello-Balsamo* (380/87) [1989] E.C.R. 2491.

[44] See, e.g. Reg.3280/92 [1992] OJ L327/3.

[45] Paris Convention for the protection of the marine environment in the North-East Atlantic (OSPAR), see Dec.98/249 [1998] OJ L104/1; see also para.7–34, below.

[46] As regards PVC, see also para.6–44, below.

it seems rather unlikely that the air pollution is caused more by diesel and petrol-driven cars than, for example, by industrial emissions, other economic activities and household heating. As long as a significantly higher participation of diesel cars emissions is not established, the restriction on the use of diesel, but not on petrol-driven, cars is discriminatory; furthermore, the measure as such is disproportional, since it appears that it is not capable of reaching the objective, i.e. the reduction of environmental pollution.

In 2014, discussions started in Paris to restrict the use of diesel cars, as they were blamed for the increase the presence of nitrogen oxides (NOx) beyond the limits permitted under Dir.2008/50.[47] This discussion which turns on fiscal incentives to buy a non-diesel car, restrict access to the city for diesel cars and higher taxation for diesel cars, has not yet come to an end.

In 1998–1999, Denmark announced and adopted draft national legislation which intended to limit considerably the marketing of lead in Denmark, and of products which contained lead; these products were expressly listed in an annex. Products which complied with EU directives were exempted from this ban. The essential question in this case is whether Denmark was entitled, in the absence of EU law, to decide that it does not wish to see lead in its environment. In my opinion, this is indeed the case and it cannot be argued, in the name of proportionality, that less restrictive measures could be taken. The Commission did not object to the Danish legislation.

In 1998, Sweden prohibited the export of products containing mercury, including dental amalgams, for reasons of human health and of environmental protection. The Court of Justice held[48] that this export ban was incompatible with Directive 93/42 concerning medical devices,[49] though this Directive is aimed at the protection of human health, but not at the protection of the environment. Article 34 TFEU would thus have allowed Sweden to provide for this export ban.[50]

3–24   **Protecting the environment outside the national territory.**   It has been argued in legal texts that a Member State's environmental measure under art.34 TFEU may also be taken in order to protect the environment outside its own jurisdiction. The Court of Justice has not yet formally decided on this issue. The first argument which is relevant in this context is the fact that the requirements of environmental protection are not limited to the EU territory. If the point of departure defended in this Chapter is correct—that in the absence of EU measures, the task of ensuring environmental protection is with the Member States—it cannot seriously be argued that such measures are not allowed under arts 34 or 36 TFEU. Indeed, measures to combat climate change or to protect the ozone layer, tropical forests, elephants, whales, tigers or rhinos do affect the environment outside the EU territory—and yet have been taken by the European

---

[47] Directive 2008/50 on ambient air quality and cleaner air for Europe [2008] OJ L 152/1.

[48] Court of Justice, *Kemikalieinspektionen* (C-288/08), judgment of 19 November 2009; see note L. Krämer, *Journal of European Environmental and Planning Law* (2010), 124.

[49] Directive 93/42 concerning medical devices [1993] OJ L169/1.

[50] In 2008, the EU adopted Reg.1102/2008 on the banning of exports of metallic mercury and certain mercury compounds and mixtures [2008] OJ L 304/74. This Regulation exempted dental amalgams from the export ban. The Swedish ban then became incompatible with this Regulation.

Union, without ever having seriously been questioned under art.34.[51] In the absence then of any EU measures, this competence is with Member States.

The possibility of protecting the environment outside the national jurisdiction of a Member State finds its limits in the general Treaty provisions, in particular in that of art.4(3) TEU which lays down the principle of sincere cooperation.[52] Thus, the protection of the environment in another Member State will normally have to be left to that other Member State. However, the individual case will have to be weighed carefully. For instance, where a Member State decides to enact a national import ban on ivory in order to protect the African elephant,[53] this measure also affects the imports of ivory from other Member States. And yet this measure may be upheld under art.34 where the principles of non-discrimination and proportionality have been respected.

A similar reasoning may apply for the protection of an endangered species that lives in another Member State. Normally, under art.4(3) TEU, it would be up to that Member State to protect this species. But there may be circumstances (e.g. political, economic or other reasons) where such a measure is not taken. In such a case, another Member State may decide to take measures to protect that species. An example is the German ban in the mid-1980s of imports for products made from corallium rubrum: corallium rubrum is a coral which lives in the Mediterranean and which is used in some Member States to produce jewellery. Weighing the arguments, the Commission did not see in that import ban a breach of Germany's obligations under arts 34–35 TFEU.[54]

The Court of Justice has not accepted export restrictions which France and the Netherlands[55] had introduced for specific wastes and for which they had invoked, amongst other arguments, the necessity of protecting the environment in other Member States. The Court considered that nothing indicated that the other Member States did not or could not protect themselves and their environment. In case C-203/96,[56] the Court was of the opinion that a Dutch provision which prohibited the export of specific waste to Germany, unless the processing abroad was "superior" to the processing in the Netherlands, was illegal; the Court considered that the treatment methodology in both countries was equivalent, and that therefore the export restriction was not justified.

3–25

---

[51] In *Safety Hi-Tech* (C-284/95) [1998] E.C.R. I-4301, the Court of Justice assessed the validity of EU measures to protect the ozone layer against art.34 TFEU, but found no breach of the Treaty provisions; see also paras 9–20 et seq., below.

[52] Article 4(3) TEU: "Pursuant to the principle of sincere cooperation, the Union and the Member States shall in full mutual respect, assist each other in carrying out tasks which flow from the Treaties ... The Member States shall ... refrain from any measure which could jeopardise the attainment of the objectives of this Treaty."

[53] Regulation 2496/89 [1989] OJ L240/5 introduced an EU-wide import ban on ivory. However, a number of Member States had already decided, at national level, to introduce such a ban prior to the EU action.

[54] Since then, corallium rubrum has been the subject of Community measures to restrict its trade, see Reg.338/97 on the protection of species of wild fauna and flora by regulating trade therein [1997] OJ L61/1.

[55] *Inter-Huiles* (172/82) [1983] E.C.R. 555: "The environment is protected just as effectively when the oils are sold to an authorised disposal or regenerating undertaking of another Member State as when they are disposed of in the Member States of origin"; *Nertsfoederfabriek* (118/86) [1987] E.C.R. 3883; the case concerned poultry waste.

[56] Court of Justice, *Dusseldorp* (C-203/96) [1998] E.C.R. I-4075.

In case C-169/89,[57] the Court decided that the Netherlands could not lawfully prohibit the marketing of a bird which had been legally marketed in the United Kingdom. The details of this judgment appear questionable, as the EU legislation expressly required to protect *all* birds and constructed national hunting provisions as exceptions to that rule; however, this case will not be discussed here,[58] since the judgment mainly dealt with the interpretation of Directive 2009/147 on the conservation of wild birds.

In 2007/2008, Belgium and the Netherlands adopted legislation to prohibit the trade in seal furs and seal products. The measures also affect the trade with other EU Member States; they are envisaged to counteract the large-scale and frequently inhumane killing of seals which the Canadian government had authorised. Canadian seals are not an endangered species. Nevertheless, as measures to protect wild animal welfare are environmental measures (see para.1–02, above), such measures could be justified under EU law as well as under WTO law. In order to preserve the unity of the EU market, the European Union introduced legislation to prohibit trade in seal products for the whole of the European Union.[59] Appeals against the Regulation were unsuccessful before the Court of Justice.[60] In contrast, in 2014 the WTO Appellate Body found that while the EU ban could, in principle, be justified for moral concerns regarding the welfare of seals, the two exceptions which the EU had provided for indigenous communities and for the sustainable management of marine resources were not justified and contradicted WTO law (art.XX(a) GATT-Agreement).[61] In February 2015, the Commission therefore proposed a regulation in order to adapt these exceptions to the WTO-requirements; the ban of seal imports as such was maintained.[62]

3–26   In conclusion, Member States may, in the absence of EU provisions on specific products, take those measures to protect the environment against the risk arising from the products which they consider appropriate. However, arts 34 and 36 TFEU and the very sophisticated and detailed case law of the Court of Justice require that a very careful assessment is made between the environmental advantage and the restriction of the free circulation of goods. Any national measure which restricts the circulation constitutes an arbitrary discrimination between national producers or traders and producers or traders from other Member States. The national measure must be capable of reaching the envisaged aim and not go beyond what is necessary to reach it (proportionality). The different criteria—arbitrary discrimination, proportionality, a non-economic objective—leave a considerable amount of discretion to the Court of Justice, which is the final place for deciding on the legality of the national environmental measure. Therefore, a case-by-case assessment is necessary, which carefully considers all aspects of a national measure.

---

[57] *Gourmetterie van den Burg* (C-169/89) [1990] E.C.R. 2143.

[58] See for a detailed discussion, Krämer, *European Environmental Law Casebook* (London, 1993), p.149.

[59] Regulation1007/2009 on trade in seal products [2009] OJ L286/36.

[60] *Inuit Katanami a.o v European Parliament and Council* (T-18/10) [2011] E.C.R. II-5599; *Inuit Katanami v European Parliament and Council* (C-583/11P) ECLI:EU:C:2013:625.

[61] WTO, Document WT/DS400 and DS401/AB/R of 29 April 2014.

[62] Commission, COM(2015) 45.

(b) National measures affecting exports

Similar requirements apply to measures which concern the export of products.   3–27
Article 35 TFEU prohibits quantitative restrictions on exports as well as measures
having an equivalent effect; art.36 also constitutes an exception to this principle
and allows export restrictions, amongst other things, for reasons to protect life
and health of humans, animals or plants. The Court of Justice interpreted art.35 in
a way that this prohibition "concerns all national measures which have as their
specific object or effect the restriction of patterns of exports and thereby ...
provide a special advantage for national products or for the domestic markets".[63]

A frequent way of prohibiting exports is the requirement to deliver waste to
specific (national) plants. The Court of Justice considered that such an obligation
constituted an indirect export ban and was therefore incompatible with art.35.[64]
In contradiction to these judgments is the decision in case C-422/92 where the
Court of Justice declared that the requirement to dispose waste generated in
Germany only in that country was compatible with EU law.[65]

It should be noted that, on the one hand, waste is a product of a specific nature
which as a consequence different provisions may apply.[66] On the other hand, in
2006 the European Union adopted new and specific provisions on the shipment
of waste within the European Union, which have been substituted for previous
provisions.[67] Member States may, under these provisions, oblige waste generators
or holders to deliver their waste to specific plants, provided that the activity is a
disposal activity. However, where waste is shipped for recovery to another
Member State, it is not possible to prohibit such a shipment by a provision which
obliges the waste holder to supply it to a specific waste recovery plant. Such a
provision contradicts art.35 and the above-mentioned Regulation on waste
shipments.[68]

In Germany, in particular, local authorities which have set up waste treatment   3–28
(incinerators) or disposal installations, often try to prohibit the export of
municipal waste to other municipalities or abroad, establishing an obligation to
deliver the waste to the local installation (Anschluss-und Benutzungszwang). The
compatibility of such measures with art.35 TFEU is doubtful, in particular where
waste is exported for recovery purposes.[69] Spanish waste legislation of 2012
provides that recyclable waste shall, as a priority, be offered to a recycling
installation within the European Union. This provision is used by local
administrations to put into public tenders the requirement of offering recyclable
waste to Spanish or EU installations. Under the Dassonville formula of the Court

---

[63] *Inter-Huiles* (172/82) [1983] E.C.R. 555.
[64] *Inter-Huiles* (172/82) [1983] E.C.R. 555; *Vanacker* (C-37/92) [1993] E.C.R. I-4947; *Nertsvoeder-fabriek* (118/86) [1987] E.C.R. 3883.
[65] *Commission v Germany* (C-422/92) [1995] E.C.R. I-1097; in that judgment, the Court did not expressly discuss art.35 but examined the German legislation under Dir.84/631 on the shipment of waste [1984] OJ L326/31.
[66] See para.2–78, above.
[67] Regulation 1013/2006 on shipments of waste [2006] OJ L190/1.
[68] See, however, now Dir.2008/98 on waste [2008] OJ L312/3, art.16(1), where Member States were authorised to restrict imports of waste for recovery, in order to protect their national incineration network.
[69] See for more details paras 10–35 et seq., below.

of Justice,[70] such a provision undoubtedly constitutes an indirect restriction of exports and is therefore not compatible with art.35.

Apart from waste issues, there has not yet been any Court decision to allow or disallow export restrictions for environmental purposes. In practice, therefore, the export ban for environmental purposes does not play a significant role.

(c)   Measures under other policies

(i)   Agricultural policy

3–29   Since the entering into force of the Lisbon Treaty at the end of 2009, agricultural policy is no longer the exclusive competence of the European Union; rather, the competence is shared (art.4(2d) TFEU). Member States' measures in environmental matters that would affect the common agricultural policy and its legislation which were, in the past, not allowed, are now permitted, provided they follow the general lines which were indicated above.

Thus, Member States may only take measures to the extent that the European Union has not taken action; such measures are under a permanent threat of being replaced by EU action. An example is the setting up of national criteria for organic farming and food therefrom: as the European Union has regulated this matter,[71] there is no competence for national measures in this area.

Measures which had been taken in the past include, in particular, the ban on certain agricultural pesticides. Since 1991, this subject has been regulated at EU level, presently by Regulation 1107/2009[72]; however, since the implementing provisions have not yet all been established, the European Union accepts that Member States continue to maintain national bans or restrictions of the marketing or use of pesticides. Once the EU system is fully established, this practice will have to be abandoned.

Environmental measures which Member States may take under these restricted conditions concern, for instance, the handling of manure,[73] the limitation of the size of industrial feedstock installations, irrigation measures, action on the management of water resources and limiting the use of fertilisers or the number of cattle per km^2.

(ii)   Transport policy

3–30   Transport policy (arts 90 to 100 TFEU) has also become, under the FEU Treaty, a common policy with shared competence (art.4(2g) TFEU), though EU measures are less comprehensive than the common agricultural policy. For this reason, Member States have a much greater likelihood of adopting environmental measures affecting transport. An important limitation, however, is art.92 TFEU,

---

[70] *Dassonville* (8/74) [1974] E.C.R. 837 at [5]: "all trading rules . . . which are capable of hindering, directly or indirectly, actually or potentially" trade, are incompatible with arts 34 and 35.

[71] Regulation 834/2007 on organic production and labelling of organic products [2007] OJ L189/1; see for more details para.6–50, below.

[72] Regulation 1107/2009 concerning the placing of plant protection products on the market [2009] OJ L309/1; this Regulation replaced Dir.91/414 [1991] OJ L230/51.

[73] Court of Justice, *Orgacom* (C-254/13) ECLI:EU:C:2014:2251: a tax on the import of manure into the Belgian region of Flanders discriminates non-Flemish traders and is therefore inadmissible.

which prohibits direct or indirect discrimination of carriers from other Member States. In 1992, the Court of Justice had to decide on a tax on the use of roads by heavy goods vehicles which Germany had introduced.[74] While this road tax was the same for all carriers, Germany had, at the same time, provided for a reduction in the motor vehicle tax to the same amount; thus, the charge of the tax on the use of roads only affected carriers from other Member States. The Court did not accept the German Government's argument that the tax on the use of roads had an environmental objective because it was intended to increase the rate of goods transported by railway. Instead, it was of the opinion that there was no encouragement for German carriers to move to railway transport and that, therefore, the effect of the German measures contradicted art.92 TFEU. The Court came to a similar conclusion in case C-205/98. Austria had raised, in 1995 and 1996, the toll rates for use of the Brenner motorway, but had provided that Austrian hauliers were charged less than foreign hauliers who were thus, in the opinion of the Court, discriminated against.[75]

A German plan, discussed in 2015, to introduce a motorway toll for all cars, but to reduce, at the same time, the tax for cars paid by Germans, would, in view of this case-law, be an indirect discrimination of non-German cars and be incompatible with EU law.

Member States may therefore take, in the absence of EU measures, non-discriminatory environmental measures, as regards, for instance, provisions on night flights at airports,[76] taxes or charges on the use of roads of all types of cars or provisions on ships. Since the European Union has, up until now, not taken many measures to integrate environmental requirements into the transport policy, arts 90 et seq. leave, in theory, large scope for national measures, although Member States do not seem inclined to make extensive use of this possibility.

(iii)   State aids

Under the FEU Treaty, state aid is a measure which provides a company or business with an economic or financial advantage, which must be granted by the state or through state resources; it must favour certain undertakings or the production of certain goods and it must affect the trade between Member States (art.107 TFEU). State aid is in principle prohibited. The intention of granting state aid has to be notified to the Commission (art.108(3) TFEU) in order to allow the assessment of its compatibility with the FEU Treaty, as art.107(2) and (3) TFEU allows state aid under certain conditions.   **3–31**

The connection with the Treaty's provision on competition needs to be underlined. Indeed, where consumers or users receive financial advantages to buy environmentally better products, there is normally no question of state aid, since financial benefits are not given to particular firms.[77] Where this is the case, aid

---

[74] *Commission v Germany* (C-195/90) [1992] E.C.R. I-3141; see also *Commission v Germany* (C-195/90R) [1990] E.C.R. I-3351, which dealt with interim measures.

[75] Court of Justice, *Commission v Austria* (C-205/98) [2000] E.C.R. I-7367.

[76] See on the interrelationship between airplane noise and environmental protection, Court of Justice, *European Air Transport* (C-120/10) [2011] E.C.R. I-7865.

[77] See e.g. Court of Justice, *PreussenElektra* (C-379/98) [2001] E.C.R. I-2099. The case concerned price advantages which were granted to small German producers—mainly private persons—of renewable energy.

may be authorised where it is granted without discrimination and does not exceed 100 per cent of the extra environmental costs. Small amounts of aid—up to €200,000 per firm over a period of three years—are considered not to affect trade and need not be notified to the Commission.[78] The financial support of environmental organisations which manage habitats or other pieces of land etc, constitutes state aid, though such aid may normally be authorised.[79]

In the same way, financial assistance which is granted to every undertaking is not aid, but may, of course, be seen as such where the receiving companies are in competition with other companies that do not have access to this assistance.

3–32   The Commission has, since 1974, established guidelines for national aid with environmental objectives,[80] which were reviewed and published several times, most recently in 2008.[81] Legally, these guidelines are not rules of law, but a communication to Member States and the other institutions, which indicate the criteria which the Commission uses to exercise its discretion for authorising national aids; they limit the Commission's discretion, as the Commission may not depart from them without reasons that are compatible with the principle of equal treatment.[82]

The basis for authorising national environmental aid is now art.107(3c)[83]; however, in specific cases, art.107(3a) or (3b) might be applicable. Under certain conditions, some environmental aid is block-exempted from notification and assessment by the Commission.[84]

Under the 2008 guidelines, aid for investment—in land, buildings, plants and, under certain conditions, technology transfer—may be authorised up to 70 per cent of the eligible costs where aid is given in order to help firms adapt to new mandatory standards. For small enterprises, the normal investment aid is 70 per cent, but may reach up to 100 per cent. For medium-sized enterprises, the normal investment aid is 60 per cent, for large enterprises 50 per cent. In specific circumstances, this aid may even be increased. The guidelines differentiate between aid for undertakings which go beyond or which anticipate EU environmental standards, environmental studies, waste management, renewable

---

[78] Commission Reg.1998/2006 on de minimis aid [2006] OJ L 379/5.

[79] General Court, *Germany v Commission* (T-347/09) ECLI:EU:T:2013:418.

[80] Commission, 4th report on competition policy (Brussels and Luxembourg, 1975), para.175; 10th report on competition policy (Brussels and Luxembourg, 1981), para.222; 16th report on competition policy (Brussels and Luxembourg, 1986), para.259; Guidelines 1994 [1994] OJ C72/3.

[81] Guidelines for state aid for environmental purposes [2001] OJ C37/3; Community guidelines on state aid for environmental purposes [2008] OJ C82/1; these guidelines applied until the end of 2014; Guidelines on state aid for environmental protection and energy 2014–2020 [2014] OJ C200/1..

[82] Court of Justice, *Archer Daniels Midland v Commission* (C-397/03P) [2006] E.C.R. I-4491 at [91]: "whilst rules of conduct designed to produce external effects as it is the case of the Guidelines [Guidelines on the method of setting fines in competition law, L.K.] which are aimed at traders, may not be regarded as rules of law which the administration is always bound to observe, they nevertheless form rules of practice from which the administration may not depart in an individual case without giving reasons that are compatible with the principle of equal treatment".

[83] Article 107(3c) TFEU: "[The following may be considered to be compatible with the common market:] aid to facilitate the development of certain economic activities or of certain economic areas, where such aid does not adversely affect trading conditions to an extent contrary to the common interest."

[84] Commission Reg.800/2008 on general block exemptions [2008] OJ L214/3.

energies, energy saving, district heating with conventional energy, the remediation of contaminated sites—here the aid for any enterprise may reach 100 per cent—and the relocation of undertakings.

Member States shall report annually on the environmental aid which they grant. The Commission publishes this information on the internet.[85] These provisions thus open up a large range of possibilities to financially assist companies which invest in clean technologies or otherwise improve the environment.

3–33

When it assessed the legality of a Spanish support scheme for indigenous coal, the General Court held that the Commission was not obliged, when it examined such aid, to examine, whether the scheme was compatible with EU environmental law. The Court was of the opinion that the protection of the environment was not part of the internal market, and as the Spanish scheme was intended to be applied within the context of the internal market, it was irrelevant, whether it complied with environmental protection provisions. The Commission might well start proceedings against Spain under art.258 TFEU, if it considered this necessary.[86] In view of arts 3 TEU, 11 and 114 TFEU and the extended jurisprudence of the Court of Justice, this judgment appears to be wrong.

(iv) Taxes and charges

Member States' possibilities of adopting environmental taxes and charges are equally great. They find their limitation in art.110 TFEU which is limited to goods and which prohibits any direct or indirect discrimination. The very existence of this provision shows that national fiscal measures are not to be assessed under art.34 TFEU. Indeed, art.110 is *lex specialis* to art.34.[87] The essential difference between the two provisions is that art.110 prohibits discriminating taxation measures, but does not refer to disproportionate taxes; and as the primary function of taxes is to ensure income there cannot be a question of environmental taxes being allowed only for non-economic reasons. Hence, Member States may fix taxes on whatever topic they wish and at whatever level they wish, as long as they do not discriminate against products from other Member States. No notification of a national measure to the Commission is necessary under art.110.

3–34

Environmental taxes are generally divided into taxes in the energy or the transport sector, with regard to pollution and concerning natural resources. By far the most frequent taxes are those in the energy sector. The Court of justice is rather strict in assessing direct and indirect discrimination: for example, a tax on the first registration of (new or second-hand) cars which takes into consideration the age and the state of the car discriminates, because the tax on the purchase of not imported second-hand cars is not influenced by such characteristics.[88] An

---

[85] Commission, Community guidelines on state aid for environmental purposes [2008] OJ C82/1, no.195.

[86] General Court, *Castelnou v Commission* (T-57/11) ECLI:EU:T:2014:1021; see in the same sense already, *Thermenhotel Stösner v Commission* (T-158/99) ECLI:EU:T:2004:2.

[87] Court of Justice, *Iannelli and Volpi* (74/76) [1977] E.C.R. 557; *Compagnie Commerciale de l'Ouest* (C-78–83/90) [1992] E.C.R. I-1847.

[88] Court of Justice, *Tatu* (C-402/09) ECLI:EU:C:2011:219.

environmental tax in the United Kingdom which provided for some exemptions for Northern Irish companies was considered to be discriminating against Irish companies.[89]

Denmark had fixed the registration tax on new vehicles at between 105 and 180 per cent of the net sales price. The Commission was of the opinion that this provision was incompatible with art.110, since it impeded the free movement of goods. However, the Court of Justice decided that art.110 only applied where tax measures were meant to protect domestic production; and since Denmark did not have a national car production industry there was no question of a breach of art.110.[90] Article 34 could, in such a case, become applicable only where a tax is so high that the import of products from other Member States would be effectively barred. Even in such cases a national tax may be compatible with art.34, namely in those cases where a Member State has legitimate environmental or other grounds for raising such a tax. Where, for instance, a Member State would not like to see a *Concorde* airplane, a pesticide, metal cans or other products on its market or in its environment, it would be entitled, instead of prohibiting the use of that product, to levy a high, dissuasive tax on the product.[91]

3–35   National eco-taxes on CFCs, energy use, packaging, groundwater and so on, are to be examined initially under art.110, not under art.34. Besides the objective of creating income, they aim at influencing economic operators', users', consumers' and tax-payers' behaviour to reduce pollution, ensure prudent use of natural resources and encourage a preference for environmentally friendly products. In 1993, Belgium adopted legislation providing for an environmental tax on a number of products, in particular packages for drinks, disposable cameras and razors, batteries, pesticides and paper. Products on which the tax was levied had to carry a distinctive sign, showing that they were eco-taxed. The Court of Justice considered the tax to come under art.110[92]; however, since the distinctive sign was to be applied on the products, it directly affected the circulation of goods and had therefore to be assessed under art.34.

In 1996, France informed the Commission of its intention to introduce tax exemptions for biofuels. The Commission at first refused to accept the French measures, since they benefited French products and thus were in conflict with art.110.[93] France then amended its legislation; the Commission was of the opinion that the new system eliminated the discrimination between the types of vegetable matter or crops which produce the biofuel and between French producers and those from other Member States. It therefore approved the system. However, the General Court considered the French measures incompatible with EU law as they gave competitive advantages to French producers.[94]

---

[89] General Court, *British Aggregates Association a.o. v Commission* (T-359/04) ECLI:EU:T:2010:366.

[90] *Commission v Denmark* (C-47/88) [1990] E.C.R. I-4509.

[91] As regards metal cans, see paras 3–11 and 3–12, above. Sweden had introduced a rather high tax for such cans. And while the Commission had tackled the Danish ban, it had not taken measures against Sweden.

[92] *Bic* (C-13/96) [1997] E.C.R. I-1753.

[93] Decision 97/542 [1997] OJ L222/26.

[94] General Court, *BP v Commission* (T-184/97) [2000] E.C.R. II-314 at [13]: "That decision was adopted without any communication being published in the Official Journal to allow interested third parties to submit their comments ... the decision was not published in the Official Journal".

A number of German local authorities taxed single-use packaging in order to promote reusable packaging. The Commission, seized with complaints from several economic operators, decided in 1996 that no infringement of the Treaty provisions was visible. In the meantime, these taxes were held to be incompatible with internal German law. In 1997, the Commission made a communication to the other institutions, in which it discussed environmental taxes and levies in the internal market.[95] The Communication examined several aspects of eco-taxes, with the implicit intention of bringing as many of the national taxes and levies as possible under the control of art.34 TFEU. This is understandable since with the progressive elimination of technical barriers to trade by art.34, barriers with similar effect may result by virtue of the introduction of national taxes and charges.

Several Member States introduced taxes for plastic bags in order to reduce their use. The Commission accepted this and even encouraged Member States to take this or other measures to reduce environmental pollution by plastic bags.[96]   **3–36**

Since the mid-1990s, Germany tried to promote alternative energies. National legislation obliged electricity companies to buy electricity from alternative energies produced in Germany at a fixed price which was determined by legislation, and to put the electricity into their grid. Seized with the question, whether this legislation was compatible with EU law, the Court decided[97] that the measures did not constitute state aid, as no public funds were made available to competitors. It also decided that in view of the present state of integration of the electricity market, the German legislation did not contradict art.34 TFEU. The discriminative character of the measure, which aimed at the promotion of German alternative energy, but excluded electricity produced from alternative energy from other Member States, could not really be put in doubt. The only explanation of this is that the Court considered the legislation to be a discrimination, but not an arbitrary discrimination. It is clear that such a differentiation can only be made by the Court—which does not increase transparency and legal certainty. In 2014, the Court of Justice confirmed its ruling of 2001, despite the development of the EU energy market.[98]

Eco-taxes are a useful tool in the promotion of environmentally sound behaviour; they help to keep environmentally unwelcome products off the market.[99] Member States have always used taxes to influence the behaviour of economic operators or private persons; examples are the taxation of petrol and diesel, of spirits and cigarettes, water, electricity and heating. Examples of past eco-taxes are differential taxes for leaded and unleaded petrol, tax relief for nuclear energy, natural gas, lignite or coal, or landfill taxes.

---

[95] Commission, COM(97) 9, [1997] OJ C224/4.
[96] Commission, COM(2013) 761.
[97] Court of Justice, *PreussenElektra* (C-379/98) [2001] E.C.R. I-2099.
[98] *Aaland Vindcraft* (C-573/12) ECLI:EU:C:2011:556; *Essent* (joined cases C-204/12 to C-208/12), ECLI:EU:C:2014:2192. See, however, also *Vent de Colère* (C-262/12) ECLI:EU:C:2013:851, where a national system was considered to imply state aid.
[99] See also European Environment Agency, *Environmental Taxes, Implementation and Environmental Effectiveness* (Copenhagen, 1996).

3. EXISTENCE OF UNION LEGISLATION AND THE TAKING OF NATIONAL MEASURES

(a) General aspects

3–37 As mentioned above, Member States' competence to deal with environmental measures does not end once the European Union has adopted an environmental measure. However, it is "superseded" by the EU measure, as far as the EU measure reaches. Member States' possibility of acting therefore depends both on the content of the EU legislative act, and on the legal basis on which that legislative act was based.

In order to assess the legal content of an EU measure, it is important to examine exactly what the measure intends to cover. For instance, the EU measure might, for product standards, cover only the standards for those products which participate in the trade between Member States, but leave the standards for products which remain on the national market to Member States. EU terminology speaks, in such cases, of optional harmonisation, since Member States may decide to set up two different types of standards for products.[100] In contrast, total harmonisation exists where an EU measure intends to set standards for all products which are put into circulation within the Union, whether they cross a border or not.[101] Partial harmonisation only concerns some products, but not all of a given type.[102] Minimum harmonisation sets standards at EU level, but leaves the possibility to Member States to fix more stringent requirements.[103] Combinations of these types of harmonisation are possible; thus, an EU directive may well fix standards for some products only (partial harmonisation), deal with all products that are on the EU market (total harmonisations) and leave Member States the opportunity to adopt more stringent standards (minimum harmonisation).

The different approaches find their source in the EU Treaties themselves. Indeed, the FEU Treaty provides for differences in Member States' rights according to the legal basis on which an EU environmental measure is grounded. For this reason, it is important to examine what the objective of a specific EU legislation is, in order to determine the possibilities for Member States to legislate.[104]

(b) Rights under art.193 TFEU

3–38 Where an EU measure was based on art.192 TFEU, the relationship between the Member States' and the Union's right to legislate is governed by art.193.[105] The provision only refers to protective measures and it may thus be doubtful whether

---

[100] Examples are the limit values for noise emissions from construction equipment, see para.8–31, below.

[101] Examples are the limit values for air emission from cars since 1988, see para.8–37, below.

[102] An example is Reg.1102/2008 [2008] OJ L 304/74.

[103] Examples are standards for waste incineration plants, see para.8–28, below.

[104] See, e.g. Court of Justice, *VAG Sverige* (C-329/95) [1997] E.C.R. I-2675.

[105] Article 193 TFEU: "The protective measures adopted in common pursuant to Art.192, shall not prevent any Member State from maintaining or introducing more stringent protective measures. Such measures must be compatible with the Treaties. They shall be notified to the Commission."

measures that aim at preserving or improving the quality of the environment (see art.191 TFEU) are also covered. However, such a differentiation would make no sense, all the more since no clear distinction can be drawn between protective, preserving and improving measures. "Protective measures" must therefore be interpreted as including all measures adopted under art.192, even where only the main objective of a measure—say 55 per cent—is environmentally oriented and a considerable part—say 45 per cent—is aimed at the achievement of internal market objectives.

Article 193 says nothing about the form which the EU provision under art.192 must take. It is therefore irrelevant whether the provision is set out in a directive, a regulation or a decision—for instance, whether to adhere to an international convention—whether the measure was adopted unanimously or by majority vote, whether it is a partial or an optional or a total harmonisation measure.

Article 193 only allows stricter measures to be taken. Consequently, the Member States may not adopt different measures from those adopted by the European Union. On the contrary: the more stringent national measure must follow the same direction and come closer than the European Union to attaining the objectives of art.191(1) TFEU. It is important that the rules adopted by the individual Member State are of the same type as the EU provisions, because then the European Union and other Member States have the possibility of catching up and aligning with the more protective measure taken by one Member State, re-establishing in this way uniform legislation throughout the European Union.[106]

For example, if the European Union decides in a measure based on art.192, to halve the production and consumption of chlorofluorocarbons (CFCs) because of its ozone-depleting potential, any Member State may still propose an outright ban on the production and consumption of CFCs. However, it may not ban, on the basis of art.193, the use of aerosol cans which contain CFC gas: this is not a more stringent protective measure, but another, different measure: an *aliud*. The legality of such a measure is therefore determined according to general Treaty provisions, in particular by arts 34 and 36 TFEU.

3–39

If the European Union introduces a system of strict, unlimited liability for environmental damage, but excludes the compensation of bodily injury, each Member State may impose strict liability and provide for the inclusion of compensation for bodily injury of individual persons. However, it may not provide for unlimited liability only for damage that was caused by negligence instead, since this is a different system. Nor could the Member State in that case, argue that experience had shown that certain industrial activities too often give cause for environmental liability and then prohibit that specific industrial activity altogether.

When the European Union introduced an eco-label for products and took a flower as its symbol, it expressly allowed Member States to maintain their national ecolabel systems.[107] Without this express authorisation, Member States would not have been able, based on art.193, to maintain their national systems.

---

[106] See also Court of Justice, *Deponieverband Eiterköpfe* (C-6/03) [2005] E.C.R. I-2753, where the Court requires the national measure to pursue "the same objectives".

[107] Regulation 66/2010 on the Community ecolabel [2010] OJ L27/1, art.11 and Recital 15; see para.6–47, below.

Indeed, the symbols as well as the selection and assessment criteria being different, these national systems are not "more protective" systems under art.193, but rather different systems.

3–40 A more protective system is a system which establishes stricter limit values for the emission of pollutants into the environment, which reduces emissions more quickly than the EU measure or which regulates, for emissions from an industrial plant, more pollutants than the EU measure.

The nationally more protective measures must be compatible with the Treaties. Consequently, they may not conflict with any provision of the Treaties, particularly with the provisions on the free circulation of goods or on undistorted competition. The measures must not constitute a means of arbitrary discrimination or a disguised restriction on trade between Member States (arts 34 and 36 TFEU). Reference to the Treaties means, of course, reference to the interpretation given to the different Treaty provisions, by the Court of Justice in particular. Therefore, a national, more protective measure may neither be discriminatory nor disproportionate with regard to the objective that is pursued with it. Protectionism is still protectionism, even if the aim is to protect the environment.

"Treaties" refers also to secondary EU law, since this is based on the FEU Treaty.[108] This theory is contested mainly by German writers who argue that otherwise the right to take more protective measures would be undermined by EU secondary legislation and become meaningless. However, this opinion does not take into consideration the fact that EU secondary legislation is also based on the Treaties. As regards art.36 TFEU, it is well established Court jurisdiction, and in the meantime is no longer contested, that this provision no longer applies where the European Union has adopted secondary legislation—whether such EU measures were based on arts 114, 192 or any other provision.

3–41 Furthermore, it has already been discussed above[109] that the Council considers arts 114 and 192 as being equally valid grounds on which to base environmental legislation and that it differentiates the legal basis, supported in this by the Court of Justice and the Commission, according to the "centre of gravity" of a measure. This means that up to 49 per cent of a measure that is based on art.192 may be provisions which deal with internal market issues. In such a case, Member States may also take more protective measures with regard to the provisions concerning the 49 per cent of the measures. An example is Directive 2000/53 on end-of-life vehicles[110] which prohibited, in new cars, the use of certain heavy metals. Member States are allowed, under art.193, to provide for further restrictions, of course, under the condition that these measures were also justified under other Treaty provisions, in particular arts 34 and 36 TFEU. In order to prevent Member States from taking such measures, the legislation on electrical and electronic waste was split up: the ban of heavy metals was regulated in Directive 2002/95 which was based on art.114,[111] whereas the other provisions concerning such waste were regulated by Directive 2002/96 which was based on art.192[112] and

---

[108] In this sense also Pagh, *E.U. Miljoeret* (Copenhagen 1996), p.242; cf. Epiney, *Umweltrecht in der Europäischen Union* (fn.20, above), p.126 quoting other German authors.

[109] See paras 2–75 et seq., above.

[110] Directive 2000/53 on end-of life vehicles [2000] OJ L269/34.

[111] Directive 2002/95 on the restriction of the use of certain hazardous substances in electrical and electronic equipment [2003] OJ L37/19.

[112] Directive 2002/96 on waste electrical and electronic equipment (WEEE) [2003] OJ L37/24.

thus allowed to recur to art.193. The opposite example is Directive 94/62 on packaging and packaging waste which is based on the present art.114.[113] In order to allow Member States to fix more demanding recycling targets than those provided for by the Directive, art.6(6) of that Directive had to introduce an express provision allowing Member States to adopt more stringent targets.

The problem is of considerable practical importance. For example, Regulation 66/2010, based on art.192, introduced an EU ecolabel.[114] The EU criteria for attribution of an ecolabel are set for product groups by EU decisions which are based on Regulation 66/2010 and, finally, on art.192 TFEU. The specific decisions, to grant the ecolabel for a specific product, are taken at national level.[115] It seems an impossible idea to establish EU-wide criteria for specific product groups and then, when a producer asks a national authority to obtain the ecolabel, inform him that the Member State in question has adopted more protective provisions so that he could not obtain the ecolabel. Such a solution would be all the more contradictory as the same producer could obtain the ecolabel in another Member State that had not adopted such "more protective measures" and could then circulate his product freely within the European Union. Thus, within one and the same Member State, products could circulate with the same ecolabel, but with different eco-criteria: this result is absurd.

Another example is the regulation on the shipment of waste, which is based on art.192.[116] The Regulation establishes lists of non-hazardous and hazardous waste, for which different surveillance and control systems as regards shipments apply. Non-hazardous waste may be shipped practically without restriction. The question is whether Member States are allowed, under art.193, to classify a non-hazardous waste as hazardous and then apply stricter controls to such shipments. I am of the opinion that this is not allowed.

A last example again concerns the shipment of waste. Regulation 1013/2006 differentiates, for hazardous wastes, between shipments that are made for disposal and shipments that are made for recovery purposes. While Member States may prohibit shipments of hazardous waste for disposal altogether,[117] they may object to shipments for recovery only in specific cases which are listed in art.12 of Regulation 1013/2006.

3–42

Article 12(1.g) allows objection to shipments:

> "if the ration of the recoverable and non-recoverable waste, the estimated value of the materials to be finally recovered or the cost of the recovery and the cost of the disposal of the non recoverable fraction do not justify the recovery under economic and environmental considerations."

Could a Member State, invoking art.193, also generally prohibit shipments of waste for recovery?

The answer must be in the negative. Indeed, there is no sense in differentiating between waste for disposal and waste for recovery at all, if Member States could

---

[113] Directive 94/62 on packaging and packaging waste [1994] OJ L365/10.

[114] Regulation 66/2010 on the Community ecolabel [2010] OJ L27/1.

[115] For more details see para.6–40, above.

[116] Regulation 1013/2006 on shipments of waste [2006] OJ L190/1; this Regulation replaced Reg.259/93 [1993] OJ L30/1.

[117] Regulation 1013/2006, art.11(1).

adopt provisions which would lead to an equal treatment of waste in both cases. Why should there be the necessity for very carefully considering environmental and economic aspects of a waste shipment under art.12 of Regulation 1013/2006, if a Member State could ensure, as a general rule, that shipments of waste would be prohibited even if the weighing up of arguments showed that such a shipment was environmentally sound? Listing specific grounds for objecting to waste shipments in art.12(1) and then admitting an unlimited number of supplementary objections does not really make sense.

3–43   This question was, under the previous Regulation on the shipment of waste, Regulation 259/93, submitted to the Court of Justice in case C-203/96,[118] the Court found that neither Regulation 259/93 nor Directive 75/442 on waste[119] allowed the application of the principles of self-sufficiency and proximity to shipments of waste for recovery. However, it did not answer the question of whether art.193 allowed such an application and, thus, whether Member States could go beyond Regulation 259/93 by invoking art.193. Instead, it examined the grounds invoked by the Dutch Government for its national measure which went beyond Regulation 259/93 and found that the justification—to ensure the continuity of supply of Dutch undertakings and increased risks for the environment by waste shipments—did not justify, in this specific case,[120] the restriction under art.36 TFEU.

This judgment might well be claimed by both sides. Indeed, if a Member State could have recourse to art.193 and generally object to waste shipments, an examination of whether such a restriction is contrary to art.35 TFEU would not have been necessary. On the other hand, if the objections listed in art.12(1) of Regulation 1013/2006 were exhaustive, should the Court have entered into an examination of supplementary objection grounds?

In my opinion, it should first of all be noted that the problem only appears as regards product standards, where the EU principle of free circulation of goods interferes. Indeed, where EU secondary legislation establishes limit values for emissions from installations, or quality standards for concentrations of pollutants in water, there is general agreement that Member States may, on the basis of art.193, set stricter provisions at national level.

As regards product-related secondary EU legislation, the solution lies in the necessity of reading the two criteria of art.193 together—i.e. "more protective measure" and "compatible with the Treaty": any EU environmental legislation, including the legislation that is based on art.192 must respect the provisions of arts 34 and 36—this is established case-law of the Court of Justice.[121] Thus, EU legislation also has to respect the principles of non-discrimination and proportionality,[122] although the EU legislature enjoy a large degree of discretion as to how to draft legislation in a specific case. The more the EU legislature has weighed up the different economic, ecological, social, political and other

---

[118] *Dusseldorp* (C-203/96) [1998] E.C.R. I–4075.

[119] Directive 75/442 as amended by Dir.91/156 [1991] OJ L78/32. This Directive is now replaced by Dir.2008/98 on waste [2008] OJ L312/3.

[120] It is not clear why the Court entered into the discussion of this specific case, although it was a question which was put to the Court under the procedure of art.267 TFEU.

[121] *Denkavit Nederland* (15/83) [1984] E.C.R. 2171; *Meyhui* (C-51/93) [1994] E.C.R. I-3879; *Safety Hi-Tech* (C-284/95) [1998] E.C.R. I-4301.

[122] The proportionality principle is also laid down in art.5(4) TEU.

arguments in detail and has elaborated detailed, balanced and sophisticated provisions (such as decisions on ecolabel criteria, waste lists, objection grounds) the more the principles of arts 34 and 36 are "filled up"; in such a case of total harmonisation—on this notion see para.3–37, above—there is thus no room left for the principles of arts 34 and 36. Therefore, when a Member State, based on art.193 TFEU, wants to take more protective measures, its legislative discretion is reduced in proportion to the concretisation which EU secondary legislation has given to the balance between environmental and economic interests in a specific situation. A national measure which deviates from the solutions set by EU secondary legislation would thus be disproportionate and therefore not compatible with the Treaties.

This means in the concrete case of waste shipments that Regulation 1013/2006—and its predecessor, Regulation 259/93—constitute, as regards objects to waste shipments for recovery—total harmonisation measures. Member States may not go further than Regulation 1013/2006 and invoke other grounds for objecting to shipments.

The problem has only been seen in practice in one case up until now. Directive 87/416 allows Member States to prohibit the use of leaded petrol, but requires that the intention of such a ban be published and notified to the Commission six months in advance.[123] Germany wanted, based on art.193, to disregard the six-month delay and ban leaded petrol four months after notification. Finally, however, it accepted the Commission's request that the six-month delay be respected, which safeguarded the interests of producers, importers, traders and users of petrol and cars.

Another example is that of sewage sludge in agriculture. Directive 86/278 on protecting the environment and soil against the use of sewage sludge[124] fixed maximum permitted concentrations of some heavy metals in sewage sludge and in the soil. Where these concentration values are exceeded, the use of sewage sludge is prohibited. In view of the accumulation of heavy metals in the soil and the possible residues in food, Austrian and German regions prohibited the use of sewage sludge on or in soil altogether. In my opinion, such a measure is justified under art.193 TFEU. Article 34 does not stand against this solution, as sewage sludge may nevertheless be traded within the European Union. It is not forbidden to trade in sewage sludge, only to use it on or in the soil. And as sludge contains heavy metals, it must remain the decision of Member States to fix for themselves the degree of protection which they want to apply for their soils.

When the European Union introduced a greenhouse gas emissions trading scheme, it amended Directive 96/61 and provided that industrial installations which participated in the trading scheme were not obliged to apply, with regard to CO_2-emissions, the best available techniques.[125] The question is whether a Member State may, on the basis of art.193 TFEU, introduce the requirement of using the best available techniques at national level. This is, in my opinion, certainly the case. Each Member State is entitled to discriminate against its own

3–44

3–45

[123] Directive 87/416 [1987] OJ L225/1.

[124] Directive 86/278 on the use of sewage sludge in agriculture [1986] OJ L181/6.

[125] See now Dir.2010/75 on industrial emissions [2010] OJ L334/17, art.9(1): "Where emissions of a greenhouse gas from an installation are specified in Annex I to Directive 2003/87 in relation to an activity carried out in that installation, the permit shall not include an emission limit value for direct emissions of that gas, unless necessary to ensure that no significant local pollution is caused."

national installations.[126] If the Council and the European Parliament wanted to provide for a total harmonisation, they should have based the legislation on industrial installations on art.114 TFEU, instead of art.192 TFEU.

Measures adopted under art.193 must be notified to the Commission. There is no time limit for such notification and the measures need not be notified to the Commission in draft form; neither is the Member State obliged to wait for a certain period after the notification before adopting the measures. However, the situation is different where the national measure comes into the field of application of Directive 98/34.[127] Indeed, that Directive provides that all product-related measures shall be notified to the Commission in draft form in order to allow an examination of whether or not they could create new barriers to trade. Therefore, where a more protective measure could have an influence on art.34 TFEU, the Commission must be notified of it in draft form. Under Directive 98/34, there is then a standstill period of at least three months during which the Commission and all other Member States may question the compatibility of the draft measure with art.34 or secondary EU legislation. Omitting to notify the Commission of the draft makes the national provision unenforceable.[128]

Article 193 does not contain any procedural provisions for checking whether the national measure fulfils the conditions that are laid down in this provision. Where the Commission is of the opinion that a national measure is not a more protective, but a different measure (an "*aliud*"), or where it believes that the measure is not compatible with primary or secondary EU law, it has, in the last instance, to recur to procedures under art.258 TFEU. The same possibility is open to any Member State under art.259 TFEU, though Member States have never used that provision.

(c) Rights under art.114(4)–(8) TFEU

(i) General aspects

3–46   Article 114(4)–(8) TFEU deals with the right of Member States to maintain existing or introduce new legislative measures where the Union has legislated on the legal basis of art.114.

The present art.114 was introduced, as art.100a, into the Treaty in 1987. Its para.4 allowed Member States, in the case of decisions according to that provision and under certain conditions, to "apply" diverging national legislation. Between 1987 and 1997, the Commission took three decisions under art.95(4)[129]; in one case, the Court of Justice issued a judgment,[130] where it stated in particular

---

[126] J. Jans and H. Vedder, *European Environmental Law*, 3rd edn (Groningen, 2008), p.108 appear to deny such a right of a Member State under art.193. They hold that the EU legislature could make such a "self-binding" commitment to exclude such a possibility. This would mean that the legislature could make a commitment to prohibit the application of a provision of the EU Treaties.

[127] Directive 98/34 laying down a procedure for the provision of information in the field of technical standards and regulations [1998] OJ L204/37. This Directive replaced Dir.83/189 [1983] OJ L109/8.

[128] Court of Justice, *CIA Security International* (C-194/94) [1996] E.C.R. I-2201.

[129] [1992] OJ C334/8 (*Pentachlorophenol Germany*); [1994] OJ L316/43 (*Pentachlorophenol Germany*); [1996] OJ L68/32 (*Pentachlorophenol Denmark*).

[130] *France v Commission* (C-41/93) [1994] E.C.R. I-1829.

that the national measure would only become applicable once the Commission had authorised it. However, this created problems, because the Commission sometimes did not take a decision for several years: on two notifications from the Netherlands, dated 1992 and concerning restrictions on the use of cadmium and pentachlorophenol, the Commission took more than six years for a decision, though it tolerated the application of the restriction in the Netherlands; this was not quite in line with the Court's judgment in case C-41/93.

In case C-319/97,[131] the Court decided that where the Commission failed to take a decision within a reasonable time, a Member State could only take court action against the Commission under art.265 TFEU, but had, in the meantime, to apply the EU measure. The Amsterdam Treaty then solved this problem by introducing art.114(6) according to which the Commission had to take a decision under art.114 within six months; otherwise, the national measure would be deemed to have been approved.[132]

The Amsterdam Treaty modified art.114 considerably, and, in particular, explicitly provided for the possibility for Member States to *maintain or introduce* national measures after the European Union had adopted a measure under art.114. This ended the extensive legal discussion on the former wording, whether "apply" was to be understood as "continue to apply"—this had always been the Commission's understanding—or was equivalent to "maintain or introduce". In 2003, the Commission resumed its practice under art.114 in a communication[133]; it also started to report on its decisions under that provision, but gave up this initiative again.[134]

(ii) Maintaining national legislation (art.114(4))

For a Member State to maintain national environmental legislation, according to art.114(4), despite EU legislation a number of conditions must be fulfilled: **3–47**

1. the European Union must have adopted a harmonisation measure;
2. a Member State must deem it necessary to maintain its national legislation on grounds that relate to the protection of the environment;
3. the Member State notifies the Commission of these provisions as well as of the grounds for maintaining them;
4. the Commission approves of the national measures (art.114(6)).

These different conditions will be examined one by one.[135]

---

[131] *Kortas* (C-319/97) [1999] E.C.R. I-3143.

[132] See for a case, where the six-month delay had been exceeded, General Court, *Poland v Commission* (T-69/08), ECLI:EU:T:2010:504.

[133] Commission, Communication concerning Article 95 (paras 4, 5 and 6) COM(2002) 760 of 23 December 2002.

[134] See Commission, 19th annual report on monitoring the application of Community law (2001) COM(2002)324; 27 the report, COM(2010) 538.

[135] The Commission has, in the meantime, adopted a number of environmental decisions concerning the application of art.95(4), in particular: Dec.99/831 (Netherlands—PCP) [1999] OJ L329/15; Dec.99/832 (Netherlands—creosote) [1999] OJ L329/25; Dec.99/833 (Germany—creosote) [1999] OJ L329/43; Dec.99/834 (Sweden—creosote) [1999] OJ L329/63; Dec.99/835 (Denmark—creosote) [1999] OJ L329/82; Dec.2000/59 (Belgium—organo-stannic compounds [2000] OJ L205/7; Dec.2002/3999 (Sweden—cadmium in fertilisers) [2002] OJ L138/24; Dec.2006/347 (Sweden—

3–48   **Adoption of a harmonisation measure.**   The express inclusion of measures taken by the Commission clarifies that the adaptation of EU measures to scientific or technical progress or by other means of delegated or implementing acts (arts 290 and 291 TFEU), may also lead to the right of Member States to maintain national legislation; such cases may well occur where technical annexes of directives are adapted to technical progress.

"Harmonisation measures" are measures adopted under art.114 TFEU. Such a measure need not have been adopted by majority decision; even in the case of a unanimous decision, the right of a Member State to maintain its national legislation exists. It is not contradictory to vote in favour of an EU measure and then decide to maintain more stringent national legislation. Indeed, a Member State may well vote in favour of an EU measure because it wishes to see the level of environmental protection increased throughout the European Union, even if the EU measure does not go as far as its own national legislation.

3–49   **Necessity of maintaining national legislation.**   It is doubtful whether any national legislation may be maintained. These doubts stem from art.114(7),[136] which demonstrates the aim of the Treaty legislature to ensure that uniform legislation applies throughout the European Union. Therefore, the EU measure shall, if at all possible, be adapted to that of the derogating Member State in order to ensure the continuous free circulation of goods in the Union's internal market.

These questions will be discussed below, when the Commission's options are examined for approving or of refusing the Member State's maintaining its national legislation. It is certain that a Member State may notify any national measure under art.114(4); it is not necessary that the legislation is adopted at national level; regional measures may also be notified.[137]

3–50   **Notification and justification of the national measure.**   The Member State which wishes to maintain its national legislation must formally inform the Commission of its intention to do so. There is no time limit for this notification; terms that require such notification to be addressed to the Commission within a specific time-span after the adoption of the EU legislation or within the time-span which was provided for in the EU measure for transposition into national legislation, have not been retained. Usually, therefore, a Member State is free to notify the Commission when it seems fit to do so.

However, it is clearly in the self-interest of the notifying Member State to notify as early as possible. On the one hand, provisions of EU law prevail over national law and may have a direct effect, even where they are not transposed into national law; this means in practice that national law which is in conflict with an

---

cadmium in fertilisers), [2006] OJ L129/19; Dec.2006/348 (Finland—cadmium in fertilisers) [2006] OJ L129/25; Dec.2006/349 (Austria—cadmium in fertilisers) [2006] OJ L129/31; Dec.2006/390 (Czech Republic—cadmium in fertilisers) [2006] OJ L150/17; Dec.2007/955 (Netherlands—paraffin) [2007] OJ L148/17.

[136] Article 114(7) TFEU: "When ... a Member State is authorised to maintain or introduce national provisions derogating from a harmonisation measure, the Commission shall immediately examine whether to propose an adaptation to that measure."

[137] See, e.g. the legislation referred to in General Court, *Austria v Commission* (T-366/03) [2005] E.C.R. II-4005, which originated from the Land (region) Ober-Österreich. The appeal was rejected, *Austria v Commission* (C-439/05) [2007] OJ LI-7141.

EU provision may not be applied—and not be enforced either.[138] On the other hand, the notification puts into operation a six-month delay within which a decision on the national measure must be taken (art.114(6)).

And, finally, the Court of Justice has decided[139] that a Member State may only apply its national legislation which deviates from the EU harmonisation measure, once it has received an approving decision from the Commission. It is doubtful whether this decision, which was taken at a time when the Treaty text did not yet differentiate in art.114 between "apply" and "maintain/introduce", is of much relevance now. Indeed, it would constitute a considerable disturbance of economic operations and administrative practice if a Member State would have to suspend the application of national legislation which might have existed for years, and wait for a Commission decision. The reasonable, and largely logical, consequence is therefore to consider the Court's statement remaining valid only for the cases of art.114(5), i.e. for cases where new national legislation is introduced. Anyway, the uncertainty of the described legal situation suggests that the Member State has a strong interest in trying to obtain the Commission's decision as quickly as possible and before the transposition period for the harmonisation measure has ended.

The notifying Member State will also have to give the grounds for its decision to maintain national legislation. It has to indicate the factual and legal aspects in sufficient detail to allow the Commission to reach a decision on the notification within six months. The requirement of providing the grounds for the decision is new and constitutes, without doubt, a considerable supplementary burden for the notifying Member State.

3–51

Commission approval.   The Commission must "approve" of the environmental measure; this wording of art.114(6) is more precise than that of the previous version of the Treaty which provided that the Commission should "confirm" the national measure, since it is now—since the judgment in case C-41/93, quoted above—clear that the approval must be made in the form of a decision under art.288 TFEU.

3–52

Approval has to be given if the national measure does not constitute a "means of arbitrary discrimination or a disguised restriction on trade between Member States". This wording is identical to that of art.36(2) TFEU. Thus, the interpretation of art.36(2) may be used to interpret this provision. Arbitrary discrimination or disguised trade restrictions are cases of abuse, where a formally legitimate objective—the protection of the environment—is used to discriminate against goods from other Member States or to pursue protectionist goals.

To these two goals, which were already contained in the previous versions of art.114, a third one has been added: the national measure "shall not constitute an obstacle to the functioning of the internal market".

It is clear that any national measure which is maintained, despite a harmonisation measure taken by the European Union, constitutes an obstacle to the functioning of the internal market; the two bans on pentachlorophenol in

---

[138] *France* (C-41/93) [1994] E.C.R. I-1829 at [30].

[139] *France* (C-41/93) [1994] E.C.R. I-1829 at [30], Opinion of Advocate-General Tesauro at [9], who argued that this interpretation is the only one which is compatible with the supremacy of EU law and which avoids legal insecurity.

Germany and Denmark, on which the Commission had decided, constitute a clear example, since products containing that substance were not allowed to circulate in these countries. It is thus not quite clear what the provision intends to achieve.

3–53 Where, for instance, the European Union decides to create a uniform ecolabelling system throughout the European Union, such a measure would have to be based on art.114. Supposing that Germany then wanted to maintain its national eco-symbol, which is a blue angel—and not a flower, as is the EU symbol—could this be done by invoking art.114(4)? The answer seems clearly to be in the negative. Indeed, it is possible to have either a system based on the flower or on the blue angel, but one cannot have both systems inside an internal market. In fact, the German system, in this example, would be a different system. Also, it is not clear what the environmental grounds would be which would make it "necessary" to maintain the blue angel system; greater efficiency cannot be a valid ground, because the EU system is just meant to create an equivalent system. Thus, in conclusion, the maintaining of the blue angel system would be a different system where the environmental grounds that would make its maintenance necessary are not visible.

Where the European Union provides for a certain limit for noise emissions from coaches, any more stringent national limit would, if properly enforced, create an obstacle to the free circulation of coaches and would thus have to be disallowed. This solution could be avoided where the Member State that wishes to maintain the more stringent national emission limit would at least allow the circulation of coaches on its territory, which are registered in other Member States and only occasionally circulate within the Member State with the more stringent limit. This consideration demonstrates that the assessment of whether the maintaining of a national measure is necessary, requires a detailed consideration of the pros and cons under internal market and ecological auspices. Sevenster[140] goes so far as to generalise this position: she is of the opinion that the necessity of considering whether the national measure constitutes an obstacle is a badly drafted expression of the proportionality principle.

In conclusion, the new addition to art.114 does not mean that the national environmental measure may not, under any circumstances, constitute an obstacle to the free circulation of goods. It is only meaningful when it is completed by a word such as "inadequate", "inappropriate" or "disproportionate".[141] This would mean that, in each individual case, the Commission would have to weigh up the protection of the environment against the proper functioning of the internal market. Thus, a national measure must be proportional to the objective pursued by it; where a less restrictive measure is available, the Member State may be asked to recur to that measure even where this would mean a change in its national rules. Also, a measure that constitutes a significant obstacle to the functioning of the internal market and where the environmental advantage is insignificant, could be rejected by the Commission.

This interpretation would bring the principle of proportionality from art.5 TEU into the assessment process of art.114(6): while it is legitimate to protect the environment and not to see the national level of environmental protection

---

[140] H. Sevenster, *European Yearbook of Environmental Law* (Oxford, 1999), p.116.
[141] See in the same sense Commission, Dec.1999/831 (Netherlands—PCP) [1999] OJ L329/15 at [23].

lowered by a harmonisation measure from the European Union, the national measure must not go beyond what is necessary to achieve appropriate environmental protection.

Procedure. The Treaty does not fix a delay, when the national measure has to be notified or approved. As mentioned, it would make sense to have it notified after the adoption of the EU measure, but before the period for transposing the EU measure into national law has expired. However, it will be impossible not to approve a national measure exclusively with the argument that it was notified too late, though the Court of Justice stated that the principle of sincere cooperation of art.4(3) TEU obliges Member States to notify a national measure "as soon as possible".[142]

3–54

The Commission is required to approve—or reject—the national decision to maintain national legislation within six months of notification; in particularly complex cases it may prolong this period by a maximum of six months more. As mentioned, this provision was introduced by the Amsterdam Treaty as a reaction to the fact that some national notifications under art.114(4) had not been decided upon for several years.[143] It is not possible to prolong this delay, for instance when the Commission argues that the Member State's decision has not been sufficiently argued. The Commission may then refuse to authorise the measure; but it may not ask for further documentation, evidence or other justification, since this would introduce supplementary conditions for the application of the six-month period, for which the Commission has no mandate in the Treaties.[144]

The time given for approval may appear short. It should be noted, however, that the legal and environmental situation in the different Member States has normally been discussed at EU level during the elaboration of the harmonisation measure. The subject-matter of national legislation is thus not entirely new to the Commission.

The sanction for failing to decide within six months is tough: the national measure "shall be deemed to have been approved". The national measure has, in such a case, an effect on all other Member States as well as on all economic operators, even though they did not have the possibility of influencing the speed of decision-making within the Commission. Where a Member State is of the opinion that the Commission has made a wrong decision, either by approving or rejecting the national measure within six months or by letting the six-month period elapse, it may bring the matter before the Court of Justice directly (art.114(8)). The procedure is governed by art.263(2) TFEU if the action is directed against the Commission, and by art.259 TFEU, if the action is directed against another Member State. The two-month delay of art.263(6) TFEU starts, in the case of the absence of a Commission decision within six months, at the end of this six-month period. Until the end of 2014, no Member State ever took such an action against another Member State or against the Commission.

3–55

Private operators may take action against the Commission under art.263(4) TFEU if they are directly and individually concerned by the decision, for instance when their exports or imports are affected. They may also try to conform to the

---

[142] Court of Justice, *Kortas* (C-319/97) [1999] E.C.R. I-3143 at [35].

[143] For an example, see Dec.2001/59 [2001] OJ L210/46.

[144] See General Court, *Poland* (T-69/08), ECLI:EU:T:2010:504..

EU harmonisation measure and, where they see their trade affected, bring the matter before the competent national court and then ask for a preliminary ruling by the Court of Justice under art.267 TFEU, in order to have the Commission's decision checked.

(iii)   Introducing new national legislation

3–56   The new provision of art.114(5) clarifies that Member States may, under certain conditions, introduce new legislation in cases where the European Union has adopted a harmonisation measure.[145] The possibility of introducing new measures exists only for measures relating to the environment and the working environment. The different grounds of art.36 TFEU which allow Member States, under art.114(4), to maintain existing more stringent national provisions, may not be invoked for the introduction of new measures.

The conditions for introducing new national environmental measures are relatively strict. They are as follows:

1. the new national measure must be based on new scientific evidence;
2. the problem must be specific to the Member State that wishes to introduce the measure;
3. the problem must have arisen after the adoption of the harmonisation measure.

The three conditions must be fulfilled cumulatively. Their likely effect will make it very rare for a Member State to demonstrate the necessity to opt out of the common EU measure, although the acting Member State has a certain amount of discretion to assess whether the new situation requires the opting out of the EU measure ("deems it necessary"). Its decision is, in turn, assessed by the Commission and, in case of litigation, by the Court of Justice.

3–57   **New scientific evidence.**   New scientific evidence may consist of studies, reports or other documentation, showing that there is a real risk to the environment and that, therefore, it is necessary to introduce a more protective national measure. It is not easy to comply with this criterion. For instance, the fact that benzene, an additive in petrol, is carcinogenic, has been known for years; thus, a Member State would not be allowed to lower the maximum admissible content of benzene in petrol below the level that was fixed by the European Union. It might be argued that the cancer statistics which show the effects of benzene, constitute "new evidence". This seems doubtful, though, in the end, acceptable; in any case, however, such a discovery would not be specific to an individual Member State, but would concern the whole of the Union. For such cases, the new formulation of art.114(3) suggests that the Commission make a new proposal for a harmonisation measure "taking account in particular of any

---

[145] Article 114(5) TFEU: "… if, after the adoption of a harmonisation measure by the European Parliament and the Council, by the Council or by the Commission, a Member State deems it necessary to introduce national provisions based on new scientific evidence relating to the protection of the environment or the working environment on grounds of a problem specific to that Member State arising after the adoption of the harmonisation measure, it shall notify the Commission of the envisaged provisions as well as the grounds for introducing them."

new development based on scientific facts". To take another example: the continuing global climate problem would not justify a Member State introducing national standards for air emissions from cars which deviate from EU standards; again, this is neither a "new" scientific evidence nor is the problem specific to one Member State alone.

Scientific evidence is new where the EU legislature was not able to take it into account at the moment of adopting the harmonisation measure. The word "evidence"[146] will, also in the light of the precautionary principle, have to be interpreted broadly and will be considered to include data, the accumulation of existing studies which bring to light a specific problem, and other factual aspects which will conclude that there is the probability of environmental risks. It is not to be understood as requiring "proof" of new risks or damage.

Specific problem. The condition that the problem must be specific to a Member State is probably the most difficult to comply with. Indeed, since art.114 refers to the internal market and thus mainly to product-related measures, it is difficult to imagine the effects of a product causing environmental problems that are specific to the national territory of a single Member State. Neither would the effect of a product on global warming, on the ozone layer, or on water or fauna and flora be sufficient, since, normally, all these effects affect more than one Member State.

3–58

When the Commission decided to allow Denmark to apply more restrictive measures on the use of the biocide pentachlorophenol (PCP), it declared that PCP easily migrated to groundwater, that Denmark took most of its drinking water from groundwater and that therefore Denmark should be allowed to deviate from the EU harmonisation measure.[147] The decision to allow Germany to deviate from the harmonisation measure was essentially justified by the argument that Germany had built a lot of buildings after 1945 and had extensively used PCP for wood preservation.[148] This may be the case; however, in most Member States, drinking water is taken from groundwater and the use of PCP for wood preservation was widespread in the European Union, although not necessarily as widespread as in Germany. Taking the criterion seriously would mean that in either case the new art.114(5) would not have allowed the introduction of new national legislation in derogation from the EU measure. More generally, a derogation under that provision could not be granted where an environmental problem appeared in several Member States.

The result is not as strange as it might appear at first sight: indeed, under art.114(7) the Commission is obliged to examine whether a new proposal for EU action shall be made; furthermore, where a definite risk to man or the environment becomes apparent, national action under the safeguard clause of art.114(10) remains possible.[149]

In 2005 the Netherlands wanted to introduce legal requirements to reduce the emissions of particulates from diesel cars, in deviation from Directive 98/69. The measure would have required, under the present state of technical knowledge,

3–59

---

[146] At least in some EU languages the word which is used has the connotation of "findings", such as in Dutch (*gegevens*), German (*Erkenntnisse*), Portuguese (*novedades*) and French (*preuves*).

[147] Commission, Dec.94/783 [1994] OJ L316/43.

[148] Commission, Dec.96/211 [1996] OJ L68/32.

[149] See para.3–64, below.

having to equip diesel cars with specific filters which are presently not required under EU legislation. The Commission accepted that the numerous studies which had been published on the problem constituted new scientific evidence. However, it compared the emissions of particulates in the Netherlands with those in other Member States and, furthermore, the number of diesel cars in the Netherlands. On that it concluded that the health problems caused by diesel particulates were not particularly acute in the Netherlands, but existed also in other Member States.[150] This decision is bitter and absurd: overall, the annual number of premature deaths in the European Union due to diesel particulates in the air is estimated to be more than 100,000. Filters for diesel cars have been available on the market for years and are in particular offered by French car manufacturers. However, the Commission hesitates to propose amendments to the existing legislation and prescribing their use because it made arrangements in the 1990s with the car industry, according to a time plan, for air pollution reduction. Then, in the name of law, it even prevents individual Member States from taking measures.

The Commission furthermore rejected a number of attempts by Member States to prevent the cultivation or placing on the market of genetically modified products, arguing that the national environment was not specifically different from the environment in other Member States. It was confirmed in this interpretation by the Court of Justice.[151]

3–60 **New problems.** The condition that the problem must have arisen after the adoption of the harmonisation measure may concern cases in which environmental effects of a specific problem become evident, such as the effect of a biocide, a pesticide or another chemical product which suddenly shows serious environmental problems to have been caused in a specific region. A simple change in the environmental policy in a Member State would not justify the introduction of new legislation. In the same way, this condition would not be fulfilled where an environmental problem—gradually or suddenly—appears before the adoption of the harmonisation measure and the Member State wishes to introduce "opt out" legislation after the adoption of the harmonisation measure.

3–61 **Procedure.** The procedure for measures under art.114(5), including the time delays, verification, approval or rejection of the national measure, is the same as in the case of the maintaining of a national measure. In the case of the introduction of new legislation, however, the standstill period stipulated by the Court of Justice will apply; thus, a Member State may only introduce its legislation after the Commission has approved of it. For the rest, reference is made to para.3–61, above.

In Decision 1999/836,[152] the Commission rejected a German request to introduce new national legislation on the classification and labelling of certain

---

[150] On appeal, the Court of Justice quashed the Commission's decision for formal reasons: the Commission had not examined all the data that had been submitted by the Netherlands, *Netherlands v Commission* (C-405/07P) [2008] E.C.R. I-8301.
[151] Commission Dec.2003/653 (Austria) [2003] OJ L230/34; Dec.2006/255 (Cyprus) [2006] OJ L92/14; Dec.2008/62 (Poland) [2008] OJ L16/17; Dec.2009/828 (Portugal) [2009] OJ L294/16. Court of Justice, *Austria v Commission* (C-439/05P) [2007] E.C.R. I-7141.
[152] Commission Dec.1999/836 [1999] OJ L329/100.

hazardous chemicals. The Commission held that the scientific and technical grounds, on which Germany had based its request, had been discussed during the elaboration of the EU legislation in question, and thus did not constitute new evidence. The Court rejected the German appeal against that decision, arguing that Germany had not submitted "new" scientific evidence.[153] By Decision 2001/570,[154] the Commission rejected another German request to introduce new national legislation on organo-stannic compounds that went beyond Directive 1999/51,[155] arguing again that Germany had not submitted new scientific evidence. The Commission maintained, amongst others, that in the framework of art.114(5) only human health arguments related to the working environment are relevant. This opinion overlooks the fact that art.191 TFEU explicitly states that environmental measures also aim at protecting human health.[156] Furthermore, the concept of the "centre of gravity" to determine the legal basis for a measure would exclude the mentioning of a human health-related Treaty provision next to art.192, where the EU measure covers, for instance, 60 per cent environmental matters and only 40 per cent health protection issues. Refusing Member States in such cases the recourse to art.114(5), as the Commission suggests, cannot therefore be correct.

In Decision 2002/570,[157] the Commission approved for the first time the introduction of new national legislation under art.114(5). This decision concerned a request by the Netherlands aiming at the ban of creosote-treated wood. The Commission considered that detailed studies made in the Netherlands on the effects of creosote constituted new scientific evidence. It stated that the environmental concerns were *not* specific to the Netherlands, but was of the opinion that the extent to which the problem existed in that country—which is rich in groundwater and surface water—allowed the conclusion that the conditions of art.114(5) were complied with.

(d) Rights under other Treaty provisions

Where an EU environmental measure is based on Treaty provisions other than arts 192 or 114, it is doubtful whether Member States also have the possibility of maintaining or introducing stricter national environmental measures. This applies in particular to measures based on arts 43 for agricultural policy measures, 91 or 100 on transport policy measures, 113 on tax measures or 207 TFEU on commercial policy measures.

3–62

German legal writers have developed, since 1987, a concept according to which the EC Treaty contains a legally binding principle according to which environmental protection within the European Union must be optimised. The reasoning is based on several provisions and principles of the Treaty, in particular arts 175, 95(4), 100b(2) EC Treaty which has been deleted in the meantime, and art.6 EC Treaty. The definition varies. Zuleeg, who later acted as judge at the

---

[153] Court of Justice, *Germany v Commission* (C-512/99) [2003] E.C.R. I-845.
[154] Commission Dec.2001/570 [2001] OJ L202/37.
[155] Directive 1999/51 [1999] OJ L142/22.
[156] An example is Dir.98/83 on the quality of water intended for human consumption [1998] OJ L330/32. This Directive is based on the present art.192 TFEU; it clearly aims at the protection of human health.
[157] Commission Dec.2002/59 [2002] OJ L23/37.

European Court of Justice and who "invented" that principle, defined it as "the right of Member States to maintain or introduce more protection of the environment, even where the EU has adopted a measure to protect the environment".[158] Other authors, while following Zuleeg in his approach, go even further; some declare that in the case of conflict between environmental objectives and objectives under other policies priority should, in the case of doubt, be given to the environmental objective. Others even suggest that, for EU environmental measures, the Treaty provision which optimises environmental protection should be used as a legal basis, and this is usually art.192.

For the question with which we are here concerned, these writers suggest that, generally speaking, Member States be granted the rights under art.193, whatever the legal base was on which the EU measure had been based. However, the legal concept is unconvincing. Indeed, it is not clear why the principle of optimising protection should just apply to environmental protection and not to the protection of human health, the respect of human rights and fundamental freedoms or to any of the values which are mentioned in art.36 TFEU. If ever the authors of the EU Treaties had in mind to establish such a principle, they could have inserted it in the Treaties at one of the Treaty amendments in 1993, 1999, 2003 or 2009.

3–63   Furthermore, where an EU environmental measure in the sector of agricultural policy is based on art.43 TFEU, it is not clear whether art.193 is a more protective provision than art.114(4) and (5) and, also, which of these two provisions should apply for a measure adopted under art.43. The concept of optimising environmental protection is incapable of explaining why Member States' residual rights have been organised differently under arts 193 and 114, although there would have been the possibility of finding a single, optimising solution. Also, the concept is more motivated, it seems, by concerns about national powers to legislate than about environmental optimisation, since it cares little for those Member States which do not have an elaborated, consistent, national environmental policy.

As none of the Treaty provisions on which an environmental action can be based contain provisions similar to those of arts 193 and 114, the conclusion must be that these provisions are exceptions to the general rule that EU measures cannot be derogated from by Member States, unless EU law expressly so provides. Their application to measures which had been adopted by virtue of arts 43, 91, 113 or 207 TFEU is therefore not possible, all the more so since it would not be clear whether arts 193 or 114 should apply in a specific case. Article 11 TFEU is of no help either, as the possibilities which Member States have under art.193, are not "requirements"; if one were adopting another position, one would also have to consider art.114 an environmental requirement—which again would raise the question which article should apply in a given case. As discussed in paras 2–70 et seq. above, it will still have to be decided by the Court what the Member States' residual rights are when new EU legislation is adopted on a double legal basis, such as arts 114 and 192 (no such decision exists as yet) or arts 207 and 192.

---

[158] M. Zuleeg, "*Vorbehaltene Kompetenzen der Mitgliedstaaten der Europäischen Gemeinschaft auf dem Gebiet des Umweltschutzes*", *Neue Zeitschrift für Verwaltungsrecht* (1987), p.280 (my translation).

(e) Rights under safeguard clauses

The safeguard clauses of both arts 191(2) and 114(10) TFEU apply where **3–64** secondary EU legislation expressly contains a provision which enables Member States to take safeguard measures. However, both provisions require a specific provision in secondary EU legislation; they do not give rights to Member States directly.

The specificity of safeguard clauses is that they allow Member States to object to the marketing or the circulation of goods even in those cases where these products comply with the requirements which were laid down at EU level. This basic consideration leads to the consequence, expressed in both provisions of arts 191(2) and 114(10), that the national safeguard measures may only be provisional, limited in time and subject to a decision by the Union as to its compatibility with EU law. In practice, safeguard clauses hardly play a role at all.

Safeguard clauses in EU environmental legislation existed long before arts 191(2) and 114(10) were introduced into the Treaty. A considerable number of EU directives or regulations contained safeguard clauses which allowed Member States to deviate, for health or environmental reasons, from EU standards. The conditions for having recourse to a safeguard clause were practically always the same:

- an express provision in the corresponding EU directive or regulation;
- a formal notification by a Member State that it had evidence that a product, while complying with the requirements of the directive/regulation, constituted a hazard for man or the environment and that therefore the circulation of the product was restricted or suspended;
- justifications for the national decision taken.

The Commission then had to proceed to consultation with the other Member **3–65** States and to take, on a regular basis by the committee procedure instituted by virtue of art.202 EC, an EU decision. Such a decision could consist of adapting the EU harmonisation measure to the requests of the notifying Member State, or in informing the Member State that his safeguard measure was not justified and had to be abandoned.[159]

In the highly controversial area of genetically modified organisms, a number of Member States recurred to the safeguard clause and prohibited the marketing and/or cultivation of genetically modified plants, though the Commission had authorised them. The Commission did not take legal action against this obvious misuse of the safeguard clause, but rather tried to find policy solutions.[160]

---

[159] See, e.g. Dec.90/420 [1990] OJ L22/49, informing Denmark that a specific substance which Denmark had declared carcinogenic by way of a safeguard measure, was in reality not carcinogenic.
[160] See for more details paras 6–37 et seq., below.

CHAPTER 4

Horizontal Measures

1. THE RIGHT TO A CLEAN ENVIRONMENT

(a) General remarks

The Treaty on European Union and the Treaty on the Functioning of the 4–01
European Union do not contain a catalogue on fundamental rights. However,
art.6(1) of the Treaty on European Union states:

> "The Union recognises the rights, freedoms and principles set out in the Charter of
> Fundamental Rights of the European Union of 7 December 2000, as adapted at
> Strasbourg on 12 December 2007, which shall have the same legal value as the
> Treaties ...
>   The Union shall accede to the European Convention for the Protection of Human
> rights and Fundamental Freedoms ...
>   Fundamental rights, as guaranteed by the European Convention for the protection
> of Human rights and Fundamental Freedoms and as they result from the
> constitutional traditions common to the Member States, shall constitute general
> principles of the Union's law."

Prior to the adoption of the Lisbon Treaty, all Member States had adhered to
the Convention for the Protection of Human Rights and Fundamental Freedoms;
however, the European Union as such had not adhered to the Convention, in
particular for institutional reasons.[1]

Article 6 TEU provides that the EU should adhere to the European Convention
on Human Rights and Fundamental Freedoms. A draft Agreement was negotiated
until 2014. However, when the Court of Justice was asked for its opinion on that
Agreement, it raised a number of objections, arguing in particular that its function
as the only arbiter on the interpretation of EU law would be impaired by
decisions of the European Court on Human Rights.[2] These arguments appear
largely unjustified, as the Court of Justice never accepted this kind of argument
from national supreme or constitutional courts. However, as the Court's Opinion
is binding on the other institutions (art.218(11) TFEU), it has the effect of a veto
and will have to be taken into consideration in future negotiations.

---

[1] See Court of Justice, Opinion 2/94 on the accession of the EC to the European Convention on
Human Rights [1996] E.C.R. I-1759.
[2] Court of Justice, Opinion 2/13 of 18 December 2014 on the accession of the EU to the European
Convention on Human Rights and Fundamental Freedoms, ECLI:EU:C:2014:2454.

4–02   At the end of 2000, the European Parliament, Council and Commission proclaimed a Charter of Fundamental Rights of the European Union[3]. The Charter applies to the EU institutions and bodies; it applies to Member States "only when they are implementing Union law" (art.51(1) of the Charter), which means their legislative activity and judicial and administrative practices when fulfilling obligations under EU law. The Charter is not meant to create legal rights of citizens, but by "making these rights more visible".[4] Its application within the Union is nuanced by a Protocol and some declarations annexed to the Treaties.[5]

The discussion on a fundamental right to a clean environment at EU level had some antecedents. In 1989, the European Parliament adopted a resolution on fundamental rights and fundamental freedoms which formulated that the preservation, protection and improvement of the quality of the environment was an integrative part of all Community policy.[6] In 1990, the Commission, in a contribution to the discussions on the Maastricht Treaty on European Union, suggested the insertion of such a right into the Treaty,[7] but remained unsuccessful. In 1997, the European Parliament adopted another resolution on the respect of human rights within the European Union where it submitted for discussion a catalogue of about 150 provisions concerning fundamental rights.[8] As regards the environment, the Parliament abstained from formulating a provision that gave rights to individuals, and limited itself to confirm that the right to live included a responsibility for present and future generations, that public authorities should guarantee a healthy environment for everybody and grant the possibility to influence decisions on his/her environment. National legal provisions should be harmonised and sanctions for impairment of the environment should be strengthened, according to the polluter-pays principle. Finally, Parliament asked that the export of all materials, food, drugs, etc which were forbidden to be marketed in the European Union, should be prohibited.[9] This Resolution did not lead to any concrete consequences.

The Charter that was adopted at the end of 2000 did not create a right to a healthy environment. It limits itself to formulate, in art.37:

> "A high level of environmental protection and the improvement of the quality of the environment must be integrated into the policies of the Union and ensured in accordance with the principle of sustainable development."

---

[3] Charter of Fundamental Rights of the European Union [2010] OJ C83/389.

[4] Charter of Fundamental Rights of the European Union [2010] OJ C83/389, Preamble.

[5] Protocol 30 on the application of the Charter of Fundamental Rights of the European Union to Poland and the United Kingdom [2008] OJ C115/313; Declarations no.2 [2008] OJ C115/337; no.53 [2008] OJ C115/355; no.61 [2008] OJ C115/358; no.62 [2008] OJ 115/358.

[6] European Parliament, Resolution of 12 April 1989 [1989] OJ C120/51, art.24.

[7] Commission, Contributions to the Intergovernmental Conference COM(90) 600 of 21 October 1990, art.7: "Every Union citizen shall have the right to enjoy a healthy environment and the obligation to contribute to protecting it. To this end, he shall have the right to information and the right to consultation where appropriate."

[8] European Parliament, Resolution of 8 April 1997 [1997] OJ C132/31.

[9] European Parliament, Resolution of 8 April 1997 [1997] OJ C132/31, nn.161–164.

This provision is rather misleading, as it is not clear in what sense such a **4–03** formula which largely corresponds to art.11 TFEU, creates "rights". The European Parliament, though, was satisfied with the Charter.[10]

In landmark decisions of 1991, the Court declared that air quality standards were adopted in the interest of protecting human health.[11] Therefore, a citizen must be entitled to ensure in court that the air-quality standards are actually complied with. This interpretation comes close to giving individuals which are affected by polluted air or water, a right to clean air or to clean water. Unfortunately, though, environmental organisations and individual citizens hardly ever tested the potential and the limits of this jurisprudence in other cases, such as, for example, in waste cases. Thus, the judgments of 1991 are practically being ignored by the administration. A citizen initiative, based on art.11 TEU[12] which asked the Commission to formulate a right to water, was rejected by the Commission in 2014.[13]

The academic discussion on a fundamental right for a clean and healthy environment which had started in the 1970s, had soon made it clear that a meaningful enforceable right to a clean environment could not be introduced into the constitutions of Member States or into primary EU law and where some constitutions had tried nevertheless, the contours of such a right remained unclear. The discussions therefore concentrated on formulating *procedural* rights to a clean environment which consisted of three parts, a right of access to information on the environment, the right of participating in decision-making on the environment and the right of access to the courts in environmental matters. Though the idea of a human right to a clean environment—be it procedural—was not popular with the European Commission, some elements of such procedural rights were taken up in the context of the European Union which also transposed the requirements of the Aarhus Convention on access to information, participation in decision-making and access to justice in environmental matters. The Aarhus Convention[14] was signed and ratified by all 28 EU Member States.

---

[10] European Parliament Resolution of 14 November 2000 [2001] OJ C223/74.

[11] Court of Justice, *Commission v Germany* (C-361/88) [1991] E.C.R. I-2567 at [16]: "the obligation imposed on the Member States to prescribe limit values not to be exceeded within specified periods and in specific circumstances ... is imposed 'in order to protect human health in particular'. It implies, therefore, that whenever the exceeding of the limit values could endanger human health, the persons concerned must be in a position to rely on mandatory rules in order to be able to assert their rights". See also *Commission v Germany* (C-59/89) [1991] E.C.R. I-2607. In 2008, the Court confirmed this jurisdiction, *Janecek* (C-237/07) [2008] E.C.R. I-6221.

[12] See art.11 TEU and Reg.211/2011 on the citizens' initiative [2011] OJ L65/1. An initiative must assemble 1 million signatures, from at least seven Member States. The administrative burden for such initiatives is too high.

[13] Commission, COM(2014) 177. The citizen initiative had the title: "Water and sanitation are a human right. Water is a public good, not a commodity!"

[14] Aarhus Convention of 25 June 1998. The European Union adhered to the Aarhus Convention by Dec.2005/370 [2005] OJ L124/1. The text of the Convention is reproduced in the annex to that Decision.

(b)   Access to environmental information

(i)   National level

4–04   In 1990, the European Union adopted a Directive on the "free access" to information on the environment.[15] Following the adoption of the Aarhus Convention in 1998, which the EU had signed, this Directive was substituted by a new Directive which gave "public access".[16] This Directive "guarantees the right of access to environmental information" (art.1) to any natural or legal person which is held by public authorities or by any person performing public administrative functions. The applicant does not have to prove an interest in the information or state the reason why he wishes to obtain the information. The notion of "environmental information" is very broad; it even includes "the state of human health and safety, including the contamination of the food chain" which brings a good part of food legislation into the field of application of the directive. Nuclear elements are not expressly mentioned, with the exception of radioactive waste; however, as "energy" is enumerated, information on nuclear energy, including permits, programmes, releases, etc is covered by the Directive.

The right of access to information is given against public authorities and all bodies that perform public functions; this includes transport or agricultural authorities, public research institutes, agencies, etc. The authorities need only supply information which is "available", but are not obliged to start collecting information themselves; with regard to the earlier Directive 90/313, though, the obligation for active information to be disseminated by authorities has considerably been increased (art.7). The authorities may charge reasonable costs for the supply of the information—but not for the refusal of it[17]; not all authorities resisted, in the past, the temptation to charge prices at a level that was a deterrent to applicants.

Access to information may be refused in certain, explicitly enumerated circumstances (art.4); with regard to the earlier Directive, this catalogue has been enlarged and fine-tuned. Some of these exceptions are self-evident, such as documents which had been declared confidential by law, further information relating to international relations, public security or national defence. Others might be more difficult to be interpreted with precision; to these belong in particular the possibility to refuse access to "unfinished documents or data", "internal communications" or "the course of justice".

4–05   Reasons for refusing access to information must be given in all cases. Where information can be given in part, this must be done. Where the request for access to information was refused, there must be a possibility to address the courts (art.6).[18]

As Directives 90/313 and 2003/4 placed access to information in the context of a human right, the right was not just given to citizens of the European Union,

---

[15] Directive 90/313 on the freedom of access to information on the environment [1990] OJ L156/58; see also Commission, Report on the experience gained in the application of Directive 90/313, COM(2000) 400 of 29 June 2000.

[16] Directive 2003/4 on public access to environmental information and repealing Dir.90/313 [2003] OJ L41/26.

[17] Court of Justice, *Commission v Germany* (C-217/97) [1999] E.C.R. I-5087.

[18] See also paras 4–16 et seq., below.

but to everybody, including associations. The omission to require proof of a specific interest constituted for many local, regional or national administrations a change from traditional concepts in their relationships with citizens. Many authorities will need more time before they will fully accept this concept; particular problems of this kind appeared in the 13 new Member States which adhered to the European Union since 2004, though Directive 2003/4 is fully applicable also in these countries since their accession.

As with any fundamental right, the problem with the rights flowing out of the Directive lie in their day-to-day application. Indeed, there are numerous attempts not to grant access to information in individual cases. The most frequent issues concern simple omission to give an answer to an application, or wide interpretations of the exceptions, such as the concept of "commercial and industrial confidentiality", the ability to conduct an enquiry of a criminal or disciplinary procedure or the argument that the decision-making process is not finished; the threat of terrorism is beginning to be used as a reason to refuse access to data on industrial emissions and similar information. Citizens rarely go to courts in order to enforce their rights; the Commission does not examine individual cases which are brought to its knowledge; it rather refers complainants to the national judiciary.

(ii)   European level

Directive 2003/4 is addressed to Member States and therefore does not apply to EU institutions. When making the proposal for a Directive in 1988, the Commission announced that it would take initiatives to apply the Directive's principles to the EU institutions.[19] Based on a joint Code of Conduct,[20] the Council and the Commission[21] had adopted, in 1993/1994, decisions concerning the access of the public to documents; almost all the other Community bodies and agencies had subsequently adopted similar decisions. In 1997, the Amsterdam Treaty included a new art.255 on access to EU documents into the EC Treaty (now art.15(3) TFEU) which became effective in 1999.[22]

4–06

Subsequent to that, the EU institutions adopted Regulation 1049/2001 on access to documents which became effective at the end of 2001.[23] The Regulation referred to the "right of access" established by the present art.15(3) TFEU and endeavoured to "ensure the widest possible access to documents" (art.1). The Regulation was built along the content of Directive 90/313, though provided for more exceptions. In 2006, the Union adopted Regulation 1367/2006 which

---

[19] Commission, COM(88) 484.

[20] Code of Conduct concerning public access to Council and Commission documents [1993] OJ L340/1.

[21] Decision 93/731 on public access to Council documents [1993] OJ L340/43; Commission, Dec.94/90 on public access to Commission documents [1994] OJ L46/58.

[22] Article 15(3) TFEU: "1. Any citizen of the Union, and any natural or legal person residing or having its registered office in a Member State, shall have a right of access to documents of the Union institutions, bodies, offices and agencies, whatever their medium, subject to the principles and the conditions to be defined ..."

[23] Regulation 1049/2001 regarding public access to European Parliament, Council and Commission documents [2001] OJ L145/43.

adapted EU law to the requirements of the Aarhus Convention.[24] It was marked by the Council's efforts to amend the original Regulation 1049/2001 as little as possible. As it applies to a supranational organisation, it is normal that Regulations 1049/2001 and 1367/2006 have a number of specificities, of which the most relevant are the following:

1.   Regulation 1049/2001 gives a right of access to documents to citizens of the European Union and to residents. Thus, a professor in Switzerland would not have a right of access to documents. Regulation 1367/2006 extends this right, in environmental matters, to everybody, in line with Directive 2003/4 which also gives a right of access to information to everybody.[25] In practice, though, the EU institutions give access to documents to any applicant.

2.   The possibilities to refuse access to internal documents, suggested by the Commission,[26] was not retained by Regulation 1049/2001. In contrast, Directive 2003/4 allows Member States to refuse access to "material in the course of completion or unfinished documents or data" (art.4(1.d)).[27]

3.   Except for the basic grounds for refusal—public security, defence and military matters, international relations, financial, monetary or economic policy and privacy—all other grounds for refusal must be balanced against the public interest in disclosure. This requires a case-by-case weighing of the different interests at stake. Regulation 1367/2006 provides in art.6(1) that "an overriding public interest in disclosure shall be deemed to exist where the information requested relates to emissions into the environment". In other cases, the fact that the information relates to emissions into the environment "shall be taken into particular account" when the environmental interests are weighed against other interests.

4.   The Commission's proposal not to give access to letters of formal notice and to reasoned opinions under art.258 TFEU was not accepted by the Council and the European Parliament, when they adopted Regulation 1049/2001; the Commission now applies the exception "inspections, investigations and audits" to refuse such access; this practice is not compatible with the Aarhus Convention, as will be explained below.[28]

5.   The right of access to information on the environment exists, following the amendment in art.3(2) of Regulation 1367/2006, with regard to all documents that are held by any "Community institution or body"; this includes access to those documents, of which the Member States or other

---

[24] Regulation 1367/2006 on the application of the provisions of the Aarhus Convention on access to information, public participation in decision-making and access to justice in environmental matters to Community institutions and bodies [2006] OJ L264/13.

[25] Directive 2003/4 [2003] OJ L41/26, Recital 8: "It is necessary to ensure that any natural and legal person has a right of access to environmental information held by or for public authorities without his having to state an interest."

[26] Commission proposal for a regulation on access to documents [2000] OJ C177E/70.

[27] Directive 2003/4 [2003] OJ L41/26 requests Member States to indicate, when material is in the course of completion, the estimated time needed for completion.

[28] See also L. Krämer, "Access to Letters of Formal Notice and Reasoned Opinions in Environmental Law Matters" [2003] *European Environmental Law Review* 197 as regards the procedure under art.258 TFEU. The Court of Justice apparently sides with the Commission, see *LPN and Finland v Commission* (joined cases C-514/11P and C-605/11P) ECLI:EU:C:2013:738.

persons are authors. The author of the document has to be consulted on a possible disclosure, though the EU institution has the final decision (Reg.1049/2001, art.4(4)).[29] Directive 2003/4 does not contain similar provisions.

6.   Where access to documents is refused, the applicant must first ask for a confirmatory administrative decision (Reg.1049/2001, art.8). Against that decision the applicant may address the General Court under art.263 TFEU.

Administrative practice shows that compliance with the letter and spirit of the Aarhus Convention and the Regulation is a process which will only progressively be realised. This became obvious, for example, when the Commission refused, in 2013/2014, to disclose information on the negotiations with the United States on a Transatlantic Trade and Investment Partnership, invoking the exception that disclosure would undermine the ongoing international negotiations. Only the strong protests from the public in almost all Member States and the European Parliament made the Commission slightly—though not decisively—soften its position.

Other practices are: 4–07

- The Commission interprets the exception that access to documents for "the purpose of inspections, investigations and audits" may be refused, extremely largely. It does not limit this exception to cases of criminal or disciplinary nature, as required by the Aarhus Convention. Also, other exceptions are interpreted broadly; this has as a consequence that a considerable number of applications are being rejected, mainly because the decision-making process is not yet finished, there is a commercial interest invoked, or the correspondence—in particular internal emails—is considered not to be "information on the environment"; in a proposal for a review of Regulation 1049/2001, the Commission suggested that access to all documents be refused which relate to "dispute settlement" procedures.[30] This would even further enlarge the number of documents which are not released.
- The Commission also refuses access to documents concerning comments which it makes towards Member States in reaction of the notification of draft national legislation under Directive 98/34,[31] though there is no inspection or investigation visible.
- Regulation 1367/2006 did not take up an amendment which the European Parliament had suggested and which consisted in giving access to information on "sustainable development" issues. The Council explained

---

[29] The Commission interpreted art.4(5)—"A Member State may request the institution not to disclose a document originating from that Member State without its prior agreement"—as giving a right of veto to a Member State, and was supported in this by the Court of First Instance, but not by the Court of Justice, see *Sweden v Commission* (C-64/05) [2007] E.C.R. I-11389. For access to information on the environment, Reg.1367/2006, art.6(3) now clarifies that the Commission has the final decision and that there is no veto right.

[30] See Commission, COM(2008) 229, art.4(2.c); the Commission also proposed to considerably restrict the notion of "document". No attempt to align Reg.1049/2001 to the requirements of the Aarhus Convention was made.

[31] Directive 98/34 laying down a procedure for the provision of information in the field of technical standards and regulations [1998] OJ L204/37.

that "sustainable development is outside the [Aarhus] Convention and not in line with Article 174 of the EC Treaty with regard to the objectives of environmental policy".[32] At least this remark is revealing: sustainable development is not an element of environmental policy! This is in line with the efforts to promote, at EU level, the objectives on economic growth and social cohesion. But it is neither historically correct nor compatible with arts 3(3) TEU[33] and 11 TFEU which are both based on the assumption that the environment is an integrated part of sustainable development and that sustainable development cannot be reached without appropriate environmental protection.

Article 2(6) of Regulation 1049/2001 clarifies that the provisions of the Aarhus Convention on access to information which are part of EU law, prevail over the provisions of Regulation 1049/2001.[34] This is in line with settled case-law by the Court of Justice.[35] The provisions on the exceptions to the right of information provided by the Aarhus Convention are considerably narrower than the exceptions provided for under Regulation 1049/2001: under the Aarhus Convention, authorities *may* refuse access, when one of the exceptions applies; under Regulation 1049/2001, they *must* refuse access in such a case, at least where general interests are at stake. The Aarhus Convention does not provide for an exception to protect the "financial, monetary or economic policy of the Union and of Member States" which Regulation 1049/2001 foresees.[36] The Aarhus Convention does not contain an exception of "legal advice" which is foreseen in Regulation 1049/2001. The Aarhus Convention allows non-disclosure of information in order to protect "the ability to conduct an enquiry of a criminal or disciplinary nature", whereas Regulation 1049/2001 allows this exception in order to protect "the purpose of inspections, investigations and audits".[37] The Aarhus Convention allows protection of "a legitimate economic interest where protected by national law"; Regulation 1049/2001 generally refers to the protection of "commercial interests". And the Aarhus Convention allows

---

[32] Council, Common Position 31/2005 [2005] OJ C264E/18 (p.25, no.III.2).

[33] Article 3(3) TEU: "The Union shall establish an internal market. It shall work for the sustainable development of Europe based on balanced economic growth and price stability, a highly competitive social market economy, aiming at full employment and social progress, and a high level of protection and improvement of the quality of the environment. It shall promote scientific and technological advance."

[34] Regulation 1049/2001 [2001] OJ L145/43, art.2(6): "This Regulation shall be without prejudice to rights of public access to documents held by the institutions which might follow from instruments of international law or acts of the institutions pursuant implementing them."

[35] Court of Justice, *IATA and ELFAA* (C-344/08) [2006] E.C.R. I-403 at [35]: "Article 300(7) EC [now Article 216(2) TFEU] provides that 'agreements concluded under the conditions set out in this Article shall be binding on the institutions of the Community and on Member States'. In accordance with the Court's case law, those agreements prevail over provisions of secondary Community legislation."

[36] In *IFAW v Commission* (T-362/2008) [2011] E.C.R. II-11, the General Court upheld a Commission to refuse disclosure of a document on the destruction of a natural habitat by an airport on grounds that the document served to protect Germany's economic policy. As this exception does not exist under the Aarhus Convention, the Court erred in referring to Reg.1049/2001.

[37] The Commission also applies this exception to environmental letters of formal notice and reasoned opinions under art.258 TFEU, though that procedure is neither an investigation nor an enquiry of criminal or disciplinary nature.

protection of "personal data relating to a natural person"; Regulation 1049/2001 provides for the protection of the "privacy and the integrity of the individual, in particular in accordance with Community legislation regarding the protection of personal data".

When it comes to the interpretation of the Aarhus Convention, the Court of Justice rather sides with the EU institutions and makes efforts to minimise the application of the Aarhus Convention.[38]

The amendments brought to Regulation 1049/2001 by Regulation 1367/2006 **4–08** and the Aarhus Convention did not significantly change the restricted practice of the EU institutions. The practice by the Commission, the numerous agencies, but also, for example of the European Investment Bank, continue to be marked by the effort to disclose as little information as possible. This is also evidenced by the active dissemination of environmental information which is a substantive requirement of the Aarhus Convention (art.4), but not seriously treated by the EU institutions, though arts 11–13 of Reg.1049/2001 and art.4 of Reg.1367/2006 deal with it. The general problem at EU level is that there is no European public opinion and not sufficient private groups or individuals who would try to progressively press the EU institutions and bodies to put into daily practice what the Aarhus Convention (Recital 17) describes as follows: "public authorities hold environmental information in the public interest", not in their own interest.[39]

(c)   Participation in environmental decision-making

(i)   National level

EU involvement concerning participation in decision-making in environmental **4–09** matters first dealt with participation in environment impact assessment for specific projects which come under Directive 85/337.[40] In 2011, the Directive was consolidated,[41] and in 2014 amended again.[42] Article 6 of this Directive provided that where an impact assessment is made, the public must be informed; and the "public concerned" must have the possibility of expressing its opinion on the envisaged project and its environmental impacts. The Directive lays down, in detail, how this participation can be made operational.[43] In 2003, the Directive

---

[38] See *LPN and Finland v Commission* (joined cases C-514/11P and 605/11P) ECLI:EU:C:2013:738; *Council a.o. v Milieudefensie a.o.* (joined cases C-401/12P to C-403/12P, ECLI:EU:C:2015:4; *Council and Commission v Stichting Natuur en Milieu a.o.* (joined cases C-404/12P and C-405/12P) ECLI:EU:C:2015:5.

[39] See also European Parliament, Resolution of 11 March 2014 on public access to documents, A7-0148/2014-2013/2135/INI, which severely criticises the present practice by the Commission and the Council.

[40] Directive 85/337 on the assessment of the effects of certain public and private projects on the environment [1985] OJ L175/40, as amended by Dir.97/11 [1997] OJ L73/5 and by Dir.2003/35 [2003] OJ L156/17.

[41] Directive 2011/92 [2012] OJ L26/1.

[42] Directive 2014/52 [2014] OJ L124/1.

[43] Directive 2011/92 [2012] OJ L26/1, art.5(2): The operator must submit a non-technical summary of his examination of the impact and must report on the alternatives which he studied; a consultation of the nature protection administration is mandatory, whose opinion must be publicly available (Court of Justice, *Mecklenburg* (C-321/96) [1998] E.C.R. 3809).

was amended further in order to adapt its provisions on participation in decision-making to the requirements of the Aarhus Convention.[44]

As regards permitting of industrial installations, Directive 2010/75 provides that with regard to applications for permits for industrial installations, the decision on such an application and the results of the surveillance of emissions from industrial installations shall be available to the public.[45] According to those provisions, the public shall have the opportunity of commenting on applications for a permit. The public is, furthermore, to be informed of the results of surveillance of the installations.

As regards *plans and programmes*, Directive 2001/42 which became effective in 2004 requires an environment impact assessment for plans and programmes that are likely to have significant environmental effects.[46] The Directive covers such plans which lead, at a later stage, to projects that have to undergo an environmental impact assessment under annexes I or II of Directive 2011/92 or under arts 6 and 7 of Directive 92/43.[47] The impact assessment under the Directive mainly consists in the elaboration of a written assessment and of extensive public consultation of such plans; it allows the public concerned the opportunity to give its opinion on the plan in question.

4–10   Directive 2003/35[48] provides for participation of the public in the elaboration and updating of a number of expressly enumerated plans and programmes, in particular in the waste area.[49] And in water management, Member States have to promote the participation of the public in the elaboration, monitoring and updating of water management plans.[50]

However, it is clear that these different specific measures do not give a general right to individuals to participate in environmental decision-making. First, Directives 2011/92, 2010/75, 2000/60 and the different waste Directives which are mentioned in Directive 2003/35 do not cover all decision-making in environmental matters. Rather, these Directives concern some (larger) industrial installations and projects. Most of medium-sized and small projects and installations are not covered by EU legislation but come, as regards environment impact assessment and permits, under the responsibility of Member States.

Secondly, environmental decision-making not only deals with the permitting of projects and installations and the authorisation of plans and programmes. There are many other decisions which affect the environment, such as decisions on the authorisation of products and processes, management decisions,

---

[44] Directive 2003/35 providing for public participation in respect of the drawing up of certain plans and programmes relating to the environment and amending with regard to public participation and access to justice Council Dirs 85/337 and 96/61 [2003] OJ L156/17.

[45] Directive 2010/75 on industrial emissions [2010] OJ L334/17.

[46] Directive 2001/42 on the environment assessment of the effects of certain plans and programmes on the environment [2001] OJ L197/30.

[47] Directive 92/43 on the conservation of natural habitats and of wild fauna and flora [1992] OJ L206/7.

[48] Directive 2003/35 [2003] OJ L156/17.

[49] Annex I of Dir.2003/35 [2003] OJ L156/17 enumerates the following plans and programmes which are covered by its provisions: waste management plans, plans for the recycling of batteries, plans for reducing nitrate inputs into waters, plans for hazardous waste management, plans for packaging waste and plans for the improvement of air quality.

[50] Directive 2000/60 establishing a framework for Community action in the field of water policy [2000] OJ L327/1.

monitoring methods and processes, derogations, omissions to decide, etc. These very diverse and different means of the administration which affect the environment have not been the subject of the Aarhus Convention which is thus far from granting a general right of participation. In the same way, EU law does not provide for a *general* right of participation, but limits it to *certain* projects, plans and programmes. Also, EU law very generally speaks of the "public concerned" which will be entitled to participate in the decision-making, but leaves the determination of the public concerned in any specific case to the Member States. As it is, for instance, obvious that the "public concerned" is different for the construction of a 1,000km motorway and a waste incinerator, there is a necessity to determine beforehand what a "public concerned" is. Furthermore, the question how much time should be given for the participation process is not clear, and only exceptionally has EU law laid down obligations for the administration to give an account what it has done with the opinions that were expressed during the participation process.[51]

Furthermore, the different directives do not specify how the opinion of the participating public is to be assembled (hearing, written submission, attributed time for oral representation) and how the administration shall manage the collected information: the best would probably be to require a written paper accompanying the final administrative decision which lists the results of the participation process and explains the reason of the administration for following or not following the opinion. Administrative practice in Member States at present shows little result of improved citizens' participation. An Irish provision which charges citizens to pay a fee for participating in the decision-making on projects, plans and programmes, was declared compatible with EU law by the Court of Justice[52]; in my opinion, this contradicts the character of the participation right as a fundamental right.   **4–11**

(ii) European level

In 2002, the Commission published two communications on public consultation[53] which were not limited to environmental issues. According to these communications, the consultation of interested groups should allow at least eight weeks for reception of responses to written public consultation and 20 working days' notice for meetings. However, the consultation principles referred to by these communications constitute internal instructions for Commission officials, but do not create any rights to participate for the "public concerned". The Commission expressly stated that it was opposed to giving citizens the right to participate, as this would interfere with formal consultations which were taking place after the adoption of a proposal by the Commission; this remark alludes to the participation of the European Parliament, the Economic and Social Committee and the Committee of the Regions in the legislative process. In contrast, there is no doubt that the Aarhus Convention requires contracting parties to give *rights* to   **4–12**

---

[51] See now Dir.2010/75 [2010] OJ L334/17, art.24(2) concerning the information which has to be made available once a decision on a permit has been taken; see also at paras 4–40 et seq., below.

[52] Court of Justice, *Commission v Ireland* (C-216/05) [2006] E.C.R. I-10787.

[53] Commission, Towards a reinforced culture of consultation and dialogue—proposal for general principles and minimum standards for consultation of interested parties by the Commission, COM(2002) 277 and COM(2002) 704.

citizens, not to create obligations for the administration only, though the Aarhus Convention is limited to projects, plans and programmes.[54]

Regulation 1367/2006, intended to make the principles of the Aarhus Convention applicable at the EU level, was adopted in 2006[55]; it endeavours to give a right to participate in EC environmental decision-making. The Regulation defines plans and programmes relating to the environment as:

> "plans and programmes
> which are subject to preparation and, as appropriate, adoption by a Community institution or body;
> which are required under legislative, regulatory or administrative provisions; and
> which contribute to, or a likely to have significant effect on, the achievement of the objectives of Community environmental policy, such as laid down in the Sixth Environment Action Programme, or in any subsequent general environment action programme."[56]

However, it also states in the same provision:

> "This definition shall not include financial, banking or budget plans and programmes, namely those laying down how particular projects or activities should be financed or those related to the proposed annual budget ... or emergency plans and programmes designed for the sole purpose of environmental protection."

4–13   This provision clearly contradicts the provisions of the Aarhus Convention. This Convention does not exempt any plans and programmes. There might be some wisdom in not including budget plans as such plans do not "relate to the environment" (Aarhus Convention art.7). However, the exemption of financial or banking plans and programmes which lay down how particular projects or activities should be financed, cannot be based on the Aarhus Convention, where such plans relate to the environment. The provision mainly aims at exempting activities from the European Investment Bank for which the FEU Treaty provides that EU provisions on access to documents—not on participation rights!—shall only apply where the Bank is performing administrative tasks.[57] For an exemption of participation provisions, no reason can be found. The same applies to the emergency plans of civil protection, though there has to be a line struck: it might be understandable to exempt emergency measures in the case of an actual disaster such as an industrial accident or a flood catastrophe, where no time may be wasted to save humans or property; in such cases, participation normally would take too much time. Another question is, for example, the restoration plan or programme after a forest fire or a flooding: here, the same urgency does not exist and an exemption from participation cannot be justified.

EU plans and programmes are only those that are *required* under legislative, regulatory or administrative provisions. This wording is ambiguous. Indeed, the 7th Environment Action Programme constitutes a "plan and programme", but

---

[54] Aarhus Convention art.1: "In order to contribute to the protection of the right of every person of present and future generations to live in an environment adequate to his or her health and well-being, each Party shall guarantee the rights of access to information, public participation in decision-making and access to justice in environmental matters in accordance with the provisions of this Convention."

[55] Regulation 1367/2006 [2006] OJ L264/13.

[56] Regulation 1367/2006 [2006] OJ L264/13, art.2(e).

[57] Article 15(3) TFEU.

art.192(2) TFEU does not *require* the elaboration of EU environmental action programmes. Also, when the Commission decides to launch a programme to promote alternative energies, to promote human health in environmental matters or to co-finance model projects in coastal zone management, this is an initiative of the Commission itself, and there is no requirement laid down anywhere to elaborate such plan or programme.[58] In such cases the Commission does normally not ensure that the public participates in the elaboration of the plan or programme. Generally, the Commission proceeds to consultations, not to a participation.

It is difficult to see, though, what Regulation 1367/2006 means by "participation": it limits itself to state that the public shall have early and effective opportunity to participate during the preparation of the plans or programmes. It does not contain any indication of what the EU institution or body is to do with the information received from the public[59] and no general principles are laid down in the Regulation in this regard. In this way, Regulation 1367/2006 in practice declares "participation" synonymous to "consultation"—which it is not. The Aarhus Convention provides in this regard that the public shall be allowed to submit in writing or, as appropriate at a public hearing, its comments or opinions; that in the administrative decision due account is taken of the outcome of the participation and that, after the decision has been taken, the text of the decision shall be made available to the public along with the reasons and considerations on which the decision is based (art.6(7)–(9) Aarhus Convention). Participation is thus a bilateral concept, whereas consultation is unilateral: it leaves the administration free to decide what it wants to do with the information received through consultation, and no explanation is to be given to the consulted persons or bodies.

The transposition of the Aarhus Convention is thus only partial. This conclusion is all the more obvious, as the consultations at EU level take place in one language (English) only—which is not an *effective* way of making citizens participate.[60] It is also true, though, that environmental organisations and citizens are not really claiming that their participation rights at EU level be made effective. 4–14

In the past, neither products nor production processes were authorised at EU level; rather, EU law normally determines which substances—heavy metals, chemicals, additives etc—may be used in which quantities in products. The permits then are issued by Member States. From this general statement,

---

[58] In *Inter-Environnement Bruxelles* (C-567/10) ECLI:EU:C:2012:159, the Court of Justice held that a plan is also "required", when the legislation provides details for its elaboration and content.

[59] Council, Common Position 31/2005 [2005] OJ C264E/18: "it should be left to institutions and bodies to determine how they want to take account of public participation results, on the basis of general principles laid out in the regulation".

[60] See also European Parliament, Resolution of 14 December 2012 (2012/2676//RSP), P7_TA(2012)256: "(The European Parliament) urges the Commission to ensure that every EU citizen's right to address the EU institutions in any of the EU official languages is fully respected and implemented by ensuring that public consultations are available in all EU official languages, that all consultations are treated equally and that there is no language-based discrimination between consultations." European Ombudsman, Decision of 4 October 2012 (640/2011/A): "public consultation should, as a matter of principle, be published in all official languages. Its failure to do so is an instance of maladministration").

dangerous chemical substances,[61] active substances for pesticides[62] and biocides[63] and genetically modified products[64] constitute an exception, as it is now the Commission which grants authorisations in these areas; its decision is valid for all Member States. Originally, the Aarhus Convention was concerned only with projects, plans and programmes; however, in view of the political sensitive nature of permits for genetically modified organisms (GMOs), a clause was inserted in the Convention that Contracting Parties should take care of participation in such GMO permitting procedures (art.6(11)). In 2005, the Convention was modified in order to also provide for participation in GMO permitting procedures.[65] The Council was of the opinion that this amendment did not require any changes of existing EU legislation and ratified the Convention's amendment.[66] This appears legally wrong, because at least Regulation 1829/2003 on genetically modified food and feed[67] does not provide for any participation of citizens; under this Regulation, an application for the release of GMO food or feed goes to the European Food Safety Authority (EFSA) which examines the application and is obliged to make the application available to the public. Then, members of the public may send observations—provided, they know of the application: however, this has nothing to do with participation of the decision of the Commission on the application: EFSA's proposal for a decision is submitted to the Commission which must decide on it within a specific time-span. The public may comment on EFSA's opinion within 30 days,[68] but no public participation is foreseen.

Under general interpretation rules, it is not possible either that EFSA simply amends its practice and now follows the principles of Regulation 1367/2006. Indeed, according to the Court of Justice—which referred, of course, to situations in Member States—such a change would have to be laid down expressly in a legislative text, in order to give legal security to the citizens. And at least from the appearance, there is a contradiction between Regulation 1829/2003 and Regulation 1367/2006.

4–15   Nothing different applies in general cases of the deliberate release of GMOs. Article 9 of Directive 2001/18[69] provides for a consultation of the public. And art.24 introduces the obligation to inform the public of applications and to allow it to comment to the Commission. Nothing is said about any participation rights of the public and on the subsequent treatment of the comments of the public.

---

[61] Regulation 1907/2006 [2006] OJ L396/1.

[62] Regulation 1107/2009 [2009] OJ L 309/1.

[63] Regulation 528/2012 [2012] OJ L 167/1.

[64] Directive 2001/18 on the deliberate release of genetically modified organisms into the environment [2001] OJ L106/1; Reg.1829/2003 on genetically modified food and feed [2003] OJ L268/1.

[65] Aarhus Convention (fn.14, above), art.6bis: "1. In accordance with the modalities laid down in Annex I bis, each Party shall provide for early and effective information and public participation prior to making decisions on whether to permit the deliberate release into the environment and placing on the market of genetically modified organisms ..."

[66] Decision 2006/957 [2006] OJ L386/46.

[67] See Reg.1829/2003 [2003] OJ L268/1.

[68] It should be mentioned that EFSA's opinions in GMO matters are normally given more than five years after the initial application; 30 days are thus disproportionately short.

[69] Directive 2001/18 [2001] OJ L106/1.

(d)   Access to Justice

(i)   National level

There are almost no EU provisions on access to national courts or to EU courts in   **4–16**
environmental matters. The Commission's announcements in the 5th Environment Action Programme and the 1992 working programme[70] to submit a proposal
for a Directive on access to justice was followed by a proposal for such a
directive only in 2003.[71] However, this proposal was withdrawn in 2014.

There is a Directive on access to justice for consumer organisations in
consumer matters[72] which is limited to trans-national aspects and appears to have
limited effects.

EU provisions on access to justice to national courts in environmental matters
exist in the following cases:

1.   Where the right of access to environmental information under Directive
     2003/4[73] was not respected (art.6 of Directive 2003/4). Instead of giving
     access to a court and in conformity with the Aarhus Convention, Member
     States may provide access to an "independent and impartial body
     established by law", whose decisions may become final and which are
     binding on public authorities. These provisions aim at allowing decisions to
     be taken by bodies such as an ombudsman, though it is doubtful whether
     the different environmental ombudsmen which exist in the different
     Member States, really fulfil all the conditions laid down in the Directive.
2.   Where the right of participation in decision-making concerning an
     environment impact assessment under Directive 2011/92 (art.11) or a right
     to participate in decisions concerning permits for industrial installations
     (Directive 2010/75, art.25) was not respected by an authority in a Member
     State.[74] Such a right to address courts implicitly existed already by virtue of
     these two Directives. However, it is useful that the provisions in the two
     Directives lifted any ambiguity concerning such a right.
3.   Directive 2001/42 concerning an impact assessment for plans and
     programmes[75] does not contain a provision on access to justice, where
     consultation or participation concerning a plan or programme is refused.
     This question is left to national law: as the Aarhus Convention does not
     provide for access to justice in cases, where the right of participation of
     participation in the elaboration of plans and programmes is not respected—
     art.7 of the Convention is not mentioned in its art.9(2)[76]—Member States
     are free to regulate this question.

---

[70] 5th Environment Action Programme [1993] OJ C138/1, Ch.9: "Individuals and public interest
groups should have practicable access to the courts".
[71] See para.4–17, below.
[72] Directive 98/27 [1998] OJ L166/51.
[73] See paras 4–09 et seq., above.
[74] Directive 2010/75 [2010] OJ L334/17.
[75] Directive 2001/42 [2001] OJ L197/30.
[76] Aarhus Convention art.7 on participation in plans and programmes, and art.9 which only refers to
art.6.

4. Where environmental damage was caused by one of the activities and under the conditions mentioned in Directive 2004/35 on environmental liability, a citizen or an environmental organisation may draw the attention of the public authorities to the damage and ask for remedial action. Where "the request and the accompanying observations show in a plausible manner that environmental damage exists", the administration will have to take a decision on that request. This decision may then be challenged in court in view of its procedural and substantial compliance with Directive 2004/35.[77]

Similar considerations to those of Directive 2001/42 apply with regard to Directive 2003/35 which also provides for the participation of "the public" in the elaboration of certain plans and programmes under EC environmental legislation. Again, "the public" is not defined. By virtue of art.2(b), it is "entitled" to participate. The Directive does not indicate whether the public has access to the national courts in the cases, where its entitlement is disregarded. However, it should be remembered that the Aarhus Convention contains, in art.9(3), a general clause on access to courts[78] which also refers to access to the courts in cases of art.7. As it is the declared objective of Directive 2003/35 to implement the Aarhus Convention,[79] and the Aarhus Convention intends to give rights to individuals, there is a right to look for judicial remedy for all those whose participation entitlement is not respected. The details of this right to access to the courts are determined by national law.

4–17   In 2003, the Commission made a proposal for a Directive on access to justice in environmental matters.[80] The proposal intended to put the relevant pillar of the Aarhus Convention into EU law. It suggested giving environmental organisations a right of standing in the courts where EU environmental law is breached. Environmental law was defined in a rather broad way. The proposal, which was based on the present art.192 TFEU, was supported by the European Parliament which even wanted to further strengthen it.[81] However it met, in Council, considerable objections from Member States which were of the opinion that access to national courts was, under the principle of subsidiarity, their competence and that the European Union should not interfere in this area. They hardly discussed the proposal which has, in the meantime, become obsolete and was withdrawn by the Commission in 2014.

In 2011, the Court of Justice decided that the Aarhus Convention, including its art.9(3), were part of EU law.[82] However, the Court declared that art.9(3) was not

---

[77] Directive 2004/35 on environmental liability with a view of prevention and remedying environmental damage [2004] OJ L143/56, arts 12 and 13.

[78] Aarhus Convention art.9(3): "In addition and without prejudice to review procedures referred to in paragraphs 1 and 2 above, each Party shall ensure that, where they meet the criteria, if any, laid down in its national law, members of the public have access to administrative or judicial procedures to challenge acts and omissions by private parties and public authorities which contravene provisions of its national law relating to the environment."

[79] See the Recitals of Dir.2003/35 [2003] OJ L156/17.

[80] Commission, proposal for a directive on access to justice in environmental matters, COM(2003) 624.

[81] European Parliament, Legislative Resolution [2004] OJ C103E/626.

[82] Court of Justice, *Lesoochranárske zoskupenie* (C-240/09), [2011] E.C.R. I-1255; confirmed in C-401/12P (fn.38, above).

directly applicable, because members of the public or environmental organisations only had access to the courts, where they complied with the requirements
that were laid down in national law. However, this reasoning which was based on
the words "if any" in art.9(3), did not (wish to) see that "if any" gives an option to
the Contracting Parties to take national measures, but does not require them to do
so. The Court continued by inviting the national courts to give the fullest possible
effect to art.9(3) with regard to standing of members of the public.

This decision is certainly also politically motivated. It would have been
possible to declare the provisions as of direct effect and give standing to every
member of the public, until the Member State in question had laid down
conditions to restrict such an *actio popularis*. The Court of Justice preferred to
ignore that the burden of legislating was with the Member States and that it
allowed them practically to take advantage of their own passivity to lay down
specific conditions; in other cases on the direct effect, the Court had argued that a
Member State should not be allowed to invoke its own omission to act and then
oppose the direct effect of an EU provision.

The judgment means that, in each individual case, applicants will have to   **4–18**
persuade local, regional or national courts of the wording, the objective and the
spirit of art.9(3), in order to obtain standing. As courts are, by nature,
conservative, this means that, in practice, not much will be changing in the future.
Article 9(3) will remain nice in words, but not very relevant in practice. Also, it is
not likely that the Court of Justice will in future change its opinion, as it decided,
in case C-240/09, in the composition of a Grand Chamber (13 judges) which
gives a particular weight to the judgment.

(ii)   European level

EU law gives persons a right of access to the European Courts, where an EU   **4–19**
measure is addressed to that person or where the person is directly and
individually concerned by the measure.[83] This right was enlarged in 2009 by
allowing access to the EU courts where a person was directly concerned by a
regulatory act which did not require the taking of implementation measures.

As regards access to information, persons have under Regulation 1049/2001 a
right to ask for access to documents. In such a case, the EU institution is obliged
to formally respond to that person. Against this formal answer, access to the EU
courts is possible, as the applicant is addressed by the formal decision.

As far as participation in environmental decision-making at EU level is
concerned, there was, prior to the adoption of Regulation 1367/2006, only soft
law which obliged Commission officials to involve individuals in measures
which they are preparing. A breach of this obligation did not lead to the
possibility to recur to the application of art.263(4) TFEU. Regulation 1367/2006,
adopted in 2006, now gives citizens a right to participate in environmental plans
and programmes which are elaborated at EU level (see paras 4–09 et seq., above).
If this right is not granted, there is a possibility for the affected public to apply,
under art.263(4) TFEU, to the Court of Justice. The same applies, in my opinion,

---

[83] Article 263(4) TFEU: "Any natural or legal person may ... institute proceedings against an act
addressed to that person or which is of direct and individual concern to them, and against a regulatory
act which is of direct concern to them and does not entail implementing measures."

where the EU institutions and bodies only provide for consultation of the public, instead of a full participation—and this difference requires a definition of the two notions. Participation clearly goes further than a mere consultation. It gives the participating persons a guarantee that his/her opinion is received, weighed and considered during the decision-making process and that the administration explains, once a decision has been taken, for which reason it followed or did not follow the opinion which was issued.

4–20 As regards access to the European Courts in other areas, Regulation 1367/2006 introduced the possibility for environmental organisations to "make a request for internal review to the Community institution of or body that has adopted an administrative act under environmental law or, in case of an alleged administrative omission, should have adopted such an act" (art.10(1)). In such a case, a written reply shall be given within a specific time-span. The environmental organisation then may institute proceedings before the Court of Justice "in accordance with the relevant provisions of this Treaty" (art.12). However, this possibility only exists with regard to "an individual administrative act adopted under environmental law" (art.10)—which excludes in practice Commission delegated or implementing acts and the majority of other acts. The Court of Justice refused to assess the compatibility of this approach with art.9(3) of the Aarhus Convention, as it held that provision to be not directly applicable.[84]

The Council's Common Position which was not changed by the final adoption of Regulation 1367/2006, expressly stated that "the Common Position carefully sticks to the provisions contained in Articles 230(4) and 232(3) of the EC Treaty, which are sufficient to ensure compliance".[85]

This means in clear terms that there is an internal review procedure, but that access to the European Courts has not changed in substance. Contrary to the Council's Opinion, I consider this not to be compatible with the Aarhus Convention. Article 9(3) of the Convention gives members of the public, including environmental organisations, a possibility of adequate remedies against acts and omissions which contravene environmental law and with the means to have existing environmental legislation enforced and made effective.

4–21 The Compliance Committee, set up under the Aarhus Convention, considered that Contracting Parties of the Convention were not obliged to introduce an *actio populars*. However, it was of the opinion that neither were they entitled to introduce or maintain "so strict criteria that they effectively bar all or almost all environmental organisations from challenging acts or omissions that contravene national law relating to the environment".[86] The Compliance Committee found in 2011 that the restrictive access to EU courts, which is granted under arts 263 and 267 TFEU, is not in compliance with the requirements of the Aarhus Convention.[87]

It is true that, at present, access to the European Courts is practically barred for environmental organisations and very largely also for citizens. There is not one single case where an environmental organisation was given standing in

---

[84] Court of Justice, C-240/09 (fn.82, above).

[85] Council, Common Position 31/2005 [2005] OJ C264E/18.

[86] Aarhus Convention, Compliance Committee, Compliance by Belgium, Doc.ACCC/C/2005/11 of 14 June 2005.

[87] Aarhus Convention Compliance Committee, Decision of 14 April 2011 in case ACCC/C/2008/32. This Decision was approved by the Meeting of the Parties of the Aarhus Convention.

environmental cases until now—except, of course, under the provisions on access to information. The Court is extremely restrictive in its interpretation in this regard.[88] And the introduction of an internal review procedure under Regulation 1367/2006 does not change the rules on access to justice.

Furthermore, the internal review procedure is not sufficient to comply with the requirements of art.9(3) of the Aarhus Convention, in particular because such a review is only possible with regard to "administrative acts under environmental law", because no possibility is foreseen to take action against private persons that do not respect EU environmental law and because, under art.10 of Regulation 1367/2006, the internal review procedure is limited to some environmental organisations. Furthermore, it follows from art.9(4) of the Aarhus Convention which requires the procedure under art.9(3) to "provide adequate and effective remedies, including injunctive relief as appropriate, and be fair, equitable, timely and not prohibitively expensive", that art.9(3) intends to introduce court procedures, not internal review procedures by the same body that adopted or should have adopted the incriminated measures. A review by the same body is neither fair nor equitable, and no injunctive relief is foreseen.

2.   FUNDING

(a)   General remarks—Environmental Fund

The European Union has not set up a general environmental fund. Attempts to introduce such a fund failed in the beginning of the 1980s. In 1987, a clause was inserted into art.175(4) EC Treaty (now art.192(5) TFEU) that, as a rule, "Member States shall finance ... the environment policy". The reasons for this basic decision were more political than legal. Title XVIII TFEU (arts 174–178) mentions economic and social cohesion; however, it is not clear why this Title does not read "Economic, social and environmental cohesion" which would parallel the objective of "sustainable development" of art.3(3) TEU. Indeed, if one looks at the three pillars of sustainable development, the European Union has established funds for economic—Agricultural Fund (art.40(3) TFEU), Regional Fund (art.176(1) TFEU), Cohesion Fund (art.177(2) TFEU)—and social problems (art.162 TFEU), but not for environmental problems. One might well reflect whether, under the auspices of the European Union, this basic decision remains justified: for damage caused by the sea transport of petrol and by nuclear accidents, systems are set up under public international law which provide a solution in order to ensure that, in any case, the damage caused to the environment is compensated, at least as far as the system—which operates under considerable influence of multinational companies—reaches.

The absence of an EU Fund for the environment would be less dramatic if, at the level of Member States, financial means were made available to address the environmental problems. This, however, is almost never the case and the result is that environmental damage is frequently not repaired or compensated. The infrastructural inferiority of environmental protection with regard to the

4–22

---

[88] See the leading case *Greenpeace v Commission* (C-321/95P) [1998] E.C.R. I-1651; see also paras 12–37 et seq., below.

protection of economic and social interests—the environment does not vote and has no voice—becomes all the more visible by this constellation. As the environment disappears in silence, the issue raises only a limited amount of concern.

An EU Fund for the environment would certainly need an amendment of the TFEU, as all existing funds are explicitly mentioned in the Treaty. In substance, a Fund would have the potential to cover a great number of areas such as aspects of climate change, renewable energies, contaminated land remediation, environmental catastrophes, biodiversity and natural habitat protection and monitoring, awareness-raising for environmental matters, clean technologies, and implementation of environmental legislation.[89] The problem of a Fund for the environment is that Member States might cede to the temptation and ensure environmental protection only to the extent that EU finances are made available. This was the main reason why, in the 1980s, the creation of an EU Fund had been rejected.

4–23
Weighing all the pros and cons of a Fund, it seems more appropriate to use existing funds—the Regional Fund and the Cohesion Fund—to support the protection of the environment. The reason for this is that the environment cannot hope to be protected "by its own". Rather, environmental concerns must be integrated into all kinds of human and economic activities such as energy, leisure, transport and the corresponding EU policies (art.11 TFEU). Greening other policies seems, in the long term, more promising to achieve environmental objectives than letting environmental policy try to fight its own fund which would always have insufficient resources. Financial instruments which concentrate on specific environmental aspects such as habitat protection or environmental catastrophes will continue as necessary. The sheer amount of financial means that would be necessary for the protection, the preservation and the improvement of the quality of the environment at a high level—these are the requirements of art.191 TFEU—will exceed the means of any environmental fund that could be set up.

Following a major flood in parts of the European Union in 2002, the European Union decided on the establishment of an EU solidarity fund.[90] The Fund is to intervene in cases of "major disasters, mainly natural disasters" which have serious repercussions on living conditions, the natural environment or the economy. The damage shall normally exceed €3 billion. Next to flooding, one might think, in the area of the environment, of droughts, forest fires, major industrial disasters or pipeline incidents. The amounts which are available under the funds are rather limited.

(b) Structural funds and cohesion fund

4–24
In the context of the EU Regional Policy which takes about one-third of the overall EU budget, financial means under the structural funds are made available to Member States for agricultural, social and regional concerns. The funds will

---

[89] A Commission study of 2003 estimated that about €110 billion would be necessary to ensure the application of existing legislation in the accession countries, and in spring 2003 the Commission published a study which indicated that the habitat network Natura 2000 set up under Dirs 79/409 and 92/ 43 (see para.5–13, below) would cost between €3.4 and €5.7 billion per year till 2013, see Commission COM(2004) 431.

[90] Regulation 2012/2002 establishing the EU solidarity fund [2002] OJ L311/3.

distribute, between 2014 and 2020, €325 billion, which means about €45 billion per year[91]; to these sums have to added some €5.7 billion of the European Maritime and Fisheries Fund.[92] The general priorities for the different funds are laid down in the relevant EC regulations.[93] Under the regional policy, programmes for the different measures are elaborated by Member States which follow the priority objectives that had been laid down at EU level. These programmes are in some form approved by the Commission which has, however, neither sufficient time nor sufficient personal resources to make a serious assessment. The individual projects are then decided by Member States. How many environmental projects are co-financed by the structural funds is also dependent on the definition of "environmental project". In 2006, the Commission estimated that some 10 per cent of the measures that are co-financed by the Regional Development Fund and 50 per cent of the Cohesion Fund were in the past spent for environmental purposes[94]; the 10 per cent figure appears to be much too optimistic.

For the coming years, Regulation 1301/2013 on the Regional Funds mentions the possibility to finance measures to shift towards a low-carbon economy; measures for climate change adaptation and mitigation; waste and water measures, investments in natural and cultural heritage projects and on biodiversity; measures to improve the urban environment and to support innovative technologies; green economy measures; investments in energy efficiency and renewable energies, environmentally friendly transport systems and noise reduction measures.[95] Elsewhere, the prevention of risks, including the development and implementation of plans to prevent and cope with natural and technological risks, and sustainable tourism are mentioned.

How much of the sums which are available are spent on the construction of roads or other infrastructure projects and how much is spent for the environment, is decided by the Member States. Long-term effects of the regional policy—impacts of motorway construction or other infrastructure projects—on the state of nature such as biodiversity or land use are difficult to assess, as many other factors also play a role. However, it seems obvious that many projects in Member States which would never have been realised without the support of EU funds, are detrimental to the protection of the environment. Environmental organisations often tried to stop such projects, normally, though, without success.[96] The influence of such organisations on the elaboration of the national plans under the Structural Funds is very limited.

---

[91] See Reg.1303/2013 concerning general provisions for the structural funds [2013] OJ L347/320, art.91 and annex VI.

[92] Regulation 508/2014 [2014] OJ L149/1, art.13.

[93] Regulation 1301/2013 on the Regional Development Fund [2013] OJ L347/289; Reg.1304/2013 on the Social Fund [2013] OJ L347/470; Reg.1300/2013 on the Cohesion Fund [2013] OJ L347/281; Reg.1305/2013 concerning the Agricultural Fund for Rural Development [2013] OJ L347/487; Reg.508/2014 [2014] OJ L149/1.

[94] Commission, COM(2004) 621.

[95] Regulation 1301/2013 [2013] OJ L347/289, art.5 nos 4 to 6.

[96] See, e.g. the facts underlying Court of Justice, *An Taisce* (C-325/94) [1996] E.C.R. I-3727; *Greenpeace v Commission* (C-321/95P) [1998] E.C.R. I-1651; *WWFUK v Council* (C-355/08P), ECLI:EI:C:2009:286; General Court, *Apiculteurs v Commission* (T-403/07), ECLI:EU:T:2008:469.

4–25   The Cohesion Fund,[97] established under art.177(2) TFEU did not, until 2006, work with programmes; rather, it made money available for specific transport and environmental projects in countries which have a gross national product per capita of less than 90 per cent of the EU average. As of 2007, the Cohesion Fund followed the model of the other funds: Member States which benefit from the Cohesion Fund, originate programmes and then obtain sums to implement these programmes. Which projects are then co-financed, is up to the Member States.

Article 177(2) TFEU provides only for the co-financing of trans-European transport and of environmental measures. Regulation 1300/2013 states that the Fund shall finance "investment in the environment, including areas related to sustainable development and energy which present environmental benefits" (art.2(1); this is an elegant way to finance energy projects which, under art.177 TFEU, may not be financed by the Cohesion Fund. The Investment priorities for the Cohesion Fund are word by word the same as for the Regional Development Fund, mentioned above.

The Cohesion Fund shall not co-finance the construction or the decommissioning of nuclear power plants, the reduction of greenhouse gas emissions of activities covered by Directive 2003/87, housing, except for promoting energy efficiency or renewable energy use, and the investment in airport infrastructure, unless related to environmental protection (art.2.(2)). Caution has to be used for the application of this provision—which mirrors an identical provision in Regulation 1301/2013 on the Regional Fund, as the 2014 budget of the Commission provides the sum of €154 million for the decommissioning of nuclear installations.[98]

4–26   Between 2014 and 2020, the Fund will distribute €63.4 billion. The Member States that will benefit from the Cohesion Fund between 2014 and 2020 are Bulgaria, Croatia, Cyprus, Czech Republic, Estonia, Greece, Hungary, Latvia, Lithuania, Malta, Poland, Portugal, Romania, Slovenia and Slovakia.

Regulation 1303/2013 provides in art.8 that all projects which are co-financed with EU money must be in keeping with the provisions of EU law.[99] However, the European Union normally relies on the affirmation of the national authorities that a project conforms with EU environmental legal provisions. Local groups and environmental organisations often protest, arguing for example that no environment impact assessment had been made before an infrastructure project was started. However, Regulation 1303/2013 enumerates in art.142 the cases under which the Commission may suspend payments to a Member State; and non-compliance with applicable EU (environmental) law does not figure on this list. This means in clear terms that when a Member State does not comply with EU environmental law the Commission would have to start proceedings under art.258 TFEU[100]; but the Commission would not be allowed to retain funds, when, for example, a motorway is being built without an environment impact assessment. The underlying idea of the present provisions is presumably that protesters might go to the national court. However, there is some value in a

---

[97] Regulation 1300/2013 [2013] OJ L347/281.

[98] EU budget 2014 [2014] OJ L51/1, Ch.32 on energy, p.II/1197.

[99] Regulation 1303/2013 [2013] OJ L347/320, art.6: "Operations supported by [the Structural Funds] shall comply with applicable Union law and the national law relating to its application."

[100] See for an example of such a (lengthy) procedure, *Italy v Commission* (C-385/13P) ECLI:EU:C:2014:2350.

legislative provision that the European taxpayer's money should only serve to finance projects which are in compliance with the European legislation.

Overall, regional policy goes more and more in the direction that Member States receive lump sums and spend them at their discretion, being loosely fenced in by the national priority programmes which they fix and which are a little bit controlled and then approved by the Commission. This trend makes the financing of environmental policies and projects increasingly dependent on the political rank that environmental policy has within the different Member States. And as the environment is not voting in elections, this rank is not high in many Member States. For a politician, who wants to be re-elected, it is much more popular to build a new road than a waste water treatment installation, to protect farmers and hunters rather than the soil and the birds. European regional development policy is quite problematic for the European environment.

(c) LIFE—Financial Instrument for the Environment

Following earlier measures to support environmental projects in the Mediterranean, Baltic and North Sea regions, a financial instrument, LIFE, was created in 1992 in order to support some environmental activities in Member States and beyond. Between 1992 and 2013, some 3,500 projects were financially supported with an overall value of €3 billion. For the period 2014–2020, under the new LIFE Regulation[101] €3.456 billion are made available for two sub-programmes, one for the environment (€2.6 billion)[102] and one for climate action (€864 million).[103] The environmental sub-programme allow support of measures on environmental and resource efficiency, environmental governance and information—this aims mainly at supporting environmental organisations—and nature and biodiversity which shall receive at least 55 per cent of the sums available under the sub-programme. The sub-programme on climate action shall support projects on climate change mitigation, climate change adaptation and governance and information in climate matters. Beneficiary countries are the EU Member States, countries in the different stages of accession, countries which are partners of the EU neighbourhood policy and those which adhered to the European Environment Agency—overall more than 35 countries. Under the environment programme, pilot and demonstration projects in particular are co-financed.

A critical look at this result must begin with the sums that are made available for the protection of nature and biodiversity. The policy target of the European Union was to stop the loss of biodiversity by 2010; the new target is 2020. As mentioned, the Member State experts on nature protection estimated that for the setting up of the Natura 2000 network alone, between €3.4 and 5.7 billion per year would be needed (15 countries). Even if one takes the lower figure and

4–27

---

[101] Regulation 1293/2013 establishing a programme for the environment and climate change [2013] OJ L347/185.

[102] See Commission Implementing Dec.2014/203 for a LIFE multiannual work programme 2014–2017 [2014] OJ L116/1.

[103] For LIFE+ (2007–2013) where €2.1 billion were made available, the EU Court of Auditors observed: "This is a modest budget for an ambitious objective: to contribute to the development, updating and implementation of EU environmental policy and legislation." Court of Auditors, Special Report 15/2013: Has the environmental component of the LIFE programme been effective?

considers it to be exaggerated, the difference of the amount which Regulation 1293/2014 provides—about €1.5 billion for seven years, which means €210 million per year, divided by some 35 countries—remains enormous. It is likely that the Commission will argue in future that Member States should provide for the financing of nature protection measures under the regional policy funds, while Member States will argue that it is LIFE which has to finance the protection of nature and biodiversity. The loser is the environment. And it must also be pointed out that the protection of nature and biodiversity cannot be limited to the designated habitats of EU interest, the Natura 2000 network.

There are other problems with LIFE. Member States take great care to ensure that every Member State gets a more or less equal share of the available money. Annex I to Regulation 1293/2013 goes so far as to fix indicative national allocations which are then, in Decision 2014/203, broken down to precise percentages. Thus, it is not necessarily the best project that is supported. The new art.24 of Regulation 1293/2013 mandates the Commission to adopt two multiannual work programmes (four years and three years) where priorities for specific projects are set. The method of project approval via comitology-like procedures appeared, led in the past to some concerted practices among Member States. Also in the past, there was a limited pilot effect of the specific project that was co-financed: the innovative measures were not easily made operational in the whole of the European Union. In 2013, the Court of Auditors concluded in a report on the environmental component of LIFE+ (2007–2013) "that, overall, the LIFE environment component was not operating effectively because it was not sufficiently well designed and implemented".[104]

3. PLANNING AND LAND USE

(a) Town and country planning; land use

4–28   Article 192(2) TFEU provides that measures concerning town and country planning and land use require unanimous adoption in the Council. The provision thus parts from the idea that such measures may also be adopted at EU level, though questions of subsidiarity are of particular relevance here. Until now, though, almost no such measures have been taken. The Commission issued some communications which concern basic aspects of town and country planning,[105] the urban environment,[106] integrated coastal zone management,[107] and wetlands.[108] On coastal zone management, the European Parliament and the Council

---

[104] Court of Auditors, Special Report 15/2013 (fn.103, above); see also the much less critical Commission report on the final assessment of LIFE (2007–2013), COM(2013) 478.

[105] Commission, Europe 2000: perspectives of future town and country planning of the Community COM(90) 544; Commission, Europe 2000: outlook for the development of the Community's territory COM(91) 452.

[106] Commission, Green Paper on the urban environment, COM(90) 218; Council Resolution of 28 January 1991 [1991] OJ C33/4; see further, Court of Auditors, Special Report on urban environment in the European Union [1994] OJ C383/1; Commission, Communication on urban development in the European Union, COM(97) 197.

[107] Commission, Communication on integrated coastal zone management, COM(2000) 547.

[108] Commission, Communication on the wise use and conservation of wetlands, COM(95) 189.

adopted a recommendation which gives guidelines for an "environmentally sustainable, economically equitable, sociable responsible and culturally sensitive management of coastal zones".[109] Despite these words, the individual recommendations are of a very general nature and not really operational. And a look at coastal zones in the European Union shows that the Recommendation is largely ignored, the most obvious example being the destruction of the Spanish coast by construction projects.

In execution of Decision 1600/2002 on the 6th Environment Action Programme the Commission published in early 2006 a thematic strategy—i.e. a sectoral action programme—on the urban environment[110] which addressed in particular problems of transport in urban agglomerations. Concrete actions on implementing the strategy were almost completely lacking. Under the Regional Policy, some pilot projects were financially supported, greater cooperation among agglomerations is promoted and awareness campaigns were initiated; the main activities, however, stem from interested cities themselves. In general, though, problems of the urban environment are much too large and too diversified to be handled at EU level.

The 7th Environment Action Programme[111] wants to "ensure" that by 2020

> "a majority of cities in the Union are implementing policies for sustainable urban planning and design, including innovative approaches for urban public transport and mobility, sustainable buildings, energy efficiency and urban biodiversity conservation."

The programme indicates what would be necessary to reach this objective, but suggests no action whatsoever on how to get there.

Article 13 of the Directive on the prevention of major accidents[112] requires **4–29** Member States to ensure that the objective of preventing major accidents and limiting the consequences of such accidents are taken into account in their land-use policies. In the long term, there will have to be appropriate distances between such establishments and residential areas, areas of public use and natural value and interest. The implementation of these provisions is to be ensured by consultation procedures. Industrial accidents in Enschede (the Netherlands) and Toulouse (France) in 2000 demonstrated the necessity of such measures, though it is rather difficult to relocate industrial installations once they come too close to urban agglomerations or newly built residential areas. In practice, art.13 of Directive 2012/18 is hardly enforceable. When the Frankfurt airport wanted to enlarge, work was upheld in 2004/2005, because a chemical plant was located exactly in the projected new landing line. After years of negotiations, the plant was relocated.

Apart from these few measures, the different communications—including the 7th Environment Action Programme—aim at focusing the attention on some

---

[109] Recommendation 2002/413 concerning the implementation of integrated coastal zone management [2002] OJ L148/24.

[110] Decision 1600/200/laying down the 6th Environment Action Programme [2002] OJ L242/1, art.7(2.g) and Commission, COM(2005) 718.

[111] Decision 1386/2013 [2013] OJ L 354/171, section 95.

[112] Directive 2012/18 on the control of major-accident hazards involving dangerous substances [2012] OJ L197/1.

specific aspects of development within the European Union or showing the environmental problems of specific areas, rather than determining legal measures for town and country planning or land use. Indeed, these measures do not announce or propose new legal measures at all to contribute to the solutions of problems. They have to be viewed alongside the European Union's policies which affect planning and land use, in particular regional, transport and agricultural policy. Sometimes the communications also serve to start a discussion whether EU financial assistance for some specific topics should be envisaged, notably in the framework of the Structural Funds. Also, measures concerning the protection of the architectural and natural heritage of the European Union[113] increasingly come under the provision on culture of art.167 TFEU.[114]

(b) Environment impact assessment

(i) Projects

4–30   **National level.**   A Directive on the assessment of the effects of certain public and private projects on the environment was adopted in 1985, substantially amended in 1997, consolidated in 2011 and again amended in 2014.[115] According to that Directive, public authorities, before they give a permit (development consent) for specific public and private projects, shall make an assessment of the direct and indirect effects which the project may have on humans and the environment. Specific procedural provisions are laid down for such an assessment, such as the requirement for the developer to submit factual information on the project and its likely impact as well as measures to reduce negative impacts, the participation of administrative bodies dealing with nature protection and the possibility for the public concerned to express an opinion. The administrative decision on the application shall take into consideration all these comments.

For a first group of projects, listed in annex I to the Directive, such as large refineries, large power stations, radioactive waste disposal installations, motor-ways, lines for long-distance railway traffic, larger airports, an environment impact assessment always has to be made. For a second group of projects (annex II) an impact assessment has to be made where the project is likely "to have significant effects on the environment by virtue, in particular, of its nature, size or location" (art.2). Member States have a large amount of discretion in deciding whether a project has such a significant impact or not. However, the Court of Justice has considerably narrowed down this discretion, by requiring, de facto that for any project that is (objectively) likely to have a significant impact on the

---

[113] See Rec.74/65 on the protection of the architectural and natural heritage [1975] OJ L21/22; Resolution of the Council and of Member States meeting in Council on the conservation of the European architectural heritage [1986] OJ C320/1; Dec.1194/2011 establishing an EU action for the European heritage label [2011] OJ L303/1.

[114] Decision 2228/97 on an action programme for the conservation of cultural heritage [1997] OJ L305/11.

[115] Directive 85/337 [1985] OJ L175/40; Dir.97/11 [1997] OJ L73/5; Dir.2011/92 [2012] OJ L26/1; Dir.2014/52 [2014] OJ L124/1.

environment, an environment impact assessment is necessary.[116] In daily practice at local and regional level, this jurisdiction is rather frequently ignored, though.

Commission attempts in the 1980s to have an environmental impact assessment made for any project co-financed by EU funds—in particular the Structural Funds or the Cohesion Fund—failed, as those Member States from Southern Europe which were mainly involved successfully argued that this would be discriminatory. This is not convincing, since the taxpayers in the different Member States, which contribute to the Funds, are certainly entitled to be assured that their money is being properly used.

Directive 2011/92 has been implemented in all Member States, although in some states with considerable delay; not all legislation conformed to the Directive's requirements and the Court had sometimes to state on the non-conformity of national legislation decades later.[117] A particular problem is the practical application of the Directive: even after a number of years of the Directive's application, most of the complaints, petitions and infringement procedures under art.258 TFEU deal with Directive 2011/92.[118] The main concerns are the policy decisions to realise a project independently from its, potentially very negative, impact on the environment; the exclusion of annex II projects from an impact assessment; the poor quality or the incomplete impact assessment; the beginning of realising the project before the end of the impact assessment procedure; the attempt to cut a project into several pieces, which are each below the thresholds or without significant impact, whereas the cumulated effects of the whole project would be significant (slicing);[119] and omissions to properly consult the public concerned.[120] The transboundary effects of a project are, under art.7 of the Directive, to be discussed and settled in an intergovernmental cooperation procedure. This is neither compatible with the right of the public concerned—even when it lives in a neighbouring country—nor with art.6 of the Aarhus Convention which gives a right to participate to persons concerned.

4–31

Directive 2011/92 has undoubtedly influenced the development of permitting procedures in all Member States, by imposing the taking into consideration of environmental aspects into this procedure. In a number of regions, it was possible to limit and reduce the almost total discretion given to local or other authorities to decide on a project.

The main problems of the Directive are:

---

[116] Court of Justice, *WWF* (C-435/97) [1999] E.C.R. I-5613; *Kraaijeveld* (C-72/95) [1996] E.C.R. I-5403; *Commission v Germany* (C-431/92) [1995] E.C.R. I-2189; *Commission v Belgium* (C-131/94) [1996] E.C.R. I-2323; *Commission v Germany* (C-301/95) [1998] E.C.R. I-6135; *Commission v Ireland* (C-392/96) [1999] E.C.R. I-5901.

[117] Court of Justice, *Commission v Ireland* (C-50/09) [2011] E.C.R. I-873; *Trianel* (C-115/09) [2011] E.C.R. I-3673; *Poumon Vert Hulpe* ECLI:EU:C:2011:738; *Solvay* ECLI:EU:C:2012:82; *Salzburg Airport* ECLI:EU:C:2013:203.

[118] Commission, Monitoring the application of Community law 13th report [1995] OJ C250/1, p.175; 17th report (1999) [2001] OJ C30/1, p.45; 19th report, COM(2002) 324, p.45.

[119] This slicing is not allowed under the Directive, see Court of Justice, *Commission v Ireland* (C-326/92) [1999] E.C.R. I-5901; *Abraham* (C-2/07) [2008] E.C.R. I-1197; *Strasswalchen* (C-531/13) ECLI:EU:C:2015:79.

[120] See the cases mentioned in fn. 116, above and furthermore *Bund Naturschutz Bayern* (C-396/92) [1994] E.C.R. I-3717.

- its loose drafting and the large discretion given to administrations often lead to the non-application of some of its principles;
- it does not oblige a developer to study or have studied alternatives to the project for which he looks for a permit[121];
- the administration is not in any way obliged to avoid and/or minimise the negative effects of a project on the environment, and may give development consent where serious negative effects are to be expected[122];
- the impact assessment need not, according to general understanding, be made in writing, though it is difficult to see how one can "describe" (art.3) the effects of a project otherwise than in writing;
- no regular national reports and no Commission report on the application of Directive is foreseen[123];
- it does not provide for consequences when an environment impact assessment has not been made. This leads to large differences. While, for example, in the United Kingdom, where an environment impact assessment has not been made, the planning consent is void and the whole procedure has to start anew, German courts consider the omission to make an environment impact assessment an administrative error which is only relevant, where it can be proven that the impact assessment would have led to another decision. Recent Court decisions clarified that the complete omission of an impact assessment made the permit procedure defective, and that a significant defect of the procedure normally would have the same effect. The Court also clarified that the burden of proof that an impact assessment would have led to another decision regarding a project, may not be placed on the applicant.[124]

4–32   The amendments brought to the Directive by Directive 2014/52, will become applicable in mid-2017. They concern in particular the screening procedure, i.e. the examination whether an annex II project shall be subject to an impact assessment, as well as the question of the scope and the details of the impact assessment report which the operator has to deliver (scoping procedure).

---

[121] See Dir.2011/92 [2012] OJ L26/1 which provides in art.5(3) and Annex IV n.2 that the developer has to submit, together with his application "an outline of the main alternatives studied by the developer". However, this clause is generally understood in the sense that the developer is not obliged to study alternatives; only where he has done so, he must submit information on them. Under the Espoo Convention which has also been concluded by the European Union (see para.4–36, below), the developer of a project which has impacts on another state, must examine "reasonable alternatives". This provision is binding on EU Member States.

[122] A good example is *Acheloos* (C-43/10) ECLI:EU:C:2012:560, where the Court of Justice sent the decision, whether the project to divert the river Acheloos was compatible with EU law, back to the Greek authorities.

[123] Directive 2011/92 [2012] OJ L26/1 only provides in art.11(3) that the Commission shall publish an implementation report five years after the adoption of the Directive. This report was published in (1993) COM(93) of 2 April 1993. The Commission occasionally published further reports, at an interval of about five to eight years. Directive 91/692 standardising and rationalising reports on the implementation of certain directives relating to the environment [1991] OJ L377/48 omitted to provide for regular reports on Dir.85/337.

[124] Court of Justice, *Altrip* (C-72/12) ECLI:EU:C:2013:712; *L. v M.* (C-463/11) ECLI-:EU:C:2013:247.

European level.   The Commission does not itself authorise projects which are realised at national level. There are thus no provisions at EU level corresponding to those of Directive 2011/92. There is considerable discussion on whether there should be an EU assessment before the Commission agrees to co-finance Member States' projects.[125] This idea was rightly rejected, as this would inevitably lead to two environmental impact assessments being made; and there is no reason to duplicate these assessments which are expensive and time-consuming. The problem would probably be less if Member States were required to make such an assessment for all projects that are co-financed out of the EU budget, and if the Commission were more systematically checking whether a necessary national environmental impact assessment was made.

The European Investment Bank requires the application of Directive 2011/92 when it co-finances a project within the EU. For projects outside the European Union, where no legislation on environmental impact assessments might exist, it takes EU legislation as a base—without it being clear whether it systematically asks for an environmental impact assessment.

(ii)   Plans and programmes

National level.   Directive 2001/42[126] requests Member States to make an   4–33
environment impact assessment for plans and programmes which are likely to have significant environment effects. Plans and programmes for which such an impact assessment is always required are listed in art.3(2); this requirement is, however, limited to plans or programmes which are the basis for subsequent project-related environmental impact assessments.[127] For plans and programmes which determine the "use of small areas of local level" and minor amendments to existing plans and programmes an assessment is only necessary where Member States determine that they are likely to have significant environmental effects; a general exemption of small areas is, however, not allowed.[128] For other plans which "set the framework for future development consent of projects", Member States shall determine whether they are likely to have such effects, either through case-by-case examination or by specifying types of plans and programmes. Plans for national defence, civil emergency and financial or budget plans or programmes are not covered by the Directive.

The definition of "environment assessment" is different from that under Directive 2011/92. Under Directive 2001/42 it means "the preparation of an environment report, the carrying out of consultations, the taking into account of the environment report and the consultations in decision-making and the

---

[125] Possible candidates could be the so-called "major projects" (art.100 of Reg.1303/2013 [2013] OJ L347/320) with a volume of €50 million or even €75 million; here the Commission surveillance is particularly intense. However, the responsibility to authorise remains with the Member State in question.

[126] Directive 2001/42 [2001] OJ L197/30.

[127] Directive 2001/42 [2001] OJ L197/30, art.3(2): "… an environmental assessment shall be carried out for all plans and programmes (a) which are prepared for agriculture, forestry, fisheries, energy, industry, transport, waste management, water management, telecommunications, tourism, town and country planning or land use which set the framework for future development consent of projects listed in Annexes I and II to Directive 85/337, or (b) which, in view of the likely effect on sites, have been determined to require an assessment pursuant to Article 6 or 7 of Directive 92/43."

[128] Court of Justice, *Valciukene* (C-295/10) [2011] E.C.R. I-8819.

provision of information on the decision" that is finally taken. The environment report must describe and evaluate the likely environmental impacts and reasonable alternatives. Consultation[129] must be made early and in any time before the adoption of the plan or programme or its submission to the legislative procedure. It must include consultations on the draft plan and on the environmental report. The public which is to be consulted includes the public affected or likely to be affected by, or having an interest in, the decision, "including relevant non-governmental organisations, such as those promoting environmental protection".

Once a decision on the plan or programme has been taken, (a) the public that was consulted shall be informed, and (b) the relevant plan or programme and a statement must be made available, summarising how environmental considerations were taken into consideration, as well as the results of the consultation and "the reason for choosing the plan or programme as adopted". The Directive also covers plans and programmes that are co-financed under the EU structural funds, though the wording is not entirely clear in this regard.[130] The Directive will hopefully ensure that public discussions on the environmental effects of plans and programmes take place and it may be hoped that this progressively benefits the environment. The necessity to explain why a specific solution for a plan was taken, might also reduce the administrations' discretion which, in some parts of the European Union, is in need of more democratic discussion. It is problematic, though, whether enough interested persons will participate in the impact assessment and how an interested public or an environmental organisation will be able to assess the environmental impact of any such plan.

4–34   National plans which were adopted without an environmental assessment, must in principle be annulled by the national courts.[131] National legislation may not either foresee that a plan which was adopted without a proper environment impact assessment, remains nevertheless valid.[132]

European level. In the context of the International Convention on Environment Impact Assessment in a Transboundary Context, signed in Espoo (Finland) in 1991, and to which the EC adhered in 1993,[133] a Protocol was signed in May 2003 in Kiev (Ukraine) which provides for a strategic environmental assessment of plans and programmes which will come into effect in the coming years; the Protocol was signed by all EU Member States and by the European Union itself. The Protocol's content is very similar to that of Directive 2001/42.[134] The most important difference is that plans and programmes for which a strategic environmental assessment is required, are those that are required by legislative, regulatory or administrative provisions and are subject to preparation or adoption by an authority (art.2(5) of the Protocol).

---

[129] Directive 2001/42 uses the words "participation" and "consultation" synonymously. As to the difference between these notions, see paras 4–13 and 4–19, above.

[130] Directive 2001/42 [2001] OJ L197/30, arts 3(9), 11(3) and 12(4).

[131] Court of Justice, *Inter-Environnement Wallonie* (C-41/11) ECLI:EU:C:2012:103.

[132] Court of Justice, *L. v M.* (C-463/11) ECLI:EU:C:2013:247.

[133] Decision of 15 October 1996. The Decision appears never to have been published.

[134] See on that Directive, para.4–33, above.

The Council approved the Protocol in 2008.[135] The problem of the Protocol's application to the EU institutions is whether there are plans or programmes elaborated by the EU institutions—not just co-financed by them, as these remain Member States' plans and programmes—that would come under the field of application of the Protocol. This is undoubtedly the case. Indeed, already the different thematic strategies which were elaborated under the 6th Environment Action Programme[136] fulfilled the conditions of art.2(5) of the Protocol. Other plans and programmes which exist and which will be covered by the provisions of the Protocol are plans for energy-saving, programmes in the agricultural sector, on trans-European networks under arts 170 et seq. TFEU, on standardisation etc. No environment impact assessment is made for any of these plans or programmes. As access to the European Court is not possible for individuals or environmental organisations—they are not directly and individually concerned by such plans or programmes—this practice is not sanctioned.

(iii) Policies and Legislation

National level. There are no specific EU provisions which require Member States to make (environment) impact assessments of national policies or legislation, before such policies or legislations are adopted. The above-mentioned Aarhus-Convention mentions public participation in policies and legislations, but in a form of soft law which does not provide for an obligation of Contracting Parties to take implementation measures (art.8).

4–35

A certain form of consultation obligation for national legislation is created by EU law, however, not for environmental, but rather opposing purposes. Directive 98/34,[137] which is based on the actual arts 114, 337 and 43 TFEU, aims at the removal or reduction of any barriers which national legislation might create to the free movement of goods. It requests Member States to notify the Commission of draft product-related legislation. Where a restriction on use or a ban of a substance or a product is in question, the Member State is asked to add, "if available", data on production, substitution products as well as "in appropriate cases" the conclusions of a risk evaluation made in accordance with the principles of chemical legislation. The national draft measure is sent to all other Member States and the notifying Member State may adopt the draft measure only after a standstill period of three months following notification. Where the Commission or another Member State indicate that the draft measure may create barriers to the free movement of goods, the standstill period is extended to six months. Where the Commission indicates its intention to propose a legally binding Community measure or where there is already a proposal on the subject-matter in question before the Council, the standstill period is 12 months.

Where a Member State adopts a national measure without having complied with the procedure under Directive 98/34, the national provision is unenforceable on economic operators, and national courts are obliged not to apply the national provision in question.[138] This "sanction", which follows from the direct effect of

---

[135] Decision 2008/71 [2008] OJ L308/34; the Protocol is published on p.35.
[136] See para.2–17, above.
[137] Directive 98/34 [1998] OJ L204/37.
[138] Court of Justice, *Security International v Signalsson* (C-194/94) [1996] E.C.R. I-2201.

the Directive's provisions,[139] is very effective, since penalties, fines or other sanctions which were pronounced under the national provision, could not be enforced either. Directive 98/34 affects numerous environmental measures[140] and has de facto replaced a standstill agreement in environmental matters which was adopted in 1973 in the form of a gentlemen's agreement.[141] The decisive criterion for the Directive's application is whether the national measure may, directly or indirectly, influence the free circulation of goods; EU environmental considerations do not really come into this assessment, and hardly any weighing of the different interests takes place. With this proviso, measures which fix air or water quality standards normally do not come within the field of application of Directive 98/34. Likewise, nature protection measures, provisions on the storage of products or on the establishment and operation of industrial installations are not normally affected.

4–36 The public is not consulted during this procedure, though it may be assumed that Member States which are informed of draft legislation of another Member State, consult their economic operators to see whether there is a potential impact on the free circulation of goods. The Commission considered the procedure to come under the "investigation" exception of Regulation 1049/2001[142] and tried not to grant access to the comments which are made under the procedure of Directive 98/34; the General Court rejected this opinion and granted access[143].

European level. There are no binding provisions concerning impact assessments for policies and legislation at EU level. During the inter-governmental discussions on the Maastricht Treaty on the European Union, the United Kingdom suggested that EU legislative measures should undergo an environmental impact assessment; the suggestion was taken up in a declaration to the Final Act of the Conference. The Inter-governmental Conference for the Amsterdam Treaty 1997 adopted another declaration on this question, without immediate consequence.[144] The Commission had, until then, made assessments of the impact of its proposals on small and medium-sized companies and on the EU finances.

Since 2002, it submits to an impact assessment:

- legislative proposals that have an economic, social or environmental impact;
- non-legislative initiatives which define future policies;

---

[139] See para.12–21, below.

[140] In 1997, out of 900 national draft regulatory measures that were notified by Member States, 63 might be qualified as environmental measures, Commission Communication [1998] OJ C281/3.

[141] Agreement of the Representatives of the Governments of the Member States meeting in Council on information for the Commission and for the Member States with a view to possible harmonisation throughout the Communities of urgent measures concerning the protection of the environment [1973] OJ C9/1; amended [1974] OJ C86/2.

[142] See Reg.1049/2001 [2001] OJ L145/43 and paras 4–06 et seq.

[143] General Court, case T-402/12, *Schlyter v Commission*, ECLI:EU:T:2015:209.

[144] Declaration No.12 [1997] OJ 340/133: "The Conference notes that the Commission undertakes to prepare environment impact assessment studies, when making proposals which may have significant environmental implications."

- certain implementing measures which are likely to have significant impacts.[145]

This impact assessment is not limited to the environmental impact, but examines the economic, social and environmental impact; it focuses on the examination of whether the impact of a proposal "is sustainable and conforms to the principles of Better Regulation".[146] The impact assessment examines, possibly with the help of studies, the impact of a project, and provides for consultation with interested parties and relevant experts, including consultations on ethical and political issues. The results of the assessment which also have to include an assessment of alternatives, are laid down in an assessment report which forms a basis for the Commission's decision on the proposal. The assessment reports are made available by the Commission in the form of SEC- or SWP-documents, once the Commission has formally adopted its proposal.

4–37

Practice since 2003 shows a limited value of the assessments. The main issue of the examination is the cost of the planned measure for economic operators. In the area of agriculture, internal market, industry and regional policy, the impact assessment procedure often just gives a rubber-stamp to political decisions which were taken elsewhere; here, the environmental impact is rarely examined and assessed in any detail. In contrast, most proposals in the environmental sector are very strictly scrutinised as to their impact on vested interests—frequently in the name of "better regulation"—and then watered down or completely rejected, before they even reach the Commission's decision-making level. The methodology of making the impact assessments is not laid open. Frequently, the options which are examined are pre-determined by the result which the Commission wishes to obtain.

To take two concrete examples: Regulation 1300/2013 and 1302 on the Regional and the Cohesion Fund[147] were the subject of one single impact assessment which considered shifting the EU support in a different way.[148] But the impact assessment did not examine the effects of these structural funds on the environment within the European Union, though this impact is enormous; an examination of the likely environmental impact of the Regulations would require detailed studies which the Commission is neither able nor ready to finance and for which there is not either the time. And the Commission proposal to allow Member States, under certain conditions, to restrict the cultivation of GMOs in their territory, was not based on an impact assessment.[149]

Such examples could be multiplied.[150] The impact assessment requirement, though acceptable in its theoretical concept, thus turns in practice into an instrument of environmental deregulation. This is further strengthened by the fact

4–38

---

[145] Commission, Communication on Impact Assessment COM(2002) 276; see also the Commission's website on impact assessment, *http://ec.europa.eu/governance/impact/index_en.htm* [Accessed 3 August 2015]. The impact assessment reports are published on this site, once the Commission has adopted a proposal.

[146] Commission, Communication on Impact Assessment COM(2002) 276, n.1.3; as regards "Better Regulation" see COM(2002) 278 and now COM(2015) 215.

[147] Regulation 1300/2013 [2013] OJ L347/281; Reg.1303/2013 [2013] OJ L347/320.

[148] Commission, SEC(2011) 1138.

[149] Commission, COM(2010) 375.

[150] See L. Krämer, "Impact Assessments and Environmental Costs in EU Law" [2014] *Journal for European Environmental Policy and Law* 201.

that the impact assessment is made, under the political responsibility of the Commission's President, by the Secretariat General. In this way, the Secretary General can easily signal to the different departments that this or that legislative proposal is unwelcome and would receive a stiff reception with the Secretariat General. Examples in the past were the proposals for a directive on access to justice, on soil protection or considerations to have a directive on biodiversity elaborated. The assessment process thus strengthens centralising activities inside the Commission, a tendency which is not favourable to the protection of the environment.

4. MEASURES CONCERNING INDUSTRIAL INSTALLATIONS

(a) Corporate environmental responsibility

4–39   Since 2001, the Commission published four communications on corporate social responsibility (CSR).[151] It expressly stated that the responsibility of companies not only included social, but also environmental matters. The main signal of the Commission was that it did not intend to provide for any binding legislation in this regard, but that it expected companies to assume their responsibility on a voluntary basis. In line with the neo-liberal tendencies which the Commission has pursued for about ten years, the change of the definition of corporate social responsibility is remarkable: while in 2001, the Commission defined CSR as "a concept whereby companies integrate social and environmental concerns in their business operations and in their interaction with their stakeholders on a voluntary basis", the definition of 2011 now reads: "(CSR is) the responsibility of enterprises for their impacts on society". In this way, the term "environment" is removed from the definition.[152]

As companies are, within the European Union, submitted to legislative requirements with regard to their emissions, waste generation and treatment, waste water requirements etc, the corporate environmental responsibility aims in particular at EU companies that are active in developing countries. I would consider it normal that no EU-based company would anywhere in the world dispose of its waste in other places than authorised landfills, even if the political, economic and environmental situation in the host country does not require or enforce such behaviour; in the same way, any company should not discharge its waste water into rivers, lakes or coastal waters without prior treatment, wherever its installation is located; it should respect human and workers' rights and take adequate measures to prevent industrial accidents. This kind of example could be multiplied. Whether, however, voluntary measures are really sufficient to make

---

[151] Commission, Green Paper: towards a European framework for corporate social responsibility, COM(2001) 366; Communication concerning corporate social responsibility, COM(2002) 347; see also Council Resolutions [2002] OJ C86/1 and [2003] OJ C39/3; COM(2006) 136: Implementing the partnership for growth and jobs: making Europe a pole of excellence on CSR 136; COM(2011) 681: A renewed EU strategy 2011–2014 for Corporate Social Responsibility.

[152] The Commission adds, but outside the definition: "To fully meet their corporate social responsibility, enterprises should have in place a process to integrate social, environmental, ethical, human rights and consumer concerns into their business operations."

companies follow basic environmental protection standards is doubtful. An international convention on corporate social-environmental responsibility appears necessary and, pending EU binding measures with regard to EU companies' environmental behaviour, wherever they act, highly desirable. Politically, though, there is little chance of seeing any initiative from the EU institutions in this regard for the next few years.

(b) Permitting

Directive 76/464[153] provided that EU-wide emission limit values for the industrial discharge of some dangerous substances into the water were to be fixed, based on the "best technical means available". As regards air emissions from industrial installations, Directive 84/360 stipulated that for new installations permits should be issued for preventing air pollution, based on the best available technology not entailing excessive costs; for existing installations, Member States had to "implement policies and strategies, including appropriate measures, for the gradual adaptation of existing plans ... to the best available technology".[154]

4–40

The putting into operation of the principle of introducing the best available technology largely failed, among other reasons, because no consensus was reached as to which technology, in a given case, was the best available technology. Under Directive 76/464, the EU-wide emission standards were fixed by way of a political compromise, not by having recourse to an analysis of the application of the best available technology. Furthermore, Member States were allowed to use, instead of emission limit values, EU quality standards.[155] Under Directive 84/360, technical notes were elaborated and published to determine what constituted, for specific sectors of industry, the best available technology. However, these notes did not have any significant impact, since they had no binding legal nature and it was neither controlled nor publicised, whether they were complied with or not. Both Directives, therefore, did not lead to a significant change in technologies used in industrial installations. Furthermore, Member States did not really favour uniform emission standards for industrial installations, but rather proposed a non-harmonised approach within the European Union.

In an attempt to accommodate this concern, improve at the same time the present situation and deregulate, decentralise and take into consideration the subsidiarity principle of the EC Treaty, the Council adopted Directive 96/61 concerning integrated pollution prevention and control,[156] which became applicable, for new installations, in 1999; existing installations had to comply with its requirements since 2007. In 2008, this Directive was replaced by Directive 2008/1 which, in turn, was replaced by Directive 2010/75.[157] Directive 2010/75 concerns a number of large industrial installations, the categories of

---

[153] Directive 76/464 on pollution caused by certain dangerous substances discharged into the aquatic environment of the Community [1976] OJ L129/23, art.6(1). This Directive ceased to exist in 2013.

[154] Directive 84/360 on the combating of air pollution from industrial plants [1984] OJ L188/20, arts 4 and 13.

[155] Directive 76/464 [1976] OJ L129/23, art.6.

[156] Directive 96/61 concerning integrated pollution prevention and control [1996] OJ L257/26.

[157] Directive 2008/1 concerning integrated pollution prevention and control [2008] OJ L24/8; Dir.2010/75 [2010] OJ L334/17.

which are listed in an annex I. It also covers large combustion plants, waste incineration and co-incineration installations and activities using organic solvents, finally also installations producing titanium dioxide; these activities were, until 2010, regulated in different specific directives. Directive 2010/75 is thus a real framework directive on industrial emissions. It entered into effect in 2013, though the entry into effect of several provisions was postponed until 2014, 2015 and even 2016.

4–41   For some time the Commission had also pursued the idea of a similar, though less stringent, directive for smaller industrial installations. In 1997, environmental ministers of Member States concluded that, from an environmental point of view, there was no reason to apply environmentally less stringent standards to small enterprises,[158] but it took the Commission until 2013 before it made, as a measure to fight climate change, a proposal for a directive on medium combustion plants.[159] This proposal is at present being discussed by the other institutions.

Despite its rather ambitious title, Directive 2010/75 essentially lays down framework rules for the national permitting systems with regard to large industrial installations. It provides that, as a rule, emission limit values are to be fixed in the individual permits. These permits must include emission limit values for pollutants which are likely to be emitted from the installation into water, air or land. The emission limit values "shall be based on the best available techniques". A technique is available when it is:

> "developed on a scale which allows implementation in the relevant industrial sector, under economically and technically viable conditions, taking into consideration the costs and advantages, whether or not the techniques are used or produced inside the Member State in question as long as they are reasonably accessible to the operator (art. 3(10))."

Thus, the best available technique depends also on economic considerations. Furthermore, the conditions in the permit on emissions into the environment may be less strict than according to the best available technique, and take into consideration the geographical location, the local environmental conditions and the technical characteristics of the installation concerned (art.15(4)).

4–42   The requirement to use the best available techniques does not exist for the emission of greenhouse gases, when the installation participates in the EU emission trading scheme (art.8); the reason for this is that it was considered that it was impossible to ask installations to use the best techniques and at the same time give them the possibility to buy rights for emitting more greenhouse gases than the best technique would allow. This provision is, though, not able to eliminate Member States' rights under art.193 TFEU to fix such emission limit values for

---

[158] President's conclusions, informal meeting of EU Environmental Ministers, Amsterdam, 18–20 April 1997, para.3: "Environmental requirements should be related to the nature and magnitude of environmental pollution and not to the size of the enterprise. Therefore, in principle similar requirements should apply to larger and smaller enterprises." The conclusions are not published. The reference is taken from M. Pallemaerts, *Production, Toxics and Transnational Law; An Inquiry into the Effectiveness of International and European Community Environmental Law* (Oxford, 2003), p.337.

[159] Commission COM(2013) 919. According to the Commission, that proposal covers some 143,000 installations.

greenhouse gases at national (or local) level or even in individual permits, as a directive cannot amend the TFEU.[160] Article 8 is thus mainly a policy concession.

In order to find the best available techniques, the Commission, under Directive 2010/75, has to organise an exchange of information with Member States, the industry sectors concerned, environmental organisations and the Commission. This exchange is to take place in a forum. The opinion of the forum shall be taken into account for the drafting of a "best available technique reference document" (BAT reference document) which shall contain, among others, emission limit values for the sector concerned (art.13).[161] Such documents—called BREFs (Best Available Technique Reference Documents)—are produced by a Bureau which is part of the Commission's Joint Research Centre and is based in Sevilla. Working groups, composed of experts from industry, administrations, research institutes and non-governmental organisations create the documents. At present, BREFs are produced only in English and are published on the internet. By the end of 2010, 35 BREFs had been produced for iron and steel, cement and lime, pulp and paper, non-ferrous metals, glass, textiles, tanning of hides and skins, refineries etc.

On the basis of the BAT reference document, a committee, composed of Member States and the Commission, decides the so-called "BAT conclusions"[162] which contain, among others, "the emission levels associated with the best available techniques" (art.3.12). The BAT conclusions adopted so far, are so general in nature that it is difficult to consider them legally binding. In any way, it appears that they are not enforced.

The fixing of binding emission limit values in the individual permit had led, under Directive 2008/1, to different emission limit values being fixed for the same type of industrial installation, according to its location, economic situation (costs and benefits) and other circumstances. The possibilities for the competent authorities in the Member States to deviate from BAT conclusions in this regard and fix less stringent requirements, have been made more difficult, but continue to exist. Therefore, the present situation will probably not change under Directive 2010/75. For example two cement kilns at a distance of five miles from each other, might still have different emission limit values fixed in their permits.[163] Also, the bargaining on less stringent conditions for emission limit values for the location of new installations is likely to increase, since the installations are able to threaten that they might look for another location with more favourable permit conditions. The words of Recital 3 of Directive 2010/75 that the chosen approach "will also contribute to the achievement of a level playing field in the Union by

4–43

---

[160] This opinion is, obviously, heavily contested.

[161] Article 11(6) of Dir.2010/75 provides that the BREF document shall be published after the adoption of BAT conclusions. This provision contradicts the provisions on access to environmental information, in particular those of the Aarhus Convention, see paras 4–09 et seq., above.

[162] See Commission Implementing Decisions on best available techniques; 2012/135 [2012] OJ L70/63 for emissions from the iron and steel production; 2013/84 [2013] OJ L45/13 for emissions from tanning of hides and skins; 2013/163 [2013] OJ L100/1 for emissions for cement, lime and magnesium oxides; 2013/732 [2013] OJ L332/34 for production of chlor-alkali; 2014/134 [2014] OJ L70/1 for emissions from the manufacture of glass; 2014/687 [2014] OJ L284/76 for the production of pulp, paper and board; 2014/738 [2014] OJ L307/38 for emissions from the refining of mineral oil and gas.

[163] For example, the air emission limit values for cement kilns, laid down in Dec.2013/163 [2013] OJ L100/1 go from 1 to 2.

aligning environmental performance requirements for industrial installations" are rather wishful thinking, as long as the different emission limit values are not fixed EU-wide.

Instead of fixing emission limit values for individual installations, Member States may also provide for "general binding rules", provided that the same results are achieved (arts 6 and 17). This possibility, which was inserted into the text at the request of Germany, is of limited assistance; indeed, competition among industrial installations within the European Union and its internal market is likely to be effective across national frontiers, not only within the individual Member States.

Member States must send to the Commission "representative data on emissions" and on emission values which were fixed (art.72); the frequency and other details of reporting are decided by comitology decision.[164] The Commission shall, every three years, submit a report on the implementation of the Directive which also assesses the need for setting minimum requirements for EU-wide emission limit values and is accompanied, "where appropriate", with a legislative proposal (art.73).

4-44 In 2006, the European Union set up a European Pollutant Release and Transfer Register[165] which requires Member States to report, for some 29,000 individual industrial installations, the emission of some 90 pollutants into the air and the water; releases to land and noise emissions are not part of the Register. The emission data are regularly published, though with considerable delay: the latest data which were available in early 2015 refer to 2012.[166] However, it seems that no consequences are drawn from the published data; in particular, environmental organisations, local authorities and individuals have not yet linked the available data on emissions to the (non-)use of the BAT by a specific installation, an approach which had been very successful in the United States.

To what extent Directive 2010/75 and its predecessors, 96/61 and 2008/1, will lead to a high level of protection of the environment as a whole, an objective which is announced several times in Directive 2010/75,[167] will have to be seen; since 1996, the date of adoption of Directive 96/61, progress was limited in this regard. It is to be welcomed that all installations covered by the Directive must have a permit and that this permit must fix emission limit values; also, the provisions of Directive 2010/75 have become significantly stricter than those of Directive 2008/1.

The Directive does not provide that there be at least a central register for all permits and the conditions fixed in these permits, although such a register would have been easy to set up in the computer age. Individuals or environmental organisations could themselves set up a register of permits and conditions, since the decision on a permit, the reasons for setting the emission limit values and a considerable number of other information must be made available to the public (art.24). The organisational capacity for such a private register appears, however, not to be available within environmental organisations or institutes.

---

[164] See Commission Implementing Dec.2012/119 on rules concerning guidance on the collection of data [2012] OJ L63/1.

[165] Regulation 166/2006 concerning the establishment of a European Pollutant Release and Transfer Register [2006] OJ L33/1.

[166] See *http://prtr.ec.europa.eu* [Accessed 3 August 2015].

[167] See, e.g. Dir.2010/75 [2010] OJ L334/17, arts 1, 3(10), 15(4) and 73.

In 2005, the Commission published a first, and in 2010 a second, implementation report regarding Directive 96/61–2008/1.[168] It reported that some 50,000 installations came under the Directive. Member States had been late—as usual—in transposing Directive 96/61 into national law[169]; furthermore, the Commission had initiated infringement action under art.258 TFEU against 16 Member States for incorrect transposition of the Directive. The same situation was repeated, when, in October 2007, Directive 96/61 became applicable to existing installations: the Commission started legal action against Belgium, Denmark, Estonia, Greece, Spain, Italy, Lithuania, Malta, Portugal, Slovenia, Austria, France, Ireland and Sweden; by the end of 2010, action against Lithuania and Estonia continued.[170] Generally, the Commission stated that more than half of all permits were not sufficiently based on BAT. The Commission proposal to replace Directive 96/61–2008/1 with a new directive—which later was adopted as Directive 2010/75—was made at the end of 2007,[171] thus before any experience was available with permits for existing installations. No implementation report exists as yet for Directive 2010/75.

4–45

(c) Individual industrial sectors

At the launch of EU environmental policy in the 1970s, there was a general consensus on the necessity of regulating environmental emissions from specific industrial installations.[172] Although the general usefulness of this concept was confirmed in 1987,[173] it did not lead to many concrete results.

4–46

Titanium dioxide (TiO$_2$).   In 1978, the Council adopted Directive 78/176 on waste from the titanium dioxide industry[174] which was followed by a directive on monitoring of TiO$_2$ installations[175] and another one on the uniform reduction of waste discharges from such installations.[176] The origins of these Directives go back to discharges of waste in the early 1970s, from a Montedison factory at

---

[168] Commission, COM(2005) 540; COM(2010) 593.

[169] Spain, United Kingdom and Greece were found of not having transposed the Directive in time, see Court of Justice, *Commission v Spain* (C-29/01) [2002] E.C.R. I-2503; *Commission v United Kingdom* (C-3901) [2002] E.C.R. I-2513; *Commission v Greece* (C-64/01) [2002] E.C.R. I-2523. Austria was found to have incorrectly transposed the Directive, *Commission v Austria* (C-78/04), ECLI:EU:C:2004:735. See also *Commission v Belgium* (C-258/09) ECLI:EU:C:2010:122; *Commission v Greece* (C-534/09) ECLI:EU:C:2010:735; *Commission v Slovenia* (C-48/10) ECLI:EU:C:2010:704; *Commisison v Spain* (C-49/10) ECLI:EU:C:597; *Commission v Italy*(C-50/10) ECLI:EU:C:2011:200; *Commission v Sweden* (C-607/10) ECLI:EU:C:2012:192; *Commission v Austria* (C-352/11) ECLI:EO:C: 2012:315; *Commission v Ireland* (C-158/12) ECLI:EU:C: 2013:234; *Commission v Sweden* (C-243/13) ECLI:EU:C:2014:2413.

[170] Commission, COM(2010) 593, p.3.

[171] Commission, COM(2007) 843.

[172] See 1st Environment Action Programme [1973] OJ C112/1, p.20, where measures for the paper and pulp industry, the iron and steel industry and the manufacture of TiO$_2$ are announced and measures for the chemical, leather, food and textile industry are envisaged.

[173] See 4th Environment Action Programme [1987] OJ C328/1, no.3.4.

[174] Directive 78/176 on waste from the titanium dioxide industry [1978] OJ L54/19.

[175] Directive 82/883 on procedures for the surveillance and monitoring of environments concerned by waste from the titanium dioxide industry [1982] OJ L378/1.

[176] Directive 92/112 on procedures for harmonising the programmes for the reduction and eventual elimination of pollution caused by waste from the titanium dioxide industry [1992] OJ L409/11. This Directive took nine years between its proposal and adoption.

Scarlino (Italy) into Mediterranean waters, which caused concern in Corsica and led to discords between Italy and France.

The Directive's main aim was the progressive reduction of pollution caused by waste from the TiO_2 industry. The manufacture of TiO_2 which is a white pigment used principally in paints, normally results in a larger quantity of waste than of the product.

4-47   The implementation of the different Directives raised problems and was poorly monitored by the Commission. The Commission was incapable of checking the actual discharges, and soon abandoned the attempts to have regular national reports and an EU-wide horizontal report on waste from the TiO_2 industry. The progressive reduction of the discharge of TiO_2 waste into sea and coastal waters was influenced more by debate from international conventions, the North Sea conferences and in particular by the technological possibility of recycling TiO_2 waste which has progressively developed over the past 20 years.

In 2010, the provisions of the three Directives were incorporated into Directive 2010/75. TiO_2-producing installations need a permit, but are not obliged to apply the best available technique. Instead, the discharge of solid waste into waters was prohibited, and limit values were fixed for air and water emissions. These emission limit values differentiate according to the technical process being used (sulfate or chloride process), a clear sign that the economic concerns prevail, not the environmental concerns.

Other industrial sectors.   In 1975, the Commission submitted a proposal for a Directive on the reduction of water pollution caused by wood pulp mills.[177] The proposal limited itself to proposing emission limit values for some pollutants. Since the United Kingdom and some other Member States were opposed to the fixing of EU-wide limit values for emissions into the environment, the proposal was not discussed in Council and has in the meantime become obsolete. A Commission announcement on a Directive concerning environmental pollution by the paper industry was not followed by concrete action.[178]

4-48   The sector-oriented approach was partly used with the adoption of "daughter" directives for Directive 76/464,[179] such as discharges by the chlor-alkali electrolysis industry. However, these Directives all provided for quality objectives next to emission limit values, thus leaving it to Member States not to follow the sector-oriented approach. Since 1991, legislative initiatives for "daughter" directives under Directive 76/464 were stopped.

In other parts of environmental policy, indications of sectoral approaches were found in air pollution, where legislation on large combustion plants was adopted in 1988 and confirmed in 2001.[180] It is noticeable that the 2001 Directive repeated emission reduction targets for 1998 and 2003 which were thus already outdated when the Directive entered into effect; the reason for this erroneous approach was the objection in particular by France, to have new targets fixed for

---

[177] [1975] OJ C99/2.

[178] See Written Questions 1491/91 (Van Hemeldonck) [1992] OJ C242/4 and E-2849/95 (De Coene) [1995] OJ C109/11.

[179] See, e.g. Dir.82/176 on limit values and quality objectives for mercury discharges by the clor-alkali electrolysis industry [1982] OJ L81/29.

[180] Directive 1988/609 [1988] OJ L336/1; Dir.2001/80 on large combustion plants [2001] OJ L309/1; see also para.8-20, below.

large combustion plants. France rather preferred to see such plants also coming under the system of Directive 2008/1 which required "best techniques" instead of precise emission targets. In 2010, the provisions on large combustion plants were incorporated into Directive 2010/75. Emission limit values for sulphur dioxide, nitrogen oxides, carbon monoxide and dust were maintained, according to the type of installation and the fuel used. Very extensive transition periods and derogations were fixed, also, for installations which used indigenous coal or fuel and could, therefore, not respect the emission limit values.

Emissions from waste incinerators were originally grouped in several directives, later placed in one piece of legislation, as the objective was to limit the emissions into air and water, whether they came from installations for municipal or for hazardous waste.[181] In 2010, these provisions were incorporated into Directive 2010/75. Waste incinerators and co-incineration installations need a permit. Directive 2010/75 maintained the system of emission limit values for such installations. A permit is also required for waste disposal facilities.[182]

Safety measures for nuclear installations that come under the Euratom Treaty, are regulated by Decision 99/319/Euratom, by which the European Union adhered to the international Convention on nuclear safety, and Directive 2009/71.[183] While Recital 3 of Directive 2009/71 recognises that the provisions of arts 31 and 32 Euratom Treaty, on which the Directive was based, aim at protecting workers, the general public *and the environment* against risks of nuclear installations, there was not one single provision in the Directive which concerned the protection of the environment. Generally, the Directive remained extremely general. It asked Member States to ensure a high level of nuclear safety, recognising that Member States had already done so to a very large extent. No provisions on the participation of the public in the authorisation of nuclear installations was foreseen. No measures on accident prevention—for example on the model of Directive 96/82 (now Directive 2012/18), providing for internal and external emergency plans—were foreseen. The only concrete measure introduced was the requirement to set up a competent national authority which was responsible for nuclear safety of installations—a measure which all Member States that had nuclear installations, had already put in place. Member States were responsible for ensuring a high level of safety of nuclear installations, but the Directive underlined that the primary responsibility in this regard rested with the licence holders. The added value of this Directive to nuclear safety is not easily seen.

Following the nuclear accident in Fukushima (Japan) in 2011, Directive 2009/71 was amended, as a stress test had revealed that necessary safety measures had not been implemented over the years.[184] The new Directive provides for an effective independence of the regulatory authority and a functional separation of its tasks from that of any other nuclear or energy-related authority (art.5). The safety of nuclear installations shall constantly be improved,

4–49

---

[181] Directive 89/369 [1989] OJ L163/32; Dir.89/429 [1989] OJ L203/50; Dir.94/63 [1994] OJ L365/24; Dir.2000/76 on waste incinerators [2000] OJ L322/91; see also para.8–28, below.
[182] Directive 1999/31 on the landfill of waste [1999] OJ L182/1.
[183] Commission Dec.99/318/Euratom [1999] OJ L318/20; the Convention is published on p.21; Dir.2009/71/Euratom establishing a Community framework for the nuclear safety of nuclear installations [2009] OJ L172/18.
[184] Directive 2014/87 Euratom [2014] OJ L317/35.

when this is "reasonably possible" (art.6). At least every 10 years, the national regulatory frame shall undergo an international peer review. The statement in Recital 5 of the Directive that decisions on nuclear safety are exclusively a national responsibility, appears wrong, in view of the considerable transboundary impact on humans and the environment which a nuclear accident within the European Union would have.

Unless there is a new policy approach, the sector-oriented approach can now be considered to be no longer pursued as a central part of EU environmental policy. The trend rather goes in the direction of fixing permit requirements, asking for the use of BATs and fixing, where unavoidable, emission limit values at EU level. This does not exclude that specific activities are regulated by way of fine-tuned provisions, in particular to make a specific technology more acceptable to the public. Examples of this approach were safety measures for mining activities which were regulated in Directive 2006/21, after several severe environmental accidents had occurred in the European Union.[185] Another example is a directive on carbon capture and storage which was adopted in the context of the EU climate change policy and had the objective to promote this technology for coal-fired and other conventional power plants.[186]

4–50   Also to be mentioned is Directive 2013/30 on offshore gas and oil extraction[187] which was adopted following a serious accident of the oil platform *Deep Horizon* in the Gulf of Mexico. The main content of the Directive deals with the prevention of accidents; emissions and discharges are not dealt with in detail. The Directive requires an authorisation for the activities which it covers. These activities shall be controlled by independent verifiers. The European Agency for Maritime Safety shall assist the Commission in monitoring the activities. The Directive will enter into effect in 2016.

No legislative measures have yet been taken on gas or oil pipelines.

Asbestos.   Asbestos was the subject of EU legislation since the early 1980s which, based on the present art.114 TFEU, restricted the use of a large number of asbestos fibres which are classified as carcinogens. Though several Member States decided on a total ban on asbestos fibres, the Commission did not take action against them. Instead, it prepared for a larger ban at EU level which was finally adopted in 1999.[188] As regards asbestos which is already on the market and in the environment, Directive 87/217 tried to establish integrated provisions.[189] Member States must use the best available technology not entailing excessive costs and take general measures to reduce asbestos emissions into the air—where a general emission limit value of 0.1mg per cubic metre is fixed—and the water; here, a complete recycling of waste water is required, unless this is "economically not practicable", which makes this provision unenforceable. Measures shall also be taken during the demolition of asbestos-containing

---

[185] Directive 2006/21 on the management of waste from the extracting industries [2006] OJ L102/15 (see also para.10–61, below).
[186] Directive 2009/31 on the geological storage of carbon dioxide [2009] OJ L140/114 (see para.9–22, below).
[187] Directive 2013/30 [2013] OJ L178/66.
[188] Directive 1999/77 on asbestos [1999] OJ L207/18.
[189] Directive 87/217 on the prevention and reduction of environmental pollution by asbestos [1987] OJ L85/40.

buildings and transport as well as at the disposal. The Directive's loose drafting and the absence of constant monitoring of its application in and by Member States means that, as a consequence, its real impact is limited.

(d) Environmental auditing

In 1993 and after a rather short discussion, the Council adopted a Regulation which established a voluntary system of eco-auditing for industrial installations.[190] In 2001 and 2009, the system was revised and also opened to any form of organisation, such as administrations, universities, funds, etc which wishes to improve its environmental performance (EMAS).[191] An organisation that intends to participate in the scheme for its sites—one site at a time or all together—must establish an environmental policy for that site which must provide for the respect of all existing environmental provisions and a continuous improvement of the environmental performance. The site must then be submitted to an environmental review which concerns the environmental conditions such as water and energy use or waste treatment. The organisation then has to develop an environmental programme for all its activities on the site in order to reach its policy objectives and must ensure that at management level the necessary measures are taken to realise the programme. The site shall be audited, either by auditors belonging to the organisation or by external auditors.

    4–51

The organisation finally has to report (environmental statement) on its activity, its policy programme, strategy and management system. This report is validated by an independent, accredited verifier and published; following that, the site is listed on a register. The organisation is allowed to inform, in its correspondence and papers—though not on products, product advertising or packaging—of its participation in the EMAS scheme.

Although participation in the scheme is voluntary, an organisation which decides to join in must comply with all the requirements of EMAS. The EMAS scheme is at present operational in all Member States. In March 2015, some 4,500 organisations with more than 8,100 sites—mostly of industrial installations, as the system, until 2001, was open only to industrial installations—were registered.

About 40 per cent of all organisations are small and medium-sized companies, though the costs of participation are sometimes significant. A plan to have less stringent requirements for small companies is not being pursued. For the participating organisation, there are clear advantages in participation, in particular better motivation of the personnel and improved competitiveness and, generally, better environmental performance. Furthermore, credit institutes and insurance companies have started to make their intervention dependent on the existence of an auditing scheme. Some governments of Member States started to adapt their control system of companies to whether or not they take part in EMAS, or to relieve them from reporting or other obligations.[192]

    4–52

---

[190] Regulation 1836/93 allowing voluntary participation by companies in the industrial sector in a Community eco-management and audit system [1993] OJ L168/1.

[191] Regulation 761/2001 [2001] OJ L114/1; Reg.1221/2009 on the voluntary participation by organisations in a Community eco-management and audit scheme [2009] OJ L342/1.

[192] See also Commission, SEC(2010) 59 on incentives for EMAS registered organisations.

At international level, EMAS is competing with ISO 14001:2004, an Environmental Management Standard, developed in 1996 by the International Standardisation Organisation (ISO). This voluntary standard differs from EMAS in particular in that it applies worldwide, that it is open to the participation of all economic sectors—the EMAS revision of 2001 eliminated this difference—and also refers to products, not only to sites. Furthermore, there is no necessity for an organisation to comply with all environmental legislation, a requirement that exists under EMAS. EMAS also requests the registration of companies or organisations by public authorities, provides for a strong involvement of the employees, contains stricter requirements on the measurement and evaluation of the environmental performance, asks for continuous improvement of such performance, and allows multi-annual comparability within and between organisations. Finally, the publication of an environmental statement is not necessary; the organisation need not respect transparency as regards its environmental performance.

The Commission recognised some elements of ISO 14001 to be equivalent to EMAS.[193] Thus, an organisation may use ISO 14001 as a first step towards adherence to EMAS and thereby avoid duplication of work.

4–53   Generally, EMAS is seen as an effective tool where an organisation tries to improve its environmental performance; its impact on the competitiveness of companies appears limited. Companies which adhere to the system sometimes feel, though, that their efforts are not sufficiently rewarded by the EMAS-system, for instance by a sort of rebate during the permitting or operating process. As the ISO-system is less ambitious, less demanding, but also less expensive and less exposing, but almost as capable as EMAS to be used for image purposes, the ISO system is favoured by economic operators.

(e)   Accident prevention

4–54   In 1976, a serious industrial accident occurred in Seveso (Italy), where dioxin was emitted into the air; some 600 people had to be evacuated from their homes and about 2,000 were treated for dioxin poisoning. Subsequently, the European Union drew up and adopted, in 1982, a directive on accident prevention from industrial installations.[194] Following two major accidents in Bhopal (India—1984), where more than 2,500 people were killed and Basel (Switzerland—1986), where a massive pollution of the Rhine occurred, this Directive was amended twice in 1987 and 1988.[195] A complete revision took place in the early 1990s; this led to the replacement of Directive 82/501[196] by Directive 96/82.[197] In 2012, a new Directive on accident prevention was adopted (Seveso III).[198]

The structure and concept of Directive 82/501 were largely maintained. Directive 2012/18 aims at preventing major industrial accidents which involve dangerous chemicals, and at limiting the consequences of such accidents. It

---

[193] Commission Dec.97/265 [1997] OJ L104/37.
[194] Directive 82/501 on the major accident hazards of certain industrial installations [1982] OJ L230/1.
[195] Directive 87/216 [1987] OJ L85/36; Dir.88/610 [1988] OJ L336/14.
[196] Directive 87/216 [1987] OJ L85/36; Dir.88/610 [1988] OJ L336/14.
[197] Directive 96/82 [1997] OJ L10/13.
[198] Directive 2012/18 [2012] OJ L197/1.

concerns installations where dangerous chemicals are present in quantities that are laid down in an annex. The operator of the installation has to produce a safety report which gives details of the establishment, the dangerous chemicals present, major risks for accidents and the management systems which are available. This last requirement is justified by the fact that "analysis of the major accidents reported in the EU indicates that the majority of them are the result of managerial and/or organisational shortcomings".

Establishments must furthermore have an internal emergency plan and must inform the public authorities in such a way that the public authorities are able to draw up an external emergency plan. Persons inside and outside the installation who are likely to be affected by an accident must be informed of the safety measures and of the requisite behaviour in the event of an accident. After an accident, the operator has to provide comprehensive information to the authorities on the accident and on the measures taken to prevent recurrence.

Directive 2012/18 provides for detailed rules on the inspection of the establishments by competent authorities, which is a rather innovative provision in environmental law. Also, it introduced national and EU reporting provisions, which did not exist before. **4–55**

In 1995 a report on the 10-year-functioning of Directive 82/501 was published which reported a total of 178 accidents that had been notified to the Commission between 1984 and 1993. Furthermore, between 2000 and 2008, Member States reported 245 major accidents; the study estimated that 50 to 80 major accidents occurred annually in the European Union. The European Environment Agency reported 339 major accidents between 1998 and 2009 in Europe, and quoted a figure of about 28 such accidents per year.[199]

The Directive, which affects about 4,500 installations, does not cover pipelines, which have an estimated length of some 150,000km for gas transmission, 35,000km for oil and 10,000km for chemicals. It also does not cover: transport activities; military establishments; hazards created by ionising radiation[200]; mines; quarries; boreholes; and landfills. Since the Directive is based on art.192 TFEU, Member States are of course free to extend its application to such installations, but did not make use of that possibility. Following spectacular accidents linked to mining activities in Aznalcollar (Spain—1988) and Baia Mare (Romania—2000), the Directive was amended in order to have risks arising from storage and processing activities in mining included in its scope of application.[201]

Overall, the system which was set up by Directive 82/501 and was improved and fine-tuned by Directive 2012/18 seems to work well, though it is obviously not possible to assess the exact impact of the prevention measures. The EU accident prevention scheme, set up by the Directives, was taken over by a number of third countries and was at the origin of the International Convention of **4–56**

---

[199] K. Rasmussen, *The Experience with the Major Accident Reporting System from 1984 to 1993* (Luxembourg, 1995); see also C. Kirchsteiger (ed.), *Lessons Learnt from Accidents* (EUR 17733), (Ispra, 1998); European Environment Agency, *Mapping the Impacts of Natural Hazards and Technological Accidents in Europe*, Technical Report 13/2010 (Copenhagen, 2010); Commission, C (2010) 5422. The different figures are not really comparable.

[200] This clause means that nuclear installations which process dangerous chemicals are covered by the Directive.

[201] Directive 2003/105 [2003] OJ L345/97.

Transboundary Effects of Industrial Accidents of 1992 to which the European Union and its Member States adhered.[202]

The prevention of accidents was also the main objective of Directive 2013/30 on offshore gas and oil activities which was adopted after the accident in 2010 in the Gulf of Mexico.[203] In contrast, a Commission announcement of an accident prevention initiative for nuclear installations, made shortly after the nuclear accident in Chernobyl,[204] was not followed by action after the Fukushima accident of 2011.

5. ENVIRONMENTAL LIABILITY

4–57   The efforts of the European Union to tackle issues on environmental liability took about 30 years to mature. As regards damaged caused by waste, the Commission submitted proposals in 1976, 1983 and 1989,[205] but none of these proposals was adopted. Whether damage caused by waste comes under Directive 85/374 on product liability,[206] is doubtful. In my opinion, this is the case, as waste material is also deliberately "produced" and put into circulation. Regulation 2027/97 concerns the liability of air companies in cases of accidents, but only deals with personal injury and economic loss, not with environmental damage.[207]

Subsequent to the Sandoz accident in Basel (Switzerland) in 1986, the Council asked the Commission to consider whether it was appropriate to introduce an EU system on environmental liability. In pursuance thereof, the Commission submitted, in 1993, a Green Paper on environmental liability.[208] The European Parliament organised a hearing on the Green Paper and then asked, under art.225 TFEU, for the drawing up of a proposal for a Directive.[209] In 2000, the Commission published a White Paper on the question, with options for future legislation.[210] In 2002, the Commission made a proposal for a directive on "environmental liability with regard to the prevention and remedying environmental damage" which the Council and Parliament adopted in 2004, 10 days before the accession of 10 new Member States to the European Union. The Directive became effective on 30 April 2007 and only concerns damage which was caused after that date.[211]

The Directive constitutes a relatively drastic departure from the classical concept of environmental liability including from the Commission's White Paper. Indeed, while liability normally parts from the idea that a person suffers bodily

---

[202] Decision 98/685 [1998] OJ L326/1.

[203] Directive 2013/30 [2013] OJ L178/66.

[204] 4th Environment Action Programme [1987] OJ C328/1, paras 4.3.8 and 4.6.4.

[205] Commission [1976] OJ C194/2; [1983] OJ C186/3; [1989] OJ C251/3, amended [1991] OJ C192/6.

[206] Directive 85/374 on the approximation of laws, regulations and administrative provisions of the Member States concerning liability for defective products [1985] OJ L210/29; amended by Dir.1999/34 [1999] OJ L141/20.

[207] Regulation 2027/97 on liability of air companies in case of accidents [1997] OJ L285/1.

[208] Commission, Green Book on remedying environmental damage [1993] OJ C149/12.

[209] European Parliament [1994] OJ C149/6.

[210] Commission, White Paper on environmental liability, COM(2000) 66.

[211] Directive 2004/35 on environmental liability with regard to the prevention and remedying of environmental damage [2004] OJ L143/56.

injury or economic damage which he tries to get compensated from the wrongdoer by way of a civil law action, the Directive does not deal with this civil law damage, but leaves legislation on this "traditional damage" (Recital 11) to Member States' law: "This Directive does not apply to cases of personal injury, to damage to private property or to any economic loss and does not affect any right regarding these types of damages" (Recital 14, see also art.3(3)).

The Directive rather deals with environmental damage.[212] Where such damage occurs, it is the public authorities which shall ensure the restoration of the environment. The Commission's proposal had placed the task of restoration on the public authorities, starting from the concept that the environment is a public, not a private interest good; and as the public authorities were mandated to protect, preserve and improve the quality of the environment, the primary task to restore the impaired environment should be incumbent on them.[213] However, the Council did not like this suggestion and amended it. The final text invokes at several occasions the polluter-pays principle and places the obligation of restoration on the polluter (art.8). Where the public authorities voluntarily restore the environment without having an obligation to do so, they may ask for compensation of the money which they extended, from the polluter; however, where the polluter does not pay, because he has gone out of business, is insolvent or cannot be identified, there is no obligation on the public authorities, contrary to the Commission's proposal. This means that in such cases it is likely that the environment is not restored.

4–58

The Directive's concept needs, of course, a number of qualifications, as environmental impairment is ubiquitous. The following limitations to the obligation of restoration were introduced:

1. No environmental impairment is to be restored, but only damage which is expressly mentioned in the Directive[214]; air pollution was excluded as air contamination sooner or later leads to depositions on the ground— acidification of the soil, fauna and flora damage etc (Recital 4). Also, the most serious environmental accidents of the past—nuclear accidents and marine pollution by hydrocarbons from tanker accidents—were excluded from the Directive, with the argument that international conventions covered these aspects. However, the international conventions do not provide for restoration of the impaired environment; also the sums which are available under their systems are not sufficient. Damage caused by

---

[212] Note that in continental Europe, "damage" normally supposes that there is a damaged person; it is thus considered to be a civil law notion.

[213] Directive 2004/35 [2004] OJ L143/56, art.2(1): "'environmental damage' means: (a) damage to protected species which is any damage that has significant adverse effects on reaching or maintaining the favourable conservation status of such habitats or species ...; (b) water damage, which is any damage that significantly adversely affects the ecological, chemical and/or quantitative status and/or ecological potential, as defined in Directive 2000/60/EC ...; (c) land damage which is any land contamination that creates a significant risk to human health being adversely affected as a result of the direct or indirect introduction, in, on or under land, of substances, preparations, organisms or micro-organisms. 'Damage' means a measurable adverse change in the natural resource or measurable impairment of a natural resource service which may occur directly or indirectly."

[214] Directive 2004/35 [2004] OJ L143/56, art.4(5): "This Directive shall apply only to environmental damage or to an imminent threat of such damage caused by pollution of a diffuse character, where it is possible to establish a causal link between the damage and the activities of individual operators."

genetically modified products such as seeds, is also included, because the concept starts from the impaired environment, and the deliberate release of GMOs is expressly mentioned as one of the sources of pollution (annex III, no.11).

2. Diffuse pollution, that means pollution caused by a multiplicity of polluting sources is excluded. Indeed, this diffuse pollution is everywhere and it was considered that an inclusion of such pollution would overcharge the public authorities' budgets, all the more as recourse against a specific polluter would not be possible.

3. The implementing legislation of Member States shall decide whether polluters who comply with the conditions laid down in a permit shall be liable to compensate public authorities for the restoration of the environment or not.[215] Such a clause would practically introduce polluters' liability for negligence, as exceeding the conditions of a permit is normally due to a deliberate or negligent action.

4. Member States shall also decide whether they allow the defence for development risks which intend to limit economic operators' risk in areas of new technologies, in particular for damage caused by biotechnology products.[216]

5. Finally, it is up to Member States to decide whether they provide for compulsory insurance in the cases covered by the Directive or not (art.14). Member States were not able to agree on a solution for or against such compulsory insurance.

Leaving aside the difference of opinions among Member States and the heavy opposition of economic operators to any liability system, the concept of compensating for environmental damage seems too far removed from environmental needs. In short, the environment is sick, rather than suffering from specific punctual accidents, pollutions or catastrophes. The liability concept which stems from compensating for physical injury and was extended to economic loss, and later to damages for pain and suffering, only adapts with difficulty to the progressive deterioration, legalised contamination and the disappearance of species.

4–59 This is the reason why, until now, national environmental liability legislation had only limited success. The Directive's approach to set up a system which places the restoration of environmental damage in the centre, is a step in the right direction. The future will show whether this direction will be pursued: as neither the environment nor future generations have a lobby or a voice, realism rather

---

[215] Directive 2004/35 [2004] OJ L143/56, art.8(4.a): "The Member States may allow the operator not to bear the cost of remedial actions taken pursuant to this Directive where he demonstrates that he was not at fault or negligent and that the environmental damage was caused by: (a) an emission or event expressly authorised by, and fully in accordance with the conditions of, an authorisation conferred by or given under applicable national laws."

[216] Directive 2004/35 [2004] OJ L143/56, art.8(4.b): "The Member States may allow the operator not to bear the cost of remedial actions ... where he proves ... that the damage was caused by: (b) an emission or activity or any manner of using a product in the course of an activity which the operator demonstrates was not considered likely to cause environmental damage according to the state of scientific and technical knowledge at the time when the emission was released or the activity took place."

than optimism with regard to the effective benefit to the environment—and this is, finally, the objective of environmental legislation—is appropriate.

The Directive enumerates in an annex III those operational activities, the operator of which may be held strictly liable if they cause environmental damage. This annex lists a number of—mainly dangerous—activities which are regulated by EU directives and regulations. As the EU legislation covers in particular large installations, many small or medium-sized companies do not come under the scope of application of Directive 2004/35, unless they act negligently, as the Directive includes liability for negligent actions (art.3(1.b)).

The Directive does not cover oil pollution damage or damage caused by the transport of dangerous substances by sea or inland waterways which are in force in the Member State concerned (art.4(2) and annex IV) and does not cover nuclear damage either (art.4(4) and annex V).

The overall impression of the Directive is that it has a rather limited field of application.[217] It aims more at the restoration of the environment after an industrial accident—with the exception of the most important cases, oil transport and nuclear accidents—than of restoring the damaged environment, despite the fact that the environment does not suffer mainly from accidents, but from the fact that it is sick. The Directive's actual application therefore risks being rather limited. The numerous exemptions, possibilities for Member States to provide for national different provisions and the absence of regulating the burden of proof—this works in favour of the polluter—make it a directive which does not lead to some sort of unified or harmonised system in the European Union. **4–60**

There are a number of efforts at international level to introduce liability for environmental damage which, however, essentially concern traditional damage (physical damage and economic loss). These efforts concern in particular:

- A Protocol under the Basel Convention on the shipment of hazardous waste. This Protocol was elaborated in 1999–2000 and covers personal injury and economic loss caused by hazardous waste. The European Union adhered to the Basel Convention, but has not yet signed the Protocol.
- A Protocol, signed in Spring 2002 under two international conventions which deals with liability that is caused by industrial accidents in international watercourses. The Protocol covers traditional damage and, in supplement, the restoration of the impaired environment. The European Union did not sign the Protocol, as it is not yet clear, how the dividing line between this Protocol and Directive 2004/35 on environmental liability will be drawn.
- A Protocol on damage caused by GMOs, adopted in 2010 under the Cartagena Protocol on Biological Safety.[218] The Protocol applies to damage "resulting from living [genetically] modified organisms which find their origin in a transboundary movement". It requests a link of causation between the damage and the wrongful act, but otherwise provides for strict liability. The European Union has not yet adhered to this Protocol.

---

[217] See also Court of Justice, *ERG* (joined cases C-378/09 and C-379/09) [2010] E.C.R I-1919; *Fipa Group*(C-534/13) ECLI:EU:C:2015:140. In both cases, the Directive was held to be inapplicable.
[218] Nagoya-Kuala Lumpur Supplementary Protocol on Liability and Redress to the Cartagena Protocol on Biosafety, adopted on 15 October 2010 in Nagoya (Japan).

6.   TAXES AND CHARGES

4–61 Already, the 1st Environment Action Programme of 1973 pleaded in favour of economic instruments in the shaping of environmental policy.[219] Subsequent programmes repeated the usefulness of developing economic instruments and the 4th Environment Action Programme was the first to mention that, besides legal "command and control" provisions taxes, charges and tradable pollution permits could also be an appropriate instrument for improving or preserving the quality of the environment from GMOs.[220] In order to combat climate change, the Commission submitted a proposal in 1991 for the EC-wide introduction of a combined CO_2 energy tax.[221] The proposal was based on art.93 and 175(2) EC (now arts 113 and 192(2) TFEU), which both require unanimous decisions in Council. This unanimity could not be reached since a number of Member States, in particular the United Kingdom, opposed for principal reasons the adoption of provisions on taxes and charges at EU level. The Commission therefore amended its proposal in the sense that Member States remained free to decide whether they wanted to introduce a CO_2 energy tax; where they so decided, they had to comply with certain conditions fixed in the proposal.[222] This proposal, which again required unanimous adoption in Council, was not adopted either. It is now outdated, though reflections on the introduction of fiscal measures at EU level continue in the context of the discussions on climate change.

In view of the obvious difficulties linked with this proposal, the Commission has not made other proposals for the introduction of an eco-tax. Scattered in directives or regulations there exist references that taxes or charges will be fixed at EU level[223]; however, such provisions neither introduce such taxes nor do they have any other legal effect or restrict the possibility of Member States to decide on their own whether to introduce eco-taxes or charges.

Taxes and charges play a considerable role in the environmental policy of Member States. Since they aim to influence, via pricing, the economic behaviour of economic operators and others, their competitiveness and market position, the European Union cannot remain unconcerned about developments at national level. Therefore, EU measures with regard to national eco-taxes try to limit their use, in order to avoid their influence on the circulation of goods.

4–62 The most obvious example of attempts to limit national tax initiatives are the provisions in the car sector. When the catalytic converter for cars was introduced, the Netherlands and Germany in particular considered encouraging the introduction of cars with catalytic converters by means of tax incentives. The

---

[219] 1st Environment Action Programme [1973] OJ C112/1, p.31: "careful analysis should be made of the economic instruments which can be used in the context of an environmental policy, their various functions, the advantages and drawbacks of using them, their relative effectiveness with regard to the objectives in view and their compatibility with the rules of cost allocation."

[220] 4th Environment Action Programme [1987] OJ C328/1, no.2.5.1.

[221] [1992] OJ C196/1.

[222] Commission, COM(95) 172.

[223] See, e.g. Dir.94/62 on packaging and packaging waste [1994] OJ L365/10, art.15: "Acting on the basis of the relevant provisions of the Treaty, the Council adopts economic instruments to promote the implementation of the objectives set by this Directive. In the absence of such measures, the Member States may, in accordance with the principles governing Community environmental policy, inter alia, the polluter-pays principle, and the obligations arising out of the Treaty, adopt measures to implement those objectives."

objection of other Member States that were afraid of a competitive disadvantage finally led to a provision which has since become standard for car emission directives[224]:

"Member States may make provision for tax incentives for the vehicles covered in this Directive. Such incentives shall meet the provisions of the Treaty as well as the following conditions:
they shall apply to all domestic car production and to vehicles imported for marketing in a Member State and fitted with the equipment allowing the European standards to be met in 1992 to be satisfied ahead of time; they shall cease upon the date set in Article 2(3) for the compulsory entry into force of the emission values for new vehicles;
they shall be of value, for each type of vehicle, substantially lower than the actual cost of the equipment fitted to meet the values set and of its fitting on the vehicle."

In 2005, the Commission made a proposal for a directive to restructure car taxes on the basis of the annual circulation of the car, in order to make passenger car taxes more CO_2-efficient.[225] This proposal which was based on art.113 TFEU and therefore required unanimity for its adoption, would abolish the registration tax for cars and increase instead the circulation taxes; these would take into account the CO_2-emissions from cars. As by the end of 2014 the Council had not adopted this proposal, the Commission withdrew it in 2015.

Another example for the interplay between national and EU rules is that of Directive 2003/96 which replaced Directive 92/81.[226] This Directive, based on art.113 TFEU, introduced a minimum rate of taxation on electricity and energy products. The minimum rates are differentiated according to the use of the products. As the Directive required unanimity, it contains a long list of possibilities for Member States to apply reduced rates for specific uses; and Member States may exempt electricity produced from alternative energies altogether. The Directive prolonged the possibility for 11 of the then 15 Member States—except Sweden Denmark, Greece and Netherlands—to apply reduced tax rates for the use of waste oils in production installations such as cement kilns or steel or power plants, though such a practice openly contradicted the requirements of Directive 75/439[227] which imposed a priority for the regeneration (recycling) of waste oils. However, in the past, the Commission did not take action against the national fiscal practices. In order to ensure consistency of EU law, Directive 75/439 was repealed altogether—to the advantage of economic operators, but to the detriment of the environment.[228]

A typical example of the approach to taxes and charges is to be found in the **4–63** Water Framework Directive.[229] It provides in art. 9 that "Member States shall take account of the principle of recovery of the costs of water services, including environmental and resource costs". However, it then continues: "Member States

---

[224] Text from Dir.89/458 [1989] OJ L226/1 art.3.

[225] Commission, COM(2005) 261.

[226] Directive 2003/96 restructuring the Community framework for the taxation of energy products and electricity [2003] OJ L283/51, replacing Dir.92/81 on the harmonisation of the structures of excise duties on mineral oils [1992] OJ L316/12.

[227] Directive 75/439 on used oils [1975] OJ L194/31; amended by Dir.87/101 [1987] OJ L42/43.

[228] Directive 2008/98 on waste [2008] OJ L312/3.

[229] Directive 2000/60 establishing a framework for Community action in the field of water policy [2000] OJ L327/1.

in so doing have regard to the social, environmental and economic effects of the recovery as well as the geographic and climatic conditions of the region or regions affected." This means in clear terms that Member States should provide for rules according to which the user of water shall pay for that use. However, the added phrase allows every Member State to maintain its system of water charges, with the argument that social, environmental and economic considerations as well the geographical situation of the affected regions so require.

A Commission communication of 1997 tried to determine generally the limits for "environmental taxes and charges in the Single Market".[230] Recommendations for optimising environmental taxes and charges were not given, probably because there are also diverging opinions within the Commission.

In the context of the European Union's climate change and energy policy, considerations are here and there made to introduce some form of taxes in order to accelerate the transition to a low-carbon, less greenhouse gas emitting economy. These considerations have not matured, though, in particular due to the requirement of unanimity for any tax legislation.

---

[230] Commission, COM(97) 9; see also Commission, Database on environmental taxes in the European Union Member States, plus Norway and Switzerland. Evaluation of environmental effects of environmental taxes (Luxembourg, 1999); European Environmental Agency, *Recent Developments in the Use of Eco-taxes in the European Union* (Copenhagen, 2000); European Environment Agency, *Market-based Instruments for Environmental Policy in Europe*, Technical Report 8/2005 (Copenhagen, 2006).

CHAPTER 5

Biodiversity and Nature Conservation

Nature conservation measures within the European Union were, until about the mid-1980s, influenced by the fact that the majority of Member States were of the opinion that nature protection came within their exclusive competence. Since environmental legal acts had, prior to 1987, to be agreed unanimously, this attitude considerably influenced the number and the content of the measures adopted; indeed, Member States favoured the negotiation and conclusion of international conventions. Another consequence was that all nature conservation measures that the Council was ready to adopt were based on art.308 EC (now art.352 TFEU).

5–01

When the present arts 191 to 193 TFEU were, in 1987, introduced into the Treaty to give an explicit environmental competence to the European Union, which included nature conservation, matters only gradually changed. The main reasons were that Member States were very keen to keep their responsibility in land-use planning matters, which they saw at least partly threatened by EU nature conservation measures; that transfrontier management of wildlife and nature protection was hardly practised; and that national and EU enforcement mechanisms for nature conservation measures were structurally too weak to properly enforce the different provisions, let alone initiating new measures.

The most recent assessment of the biodiversity in the European Union is the Report from the European Environment Agency (EEA) "European Union biodiversity baseline" of 2010.[1] A new report is foreseen for 2015; art.4(4) of Regulation 1367/2006[2] requires the Commission to publish and disseminate every *four* years a report on the state of the EU environment. The Commission delegated this task to the EEA, but both institutions ignore the four-year requirement.

1.   GENERAL MEASURES

(a)   International conventions

The European Union adhered to a number of international conventions which aim, as a general objective, at the protection of nature or of parts of it. For the majority of these conventions, however, the European Union did not take measures of secondary EU law to implement these international conventions. In

5–02

---

[1] European Environment Agency, Technical Report 12/2010 [2010] Copenhagen.
[2] Regulation 1367/2006 [2006] OJ L264/13.

law, an international convention to which the European Union adheres becomes part of European Union (art.216(2) TFEU)—at least, where the area covered by the convention comes into EU competence—and is thus also binding for those Member States which have not ratified the international convention.[3] As regards the hierarchy, the provisions of the convention rank between primary and secondary EU law, which means that they prevail on EU regulations and directives. The application and enforcement of the provisions of the convention is shared between the European Union and its Member States, according to their internal repartition of competence.

In practice, the application and enforcement of international environmental conventions to which the European Union adhered, without adopting a regulation or directive to implement its provisions in EU law, does not take place as far as the EU level is concerned; in particular, the Commission does not "ensure" that the legal provisions of the international measure are applied, as art.17 TEU requires. Rather, the Commission leaves it to Member States to apply the provisions of the convention. The EU institutions apply a provision of an international environmental convention only in those cases where the provision is sufficiently precise and concrete (direct effect).[4] Individual persons or environmental organisations may rely on the provision of an international environmental convention only when the provision is sufficiently precise and unconditional, the Court is rather restrictive in this regard.[5] And in cases initiated by individuals, the Court does not look at the *effet utile* of a provision of a convention.

As a consequence, the decision to adhere to the international environmental convention is marked by the participation of the European Union, but as such does not bring an added value to the protection of the environment.

5–03   The following environmental conventions belong to this group of conventions on nature conservation:

1.   Bonn Convention of 23 June 1979 on the conservation of migratory species of wild animals[6];
2.   Rio de Janeiro Convention of 5 June 1992 on biological diversity[7];
3.   Salzburg Convention of 7 November 1991 on the protection of the Alps[8];
4.   Canberra Convention of 20 May 1980 on the conservation of Antarctic marine living resources[9];
5.   Paris Convention of 17 June 1994 on combating desertification.[10]

On biological diversity, the European Union adopted a communication on an EU strategy for biological diversity[11] which contained four areas of activity: on

---

[3] See Court of Justice, *Pêcheurs de l'Etang de Berre* (C-213/03) [2004] E.C.R. I-7357; *Commission v France* (C-239/03) [2004] E.C.R. I-9325.
[4] See Court of Justice, *Council a.o. v Milieudefensie a.o.* (joined cases C-401/12P to C-403/12P) ECLI:EU:C:2015:4.
[5] See *Lesoochranárske zoskupenie* (C-240/09) [2011] E.C.R. I-1255; *Milieudefensie* (joined cases C-401/12P to C-403/12P) ECLI:EU:C:2015:4.
[6] Decision 82/461 [1982] OJ L210/10.
[7] Decision 93/626 [1993] OJ L309/1.
[8] Decision 96/191 [1996] OJ L61/31.
[9] Decision 81/691 [1981] OJ L252/26.
[10] Decision 98/216 [1998] OJ L83/1.
[11] Commission, COM(98) 42.

conservation and sustainable use of biological diversity; the sharing of genetic resources; research, control and exchange of information; and education, training and sensibilisation. No specific legislative measures were announced; instead, the objectives of the strategy were to be reached within the context of the different ongoing EU activities.[12] Decision 1386/2013 on the 7th Environment Action Programme repeated earlier commitments to stop the loss of biodiversity and the degradation of ecosystems by 2020.[13] This objective had already been fixed for 2010;[14] in 2006, the Commission made a communication suggesting measures, identifying a number of possible measures, but limiting itself largely to suggest measures at the national level.[15] When it turned out, in 2010, that the loss of biodiversity was not stopped, the Commission adopted a new communication, on the basis of which the Council concluded that by 2050 the EU biodiversity and the ecosystem services it provides should be protected and that, by 2020, the biodiversity loss should be halted.[16] Again, no specific measures were suggested, and the 7th Environment Action Programme did not provide for such measures either.

The Commission recognised that more needed to be done to integrate the biodiversity considerations into other sector policies, to make available the necessary funding and to fill the existing policy gaps.[17] It did not consider, though, suggesting a framework directive on biodiversity[18] which could, among other things, transpose the requirements of the conventions mentioned above into EU law, incorporate the provisions of the Council of Europe Landscape Convention, make available the necessary funding and put into binding legal rules the biodiversity targets which had been agreed under the auspices of the Biodiversity Convention—included by the European Union and its 28 Member States—in Nagoya/Japan in October 2010. A model for putting such precise, binding targets agreed at international level into EU law were the commitments to reduce greenhouse gas emission reductions laid down in the Kyoto Protocol of 1997 and Decision 2002/358.[19]

Forestry is not part of the Common Agricultural Policy, as trees and forestry products do not normally come under the notion of "agricultural products". When the Council tried to integrate forestry measures into the Common Agricultural

5–04

---

[12] See also Commission, First report on the implementation of the Convention on biological diversity by the European Community (Luxembourg, 1998) European Parliament, Resolution of 20 October 1998 on biodiversity [1998] OJ C341/41.

[13] Decision 1386/2013 on a Seventh Environmental Action Programme [2013] OJ L354/171, sections 20 and 28.

[14] Decision 1600/2002 [2002] OJ L242/1, art.6

[15] Commission, COM(2006) 216; see also COM(2010) 548 concerning the assessment of implementing this Action Plan.

[16] See Commission, COM(2010) 4 and Council, conclusions of 15 March 2010, Doc.7536/10 of 16 March 2010. See also Commission, The 2010 assessment of implementing the EU Biodiversity Action Plan (2010) 548 and SEC 82010 1164.

[17] Commission, COM(2010) 548, p.14.

[18] A piece of new EU legislation is also suggested by Van Hoorick, "Biodiversity outside protected areas: an outlaw waiting to be saved?", in C. Born a.o. (eds), *The Habitat Directive in its EU Environmental Law* Context (Abingdon, 2015), p.452.

[19] Decision 2002/358 [2002] OJ L130/1; Dec.1386/2013 [2013] OJ L354/171, section 20.

Policy by basing such measures on the present art.43 TFEU, the Court of Justice opposed this and declared the measures in question to be part of the EU environmental policy.[20]

In 1998, the Commission published a non-binding forest strategy which got a prudent welcome from the Council which underlined the primary responsibility of Member States on forest management.[21] No concrete measures were suggested or decided. In 2003 a regulation was adopted which brought two earlier regulations on the protection of forests against air pollution and against fire[22] into one single instrument, based on art.192 TFEU.[23] However, four years later, this Regulation was repealed, and measures for protection forests were integrated into the LIFE regulation.[24]

In 2005, a regulation on the establishment of a Forest Law Enforcement, Governance and Trade (FLEGT) licensing scheme for imports of timber into the EU was adopted.[25] The Regulation provides that the conclusion of non-binding, voluntary agreements with partner countries "place a legally binding obligation on a partner country to implement the licensing scheme". Under such agreements, only the import of "legally" harvested timber into the European Union will be allowed which is timber that corresponds to the national legislation or standards in force. The Regulation tries to progressively reduce the import of illegally logged timber, as at present, it is estimated that between one-third and one-half of tropical timber imports into the European Union stems from illegal logging. However, whether bilateral agreements—by March 2015, such agreements were concluded with Ghana, the Republic of Congo, Cameroon, Liberia, the Central African Republic and Indonesia[26]—can be enforced in the wood exporting country, is not clear; also, an export, for example of Indonesian timber to China which then produces wood products and exports them to Europe, would not be reached by such agreements.

5–05   In 2010, the Union adopted a Regulation to prohibit the placing on the EU market of illegally harvested timber and timber products.[27] The operators have to apply due diligence measures in order to ensure that timber and timber products come from legally harvested wood. The Regulation became fully operational in 2013; it considers that timber in countries with which a voluntary agreement under Regulation 2173/2005 had been concluded, was legally harvested.

Following some earlier communications, in 2013 the Commission presented a new strategy on forests which mainly addressed the forest-based industries in the

---

[20] Court of Justice, *European Parliament v Council* (joined cases C-164/97 and C-165/97) [1999] E.C.R. I-1139.

[21] Commission COM(98) 649; Council Resolution of 15 December 1998 [1999] OJ C56/1.

[22] Regulation 3528/86 [1986] OJ L326/2 (air pollution); Reg.2158/92 [1992] OJ 217/3 (fire).

[23] Regulation 2152/2003 concerning monitoring of forests and environmental interactions in the Community (forest focus) [2003] OJ L324/1.

[24] Regulation 614/2007 concerning the Financial Instrument for the Environment (LIFE+) [2007] OJ L149/1.

[25] Regulation 2173/2005 on the establishment of a FLEGT licensing scheme for imports of timber into the European Community [2005] OJ L347/1.

[26] Agreement with Ghana [2010] OJ L70/3; Agreement with the Republic of Congo [2010] OJ L271/1, Agreement with Cameroon [2011] OJ L92/3; Agreement with Liberia [2012] OJ L191/1; Agreement with Central African Republic [2012] OJ L191/102; Agreement with Indonesia [2014] OJ L150/250.

[27] Regulation 995/2010 laying down the obligations of operators which place timber and timber products on the market [2010] OJ L295/23.

European Union.[28] The Commission indicated that the EU Agricultural Fund for Rural Development had spent, between 2007 and 2013, some €5.4 billion in support of forests and that a similar amount was expected to be spent until 2020. The strategy remained rather general and did not suggest new environmental protection measures, though the term "sustainable forest management" was continuously used. It did not address the tensions between environmental interests and the interests of the (private) owner of forests which do not always coincide.

(b)   Land use and soil protection

There are no general EU measures which directly concern soil protection, although agricultural measures generally may have an impact on land use.[29] A regulation from 1992, several times amended and replaced[30] provided for financial assistance to farmers who voluntarily agree to substantially reduce the use of fertilisers or pesticides, to use organic farming methods, to set aside land—for at least 20 years—for environmental purposes, or to pursue other ways of environmentally acceptable farming practices. At present, more than 20 per cent of EU farmland is covered by such measures, with about 1.5 million agreements.

5–06

In the 7th Environment Action Programme, the European Union considered measures on land use to be necessary in the areas of habitat and ecosystem protection and restoration, management of the countryside, of landscapes, sustainable forest management, fight against soil erosion and remediation of contaminated sites.[31] Measures on a sound use of pesticides were presented in the form of a communication (thematic strategy) in 2006.[32] It suggests in particular that Member States establish national plans to reduce the risks of pollution from pesticides. In environmentally friendly areas, the use of pesticides is to be limited and other accompanying measures are proposed. Following this, in 2009, a directive was adopted which obliged Member States to adopt national action plans for the use of plant protection products and to set up targets for the reduction of the use of pesticides; some accompanying measures also aim to progressively reduce the use of such products.[33]

The use of some pesticides throughout the European Union had already been forbidden throughout the European Commission.[34] In 2009, a new regulation[35]

---

[28] See, e.g. COM(2006) 302 (forest action plan); COM(2008) 645 (forests and climate change); COM(2010) 66 (forest protection); Commission COM(2013) 659 and SWD(2013) 342 and 343.

[29] The Commission's Communication on sustainable agriculture [1999] OJ C173/2 indicates that some 156 million hectares of soil are suffering from water or wind erosion and that soil erosion is increasing (pt 2.3).

[30] See last Reg.1307/2013 establishing rules for direct payments to farmers under support schemes [2013] OJ L347/608.

[31] Decision 1386/2013 [2013] OJ L354/171, sections 17–28.

[32] Commission, Communication on a Thematic Strategy on the sustainable use of pesticides, COM(2006) 372.

[33] Directive 2009/128 establishing a framework for Community action to achieve the sustainable use of pesticides [2009] OJ L309/71.

[34] Directive 79/117 prohibiting the placing on the market and use of plant protection products containing certain active substances [1979] OJ L33/36; this Directive had been updated at regular intervals, but was finally repealed in 2006.

was adopted concerning the placing of plant protection products on the market which repealed, among other things, Directive 79/117. Under this Regulation, the EU adopts a list of active substances which may enter pesticides. Plant protection products need a national authorisation in order to be put on the market (art.28); the withdrawal of the authorisation is also in the hands of the Member States (art.44).

5–07   In 1995, the Commission launched an Integrated Coastal Zone management demonstration programme.[36] This programme, however, only explored ways for an effective management; it did not affect decisions on land use, which are taken at the level of Member States. In 2001 it was followed by a Recommendation with a similar limitation.[37]

In 2006, the Commission presented, in the form of a communication, a thematic strategy on the urban environment[38] which has the ambitious aim of improving the environmental performance and quality of urban areas, where three-quarters of the EU population live. The communication provides for integrated management of urban areas, sustainable transport, the exchange of best practices and similar measures. The 7th Environment Action Programme suggests that the European Union should, by 2020 "enhance the sustainability of the Union's cities".[39] This is further specified in sections 90–95 which indicates that this objective requires the agreement on a set of criteria to assess the environmental performance of cities, the improvement of information on and better access to the financing of measures to improve urban sustainability, the sharing of best practices between cities and to develop a common understanding of how to improve urban environments. These general and vague indications leave, in practice, everything to Member States and to cities.

It is clear that the progressive ban on uncontrolled discharges to rivers, lakes or coastal waters also contributes to the protection of land. The siting of industrial installations or infrastructure measures is decided by Member States at their discretion; eventual negative impacts on the environment, demonstrated for instance by an environmental impact assessment,[40] do not restrict this right.

5–08   Directive 2009/147[41] requires Member States to classify the most suitable territories as special protection areas for some particularly threatened bird species. Within these areas, they shall take "appropriate steps to avoid pollution or deterioration of habitats or any disturbances affecting the birds, in so far as these would be significant".[42] In individual cases, this can lead to restrictions of the use of land: in case C-355/90,[43] the construction of roads and other infrastructure measure within a birds' habitat was declared incompatible with

---

[35] Regulation 1107/2009 concerning the placing of plant protection products on the market [2009] OJ L309/1; see also paras 6–33 et seq., below.

[36] Commission, COM(95) 511; progress report COM(97) 744.

[37] Recommendation 2002/413 concerning the implementation of Integrated Coastal Zone Management in Europe [2002] OJ L148/24.

[38] Commission, a thematic strategy on the urban environment, COM(2006) 718.

[39] Decision 1386/2013 [2013] OJ L354/171, art.2(1)(h).

[40] See more closely para.4–09, above.

[41] Directive 2009/147 on the conservation of wild birds [2010] OJ L20/7; this Directive replaced Dir.79/409 [1979] OJ L103/1.

[42] Directive 2009/147, art.4(4).

[43] *Commission v Spain* (C-355/90) [1993] E.C.R. I-4221 (*Santona*); in the same sense, for a case under Dir.92/43, *Commission v Cyprus* (C-340/10) ECLI:EU:C:2012:143.

art.4 of Directive 2009/147; that specific habitat had not been classified under that provision even though it should have been. In case C-44/95,[44] the United Kingdom had classified a specific area under art.4, but had exempted a specific part, since it considered that at a later stage this part could be needed for the extension of a nearby commercial port. The Court of Justice held that this was not allowed, although, obviously, it did not discuss whether the port extension was compatible with the designation of the habitat.

A similar provision to art.4 of Directive 2009/147 was introduced in an article of Directive 92/43.[45] However, in reaction to Court jurisdiction, which was considered too restrictive,[46] a provision was inserted that despite its negative effects a measure could be carried out "for imperative reasons of overriding public interest".[47] This provision considerably facilitates the carrying out of measures even in a classified habitat, in particular in the light of the Commission's wide interpretation and loose handling of art.6(4).[48] The Court of Justice continues to allow only a restricted application of art.6 of Directive 92/43.[49]

The protection of habitats, granted by Directives 2009/147 and 92/43, also applies when activities outside a habitat have effect within such areas.[50] As regards, more generally, areas other than habitats, Directive 92/43 invites Member states to "encourage the management of features of the landscape which are of major importance for wild fauna and flora" (art.10); the Directive mentions rivers, field boundaries, ponds and small woods as examples. This invitation is not more than a recommendation to Member States. The European Union has not yet taken any steps to adhere to the Council of Europe Convention on Landscapes which was signed in Florence in 2000.

Directive 2008/98[51] prohibits the abandonment, dumping or uncontrolled management of waste. The Court of Justice clarified that this provision also included the obligation to clean up the land when an unauthorised discharge of waste had taken place.[52] The Court, though, did not discuss the borderline between the obligations flowing out of EU waste law and the contamination of land by waste materials that had been discharged on land prior to 1977, when EU

5–09

---

[44] *RSPB* (C-44/95) [1996] E.C.R. I-3805 (*Lappel-Bank*); see also *Commission v Germany* (C-57/89) [1991] E.C.R. I-883 (*Leybucht*).

[45] Directive 92/43 on the conservation of natural habitats and of wild fauna and flora [1992] OJ L206/7, art.6(2): "Member States shall take appropriate steps to avoid, in the special areas of conservation, the deterioration of natural habitats and the habitats of species as well as disturbance of the species for which the areas have been designated, in so far as such disturbance could be significant in relation to the objectives of this Directive."

[46] Court of Justice, *Commission v Germany* (C-57/89) [1991] E.C.R. I-883.

[47] Directive 92/43 [1992] OJ L206/7, art.6(4).

[48] See L. Krämer, "The European Commission's opinions under art.6(4) of the Habitats Directive" [2009] *Journal of Environmental Law* 59; D. McGillivray, "Compensatory measures under Article 6(4) of the Habitats Directive: no net loss for Natura 2000?", in Born a.o., *The Habitat Directive in its EU Environmental Law Context* (2015), p.101.

[49] Court of Justice, *Sweetman* (C-258/11) ECLI:EU:C:2013:220; *Briels* (C-521/12) ECLI:EU:C:2014:330.

[50] See, e.g. Court of Justice, *Alta Sil* (C-404/09) ECLI:EU:C:2011:768.

[51] Directive 2008/98 on waste [2008] OJ L312/3, art.36. This Directive repealed Dir.75/442 and its later version Dir.2006/12.

[52] Court of Justice, *Commission v Greece* (C-378/13) ECLI:EU:C:2014:2405; *Commission v Italy* (C-196/13) ECLI:EU:C:2014:2407.

waste legislation became applicable. In my opinion, waste discharges prior to 1977 are not covered by the clean-up obligation.

Directive 86/278[53] prohibits, under certain conditions, the use of sewage sludge on certain land, in particular where there are overly high concentrations of heavy metals, on grassland or forage crops, on soil in which fruit and vegetable crops are growing and on ground for the cultivation of fruit and vegetable crops which are normally eaten raw.

There are no specific EU provisions for protecting the soil, in particular against soil erosion, although EU funds may assist national measures. The same can be said with regard to questions of desertification. Following an announcement in the 6th Environment Action Programme on measures concerning the protection of soil,[54] a first communication, identifying the main problems of the soil within the Member States was published in 2002.[55] This was followed by a further communication and a proposal for a directive on soil protection in 2006.[56]

5–10   The proposal for a directive was based on art.192(1) TFEU, as the Commission considered that it deals with the protection of the environment and not with land use. It identified as the following eight main aspects of the soil degradation process: erosion, organic matter decline, contamination, salinisation, compaction, soil biodiversity loss, sealing, landslides and flooding. With the exception of flooding, for which the Commission had proposed a separate directive, it suggested that Member States identify areas at risk and draw up national programmes. Of considerable interest was also the proposal to establish a national inventory of contaminated sites and to progressively start remediation work.

The Council discussed this proposal on several occasions. However, a blocking minority of Member States which included Germany, France and the United Kingdom, opposed any legislative measure on soil protection at EU level, for reasons of subsidiarity.[57] As there were no signs that this attitude would change in a foreseeable future—though it is not contested that EU regional, agricultural and transport policies contribute to the problems of soil in practically all Member States—the Commission withdrew its proposal in 2014, while the 7th

---

[53] Directive 86/278 on the protection of the environment and in particular of the soil, when sewage sludge is used in agriculture [1986] OJ L181/6, arts 5 and 7.

[54] Decision 1600/2002 [2002], OJ L 242/1, art.7(2c).

[55] Commission, Towards a Thematic Strategy for Soil Protection, COM(2002) 179.

[56] Commission, COM(2006) 232.

[57] Twenty-two Member States pleaded in favour of an EU directive. The Member States opposing the directive were all states which disposed of national legislation on soil protection.

Environment Action Programme called for more measures to protect soil.[58] In 2012, the Commission adopted guidelines on soil sealing.[59]

Any land use measure by the European Union would have to be adopted by virtue of art.192(2) TFEU. In legal texts, it is sometimes argued that this provision also applies to amendments of Directives 2009/147 and 92/43.[60] However, both Directives concern general measures which give a specific status to land, but do not directly deal with the use of the land. Indeed, land use is not outlined in a specific way by either Directive. Their correct legal basis is therefore art.192(1) TFEU.

(c)   Habitat protection

The Commission stated in 2001 that: **5–11**

> "Pollution from transport, industry and agriculture continues to threaten natural areas and wildlife ... Pressure is coming from the changes in how we utilise land ... The building of new roads, houses and other developments is fragmenting the countryside into ever-smaller areas, making it harder for species to survive. All the trends suggest that the loss of open countryside to development will continue in the future ... As habitats are degraded or lost, wildlife is frequently under pressure or even the threat of extinction."[61]

(i)   Birds' habitats

In 1979 the Union adopted Directive 79/409 on the conservation of wild birds,[62]   **5–11**
following considerable public pressure in favour of such a measure; in 2009, this Directive was renumbered as Directive 2009/147.[63] That Directive aimed at comprehensive protection of *all* wild birds within the European Union and outlined detailed provisions, in particular on hunting, capturing and trading of birds. Member States were required to take necessary measures "to preserve, maintain or re-establish a sufficient diversity and area of habitats" for all birds (art.3) by the creation of protected areas or biotopes and the upkeep, management and re-establishment of biotopes. For particularly threatened bird species, listed in an annex I, they were asked to classify habitats as special protection areas for the conservation of these species (art.4). The different designated habitats were to

---

[58] See 7th Environment Action Programme [2013] OJ L354/171, sections 23 and 25: "The degradation, fragmentation and unsustainable use of land in the Union is jeopardising the provision of several key ecosystems, threatening biodiversity and increasing Europe's vulnerability to climate change and natural disasters. It is also exacerbating soil degradation and desertification. More than 25% of the Union's territory is affected by soil erosion by water, which compromises soil functions and affects the quality of freshwater. Soil contamination and sealing are also persistent problems ... Every year more than 1000 km² of land are taken for housing, industry, transport or recreational services ... The Union and its Member States should also reflect as soon as possible on how soil quality issues could be addressed using a targeted and proportionate risk-based approach within a binding legal framework. Targets should also be set for sustainable land use and soil."
[59] Commission SWD(2012) 101.
[60] See para.2–90, above.
[61] Commission, Communication on sustainable agriculture [1999] OJ C173/2, pt 4.1.
[62] Directive 79/409 (see fn.41, above).
[63] Directive 2009/147 (see fn.41, above).

form a "coherent whole",[64] which met the protection requirements for birds all over the European Union. Inside these special protection areas, appropriate conservation measures had to be taken.

The provision of art.3 has, as far as can be seen, not led to any significant change at national level; the provision was scarcely monitored by the Commission, though it has undoubtedly a legally binding content; the Court of Justice found only one case where art.3 had not been respected by a Member State.[65] As regards art.4, designation of special protection areas advanced only slowly. While the Directive required the classification to be completed by 1981, the following actual development took place[66]:

1986: 309 areas (10 Member States);
1990: 450 areas (12 Member States);
1995: 1,247 areas covering 71,679 km^2 (15 Member States);
1998: 1,842 areas;
2002: 2,885 areas covering 232,062 km^2;
2006: 4,523 areas covering 444,108 km^2 (25 Member States);
2010: 5,315 areas covering 593.486 km^2 (27 Member States);
2013: 5,491 areas (28 Member States).

5–12   The Commission stated in 1991 and in 1998 that only Denmark and Belgium[67] had fully complied with their obligations under art.4 of Directive 2009/147.[68] In 2002, the Netherlands was added as the third Member State,[69] a remarkable change that had obviously been induced by a Court judgment against the Netherlands.[70] In 2010, the Commission indicated that the designation of areas was "largely completed" for Belgium, Denmark, Germany, Estonia, France, Italy, Luxemburg, Malta, Netherlands, Poland, Portugal and Finland.[71] Since then, the Commission did not further disclose information on implementation.

In a number of cases, the Commission tried to ensure through legal proceedings the habitat status of specific zones where it was of the opinion that Member States had not fully complied with their obligations. These procedures

---

[64] Directive 2009/147, art.4(3); the French and German texts talk of a "coherent network", which is certainly more precise.
[65] Court of Justice, *Commission v Ireland* (C-117/00) [2002] E.C.R. I-5335. Generally, see Commission, *Information sur l'application de la directive 79/409/CEE* (Brussels and Luxembourg, 1990), pp.35 et seq.; Report on the application of Directive 79/409 (1993–1995), COM(2000) 180 of 29 March 2000; Report on the application of Directive 79/409 (1996–1998), COM(2002) 146 of 25 March 2002.
[66] Commission, *Information sur l'application de la directive 79/409/CEE* (1990), p.46; Commission, 2nd report on the application of Directive 79/409 on the conservation of wild birds, COM(93) 572 of 24 November 1993, p.115; Commission (DG ENV) *Natura 2000* Newsletter, May 1996, p.6; February 1998, p.6; November 1998, p.6; May 2002 p.8; European Topic Centre on Biological Diversity, *Natura 2000* Database, June 2006.
[67] As regards Belgium, see however Court of Justice, *Commission v Belgium* (C-415/01) [2003] E.C.R. I-2187, where the Belgian measures were considered as not being legally precise enough.
[68] Commission, 8th report on monitoring application of Community law (1990) [1991] OJ C338/1, p.220; Commission, *Natura 2000* Newsletter, February 1998, p.6.
[69] Commission, *Natura 2000* Newsletter, May 2002, p.8.
[70] Court of Justice, *Commission v Netherlands* (C-3/96) [1998] E.C.R. I-3031; WWF, *Spotlight on Natura 2000 No.4/1997*, p.8 reports that the Commission stated during the public hearing before the Court that proceedings had been initiated against the Netherlands, because these had not, contrary to other Member States, "shown any interest in settling the matter bilaterally".
[71] Commission, *Natura 2000* Newsletter, June 2010, p.6.

are rather time-consuming, in particular where the dispute has to be decided by the Court of Justice.[72] The Commission announced in 2002 that it was developing a strategy to initiate general infringement proceedings, rather that beginning *proceedings* on a site-by-site basis.[73] This strategy practically had the consequence that the Commission did not bring cases any more before the Court of Justice.[74]

Generally, however, not much can be said on the practical application of the Directive, as the Commission is remarkably—and unacceptably so—discrete in reporting on Member States' failure to transpose or actually apply the Directive's provisions. Its implementation reports became more and more vague and general over the years. The last one which was made public was dated 2006.[75] A 2011 report, covering the years 2005–2007, was not made public, and no reason was given. Since then, no information has been disclosed on the Directive's application, which is a scandal. The Commission's annual reports on monitoring EC law limit themselves to indicate those cases which the Commission has brought to the Court or which the Court decided. The statement that more efforts are needed is, 35 years after the entry into effect of the Directive and as a means to inform and interest the public on the Directive's application, a poor one; it resembles more a non-information.

(ii) Fauna and flora habitats

Habitats are also protected by virtue of the provisions of Directive 92/43.[76] This Directive protects over 200 different types of habitats of particular ecological value[77] which are listed in an annex I; furthermore, it requires that habitats for those fauna and flora species which are listed in an annex II be designated by Member States. The procedure of designating these habitats is slightly different from that of Directive 2009/147. First of all, Member States have to establish national lists of sites which are important for the conservation of habitat types or fauna or flora species; where the Commission disagrees, the matter is finally decided by a unanimous Council decision. Out of these national lists, the Commission, in agreement with the Member State concerned, establishes a list of sites of EU importance. Member States shall then, within six years, designate the

5–13

---

[72] See, e.g. *Commission v Germany* (C-57/89) [1991] E.C.R. I-883; *Commission v Spain* (C-355/90) [1993] E.C.R. I-4221 (*Santona*); *RSPB* (C-44/95) [1996] E.C.R. I-3805; *Commission v France* (C-166/97) [1999] E.C.R. I-1719; *Commission v France* (C-96/98) [1999] E.C.R. I-8531; *Commission v France* (C-374/98) [2000] E.C.R. I-10799.

[73] Commission, 19th Report on monitoring application of Community law (2001), COM(2002) 324, no.2.8.6.

[74] Between January 2010 and March 2015, the Commission brought only two cases before the Court, one on incorrect transposition of Dir.2009/147 *Commission v Poland* (C-192/11) ECLI-:EU:C:2012:44) and the other for not making a correct environmental impact assessment (*Commission v Spain* (C-461/14); the case is pending).

[75] Commission, COM(2006) 164.

[76] Directive 92/43 [1992] OJ L206/7; Commission proposal [1988] OJ C247/3; European Parliament Opinion [1991] OJ C75/12; Economic and Social Committee Opinion [1991] OJ C31/25.

[77] See also Commission, Interpretation manual of Environmental Habitats, April 2013, *http://ec.europa.eu/environment/nature/legislation/habitatsdirective/docs/Int_Manual_EU28.pdf* [Accessed 30 September 2015].

sites on this list as Special Areas of Conservation, which form, all together, "a coherent European ecological network" or Natura 2000.[78]

By the end of 1997, Belgium, Germany, Greece, France and Finland had not even transposed the Directive into national law. This transposition has taken place in the meantime, and the emphasis has concentrated, over recent years, to see the provisions of the Directive completely and correctly transposed and effectively applied.

The national lists had to be drawn up by June 1995. In April 1996, five Member States had transmitted complete national lists, two others partial lists. In 1999, the Commission warned Member States that if they did not transmit adequate lists for the setting up of the Natura 2000 network, the Commission might not be able to evaluate and co-finance plans and programmes under the Structural Funds; accordingly, it might not be able to attribute the corresponding financial means to Member States.[79] Though this letter raised an outcry, especially in Germany, together with a number of Court judgments it had the effect that the lists of sites under art.6 of Directive 92/43 arrived more regularly. In particular the German *Länder* abandoned their fundamental opposition to the Directive.

5–14   By the end of 2014, the Commission had published EU lists for the bio-geographical areas of Macaronesia (Azores, Madeira and Canary Islands), Alpine (mountain), Continental, Atlantic, Boreal, Mediterranean, Steppic, Pannonian and Black Sea regions.[80] Overall, the 28 Member States designated, by March 2015, 23,608 areas, covering 1,106,610 km², 18.14 per cent of their terrestrial area.[81] The designations by Belgium, Denmark, Germany, Greece, Italy, Malta, Netherlands and Portugal were considered "largely complete". The Commission does not disclose information on whether the Member States proceeded to the definite classification of "special areas of conservation" at national level. Following a judgment by the Court of Justice, according to which Directive 92/43 applies also to the marine environment,[82] Member States progressively also designate marine habitats, though much less than terrestrial habitats.[83]

The largest part of the terrestrial area was designated by Slovenia (37.85 per cent of its territory), Croatia (36.53 per cent), Bulgaria (34.46 per cent), Cyprus (28.39 per cent) and Spain (27.23 per cent); the smallest parts were designated by Denmark (8.34 per cent), United Kingdom (8.53 per cent), Latvia (11.53 per

---

[78] The special protection areas classified under Dir.2009/147 are also included in this network, see arts 6 and 7 of Dir.92/43 [1992] OJ L206/7.

[79] *Commission v Greece* (C-329/96) [1997] E.C.R. I-3749; *Commission v Germany* (C-83/97) [1997] E.C.R. I-7191 and Commission, Monitoring application of Community law—15th report (1997) [1998] OJ C250/1, p.178.

[80] Commission, Decisions 2013/736 (2nd list Steppic region) [2013] OJ L350/36; 2013/735 (5th list Pannonian region) [2013] OJ L350/10; 2013/734 (2nd list Black Sea region) [2013] OJ L350/40; 2013/734 (4th list Macaronesian region) [2013] OJ L350/1; 2013/738 (7th list Alpine region) [2013] OJ L350/44; 2013/740 (7th list Atlantic region) [2013] OJ L350/201; 2013/741 (7th list Continental region) [2013] OJ L350/287; 2013/739 (7th list Mediterranean region) [2013] OJ L350/101; 2013/742 (7th list Boreal region) [2013] OJ L350/555.

[81] As there might be an overlapping with the percentages which were given for bird areas, these figures may not be accumulated with those given in para.5–11, above.

[82] Court of Justice *Commission v United Kingdom* (C-6/04) [2005] E.C.R. I-9017.

[83] In January 2015, the Member States had designated a total of 3,024 marine sites, covering a surface of 318.133 km², see Commission, *Natura 2000* Newsletter, January 2015.

cent), Lithuania (12.15 per cent) and France (12.64 per cent). The Commission indicated that the designation of habitats—Birds and others together—was "sufficient for Denmark, Ireland and Hungary, and nearly sufficient for Finland, United Kingdom, France, Netherlands, Sweden, Malta, Bulgaria and Estonia.[84] Of course, the designation of a habitat does not say anything about the actual conservation measures which are applied.

One of the main reasons for the considerable delay in the setting up of national lists was the provision of art.6(2) of Directive 92/43, which requested Member States to avoid:

> "the deterioration of natural habitats and the habitats of species as well as disturbance of the species for which the areas have been designated, in so far as such disturbance could be significant in relation to the objectives of this Directive."

Although this provision was completed by the above-mentioned provision of art.6(4) and although the Commission decisions even showed a wide interpretation of this exemption, there was considerable concern at local level in many Member States that, on a site which would come under Directive 92/43, economic or leisure activities would be severely restricted. Under pressure from hunters, fishermen, farmers and other groups, France went even so far, in the summer of 1996, as to freeze its work on a national list for several months, arguing that it was neither clear who would finance the managing of the habitats,[85] nor exactly what activities would be forbidden within a habitat; some months later, France abandoned this attitude again.

5–15

The question of what is allowed and what is not allowed in a designated habitat is one of the most intricate ones.[86] (Bird) hunting in a habitat is often accepted—although heavily contested by environmental organisations. Other, more relevant, economic measures such as irrigation, urbanisation and road construction are often undertaken within habitats without systematic monitoring by local, regional, national or EU authorities. Generally, economic development prevails over conservation, and cases where the development of a project was stopped because of the existence of a habitat or a threatened species are extremely rare in the European Union. The Commission attempted twice to have a rule adopted that all projects listed in annex II of the environmental impact assessment Directive[87] should, before development consent is given, be preceded by an environmental impact assessment; however, the Council twice rejected this approach.[88] Directive 2001/42 now provides that any plan—though not a project!—which might significantly affect a designated natural habitat or a bird habitat, must be preceded by an environment impact assessment.

The dilemma is that, on the one hand, it is hardly possible to transform designated habitats into nature museums, where no change may take place; this is the reason why local people or authorities so often oppose the designation of a

---

[84] Commission, *Natura 2000* Newsletter, January 2015.

[85] Commission, Monitoring the application of Community law, 17th Report (1999), p.53.

[86] See as examples Court of Justice, *Commission v Spain* (C-308/08) [2010] E.C.R. I-4281; *Eolica Franchini* (C-2/10) [2011] E.C.R. I-6561.

[87] Directive 2011/92 on the assessment of the effects of certain public and private projects on the environment [2012] OJ L26/1.

[88] Commission, proposal for Dir.92/43 [1988] OJ C247/7, art.10; proposal for Dir.97/11 [1994] OJ C130/8; the Council's decision is found in Dir.97/11 [1997] OJ L37/5, Recital 10.

habitat. On the other hand, the Commission itself stated[89] that almost everywhere in Western Europe habitats and nature protection sites are shrinking slowly, but dramatically, due to road and other infrastructure construction, urbanisation, intensive farming activity, irrigation and holiday and leisure activities.[90]

5–16   To date, there are only two implementation reports, which are of limited informative value as regards the legal questions of transposition and application of Directive 92/43.[91] The Commission shows a growing disinterest in the practical application of the legislation to specific cases and concentrates on transposition and designation of habitats. Fortunately, the Court of Justice has taken on a very considerable role in defending the degree of protection reached by Directive 92/43 against attempts of reducing this protection in favour of vested interests.[92]

With all the delays and difficulties in designating habitats and conserving them, Directives 2009/147 and 92/43 constitute the first serious attempt in Western Europe to conserve nature protection sites. As such, they go far beyond what individual Member States had done at national level in this area. The experience of 35 years of application of Directive 2009/147, which has neither led to sufficient designation of habitats and adequate conservation measures nor generally stopped the shrinking of individual habitats, does not promote optimism. In Western Europe, which is a small area that is densely populated, that has great economic activity and an impressive transport and energy infrastructure network, nature is in retreat because it conflicts with demographic and economic evolution. For this reason, in almost all cases where economic interests in building a bridge, a port, an airport, a motorway or a new high-speed train clash with the environmental interests of preserving a habitat, the environmental interests lose. It is not likely that the application of Directive 92/43 will change this situation significantly, all the more as the Commission apparently neglects problems of specific, individual habitats.[93]

Habitats of wild flora and fauna species are also protected under art.4 of the Berne Convention on the conservation of European wildlife and natural habitats of 1979, to which the Union had adhered by a decision of 1981.[94] However, as is explained above,[95] the Commission does not monitor the application of international conventions to which the European Union has adhered, but leaves their application entirely to Member States: an exception is only made in those cases where the European Union enacts legislation which transposes the convention requirements into Union environmental law. In those cases, the implementation of the transposing act is monitored under art.258 TFEU; indeed,

---

[89] Commission, Communication on rational use and conservation of wetlands, COM(95) 189 of 29 May 1995.

[90] Perhaps the most eloquent example is the French habitat Camargue which lost, between 1942 and 1984, about 1,000 hectares per year of its natural surface, see A. Tamisier, *Camargue, milieux et paysages évolution de 1942 à 1984* (Arles, 1992).

[91] Commission, COM(2003) 845 and COM(2009) 358.

[92] Since 1994 until the end of 2014, the Court of Justice delivered 55 judgments on the interpretation of Dir.92/43.

[93] See generally on the application of Dir.92/43 in the EU, A.García Ureta (ed.), "La directive de Habitats de la Unión Europea. Balance de 20 anos" [2012] *San Sebastian*; Born a.o., *The Habitat Directive in its EU Environmental Law* Context (2015).

[94] Decision 82/72 of 3 December 1981 [1982] OJ L38/1.

[95] See para.5–02, above.

the Commission justified the proposal for Directive 92/43 amongst others with the argument that it transposed the Berne Convention into EU law.

A specific problem is that of (habitats of) species which are protected under the Berne Convention, but not under Directives 2009/147 or 92/43; an example of this is the badger. Supposing a Member State were infringing the obligation adequately to protect the badger's habitat: would this constitute a breach of the European Union's obligations under the Convention? In my opinion, the European Union undertakes, by adhering to an international convention, to ensure that the convention is respected all over the EU territory. EU Member States are obliged, under art.4 TEU, to take all measures in order to allow the European Union to respect this obligation; such an obligation even exists where a Member State itself is not a contracting party of the Convention, and the Commission has the obligation to ensure, under art.17 TEU, that Member States fulfil their obligations. The problem is, though, that the Commission is not willing to pursue such cases, and members of the public do not normally have standing to bring such cases before the Court of Justice.

The opinion, which is defended here, was supported by the Aarhus Convention Compliance Committee in 2012. The case concerned a lack by Ireland to properly apply art.7 of the Aarhus Convention on access to information, public participation in decision-making and access to justice in environmental matters. At the time of the decision, Ireland had not ratified the Aarhus Convention, but the European Union had. The Compliance Committee decided that the European Union had breached its obligations under the Convention, as it had not taken the necessary measures to ensure that the provisions of the Convention were properly applied and enforced in Ireland.[96]

Directive 78/659[97] tried to protect the habitats of fish. Member States were asked to designate fresh waters to support fish life. For these waters they had to establish programmes which had to ensure that the waters corresponded to specific quality requirements which were laid down in the Directive. A similar approach was followed by Directive 79/923 for shellfish.[98]

Both Directives completely failed to reach their objective.[99] The main reasons were that Member States were also allowed to designate waters which already complied with the requirements so that no clean-up programme was necessary. Furthermore, the number of waters which were to be designated was not fixed which led several Member States to designate only very few waters; a decision by the Court of Justice in 1988, stipulating that Member States had to designate and clean up waters throughout their territory,[100] did not lead to substantial changes. Finally, the Commission did not closely monitor the application of these Directives.

5–17

5–18

---

[96] Aarhus Convention Compliance Committee, communication ACCC/C/2010/54 of 24 June 2012.
[97] Directive 78/659 on the quality of fresh waters needing protection or improvement in order to support fish life [1978] OJ L222/1.
[98] Directive 79/923 on the quality required of shellfish waters [1979] OJ L281/47.
[99] See for the factual details Commission, Quality of fresh water for fish and of shellfish water; summary report on the state of application of the Directives 78/659 and 79/923 (Luxembourg, 1995) (EUR 14118).
[100] *Commission v Italy* (C-322/86) [1988] E.C.R. 3995.

Both Directives were repealed in 2013 by Directive 2000/60[101] which intends to take over the attainment of the objectives of these Directives, though it deals with water quality, not with habitat protection.

(d)   Financial measures to support nature conservation

5–19   The different EU financial means, given to Member States in particular in the context of the agricultural or regional policy, may also contribute, as the case might be, to the conservation of nature; examples are the setting aside of land or the construction of walls alongside a road. However, the main purpose of such measures is not the protection of the environment, but rather the achievement of an objective of agricultural or regional policy.

This also applies to the financial assistance given under Regulation 1305/2013 and its predecessor, Regulation 1698/2005[102] which aim at ensuring income to farmers who practise environmentally responsible farming practices.[103] The regional policy objective is also visible with the financial means which are made available under the Cohesion Fund.[104] For the period 2014–2020, all Member States which adhered to the EU since 2004, benefit from the Cohesion Fund, plus Greece and Portugal. The Fund now no longer co-finances individual projects, but gives lump sums to the entitled Member States, according to programmes which these states have elaborated and which have been previously approved by the Commission (see details in para.4–22, above). To what extent the Fund will in future co-finance nature protection projects, depends thus on each of the entitled Member States. The overall amount for all regional funds is of €63.4 billion (2013–2020).

One of the principal objectives of the financial instrument LIFE, which was set up in 1992 and reviewed in 1996, 2000 and 2007, was the protection of "habitats and of nature".[105] LIFE disposed, between 1992 and 1995 of €400 million, between 1996 and 1999 of €450 million, between 2000 and 2004 of €640 million, between 2004 and 2006 of €317.2 million and between 2007 and 2013 of €840 million (27 Member States). For the period 2014–2020, some €1.43 billion are earmarked for the protection of habitats, applying, though, to some 35 EU countries (plus accession and neighbouring countries).

5–20   Since the time span imposed on Member States to submit national lists for habitats under Directive 92/43[106] elapsed in 1996, LIFE, since then, only

---

[101] See Dir.2000/60 establishing a framework for Community action in the field of water policy [2000] OJ L327/1, art.22(2).

[102] Regulation 1305/2013 on the support for rural development by the European Agricultural Fund for Rural Development (EAFRD), [2013] OJ L347/487; Reg.1698/2005 [2005] OJ L277/1.

[103] The Court of Justice clarified that this money is reserved for farmers, not for other persons or bodies which set aside land, *Agrooikosystema* (C-498/13) ECLI:EU:C:2015:61.

[104] Regulation 1164/94 setting up a Cohesion Fund [1994] OJ L130/1; Reg.1084/2006 on the Cohesion Fund [2006] OJ L210/79; Reg.1300/2013 on the Cohesion Fund [2013] OJ L347/281.

[105] Regulation 1973/92 establishing a financial instrument for the environment [1992] OJ L206/1 (LIFE I); the explanatory memorandum, COM(91) 28 of 31 January 1991 contains detailed figures on Community expenditure for the environment prior to 1991; Reg.1404/96 [1996] OJ L181/1 (LIFE II); Reg.1655/ 2000 [2000] OJ L192/1 (LIFE III); Reg.1682/2004 [2004] OJ L 308/1; Reg.614/2007 [2007] OJ L149/1.

[106] Commission, COM(97) 633 of 12 December 1997; *Natura 2000*, February 1999, p.2; see also Commission, COM(95) 135 of 12 April 1995: Progress report on implementation of the LIFE

co-financed projects for sites which had been listed in these national lists or, in the case of bird habitats, had already been classified under Directive 2009/147. The EU funds were mainly used to buy or to hire the ground—most of the acquisition is done by local or regional nature conservation groups or bodies—to assist in the establishment of national, regional or local inventories or to pay for conservation or improvement measures at the site.[107]

The Commission gave up earlier attempts to have nature protection measures financed by the Regional Fund and/or the Cohesion Fund, as the European Parliament and the Council did not accept this approach.

The European Union also financed measures to protect forests. As regards forests within the European Union, the Council adopted, in 1986, a Regulation on the protection of forests against atmospheric pollution.[108] This Regulation provided for the setting up of inventories for forest damage, a network in order to obtain a coherent network of data, regular national reports on that data and for EC financial support for protection measures. Though damage levels have been stabilised from 1995 onwards, the Commission estimated that in 2002 almost one-quarter of Europe's trees suffered damage from atmospheric pollution.[109] A Regulation of the same year on the protection of forests against fire provided for technical and financial assistance to prevent forest fire, in particular in the Mediterranean area.[110] Between 1983 and 2003, more than €2 billion were spent on the conservation, improvement and protection of EU forests.[111] As mentioned above, all measures to finance forest conservation by the European Union, are, since 2006/2007, integrated into the Regional Funds and into LIFE; it is thus up to Member States to decide on financial allocations for forestry.[112] The Commission estimated that between 2007 and 2013, €5.4 billion had been made available from EU funds for the protection of forests.[113]

As regards tropical forests, a regulation of 2000 which replaced earlier provisions[114] provided for financial assistance—€249 million for the period 2000–2006—in sustainable forestry and generally in sustainable development measures. It also planned to assist in the development of an international labelling

5–21

Regulation and evaluation of the action by the Community relating to the environment ACE, MEDSPA, NORSPA and ACNAT; European Environment Agency, *Ecosystem Accounting and the Cost of Biodiversity Losses. The Case of Coastal Mediterranean Wetlands*, Technical Report 3/2010 (Copenhagen, 2010).

[107] See para.5–19, above.

[108] Regulation 3528/86 [1986] OJ L326/2.

[109] Commission, 2nd Report on Biological diversity; Thematic Report on Forests and Biodiversity (Luxembourg, 2003), no.2.6.

[110] Regulation 3529/86 [1986] OJ L326/5; this Regulation was replaced by Reg.2158/92 on protection of the Community's forests against fire [1992] OJ L217/3; the Committee of the regions had indicated in its opinion of 15 October 1997 [1998] OJ C64/27 at pt.2.1.18 that out of 300,000–500,000 hectares of forest which are burnt every year in the EC, 97 per cent concerned Spain, France, Italy, Greece and Portugal.

[111] Commission, 2nd Report on Biological diversity; Thematic Report on Forests and Biodiversity (2003), no.2.7.

[112] See para.5–04, above.

[113] See para.5—06, above.

[114] Regulation 2494/2000 on measures to promote the conservation and sustainable management of tropical forests and other forests in developing countries [2000] OJ L288/6; this Regulation replaced Reg.3062/95 [1995] OJ L327/9; both Regulations were based on arts 175 and 179 EC.

system for tropical wood that comes from sustainable forestry,[115] though the later FLEGT Regulation—see para.5–05, above—did not take the issue up. Regulation 2000/494 was repealed, when a more general financial instrument for development cooperation was set up in 2006 and repeated in 2014.[116] At present, no specific instrument exists for EU assistance to tropical forest conservation.

In 2003, a working group set up by the Commission on "Financing Nature 2000" concluded that from 2003–2013, between €6.1 billion would be needed per year within the then 15 Member States to ensure proper management of the different zones that come under the network of habitats of Nature 2000, established under Directive 92/43.[117] The amount which LIFE will make available between 2014 and 2020 for some 35 states is about €149 million per year (see also para.4–22, above).

2. PROTECTION OF THREATENED SPECIES

(a) Fauna and flora species

5–22   Directive 92/43[118] established a general system of protection for European endangered species, which it lists, in Latin only, in an annex; these lists cover some 1,180 animal and plant species, apart from the some 200 bird species protected under Directive 2009/147; the accession of 13 new Member States since 2004 had led to enlargement of the lists. As the Directive is based on art.192 TFEU, Member States may, at national level, provide for other species to be protected. Deliberate capture or killing, the deliberate disturbance, taking eggs or deterioration or destruction of breeding sites or resting places of fauna species are prohibited. For some particularly endangered species, Member States must provide for supplementary measures, for example to prevent the unintentional capture or killing (art.12). Derogations from the protection rules are, under relatively loosely drafted provisions, possible (art.16). Reports on derogations granted shall be sent to the Commission every two years; however, the experience with the similar derogation provision of art.9 of Directive 2009/147 does not inspire optimism.[119] And it is surprising to find that the Commission's comments on these national derogations shall only be submitted to the Committee under Directive 92/43, but shall not be published (art.9(2)).[120] The first implementation

---

[115] See generally on tropical forests, Commission, Communication on the role of the Community in the conservation of tropical forests [1989] OJ C264/1.

[116] Regulation 1905/2006 [2006] OJ L378/41; Reg.233/2014 establishing a financing instrument for development cooperation 2014–2020 [2014] OJ L77/40. Regulation 233/2014 provides for an amount of €19.661 billion, but refers to all forms of development cooperation. An indicative financial allocation (annex IV) provides for 27% of the total amount to be spent on environment and climate change. Which programmes and projects are cofinanced by the EU, depends on the applicant states and regions.

[117] Commission, COM(2004) 431.

[118] Directive 92/43 [1992] OJ L206/7.

[119] See on this and general application questions, L. Krämer, "Monitoring the Application of the Birds and the Habitats Directive" [2013] *Journal for European Environmental and Planning Law* 209.

[120] See also Commission, 8th report on monitoring application of Community law (1990) [1991] OJ C338/1, p.220, where the Commission stated that the reports on the derogations under Dir.79/409 were so general that they did not allow any control.

report of the Commission showed that numerous Member States just enumerate their protection legislation, but do not report on the concrete measures which they have undertaken to protect endangered species; probably, in most cases, Member States satisfied themselves with the adoption of legal requirements without trying to make them effective.

The problems with the designation and management of habitats under Directive 92/43 are so considerable that measures to ensure the protection of individual species were hardly taken, apart from measures for big animals such as the bear or the Mediterranean seals which were then financed under LIFE. Reacting to complaints from individuals, the Commission took court action to protect the sea turtle *caretta caretta* on the Greek island of Zakynthos, the red grouse in Ireland, the wood pigeon in Spain, the viper in Greece, the wolf in Finland the corncrake in Austria, the hamster in France and the grass snake in Cyprus.[121]

(b)   Birds

Directive 2009/147 lists in an annex some 200 particularly threatened bird species which require special protection measures. The most important of these measures are the designation of special protection areas under art.4[122] and the taking of conservation measures within these areas. The list of threatened bird species has constantly been prolonged, in particular due to the subsequent accession of Greece, Spain, Portugal, Austria, Finland and Sweden and then of 13 new Member States in 2004, 2007 and 2013 to the European Union. Only one species was, until now, deleted from the list: in 1997, the Commission decided to delete the cormorant from the list of threatened species, in particular due to pressure from fishermen.[123]

Directive 2009/147, however, does not only protect threatened birds, but all wild birds within the European Union; the reason for this overall protection was most likely the fact that "a large number of wild birds … are declining in number".[124] The Directive thus provides for restrictive measures such as hunting times restrictions, prohibitions on killing or capturing birds or on the taking of eggs. Furthermore, it bans a number of means for large-scale or non-selective capture or killing of birds (snares, limes, hooks, mirrors, explosives, nets, traps or motor vehicles). Derogations are possible "where there is no other satisfactory solution" (art.9).

Directive 2009/147 meant to improve the conditions of birds in Western Europe. This also implied a considerable change in people's habits. Apart from the designation of birds' habitats, the different provisions, including hunting

5–23

---

[121] Court of Justice, *Commission v Spain* (C-135/04) [2005] E.C.R. I-5261 (wood pigeon); *Commission v Greece* (C-518/04) [2006] E.C.R. I-42 (sea turtle); *Commission v Finland* (C-342/05) [2007] E.C.R. I-4713 (wolf); *Commission v Ireland* (C-117/00) [2002] E.C.R. I-5335; *Commission v Austria*(C-209/02) [2004] E.C.R. I-1211 (corncrake); *Commission v France* (C-383/09) [2011] E.C.R. I-4869 (hamster); *Commission v Cyprus* (C-340/10) ECLI:EU:C:2012:143 (grass snake).

[122] See para.5–12, above.

[123] Directive 97/49 [1997] OJ L223/9.

[124] *Commission v Poland* (C-192/11) ECLI:EU:C:2012:44, second Recital.

provisions, proved difficult to enforce.[125] In particular in, but not restricted to, France, Spain, Italy, and Malta hunting is perceived as a *right* by hunters, farmers and others. When Malta acceded to the European Commission in 2004, it even obtained a transition period to continue bird hunting with means that are normally forbidden under Directive 2009/147. National hunting provisions often did not correctly transpose the Directive[126]; hunting seasons were generously allowed and little restricted. To what extent the hunting of migrating birds, which art.7(4) of the Directive expressly forbids, has really been reduced, in particular in southern Europe—nobody can argue that it has stopped in reality—is very doubtful.[127]

5–24   In 1994, the Commission gave in to the pressure from (French) hunting interests and suggested an amendment of the Directive's hunting provisions which would have prolonged hunting seasons,[128] but was stopped by the European Parliament and the Council. In 1998, the French Parliament adopted legislation which extended the hunting period for birds into the time of migration and breeding, in deliberate and open defiance of Directive 2009/147. In 1999, France was condemned by the European Court of Human Rights because some of its hunting provisions were in conflict with the individual right of property. And in 2000, the Court of Justice gave a judgment on the French hunting rules[129] which once more stated that they were not compatible with EU rules. In 2004, hunters and environmental organisations signed, on the initiative of the Commission ("sustainable hunting") an agreement on hunting. Since then, the Commission practically stopped to take action against Member States' hunting legislation or practice.

Generally, implementation of Directive 2009/147 was slow. Until 2012, the Commission had to take court action, because national legislation did not fully comply with the Directive And until 2015, the Commission had only published five of the composite reports which it should have published under art.12(2) of the Directive every three years, limiting these reports largely to reproducing Member States' comments, without analysing and assessing the situation itself.

---

[125] *Commission v Belgium* (C-247/85) [1987] E.C.R. 3073; *Commission v Italy* (C-262/85) [1987] E.C.R. 3073; *Commission v Germany* (C-412/85) [1987] E.C.R. 3503; *Commission v Netherlands* (C-236/85) [1987] E.C.R. 3989; *Commission v France* (C-252/85) [1988] E.C.R. 2243; *Gourmetterie van den Burg* (C-169/89) [1990] E.C.R. 2143; *Commission v Italy* (C-334/89) [1991] E.C.R. 93; *Commission v Germany* (C-345/92) [1993] E.C.R. I-1115; *Association des Animaux v Préfet Maine et Loire* (C-435/92) [1994] E.C.R. I-69; *Ministère public v Vergy* (C-149/94) [1996] E.C.R. I-299; *V.D. Feesten* (C-202/94) [1996] E.C.R. I-355; *Ligue belge des oiseaux* (C-10/96) [1996] E.C.R. I-6775; *Commission v Austria* (C-507/04) [2007] E.C.R. I-5939; *Commission v Greece* (C-293/07) ECLI:EU:C:2008:706; *Commission v Greece* (C-259/08) ECLI:EU:C:2009:13; *Commission v Italy* (C-164/09) ECLI:EU:C:2010:672; *Commission v Poland* (C-192/11) ECLI:EU:2012:44.

[126] See the different cases on national hunting rules: *Commission v Netherlands* (C-339/87) [1990] E.C.R. 851; *Commission v Germany* (C-288/88) [1990] E.C.R. 2721; *Commission v Italy* (C-157/89) [1991] E.C.R. 57; *Association des Animaux v Préfet Maine et Loire* (C-435/92); *WWF v Veneto* (C-118/94) [1996] E.C.R. I-1451; *Commission v Spain* (C-79/03) [2004] E.C.R. I-11619; *Commission v Finland* (C-344/03) [2005] E.C.R. I-11033; *Commission v Spain* (C-221/04) [2006] E.C.R. I-4515; *WWF v Lombardia* (C-60/06) [2006] E.C.R. I-5083; *Commission v Italy* (C-503/06) ECLI:EU:C:2008:279; *Commission v Malta* (C-76/08) [2009] E.C.R. I-8213.

[127] See, as an example, Written Question E-012160/13 (Kamall) [2014] OJ C221/254.

[128] Commission [1994] OJ C100/12.

[129] Court of Justice, *Commission v France* (C-38/99) [2000] E.C.R. I-10941; see also the earlier judgment, *Commission v France* (252/85) [1988] E.C.R. 2243.

The last report of 2011 covered the period 2005–2007, thus came four years late; one might imagine that a report which is delayed for such a long time and then reports only on generalities, has not much more than academic value.

The conclusion after 35 years of operation of Directive 2009/147[130] is that it has undoubtedly had positive effects. Its legally binding provisions, which markedly contrast with international conventions that are considered as soft law and are neither enforceable nor enforced, have alerted administrations concerned, public opinion and research and caused them to seriously consider the state of birdlife in Europe. Habitats have been designated and concern for ensuring the survival of the different species of birds has been raised. No international convention was capable of achieving similar results, in particular as the Commission acted and continues to act as a coordination and enforcement body. While about 12 per cent of European birds are threatened with extinction,[131] some species have even increased in number. The problems of applying the Directive are the same that apply to nature conservation and to biodiversity generally: the overall decline of birds has not yet been stopped in Western Europe.

Generally, on biodiversity protection by the European Union, the following statement appears pertinent[132]:   5–25

> "The absence of a political will, the lack of financial resources, the predominance of traditional interests over ecological interests, outdated systems of criminal law, the inability of environmental associations in many Member States to bring court actions, and the ambiguity of the applicable legal provisions are just a few of the factors undermining the application of harmonised EC rules. It comes as no surprise that despite the number of laws that now exist with respect to nature conservation, and the many positive impacts that they had, these positive steps are falling short of preventing Noah's Ark to sink."

(c) Trade restrictions

Internationally, the trade in endangered species is regulated by the Convention on   5–26
International Trade in Endangered Species of fauna and flora (CITES) which covers some 30,000 species of animals and plants.[133] The European Union is not a member of CITES, since that Convention was, in the past, only open to states, not to international institutions. A 1983 amendment of the Convention, which would enable the European Union to adhere, entered into force only in 2013.[134] The European Union adhered to the Convention in 2015.[135] Since 1982, the European Union applied the provisions of that Convention within the European

---

[130] See N. de Sadeleer, *"Bilan d'une décennie d'efforts législatifs en droit communautaire de la protection de la nature"* in P. Renaudière and P. van Pelt (eds), *Développements récents du droit communautaire de l'environnement* (Diegem, 1995), pp.199 et seq. (at p.259); C. Mayr, *"Vierzehn Jahre EG-Vogelschutzrichtlinie. Bilanz ihrer Umsetzung in der Bundesrepublik Deutschland"*, *Berichte zum Vogelschutz* 31 (1993), p.13; P. Pagh, *"EU's beskyttelse af vilde fugle og fisk: indgribende betydning for arealanvendelsen"*, *Ugeskrift for Retsvaesen* (1997), pp.511 et seq.
[131] European Environment Agency, Technical Report 12/2010 [2010] Copenhagen, p.14.
[132] N. de Sadeleer, "EC law and biodiversity", in R. Macrory (ed.), *Reflections on 30 Years of EU Environmental Law* (Groningen, 2005), p.369.
[133] CITES Convention of 3 March 1973 [1982] OJ L384/8.
[134] The so-called Gaborone amendment.
[135] Decision 2015/451 [2015] OJ L75/1.

Union. The last update is from 1997, Regulation 338/97.[136] This Regulation is regularly aligned to decisions by the CITES institutions.[137]

Regulation 338/97 deals only with conservation measures. Provisions in earlier regulations and also in the Commission's proposal for Regulation 338/97,[138] which aimed at dealing with questions of public safety and animal welfare, were removed from the final version of the Regulation, which led, at the same time, to the taking of art.192 TFEU as a legal basis, rather than arts 114 and 207 TFEU, as proposed by the Commission. The Regulation treats the European Union as one territory. It introduces a differentiated system of protection. Annex A contains all endangered species which are under the total protection of the CITES Convention and, in addition, a number of other species which are considered threatened under the stricter criteria of the Regulation. Trade in these species for primarily commercial purposes is prohibited; also, within the European Union only very narrow derogation possibilities exist. The Commission's proposal generally to prohibit any possession of species listed in annex A was not accepted by the Council.

Annex B contains species which are not actually threatened by trade; however, trade in these species should take place under strict conditions in order to avoid them becoming threatened. Again, the Regulation goes considerably beyond the requirements of the CITES Convention. Importing these species into the European Union requires an import licence from the country of destination, which must be presented at the time of importation.

5–27 The import of species listed in annex C into the European Union is subject to the presentation of an import notification rather than a licence. Finally, annex D includes species that are imported into the European Union in such quantities that an import notification is considered necessary.

Under arts 4(6) and 19(2) of Regulation 338/97, the Commission may, under certain ecological conditions, restrict the introduction of certain specimens of species into the European Union, because of reasons in the country of origin. Several Commission decisions, the last one of 2014, contained a list of species which may not be imported into the European Union.[139] This list and also the amendments to the annexes of the Regulation are drawn up by way of a committee procedure, which allows a speedy reaction to decisions of the contracting parties of the CITES Convention.

Trade transactions which are covered by CITES concern mainly imports. In 2012, some 100,000 such import transactions were reported by Member States, while 225 exports took place.[140] Illegal trade in endangered species is high; the European Union often serves as a transit region.

---

[136] Regulation 338/97 on the protection of species of wild fauna and flora by regulating trade therein [1997] OJ L61/1; this Regulation replaced Reg.3626/82 [1982] OJ L384/1.
[137] See, e.g. Commission Regs 101/2012 [2012] OJ L39/153; 1158/2012 [2012] OJ L339/1; 720/2013 [2013] OJ L212/1; 1320/2014 [2014] OJ L361/1; 2015/56 [2015] OJ L10/1.
[138] Regulation 338/97 [1992] OJ C26/1.
[139] Commission, Reg.888/2014 suspending the introduction into the Union of specimens of certain species of wild fauna and flora [2014] OJ L243/21.
[140] UNEP, analysis of the 2012 EU annual reports to CITES, *http://euanalysis2012unep.wcmc.org/overview-of-eu-trade* [Accessed 30 September 2015]. The ten mostly imported commodities in 2012 were: live plants; plant leaves; plant stems; reptile skins; small leather products; plant wax; plant roots; timber; live corrals; and raw corrals.

Prior to adopting the different CITES Regulations since 1982, the European   **5–28**
Union had already, in 1981, adopted a regulation to protect whales.[141] The
Regulation strictly prohibited, without derogation, the commercial import of
whale and other cetacean meat, bones, fats and oils, leather and furs. Since this
ban was in line with international decisions on the protection of whales, this
Regulation, which was later largely superseded by the provisions of Regulation
338/97,[142] raised few concerns. Trade restrictions on seals which are not an
endangered species will be discussed at para.5—38, below.

The trade restrictions with regard to timber and timber products, mentioned
above,[143] also have the purpose to protect tropical forest species.

(d)   Invasive species

In 2014, the European Union adopted a Regulation in invasive alien species.[144]   **5–29**
Under this Regulation, a species is considered alien when it is introduced, by
human intervention, outside its natural range. It is considered to be "invasive"
when its adverse impacts are found to threaten on biodiversity or related
ecosystem services (art.3). Invasive alien species may have

> "severe impacts in native species and the structure and functioning of ecosystems,
> through the alteration of habitats, predation, competition, the transmission of
> diseases, the replacement of native species throughout a significant proportion of
> range and through genetic effects by hybridisation. Furthermore, invasive alien
> species can also have a significant adverse impact on human health and the
> economy" (Recital 3).

The Commission is asked to establish a Union list of invasive alien species,
based on scientific evidence, a risk assessment and a consideration of the cost
impact. Article 5 provides for an import, trade, use etc ban for such species.
Regional and national invasive alien species are subject to specific provisions of
information and cooperation.

Member States may inform the Commission of invasive alien species in order   **5–30**
to have them included in the Union list, which shall be regularly updated.
Member States are further requested to adopt an action plan in order to identify
the pathways of the introduction of invasive alien species. They then have to set
up a national surveillance and control system. Whenever they detect new invasive
alien species, they are to notify the Commission. Then, within three months, they
are to take eradication measures. Furthermore, they are to set up a management
system for widely spread invasive alien species. National emergency measures
may be taken under certain conditions. All EU or national measures are subject to
scientific advice and shall take the cost of the envisaged measure into
consideration. The Regulation does not apply to genetically modified organisms
and to alien species which invade the Union without human intervention.

---

[141] Regulation 348/81 on common rules for imports of whales or other cetacean products [1981] OJ
L39/1.
[142] Regulation 338/97 [1992] OJ C26/1.
[143] See para 5–04, above.
[144] Regulation 1143/2014 on invasive alien species [2014] OJ L317/35.

The first Union list is to be published before the end of 2015. In view of the fact that the Regulation estimates the presence of some 12,000 alien species in the European Union, of which 10 to 15 per cent are thought to be invasive (Recital 1), it remains to be seen whether the measures adopted will, in times of globalisation and climate change (both effects of human activity!), be effective

(e) Other measures

5–31   Among the other measures to be mentioned, methods for capturing animals should be particularly noted. Directives 2009/147 and 92/43 both contain a specific annex to prohibit the use of large-scale or non-selective capturing methods, without having been able to stop completely the use of such means within the European Union, in particular for bird hunting.

Regulation 894/97, which replaces a number of earlier legislative acts and which was later amended by Regulation 1239/98, prohibited the use of fishing driftnets of more than 2.5km in length;[145] this ban applied since 1 January 2008 over all the EU waters, as by then a derogation for the Baltic Sea ended. The reason for this ban is the non-selective character of capturing with driftnets, which may reach 100km in length; the problem first appeared when dolphins were captured during the fishing of tuna. Besides this problem, the use of driftnets leads to overfishing and has contributed to the serious depletion of fish resources worldwide and in EU waters.

As the ban was "easy to circumvent" and Member States' enforcement systems were not functioning well,[146] in 2014 the Commission proposed a total prohibition on the carrying on ships or the use of any kind of driftnets.[147] The European Parliament and the Council have not yet decided on this proposal.

3.   ANIMAL WELFARE

(a) Animal welfare and the EU Treaties

5–32   Animal welfare concerns animals as living beings. It tries to protect animals independently from the question of whether a species is endangered or not. It is obvious that such a concept is strongly influenced by ethical, religious and similar considerations. The EU Treaties treat animals differently from goods, as appears clearly in art.36 TFEU, which allows restrictions for the free circulation of goods in order to protect life and safety of animals and plants; furthermore, trade measures for animals are based on art.192 TFEU or, in agricultural matters, on art.43, rather than on art.114 TFEU.

At EU level, the idea that animals could or should have rights of their own, or that trees should be important in their own right, has never seriously been discussed: such considerations appear too distant from the anthropocentric

---

[145] Regulation 894/97 on technical measures to preserve fish resources [1997] OJ L32, p.1, art.11. The Regulation was based on art.43 TFEU. It was replaced by Reg.1239/98 [1998] OJ L171/1.
[146] See Court of Justice, *Commission v France* (C-479/07) ECLI:EU:C:2009131; *Commission v France* (C-556/07) ECLI:EU:C:2009:153; *Commission v Italy* (C-249/08) ECLI:EU:C:2009:672.
[147] Commission COM(2014) 265.

concept of nature, in particular in Roman law Member States. A mention of consideration for animals in the 4th Environment Action Programme 1987 did not lead to the development of a coherent approach.

Attempts by animal welfare groups, supported in this also by the European Parliament,[148] to have a specific provision on animal welfare inserted into the EU Treaties were only successful in 2009. At the conclusion of the Maastricht Treaty, a declaration was made by the Intergovernmental Conference that animal welfare aspects should be taken into consideration in the context of some EU policies.[149] The Amsterdam Treaty on European Union added a Protocol to the Treaty,[150] which provided that EU policy should take animal welfare fully into consideration in its policies on agriculture, transport, internal market and research.[151] In 2009, this provision was included in the TFEU, where animals were called "sentient beings".[152] It is not quite clear why environmental policy was not also enumerated.

Wild animals are part of the natural resources; measures to protect them, to provide for their welfare when captured and so on, are environmental measures. Indeed, the preservation and protection of natural resources is not limited to protecting endangered species, but applies to all natural resources. Measures regarding wild animals, even where they do not belong to an endangered species, therefore come under arts 191–193 TFEU. This approach was recognised in 1999, when the European Union adopted a Directive on the keeping of wild animals in zoos, based on art.192 TFEU,[153] though it was explicitly mentioned that this Directive intended to protect species of animals, not individual animals. However, it is obviously erroneous to consider all animals in zoos to be endangered species.

5–33

The main legal problem is that the rules of international trade, established by the General Agreement of Tariffs and Trade (GATT) and the World Trade Organisation (WTO), are generally interpreted as prohibiting measures which restrict trade because of the production methods used. Debate about these issues is not very thorough, as the examples of products made by working children or those produced in jail demonstrate; indeed, trade in such products may be prohibited under GATT/WTO rules. As further discussed below, though, WTO accepted, in 2014, an EU ban on trade in seals as justified on moral grounds, even though seals are not an endangered species.

---

[148] See 4th Environment Action Programme 1987–1992 [1987] OJ C328/1, no.5.1.9: "An improvement in the quality of life also entails respect for animals in the Member States and in the Member States' dealings with the rest of the world. The regular debates concerning the hunting of seal pups should not conceal the many questions raised by the exploitation of animals in Europe: the use of animals for experiments, factory farming, trading in animals and the processing of animals for consumption. The Commission will examine all possible steps which it can take in this connection."

[149] See European Parliament, Resolution of 21 January 1994 [1994] OJ C44/206; the European Parliament in particular wanted animals to be no longer called, within the context of agricultural policy, "agricultural products".

[150] [1992] OJ C191/1, Declaration No.12.

[151] [1997] OJ C340/110.

[152] Article 13 TFEU: "In formulating and implementing the Union's agricultural, fisheries, transport, internal market, research and technological development and space policies, the Union and the Member States shall, since animals are sentient beings, pay full regard to the welfare requirements of animals, while respecting the legislative or administrative provisions and customs of the Member States relating in particular to religious rights, cultural traditions and regional heritage."

[153] See para.5–37, below.

The discussion on environmentally sustainable production methods—an example is the consideration on import restrictions for tropical wood that does not stem from sustainable production—has only just started. The European Union began, since the early 1990s, to take measures in order to prevent possible conflicts with WTO or trading partners, which might end in formal WTO proceedings.[154] This explains why the full implementation of animal welfare measures is often delayed.

(b)   Tests on animals

5–34   Directive 2010/63[155] limits the use of animals for experimental or scientific purposes, in order in particular to avoid unnecessary experiments and to avoid pain, suffering distress and lasting harm. The Directive is based on art.114 TFEU, but allows Member States to maintain or introduce stricter measures at national level (art.2). It lays down detailed provisions on the authorisation of animal testing, the persons responsible for experiments, the keeping of animals, the establishments, etc; detailed guidelines for accommodation and care of animals are annexed to the Directive. Particular restrictions apply to endangered animals. The Directive does not apply to non-experimental agricultural practices.

Whether the Directive applies where animals are used to "produce", for instance a secretum, blood or anti-bodies, etc, was doubtful and, since 1986, answered differently by Member States. The limitation of animals for experimental or other scientific purposes (art.3(1)) and the limitation of "procedures" to basic, translational or applied research with specific aims (art.5) indicates that the new Directive 2010/63 does not allow animals to be used for such production purposes.

Animals may not be used where another scientifically satisfactory method or testing strategy is available (art.4). Endangered species and non-human primates may not normally be used for scientific purposes (arts 7 and 8); animals taken from the wild may not be taken either, though national authorities may grant derogations (art.9).

5–35   Since 1994, the Commission published overall seven reports on statistical data concerning the practical application of Directive 86/609, the predecessor of Directive 2010/63.[156] The figures in these reports are not comparable, as the number of EU Member States changed and as the statistical methods for calculation had been amended. The 7th report of 2013, which covers the year 2011, gives for the first time data on 27 EU Member States.

According to that report, there were about 11.5 million animals used for scientific or experimental purposes. Mice (61 per cent), rats (14 per cent), cold-blooded animals—reptiles, amphibians and fish (12.5 per cent) and birds (5.9 per cent) were the most used animals. No Great Apes were used. The report for 2008 had indicated the use of 12 million animals.

---

[154] See also paras 5–40 and 11–30, below.

[155] Directive 2010/63 on the protection of animals used for scientific purposes [2010] OJ L276/33; this Directive replaced Directive 86/609 [1986] OJ L358/1.

[156] Commission, COM(95) 195; COM(1999) 191; COM(2003) 19; COM(2005) 7; COM(2007) 675; COM(2010) 511.

The European Union adhered in 1998 to the Council of Europe Convention for the protection of vertebrate animals used for experimental and other scientific purposes.[157]

In 1993, the Directive on cosmetic products[158] was amended with a view to ban, as of 1 January 1998, cosmetic products containing ingredients or combinations of ingredients tested on animals.[159] Subsequently, this date was extended several times and only became effective in 2013.[160]

5–36

Regulation 1907/2006 on chemicals[161] contains specific provisions in order to reduce and avoid the duplication of testing on vertebrate animals and even imposes, under certain conditions, the sharing of test studies.[162] Provisions with the same objective are contained in the Regulations on pesticides and biocides.[163]

(c) Seals

Beginning in 1982, the killing of baby seals, particularly in Canada, attracted considerable attention from the Western European media. The European Parliament asked for an import ban on baby seal furs[164] and environmental organisations urged action. Although the Council strongly doubted the possibility of adopting a Commission proposal to ban imports of baby seal furs,[165] it finally adopted such an import ban for two years.[166] After an initial prolongation for four years, in 1989 the import ban was extended for an undetermined time.[167] The Directive did not argue that seals are an endangered species. For that reason alone, the only justification for the import ban on furs and other seal products were the killing methods which were used, thus animal welfare considerations.

5–37

Since 2002/2003, Canada has allowed the hunting and killing of several million seals per year that were not considered to be endangered species. In reaction to that, Belgium and the Netherlands adopted legislation which prohibited the trade in seal products, pointing to the fact that such a ban was effective in the United States for decades and that Mexico had introduced a similar ban in 2005. Several other Member States considered similar action. In view of this, the Commission proposed a regulation on banning trade in seal products which the European Parliament and the Council adopted in 2009.[168] Canada and Norway submitted the matter to the WTO, arguing that this was an

---

[157] Decision 1999/575 (1999) OJ L222/29; the Convention is published in the annex to this Decision.
[158] Directive 93/35 [1993] OJ L151/32.
[159] See Dir.76/768 on cosmetic products [1976] OJ L262/169, art.4(1.i) as amended by Dir.93/35 [1993] OJ L151/32 and Dir.2000/41 [2000] OJ L145/25.
[160] See Written Question 3223/13 Motti, [2014] OJ C11e/548.
[161] Regulation 1907/2006 [2006] OJ L396/1.
[162] Regulation 1907/2006 [2006] OJ L396/1, Recitals, 33, 47 and arts 26 et seq.
[163] See Reg.1107/2009 on pesticides [2009] OJ L309/1, art.62; Reg.528/12 on biocides [2012] OJ L167/1, art.62: "In order to avoid animal testing, testing on vertebrates for the purposes of this Regulation shall be undertaken only as a last resort. Testing on vertebrates shall not be repeated for the purposes of this Regulation …"
[164] European Parliament, Resolution of [1982] OJ C87/87 and 11 March 1982 [1982] OJ C267/47.
[165] Resolution of [1983] OJ C14/1; France, the United Kingdom, Belgium, Denmark and Greece were reported to have opposed measures, since these would be motivated by purely moral motives.
[166] Directive 83/129 concerning the importation into Member States of skins of certain seal pups and products derived therefrom [1983] OJ L91/30.
[167] Directive 85/444 [1985] OJ L259/70 and Dir.89/370 [1989] OJ L163/37.
[168] Regulation 1007/2009 on trade in seal products [2009] OJ L286/36.

unjustified barrier to the free trade in products. Their application was rejected, as the WTO considered the EU measures justified on public moral grounds.[169] On some minor points, the EU lost, but started to amend the seals Regulation, in order to bring it fully into line with the WTO requirements.[170] Canadian groups also attacked the Regulation before the Court of Justice, however without success.[171]

This clarifies that such a ban is, for animal welfare reasons, compatible with art.36 TFEU, as well as with the corresponding WTO/GATT rules. Indeed, public opinion in the European Union does not accept the methods which are used in Canada for the hunting of seals which frequently lead to the skinning of live animals. Public morals and animal welfare considerations cannot be the same all over the world; it must be thus a decision of each individual State—or, in this case, the European Union—whether it considers public morals to be affected or not.

(d)　Leghold traps

5–38　Regulation 3254/91 prohibited, as of 1995, the use of leghold traps within the European Union.[172] Leghold traps, which hold the leg of a captured animal until the hunter arrives or the animal dies, are considered non-selective[173] and cruel (not "humane"). Bans or restrictions on the use of leghold traps are in use in about 60 states all over the world.[174]

While this ban is undisputed, the Commission had—subsequent to a petition of 272 Members of the European Parliament—proposed and the Council had adopted an import ban on the furs of 13 animal species (beaver, otter, coyote, wolf, lynx, bobcat, sable, raccoon, musk rat, fisher (martes pennanti), badger, marten and ermine) from those countries which continued to use leghold traps.[175] The import ban was to come into effect in 1995[176]; the Council expected that by then internationally "humane trapping standards" would be agreed.

---

[169] WTO Document WT/DS 400 and DS 401/AB/R of 29 April 2014. The relevant provision of the WTO/GATT Agreement reads: "Article XX: Subject to the requirement that such measures are not applied in a manner which would constitute a means of arbitrary or unjustifiable discrimination between countries where the same conditions prevail, or a disguised restriction on international trade, nothing in this Agreement shall be construed to prevent the adoption or enforcement by any contracting party of measures (a) necessary to protect public morals; . . ."

[170] Commission, COM(2015) 45.

[171] Court of Justice, *Inuit Katanami a.o. v European Parliament and Council* (C-583/11P) ECLI:EU:C:2013:625.

[172] Regulation 3254/91 prohibiting the use of leghold traps in the Community and the introduction into the Community of pelts and manufactured goods of certain wild animal species originating in countries which catch them by means of leghold traps or trapping methods which do not meet international humane trapping standards [1991] OJ L308/1.

[173] According to figures quoted by ECOSOC, Opinion of 26 April 1990 [1990] OJ C168/32, no.1.6.3, about 10% of animals caught in leghold traps are caught unintentionally.

[174] Written Question 1936/88 (Zarges) [1989] OJ C255/15.

[175] The Commission's proposal [1989] OJ C134/5 did not contain a ban on leghold traps, since such a ban had been proposed in the directive on habitats [1988] OJ C247/3; since it thus only contained an import ban, it was based on art.207 TFEU. The Council Regulation is based on arts 207 and 192 TFEU.

[176] Subsequently, there was a controversy whether the ban did indeed become effective. Article 3(1) of Reg.3254/91 stipulates: "The introduction into the Community of the pelts ... shall be prohibited as of 1 January 1995, unless the Commission ..." (states that in a third country leghold traps or

However, this was not the case. In particular, the United States, Canada and Russia heavily opposed the import ban, arguing that it was contrary to the rules of the GATT/World Trade Organisation and disadvantaged indigenous populations. In view of this, the Commission proposed, in December 1995, to replace the import ban by a mandate to be given to the European Union in order to negotiate an agreement with third countries on humane trapping standards.[177] The Council did not adopt the proposal, but agreed to negotiations. An agreement with Canada and Russia was reached in 1997, with the United States in 1998.[178] The agreements provided essentially for the fixing of some trapping standards and the phasing out, within four years, of some leghold traps for two species, without containing a legally enforceable commitment. In substance, the European Union abandoned its import ban with regard to these three countries. Regulation 3254/91 has not yet been amended. Thus, for other third countries, the import ban entered into effect in 1997.[179]

In 2004, the Commission proposed a directive in order to implement the two international agreements.[180] However, the European Parliament rejected the proposal with its absolute majority, arguing that the proposal intended to consider the actual practice of Canadian, US and Russian trappers as "humane" trapping methods, without having made scientific research as to less painful trapping methods. The proposal is thus politically dead.

5–39

(e)   Animals in zoos

In 1991, the Commission proposed a directive on the keeping of animals in zoos, of which there are about 1,000 within the European Union (EU 15).[181] Following the extensive discussion on subsidiarity and deregulation which followed the signing of the Maastricht Treaty on European Union in 1991, the proposal was listed, by the Edinburgh summit meeting of the European Council and with pressure from the United Kingdom, as one of the instruments for which the subsidiarity clause should apply; this meant that the European Union should leave the matter to Member States to deal with. The Commission thus withdrew its proposal and replaced it by a proposal for a Council recommendation which contained detailed guidelines on the accommodation and care of animals in zoos.[182]

5–40

The European Parliament and the Economic and Social Committee both pleaded in favour of a directive. The Council first agreed unanimously on a common position concerning a recommendation. However, upon the instigation of the United Kingdom, which completely changed its position adopted in 1992

---

inhumane trapping methods are forbidden). This wording indicates, in my opinion without any legal doubt, that the ban became effective as of 1 January 1995, since the Commission has not made any such statement.

[177] [1996] OJ C58/17.

[178] Decision 98/142 [1998] OJ L42/40 (Canada and Russia); Dec.98/487 [1998] OJ L219/24 (United States); the Decisions were based on arts 207 and 114 TFEU; see also European Parliament [1998] OJ C210/31, which had rejected the agreements.

[179] See Dir.97/602 [1997] OJ L242/64; see also Written Question E-294/98 (Pollack) [1998] OJ C223/160.

[180] Commission COM(2004) 532.

[181] [1991] OJ C241/14.

[182] Commission, COM(95) 619 of 12 December 1995.

at the Edinburgh summit, it changed the principal objective of the instrument, to make it an instrument for the conservation of biodiversity; the detailed rules on accommodation and care of animals were deleted. Zoos were mainly considered to have a role in the conservation of biodiversity, though it was obvious to everybody that the animals kept in zoos were not all endangered. Zoos had to have a permit and were to be regularly inspected by the national competent authorities. On this basis, a Directive was adopted in 1999 based on art.192(1) TFEU.[183] It is remarkable, though, that the Commission does not monitor its application.

---

[183] Directive 1999/22 on the keeping of wild animals in zoos [1999] OJ L94/24.

CHAPTER 6

Products

1. GENERAL QUESTIONS

There is no consistent and coherent EU policy on products. Most of the product-related measures adopted are meant to establish common rules for the establishment and functioning of the internal EU market and thus enable the free circulation of goods. Aspects of health, safety, consumer protection and, at a later stage, environmental protection, were not systematically tackled at EU level, but were, rather, left to be regulated at Member State level; hence, common rules became necessary in order to ensure a level playing field. The so-called "new approach" to product standards' harmonisation, introduced in the 1980s by a Council Resolution,[1] where EU legislation only fixes the essential requirements for a product, leaving the details to industrial standardisation by European standardisation organisations, has not changed this situation. Indeed, these "essential requirements" normally refer to health and safety aspects of a product, but not to its impact on the environment. The Directive on general product safety[2] refers to the "safety and health of persons", but does not mention the environment at all. And legislation on the protection of workers at the working place is limited to that area, but has no general application.

In a judgment of 2009, the Court of Justice held that, as regards mercury, references to "health" also included environmental concerns. Thus, where the European Union had regulated health aspects of products containing mercury, Member States were barred from adopting measures at national level which concerned the environmental aspects of mercury.[3] This judgment ignores the dividing line which primary and secondary EU law draws between the protection of health and safety on the one side, on the protection of the environment on the other side.[4]

In 2013, the Commission proposed a Regulation on the market surveillance of products.[5] This surveillance was to be done by the Member States. Where a Member State was of the opinion that a product presented a risk to humans or to the environment, it had to make a risk assessment. Measures which eventually

6–01

---

[1] Council Resolution of 7 May 1985 [1985] OJ C136/1.

[2] Directive 2001/95 on general product safety [2002] OJ L1/4; this Directive replaced Dir.92/59 [1992] OJ L228/4; proposal for a regulation to replace Dir.2001/95, COM(2013) 78.

[3] Court of Justice, *Kemikalieinspektionen v Nordiska Dental* (C-288/08) [2009] E.C.R I-11031.

[4] See for more details L. Krämer, comment on *Journal of European Environmental and Planning Law* (C-288/08) 2010, p.124. The proposal mentioned in fn.2, above, does not refer to environmental safety at all.

[5] Commission, COM(2013) 75.

were taken at national level were to be confirmed or disapproved by an EU procedure. The proposal is at present discussed by the other EU institutions.

6–02   Different scientific committees, which the Commission had set up in the 1970s, have played some role in determining the effects of products on humans and the environment. Only the Scientific Committee on Human Consumption achieved, in the past, an authoritative reputation; some of the other committees do not seem to have always been completely neutral towards vested interests. In 1997, following the BSE scandal where concern was voiced that the Commission had hidden information on "mad cow disease" and its influence on humans, the Commission restructured the six different scientific committees, renamed them and placed them under the responsibility of the Commissioner on consumer affairs. Thus, the Scientific Committee for the Toxicity and Ecotoxicity of Chemical Substances became the Scientific Committee for Toxicity, Ecotoxicity and the Environment with the task to look into the effects of chemical, biochemical and biological compounds on human health and the environment.[6]

Product policy inevitably affects health and safety, consumer protection and environmental impairment, aspects which cannot clearly be dissociated from each other. EU efforts concentrate on the attempts to find a balance between health and safety of humans on the one hand, and on the free circulation of goods, their export and import on the other hand. Environmental concerns play a secondary role. The fact that substances or products—in the form of emissions, goods, wastes, residues, etc—exist everywhere in the environment and present considerable risks to biodiversity, soil, fresh and marine waters, or buildings has not really led to the setting up of a product policy which is less anthropocentric and more integrated.

The Commission's attempt to launch an "integrated product policy"[7] did not really contain what the title promises. The Commission defined integrated product policy "as an approach which seeks to reduce the life cycle environmental impacts of products from the mining of raw materials to production, distribution, use and waste management".[8] This approach was thus limited to try to integrate environmental requirements into product-related aspects. The Commission favoured non-binding instruments under this approach, and published in 2005 and 2006 the results of two pilot projects on mobile phones and teak garden chairs; there was no further follow-up on these projects. Since then, the whole discussion on integrated product policy largely came to a standstill, as also proven by the Commission's poor implementation report of 2009 and a new communication of 2010 which is full of commonplaces.[9]

6–03   The discussion on an environmentally oriented product policy at national level is strongly influenced by the Treaty provisions on the free circulation of goods and the interpretation that, under these provisions, a product that is lawfully produced and marketed in one Member State must in principle also be allowed to circulate in the other Member States. It should be noted, though, that this general

---

[6] Decision 97/579 [1997] OJ L237/18; see also Dec.97/404 setting up a Scientific Steering Committee [1997] OJ L169/85.

[7] Commission, Green Paper on Integrated Product Policy COM(2001) 68; COM(2003) 302.

[8] Commission, COM(2001) 68, p.2.

[9] Commission, Report on the state of implementation of integrated product policy, COM(2009) 693; Commission, An integrated industrial policy for the globalisation area; putting competitiveness and sustainability at centre stage, COM(2010) 614.

provision does not prevent the introduction of an environmental product policy at Member State level. Indeed, the Court jurisdiction regarding the interdependency between art.34 TFEU and environmental protection may be summarised in the statement that in the absence of EU provisions concerning a product a Member State may adopt any environmental provision it wishes, as long as there is no discrimination of producers and traders from other Member States and as long as the national measure is not disproportionate to the environmental objective pursued; furthermore, the measures taken by a Member State must be proportionate.[10]

Discussions on product policy at Member State level are considerably further advanced than that at EU level. The Netherlands Government formulated its product-oriented environmental policy as[11]:

"to bring about a situation whereby all market actors—producers, traders and consumers—are involved in an ongoing effort to reduce the impact which products have on the environment."

Germany defined, in 1999, the integrated product policy as "public policy which aims at or is suitable for continuous improvement in the environmental performance of products and services within a life-cycle context". The most advanced approach is, however, that of the Swedish Government which declared as the aim of an integrated product policy[12]:

"to produce products and services that make the smallest possible impact on human health or the environment at each stage of their life-cycle. Products should be material—and energy—efficient, at the same time as they should not contain or require the use of substances that may involve adverse effects on human health or the environment."

More important perhaps than the conceptual differences are the concrete actions which are undertaken. Almost all depends on the political determination to bring the concept of integrated product policy into reality. An important principle in this concept is the substitution principle, which the EU 6th Environment Action Programme described as follows[13]:

6–04

"Chemicals that are dangerous should be replaced by safer chemicals or safer alternative technologies not entailing the use of chemicals, with the aim of reducing risks to man and the environment."

---

[10] See in particular Court of Justice, *Mickelsson and Roos* (C-142/05) [2009] E.C.R. I-4273 and *Sandström* (C-433/05) [2010] E.C.R I-2885, where the Court laid down the conditions under which national measures which restricted the use of personal watercraft on Swedish waters were compatible with arts 34–36 TFEU; these products were, by virtue of EU legislation, allowed to circulate freely within the European Union.

[11] (Netherlands) Department of Environmental Affairs (VROM), Policy paper on products and the environment (The Hague, 1994).

[12] Swedish Government Communication 1999/2000:114 (Stockhom, 2000).

[13] Decision 1600/2002 laying down the 6th Environment Action Programme [2002] OJ L242/1, Recital 25 and art.7(1). Such a commitment is, however, *not* repeated in Dec.1386/2013 on a general Union environment action programme to 2020 [2013] OJ L354/171.

Though the principle's application is limited, in this context, to chemicals, its application is much broader and applies, it is submitted, to all products.[14] The substitution principle is also expressed in Directive 2011/65 which limits the use of certain dangerous substances in electrical and electronic equipment and which provides that other substances than those mentioned in the Directive shall be regulated in view of their substitution by environmentally more friendly substances, as soon as sufficient scientific information is available.[15]

In 2001, a judgment of the Court of Justice showed strong sympathy for the substitution principle in environmental law.[16] Regulation 1907/2006 on chemical products, REACH (see paras 6–32 et seq., below), tries to make the substitution principle one of the cornerstones of the new system on chemicals.[17] Also Regulation 1107/2009 concerning the placing on the market of pesticides provides for extensive recurrence to the substitution principle.[18]

6–05   The integrated product policy approach at EU level has never mentioned the substitution principle as one that would be guiding action in this area. It is not clear either, up until now, which other principles apply and whether there will be any attempt to systematically address environmental issues caused by products. In my opinion, an integrated product policy must base itself, in particular, on the following four principles:

1.   The substitution principle, according to which dangerous substances should not be used in products where substances are available that are less dangerous for humans or the environment.
2.   The precautionary principle, according to which the absence of scientific certainty does not prevent the taking of action, where a presumption of a risk to humans or the environment exists.
3.   The minimisation principle, according to which a product should make the smallest possible impact on humans and the environment.
4.   The principle of producer responsibility, according to which the producer shall be responsible for his product from the selection and choice of the raw materials to the responsibility for the product when it has finished its useful lifetime and becomes waste.

Efforts in an EU product policy are also hampered by the fact that products (goods) are the subject of trade, and EU-wide and international efforts are dominated by the attempt to ensure free trade in goods. From this objective stems the request that the taking of any measure in the product-related area be allowed only where it is scientifically proven that the product or production method that is used presents a risk to human health or safety or to the environment. Free trade in goods should therefore only be affected where the risk assessment for substances

---

[14] See also Court of Justice, *Kemikalieinspektionen* (C-473/98) [2000] E.C.R. I-5681.

[15] Directive 2011/65 on the restriction of the use of certain dangerous substances in electrical and electronic equipment [2011] OJ L174/88, Recitals 16 and 18 and art.5. This Directive replaced Dir.2002/95 [2003] OJ L37719.

[16] Court of Justice, *Kemikalieinspektionen* (C-473/98) [2000] E.C.R. I-5681.

[17] Regulation 1907/2006 concerning the registration, evaluation, authorisation and restriction of chemicals (REACH), establishing a chemicals agency [2006] OJ L396/1.

[18] Regulation 1107/2009 concerning the placing on the market of plant protection products [2009] OJ L309/1.

or products demonstrates an unacceptable risk to health or the environment. Where such risk assessment also includes a cost-benefit analysis, the objective is no longer to minimise the impact of products on humans and the environment—see the above-mentioned Swedish approach—but rather to minimise the impact of environmental measures on trade in goods.

At EU level, the attempts to minimise the impact of products on humans and the environment are still at their beginnings and not systematic. The 6th and 7th Environment Action Programmes do not mention a policy approach on products. Only in the chapter on natural resources and waste management of the 6th Programme is the integrated policy approach mentioned, however, in a rather marginal way. In contrast, the attempts to minimise the environmental impact on the free circulation of goods are more systematic: Member States must, before adopting any product-related legislation that might affect the free circulation of goods, transmit their draft legislation together, "if available", with a risk analysis, to the Commission and to all other Member States.[19] For chemicals, Regulation 1907/2006 now requires producers and importers to deliver the results of safety tests to the European Chemical Agency which means that they have to make a sort of impact assessment; the difference to the previous legislation is that it is no longer the public authorities which have to test the safety of chemicals.[20] This is the consequence of the general understanding that risk assessment was slow and resource-intensive and did not allow the system to work efficiently and effectively.[21] In the past, the Commission had committed itself to carry out risk assessments and adequate analyses of the costs and benefits prior to any proposal or adoption of a regulatory measure affecting the chemical industry.[22]

This policy of requiring that any action on the restriction of use of a substance is preceded by a risk assessment contradicts the precautionary principle of art.191 TFEU, which asks EU institutions to act even in cases where there is scientific uncertainty as to the harmfulness of a substance for humans or the environment. In the case of doubt, these principles suggest EU action, so that, in the case of an error, free trade is affected rather than human health or the environment: where a product or a substance is suspected to be dangerous, it is appropriate to act and not to wait for definitive scientific evidence.

6–06

It is comforting that, in the past, the Commission itself has not systematically provided for a risk assessment on specific substances, in particular in those cases where either public opinion was concerned about the risks of a substance for humans or when Member States took action to restrict the use of a substance. Cases dealt with since 1997, where the results of a risk assessment were not available before EU legislative action was started, concern phthalates,[23] asbestos,[24] greenhouse gases,[25] ozone-depleting substances,[26] the restriction of

---

[19] Directive 98/34 laying down a procedure for the provision of information in the field of technical standards and regulations [1998] OJ L204/37, art.8(1).

[20] Regulation 1907/2006 [2006] OJ L396/1.

[21] See in more detail paras 6–25 et seq., below.

[22] Commission, White Paper on Chemical Policy (1998) 88, no.2.1.

[23] See para.6–51, below.

[24] See para.4–50, above.

[25] See para.9–22, below.

[26] See paras 6–24 and 9–30, below.

heavy metals in cars[27] or in electrical and electronic equipment,[28] the measures in reaction to the accident of *The Prestige* tanker off the Spanish coast in November 2002[29] or cadmium in batteries and accumulators.[30] Requesting in all cases a risk analysis and a cost-benefit analysis neglects the fact that the environment suffers from the presence of too many pollutants. Accident prevention and remediation procedures are very important for the environment; however, the primary aim of any environmental policy should be to prevent environmental impairment and therefore to reduce the placing of environmentally hazardous substances into the environment.

The Court of Justice in its judgment C-180/96, confirmed the possibility for preventive action, without putting as a condition that a risk assessment or cost-benefit analysis must be undertaken beforehand.[31] Nothing else can apply to the protection of the environment, all the more as the Court of Justice, in its above-mentioned judgment and in later decisions, expressly referred to the necessity of preventive action, laid down in art.191(2) TFEU.

6–07   It is to be expected that the battle will continue between supporters of a wide application of the precautionary and prevention principles in order to promote an active, environmentally sound EU product policy, and the supporters of an unhampered circulation of goods which try to introduce risk analyses, life-cycle assessments, cost-benefit calculations into any decision-making, limit precautionary measures to provisional action, etc. This discussion will be of particular importance in the context of the increasing number of free trade agreements which the EU concluded or intends to conclude with South Korea, Vietnam, Canada, the United States and other countries.

2.   COMPOSITION AND MARKETING OF PRODUCTS

6–08   There are only a few EU provisions on the making of products. It is general EU policy that a certain technology for products should not be prescribed in order to reach environmental results and that EU legislation should set targets (results) to be achieved, such as emission limits, and leave it to manufacturers how to achieve these results. Obviously, this principle applies more to machinery than to other products. Indeed, chemical legislation does provide, via the establishment of lists of substances that may or may not be used in a product, for direct influence on the product; an example is the sector of pesticides, where EU legislation is setting up a list of active substances that may be used in pesticides, while leaving the composition of pesticides to the producer.[32] Also, the legislation

---

[27] Directive 2000/53 on end-of-life vehicles [2000] OJ L269/34.
[28] Dirctive 2011/65 [2011] OJ L174/88.
[29] See Commission, Report on actions to deal with the effects of the Prestige disaster, COM(2003) 105.
[30] Directive 2006/66 on batteries and accumulators and waste batteries and accumulators [2006] OJ L266/1.
[31] Court of Justice, *United Kingdom v Commission* (C-180/96) [1998] E.C.R. I-2265; see also para.1–33, above; see, further, European Parliament Resolution of 20 October [1998] OJ C341/31 on endocrine disruptors.
[32] See paras 6–33 et seq., below.

on end-of-life vehicles and electrical and electronic products which prohibits the use of certain heavy metals in these products belongs to this category.[33]

In contrast, the European Union has never applied the principle of art.191(2) TFEU according to which environmental impairment should be rectified at source, to its general product-related legislation. It did not request cars to be equipped, from a certain time onwards, with catalytic converters, but rather fixed emission limit values that could, at the time when they were fixed, only be reached when a catalytic converter was used. In the same way, it is unthinkable that EU legislation would ever require cars to be built in a way that they cannot run quicker than 100km/hour or that they use not more than three litres of petrol per 100km; at least this last legislation is partly in force in California. Within the European Union and in Germany, France, Italy, etc, the car industry is much too influential to ever accept such legislation.

In 2005, the Council and Parliament adopted Directive 2005/32 on the eco-design of energy using products, which was, in 2009, updated by Directive 2009/125.[34] The Directive was based on art.114 TFEU; it was part of the European Union's policy to fight climate change by increasing energy efficiency. It provided for measures at EU level to reduce energy consumption of products, relying to a considerable degree on self-regulation, industrial standardisation, etc. As a first step, stand-by losses and products that offer a high potential for cost-effective reduction of greenhouse gas emissions, such as heating and water heating equipment, electric motor systems lighting, domestic appliances, office equipment, consumer electronics and heating ventilating air conditioning systems were tackled. Overall, the work programme under this Directive provided for regulations for 57 product groups. The instruments used are Commission regulations, adopted in the form of comitology decisions. Voluntary agreements by producers and industrial standards which should, according to the Directive, be preferred to regulatory measures, only play a very minimal role: economic operators appear to be too much afraid of free-riders and third-country producers who would not be subjected to voluntary provisions. Though the Directive also allowed in the Recitals for the tackling of other issues of eco-design, such as water consumption, noise levels or material use, it was clarified that the (only) priority would be to reduce the emission of greenhouse gases.[35]

At the end of 2005, the Commission made a communication on a thematic strategy on the sustainable use of natural resources.[36] The communication underlined the necessity of life-cycle thinking for products, from raw materials to the waste stage. The objective is to reduce the environmental impacts of using natural resources. The measures announced mainly address Member States and do not anticipate the promotion of legally binding instruments to ensure "ecologically sound and sustainable product design". The Commission expressly

6–09

---

[33] See Dir.2000/53 [2000] OJ L269/34 and Dir.2011/65 [2011] OJ L174/88.

[34] Directive 2005/32 [2005] OJ L191/29; in 2009, this Directive was replaced by Dir.2009/125 establishing a framework for the setting of eco-design requirements for energy-related products [2009] OJ L285/10.

[35] Directive 2009/125 [2009] OJ L285/10, Recital 14: "Although a comprehensive approach to environmental performance is desirable, greenhouse gas mitigation through increased energy efficiency should be considered a priority environmental goal, pending the adoption of a working plan."

[36] Commission, COM(2005) 667.

clarified that it had no intention to phase out bad materials for the making of products. The announcement of measures to prevent waste generation was not to propose binding instruments either.[37] Overall, the strategy[38] was not really a strategy, but a—rather superficial—description of the present situation and the expression of hope that something will change in the future. And the strategy was not followed by concrete action.

Environmental directives and regulations have established some lists of substances or products[39] that were considered dangerous for the environment, frequently taking inspiration from international environmental conventions.

As regards water discharges, Directive 76/464 which was, in 2006, codified under the number of Directive 2006/11, created a black list of substances and products, which were selected because of their toxicity, persistence and bioaccumulation; a second list of substances was fixed, which have "a deleterious effect on the aquatic environment".[40] For list I, a priority list of 129 substances was then agreed, which should be regulated by Community emission standards[41]; these measures were brought to a halt in 1991, after only 17 substances had been regulated. Under Directive 2000/60[42] which repealed Directives 76/464 to 2006/11 by 2013, a list of hazardous substances was established in 2001 which were to be further examined in view of a prohibition to discharge them into waters.[43] This list included substances—for instance atrazine, benzene, naphtaline, pentachlrophenol or simazine—and groups of substances such as cadmium, mercury, nickel, lead and their compounds. In 2008, a directive fixed environmental water quality standards and pollution controls for the substances of the 2001 list as well as for eight new substances, and abandoned the objective of prohibiting their discharge.[44] A new Directive of 2013 brought further amendments and prolonged the date for compliance until 2021 and 2027.[45]

6–10   For air pollutants, Directive 84/360 on air emissions[46] contained another list of pollutants the emissions of which were to be limited; no indication was given as to how these substances had been selected. The pollutants were not systematically tackled. This list was practically replaced by another list of air pollutants which was laid down in Directive 96/62 on ambient air quality for which air quality

---

[37] Commission, COM(2005) 667.

[38] Commission, Communication: Taking sustainable use of resources forward: a thematic strategy on the prevention and recycling of waste, COM(2005) 666.

[39] EU terminology is not consistent. Sometimes, the word "substances" is used, where clearly a preparation, i.e. a mixture or composition of two or more substances, is meant.

[40] Directive 76/464 on pollution caused by certain dangerous substances discharged into the aquatic environment of the Community [1976] OJ L129/23, in particular art.6 and annex, list I; codification of Dir.76/464 by Dir.2006/11 [2006] OJ L64/52.

[41] Council Resolution of February 1983 [1983] OJ C46/17. For details on the monitoring of Dir.76/464, see paras 7–24 et seq., below.

[42] Directive 2000/60 establishing a framework for Community action in the field of water policy [2000] OJ L327/1.

[43] Decision 2455/2001 establishing the list of priority substances in the field of water policy [2001] OJ L331/1.

[44] Directive 2008/105 on environmental quality standards in the field of water policy [2008] OJ L348/84.

[45] Directive 2013/39 [2013] OJ L226/1.

[46] Directive 84/360 on the combating of air pollution from industrial plants [1984] OJ L188/20; for more details see paras 8–23 et seq.

standards were to be elaborated[47]; on pollutants in general, Directive 96/61—in 2008 replaced by Directive 2008/1 and in 2010 by Directive 2010/75—on integrated prevention and pollution control laid down a list for air and water pollutants which were emitted by industrial installations.[48]

The Stockholm Convention on Persistent Organic Pollutants (POP) which was signed in 2001, by the European Union and all its Member States and which was transposed into EU law by way of a Regulation 850/2004, provides for a list of persistent organic pollutants which are internationally banned.[49]

All these lists had no direct influence on product-related provisions adopted at EU level, but were, rather, aimed at framing EU policy for the limitation of the emission of pollutants into the environment. The EU institutions did not take them as binding either, but were quite loose in working according to the frame which was set by them, sometimes just not following the list and elaborate detailed emission limit or concentration values.

Restrictions concerning the composition of products had been mainly—but by no means exclusively—inserted into Directive 76/769[50] which had, up to mid-2006, been amended more than 30 times. This Directive is now replaced: the restriction of chemicals are regulated under the REACH-system for chemical substances and inserted in its annex XVII.[51]

6–11

Most initiatives for introducing EU-wide restrictions came from Member States, which introduced bans or restrictions of substances or products in order to protect humans or the environment. This then initiated the restriction procedure at EU level, since the Commission wished to preserve the unity of the internal market, which requires uniform product standards. It is likely that also in future the majority of initiatives to restrict the use of substances will come from Member States; only gradually will the new Chemical Agency assume a leading role and propose restrictions, based on the safety assessments that it receives.

There are only very limited possibilities to provide for interim EU-wide measures that take a substance or a product from the market. When, in 2000, the Commission was of the opinion that six phtalates presented a risk in children's toys and made a proposal for a directive to have the use of these phtalates restricted, it had to recur to Directive 92/59 on general product safety[52] which allowed for interim measures to be taken for a period of three months. As the

---

[47] Directive 96/62 [1996] OJ L296/55; this Directive was, in 2008, replaced by Dir.2008/50 on ambient air quality and cleaner air for Europe (2008), L152/1.
[48] Directive 96/61 on integrated pollution prevention and control [1996] OJ L257/26; Dir.2008/1 on integrated pollution prevention and control [2008] L24/8; Dir.2010/75 on industrial emissions [2010] OJ L334/1.
[49] Regulation 850/2004 [2004] OJ L158/7, amended by Commission Reg.519/2012 [2012] OJ L159/1. The pollutants are: Polychlorinated biphenyls PCB, dioxins, furans, aldrin, dieldrin, endrin, DDT, chlordane, hexachlorobenzene, mirex, toxaphene, heptachlor, endosulfan, hexachlorobutadiene, polichlorinated naphtalenes and alkanes C10-C13. See also Dec.2006/597 by which the EC adhered to the Stockholm Convention [2006] OJ 209/1; the text of the Convention is reproduced there at p.3.
[50] Directive 76/769 relating to restrictions on the marketing and use of certain dangerous substances and preparations [1976] OJ L262/201.
[51] Regulation 1907/2006 [2006] OJ L396/1; see in particular Commission Reg.552/2009 [2009] OJ L164/7 which transferred the restrictions of Dir.76/769 into annex XVII of Reg.1907/2006; furthermore, Commission Reg.276/2010 [2010] OJ L86/7.
[52] Directive 92/59 [1992] OJ L228/4.

Commission's proposal on phtalates was only adopted in 2005,[53] the interim measures had in the meantime been prolonged more than 10 times.[54]

(a) Detergents

6–12   The first provisions that regulated the composition of products concerned those products where diverging national provisions risked the creation of barriers to the free circulation of goods. Thus, from 1973, a Directive prohibited the placing on the market of detergents which were less than 90 per cent biodegradable[55]; since that Directive had to be adopted unanimously and no real consensus was reached as to whether a percentage of 80 or 90 per cent should apply, a compromise was found that the detergent could be placed on the market, as long as the harmonised test methods showed that it was biodegradable by 80 per cent.[56]

In 2005, a completely new regulation on detergents was adopted which replaced the existing legislation[57] and dealt with the biodegradability of all surfactants in detergents, not only that of anionic and non-ionic surfactants. The Regulation provided for the use of different test standards, which may be used alternatively, as obviously no consensus on the use of one standard exists. The biodegradability must normally be 60 per cent (five test methods, annex III A) or 70 per cent (two other test methods, annex III B). Where this biodegradability is not reached, the producer may ask for a derogation, which may, under certain conditions, be granted by the EU Commission (comitology procedure), provided the biodegradability does not exceed 80 per cent (annex II).[58]

In order to reduce the eutrophication of waters, Regulation 259/2012 amending Regulation 648/2004, limited the content of phosphates and phosphorous compounds in consumer detergents as of 2013/2017.[59]

(b) Fuels and biofuels

6–13   The combustion of fuels releases pollutants that contaminate the environment—the damage caused by one tonne of sulphur dioxide is estimated at €4,000.[60] Measures concerning the composition of fuels concentrated on the reduction of

---

[53] Directive 2005/84 [2005] OJ L344/40. These restrictions are now found in Reg.1907/2006 [2006] OJ L396/1, annex XVII, no.52.

[54] Directive 2001/95 [2002] OJ L1/4, art.13, prolonged in the meantime the validity of a Commission measure to one year. The Commission proposal (fn.2, above), art.12 provided for a validity of two years

[55] Directive 73/404 on the approximation of the laws of the Member States relating to detergents [1973] OJ L347/51.

[56] Directive 73/405 on the approximation of the laws of the Member States relating to methods of testing the biodegradability on non-ionic surfactants [1973] OJ L347/53; subsequently, Dirs 82/242 [1982] OJ L109/1 and 82/243 [1982] OJ L109/18 completed the provisions for testing methods.

[57] Regulation 648/2004 on detergents [2004] OJ L104/1.

[58] As to the equivalence of results, see Reg.648/2004 [2004] OJ L104/1, annex IIIB: "It should be noted that the pass criterion of at least 70 percent of these methods is to be considered as equivalent to the pass criterion of at least 60 percent referred to in the methods listed in point A."

[59] Regulation 259/2012 [2012] OJ L94/16.

[60] Commission, COM(1997) 88, p.44.

pollutants. As Member States had different perceptions of environmental problems, it is not surprising that such differences reappeared when fuels were regulated.

EU legislation started with regulating the sulphur content of gas oil which was fixed between 0.5 and 0.8 per cent.[61] In 1987, a general level of 0.3 per cent was introduced.[62] However, Member States were allowed to require the use of gas oil with a sulphur content of 0.2 per cent in regions with high pollution or "where damage to the environment or to the national heritage caused by total sulphur dioxide emissions requires" a lower sulphur content than 0.3 per cent. In 1993, Directive 93/12, based on the present art.114 TFEU, introduced a level of 0.2 per cent sulphur as of the end of 1994 and 0.05 per cent as of the end of 1996; the Directive stated expressly that this was necessary in order to reach the emission limit values fixed in other EU provisions.[63] Then, a Directive of 1999 fixed the maximum permissible sulphur content in gas oil at 0.2 per cent as of 1 July 2000 and at 0.1 per cent as of 1 January 2008.[64] Member States were allowed to use, until 2013, gas oil with a sulphur content between 0.1 and 0.2 per cent, if the quality standards of Directive 80/779 were respected and the emissions did not lead to an exceeding of the critical quantities in other Member States; of course, these latter requirements cannot really be controlled: how could the Commission prove, in a litigation under art.258 TFEU, that the quality standards were respected? Furthermore, Spain (for the Canary Islands), France (for its overseas departments), Greece and Portugal (for Madeira and the Açores) were allowed, for an unspecified time, to use gas oil with a higher sulphur content than 0.2 per cent.

As regards heavy fuels which are used in particular by ships, the Commission published, in 1997, figures according to which most sulphur dioxide emissions in the European Union stemmed from the burning of coal (62.9 per cent), heavy fuel (18.4 per cent), gas oil/diesel (7.0 per cent) and refinery fuels (6.5 per cent).[65] As part of the EU strategy to combat acidification, Directive 1999/32 reduced the sulphur content of heavy fuel oils as of 2003 to 1 per cent. However, Member States obtained the possibility of allowing the use of heavy fuels with a sulphur content of up to 3 per cent, provided that the air-quality standards for sulphur dioxide laid down in Directive 80/779[66] and other EU provisions were respected and that the contribution to transboundary pollution was negligible. It should be noted again that the respect of quality standards under Directive 80/779 are not and cannot really be monitored, as it was not indicated for how much time compliance with standards must have existed, whether transboundary pollution also referred to non-EU regions and how this kind of pollution was assessed.

Directive 2005/33, based on art.114 TFEU, amended Directive 1999/32.[67] It fixed the sulphur level of heavy fuels at 1 per cent as of 1 January 2003—thus retro-actively!—and of marine fuels for ships which sail under a flag of Member States or use Member States' ports at 1.5 per cent. However, this last restriction

6–14

---

[61] Directive 75/716 [1975] OJ L307/22.

[62] Directive 87/219 [1987] OJ L91/19. This Directive was based on the present art.115 TFEU.

[63] Directive 93/12 on the sulphur content of certain liquid fuels [1993] OJ L74/81.

[64] Directive 1999/32 [1999] OJ L121/13.

[65] Commission, COM(91) 154.

[66] Directive 80/779 [1980] OJ L229/30.

[67] Directive 2005/33 [2005] OJ L191/59.

applied only to the Baltic Sea and the North Sea. A further Directive of 2012 limited the sulphur content of marine fuels generally to 3.5 per cent, in sulphur oxide emission control zones—Baltic Sea and North Sea—to 1.0 per cent.[68] The European Union thus clearly wanted to let sea transport provisions prevail over environmental considerations and leave the decision of generally limiting the sulphur content of marine fuels to the international maritime organisations. For inland waterway vessels the sulphur content was fixed at 0.1 per cent as of 2010, with some exceptions for some Greek vessels.

Directive 98/70[69] fixed the maximum sulphur content of diesel fuel (and petrol) at 350mg/kg; this level was to be reduced to 50mg/kg by 2005. Member States were allowed to introduce more stringent requirements for sensitive areas, subject to Community authorisation. The limit was amended by Directive 2003/17[70] and lowered to 10 mg/kg as of 1 January 2005.

Member States were likewise divided on the lead content of petrol. Directive 78/611[71] fixed the lead content to 0.4g per litre, but allowed Member States to lower this level down to 0.15g. Until 1986, Ireland was allowed to apply a level of 0.64g.[72]

6–15   In the early 1980s, campaigns on reducing the lead content in the air—for health reasons in the United Kingdom, for environmental reasons (Waldsterben— the problem of dying forests) in Germany—led the European Council to ask for the introduction of lead-free petrol,[73] which was proposed in May 1984 and adopted in March 1985, almost a record time.[74] The Directive required Member States to "take the necessary measures to ensure the availability and balanced distribution within their territories of unleaded petrol from 1 October 1989" (art.3). Unleaded petrol was defined as petrol that contained less than 0.013g of lead per litre, leaded petrol as containing between 0.15g and 0.40g of lead per litre. Member States were also authorised to prohibit leaded regular petrol,[75] which eliminated the free circulation of such petrol within the European Union.

Other content requirements for petrol concerned the benzene content, which was fixed at 5 per cent, the minimum motor octane number (85) and the minimum research octane number (95) of unleaded petrol. The vague wording of art.3 made any monitoring of the effective introduction of unleaded petrol practically impossible. It was the Member States' policy and the mineral oil companies that determined the speed of the introduction of unleaded petrol. Generally, this introduction advanced more quickly where a Member State had introduced a tax differentiation between leaded and unleaded petrol.[76]

---

[68] Directive 2012/33 on the sulphur content of marine fuels [2012] OJ L327/1.

[69] Directive 98/70 [1998] OJ L350/58.

[70] Directive 2003/17 [2003] OJ L76/10.

[71] Directive 78/611 [1978] OJ L197/19.

[72] The reason for this split standard was that Germany had already introduced, as of 1976, a standard of 0.15g and was not prepared to go back on this decision.

[73] See (1993) 6 *Bulletin of the European Communities* 1.5.15.

[74] Directive 85/210 on the approximation of the laws of the Member States concerning the lead content of petrol [1985] OJ L96/25.

[75] Directive 87/416 [1987] OJ L225/33.

[76] See European Environmental Agency, *Environmental Taxes: Implementation and Environmental Effectiveness* (Copenhagen, 1996), p.30 ("The tax differentiation schemes for fuels have been particularly successful") and p.55 (annex II, where the Agency reports on the Swedish tax

At the end of 1998, Directive 85/210 was replaced by Directive 98/70, which was based on art.114 TFEU.[77] This Directive prohibited the marketing of regular leaded petrol as of January 2000, reduced the benzene content to 1.0 per cent and contained a number of other specifications for unleaded petrol. In 2009, Directive 2009/30 further reduced the sulphur content of petrol and diesel[78] which was fixed, as a rule, at 10 mg/kg. Some derogations and transition provisions were fixed.

Directive 2009/28 required that by 2020, the share of energy from renewable sources in all forms of transport was at least 10 per cent of the final consumption of energy in transport.[79] "Biofuels" were defined as liquid or gaseous fuels for transport, produced from biomass. Biomass "means the biodegradable fraction of products, waste and residues from biological origin from agriculture (including vegetal and animal substances), forestry and related industries including fisheries and agriculture, as well as the biodegradable fraction of industrial and municipal waste". Detailed provisions were intended to ensure that such biofuels do not come from "land with high biodiversity value". The Directive enumerated in this regard primary forest and other wooded land; areas designated for nature protection areas or for the protection of recognised rare, threatened or endangered ecosystem or species; highly biodiverse grassland; wetlands; continuously forested areas; forests of more than one hectare; and peatland. Obviously these are also production standards which might constitute, in the eyes of the United States or others, obstacles to free trade. **6–16**

The controversy with environmental organisations on how the requirement of the production of biofuels can be ensured, whether the large-scale use of biofuels does not lead to significant environmental impairment, and how biofuels production in third countries can be effectively controlled, is in full swing within the European Union.

The different provisions on diesel and petrol fuel, based sometimes on art.114, sometimes on art.192 TFEU, and containing numerous derogations, transitions and authorisations for Member States' derogations, illustrate well the changing motivations behind the EU approach, which varies between environmental protection and internal market considerations. Recently, art.192 TFEU seems to be favoured.

The different provisions do not concern the composition of fuel for cars generally. There are numerous additives that are added to petrol in order to influence its quality, which may later, in the form of emissions, enter the environment. A new art.8a of Directive 98/70, inserted by Directive 2009/30, asked the Commission to establish by 2012, for the first time, a test methodology for metallic additives. The additive MMT was restricted in use (6 mg per litre).[80] **6–17**

---

differentiation for leaded petrol). The Commission had proposed such a tax differentiation [1984] OJ C178/5, but the Council had considered this to be a question for Member States alone.

[77] Directive 98/70 [1998] OJ L350/58.

[78] Directive 2009/30, [2009] OJ L140/88. This Directive was based on the present art.114 TFEU and, as regards the greenhouse gas emission reductions and amendments for marine fuels, on the present art.192 TFEU.

[79] Directive 2009/28 on the promotion of the use of energy from renewable sources [2009] OJ L140/16. This Directive was based on the present art.192 TFEU and, as regards the sustainability criteria of biofuels, their verification and calculation, on the present art.114 TFEU.

[80] See for MMT also Court of Justice, *Afton Chemicals* (C-343/09) [2010] E.C.R. I-7027.

(c) Cars

6–18   There are almost no EU environmental provisions on the making of cars. However, numerous provisions exist that decide on the air emissions from cars, although it is left to car manufacturers to decide how they intend to comply with the emission standards, whether they install a catalytic converter, and use an electro motor or another motor with a low consumption of fuel and thus generate only low emissions. Thus, for instance, the noise levels from cars are fixed in the form of emission-limit values, but do not require the use of particular materials, designs or tyres, etc, in order to comply with these values.

Sometimes the different objectives pursued in the car sector contradict each other. Thus, a reduction of the weight of cars, which would lead to less fuel consumption, might contradict the objective of increased safety of passengers. The increased use of plastic materials, which make a car lighter, could make the recycling of end-of-life vehicles more difficult. The use of aluminium in cars recurs to a material that is produced in a very polluting way, etc.

The European Union never considered imposing certain product standards on cars, such as, for instance, a maximum fuel consumption, the use of certain materials or fuels, or an in-built speed limitation for cars. Directive 2009/125 on the eco-design of energy using products,[81] which allows the European Union to provide for design requirements, could apply in theory also to cars and lead to provisions imposing a certain design; however, as the climate change situation is not yet perceived as being serious enough, this consideration is, for the time being, purely theoretical, and cars are expressly exempted from the provisions of that Directive. Tax provisions which are, until now, purely national,[82] do not differentiate according to the car emissions or the fuel consumption, though in most countries, diesel fuel is taxed lower than petrol, in order to indirectly subsidise the transport and the agricultural sector

6–19   The Directive on end-of-life vehicles[83] contained an article on waste prevention, but suggested measures for promotion and encouragement as regards car design and production, recycled materials and hazardous substances in cars; another provision provided for a ban of the use of lead, mercury, cadmium and hexavalent chromium, though a number of derogations were foreseen. Finally, the Directive provided for cars to be 85 per cent recyclable by 2015, which again will have an impact on the composition of cars provided the Directive is properly applied and monitored.

(d) Packaging

6–20   Directive 94/62 on packaging and packaging waste[84] provided for a reduction of the total metal content of four heavy metals—cadmium, lead, mercury and polyvalent chromium—in three steps by the year 2001. The Directive did not fix methods for the measuring of this content. Specific requirements for the

---

[81] Directive 2009/125 establishing a framework for the setting of eco-design requirements for energy-related products [2009] OJ L285/10.

[82] The Commission had proposed, in 2005, to tax cars according to the CO_2 emissions, COM(2005) 161. As no agreement could be reached in Council, it withdrew this proposal in 2015.

[83] Directive 2000/53 [2000] OJ L269/34.

[84] Directive 94/62 on packaging and packaging waste [1994] OJ L365/10.

composition of packaging were not laid down. There was, however, an interesting combination of the new approach system for product harmonisation and environmental requirements: Member States were obliged to accept on their markets all packaging that complied with the essential requirements of Directive 94/62, which were laid down in an annex II. They included the provision that "packaging shall be designed, produced and commercialised in such a way as to minimise its impact on the environment when packaging waste or residues from packaging waste management operations are disposed of", that packaging "shall be so manufactured that the presence of noxious and other hazardous substances and materials ... is minimised with regard to their presence in emissions, ash or leachate when ... packaging waste are incinerated or landfilled". These provisions would easily allow a Member State, which so wishes, to prohibit PVC packaging, restrict the use of aerosols or to provide for other restrictions on the use of packaging; this would raise difficulties, since Directive 94/62 is based on art.114 TFEU, which aims at ensuring the free circulation of packaging.

CEN (see para.6–60, below) was charged with elaborating European standards for the essential environmental requirements for packaging. As the CEN standards did not correspond to the Directive's requirements, but were drafted in a rather loose and vague way, the Commission initially refused, under the procedure of Directive 98/34,[85] to recognise four of them as harmonised EC standards[86]—which would have meant that compliance with the CEN standards created a presumption of compliance with the Directive's requirements. CEN then represented the same standards after some time, and this time got EU approval, as the environmental enthusiasm diminished in the meantime.

In 2013, the Commission proposed to amend Directive 94/62 in order to allow Member States to reduce the number of light plastic bags.[87] Member States should be able to tax such bags, to prohibit them altogether or take other appropriate measures. The Commission justified its proposal with the environmental problems caused by such bags, of which it declared about 8 billion were littered in 2008. In view of this and the almost complete freedom of Member States as regards the taking of measures, the choice of the legal basis of the proposal—art.114 TFEU—is wrong: no EU-wide standard is aimed at. The proposal was adopted in 2015[88].

(e)   Other products that contain heavy metals

The European Union regulated the composition and marketing of a considerable   **6–21**
number of products, in particular to ensure the establishment and functioning of the internal market. These include foodstuffs, animal feeding stuff, pharmaceuticals, cosmetics, textiles, toys, pesticides, fertilisers, drinking water, batteries, packaging, paints and varnishes, construction material, footwear, not to mention non-consumer goods such as ships, airplanes or office equipment. Scattered in these provisions there are sometimes provisions that prohibit or restrict the use of

---

[85] Directive 98/34 [1998] OJ L204/37.
[86] Commission Dec.2001/524 [2001] OJ L190/21.
[87] Commission, COM(2013) 761.
[88] Directive 2015/720, [2015] OJ L115/11.

this or that substance. The following examples may be given. Directive 2006/66[89] prohibited the use of certain batteries, where the mercury levels fixed in the Directive are exceeded. Lead carbons and lead sulphates may not be used in paints[90]; some derogations are allowed for the restoration of works of art and historic buildings.[91] Mercury, arsenic or organostannic compounds[92] may not be used to prevent the fouling by micro-organisms (plants or animals) of boats, in fish or shellfish farming and in the preservation of wood.[93] Cadmium and its compounds are banned from use as colourants or stabilisers for different products; also cadmium plating is forbidden in a number of expressly defined products.[94] Finally, nickel is prohibited for use in products which come in contact with the human skin.[95] In cars and in electrical and electronic equipment the use of cadmium, mercury, lead and hexavalent chromium is prohibited,[96] in electrical and electronic equipment furthermore the use of polybromated biphenyls (PBB) and diphenyls.[97] The different provisions contain each time a number of exceptions, derogations or transition provisions.

As can be seen, the restrictions are anything but systematic. Most of the provisions concern heavy metals, in particular lead, mercury or cadmium. In recent times, substances that deplete the ozone layer or lead to the emission of greenhouse gases are also regulated. It is true that a small number of products such as PCBs[98] or asbestos[99] were forbidden by the European Union, mainly in reaction to national bans. However, the phase-out periods were extremely long.

Until now, there were only two attempts to systematically tackle the problem of dangerous substances in products; these were the attempts to regulate cadmium and mercury. The first environmental action programme designated cadmium, together with other substances, as a substance that should be examined as a priority, because of its toxicity and its effect on human health and on the environment.[100] The Council confirmed in 1975 that an examination into the effects of cadmium on water was already ongoing and asked for an examination of air emissions of cadmium.[101] In 1981 the Commission asked the Consultative

---

[89] Directive 2006/66 [2006] OJ L266/1.

[90] Directive 76/769 [1976] OJ L262/201.

[91] As regards lead, see also Written Question E-0837/96 (Muscardini) [1996] OJ C297/35.

[92] For these substances, see Written Question 1139/89 (Adam) [1990] OJ C328/4.

[93] Directive 76/769 [1976] OJ L262/201, nos 19, 20 and 21.

[94] Directive 76/769 [1976] OJ L262/201, no.24.

[95] Directive 76/769 [1976] OJ L262/201, no.28.

[96] Directive 2000/53 [2000] OJ L269/34.

[97] Directive 2011/65 [2011] OJ L174/88.

[98] As regards PCB, Dir.76/769 [1976] OJ L262/201 prohibited the marketing in 1983. However, Dir.96/59 on the elimination of PCB/PCT [1996] OJ L243/31 provided for the final elimination of these materials until 2010.

[99] Asbestos was partly prohibited in the European Union by Dir.83/478 [1983] OJ L263/33 which amended Dir.76/769 [1976] OJ L262/201; in 1999, Dir.1999/77 [1999] OJ L207/18 introduced an almost total ban.

[100] 1st Environment Action Programme [1973] OJ C112/1, p.13.

[101] Resolution of 24 June 1975 [1975] OJ C168/4.

Scientific Committee on the toxicity and ecotoxicity of chemical compounds for an opinion on cadmium, which recommended the reduction of cadmium emissions wherever possible.[102]

In 1987, the Commission sent a communication to the Council, in which it listed 20 directives which limited the use of cadmium, suggested an action programme consisting of nine points to eliminate cadmium from the environment[103] and announced that it would, within two years, submit proposals for all nine points. The Council approved the strategy.[104] In 1991, the Council adopted a Directive to reduce the cadmium content as colourant, stabiliser or surface coating for a number of products,[105] and this Directive was to be reviewed "at regular intervals" —though this was never done.

6–22

Nevertheless, the Commission considered it necessary to include cadmium and its different compounds in its priority lists for existing chemicals,[106] which were established under Regulation 793/93[107] and which are designed to assess the effects of substances on man and the environment. This assessment, for which Belgium took the lead, started in 1996 and finished in 2008. The Commission adopted a recommendation on cadmium which had a very limited content— resuming 35 years of attempts to reduce the presence of cadmium in the environment.[108]

The main source of the presence of cadmium in the environment is the cadmium content of fertilisers that are used in agriculture. EU law does not contain limit values for cadmium concentrations in fertilisers, but the national legislation of the three acceding Member States—Sweden, Austria and Finland—did. The Accession Treaty therefore provided that this legislation could be maintained for four years; in the meantime, a re-examination of the EU provisions would take place. In 2003, the European Union adopted new legislation on fertilisers, which again did not provide for a limit of cadmium.[109] The Commission announced that it would present a proposal on the cadmium content of fertilisers; until then, it granted Austria, Sweden, Finland and the Czech Republic derogations under art.114 TFEU to continue to apply their limitations; until the end of 2010, this proposal has not been presented. Overall, this transition period thus exists already for more than 15 years. This sequence of events shows that a systematic EU approach as regards cadmium simply does not exist.

In 2005, the Commission presented, at the request of the Scandinavian countries, a Communication for a strategy to reduce the emissions of mercury.[110]

6–23

---

[102] Scientific Consultative Committee on the toxicity and ecotoxicity of chemical compounds, opinion of April 1981, published in Activity Report 1979–1983 (EUR 9246) (Luxembourg, 1984), p.37.

[103] Commission, Environmental pollution by cadmium. Proposal for an action programme, COM(87) 165.

[104] Resolution of 25 January 1988 [1988] OJ C30/1.

[105] Directive 91/338 amending, for the tenth time, Dir.76/769 [1991] OJ L186/59.

[106] See Reg.143/97 [1997] OJ L25/13, nos 2 and 3.

[107] Regulation 793/93 evaluation and control of the risks of existing substances [1993] OJ L84/1.

[108] Commission, Rec.2008/446 [2008] OJ L156/22; the reference to the Belgian risk assessment is found in [2008] OJ C149/6.

[109] Regulation 2003/2003 on fertilisers [2003] OJ L304/1; see also, by way of example, the derogation granted to Sweden, Dec.2006/347 [2006] OJ L129/19.

[110] Commission, COM(2005) 20; reviewed COM(2010) 723.

The strategy listed more than 20 actions that could be taken at EU level to reduce the use and the emissions of mercury, among others also to ban its export by 2011. This was finally decided, for a number of mercury-containing products, in 2008.[111] Subsequently, further restrictions of the use of mercury in measuring devices were adopted,[112] other restrictions were inserted in the chemicals Regulation,[113] the storage of metallic mercury in landfills was regulated[114] and the mercury content in batteries reduced.[115] In contrast, no measures were adopted to reduce mercury in dental amalgams;[116] also, no limit value for mercury emissions into the air were fixed.[117] In 2013, the EU signed the UN Minamata Convention on mercury; its ratification is envisaged for 2015.

Overall, no systematic approach exists until now at EU level to substitute heavy metals or other dangerous substances, wherever this is possible.

(f) Products containing ozone-depleting substances

6–24 In order to protect the ozone layer, the European Union has adopted a number of measures as regards ozone-depleting substances.[118] The Montreal Protocol[119] deals with such substances, but only indirectly touches the question of products that contain ozone-depleting substances.[120] It is true, though, that art.2(11) of the Protocol allows Contracting Parties to "take more stringent measures" than those required by the Protocol. These provisions, incidentally, also apply to "products produced with, but not containing" ozone-depleting substances.

The European Union could thus, by virtue of the Montreal Protocol, which has been transposed into EU law by Regulation 1005/2009,[121] take measures to prohibit products that contain ozone-depleting substances or had been produced with the help of such substances, without infringing provisions of the World Trade Organisation.[122] However, it has not yet done so, but has instead limited its measures to the substances themselves. Regulation 1005/2009 also prohibits the use of ozone-depleting substances in air condition installations, refrigerators and fire extinguishers.

[111] Regulation 1102/2008 on banning the exports of metallic mercury and certain mercury compounds and mixtures and the safe storage of metallic mercury [2008] OJ L304/75.
[112] Directive 2007/51 restricting the use of mercury in measuring devices [2007] OJ L257/13.
[113] Commission Reg.847/2012 amending annex XVII of Reg.1907/2006 [2013] OJ L253/1.
[114] Directive 2011/97 [2011] OJ L328/49.
[115] Directive 2013/56 amending Dir.2006/66 [2013] OJ L329/5.
[116] See Written Question P-012141/13 (Delli) [2014] OJ C221/233.
[117] Directive 2004/107 [2005] OJ L23/3; see also paras 8–10 and 8–11, below.
[118] See for more details, paras 9–30 et seq., below.
[119] Montreal Protocol of 16 September 1987 on substances that deplete the ozone layer; the Protocol was adhered to by the European Union by Dec.88/540 [1988] OJ L297/8.
[120] Article 4(3) of the Protocol provides for rules to be elaborated that prohibit the import of products containing ozone-depleting substances from states that are not party to the Protocol; art.9(1b) invites research and development of alternatives to products that contain ozone-depleting substances.
[121] Regulation 1005/2009 on substances that deplete the ozone-layer [2009] OJ L286/1; this Regulation replaced the earlier Reg.1037/2000 [2000] OJ L244/1. For an assessment of the EU and the global efforts to reduce the emissions of ozone-depleting substances see Commission SEC(2008) 2366.
[122] The European Union adhered to WTO by Dec.94/800 [1994] OJ L336/1.

(g) Chemicals

Chemicals, in the form of substances, preparations, pesticides, fertilisers, pharmaceuticals, cosmetics and food additives, are extensively regulated at EU level, since for all these products uniform rules are necessary—from the industry's point of view—to establish a common market. Pharmaceuticals, cosmetics and food additives will not be discussed in this book, since health issues prevail and environmental elements are peripheral in these sectors. EU legislation on substances and mixtures of substances is based on art.114 TFEU and tries to achieve total harmonisation; this means that national legislation on chemicals that diverges from existing EU provisions is, in principle, not allowed.[123]

6–25

EU legislation on chemicals was introduced since 1967. It was based on directives which differentiated between substances and preparations on the one hand,[124] on chemicals which were on the EU market before 1981 and those which were put on the market later (new substances) on the other hand.[125] Existing substances were allowed to be used freely, until they were examined by the European Union, whereas new substances underwent a sort of EU-approval procedure, before they were allowed to be placed on the market. Restrictions on the use of chemicals were mainly introduced at the initiative of individual Member States, and then generalised by an EU Directive.[126]

Overall, the system was considered successful for new substances, as these had to undergo a risk assessment before they could be marketed.[127] In contrast, the system for existing substances revealed itself to be too complicated. By 2005, only about 3,500 substances had been properly regulated, while some 100,000 substances were registered as being on the EU market. Attempts to accelerate the procedure[128] remained unsuccessful.

In 2001, the Commission published a White Paper on the strategy concerning a future chemcial policy.[129] The following discussions led, in 2006, to the adoption of the so-called REACH-Regulation.[130]

6–26

---

[123] See as a good example on the discussion about total harmonisation, Court of Justice, *Kemikalieinspektionen* (C-473/98) [2000] E.C.R. I-5681.

[124] Directive 67/548 on the classification, labelling and packaging of dangerous substances [1967] OJ 196/1; Dir.1999/45 relating to the classification, packaging and labelling of dangerous preparations [1999] OJ L200/1.

[125] Directive 79/831 [1979] OJ L259/10.

[126] Directive 76/769 relating to restrictions on the marketing and use of certain dangerous substances and preparations [1976] OJ L262/201; each restriction of a substance required an amendment of this Directive.

[127] Directive 93/67 laying down the principles for assessment of risks to man and the environment of substances notified in accordance with Dir.67/548 [1993] OJ L22/79; the Commission guidance document on the making of a risk assessment (Luxembourg 1996) had a length of 700 pages. Until the end of 2005, some 3000 new substances had been notified and classified.

[128] Regulation 793/93 on the evaluation and control of the risk of existing substances [1993] OJ L84/1.

[129] Commission, COM(2001) 88.

[130] Regulation 1907/2006 concerning the registration, evaluation, authorisation and restriction of chemicals (REACH), establishing a European Chemicals Agency amending Dir.1999/45 and repealing Council Reg.793/93, Council Dir.76/769 and Commission Dir.91/155, 93/67 93/105 and 2000/21 [2006] OJ L396/1.

REACH provides that all chemical substances which are manufactured or imported into the European Union in quantities of one tonne per year or more have to be registered with the European Chemical Agency (art.6). This also applies to producers or importers of a substance which had already been registered by another person, in order to avoid an economic advantage for free-riders. Registration is also necessary for substances which are contained in products, provided the substance is present in articles in quantities of more than one tonne per year and is intended to be released under normal or reasonably foreseeable conditions of use (art.7). Where a dangerous substance is present in a product "above a concentration of 0.1 per cent weight by weight" (art.7(2)(b)), the producer or importer has to notify the Agency.[131] Several persons which put into circulation a substance may do this in common (art.11). In order to avoid the duplication of vertebrate animal testing, a registration is possible by referring to an earlier registration, without the consent of the earlier registrant, provided the costs are shared (art.27). For substances which had not been registered under the system before 2006, transitional provisions are foreseen, according to the quantities marketed (art.23). A substance which has not be registered, may not placed on the market (art.5).

A registration has to be accompanied by detailed information on the substance and its characteristics, its use and the quantities which are put on the market, and a report on the safety assessment (art.14). This safety report constitutes the risk assessment which, before 2006, had been the responsibility of the public authorities and is now the responsibility of the registrant. The Agency has to examine the completeness of the information which was submitted. If it does not require more information or otherwise object, the substance may be placed on the EU market (art.21); the Agency has no possibility of taking provisional measures in order to stop the marketing of a substance.

6–27   The evaluation of the registered substance—in particular with regard to the safety report—is made by a Member State on the basis of a rolling action plan established by the Agency (arts 44–47). The responsible Member State shall submit its conclusion to the Agency which then informs the Commission, the other Member States and the registrant.

The Agency then has to decide, how to classify the substance in question. When a substance is carcinogenic, mutagenic, toxic for reproduction, persistent, bioaccumulative or toxic, or very persistent or very bioaccumulative, the substance is placed into annex XIV.[132] The consequence of such a classification is that the placing on the market and use of the substance is prohibited after a certain date, unless an authorisation is granted (arts 57–59). The producer or importer then has to apply for an authorisation and submit certain dates. Committees for risk assessment and socio-economic analysis which are set up by Regulation 1907/2006, are consulted on the application. The Commission will then decide in a comitology procedure. An authorisation to use a substance is normally only granted where it is shown that the socio-economic benefits

---

[131] In case C-106/14, FCD and FMB, ECLI:EU:C:2015:576, the Court of Justice clarified that the 0.1% does not refer to the product as a whole (e.g. a car), but to each component of a product (e.g. the brakes of a car).

[132] See for details, art.57 of Reg.1907/2006.

outweigh the risk to human health or the environment and if there are no suitable alternative substances or technologies (art.60(4)). And the authorisation shall be subject to a time-limited review.

Articles 68–73 deal with the restriction of use of chemicals. When the Commission (art.69) or a Member State (art.70) is of the opinion that a substance poses a risk to human health or the environment, it may ask the Agency to prepare a dossier and suggest restrictions; under certain conditions, the Agency may also act on its own initiative. The committees on risk assessment and socio-economic analysis shall give an opinion. The final decision is again taken by the Commission by way of the comitology procedure. The Commission shall decide on a restriction, when "there is an unacceptable risk" to human health or the environment (art.68).

It should be mentioned again that not all the substances which are banned or restricted by EU legislation, are assembled in annex XVII. Rather, different regulations and directives, scattered all over EU law, contain other restrictions.[133]   **6–28**

The putting into operation of the REACH Regulation advanced slowly. The Chemical Agency, ECHA, situated in Helsinki, was quite absorbed by the registration of chemicals and their evaluation. It developed a rather limited number of own initiatives to restrict the use of substances or place them in annex XIV, in order to submit them to an authorisation. The Commission adopted, until the end of 2014, three Regulations which inserted chemicals in annex XIV.[134] It granted three authorisations for continued use of a dangerous chemical.[135] It adopted, until March 2015, 16 regulations which inserted chemicals into annex XVII to the REACH Regulation, restricting their use, amongst them Regulations on cadmium,[136] lead[137] and mercury.[138] In one case, it refused to follow a request by Denmark and restrict the use of four phthalates.[139]

Following work at global level, under the auspices of the United Nations, a global harmonised system (GHS) concerning the classification, labelling and packaging of chemicals was agreed in 2002, which was influenced by the less environment- and consumer-friendly system used in the transport of goods. The European Union amended its earlier system which had been established by Directive 67/548,[140] and aligned it to the new GHS system. The classification of a substance—whether it is toxic, dangerous, explosive etc—is regulated in Regulation 1272/2008.[141] Manufacturers and importers shall classify substances and mixtures, before placing them on the market (art.4). Any supplier—this includes a manufacturer or an importer who places a substance or mixture on the market—has to label and pack the substance or mixture according to its classification. The Regulation fixes in detail classes and degrees of risks; it is

---

[133] See, e.g. Reg.1223/2009 on cosmetic products [2009] OJ L342/59; Reg.850/2004 on persistent organic pollutants [2004] OJ L158/7.
[134] Commission Regs 143/2011 [2011] OJ L49/52; 248/13 [2013] OJ L108/1; Reg.895/2014 [2014] OJ L244/6.
[135] Commission Communications [2014] OJ C 260/10; [2014] OJ C461/24; [2015] OJ C91/2.
[136] Commission Reg.494/2011 [2011] OJ L134/2 and Reg.835/2011[2011] OJ L252/1.
[137] Commission Reg.836/2012 [2012] OJ L252/4
[138] Commission Reg.847/2012 [2012] OJ L253/1.
[139] Commission Communication [2014] OJ C260/1.
[140] Directive 67/548 [1993] OJ L22/79.
[141] Regulation 1272/2008 on the classification, labelling and packaging of substances and mixtures [2008] OJ L353/1.

then, in principle, up to the manufacturer or importer to classify his product according to these risks. The classification decision has to be notified to the Chemical Agency which has to verify them for correctness and keep an inventory of the classifications received (arts 40–42). The self-classification by the manufacturer/importer is in particular necessary for mixtures, as there are no lists of substances which enter such mixtures.

6–29   Some substances are subject to a harmonised classification which may also take place at the request of a Member State, a manufacturer or an importer. In such a case, the Commission decides on the harmonised classification by way of the comitology procedure, on the basis of preparatory work of the Agency. This classification is then binding on everyone. Annex VI to Regulation 1272/2008 contains the list of substances which were the subject of harmonised classification. That list is regularly updated; at the same time, the Regulation is aligned to amendments which are introduced, at global level, to the GHS system.[142]

The labelling requirements for chemicals are discussed in para.6–54 below.

In 2013, the Commission published a first report on the functioning of REACH and of Regulation 1272/2008.[143] It showed itself satisfied with the effectiveness of both instruments. It did not comment in detail on lacunae, omissions and the fact that Regulation 1272/2008 was only complied with at 70 per cent. Its examination of 155 other pieces of EU chemical legislation did not reveal major overlaps or inconsistencies. The Commission did not see the need to suggest major amendments of the REACH legislation.

6–30   Regulation 1907/2006 is based on the precautionary principle.[144] This allows the public authorities to ban or restrict the placing on the market or use of a substance which is suspected to present a risk to humans or the environment, without having to wait until the full evidence has demonstrated such a risk. The Regulation made use of this principle in several practical cases. For example, the burden of proof that a chemical substance is safe to be used, has been laid on the manufacturer/importer, who has, together the registration, to submit data on the possible hazards of the substance and the risk management measures which must be taken in order to allow a safe use of the substance. Furthermore, a substance may be restricted in use or even be banned altogether where the authorities have sufficient evidence of a possible risk. In taking a restriction decision, the authorities benefit from a very wide discretion which may only be controlled where there is a manifest error, a misuse of powers or a manifest exceeding of the limits of discretion by the EU courts.[145]

An expression of the precautionary principle is also found in the requirement that:

---

[142] See, e.g. Commission Regs 286/11 [2011] OJ L83/1; 487/2013 [2013] OJ L149/1; 944/2013 [2013] OJ L261/5; 605/2014 [2014] OJ L167/36; 1297/2014 [2014] OJ L350/1—this Regulation constituted a reaction to several incidents of poisoning and eye damage which occurred in the European Union.

[143] Commission, COM(2013) 49 and SWD(2013) 25.

[144] See Reg.1907/2006 [2013] OJ L253/1, art.1(3): "This regulation is based on the principle that it is for manufacturers, importers and downstream users to ensure that they manufacture, place on the market or use such substances that do not adversely affect human health or the environment. Its provisions are underpinned by the precautionary principle." As regards the precautionary principle, see also paras 1.31 et seq., above.

[145] See Court of Justice, *Rüttgers v ECHA* (C-288/13P) ECLI:EU:C:2014:2176.

- without data, substances may not be placed on the market[146];
- substances which are carcinogenic, mutagenic or toxic for reproduction may be supplied to the general public, because of their intrinsic hazard, without the necessity of evidence that they constitute an actual risk (arts 57 and 58);
- manufacturers or importers of substances of very high concern must submit specific supplementary information, without the public authorities being required of proving the existence of a risk.

Since 2013, negotiations have been going on between the European Union and the United States on a Transatlantic Trade and Investment Partnership (TTIP) Agreement which also intends to cover the free trade in chemicals. In the United States the precautionary principle does not apply, which means that the approach to regulation is rather different from the EU approach: a manufacturer is normally not obliged to convey information to the public authorities on a substance which he markets. The authorities may only ask for such information in order to find out whether an actual risk exists, where they already have sufficient information on a potential risk of that substance.[147] And the authorities must have similar doubts that a chemical poses a risk before they may take any regulatory action to restrict the production or use of the substance.[148] In practice, this burden for public authorities is so high, that since the adoption of the US chemical legislation in 1976, only five substances were subject to restrictions in the United States, none in the last 20 years.[149] In contrast, the European Union added new substances or updated and amended existing restrictions laid down in annex XVII not less than 16 times between 2009 and 2015.[150]

It is obvious that the precautionary principle which applies in the European Union but not in the United States, leads to different results on both sides of the Atlantic. The TTIP Agreement is likely to lead, in the name of free trade of chemical substances, to an adaption of EU regulatory system to that of the United States. This is due in particular to the planned installation of a "regulatory committee", where draft regulations are discussed by both sides. It is to be expected that the United States will resist the supply of information and the taking of precautionary measures by the European Union, supported in that by the EU chemical industry.

6–31

---

[146] See Reg.1907/2006 [2013] OJ L253/1, art.5: "substances on their own, in preparations or in articles shall not be manufactured in the Community or placed on the market unless they have been registered in accordance with the relevant provisions of this Title where this is required".

[147] See US Toxic Substances Control Act 1976, 15 U.S.C. §§2601 et seq., section 5: "If the Administrator finds that the manufacture, distribution in commerce ... of a chemical substance or mixture ... may present an unreasonable risk of injury to health or the environment ... the Administrator shall by rule require that testing be conducted on such substance or mixture with respect to the health and environmental effects for which there is an insufficiency of data and experience."

[148] See Toxic Substances Control Act 1976 15 U.S.C. §§2601 et seq., Section 6: "If the Administrator finds that there is a reasonable basis to conclude that ... a chemical substance or mixture presents ... an unreasonable risk of injury to health or the environment, the Administrators shall by rule apply (restriction provisions)."

[149] See V. Buonsante, "Regulatory Coherence in the Transatlantic Trade and Investment Partnership Agreement: The Case of Chemicals" [2014] ENLI Review 39.

[150] See last Commission Regs 2014/474 [2014] OJ L136/19; 2015/326 [2015] OJ L58/43.

(h) Pesticides and biocides

6–32   Pesticides in EU terminology are subdivided into agricultural (plant protection products) and non-agricultural (biocides) pesticides. As regards agricultural pesticides, of which some 25,000 with about 700 active substances are thought to be on the market, Regulation 1107/2009 which replaced Directive 91/414, deals with the authorisation for their placing on the market[151]; a number of directives deal with pesticide residues on and in fruit and vegetables, cereals and foodstuffs of animal origin.[152]

(i) Plant protection products

6–33   Regulation 1107/2009, based on arts 43, 114 and 169 TFEU, regulated the placing on the market of plant protection products (agricultural pesticides). The Regulation differentiates between products that have to authorised by the individual Member State and the active substances for such products (which are authorised by the European Union). An agricultural pesticide may only be authorised to be placed on the market if it contains an active substance that is listed—and is thus authorised EU-wide—in Regulation 1107/2009. The Regulation fixed a number of conditions for the authorisation of pesticides, such as the requirement that the pesticide may not have unacceptable effects on plants, does not have damaging effects on the health of humans or animals or on the groundwater or does not have unacceptable effects on the environment in general.

The authorisation of a pesticide is valid for the Member State for which it was requested. For the recognition of the pesticide in another Member State, the Regulation divided the European Union in three biogeographical zones, North, Centre and South.[153] When the recognition is asked for a Member State of the same zone, this recognition has to be given, subject to some exceptional situations. For the authorisation in another zone, a new authorisation has to be requested.

Active substances are assessed, as regards their effects, by an EU mechanism. Applicants must submit detailed dossiers, and a comprehensive risk assessment which are examined and assessed, on the basis of a Member State's report, by the Standing Committee on Plant Health[154]; the substance is, after a positive decision, registered in an annex to Regulation 1107/2009, together with

---

[151] Regulation 1107/2009 concerning the placing of plant protection products on the market [2009] OJ L309/1; this Regulation replaced Dir.91/414 [1991] OJ L230/1.

[152] Directive 76/895 relating to the fixing of maximum levels for pesticide residues in and on fruit and vegetables [1976] OJ L340/26; Dir.86/362 on the fixing of maximum levels for pesticide residues in and on cereals [1986] OJ L221/37; L221/43; Dir.90/642 on the fixing of maximum levels for pesticide residues in and on certain products of plant origin, including fruit and vegetables [1990] OJ L350/71.

[153] See Reg.1107/2009 [2009] OJ L309/1, annex I: The zone North includes Denmark, Estonia, Latvia, Lithuania, Finland and Sweden; the zone Centre includes Belgium, Czech Republic, Croatia, Germany, Ireland, Luxembourg, Hungary, Netherlands, Austria, Poland, Romania, Slovenia, Slovakia and United Kingdom; the zone South includes Bulgaria, Greece, Spain, France, Cyprus, Malta and Portugal.

[154] This Committee was set up by Dec.76/894 [1976] OJ L340/25.

restrictions of use, expiry dates for the authorisation etc.[155] The withdrawal of an authorisation, the non-renewal or the refusal to approve an active substance is organised by Commission implementing Regulations.[156] As mentioned above, active substances which qualify as persistent organic pollutants are also the subject of explicit prohibitions under Regulation 850/2004.[157]

The conditions for use, marked for each active substance in Regulation 540/2011, are not very specific; for example, as regards Glyphosate, a widely used active substance, it is stated:

6–34

> "only uses as herbicide may be authorised ... For the implementation of the uniform principles ... the conclusions of the review report on glyphosate and in particular Appendices I and II thereof, as finalised in the Standing Committee on Plant Health on 29 June 2001 shall be taken into account. In this overall assessment, Member States must pay particular attention to the protection of the groundwater in vulnerable areas, in particular with respect to non-crop uses."

Such information may be of very limited use for farmers or households who use glyphosate.

The labelling of pesticides is regulated by an implementing Regulation of the Commission,[158] which also provides for standard phrases on specific risks to humans, animals or the environment (annex II) and for standard phrases for safety precautions (annex III).

In 2009, a Directive was adopted, based on art.192 TFEU, on the sustainable use of pesticides which required Member States to adopt National Action Plans in order to reduce risks and dependence on pesticides (art.4), to provide for integrated pesticide management (art.14) and to provide for compulsory training of distributors and professional users.[159] Implementation of that Directive only advances slowly.[160]

(ii) Biocides

Regulation 528/12 which replaced an earlier Directive, deals with the authorisation and use of non-agricultural pesticides (biocides); it is based on art.114 TFEU.[161] The Regulation concerns pesticides such as disinfectants, preservatives, pest-control products, anti-foulants and insecticides—overall, some 15,000 products. These products were grouped in 22 product types (annex V). The Regulation builds on Regulation 1907/2006 on chemicals and on

6–35

---

[155] See Commission implementing Reg.540/2011 containing the list of active substances [2011] OJ L153/1. The list is regularly updated by Commission Regulations.

[156] See, e.g. Commission implementing Reg.767/2013 on bifertranol [2013] OJ L214/5; Reg.1022/2011 on cyclanilide [2011] OJ L270/11.

[157] Regulation 850/2004 [2004] OJ L158/7.

[158] Regulation 547/2011 as regards labelling requirements for plant protection products [2011] OJ L155/176.

[159] Directive 2009/128 establishing a framework for Community action to achieve the sustainable use of pesticides [2008] OJ L309/71.

[160] See Written questions E-000584 and 000585 (Ferreira and Zuber) [2014] OJ C286/170.

[161] Regulation 528/2012 on biocidal products [2012] OJ L167/1; this Regulation replaced Dir.98/8 [1998] OJ L123/1.

Regulation 1107/2009 on pesticides. Considerable monitoring tasks were delegated to the Chemical Agency, established under Regulation 1907/2006.

The Regulation contains a list of active substances which may be used in biocidal products. These substances are authorised at Union level. The authorisation for a biocidal product is normally granted by Member States (arts 29 et seq.). The manufacturer may, however, under certain conditions apply for an EU authorisation which would be valid in the whole of the Union (arts 41 et seq.). The Regulation contains detailed provisions for the mutual recognition of national authorisations (arts 32 et seq.), on articles that are treated with biocides, on the information which has to accompany any application and on the labelling of biocides.

(iv) Products from biotechnology

6–36   EU legislation on biotechnology and products derived from biotechnology, which started in the mid-1980s, is scattered, because in particular in the areas of agriculture and food on the one hand, and of pharmaceuticals on the other hand, numerous directives fix specific provisions for certain products; these provisions are not presented here, since they concern the sectors of agriculture, consumer protection, health or industrial policy. As regards the environment, two basic Directives on the contained use of genetically modified micro-organisms[162] and on the deliberate release of genetically modified organisms (GMO),[163] were adopted in 1990; the Directive on the deliberate release was substituted, in 2001, by Directive 2001/18.[164] A third directive, on the legal protection of biotechnological inventions, was adopted in 1998, after 10 years of discussion at EU level.[165] This Directive is based on art.114 TFEU. It provides for the protection of such inventions by national patent law of Member States and completes these provisions with a number of common rules. Furthermore, the European Union adopted legislation on GMOs in food and feed[166] and the transport of GMOs.[167]

Directive 2009/41 on the contained use of genetically modified micro-organisms[168] was based on art.192 TFEU. It defined micro-organisms as any microbiological entity, cellular or non-cellular, capable of replication or of transferring genetic material; this definition shows that the Directive deals with living beings, which are, for economic reasons, treated as chemicals. The Directive divided contained-use operations into those which are for teaching, research, development or non-industrial or non-commercial purposes and which are of small-scale (type A) operations and other (type B) operations. Before an installation is used, a notification has to be made to the competent authorities which describes the work, the scale of the operation and an "assessment of the

---

[162] Directive 90/219 on the contained use of genetically modified micro-organisms [1990] OJ L117/1; this Directive was, in 2009, codified under number 2009/41 [2009] OJ L175/75.

[163] Directive 90/220 [1990] OJ L117/15.

[164] Directive 2001/18 on the deliberate release of genetically modified organisms [2001] OJ L106/1.

[165] Directive 98/44 [1998] OJ L213/13.

[166] Regulation 1829/2003 on genetically modified food and feed [2003] OJ L268/1.

[167] Regulation 1946/2003 on the transboundary movement of genetically modified organisms [2003] OJ L287/1.

[168] Directive 2009/41 [2009] OJ L175/75.

contained uses as regards the risks to human health and the environment that may occur". The amount of information to be notified depends, furthermore, on the type of micro-organisms and the operations to be carried out. If new aspects become known, which might affect the risk, this information must also be conveyed. Also, information on any accident—"any incident involving a significant and unintended release ... which could present an immediate or delayed hazard to human health or the environment"—that has occurred, has to be given to the authorities.

The competent authorities must examine the completeness of the information received. In certain cases, operations may not begin before consent is given; in other cases, a waiting period of 60–90 days must be respected. The authorities may put conditions for the operations to be carried out, may provide a consultation of "groups or the public" and may generally take all measures that they consider necessary.

Since, in particular, economic operators had considered several provisions of   6–37
the original Directive 90/219 too restrictive—including the "small-scale" requirement—a major amendment of the Directive was adopted in 1998.[169] The different procedures were simplified; notably the procedures for the risk assessment of the operation were specified in more detail, and the number of micro-organisms that come into the lower categories of risky organisms was considerably increased. Directive 2009/41 maintained these simplifications.

Directive 2001/18,[170] which was based on art.114 TFEU, dealt with the deliberate release into the environment of genetically modified organisms (GMOs) and of products that contain such organisms. The Directive replaced Directive 90/220 which had been in force since 1990 and had two sections, on experimental releases of GMOs and on the release of products. Its application had led to more than 1,000 experimental releases and some 30 releases of products containing GMOs.[171]

A crisis in the application of Directive 90/220 broke out in 1996.[172] The Swiss company, Novartis, had applied in France for the authorisation to market genetically modified maize (Bt-maize). France examined the dossier that accompanied the application and considered that the risk assessment, which was part of the dossier, allowed the placing on the market of the maize. It thus sent the application with a favourable opinion to the European Commission, which transmitted the dossier to the other Member States. The Commission shared France's opinion that the placing on the market should be allowed and therefore submitted a corresponding proposal to the Committee set up under Directive 90/220. However, the great majority of the Member States (13 out of the then 15 Member States) was of the opinion that the risk assessment did not allow the placing on the market; they held that further research was necessary. Under the committee procedure of Directive 90/220, an opinion of the Committee which differed from the Commission's proposal, needed unanimity; and this unanimity could not be reached as France sided with the Commission. The dossier then went to the Council, which again needed, under the present art.293 TFEU, unanimity

---

[169] Directive 98/81 [1998] OJ L330/13.
[170] Directive 2001/18 [2001] OJ L106/1.
[171] Commission, COM(1998) 85.
[172] Part of the events are described in Court of Justice, *Greenpeace France* (C-6/99) [2000] E.C.R. I-1651, in particular, in the Advocate General's Opinion.

in order to amend the Commission's proposal. As France sided once more with the Commission, the fact that 13 Member States favoured a rejection of the application, was of no help. Under the committee procedure, the dossier therefore went back to the Commission which then decided to give a positive opinion to the application.[173]

6–38   This decision led to strong reactions from the Member States. A number of them adopted national provisions, which prohibited the placing on the market of the maize, invoking a safeguard clause of Directive 90/220. As all Member States expressed concern on the procedure and at the same time there was "growing concern on the part of the general public ... with ... this new technology", the Commission did not take legal action against Member States. Under this moratorium, no further application under Directive 90/220 was made, discussed or decided at EU level. Rather, the elaboration of amendments to Directive 90/220 was prepared. When the Commission suggested amendments, Parliament and Council agreed that it would be better to have a completely new Directive; this finally led to the adoption of Directive 2001/18. The Directive became effective in October 2002; in 2003/2004, the standstill on the placing of new GMO-containing products on the market ended, at the same time, when new legislation on genetically modified food and feed was adopted.[174]

Directive 2001/18 distinguished between releases for "any other purpose than the placing on the market"—in particular releases for research, development or experimental purposes—and the placing on the market of GMOs "as or in products". A deliberate release for "other purposes" must be notified in advance to the competent authority of the Member State in which the release is to take place, and be accompanied by a technical dossier. This dossier must in particular contain information on the GMO, the conditions of release and the receiving environment, a plan for monitoring, information on control, remediation methods, waste treatment and an environmental risk assessment, for which detailed provisions are laid down. The competent authority must, within 90 days, decide in writing on the application, provided the dossier is complete; the authorisation procedure is thus purely national. However, where the competent authority is of the opinion that sufficient experience has been obtained with such a release, it may ask the release to be admitted EU-wide. In this case, all other Member States become involved in the decision. The public "and, where appropriate, groups" (art.9) shall be consulted on deliberate releases. Furthermore, the public shall be informed of all "other-purposes" releases.

Where GMOs are placed on the market "as or in products", again the applicant has to submit a notification to the competent authority where the product is to be placed on the market for the first time. The application and a summary of the accompanying dossier is immediately transmitted to the other Member States and the Commission. The notification shall contain extensive information and documentation, in particular on the GMO, indications for use and handling, the environmental risk assessment, data on results from research and development releases, the conditions for placing on the market, a monitoring plan as well as a proposal for packaging and labelling of the product. The competent authority must react to the notification within 90 days. Where it decides that it has

---

[173] Commission Dec.97/98 [1997] OJ L31/69.
[174] See para.6–39, below.

sufficient information which indicates that a GMO release would not be a risk to humans or the environment, it shall send the dossier to the European Commission, together with an assessment report and an indication whether the GMO product should or should not be placed on the market. The other Member States who also receive the dossier, and the Commission may ask for further information; they may also comment on the application or present reasoned objections to the placing on the market of the GMO (product). The aim is to arrive at a final EU-wide decision on the application within 105 days from the date of circulation of the assessment report. The summary of the notified dossier and of the assessment report must be made available to the public. Comments from the public shall be circulated among public authorities.

Where objections are raised, the period for decision-making is prolonged to 120 days. The Commission is then obliged to consult the relevant EU Scientific Committee.[175] The Commission also may consult any committee that it has set up with a view to obtaining advice on the ethical implications of biotechnology. The Commission shall then elaborate a proposal for a decision, which is submitted to the Committee that was set up, in conformity with Decision 1999/468,[176] under art.30 of Directive 2001/18. Where the Committee agrees with the Commission proposal, the Commission takes the decision. Where the Committee does not give an opinion or disagrees, the Commission's proposal is referred to the Council, which has three months to decide. If the Council opposes the proposal with a qualified majority, the Commission shall re-examine it, re-present it anew to the Council, shall present a modified proposal or present a legislative proposal.[177] Where the Council does not raise objections, the Commission adopts its proposal and sends the dossier back to the Member State that first received the notification. That Member State finally authorises the placing on the market of the GMO (product).

6–39

In order to further mitigate concerns of consumers and public opinion, the Council adopted a regulation on novel food,[178] which required food products that contain GMOs to be authorised EU-wide or—where the risk is less great—notified and bear a corresponding label, in so far as differences to normal food products can scientifically be detected. Furthermore, Commission Regulation 1813/97[179] and Council Regulation 1139/98[180] fixed supplementary labelling requirements for the labelling of food and food additives that were produced with the help of GMOs.[181]

Regulation 1829/2003 on genetically modified food and feed[182] also applied to GMOs used for cultivation (as seeds) to produce food or feed, which thus do no longer come under Directive 2001/18.[183] It deviated, for these products, considerably from Directive 2001/18. Applications under this Regulation are now

---

[175] On this Committee, see para.6–01, above.
[176] Decision 1999/468 [1999] OJ L184/23.
[177] Decision 1999/468 [1999] OJ L184/23, art.5.
[178] Regulation 258/97 on novel food and novel food ingredients [1997] OJ L43/1; see also Commission Reg.1813/97 [1997] OJ L257/7.
[179] Commission Reg.1813/97 [1997] OJ L257/7.
[180] Regulation 1139/98 [1998] OJ L159/4.
[181] See also Commission Regs 49/2000 [2000] OJ L6/13 and 50/2000 [2000] OJ L6/15.
[182] Regulation 1829/2003 [2003] OJ L268/1.
[183] See Reg.1829/2003 [2003] OJ L268/1, Recital 34, and arts 16(7) and 18(3)(c); see also Court of Justice, *Monsanto* (C-58/10) ECLI:EU:C:2011:553.

to be made to the European Food Safety Authority (EFSA), seated in Parma; Member States only play a marginal role in the authorisation procedure. It is EFSA which evaluates the application and gives, if possible within six months, an opinion on it to the Commission. The Commission decides within three months and by Comitology procedure, whether to authorise the placing on the market of the product.

6–40   The participation of the public is almost not ensured.[184] And it is not surprising that the "club"-attitude of EFSA and the considerable secrecy surrounding the decision-making process has raised considerable suspicion with public opinion in Europe, which remains—including the majority of farmers—sceptical with regard to the new technology. Almost all authorisations that were given since the end of the moratorium were given under the new procedure of Regulation 1829/2003, no longer under Directive 2001/18. A WTO condemnation of the European Union for practising a moratorium and not authorising GMO products any more, which had examined the procedure under Directive 2001/18, did thus not raise concerns within the European Union.[185]

Regulation 1946/2003 dealt with the transboundary movement of genetically modified organisms,[186] following a requirement of the Cartagena Protocol on biosafety. The European Union adhered to the Protocol itself by Decision,[187] the Court of Justice having confirmed, at the request of the Commission, that art.192 and not art.191(4) and/or art.207 TFEU was the appropriate legal basis for that Decision.[188] The Regulation was based on the principle of prior informed consent, in order to promote trade in GMO products.

In 2015, Directive 2001/18 was amended on the basis of art.114 TFEU; in particular, a new art.26b was inserted into the Directive[189] which reads:

> "… a Member State may adopt measures restricting or prohibiting the cultivation in all or part of its territory of a GMO, provided that such measures are in conformity with Union law, reasoned, proportionate and non-discriminatory and, in addition, are based on compelling grounds such as those related to: (a) environmental policy objectives; (b) town and country planning; (c) land use; (d) socio-economic impacts; (e) evidence of GMO presence in other products …; (f) agricultural policy objectives; (g) public policy … Those grounds shall, in no case, conflict with the environmental risk assessment carried out pursuant to this Directive or to Regulation (EC No 1829/2003)."

The Member State concerned shall send a draft of its measure to the Commission and wait during a standstill period of 75 days for Commission (non-binding) comments, before they adopt measures.

6–41   Recitals 14 and 15 underline that the grounds which may be invoked by Member States to take restriction or prohibition measures, must be "distinct from

---

[184] See on participation in the decision-making procedure for authorising GMO-products, para.4–12, above.

[185] World Trade Organisation, Case DS 291 *USA v European Union*, Panel Report of 29 September 2006.

[186] Regulation 1946/2003 [2003] OJ L287/1.

[187] Decision 2002/628 [2002] OJ L201/48.

[188] Court of Justice, Opinion 2/00 [2001] E.C.R. I-9713.

[189] See Dir.2015/412 amending Dir.2001/18 as regards the possibility for Member States to restrict or prohibit the cultivation of genetically modified organisms (GMOs) in their territory [2015] OJ L68/1.

and complementary to" the risk assessment which was made under EU GMO legislation. Such environmental measures could be (Recital 14) "the maintenance and development of agricultural practices which offer a better potential to reconcile production with ecosystem sustainability, or maintenance of local biodiversity, including certain habitats and ecosystems, or certain types of natural and landscape features, as well as specific ecosystem functions and services"— whatever that means. Examples for socio-economic impacts are high costs, impracticability or impossibility of implanting coexistence, small islands or mountain zones, the diversity of agricultural production or the need to ensure seed and plant propagating material purity; also cultural traditions are mentioned by way of example.

The underlying consideration of these provisions is that health and environment aspects are already harmonised at EU level. This approach, though, appears inconsistent: objections against the planting of GMO seeds are just based on health or environmental concerns: even where such plants might impair organic agricultural production, the concern is one of health. Indeed, consumers buy organic food because they consider it to be less treated with chemicals, produced in an environmentally more friendly way, etc. The underlying reason for favouring organic food is thus the concern for health and/or the environment.

It remains to be seen how the Directive will work in practice; its compliance with WTO provisions appears doubtful. The correct way of addressing the concern of numerous Member States would have been to suggest either that the legal basis for the EU legislation were changed and art.192 TFEU became the legal basis, allowing Member States to recur to art.193 TFEU and completely prohibit GMO plants (or GMO animals), or inserting the provisions of art.193 TFEU into the existing EU legislation which is possible, even where the legislative act is based on art.114 TFEU.[190]

The 25 years of discussion on the placing of genetically modified products on the market of the European Union have thus led to a strong centralisation of the permitting procedure. As the European Union is not a state, many of the democratic safeguards which exist at the level of a Member State have disappeared or been reduced at EU level, such as full access to the scientific data which accompany the application, a public discussion of the necessity and opportunity to authorise the placing of the market, of the health and environmental risks linked to this placing on the market, etc. Opinion polls show a continued public hostility to the use of genetically modified food, feed and seeds—though much less of medical and industrial uses. An increasing concern is that of cross-fertilisation of organic farming products by GMO farming, which would make organic farming—the relevant EU provisions provide that organic farming must be GMO-free—impossible.

6-42

The health risk of GMO products seems not beyond suspicion, if one considers long-term effects, plant resistance, allergy issues and the uncertainty of animal tests. It is not clear why this technology should be introduced: it is made for industrial agriculture, brings limited benefits to farmers who already produce too much food, does not constitute a solution to the hunger in the world—which

---

[190] A recent example is Dir.2010/63 on the protection of animals used for scientific purposes [2010] OJ L276/33 which is based on art.114 TFEU and allows Member States to maintain or introduce more stringent national measures; see para.5–33, above.

is a problem of distribution, not of production—and favours patents on life of industrial companies. The environmental problem with GMOs is that once they are released into the environment, they cannot be taken back. GMO products in agriculture seem to require the increased rather than the decreased use of pesticides, because plants and pests get resistant to the new genetically modified plant. Also, the co-existence with organic food production is, in the long term, impossible. From that angle, the public request, based on the precautionary principle, to err on the side of caution, is more than understandable. However, it seems that in view of the worldwide development and expansion of this new technology—in particular in agriculture, food and pharmaceuticals—the large-scale introduction of genetically modified organisms into the environment is no longer reversible, unless new data demonstrate the long-term adverse health and environmental effects.

The difference of approach between public opinion which is afraid of and therefore opposed to biotechnology, and economic operators and EU public authorities which favour it and try to press this technology on the market, cannot be solved by providing for labelling for GMO products, at least not as long as the European Union does not introduce a label "GMO-free"—which the Commission has rejected until now. A label that informs consumers of the presence of GMOs which is meant to allow consumers to make an informed choice will have little or no effect in many situations (hotels, restaurants, catering, food aid), apart from the fact that labels are not frequently read. The placing on the market of agricultural GMOs in developing countries is not in the general interest of those countries and their economic development, as it rather increases economic dependence on industrialised countries.

6–43   Overall, GMO-technology in agriculture seems to be a technology that is superfluous, profitable to few, promoting industrial agriculture and bearing risks for humans and the environment.

(i) PVC

6–44   Polyvinyl chloride (PVC) is a chemical preparation that is at present produced in quantities of about 5 million tonnes per year within the European Union. It is mainly used as building material (about 55 per cent), packaging (14 per cent), and in toys, cars, pipes, etc. More than half of the PVC consists of chlorine, an irritant that is not found in other plastic raw material. In order to ensure the specific properties of PVC, the use of additives—plasticisers and stabilisers—is necessary. The main plasticisers are phthalates, of which several hundred exist. The European Union classified DEHP, the most commonly used phthalate, and three other phthalates (DBP, BBP and DIBP) as reproductive toxicants,[191] which means that these substances cannot be placed on the market or used as such, as constituents of other substances or in mixtures to be supplied to the general public, when the concentration of one of these phthalates is greater than 0.3 per cent. In 2014, it refused to follow a Danish request and further restrict the use of these phthalates, arguing principally that their use was decreasing anyway.[192]

---

[191] Commission Dec.90/420 [1990] OJ L222/49; Reg.1907/2006 [2013] OJ L253/1, annex XVII, no.30.
[192] Commission, Communication [2014] OJ C260/1.

Phthalates are suspected to have long-term negative effects in the aquatic environment and to be endocrine disruptors, which may disturb the hormone system of mammals and humans.[193] Stabilisers used in PVC are mainly lead and cadmium (both toxic and bioaccumulative) and organo-tin compounds (which are considered toxic to the aquatic environment). Substitutes, mainly on the basis of barium-zinc or calcium-zinc, exist, but are less often used, for economic reasons.

Manufacturing of PVC creates some environmental problems[194]; however, the main problems occur during its use, incineration (which generates hydrochloric acids, residues with high concentrations of heavy metals and dioxins) and landfill (where a risk of leaching of heavy metals exist). Recycling of PVC proves, at present, extremely difficult.

There is little EU legislation on PVC. Directive 86/280[195] established water-emission limit values of 1.2-dichlorethane (EDC), another additive of PVC; however, no air-emission standards have ever been fixed for this substance or for other componants of PVC. Cadmium is limited for use in many PVC applications. As regards incineration, Directive 2010/75 on the incineration of hazardous waste fixes air-emission standards, particularly for dioxins[196]; however, PVC waste is not classified as hazardous waste and no dioxin standards as yet exist for the incineration of non-hazardous waste.

6–45

An EU recommendation of 1998 suggested to Member States that they take the necessary measures in order to ensure a high level of health protection of toys destined to be put in the mouth by small children and which contained certain phthalates.[197] Under public pressure, this was turned into an amendment of Directive 76/769 that restricted the use of phtalates.[198]

A number of Member States and third countries have looked into the question of whether, in view of its environmental effects at the waste stage, it would not be appropriate to restrict the use of PVC generally. In its proposal on the directive for end-of-life vehicles, the Commission made some remarks on this point, though the adopted directive did not take up this point.[199] Should a restriction on the use of PVC ever come into force, this would constitute the first EU measure with regard to a product in view of its behaviour in the waste stage. Since any restriction of the use of PVC is heavily opposed by economic operators, such EU action is not very likely to succeed. Rather, it may be expected that measures are taken against some PVC additives—cadmium, lead and phthalates—and not against PVC itself.

---

[193] See also Commission, Communication on endocrine disruptors, COM(1999) 707.

[194] See Commission, Environmental issues of PVC COM(2000) 469.

[195] Directive 86/280 [1986] OJ L181/16; this Directive was in the meantime repealed.

[196] Directive 2010/75 [2010] OJ L334/17.

[197] Recommendation 98/485 [1998] OJ L217/35.

[198] See Directive 2005/84 [2005] OJ L344/40; the restrictions are now found in Reg.1907/2006 [2013] OJ L253/1, annex XVII, no.51.

[199] [1997] OJ C337/3: "the Commission will consider the evidence regarding the environmental aspects relating to the presence of PVC in waste streams; on the basis of this evidence, the Commission will review its policy regarding the presence of PVC in waste streams"; see also Dir.2000/53 [2000] OJ L269/34, Recital 12.

3.   ENVIRONMENTAL LABELLING

6–46   The European Union developed a considerable number of labels which refer to environmental aspects of products,[200] without forming a consistent and coherent whole. Mainly two groups of labels may be distinguished:

1.   environmental quality labels which present the environmental performance or an environmentally "good" composition of products and which want to incite buyers and users to make an informed choice, preferring the environmentally "better" product;
2.   labels which warn of environmental risks and dangers of a product.

(a)   Environmental Quality Labels

(i)   Regulation 66/2010 on eco-labelling

6–47   In 1992, the European Union adopted a regulation on an eco-label award scheme with the aim of promoting products which have a reduced environmental impact during their entire life-cycle and which give better information to consumers/ users. In 2000 and 2010, the system was revised, but not significantly modified.[201]

Participation in the scheme is voluntary. The scheme consists of an eco-logo—a flower with a corolla of petals in the form of the 12 EU stars surrounding an "E"—and is granted to products which satisfy certain environmental criteria. These criteria are fixed at an EU level for specific product groups, while the attribution of the label to the individual product is decided by the competent authorities of each Member State. The Regulation fixes selective criteria, organises the consultation with interest groups and other relevant matters for the functioning of the scheme.

In the follow-up of the deregulation move of 1992, economic operators tried to see the system privatised, but met with stiff opposition from the Council, led by the United Kingdom and Denmark.[202] Nevertheless, the system had difficulties to overcome in order to succeed. Indeed, it met with the opposition of economic operators' associations from the very beginning, who opposed the idea that some 15, 20 or 30 per cent of products of a specific product group should be allowed to bear an official label which qualified these products to be "better". Such objections formed themselves at national level in countries that were afraid of competition from other Member States, but reached EU level. Furthermore, procedures for determining criteria for product groups were long-lasting and complicated; consumers barely knew about the logo, so that producers did not have much to gain from using the logo which was not inexpensive. National

---

[200] See also the definition of the International Standardisation Organisation (ISO) for environmental labels: "A logo or a symbol attached to a product which is awarded by a third-party, agency or non-governmental organisation and which is based on multiple criteria and lifecycle analysis." A second type of eco-label includes claims of single attributes, such as "energy efficient".
[201] Regulation 66/2010 on the EU eco-label [2010] OJ L27/1; this Regulation replaced Reg.1980/2000 [2000] OJ L237/1; the original Regulation was Reg.880/92 [1992] OJ L99/1.
[202] Environmental Watch, 7 October 1994, p.1.

eco-label systems, in particular the Blue Angel in Germany or the Green Swan in Scandinavia, were well established, better known and accepted and quicker at producing results.

Finally, third countries—first of all the United States, but also Brazil— **6–48** complained that the scheme created barriers to international trade. Typical controversies concerned questions on whether the use of recycled toilet paper and other papers should be rated as environmentally favourable: wood-exporting countries were, of course, not of this opinion. The United States was of the opinion that, if criteria concerning the production methods were taken into consideration, this would mean that the European Union wanted to impose its production standards on third countries. In contrast, EU producers were of the opinion that production or social standards in third countries were not adequately taken into account and that this privileged imports.

For the review of the scheme, the Commission had suggested to phase out national and regional eco-labels for product groups which were covered by the EU scheme, to introduce a graded system that would allow products to obtain one, two or three flowers, depending on how environmentally superior they were, and to transfer responsibility for fixing the ecological criteria for the different product groups to an independent body.[203] All these proposals were rejected. The co-existence with national eco-label schemes was solved by allowing the co-existence of the two systems for one and the same product.

By mid-2015, criteria for some 35 product groups had been established,[204] 2,000 licences had been granted, and some 44,000 products had received the EU eco-label, still a very small number, though a considerable increase compared to 2010, when 1,073 had the eco-label. Denmark even turned away from the EU system and back to the Scandinavian eco-label system, while not less than 13 Member States set up national eco-labelling schemes—though often with limited success. The status of the eco-label scheme is still very uncertain; neither economic operators nor environmental or consumer groups are enthusiastic about it. The label is not well known and has not really reached consumer awareness.[205] A recent decision to develop eco-labels for hotels[206] and camping sites[207] could make the label better known, provided that specific regions, such as islands, systematically equip their hotels with such a label.[208]

(ii) Organic farming

Agricultural products which come from specific ecological production—the **6–49** conditions of which have been very meticulously laid down, in order to avoid abuses and, at the same time, make life for traditional farmers easier—must bear

---

[203] [1997] OJ C114/9.

[204] See last Commission Decs 2014/256 on converted paper products [2014] OJ L135/24; 2014/350 on textile products [2014] OJ L174/45; 2014/893 on some cosmetic products [2014] OJ L354/47.

[205] See also Commission Dec.2006/402 establishing the EU eco-label working plan [2006] OJ L162/78 which is relatively ambitious.

[206] Commission Dec.2009/578 on tourist accommodation services [2009] OJ L198/36.

[207] Commission Dec.2009/564 on campsite services [2009] OJ L186/36.

[208] By mid-2015, 98 hotels in the European Union had acquired the eco-label, more than half of them in Italy, see *http://www.ec.europa.eu/ecat* [Accessed 31 July 2015].

the label "organic farming".[209] Products from organic farming—which may neither be produced from GMOs nor by GMOs, reached a market share of about 5 per cent within the European Union, although the differences among Member States are considerable.[210] In 1999, the Council adopted an amendment in order to have animal farming included in the Regulation.[211] And in the same year the Commission created a specific logo which products from animal farming were allowed to display; in 2008, this logo was refined.[212] Products from third countries may bear the statement "organic product", where the production methods have expressly been recognised as being equivalent to the requirements of Regulation 834/2007.[213] The label is not well known, also because the agricultural policy tries to favour traditional farming and make life for organic farmers as difficult as possible; the refinement of 2008 tried to improve this situation.

In 2014, the Commission proposed an overall review and improvement of the provisions on organic farming, as the number of organic farmers had remained stable since about 2000[214]; the adoption of this proposal is slowed down, due to a controversy with the European Parliament and the Council on the Commission's implementing and delegated powers.

(iii) Energy consumption

6–50   The EU discussion on the labelling of energy consumption of electrical household appliances started about 30 years ago. However, attempts to obtain solutions via industrial standardisation and voluntary agreements with manufacturers failed.[215] This led the European Union to develop, since 1992,[216] environmental labels for electrical or electronic household appliances, which are somehow too narrowly called energy labels. The labels indicate, according to national standards or other provisions fixed in the annexes and in a graphically fixed scheme the energy and water consumption, performance and noise level.

In 2010, a new directive was adopted on the energy labelling of products[217] which applies to all products that consume energy. The detailed labelling requirements were subsequently elaborated for each type of products by Commission delegated regulations.[218] They consist of green, yellow or red

---

[209] Regulation 834/2007 [2007] OJ L189/1; this Regulation replaced Reg.2092/91 [1991] OJ L198/1; the labelling details were fixed by Commission Reg.889/2008 [2008] OJ L250/1.

[210] Commission, COM(2012) 759; since about 2000, this percentage has almost not changed, see European Environment Agency, *Environmental Signals 2001* (Copenhagen, 2001), Pt 7.4.

[211] Regulation 1804/99 [1999] OJ L222/1.

[212] Commission Reg.889/2008 [2008] OJ L250/1; this Regulation replaced Commission Reg.331/2000 [2000] OJ L48/1.

[213] Commission Reg.1235/2008 [2008] OJ L334/25 with later amendments.

[214] Commission, COM(2014) 180.

[215] See Economic and Social Committee [1995] OJ C155/19, no.2.7.

[216] Directive 92/75 on the conservation of energy and other resources by household appliances [1992] OJ L297/16.

[217] Directive 2010/30 on the indication by labelling and standard product information of energy and other resources by energy-related products [2010] OJ L153/1.

[218] See Commission Delegated Regs 1059/2010 on dishwashers [2010] OJ L314/1; 1060/2010 on refrigerators [2010] OJ L314/17; 1061/2010 on washing machines [2010] OJ L314/47; 1062/2010 on televisions [2010] OJ L314/64; 627/2011 on air conditioners [2011] OJ L178/1; 392/2012 on tumble driers [2012] OJ L123/1; 874/2012 on electrical lamps [2012] OJ L258/1; 665/2013 on vacuum

arrows, ranging from A+++ to G according to the energy efficiency which measures the annual energy consumption. The class to which the product in question belongs, is indicated in black. "Where relevant other resources during use" shall also be indicated;[219] this requirement refers to noise levels,[220] but no longer to water consumption. The efficiency of the label is questionable, as most of appliances range in the A+++ or A++ class. In 2015, the Commission proposed to abandon the A+++ system and return to the A to G system.

(iv) Fuel consumption of cars

Directive 1999/94, based on art.192 TFEU, introduced a requirement that all new passenger cars at the point of sale bear a label on the official fuel consumption and their average CO_2 emissions.[221] Also, a guide on fuel economy and CO_2 emissions had to be made available to consumers at the point of sale, free of charge, but "on request" only (art.4). Extending the labelling requirement in future also to used cars was under consideration (Recital 6), but has since been abandoned.   **6–51**

Such a label is not really capable of making the consumer change his intentions and buy a car that consumes or emits less, as there is no yardstick to allow the consumer to measure possible economies. The label requirement was mainly introduced at the instigation of the car industry, which wanted to be seen as contributing to the fight against climate change. There is general consensus in the meantime that the Directive did not achieve its aims.

(v) Recyclable packaging

Under Directive 94/62 on waste and packaging waste,[222] the Commission made a proposal for the marking of reusable or recyclable packaging.[223] The symbols consisted of different round circles. The proposal attempted to create new, EU-specific symbols. As economic operators, however, oriented themselves more and more to the US system for labelling of packaging which is also promoted via international standardisation organisations, the Commission proposal received a cool reception. The Council did not discuss it and the European Parliament suggested it rather take over symbols that had been developed by different sectors of the packaging industry. The proposal is now obsolete.   **6–52**

(vi) Forest label

In view of the disappearance of tropical and other forests, discussions have gone on for a considerable amount of time to create a label for wood, which indicates   **6–53**

---

cleaners [2013] OJ L192/1; 811/2013 on space heaters [2013] OJ L239/1; 812/2013 on water heaters [2013] OJ L239/83; 1254/2014 residential ventilation units [2014] OJ L337/27; 65/2015 on domestic ovens [2015] OJ L29/1.

[219] Directive 2010/30 [2010] OJ L153/1 art.4.

[220] For example, the noise level must be indicated for refrigerators and air conditioners, but not for television sets.

[221] Directive 1999/94 [1999] OJ L12/16.

[222] Directive 94/62 on packaging and packaging waste [1994] OJ L365/10.

[223] [1996] OJ C382/10.

that the wood comes from sustainable forestry. The European Union indicated on several occasions its commitment to such a label. In decisions taken in the context of the EU eco-label scheme, one of the criteria for paper products is that the wood must stem from sustainable forestry. Until now, however, no internationally recognised label for such sustainable forestry exists. The European Union has not either developed such a label. Attempts in the Netherlands to impose such a label failed, because no agreement could be found as to what exactly sustainable forestry meant. At present, illegal logging continues to be practised in many countries without trade in wood products being affected. Regulation on timber and timber products did not introduce a label to inform users and consumers that the timber was legally harvested.[224]

(b) Environmental warning labels

(i) Chemicals that are dangerous for the environment

6–54 Directive 67/548[225] on dangerous chemical substances was amended in 1979 to include a label "dangerous to the environment". The label consisted of a symbol showing a dead fish beached beside a dead tree, both in black on a yellow-orange background; the symbol was accompanied by phrases on the special risks (R-phrases) and on the safe use of the substance (S-phrases). By the end of 2007, some 200 substances were labelled with the symbol "dangerous for the environment". This seems somewhat few substances. However, some thousand substances from petrol refining, such as aromatic hydrocarbons, naphta, extracts and distillates, which are classified "toxic", did not bear this label, though they obviously appear to be dangerous for the environment. The reason for this was that a substance that was labelled "toxic", need not also be labelled "dangerous for the environment" (art.23 of Directive 67/548). The same was true for substances where the indication "may cause cancer" was obligatory.

In 2008, this labelling system was significantly amended by a new regulation, which adapted the EU labelling scheme to the United Nations Global Harmonised System of Classification and Labelling of Chemicals (GHS) which itself was considerably influenced by the global labelling scheme for the transport of goods.[226] The new Regulation ignored the fact that the risks for the consumer/user and for the environment are very different during the transport of a product and during its use in the home, in the garden, at the working place or in agriculture. The most significant change in the new system is the abandoning of the yellow-orange background of the label, which was replaced by a rhombus with a white background, sometimes surrounded by a red frame. The new label is much less visible. The pictogram—where it is required—is accompanied by signal words ("danger" or "warning") and by hazard statements and precautionary statements which are standardised by Regulation 1272/2008. The hazard statements and precautionary statements are limited to indicate risks to the

---

[224] Regulation 995/2010 laying down obligations of operators who place timber and timber products on the market [2010] OJ L295/23.

[225] Directive 67/548 [1967] OJ 196/1.

[226] Regulation 1272/2008 on the classification, the packaging and the labelling of chemical substances and mixtures [2008] OJ L250/1.

aquatic environment and to the ozone layer; all other risk phrases referring to the environment were deleted. The pictogram "dangerous to the environment" only appears for the aquatic environment; the risk to the ozone layer is symbolised by a pictogram showing an exclamation mark. The number of environment-related safety phrases (precautionary statements) was greatly reduced.

Pesticides labelling is not included in the present labelling requirements for dangerous mixtures. Its labelling is regulated by Commission Regulation 547/2011.[227] No pictograms are foreseen. The label must indicate the concentration of the active substance and contain standard phrases for special risks to humans and the environment (annex II) as well as standard phrases for safety precautions (annex III).

(ii) Separate collection

Directive 2006/66 on batteries[228] contains a symbol indicating "separate collection" of batteries, which consists of a crossed-out wheeled bin, accompanied by an indication of which heavy metal is involved (Hg for mercury, Cd for cadmium or Pb for lead). This symbol is to be placed on batteries only and indicates that they are subject to separate collection, and shall not be put in a normal waste-bin. The same symbol is used in Directive 2012/19 to indicate that electrical and electronic products shall be collected separately.[229]

6–55

(iii) Labelling of products containing GMOs

In order to meet public concern within the European Union regarding the placing on the market of products that contain GMOs, the European Union adopted a regulation[230] that requires food labels to indicate that the food contains GMOs; however, this requirement only applies to those cases where differences between such food products and normal food products can be scientifically detected. Since this label neither covers all products nor all products that contain genetically modified organisms—estimations indicate that 90 per cent of all food products will not be covered by the labelling requirements—it will not allow consumers systematically to avoid such products. The large-scale introduction of products that contain genetically modified organisms cannot be stopped by such a measure; at best it will be slowed down. Requests from environmental and consumer organisations to introduce a label "GMO-free"—this would be perceived as a quality label, not as a warning label—have so far been rejected by the European Union. Based on a recital of Regulation 1830/2003,[231] a number of Member States introduced, at national level, a label "GMO-free", without the Commission taking action against this practice.

6–56

---

[227] Commission Regulation 547/2011 [2011] OJ L155/176.
[228] Directive 2006/66 [2006] OJ L266/1.
[229] Directive 2012/19 [2012] OJ L197/38.
[230] Regulation 1830/2003 concerning the traceability and labelling of genetically modified organisms and of food and feed products produced from genetically modified organisms [2003] OJ L268/24.
[231] Regulation 1830/2003 [2003] OJ L268/24, Recital 11: "It is necessary to ensure that consumers are fully and reliably informed about GMOs and the products, foods and feed produced therefrom, so as to allow them to make an informed choice of product."

4. IMPORTS AND EXPORTS OF PRODUCTS

6–57 There are no general provisions on the import and export of products. In particular, the European Union has no general provision which provides that a product which is banned or severely restricted to be placed on the market within the European Union should not be exported, either to any third country or at least to any non-industrialised country. Rather, the European Union follows international trends which are based on the principle that any country should decide for itself, whether it wishes to have certain substances or products on its market or not. International conventions thus follow the principle of "prior informed consent" (PIC): prior to the first export, the importing state is to be informed of the existence of the ban or the restrictions that exist in the exporting country. Then it has to decide whether it allows the import.

If one takes asbestos products as an example: which reasons may exist that asbestos fibres which are known now to cause cancer, are banned within the European Union, but undergo the PIC procedure only, when they are exported to Africa or Asia? In my opinion, the PIC principle does not offer sufficient protection to humans and the environment in the developing countries, where administrative controls are often insufficient. The EU policy should rather provide that, as a rule, a substance or a product that is banned or severely restricted in use within the European Union shall have the same restriction when it is exported to non-industrialised countries.

The European Union follows a different approach. Regulation 649/2012,[232] which replaced earlier Regulations,[233] and which is based on both art.192(1) and art.207 TFEU,[234] provided that where a third country notifies an EU Member State of the export to the European Union of a chemical substance that is banned or restricted in use in that third country, that notification shall be sent to the Commission and hence to all other Member States. The Commission takes into consideration all import restrictions which may exist at national or EU level and adopts, by way of Comitology procedure, an import decision (art.13).

6–58 In 2002, the European Union decided to ratify the Rotterdam Convention of 1998 on the PIC procedure related to the export and import of chemicals[235] which had been elaborated under the auspices of the Food and Agricultural Organisation (FAO) and the United Nations Environment Programme (UNEP). Regulation 649/2012[236] adapted the EU requirements to the provisions of the Rotterdam Convention. Annex 1 of that Regulation lists different groups of chemicals which are subject to the notification procedure. The three parts of annex 1 differentiate according to the amount of information which has to accompany the notification. Part 1, comprising some 160 substances, requires information to be conveyed on the identity of the substance, the type of restriction which exists and other necessary information. Part 2 only requires the indication of the identity of the

---

[232] Regulation 649/2012 concerning the export and import of hazardous chemicals [2012] OJ L201/60.

[233] Regulation 689/2008 [2008] OJ L204/1; this Regulation replaced Reg.2455/92 [1992] OJ L251/13.

[234] See on the double legal basis Court of Justice, *Commission v European Parliament and Council* (C-178/03) [2006] E.C.R. I-107.

[235] Decision 2003/106 [2003] OJ L63/27.

[236] Regulation 649/2012 [2012] OJ L201/60.

substance. An exporter who intends to export for the first time a chemical coming under the Regulation shall notify his intention to export to the competent authorities of the Member State where he is established at least 35 days before the export takes place, and 15 days in advance for the first export of the chemical each year thereafter. The competent authority has to check whether the information is complete and then inform the European Chemical Agency of the export, which has to ensure that the importers receive notification at least 15 days prior to the first shipment. Annex V contains a list of substances and products the export of which is banned. This list includes in particular the persistent organic pollutants covered by Regulation 850/2004.[237]

It is doubtful whether these measures are sufficient. Indeed, administrations in third countries do not always seem to be able fully to assess the impact of chemicals that are to be imported. Also, the World Health Organisation estimates that every year a considerable number of persons suffer acute unintentional poisoning as a result of the misuse of pesticides; no figures exist for environmental damage caused by chemicals, the use of which is banned or restricted within the European Union.

In 2012, the European Union banned the export of metallic mercury and certain metallic compounds and mixtures, following a global initiative to eliminate mercury from the environment, as far as possible.[238]

5.   INDUSTRIAL STANDARDISATION

Environmental requirements for products—as for processes—may be fixed by legislative regulation, such as, for instance, for emissions from cars. They may also be fixed by industrial technical standards, which are elaborated by private standardisation organisations, the result of which is a technical indication for some product characteristics.   **6–59**

Industrial standards are, by definition, not mandatory. Legally, they constitute a recommendation of the authors to follow the indications laid down in the standard. Their degree of recognition depends on the readiness of producers to apply the standard. Public authorities often support the application of standards, for instance by providing in legislation that standards must be complied with or by not laying down specifications in regulations, but referring to (private) standards, etc.

At EU level, there are no specific EU standardisation organisations. Rather, the three organisations that exist are international bodies, which went, right from their beginnings, beyond the borders of the European Union. All three organisations have close relations with national standardisation bodies on the one hand, and with international bodies on the other hand, which include arrangements to avoid the duplication of work.

CEN (*Comité Européen de Normalisation*; European Committee for Standardisation) was created in 1961. It is an association under Belgian law, the members of which are national standards institutions of Western European countries and, since 1992, associate members in the form of organisations that   **6–60**

---

[237] Regulation 850/2004 [2004] OJ L158/7.
[238] Regulation 1102/2008 [2008] OJ L304/75.

represent economic and social interests at European level and which fulfil certain conditions as regards representativity and objectives. About half of CEN's budget is provided for by EU funds.

The CEN secretariat is located in Brussels. Since 1989, CEN has had an agreement with the International Standardisation Organisation (ISO), which enables one of the two organisations to allow the other to take the lead on a specific standardisation project. This avoids different standards being elaborated at global (ISO) and European (CEN) level.[239]

CEN standards are prepared by technical committees—at present numbering about 300. Programme committees and technical sector boards have the task of providing for coordination among these committees. Since the early 1990s, CEN has established a Programming Committee on the "Environment", which, in turn, has set up a working group on "Environmental Aspects in Product Standards"; this group has the task of looking into the environmental aspects of general product standards and to give guidance and make recommendations to standards writers.

6–61   CEN differentiates between direct and indirect standardisation work. Direct standardisation concerns items such as environmental assessment methods; measurement methods for environmental properties of chemicals; pollution control methods and equipment; environmental management tools; and methods for the evaluation of environmental effects of products. Indirect standardisation aspects deal with the environmental aspects of general product standards.

CENELEC (*Comité Européen de Normalisation Electrotechnique*; European Committee of Electrotechnical Standardisation) began its work in the early 1960s. Since 1972 it has been located in Brussels. Its members are national electrotechnical committees. It elaborates standards in the area of electrical and electronic equipment and roughly one-third of its budget is provided by the European Union. About three-quarters of all CENELEC standards are parallels of international electrotechnical standards.

ETSI (European Telecommunications Standards Institute) was created in 1988 for the telecommunications sector.

6–62   For the European Union, industrial standardisation is of growing importance for environmental issues, since the European Union opted, in the early 1980s, for a "new approach" to the approximation of national legal rules,[240] by which the Council

> "emphasizes the importance and desirability of the new approach which provides for reference to standards—primarily European standards, but national ones if need be, as a transitional measure—for the purposes of defining the technical characteristics of products."

The same resolution laid down four "fundamental principles" for the new approach:

---

[239] In pursuance of this agreement, CEN decided, for example, not to prepare separate environmental management systems, but to adopt the standards ISO 14001 and 14004 prepared by ISO; ISO has also taken the lead for standards on life-cycle assessments.

[240] The definition of "new approach" was first used in Commission, COM(85) and Council Resolution of 7 May 1985 [1985] OJ C136/1: On a new approach to technical harmonisation and standards.

- "legislative harmonization is limited ... to the adoption of the essential safety requirements (or other requirements in the general interest) with which products put on the market must conform";
- the task of drawing up the technical specifications of products is done by industrial standardisation organisations;
- these technical standardisations maintain their status of voluntary standards;
- products which conform to harmonised standards are presumed to conform to the essential requirements established by a Directive.

A number of product-related directives have been elaborated since the mid-1980s according to the new approach.[241] However, the essential requirements, laid down in these Directives, practically never deal with environmental issues. Thus, the impact of these directives on the environment is limited: indeed, since the protection of the environment is also an essential requirement of EU policy,[242] the omission of the regulation of environmental issues in the context of essential requirements at EU level means that Member States are free to adopt environmental measures at national level as regards these products.

The new approach is certainly not applied systematically. For a number of areas, European standards do not as yet exist, and large sectors such as food and pharmaceuticals, cars and chemicals are not covered by it at all. Its main area of application is the mechanical sector.

6–63

Up to 2015, the only environmental Directive adopted under the new approach has been the Directive on packaging and packaging waste.[243] This Directive, which is based on art.114 TFEU, contains an annex which lays down essential requirements for packaging. Thus, packaging shall be:

- so manufactured that the packaging volume and weight is limited to the minimum adequate amount to maintain the necessary level of safety, hygiene and acceptance for the packed product and for the consumer;
- designed, produced and commercialised in such a way as to permit its reuse or recovery, including recycling, and to minimise its impact on the environment when packaging waste or residues from packaging waste management operations are disposed of;
- manufactured so that the presence of noxious and other hazardous substances and materials is minimised with regard to their presence in emissions, ash or leachate, when packaging or residues are incinerated or landfilled.

Where the standards do not, in part or in full, comply with the essential requirements of the Directive, the only "sanction" is that the European Union could refuse to recognise them as harmonised standards. This has as a

---

[241] In particular Dir.73/23 on low-voltage equipment [1973] OJ 77/29; Dir.87/404 on pressure vessels [1987] OJ L220/48; Dir.87/378 on toy safety [1987] OJ L187/1; Dir.89/106 on construction products [1989] OJ L40/12; Dir.89/392 on the safety of machines [1989] OJ L183/9; Dir.90/396 on appliances burning gaseous fuels [1990] OJ L196/15; Dir.92/42 on new hot-water boilers fired with liquid or gaseous fuels [1992] OJ L167/17; Dir.94/62 on packaging and packaging waste [1994] OJ L365/11.
[242] *Procureur de la République v Association de Défense de Bruleurs* (240/83) [1985] E.C.R. 531.
[243] Directive 94/62 [1994] OJ L365/11.

consequence that the presumption—laid down in art.11(2) of Directive 94/62—according to which a packaging that complies with the standards also complies with the requirements of the Directive would not apply. Member States are then not obliged to admit a packaging on their market that they consider not to comply with their interpretation of the essential requirements, even where the packaging complies with the standards. This would mean that, for instance, Denmark might continue to refuse metal cans on its market with the argument that they do not comply with essential requirements, though Denmark repealed, in the meantime, its national restrictions for metal cans. Other candidates for national measures could be PVC packaging, aerosols or—more generally— plastic or non-biodegradable packaging, where in each case it could be argued that the packaging does not comply with the essential requirements of Directive 94/62.

6–64   Obviously, these considerations depend on the determination of Member States to ensure that the essential requirements, laid down in Directive 94/62, really are respected. However, as regards the standards for packaging, this is what the Commission did: it considered the standards that CEN had elaborated of such a poor quality that it refused to recognise them as harmonised standards.[244] As mentioned in para.6–20, above, the Commission accepted, at a later stage, the CEN standards though these had hardly been amended in the meantime.

It remains to be seen how the packaging policy within the European Union will develop. Few Member States seem prepared to pursue a policy that aims at the reduction of packaging material and the recycling/reuse of packaging material.

The problems of standards for packaging illustrate well the general environmental difficulties with industrial standardisation: the problem how industrial standards can be made greener is not yet solved. Indeed, at national level, public authorities can participate and do participate in the working groups that elaborate the technical standard. Their representative may bring environmental aspects into the discussion on the elaboration of a standard, and influence the taking into consideration of the general interest to protect the environment. Where they do not succeed in this attempt, they may suggest governmental regulation on the subject covered by the standard, which makes the industrial standard more or less obsolete.

6–65   At EU level, the representatives of economic operators in CEN/CENELEC write their own standards and are hardly influenced at all by environmental organisations, which are too weak and financially too feeble to organise themselves structurally at EU level. Commission officials do not, in practice, participate in the working groups of CEN or CENELEC, and written contributions, if they are made at all, do not significantly influence the making of standards. Until now, no horizontal structures have been set up, which would—if instigated in time—change this situation. Despite all discussion on the integration of environmental requirements into industrial standardisation, nothing significant has changed during the last 25 years. Most of the reflections on such new structures aim at the increased participation of environmental organisations in the discussion and decision-making process of CEN and, to a lesser degree, of

---

[244] Decision 2001/524 [2001] OJ L190/21.

CENELEC. Other measures discussed are an environmental impact assessment for the subject covered by a standard; the results of this assessment would be incorporated into each CEN standard.

In 2012, the Union adopted a Regulation to improve the rules on cooperation with the three above-mentioned standardisation organisations and to officialise the strong financial support which these organisations had received annually from the Commission.[245] The organisations are requested to produce an annual work programme and "encourage and facilitate" (art.5) the participation of environmental organisations and other stakeholders in their work. Public authorities are encouraged to participate at national level in the work of standardisation organisations (art.7); a corresponding provision for the Union level does not exist. The Commission shall produce an annual work programme for standardisation with priorities regarding its work and shall seek to agree the priorities with the private organisations.

The Commission work programme for 2015[246] enumerates six priority areas out of which four—bio-based products including fuels, ecodesign/energy-related products, waste recycling, and air quality and industrial emissions—are environmental-related which demonstrates the relevance of standardisation work for environmental policies.

---

[245] Regulation 1025/2012 on European standardisation [2012] OJ L316/12.
[246] Commission, COM(2015) 500.

CHAPTER 7

Water Protection

1. EU WATER POLICY AND LAW

EU water policy and law is about 40 years old. It was fixed, in the beginning, on   **7–01**
two objectives; on the one hand, it set quality requirements for specific water
uses, such as surface waters, groundwater, bathing or drinking water; on the other
hand, it tried to limit discharges of pollutants into the waters. In 1988, an
inter-ministerial meeting on water policy endeavoured to lay down the principles
of a more coherent water policy[1]; however, the objectives identified at this
seminar only very partially materialised.

The European Council in Edinburgh, in December 1992, which tried to start a
deregulation process, fixed a number of orientations for EU policy and invited the
European Union to simplify, consolidate and adapt EU environmental legis-
lation.[2] Nowhere was this statement taken more seriously than in the water sector,
probably also because the United Kingdom, which had presided over the
Edinburgh Council, had just received a judgment from the Court of Justice, which
obliged it to make considerable investments in cleaning up drinking water.[3]
Subsequent to this Council, and on the repeated insistence of the European
Parliament,[4] the Commission published a Communication in 1996 on the
"European Community Water Policy".[5] This Communication fixed as objectives
of EU water policy:

- a secure supply of drinking water;
- sufficient quality and quantity of water resources to meet other economic
  requirements;
- to protect and sustain the good ecological state and functioning of the
  aquatic environment and meet the water needs of wetland and terrestrial
  ecosystems and habitats;
- the management of water so as to prevent or reduce the impact of floods
  and droughts.

---

[1] The conclusions of this seminar were never published; a short report is found in (1988) *Bulletin of
the European Communities*, para.2.1.175; the Council adopted a resolution on the follow-up of the
seminar [1988] OJ C209/3.
[2] See (1992) 12 *Bulletin of the European Communities* 18.
[3] *Commission v United Kingdom* (C-337/89) [1992] E.C.R. I-5973.
[4] See in particular European Parliament, Resolution of 23 October 1996 [1996] OJ C347/80.
[5] Commission, COM(96) 59.

These objectives obviously refer to fresh and coastal water rather than, for instance, to oceans. They are targeted to meet, first of all, human needs. The communication stated that the "environmental quality objectives approach" and the "emission limit values approach" were complementary and not contradictory. It continued by stating that quality objectives could either fix common parametric values applicable in all Member States or could be expressed in a form such that common criteria for the establishment of parameters and values were fixed at EU level, but that the values were established at national level, in order "to allow flexibility to adapt to the very different environmental conditions in different parts of the Community". The Commission clearly indicated that it preferred this approach.

7–02   The European Parliament was of the opinion that the Communication failed in its objective to present a coherent overall concept and requested that the review of water policy should in no way lead to a lowering of standards; as a minimum the fixing of strict and uniform emission standards was necessary.[6]

The first EU water Directives and other measures were regularly based on arts 100 and 235 EC Treaty which since became arts 115/114 and 352 TFEU, and were adopted at unanimity.[7] Despite the existence of environment action programmes from the early 1970s, the adoption of these directives did not follow a political strategy; rather, the Directives were adopted where political or legal opportunities existed. They were often drafted by non-lawyers, and perceived more as guidelines than as legally binding requirements for Member States and water administrations. The Commission did not look closely into questions of their legal implementation and practical application.

Since 1987, art.192 TFEU became the legal basis for all environmental matters, including those on the protection of waters. Such measures continued to request unanimous decisions, until the Maastricht Treaty introduced, in 1993, majority decisions into art.192 TFEU. This amendment of the Treaty, however, brought some uncertainty as to the correct legal basis for EU water legislation. Indeed, while art.192(1) provided for majority decisions, art.192(2) provided for unanimous decisions by the Council for measures concerning "the management of water resources". And while art.192(1) introduced the co-decision procedure with the European Parliament under the present art.294 TFEU,[8] art.192(2) limited the role of the European Parliament to a consultative function.

7–03   The different interpretations on the delimitation between art.192(1) and (2) as regards water measures were solved by a judgment from the Court of Justice.[9] This judgment concerned Decision 97/825, by which the European Union had adhered to the Convention on Co-operation for the Protection and Sustainable Use of the River Danube[10]; the Council had based that Decision on the old art.130s(1) EC—now art.192(1) TFEU. Spain was of the opinion that the

---

[6] European Parliament, Resolution of 23 October 1996 [1996] OJ C347/80; see also Economic and Social Committee [1996] OJ C30/5; Committee of the Regions [1997] OJ C34/30.

[7] Directive 75/440 on the protection of surface waters for the abstraction of drinking water [1975] OJ L194/26; Dir.76/160 on the quality of bathing water [1976] OJ L31/1; Dir.78/659 on fresh water supporting fish life [1978] OJ L222/1; Dir.79/923 on shellfish water [1979] OJ L281/47.

[8] Between the entry into force of the Maastricht Treaty in 1993 and the Amsterdam Treaty in 1999, art.192(1) provided for the cooperation procedure according to art.252 EC Treaty.

[9] Court of Justice, *Spain v Council* (C-36/98) [2001] E.C.R. I-779.

[10] Decision 97/825 [1997] OJ L342/18.

Decision should have been based on art.192(2), as it concerned the management of water resources, and applied to the Court of Justice. The Court found that only the Dutch version of art.192(2) used the word "quantitative", while the French version also used expressions which signalled that the quantitative management of water was in question. The Court then referred to the purpose and general scheme of the provision and concluded that art.192(2) was limited to quantitative aspects of water management; this judgment conformed to the overwhelming opinion in legal literature. Two weeks after this judgment, the Treaty of Nice was signed which amended art.192(2). Unanimity is now required, where a measure concerns *quantitative* aspects of water management.

Until mid-2015, the European Union has not adopted water measures that were based on art.192(2) TFEU.

In its efforts to give greater coherence to measures on water protection and, at the same time, to follow the trend towards deregulation and the abandoning of precise provisions, the Commission submitted, in 1994, a proposal for a directive on the ecological quality of water.[11] The proposal suggested a good ecological water quality for all surface water in the European Union. Member States were to identify the sources of pollution and to fix objectives in order to reach this good ecological quality. They were then to elaborate integrated programmes to reach the objectives. The proposal met with little enthusiasm in the European Parliament, which continued to press for a more coherent approach to water policy.[12] The Commission accepted this request and presented, on the one hand, a communication on water policy[13] and, on the other hand, a proposal for a directive "establishing a framework for Community action in the field of water policy".[14] This proposal was adopted in 2000 and came into effect at the end of 2003.[15] It aimed at the protection of all waters, i.e. surface waters, groundwaters and coastal waters, but did not cover marine waters. Article 1 fixed five objectives:

1. prevention of further deterioration and protection and enhancing of aquatic and terrestrial ecosystems and halt to further deterioration;
2. promotion of sustainable water use, based on long-term protection of available water resources;
3. enhanced protection and improvement of the aquatic environment through the progressive reduction of discharges and the cessation or phasing-out of discharges, emissions and losses of priority hazardous substances;
4. progressive reduction of groundwater pollution;
5. mitigation of the effects of floods and droughts.

---

[11] [1994] OJ C222/6; explanatory memorandum COM(93) 680.
[12] European Parliament, Resolution of 23 October 1996 [1996] OJ C347/80.
[13] Commission, COM(96) 59.
[14] [1997] OJ C184/20; explanatory memorandum, Commission COM(97) 49; amendment of the proposal [1998] OJ C16/14 and [1998] OJ C108/94.
[15] Directive 2000/60 establishing a framework for Community action in the field of water policy [2000] OJ L327/1.

The Directive requested Member States to organise their waters—including groundwater and coastal water—according to individual river basin districts.[16] Where a river basin covered the territory of more than one Member State, it must be assigned to an international river basin district (art.3(3)); where non-EU countries belong to a river basin—examples are the Rhine or the Danube— Member States were asked to "endeavour to establish appropriate co-ordination". The river basin administration shall ensure the application of the Directive's rules in the river basin; for "international river basin districts the Member states concerned shall together ensure this co-ordination".

7–04   These provisions thus obliged, in regionalised or in federal countries, the water administration to organise itself in administrative units—districts—which it had not set up until then. Also, the obligation to a joint administration in international river basin districts constituted an interference with political or administrative autonomy that met—for instance in German regionalised legal literature—some concern. These provisions had, though, a number of precedents: Directive 91/271 obliged Member States to build specific waste water treatment installations.[17] Directive 85/337 on the environmental impact assessment obliged Member States to cooperate among themselves in those areas where transfrontier elements of environmental protection were in question. This obligation to administrative cooperation flows from art.10 EC—at present art.4(3) TEU— which establishes the basic principle that Member States have to cooperate. In the last instance, one might ask what the European Union is really about, if there were not even the possibility to organise environmental protection measures— which are, by nature, not limited by a national frontier—according to reasonable objective criteria such as river basins.

Article 4 of Directive 2000/60 fixed environmental objectives, separated for surface waters, groundwater and protected areas. The objective was to reach "good" surface water (groundwater) status of "good" ecological potential, and "good" water chemical status. Under certain conditions, Member States may aim to achieve less stringent environmental objectives for specific bodies of water which are so strongly affected by human activity that the achievement of the normal objectives is infeasible or disproportionately expensive (art.4(5)). And Member states were declared to be "not in breach of this Directive", when certain new sustainable human development activities or new modifications of the water body occurred (art.4(7)). The objectives had to be achieved "at the latest" by 2015, though Member States were allowed to prolong this date unilaterally until 2027 (art.4(4.c)).

The Directive defined what is "good" by reference to criteria that were laid down in an annex V. This means in practice that each river basin plan fixes itself the water quality which is to be achieved under the Directive, though the criteria of annex V may lead to some alignment. Also, the question of whether a water had a high, a good or a moderate status, whether a water was to be classified as good, poor or bad—all these classifications were introduced by the Directive—

---

[16] Article 2(13) of Dir.2000/60 [2000] OJ L327/1: "river basin means the area of land from which all surface run-off flows through a sequence of streams, rivers and, possibly, lakes into the sea at a single river mouth, estuary or delta".

[17] Directive 91/271 on waste water treatment [1991] OJ L135/40.

depended on the decisions taken within the water management bodies and could thus vary from one water basin to the other.

In order to reach the objectives of the Directive, Member States had to establish, by 2009, programmes of measures for each river basin district,[18] for which a considerable number of conditions were set in the Directive (art.11). Such programmes had to be updated every six years. Furthermore, for each river basin district, a river management plan had to be produced (art.13(1)). Member States were only obliged to produce such a plan for districts that were entirely situated within their territory. For international districts, Member States had to coordinate such plans among each other and, where third countries were involved, they had to "endeavour to produce a single river basin management plan" (art.13(4)). The "public" had to have the opportunity to comment on the production, review and updating of the river management plan (art.14). For groundwater, the adoption of a specific directive was foreseen; this Directive was adopted in 2006.[19]

7–05

In order to reduce water pollution, art.16 provided that EU measures would be taken for specific pollutants or group of pollutants. These measures aimed, for priority hazardous substances, "at the cessation, phasing-out of discharges, emissions or losses" (art.16(1)). For this purpose, a list of priority substances had to be fixed at EU level. These substances then had to undergo a risk assessment or targeted risk assessment.[20] For priority substances, EU measures for the control of the progressive reduction of discharges, emission, limits or losses were foreseen (art.16(6)). Discharges, emissions and losses should be completely stopped within a period which "shall not exceed 20 years", after the EU decision on these substances (art.16(6)).

At the end of 2001, the European Union adopted a list of priority substances.[21] The list contained 33 substances or groups of substances, out of which 25 were identified as priority hazardous substances. In 2008, the European Union fixed quality standards for the 33 substances, and for eight other substances which had already been regulated at EU level.[22] In 2013, an amendment of Directive 2008/105 revised some of the previously fixed quality standards and introduced quality standards, in the form of maximum allowable concentrations for overall 45 substances.[23] Where quality standards were amended, Member States had time

---

[18] This obligation was, for international river basin districts, limited to the territory of each Member State.

[19] Directive 2006/118 on the protection of groundwater against pollution and deterioration [2006] OJ L372/19.

[20] A targeted risk assessment focuses solely "on aquatic ecotoxicity and on human toxicity via the aquatic environment".

[21] Decision 2455/2001 establishing the list of priority substances in the field of water policy and amending Dir.2000/60 [2001] OJ L331/1.

[22] Directive 2008/105 on environmental quality standards in the field of water policy, [2008] OJ L348/84. The regulated substances were: Alachlor, Anthracene, Atrazine, Benzene, Brominated Diphenylethers, Cadmium and its compounds, Carbon tetrachlor, C_{10-13}-chloralkanes, Chlorofenvinphos, Chlorpyrifos, DDT, DEHP, 1,2-Dichloroethane, Dichloromethane, Diuron, Endosulfan, Fluoranthene Hexachlorobenzene, Hexachlorobutadiene, HCH, Isoproturon, Lead and its compounds, Mercury and its compounds, Naphthalene, Nickel and its compounds, Nonylphenols, Octylphenols, Pentachlorobenzene, PCP, Polyaromatic Hydrocarbons, Simazine, Tributyltin compounds, Trifleralin, Trichlorobenzenes, Trichloromethane. See further para.7–25, below.

[23] Directive 2013/39 [2013] OJ L 226/1.

until the end of 2021 to comply with them; where new quality standards were fixed, Member States had to comply with them by 2027.

7–06   Furthermore, Member States had to take measures to control emissions into the EU waters. The authorisations for the emission of these substances would be given by the authorities of the Member States; the emission values would be based either on existing or future EU legislation or on best available technologies. For this purpose, EU emission limit values and quality standards (quality objectives) listed in a number of EU Directives[24] had to be observed at the latest in 2012, though earlier compliance dates in those Directives remained valid.

Finally, Directive 2000/60 repealed a number of existing water directives according to a precise timetable.[25]

Several Member States were late in transposing Directive 2000/60 into their national law. The Commission took action against France, Belgium, Finland, Germany, Italy, Luxemburg, Netherlands, Portugal and the United Kingdom[26]; the Court of Justice found Belgium, Germany, Luxemburg, Italy and Portugal in breach of their obligations in this regard.[27] The Commission found, in 2008, that transposition of the Directive was poor[28] and mentioned that significant transposition problems existed in 19 of the then 27 Member States. Nothing is known on the content of the Commission's arguments, as the Commission does not publish studies which led to its findings and does not disclose any other relevant information. The public thus learns from a Member State's breach of its obligations when the judgment of the Court is published—an anti-democratic state of affairs.

7–07   Article 4(1)(a.i) of Directive 2000/60 requested Member States to "prevent deterioration of the status of all bodies of surface waters". It does not indicate though, from when on this prohibition of deterioration applies, since 2000 (date of adoption of the Directive, 2003 (date of its final transposition into national law), since 2008 (beginning of monitoring of surface water according to art.8), or 2012 (date of the beginning of measures according to art.12). The Directive does not either define what exactly deterioration means and how significant it must

---

[24] See for details annexes IX and X of the amended Dir.2000/60.

[25] The following timetable for repeal was fixed: End 2007: Dir.75/440 on surface water [1975] OJ L194/26; Dir. 79/869 on measuring methods [1979] OJ L271/44; End of 2013: Dir.78/659 on fishwater [1978] OJ L222/1; Dir. 79/923 on shellfish water [1979] OJ L281/47; Dir. 80/68 on groundwater [1980] OJ L20/43; specific repeal provisions were fixed for Dir.76/464 on the discharge of substances [1976] OJ L129/23.

[26] Commission, SEC(2005) 1055, p.11.

[27] Court of Justice, *Commission v Belgium* (C-33/05) ECLI:EU:C:2005:790; *Commission v Germany* (C-67/05) ECLI:EU:C:2005:791; *Commission v Luxemburg* (C-32/05) [2006] E.C.R. I-11323; *Commission v Italy* (C-85/05) ECLI:EU:C:2006:33; *Commission v Portugal* (C-118/05) ECLI:EU:C:2006:35. See also the later judgments *Commission v Greece* (C-264/07) ECLI:EU:C:2008:69; *Commission v Italy* (C-85/07) ECLI:EU:C:2007:522; *Commission v Spain* (C-516/07) ECLI:EU:C:2009:291; *Commission v Malta* (C-351/09) ECLI:EU:C:2010:815; *Commission v Greece* (C-297/11) ECLI:EU:C:2012:228; *Commission v Portugal* (C-223/11) ECLI:EU:C:2012:379; *Commission v Belgium* (C-366/11) ECLI:EU:C:2012:316; *Commission v Spain* (C-403/11) ECLI:EU:C:2012:612; *Commission v Spain* (C-151/12) ECLI:EU:C:2013:690; *Commission v Germany* (C-525/12) ECLI:EU:C:2104:2202.

[28] Commission, COM(2007) 128.

be[29]; a transitory deterioration does not appear relevant (see art.4(6)). Anyway, the Commission did not take any action against any Member State with regard to the prohibition of deterioration.

The Directive did not clarify whether the good surface status of waters is an objective which Member States shall have to reach, or an orientation which Member States shall endeavour to reach; this last understanding was the point of view of the Netherlands, which has now been rejected, in case C-461/13, by the Court; the Commission did not try to stop such an interpretation. Furthermore, while art.4(1)(a.ii) indicated that the good surface water status shall be achieved "at the latest 15 years" after 2000, art.4(4) allowed this delay to be extended "for the purposes of phased achievement" by, overall 12 further years. Soon after the adoption of Directive 2000/60, United Kingdom and Netherlands signalled that the achievement of a good surface water status by 2015 would be too expensive, and prolonged the delay until 2027. The Directive did not clarify what happens, when the good surface water status is not achieved in 2027. This vagueness considerably reduces the relevance of the Directive.

Artificial and heavily modified bodies of water were subjected to less stringent requirements, art.4(1)(a.iii). The definition of such bodies (art.2 no.8 and 9) was not precise. As the designation of such bodies is in the hands of Member States, these may reduce their obligations by designating more waters as artificial or heavily modified.

Member States had to adopt River Basin Management Plans by the end of 2009 and to update them every six years. A Commission map showed that by March 2011, Portugal, Spain, Belgium (Wallonia and Bruxelles Region), Greece, Slovenia and Cyprus had not yet adopted management plans. Greece, Portugal, Belgium and Spain were subsequently condemned by the Court of Justice.[30] In 2015, the Commission published a progress report on the implementation of Directive 2000/60. The data are given, though, in general terms, so that the reader cannot find out, which Member State was in compliance or in default.[31] Attached to this report were analyses of the management Plans of Belgium, Croatia, Greece, Portugal and Spain which described in detail the general characteristics, deficiencies and omissions of the different River Basin Management plans in these countries.[32]

7–08

By 2015, some 52 per cent of surface water bodies are expected to reach a "good" status – compared with 42 per cent in 2009; the chemical status of 40 per cent of surface waters is unknown.[33] The most significant improvement appears to stem from the better treatment of waste water.[34]

Over the next 20 years, this comprehensive Directive will strongly influence water management within the enlarged European Union and—in particular via

---

[29] In case C-461/13, *BUND v Germany*, ECLI:EU:C:2015:433, the Court of Justice now defined the term 'deterioration'.

[30] Court of Justice, *Commission v Greece* (C-297/11); *Commission v Portugal* (C-223/11); *Commission v Belgium* (C-366/11); *Commission v Spain* (C-403/11) (see fn.27, above).

[31] Commission, The Water Framework Directive and the Floods Directive: actions toward the "good status" of EU water and to reduce flood risks, COM(2015) 120.

[32] Commission SWD(2015) 52–56. The Report on Spain (SWD(2015) 56) is 90 pages.

[33] Figures from European Environment Agency, European waters—current status and future trends, Report 9/2012 (Copenhagen 2012), p.12; Commission, COM(2012) 673.

[34] See on that para.7–32, below.

the river basin concept—beyond. As it has not even become fully operational, it is too early to assess whether it will reach its objectives. As numerous provisions of the Directive are very loosely drafted[35] much will depend on the political will and the determination of the relevant administrations to work for the improvement of water quality rather than monitoring the status quo. It is encouraging to see that Member States decided a joint implementation plan for the Directive,[36] even though its monitoring lacks any transparency and democratic control.

7–09   The Commission has published, to date, four reports on the implementation of Directive 2000/60,[37] where it has shown itself prudently optimistic about the progressive implementation of the Directive, though it did not hide that more measures were necessary. "The pressures on Europe's waters (diffuse pollution, hydromorphological alteration and over abstraction) are driven by the way agricultural land is managed and by society's need for energy, transport and urbanisation".[38] As long as there are no substantive changes in these areas, the improvement of the water quality in the European Union will advance only slowly. Directive 2000/60 appears to serve as a framework for monitoring waters, but it does not really matter whether the fixed targets are reached by 2015, 2021 or 2027.[39]

Climate change is likely to increase the frequency of droughts in the European Union, not only in the South, but also in Central and Northern Europe. No concrete measures were taken by the European Union until now. Furthermore, problems are also to be anticipated in the management of water scarcity,[40] which mainly occurs in Southern Europe. Directive 2000/60 does not really address this problem. A good example of this problem was the Spanish National Hydrogeological Plan of 2001, which was adopted by parliamentary procedure and which provided for the transfer of about 1.05 billion m³ of water per year from the Ebro river to Southern Spanish regions which lack water. The Plan included the construction of some 900 dams, the destruction of a considerable number of natural habitats and wetlands and other considerable interferences into more traditional water management and infrastructures; it met with considerable resistance from "water exporting" regions, environmental groups and others, while the "water importing" Spanish regions generally favoured the Plan. General or specific environmental impact assessments had not been undertaken. When the government changed in Spain in 2004, the plan to transfer Ebro water was

---

[35] A good example is art.9 of the Directive. It asks Member States "to take account of the principle of recovery of the costs of water services, including environmental and resource costs", but allows them "in so doing have regard to the social, environmental and economic effects of the recovery as well as the geographic and climatic conditions of the region or regions affected". It is difficult to see in these provisions more than a policy recommendation addressed to Member States. See generally European Environmental Bureau, *10 Years of the Water Framework Directive. A Toothless Tiger?* (Bruxelles, July 2010).

[36] Common strategy on the implementation of the Water Framework Directive (2000/60) as agreed by the Water Directors under Swedish Presidency, 2 May 2001; *http://ec.europa.eu/environment/water/water-framework/objectives/pdf/strategy.pdf* [Accessed 8 April 2011].

[37] Commission (COM)2007) 128; COM(2009) 156; (2013) 670 and (2015) 120.

[38] European Environment Agency, European waters—current status and future trends, Report 9/2012 (Copenhagen 2012), p.6.

[39] This conclusion is also to be drawn from Commission COM(2015) 120 (fn.31, above).

[40] Water scarcity exists, where the abstraction of water exceeds the available water quantities.

abandoned—though many of the envisaged infrastructure projects had, in the meantime, been completed. Therefore, the plan might be reanimated in future, when the government changes again.

It is remarkable, that EU water law played hardly any role in the attempt to find, in this or in similar cases,[41] an adequate balance between economic interests and environmental concerns, a problem which will become more acute with climate change in Europe. The Commission limited itself until now to publish reports on water scarcity and droughts and indicated measures which might be taken at national or EU level.[42] It reported that the Czech Republic, Cyprus and Malta declared to have continuous problems with water scarcity; France, Netherlands, Romania and Sweden had local scarcity. Portugal, France, Hungary, Spain and the United Kingdom indicated that the rainfalls were lower than the long-term annual average, while Austria, Belgium, Estonia, Ireland, Luxembourg and Slovakia declared that they had no scarcity or drought problems.

Following a series of floods, mainly in Central Europe, the European Union adopted, in 2007, a Directive on the assessment and management of flood risks.[43] The Directive was based on art.192(1) TFEU; a suggestion by the United Kingdom, to limit its field of application to transboundary river basins was rejected by the majority of Member States in Council. The Directive covered inland and coastal waters. It mainly provided for three measures by Member States: (1) The making of a preliminary flood risk assessment. This assessment is to be made for each river basin and shall describe the factual situation, the likelihood of future floods and a forecast of their estimated consequences. Where the assessment concludes that no potential significant flood risks exist, Member States have no further obligation. (2) For basins districts with a potential significant flood risk Member States shall, by the end of 2013, elaborate flood risk maps, in order to increase public awareness, orient investments and strategies and support planning. (3) For these basin districts, flood risk management plans are to be elaborated by the end of 2015, for which some orientations were laid down in the Directive.

7–10

All data available demonstrate that with the effects of climate change, the number of floods will increase. The Commission called for a better coordination between measures under the Floods Directive and the Water Framework Directive, but did not propose concrete measures.[44]

---

[41] See the underlying facts of Court of Justice, *Acheloos* (C-43/10) ECLI:EU:C:2012:560 and *LPN and Finland v Commission* (joined cases C-514/11P and 605/11P) ECLI:EU:C:2013:738.

[42] Commission COM(2007) 414; (2008) 875; (2011) 133.

[43] Directive 2007/60 on the assessment and management of flood risks [2007] OJ L288/27.

[44] Commission COM(2015) 120.

2. QUALITY MEASURES

(a) Drinking water

7–11   Directive 80/778, adopted in 1980, five years after the proposal of the Commission, limited the presence of undesirable substances in drinking water.[45] The Directive fixed maximum admissible concentrations for 62 substances in drinking water, and gave non-mandatory guide values for some of them; Member States had to take the necessary measures to ensure compliance with the concentrations. At the request of the UK Government, which had argued that Directive 80/778 only requested Member States to take "all practicable steps" to comply with the Directive's standards, the European Court stated expressly that Member States were not only obliged to make an effort, but were obliged to reach the specific result that was required by the Directive.[46]

The Directive introduced, for the first time, objective standards for drinking water in all EU Member States, oriented investments and led to a considerable, though slow, improvement of drinking water quality.

Since there were difficulties in complying with the Directive's requirements, considerable pressure was put on the Commission to lower the standards, in particular as regards pesticides, where the agro-chemical and agro-industrial industry were particularly active. In 1995 the Commission made a proposal for replacing Directive 80/778 by a new Directive which the Council adopted in 1998.[47]

7–12   The new Directive 98/83 provided that drinking water, at the point of entry into the domestic distribution system, must be wholesome and clean; the consequence of this change from the requirement of water quality at the tap to water quality at the point of entry into the domestic supply system is that individual persons can no longer argue against the water supply companies that their tap water must be in compliance with the EU Directive; they had this right under Directive 80/778.

Drinking water is wholesome and clean when the water is free from micro-organisms, parasites and substances which may, in numbers or in concentrations, constitute a potential danger to human health, and when the requirements of some 28 parameters, laid down in annex I(A) and I(B) are respected. The parameter for lead was lowered from 50 to 10 microgrammes, with a transition period of 15 years.[48] The European Parliament succeeded in avoiding a change of the pesticide parameter, though the Commission had proposed to delete the collective parameter of 0.5 microgrammes. Where the parameters are exceeded, Member States have to take remedial action.

Annex I(C) contains a list of 20 indicator parameters for which the Member States need only fix parameters for monitoring purposes; this annex includes, among others, aluminium, ammonium, chlorides and coliform bacteria. When

---

[45] Directive 80/778 relating to the quality of water intended for human consumption [1980] OJ L229/11.

[46] *Commission v United Kingdom* (C-337/89) [1992] E.C.R. I-6103.

[47] Directive 98/83 on the quality of water intended for human consumption [1998] OJ L330/32; Commission proposal [1995] OJ C131/5 and COM(94) 612.

[48] Directive 98/83 [1998] OJ L330/32, art.4.

these parameters are exceeded, Member States shall consider whether this poses any risk to human health; if that is the case, they must take remedial action.

The grounds for derogations are no longer enumerated, so that Member States may decide themselves, where and when they derogate; the list of derogations was considerably enlarged. For the 26 parameters of annex I(B), Member States may provide for derogations "up to a maximum value to be determined by them, provided no derogation constitutes a potential danger to human health" (art.9). The derogation may not exceed three years. Where a second, prolonging derogation is intended, the Commission is to be informed—though not consulted. Any third derogation which again may not exceed three years, has to be decided by the Commission.[49] In all cases the affected population must be informed of the derogation.

7–13

Member States and the Commission must each publish a report every three years on the quality of drinking water. The first national reports were due before the end of 2005, the first EU report in 2006. The last available "synthesis report" on drinking water, published in June 2014, dealt with the drinking water between 2008 and 2010. The Commission showed itself satisfied with the quality of drinking water in general, though it pointed at some problems with small water supplies.

One might well ask about the value of a report that informs, in general terms, of the drinking water quality six years ago![50] In substance, the report only gives general data. It does not indicate where parameters were exceeded, or which derogations were granted. Compliance dates are given in percentages and refer to Member States only. With regard to earlier reports, the information which is made available has decreased.[51] To the individual citizen, the report is of no use at all. The Commission, in its conclusions (p.8), indicates that in times of information technologies, better access to information should be made available; this applies first of all to the Commission itself.

In 2013, a Directive determined the parametric levels for radioactive substances (radon, tritium and indicative doses) in drinking water.[52] Member States were asked to set up a system to monitor the presence of such substances in drinking water. Where the levels indicated in the Directive were exceeded, Member States were asked to examine, whether there was a risk to human health. If that were the case, they had to take appropriate measures.

7–14

Also in 2013, a citizen initiative, started under Article 11(4) TEU, and assembling more than 1.6 million signatures, asked the Commission to recognise water and sanitation as a human right. In its official reaction, the Commission treated the request, as if it concerned drinking water. It enumerated all legal,

---

[49] The Commission (COM(2014) 363) granted, until 2014, derogations to the Czech Republic, Italy, Hungary and Germany. It refused a derogation request by Estonia. See Commission C(2010) 7605 granting a derogation to Italy; C(2014) 2521 regarding Estonia.

[50] Commission Synthesis Report on the Member States' Reports 2008–2010, COM(2014) 363.

[51] See Commission, Quality of drinking water in the EU 2002–2004 (Bruxelles, 2007).

[52] Directive 2013/51/Euratom [2013] OJ L296/12. The Court of Justice held that art.31 of the Euratom Treaty constituted the correct legal basis for this Directive, *European Parliament v Council* (C-48/14) ECLI:EU:C:2015:91.

financial and political measures taken in the past with regard to water, but avoided carefully to recognise access to drinking water and sanitation as a human right.[53]

(b)   Bathing water

7–15   In 1975 the Council adopted, on the basis of arts 94 and 308 EC (now, arts 115 and 352 TFEU), a Directive on the quality of bathing water,[54] which fixed, for coastal and for fresh-water zones, quality requirements for bathing waters. Imperative or guide parameters were fixed for a number of pollutants. Member States were given 10 years to comply with the Directive's requirements. Within its 35 years of existence, the Directive caused a significant improvement of bathing-water quality. To this contributed the fact that annual reports were published; and that a private organisation had launched a "blue flag" campaign,[55] which identified high-quality bathing waters and beaches; and finally that, in general, the data on bathing-water quality found its way into tourism prospectuses, advertising campaigns etc. This also caused local authorities to publish data, invest in water improvement and to make specific efforts to comply with the Directive's requirements.

In 1994, the Commission made a proposal to replace Directive 76/160 by a new Directive.[56] It justified this by the need to take into account subsidiarity questions, the need to simplify the text and by scientific and technical progress. The proposal was not discussed in Council. For that reason, the Commission published a Communication and, based on the reactions to it, another proposal for a new Directive which was adopted in 2006.[57] The Directive is based on art.192(1) TFEU.

What constitutes bathing water is where public authorities expect there to be a large number of bathers, having regard to past trends and to existing infrastructure for services. Waters in swimming pools and waters for therapeutic purposes were not covered by the Directive. Contrary to requests which were made during the consultations, the Directive did not extend its scope of application to areas concerning the recreational use of waters such as surfing, kayaking etc. The number of 19 parameters which were to be sampled of Directive 76/160 was reduced to two—Intestinal Enterococci and Escherichia coli.[58]

---

[53]   Commisison COM(2014) 177.

[54]   Directive 76/160 [1976] OJ L31/1.

[55]   On the "blue flag" campaign, see Written Question P-1667/02 *Carnéro Gonzalesz* [2002] OJ C301E/208. The Commission indicates in its answer that since 1998 it no longer participated in the activities of the private body to award a blue flag nor granted financial assistance.

[56]   Commission, [1994] OJ C112/3 and COM(94) 36.

[57]   Directive 2006/7 concerning the quality of bathing water [2006] OJ L64/37.

[58]   The levels are for intestinal enterococci per 100ml, in coastal waters: 100 for excellent quality, 200 for good quality and 185 for sufficient quality; in inland waters: 200 for excellent quality, 400 for good quality and 330 for sufficient quality. For Escherischia coli in 100ml: coastal waters: 250 for excellent quality, 500 for good quality and 500 for sufficient quality; in inland waters: 500 for excellent quality, 400 for good quality and 330 for sufficient quality. The fact that the values for sufficient quality are occasionally stricter than for good quality is explained by the different calculation of the average of the sampling. Where the sampling exceeds the level of "sufficient", the water is of "poor" quality.

The Directive did not provide that bathing waters must comply with certain 7–16
quality requirements. Rather, it required Member States to make a "bathing water
quality assessment". This quality assessment is to be made at the end(!) of the
bathing season and shall take the average results of the running and of the four
preceding bathing seasons into consideration. Then the bathing water is to be
classified as "excellent", "good", "sufficient" or "poor". The maximal concentrations for the two parameters are differentiated in annex I(A), with average
methods of calculation ensuring that the results remain positive. Member States
must sample the water quality by means of taking at least four samples per
bathing water season, plus one sample before the season starts. Short-term
pollutions—up to three days—may be ignored, provided Member States have
identified the source of the pollution and addressed the issue. Where water is of
"poor" quality, it nevertheless complies with the Directive provided that Member
States pronounce a prohibition to bathe or give advice not to bathe. Only where
the water is classified as "poor" for five subsequent bathing seasons, shall there
be a permanent prohibition on bathing. The first classification of waters was to be
made in 2015; by then, all bathing waters shall attain at least "sufficient" quality.

The European Environment Agency and the Commission report annually on
the quality of bathing waters. The last report, for 2013,[59] reported that 96.8 of all
coastal waters and 89.7 inland bathing waters—overall 21,836 EU bathing waters
were covered—complied with the requirements of Directive 2006/7.

Directive 2006/7 has considerably increased the flexibility for local authorities
and makes it almost impossible for citizens and environmental organisations to
get reliable information on compliance issues. The initial classification of waters
and the possible changes during the bathing season cannot be properly controlled
and enforced by others than the (local) administrations themselves. The average
of quality of four seasons is of very limited information value for the next bathing
season. The small number of samples required is inadequate for bathing waters,
where several thousands of bathers dwell. It is to be expected that the Directive's
application will lead to reports with very good results, without the environmental
quality of bathing waters having improved.

(c) Groundwater

In 1979, the Council adopted a Directive on groundwater quality, based on arts 7–17
115 and 352 TFEU.[60] The Directive aimed to prevent groundwater pollution and
to eliminate the consequences of pollution, as far as possible. It established a list
I of substances that were considered toxic, persistent or bioaccumulative, and a
list II that groups together substances that "could have a harmful effect on
groundwater". The direct discharge of list I substances was prohibited, and the
indirect discharge—discharge after percolation through the ground or the

---

[59] European Environment Agency, *European Bathing Water Quality in 2013* (Copenhagen 2014).
[60] Directive 80/68 on the protection of groundwater against pollution caused by certain dangerous
substances [1980] OJ L20/43. As regards implementation and compliance, see Court of Justice,
Commission v Belgium (C-1/86) [1987] E.C.R. 2797; *Commission v Netherlands* (C-291/84) [1987]
E.C.R. 3483; *Commission v Italy* (C-360/87) [1991] E.C.R. I-791. In 1993, Belgium was even
censured a second time, under art.260 TFEU for not having complied with the first judgment:
Commission v Belgium (C-174/91) [1993] E.C.R. I-2275. See also *Commission v Germany*
(C-131/88) [1991] E.C.R. I-825.

subsoil—of that list was subject to investigation and authorisation. Discharges of list II substances were subject to investigation and authorisation. Furthermore, the Directive dealt with details of the authorisation procedure.

The Water Framework Directive 2000/60 also covered groundwater. Article 17 of that Directive provided that a specific directive was to be elaborated to prevent and reduce groundwater pollution. This new Directive was adopted in 2006.[61]

Directive 2006/118 provided for quality standards for groundwater that are fixed at EU level; the standards shall be for nitrates (50mg/l) and pesticides (0.1 micrograms per pesticide, 0.5 micrograms for all pesticides). Furthermore, Member States were asked to fix national threshold values—these are quality standards—for the presence of hazardous and other undesirable substances in groundwater; the Directive listed, in a non-binding provision, a number of substances for which such thresholds might be fixed. Groundwater is of "good" quality, where the quality standards and the threshold values are either not exceeded or exceeded under the conditions that are laid down in the Directive. The monitoring of groundwater quality is done at national level, mainly in the context of the river basin management activities under Directive 2000/60. Quantitative elements of water management were not covered by the Directive.

7–18   The added value of this legislation for the environment is limited. Indeed, management and monitoring is almost entirely in the hands of Member States, though it has to be mentioned that, in the past, groundwater was hardly ever monitored by the Commission. The main feature is thus that Directive 2006/118 enters into the line of re-nationalising water legislation. The national threshold values for heavy metals show differences of up to 1:1500.[62]

Information on the quality of groundwater is difficult to obtain, as there is a very general lack of data. The European Environment Agency reported in 2004 that the drinking water directive nitrate levels (50 mg/l) were exceeded in around one-third of the water bodies for which information was available. For pesticides in groundwater, it signalled a lack of reliable data.[63]

(d)   Nitrates in water

7–19   Directive 91/676, adopted in 1991 and based on art.192 TFEU, tried to protect waters against pollution by nitrates and thereby to combat eutrophication.[64] It was almost the first Directive that provided for measures against pollution from agricultural activity. "Waters" were not defined and thus referred to fresh water as well as to coastal and marine waters. Member States had to designate vulnerable zones in their territories according to criteria fixed by the Directive; the decisive criterion was whether the nitrate content of the water exceeded or risked exceeding 50mg per litre or whether the waters were eutrophic. For these vulnerable zones, Member States had to establish action programmes, for which the Directive fixed some measures, amongst which were the necessity of

---

[61] Directive 2006/118 [2006] OJ L372/19.

[62] Commission, SEC(2010) 166, Annex III: the values had a scale between 1:300 for arsenic, 1:1200 for cadmium, 1:1500 for lead and 1:500 for mercury.

[63] European Environment Agency (May 2004), *http://www.eea.europa.eu/data-and-maps* [Accessed 30 September 2015].

[64] Directive 91/676 concerning the protection of waters against pollution caused by nitrates from agricultural sources [1991] OJ L375/1.

prohibiting the use of certain fertilisers during certain periods and restricting the amount of livestock manure applied to the land per year to not more than 170kg of nitrogens, though some transitional periods were allowed.

Furthermore, Member States had to establish a code of good agricultural practice "to be implemented by farmers on a voluntary basis" with the objective of reducing nitrate pollution, for which the Directive gave a number of possible ("should contain") provisions. Member States had to report on the implementation every four years and the Commission had to establish a summary report.

Member States had to transpose the Directive into national law by the end of 1993. Spain, Italy, the United Kingdom, Luxembourg, Spain and Italy again, furthermore Germany, France, Netherlands, Belgium and Ireland were condemned by the Court of Justice for not having correctly transposed or applied the Directive or for not having sent plans, data or reports.[65] On average, Member States took the necessary measures to transpose the Directive with a delay of five years.[66]

In its most recent report on the implementation of the Directive which dates 7–20 from 2013,[67] the Commission stated that at least 30–40 per cent of rivers and lakes showed symptoms of eutrophication. Agriculture was responsible for 50–80 per cent of all nitrate inputs into waters. In order to improve this situation, effective application of the Directive would constitute the most efficient way—and is, at the same time, the biggest problem. The overall levels of nitrates in waters appear stagnant (42.7 per cent in groundwater and 38.7 per cent in surface waters) with some increasing (30.7 per cent in groundwater and 19.1 per cent in surface waters) or decreasing tendency (26.6 per cent in groundwater and 42.1 per cent in surface water). These average figures hide considerable regional differences.

The core environmental question is whether the Directive's objective to see in vulnerable zones, where the permitted level of nitrates are exceeded, the number of cattle reduced, so that the output of nitrogens per hectare does not exceed 170kg. This appears, up until now, not to be the case. Denmark, Netherlands, Germany, United Kingdom and Ireland have derogation granted by the Commission for the whole of their territory, Italy and Belgium for some of their regions. These derogations are regularly renewed: thus, for example, Denmark has this derogation since 2002. France, where a serious nitrate problems exist, in particular in the waters of the Bretagne, regularly invokes the social problems linked to a full application of the Directive. And the Commission prefers granting derogations or remaining altogether passive, rather than enforcing the Directive

---

[65] Court of Justice, *Commission v Spain* (C-71/97) [1998] E.C.R. I-5991; *Commission v Italy* (C-195/97) [1999] E.C.R. I-1169; *Commission v Spain* (C-274/98) [2000] E.C.R. I-2823; *Commission v United Kingdom* (C-69/99) [2000] E.C.R. I-10979; *Commission v Luxembourg* (C-266/00) [2001] E.C.R. I-2073; *Commission v Italy* (C-127/99) [2001] E.C.R. I-8305; *Commission v* Germany (C-161/00) [2002] E.C.R I-2753; *Commission v France* (C-258/00) [2002] E.C.R. I-5959; *Commission v Netherlands* (C-322/00) [2003] E.C.R. I-11267; *Commission v Ireland* (C-396/01) [2004] E.C.R. I-2315; *Commission v Belgium* (C-221/03) [2005] E.C.R. I-8307; see also *Standley* (C-293/97) [1999] E.C.R. I-2603.
[66] Commission, Implementation of Directive 91/676, COM(2010) 47.
[67] Commission, Implementation of Directive 91/676, COM(2013) 683.

on all Member States. The cases which it submitted to the Court of Justice do not address this core question, but touch aspects of minor importance.[68]

(e) Other directives

(i) Surface water

7–21   Directive 75/440, based on arts 115 and 352 TFEU, concerned the quality of surface water that was used for the production of drinking water.[69] It asked Member States to divide their surface waters according to their quality into three classes—class 3 was not allowed to be used for drinking-water purposes. The Directive was repealed at the end of 2007 by Directive 2000/60.[70]

Most Member States considered the Directive, right from its beginnings, as a recommendation. In particular, the clean-up plans were hardly ever drawn up and never transmitted to the Commission. The Commission, while belatedly taking some legal action against Member States, did not really monitor the application of the Directive, but instead turned its attention to Directive 80/778 on drinking water. Thus, the move to reduce discharges into surface waters was turned into the obligation to treat water in order to obtain drinking water.

(ii) Fresh fish water

7–22   Directive 78/659[71] fixed quality standards for fresh fish water. Member States had to identify those waters, which came under the Directive and had then to draw up clean-up programmes in order to make the fish waters conform, within five years, to the quality values of the Directive. The Directive suffered from the fact that Member States themselves assigned which waters were to be submitted to the Directive; they often designated waters that were unpolluted or did not designate waters that were too polluted. In 1991, the Commission reported that only three Member States had transmitted clean-up programmes.[72] A judgment by the Court of Justice, that Member States had to designate fish waters all over their territory, not only in some regions,[73] only had limited effect: Italy was, in 1994, condemned a second time and in 1996 the Court found that Germany had not designated any fish water[74]—18 years after the adoption of the Directive! In the absence of systematic monitoring of this Directive by the Commission, its effects remain modest. According to art.22 of Directive 2000/60, Directive 78/659

---

[68] Court of Justice, *Commission v Luxemburg* (C-526/08) [2010] E.C.R. I-6151; *Commission v France*(C-193/12) ECLI:EU:C:2013:394; *Commission v France*(C-237/12) ECLI:EU:C:2014:2152; *Commission v Poland*(C-356/13) ECLI:EU:C:2014:2386.

[69] Directive 75/440 [1975] OJ L194/26.

[70] See Commission statement in COM(96) 59, annex point 1.1: "This is an old Directive, adopted before the Drinking Water Directive. The parameters and classifications are now out of date and it makes little or no contribution to the safety of drinking water now that the Drinking Water Directive exists. Its value in protecting future sources of drinking water is unproven."

[71] Directive 78/659 [1978] OJ L222/1.

[72] Commission, Eighth report on monitoring application of Community law (1990) [1991] OJ C338/1, p.218.

[73] *Commission v Italy* (C-322/86) [1988] E.C.R. 3995.

[74] *Commission v Italy* (C-291/93) [1994] E.C.R. I-859; *Commission v Germany* (C-298/95) [1996] E.C.R. I-6747.

ceased to exist in 2013. This did not prevent the Community from codifying the Directive which now has the new number 2006/44.[75]

(iii)   Shellfish water

Directive 79/923[76] had a construction similar to Directive 78/659: Member States had to designate waters to which the Directive applied, then had to draw up pollution reduction programmes in order to make these waters conform to the quality requirements that the Directive had fixed. Again, implementation was slow: in 1991, four Member States had drawn up programmes[77] and the Commission monitoring was neither systematic nor whole-hearted[78]; only Italy was condemned for not having respected the Directive.[79] The Commission is now of the opinion that Directive 91/492,[80] which fixed health conditions for the production and placing on the market of live bivalve molluscs, made Directive 79/923 redundant.[81] According to art.22 of Directive 2000/60, Directive 79/923 ceased to exist in 2013.

7–23

3.   REDUCTION OF DISCHARGES INTO WATER

(a)   Dangerous substances

(i)   Directive 76/464

Directive 76/464, adopted in 1976 on the basis of arts 115 and 352 TFEU, fixed the framework conditions for discharges of dangerous substances into waters.[82] The Directive established two lists of substances and groups of substances. List I contained substances considered toxic, persistent or bioaccumulative,[83] list II other polluting substances.[84] The Directive required all discharges which contained list I or list II substances to be authorised. The authorisations had to lay down emission limit values for these substances.

7–24

Article 6 stipulated that the European Union would lay down emission limit values for list I substances "taking into account the best technical means available". At the same time, the Council was to adopt quality standards on the

---

[75] Directive 2006/44 [2006] OJ L264/20.

[76] Directive 79/923 [1979] OJ L281/47.

[77] Commission, Eighth report on monitoring application of Community law (1990) [1991] OJ C338/1, p.218.

[78] See, for instance, Court of Justice, *Commission v Italy* (C-225/96) [1997] E.C.R. I-6887, where the Commission had applied to the Court for absence of legislation in Italy in 1996, 17 years after the adoption of the Directive.

[79] Court of Justice, *Commission v Italy* (C-225/96) [1997] E.C.R. I-6887.

[80] Directive 91/492 [1991] OJ L268/1.

[81] Commission, COM(96) 59, annex point 1.6.

[82] Directive 76/464 on pollution caused by certain dangerous substances discharged into the aquatic environment of the Community [1976] OJ L129/23.

[83] Organohalogens, organophosphorous and organotin compounds, carcinogenics, mercury, cadmium, mineral oils and hydrocarbons and persistent synthetic substances.

[84] In particular, heavy metals, biocides, silicon compounds, cyanides, fluorides, ammonia, nitrites and all list I substances, for which no EU emission limits had been fixed.

basis of concentrations in living organisms and in sediment. The emission limit values were to apply all over the European Union "except in cases where a Member State can prove to the Commission … that the quality objectives … are being met and continuously maintained". The Commission had to report to the Council on cases where the quality standards were used; the Council should review every five years the cases where the quality objective method had been applied. For list II substances, Member States had to establish programmes in order to reduce water pollution, and set timetables for their implementation.

The Directive's provisions on emission limit values and quality standards constituted a compromise between the United Kingdom and the other—by then eight—Member States, which was necessary, since the Directive had to be adopted unanimously. The United Kingdom opposed the fixing of EU emission limit values, arguing that local environmental conditions were too different,[85] rivers in the United Kingdom were short and quick-flowing and, at the coast, the tide would quickly wash away any eventual polluting discharge. While the other Member States pleaded in favour of emission limits, they finally accepted the compromise, indicating in a statement that they would introduce only emission limit values.

7–25   Under the Directive, emission limit values and quality objectives were fixed for 17 substances. At no time, though, did the Commission follow the procedural provisions of the Directive. Also, the formula of using the best technical means available, remained a dead letter: instead, the values for the different pollutants were fixed on the basis of a political compromise between the institutions and Member States. The Directive was a complete failure as regards list II substances. No Member State established programmes for them in order to reduce pollution; no Member State fixed quality objectives, either. Finally, it had clearly been impossible to undertake regular comparisons of Member States' pollution reduction programmes, as such programmes either did not exist or were too vague.

The new evolution in EU water law, which started with the Edinburgh summit meeting,[86] led to a complete standstill in the monitoring of Directive 76/464 since about 1993—except as regards the procedures under art.258 TFEU that were progressively submitted to the Court of Justice.[87] The Commission and Member States relied on the fact that art.22 of Directive 2000/60 provided that Directive 76/464 ceased to exist in 2013; this date is, in practice, anticipated, all the more, as Directive 2000/60 provided that art.6 was repealed already since 2000.

---

[85] See on the history of this controversy in particular, N. Haigh (ed.), *Manual of Environmental Policy: the E.C. and Britain* (looseleaf, London), Chs 3.9 and 4.8.

[86] See para.7–01, above.

[87] The first ever judgment on Dir.76/464 was given on 11 June 1998, 22 years after its adoption; this case, *Commission v Greece* (joined cases C-232 and 233/95) [1998] E.C.R. I-3343, concerned the absence of programmes for two Greek waters. Since then the following judgments were given *Commission v Luxembourg* (C-206/96) [1998] E.C.R. I-3401; *Commission v Italy* (C-285/96) [1998] E.C.R. I-5935; *Commission v Spain* (C-214/96) [1998] E.C.R. I-7661; *Commission v Belgium* (C-207/97) [1999] E.C.R. I-275; *Commission v Germany* (C-184/97) [1999] E.C.R. I-7837; *Commission v Greece* (C-384/97) [2000] E.C.R. I-3823; *Commission v Portugal* (C-261/98) [2000] E.C.R. I-5905; *Commission v Portugal* (C-435/99) [2000] E.C.R. I-11179; *Commission v Netherlands* (C-152/98) [2001] E.C.R. I-3463; *Commission v France* (C-130/01) [2003] E.C.R. I-5829; *Commission v Belgium* (C-406/02) judgment of 12 February 2004; *Commission v Ireland* (C-282/02) [2005] E.C.R. I-4653.

(ii) Daughter directives

Subsequent to the framework that had been set up by Directive 76/464, the   **7–26**
European Union fixed emission limit values and quality standards for list I
substances. To that end, the Commission established a list of 129 substances
under list I, to which the Council agreed in a resolution.[88] A proposal for a
directive on quality standards for a list II substance (chromium) was submitted,[89]
but not adopted by the Council. Emission limit values and quality standards were
fixed for mercury,[90] cadmium,[91] HCH (lindane),[92] carbon tetrachloride, DDT,
pentachlorophenol, aldrin, dieldrin, endrin, isodrin, hexachlorobenzene, hexachlorobutadiene, chloroform, 1.2-dichloroethane, TRI, PER and trichloroben-
zene.[93]

As an example, Directive 83/513 on cadmium discharges[94] may be quoted in
more detail. It fixed emission limit values for zinc mining, lead and zinc refining,
the cadmium metal and non-ferrous metal industry, the manufacture of cadmium
compounds, pigments, stabilisers and batteries, and for electroplating. A footnote
requested Member States to fix emission limit values for other industrial sectors
and, in particular, the production of phosphoric acid and/or phosphatic fertilisers
from phosphatic rocks.[95] Member States had to institute a monitoring procedure
to check whether the actual discharges complied with the emission standards.
That procedure had to provide for the taking and analysis of samples and for
measurement of the flow of the discharge and the quantity of cadmium handled.
A sample representative of the discharge over a period of 24 hours had to be
taken. The quantity of cadmium discharged over a month then had to be
calculated on the basis of the daily quantities of cadmium discharged. These
monitoring requirements did not specify whether the industrial installation itself
was to monitor its discharges, nor whether public authorities were ever to check
the private monitoring system.

The Commission did not systematically monitor the application of the
different daughter directives by, for instance, spot checks, asking Member States
for data or comparing the monitoring procedures and the actual measuring results
reached. Comparative reports were never made; no attempt was made to find out

---

[88] Resolution of 7 February 1983 [1983] OJ C46/17.

[89] [1985] OJ C351/33.

[90] Directive 82/176 on limit values and quality objectives for mercury discharges by the chlor-alkali
electrolysis industry [1982] OJ L81/29; Dir.84/156 on limit values and quality objectives for mercury
discharges by sectors other than the clor-alkali electrolysis industry [1984] OJ L7449.

[91] Directive 83/513 on limit values and quality objectives for cadmium discharges [1984] OJ L291/1.

[92] Directive 94/491 on limit values and quality objectives for discharges of hexachlorocyclohexane
[1984] OJ L274/11.

[93] Directive 86/280 on limit values and quality objectives for discharges of certain dangerous
substances included in list I of the annex to Dir.76/464 [1980] OJ L181/6, amended by Dir.88/347
[1988] OJ L158/35 and Dir.90/415 [1990] OJ L219/49.

[94] Directive 83/513 [1984] OJ L291/1.

[95] Directive 83/513 [1984] OJ L291/1, annex I, nn.1 and 4: "Limit values for industrial sectors not
mentioned [in this Directive] will, if necessary, be fixed by the Council at a later stage. In the
meantime the Member States will fix emission standards for cadmium discharges autonomously in
accordance with Directive 76/464. Such standards must take into account the best technical means
available and must not be less stringent than the most nearly comparable limit value in this Annex ...
The absence of such limit values [for phosphatic rock utilisation] does not release the Member States
from their obligation under Directive 76/464 to fix emission standards for these discharges."

what kind of emission limit values were fixed for the different industrial installations, whether they were expressly mentioned in the directives or not. Legal action against Member States was only taken where national legislation had not been adopted or where a Member State had transposed the directives by administrative circulars rather than by binding legislation.[96]

7–27   Apart from such legal action, monitoring work on these daughter Directives as well as on setting new emission limit values and quality standards came, since 1990, to a standstill, without an express decision by the Council or the Commission. The causes for this are not clear: indeed, all published programmes, resolutions, press releases and communications pleaded instead in favour of accelerating and intensifying work at EU level. It can only be presumed that the subsidiarity discussion which had started with the adoption of the Maastricht Treaty on European Union in 1993 has led the Commission deviate from its obligations and accommodate the wishes of Member States, in particular of the United Kingdom, not to have EU-wide emission standards, but to accept that the best available technique for discharges be applied—whatever a Member State understands by this notion.

Article 22(3) of Directive 2000/60 provided that the priority list of substances that was established in 1982, was to be replaced by a new priority list. A first new list of substances was set up by Decision 2455/2001.[97] It identified 33 substances or group of substances which were considered to be of a particular risk to the aquatic environment (art.16 of Directive 2000/60) and the Commission was asked to come forward with proposals: "of controls for the progressive reduction of discharges, emissions and losses of the substances concerned and in particular the cessation or phasing out of discharges, emissions and losses of the substances …, including an appropriate timetable for doing so" (art.16(6)). Article 16(7) of Directive 2000/60 furthermore stated: "The Commission shall submit proposals for quality standards applicable to the concentrations of the priority substances in surface waters, sediments or biota." In 2006, the Commission submitted a proposal "on environmental quality standards in the field of water policy and amending Directive 2000/60".[98] The Commission proposed quality standards for 33 priority substance and explicitly referred to art.16(7) of Directive 2000/60. The proposal also aimed at repealing all the above-mentioned daughter directives by 2012 and explained that, in the meantime, Member States need no longer monitor application of emission limit values of these daughter directives (art.8(2)). With regard to the requirements of art.16(6) of Directive 2000/60, the proposal stated (Recital 5):

> "As regards emission controls of priority substances from point and diffuse sources as referred to in Article 16(6) and (8) of Directive 2000/60/EC, it seems more cost-effective and proportionate for Member States to include, where necessary, in addition to the implementation of other existing Community legislation, appropriate control measures in the programme of measures to be developed for each river basin in accordance with Article 11 of Directive 2000/60/EC."

---

[96] Court of Justice, *Commission v Portugal* (C-213/97) [1998] E.C.R. I-3289 on failure to transpose Dir.86/280 and Dir.88/347; *Commission v Portugal* (C-208/97) [1998] E.C.R. I-4017 on failure to transpose Dir.84/156.

[97] *Commission v Germany* (C-262/95) [1996] E.C.R. I-5729.

[98] Decision 2455/2001 [2001] OJ L331/1.

The proposal was adopted in 2008.[99] It meant in clear terms that the European Union does not have the intention any more to adopt legislation for emission limit values for priority hazardous substances, in view of their complete phasing out in the next 20 years, as was requested by Directive 2000/60. As at the same time the existing limit values for water discharges were repealed, this Directive signified the departure from EU emission limit values. Thus, after 30 years, the United Kingdom won the battle against EU interference in its national water policy.

The environmental problem is that water (and air) quality standards are not enforced in practice and most likely cannot be enforced. It is of course much easier and more precise to measure emissions at the point where they leave the discharging installation, and the control of point sources is also more cost-effective. Nobody would consider letting cars circulate with whatever air emissions or noise emissions they might generate, and just measure the pollution concentration or noise levels in the air. There is no difference with regard to water pollution. It is also sure that diffuse pollution sources cannot be subject of emission controls: it is physically impossible to measure the faecal emissions into the water of every cow or pig. For this reason, EU environmental policy, for the last 30 years, has underlined that emission limit values *and* quality standards were necessary in order to ensure an effective protection and reduction of pollution. This basic principle appears to have been abandoned.

7–28

(b)   Discharges from industrial installations

The EU measures on emissions, including water discharges, from the titanium dioxide industry were already discussed.[100] As regards water discharges from incinerators for hazardous waste, the Commission proposed a Directive where it suggested emission limit values for, in total, 15 pollutants, which it later withdrew.[101] Generally, however, the sector-oriented approach, where emission limit values are fixed for a specific industrial sector, has been abandoned with the adoption of Directive 96/61[102] which requests the application of the best available technique. This policy change, however, created a problem, since Directive 96/61 which was since replaced by Directive 2010/75 on industrial emissions,[103] only applied to certain large industrial installations, whereas water contamination depends on the quantity of discharges, which may also stem from cumulated emissions from smaller plants.

7–29

Directive 2010/75 required the fixing of emission limit values in the individual permits for installations that come under the Directive. The pollutants covered are those: "likely to be emitted from the installation in significant quantities, having regard to their nature and their potential to transfer pollution from one medium to the other (water, air and land)". Special attention shall be given to fixing emission limit values for 13 "main polluting substances", which are listed in annex II.[104]

---

[99] Commission, COM(2006) 397.

[100] Directive 2008/105 on quality standards in the field of water policy [2008] OJ L348/84.

[101] Commission, [1998] OJ C13/6.

[102] Directive 96/61 [1996] OJ L257/26. In 2008, this Directive was replaced by Dir.2008/1 [2008] OJ L24/8.

[103] Directive 2010/75 on industrial emissions [2010] OJ L334/17.

[104] Directive 2010/75 [2010] OJ L334/17, annex II (water pollutants):

(c) Dumping of waste; discharge of offshore installations

7–30   Legally speaking, the discharge of waste is no different from any other discharge into water; the terminology "dumping" stems from international conventions, which wanted to give a specific definition to the discharge of waste from ships and called this practice dumping. Under EU waste legislation, the discharge of waste needs an authorisation; thus, Member States may authorise the discharge of waste into waters at their discretion.[105]

In 1976, the Commission made a proposal on the dumping of waste at sea; it made another proposal in 1985.[106] However, these proposals were not extensively discussed in Council, since Member States preferred to see questions of marine pollution discussed in the context of international conventions, rather than at EU level. Waste dumping from ships is now prohibited by Directive 2008/98 on waste.[107]

Identical considerations apply to the discharge of ships themselves and of offshore installations. At the end of their useful lifetime, offshore installations become waste. Their discharge into waters thus follows the same rules. After the Brent Spar incident—in 1995, an oil company had tried to sink a rig into the North Sea/Atlantic, but had abandoned its plans after massive public protests in some (northern) EU Member States—the Commission considered the elaboration of a Directive on the decommissioning of offshore installations. However, it abandoned these plans in view of the resistance from Member States; the decommissioning of offshore installations was then addressed within the framework of the OSPAR Convention.[108]

7–31   In 2006, France wanted to send its aircraft carrier *Clemenceau* to South Asia, in order have it dismantled there. As the ship contained some 30,000 tonnes of asbestos, it was, legally speaking, hazardous waste, the export of which is prohibited under EU waste legislation (see para.10–38, below). Nevertheless, France pursued its action. When Egypt refused the transit of this hazardous waste through the Suez Canal, it obtained development aid and forgot its objections. In the Gulf States then, Greenpeace activists entered the ship and protested against the shipment. At the same time, the French Conseil d'Etat confirmed that the transport in question was indeed a shipment of hazardous waste. In view of the public protests, the French President ordered the ship to come back to France. This single case stands out, though European tankers and other commercial ships

---

1. Organohalogen compounds and substances which may form such compounds in the aquatic environment; 2. Organophosphorous compounds; 3. Organotin compounds; 4. Substances and preparations which have been proved to possess carcinogenic or mutagenic properties or properties which may affect reproduction in or via the aquatic environment; 5. Persistent hydrocarbons and persistent and bioaccumulable organic toxic substances; 6. Cyanides; 7. Metals and their compounds; 8. Arsenic and its compounds; 9. Biocides and plant protection products; 10. Materials in suspension; 11. Substances which contribute to eutrophication (in particular, nitrates and phosphates); 12. Substances which have an unfavourable influence on the oxygen balance (and can be measured using parameters such as BOD, COD, etc); 13. Substances which are listed in annex X to Dir.2000/60.

[105] Directive 2008/98 on waste [2008] OJ L312/3.
[106] [1976] OJ C40/3; [1985] OJ C245/23.
[107] Directive 2008/98 [2008] OJ L312/3.
[108] Directive 2008/98 [2008] OJ L312/3, art.36: "Member States shall take the necessary measures to prohibit the abandonment, dumping or uncontrolled management of waste". See also para.7–39, below.

are regularly shipped to South-East Asia, in order to be dismantled and shredded, under appalling social and environmental conditions. A recent regulation on ship dismantling tries to address the dismantling problems in general.[109]

(d) Waste water

In 1991, the European Union adopted a Directive on urban waste water,[110] based on art.192(1) TFEU. The Directive aimed at reducing the pollution of surface waters with nutrients, in particular nitrates and phosphates from urban waste water, and thus to combat eutrophication. It applied to domestic waste water and the mixture of domestic waste water with industrial waste water and/or run-off rainwater. The Directive required Member States to provide, by the end of 2005, a sewerage system for all agglomerations consisting of more than 2,000 people; agglomerations of more than 15,000 people have to be equipped with such a system by the end of the year 2000. The Member States which joined the European Union since 2004, obtained, at their request, transition periods.

    Before the waste water enters such a collecting system, it must undergo at least secondary (biological) treatment; this requirement was to be complied with by the end of 2005, and by the year 2000 for agglomerations of more than 15,000 people. Furthermore, Member States had to designate sensitive areas for which more stringent treatment requirements were to apply; such areas are waters that are found to be eutrophic, that are intended for the production of drinking water and could contain more than 50mg of nitrates per litre, and areas where more than secondary treatment was necessary to comply with the Directive. Member States were also allowed to designate their whole territory as a sensitive area. They could also consider certain areas as less sensitive areas (marine waters), for which less stringent requirements applied. The discharge of sludge from treatment installations into waters had to be phased out by the end of 1998.

    Member States had to establish programmes for the implementation of Directive 91/271 and to publish, every two years, situation reports on the disposal of urban waste water and sludge. Overall, it was estimated that about 40,000 water treatment plants were to be constructed or renewed for the some 23,000 agglomerations that were covered by the Directive; to this had to be added the construction of sewerage systems.[111]

    The Directive had to be transposed into national law by mid-1993. By the end of 1994, only Denmark, France and Luxembourg had done so.[112] In 1996, the Court of Justice condemned Greece, Germany and Italy for not having transposed the Directive into national law[113]; Belgium and Italy were also condemned for not having provided for waste water treatment for Bruxelles and Milano,[114] and a

7–32

7–33

---

[109] Regulation 1257/2013[2013] OJ L330/1; see for more details para.10–36, below.

[110] Directive 91/271 concerning urban waste water treatment [1991] OJ L135/40; amended by Commission Dir.98/15 [1998] OJ L67/29.

[111] Court of Auditors [1998] OJ C191/1, paras 3 and 5.

[112] Commission, 12th report on monitoring application of Community law (1994) [1995] OJ C254/1, p.128.

[113] *Commission v Greece* (C-161/95) [1996] E.C.R. I-1979; *Commission v Germany* (C-297/95) [1996] E.C.R. I-6739; *Commission v Italy* (C-302/95) [1996] E.C.R. I-6765.

[114] Court of Justice, *Commission v Belgium* (C-236/99) [2000] E.C.R. I-5657; C-396/00 *Commission v Italy* [2002] E.C.R. I-3948.

number of other Member States for incorrect transposition or application or for not cooperating with the Commission in implementing the Directive.[115] The most recent implementation report by the Commission[116] points at considerable progress, in particular the EU-15 states. The Commission hopes, that for these states, the Directive will be fully implemented by 2015/2016. In the countries which adhered since 2004, the situation is less good, all the more as some transition periods have still not expired. The Commission thinks that the Directive might be fully applied in these countries by 2027/2028.

To give just some figures, in order to illustrate the differences which hide behind general figures: in 2010, only 11 of the then 27 capitals of the Member States complied with the Directive's requirements for big cities: Bruxelles, Sofia, Nicosia, Prague, Riga, Dublin, Rome, Tallinn, Luxemburg, La Valetta, Warsaw, Lisbon and London did not satisfy the requirements of waste water treatment of the Directive.[117]

In contrast to Directive 91/676, where the Commission was not very serious about monitoring the implementation, the Commission took rather systematic infringement actions against Member States[118]—with the exception of France—for failing to implement Directive 91/271. Belgium and Luxembourg were even brought to the Court under Article 260 TFEU and were fined.[119] Overall, it seems, that the attempt to enforce the application of Directive 91/271 is more successful than working with derogations and tolerating non-compliance (Directive 91/676).

---

[115] Court of Justice, *Commission v Spain* (C-419/01) [2003] E.C.R. I-4947; *Commission v Belgium* (C-27/03) ECLI:EU:C:2004:418; *Commission v France* (C-280/02) [2004] E.C.R. I-8573; *Commission v France* (C-191/04) ECLI:EU:C:2005:393; *Commission v France* (C-280/02) [2004] E.C.R. I-8573; *Commission v Luxembourg* (C-452/04) [2006] E.C.R. I-120; *Commission v Italy* (C-293/05) [2006] E.C.R. I-122; *Commission v United Kingdom* (C-405/05) [2007] E.C.R. I-10; *Commission v Spain* (C-219/05) [2007] E.C.R. I-56; *Commission v Greece* (C-440/07) [2007] E.C.R. I-145; *Commission v Portugal* (C-233/07) [2008] E.C.R. I-79; *Commission v Ireland* (C-316/06) [2008] E.C.R. I-124; *Commission v Portugal* (C-530/07) ECLI:EU:C:2009:292; *Commission v Finland* (C-335/07) judgment of 6 October 2009; *Commission v Sweden* (C-438/07) ECLI:EU:C:2009:613; *Commission v United Kingdom* (C-390/07) ECLI:EU:C:2009:765.

[116] Commission, 7th report on the implementation of the Urban Waste Water Directive, COM(2013) 574.

[117] Commission, SWD(2013) 298.

[118] Apart from the judgments mentioned in fn.115, above, see *Commission v Portugal* (C-526/09) ECLI:EU:C:2010:734; *Commission v Portugal*(C-220/10) ECLI:EU:C:2011:558; *Commission v Spain* (C-343/10) ECLI:EU:C:2011:260; *Commission v Italy* (C-565/10) ECLI:EU:C:2012:476; *Commission v France* (C-23/13) ECLI:EU:C:2013:723; *Commission v Italy* (C-85/13) ECLI:EU:C:2014:251.

[119] *Commission v Belgium* (C-533/11) ECLI:EU:C:2013: 659. Belgium was ordered to pay a lump sum of €10 million and €859,404 every six months, until it complied with the judgment. *Commission v Luxembourg* (C-576/11) ECLI:EU:C:2013:733. Luxembourg was ordered to pay a lump sum of €2 million and €2,800 per day of non-compliance. Cases under art.260 TFEU were in mid-2015 pending against Portugal (C-557/14) and Greece (C-167/14).

4.   OCEANS AND RIVERS

(a)   Oceans

Though the EU environmental policy also has as its aim to contribute to the   7–34
solution of global or regional environmental problems (art.191 TFEU), it has not
developed a consistent policy to address the protection of the marine
environment. Until 2008, there was not one single EU environmental measure
which expressly protected the marine environment, though a number of the
above-mentioned directives also apply to marine waters. Even in those directives,
the European Union has, in its political and legal activity, only considered the
seas adjacent to EU territory, in particular the North Sea, the Baltic Sea and the
Mediterranean Sea, and to a lesser extent the Atlantic Ocean. A different approach
as regards the environment was only taken in the context of the Common
Fisheries Policy, where the Community also took an interest in fish—the "natural
resources"—in West Africa, the Caribbean Sea and the Antarctic waters; it was
also dealt with within the framework of the Common Transport Policy.

In 2006, the Commission published a Communication on an EU maritime
policy.[120] The title, indicative, better explains the ideas behind the communication which does not announce concrete measures, in particular not on
environmental issues.

In 2002, the Commission made a Communication on the protection of the
marine environment.[121] Following that, the Commission made a second
Communication on the marine environment[122] and in 2005 suggested a Directive
on the marine environment which was adopted in 2008.[123] The Directive aimed at
achieving good environmental status of the marine environment by 2021. It
limited itself to fix objectives and principles, but omitted to provide for concrete
measures. It established European Marine Regions as management units which
happen to coincide with the areas covered by the three regional water
conventions of Paris/Oslo (North East Atlantic), Helsinki (Baltic Sea) and
Barcelona (Mediterranean Sea). The Black Sea Region was mentioned in the
Directive, but only marginally, as the European Union is not a contracting party
of the Bucharest Convention on the Protection of the Black Sea; that Convention
is only open to ratification by Member States.

Member States shall develop, for each Marine Region, a Marine Strategy   7–35
which shall contain a number of measures designed to achieve good
environmental status. The Directive did not define what a good environmental
status is, or give a description of it. It rather attempted to let the regional

---

[120] Commission, Towards a future maritime policy for the Union: a European vision for the oceans
and seas, COM(2006) 275.
[121] Commission, Towards a strategy to protect and conserve the marine environment, COM(2002)
539 of 2 October 2002.
[122] Commission, Thematic strategy on the protection and conservation of the marine environment,
COM(2005) 504.
[123] Directive 2008/56 establishing a framework for Community Action on marine water quality in the
field of Marine Environmental Policy (Marine Strategy Framework Directive), [2008] OJ L164/19.

conventions' structures take care of, elaborate and monitor the future pro-grammes, limiting itself largely to provide for reporting provisions. Other aspects than marine *water* aspects—for instance on the fauna and flora or marine natural parks—were practically not covered.

It is too early to reflect on the impact of the Directive on the marine environment. As the Directive allowed and even encouraged the existing intergovernmental cooperation within the framework of the regional marine conventions, it is to be expected that not too much will change with regard to the present situation of marine waters surrounding the European Union. Rather, the state of the marine environment, as it is in 2021, is likely to be declared "good", while it will be acknowledged that improvements could still be made here or there.

In 2014, the Union adopted a Directive on maritime spatial planning, based on arts 43, 100, 192 and 194 TFEU.[124] Under this Directive, the Member States shall establish, until 2021, integrated plans for their marine waters; consequently, the Directive does not apply to landlocked Member States. The necessity for such plans is explained with the multiple activities which take place at present in marine waters and which are likely to increase in future. Recital 1 mentions in this regard installations for the production of energy from renewable sources, oil and gas extraction and exploitation, maritime shipping and fishing activities, ecosystem and biodiversity conservation, the extraction of raw materials, tourism, aquaculture installations, underwater cultural heritage and the pressures on coastal resources.

7–36   The Directives gives some rather vague and general indications of what a plan should contain, but does not impose other obligations on Member States.

The European Union adhered to the following international conventions concerning the marine environment, most of which having been completed by a number of protocols to which the European Union normally also adhered:

- Paris Convention on the prevention of marine pollution from land-based sources[125];
- Barcelona Convention on the protection of the Mediterranean Sea against pollution[126];
- Bonn Agreement for cooperation in dealing with pollution of the North Sea by oil and other harmful substances[127];
- Cooperation Agreement for the protection of the coasts and waters of the north-east Atlantic against pollution[128];
- Helsinki Convention on the protection of the marine environment of the Baltic Sea Area[129];
- Helsinki 1992 Convention on the protection of the marine environment of the Baltic[130];

---

[124] Directive 2014/89 establishing a framework for maritime spatial planning (2014) OJ L257/135.
[125] Decision 75/437 [1975] OJ L194/5.
[126] Decision 77/85 [1977] OJ L240/1.
[127] Decision 84/358 [1984] OJ L188/7.
[128] Decision 93/550 [1993] OJ L267/20.
[129] Decision 94/156 [1994] OJ L73/1.
[130] Decision 94/157 [1994] OJ L73/19.

- Paris Convention for the protection of the marine environment in the north-east Atlantic (OSPAR)[131];
- Montego Bay Convention on the law of the sea.[132]

With the adhering of the European Union to these international conventions, their legal provisions became part of EU law. Nevertheless, for each negotiation of a protocol to a convention or any other amendment, the Commission needs a mandate from the Council in order to negotiate in the name of the European Union; for the signing of such a protocol, the same procedure applies.[133]

The reasons why Member States object to the taking of EU directives or regulations on environmental problems facing the sea have never been expressly specified. They are presumed to be the following: **7–37**

1. International conventions are normally adopted unanimously. It is true that, during the last few years, public international law has developed the habit that amendments may, under certain conditions, be adopted by majority decisions; however, this possibility remains largely theoretical. Instead, the principle of international conventions remains based on consensus. Each contracting state thus has the right to veto decisions.

   In contrast, EU environmental measures are normally adopted by qualified majority, which allows measures to be taken against the will of an objecting Member State.

2. The initiative for measures at international level is, jointly or severally, in the hands of contracting states. This allows a fairly direct influence on the international agenda. For the Commission to negotiate, in the name of the European Union, at international conventions, a mandate is necessary under art.218 TFEU. In contrast to that, initiatives for measures at EU level are taken by the Commission, which has the monopoly on this.

3. At international level, media attention and the participation of environmental organisations is normally relatively limited. At EU level, the increasing importance of the European Parliament and its co-decision function make quasi-confidential discussions and decisions practically impossible.

4. For years, France and the United Kingdom have also discharged radioactive materials, which stemmed from military or private activity, into the sea. In the name of national sovereignty, such activities were always considered to remain outside the area of EU competence. This attitude has probably caused these two countries, but also other Member States where the situation was similar—though not necessarily concerning radioactive matters—not to accept EU environmental initiatives to protect seas. Generally, a number of Member States continue to consider the seas as a big sewer system, where discharges are all too often allowed to take place.

The statement that the international conventions become, with the adherence of the European Union, part of EU environmental law is legally correct. It is, however, rather theoretical, since the monitoring of these conventions is not

---

[131] Decision 98/249 [1998] OJ L104/1.
[132] Decision 98/392 [1998] OJ L179/1.
[133] See for details art.218 TFEU.

ensured by the Commission, but by the secretariat of the different conventions. At no time has the Commission tried, with regard to the different decisions incorporating the conventions into EU law, to "ensure the application of the treaties and of measures adopted by their institutions pursuant to them",[134] and thus to control the effective implementation and enforcement of these conventions. Unless there is a specific EU directive or regulation that reproduces the content of the international convention, it is left to Member States to decide if and to what extent they transpose the provisions of the conventions into their national legal order and apply them. The Commission has never explained why it applies this self-restraint.

In case C-213/03, the Court of Justice confirmed the interpretation given here. It declared that France had infringed EU law, because it did not apply a Protocol to the Barcelona Covention; this Protocol had been ratified by the European Union, but not by France.[135] However, this is up to now the only case where the Commission took action under art.258 TFEU against a Member State for infringement of provisions of an international environmental convention which had become part of EU law. The reason for bringing this case before the Court was that a French Court had submitted a preliminary question to the EU Court of Justice and the Commission did not wish to be seen as remaining passive.

7–38   The present practice by the EU institutions leads to different legal situations and, hence, to different pollution situations for the different seas. To give some examples: OSPAR took decisions to reduce the discharge of radioactive substances into the North East Atlantic (Decision 2000/1), on the use of organic-phase drilling fluids (Decision 2000/3), a control system for use and discharge of offshore chemicals (Decision 2000/2), on carbon dioxide streams in the water column, on the seabed or in geological formations (Decisions 2007/1 and 2) or on maritime protected areas (Decisions 2010/1 to 5). The EU was passive with regard to all these activities.

Most, if not all, of these measures have an impact on the functioning of the European Union. However, it is highly unlikely that in the context of the Barcelona Convention on the Mediterranean Sea similar subjects will be raised at all, not to mention the taking of binding decisions.

At the same time, this list of subjects indicate the impact that OSPAR decisions have or might have on the European Union. Indeed, the ban of products or processes will impinge on the free circulation of goods and the competitive situation of undertakings.

In the case of hexachloroethane, a substance which a decision by the OSPAR Convention had phased out, the potential conflict was solved, not without complications, by the adoption of an EU directive which took over the OSPAR decision to phase out that substance.[136] Another approach was taken in the Brent Spar incident: while the Commission had first considered making a proposal for an EU directive on offshore installations, it finally rejected this approach with legally unconvincing arguments and left the decision to OSPAR, which it took in

---

[134] See art.17 TEU.
[135] Court of Justice, *Commission v France* (C-239/03) [2004] E.C.R. I-9325; see also *Pêcheurs de Berre* (C-213/03) [2004] E.C.R. I-7357.
[136] Decision 97/16 [1997] OJ L116/31.

1998.[137] The Commission then proposed to approve, by way of a decision, this decision by OSPAR, without, however, proposing an amendment to EU law, in order to introduce provisions on offshore installations that were binding on all EU Member States.[138] However, the proposal to take over the OSPAR decision was never adopted by the Council.

It must be assumed that the Commission definitely abandoned its plan for a directive on the decommissioning of offshore installations[139] because any such proposal would have been rejected in the same way as the proposal for a directive on the dumping of waste at sea. However, this change also risks leading to a de facto loss of the Commission's right of initiative for EU action. Neither rules on subsidiarity nor on deregulation can solve the problem of decisions being taken by the regional marine conventions which have an impact on the European Union as a whole.

7–39

The Commission also submitted proposals to approve other OSPAR decisions, for example on a new annex V to the OSPAR Convention,[140] the disposal of radioactive waste,[141] and on emission limit values from the production of vinyl chloride monomers.[142] However, these proposals were, again, not adopted.

In November 2002, the tanker *Prestige* which was single-hulled and had loaded 77,000 tonnes of heavy fuel oil, had an accident off the coast of Galicia (Spain) and sank. A large quantity of fuel oil was released which polluted in particular the Spanish and French coasts. Estimation of the damage caused by the accident and the subsequent coastal and marine pollution are for more than €1 billion. The accident caused a strong activity from the European Union to improve the safety of maritime transport of fuel oils and other dangerous substances, and generally to improve maritime transport safety.[143] Similar increased legislative activities had already taken place after the accidents of the *Braer* in the Shetlands 1993 and the *Erika* in France 1999. The *Erika* accident led to the setting up of a European Maritime Safety Agency[144] which has the task of ensuring "a high uniform and effective level of maritime safety and prevention of pollution from ships" (art.1); the Decision is based on art.90(2) TFEU.

---

[137] OSPAR, Dec.98/3 on the disposal of disused offshore installations. See also Commission Communication on removal and disposal of disused offshore oil and gas installations, COM(1998) 49, para.6.2: "The disadvantage of this approach [a directive] is that only EC and EEA Member States would be bound to the common approach whereas other third countries with which we share the Seas concerned would not be bound to implement the same or similar measures without the Community taking the initiative to negotiate and adopt such rules in the relevant regional seas Conventions. Although this approach would have the advantage of applying to all EC Member States immediately, i.e. also to those Member States outside OSPAR—namely Austria, Greece and Italy—it would only apply to Norway after a Decision of the EEC Joint Committee. It could also be interpreted as prejudicial to Community interest in other OSPAR policies if the Commission were to be seen to press ahead separately for action via EC legislation rather than via the newly ratified OSPAR Convention. Furthermore, it could be seen as an attempt to exclude Norway from negotiations on any final policy."
[138] Proposal for a Council decision [1999] OJ C158/10.
[139] See, however, Dir.2013/30 on the safety of offshore oil and gas operations [2013] OJ L178/66. This Directive was a follow-up of the accident of an offshore installation in the Gulf of Mexico and is almost entirely limited to accident prevention and restoration measures.
[140] [1999] OJ C158/1.
[141] [1999] OJ C158/8.
[142] [1999] OJ C158/19.
[143] Commission, Report to the European Council on action to deal with the effects of the *Prestige* disaster, COM(2003) 105 of 5 March 2003.
[144] Regulation 1406/2002 [2002] OJ L208/1.

(b) Rivers

7–40 The European Union adhered to the following international conventions concerning the marine environment:

- Bonn Convention for the protection of the Rhine against chemical pollution[145];
- Regensburg Agreement on cooperation for management of water resources in the Danube basin[146];
- Magdeburg Convention on the International Commission for the protection of the Elbe[147];
- Sofia Convention on cooperation for the protection of the Danube[148];
- Wroclaw Convention on the International Commission for the protection of the Odra against pollution[149];
- Helsinki Convention on the Protection and use of transboundary watercourses and international lakes.[150]

The legal situation as regards rivers is similar to that of seas. While the different conventions became, with the EU decisions to adhere to them, part of EU law, they are de facto treated by the European Union and by the Commission as instruments of public international law. In particular, the Commission does not monitor the adoption of measures to incorporate the conventions into national law and their application in practice. Thus, the question that was put some years ago, particularly by Dutch lawyers, "Who shall clean up the Rhine river—the Rhine Commission or the European Community?", is in reality answered for the Rhine and for the other rivers that are the subject of conventions: it is not the European Union, but the different secretariats of the conventions, which are in charge of combating river pollution. The question of water resources goes beyond river water, since it might also apply to groundwater resources. To date, there has been not one single provision in EU water law which deals with quantitative aspects of water resources.

The above-mentioned Directive 2000/60 also requested the elaboration of river basin management plans for the Rhine, Danube, Elbe and Oder. Member States largely used the administrative structures existing for these rivers to fulfil their obligations under Directive 2000/60. The Commission's role in monitoring the application of the river basin management plans for these rivers did not, however, change in practice.

---

[145] Decision 77/586 [1977] OJ L240/35.
[146] Decision 90/160 [1990] OJ L377/28.
[147] Decision 91/598 [1991] OJ L321/25.
[148] Decision 97/825 [1997] OJ L342/18.
[149] Decision 1999/257 [1999] OJ L100/20.
[150] Decision 95/308 [1995] OJ L186/42.

CHAPTER 8

Air Pollution and Noise

1. AIR POLICY AND LAW

The first environmental action programmes of the European Union mentioned air pollution, its causes and its effects on the environment, but actions were dispersed, incoherent and limited to specific pollution sources, in particular to emissions from passenger cars. The turning point came at the beginning of the 1980s, when the state of the forests, particularly those in Germany and central Europe, raised considerable concern. The subject of air pollution was discussed, in 1983, by the Heads of State and Governments who suggested effective action against acid rain and air pollution.[1] This led, in the same year, to proposals for a general directive on air pollution from industrial installations,[2] for a directive on large combustion plants[3] and for a directive for quality objectives for NOx.[4] Other measures concentrated on the introduction of a catalytic converter for cars, which had been discussed since 1984 and had been progressively introduced since 1988 for new cars; since 1993, all new cars have had to be equipped in this way.

8–01

Since the mid-1980s, the depletion of the ozone layer and climate change entered more and more into the foreground of discussions. These aspects will not be dealt with here, but in a separate chapter.[5]

EU legislative measures on air emissions from industrial installations were based, in the early 1980s, on the concept of emission limit values which was in use mainly in legislation in Germany.[6] Large industrial installations in specific sectors were to operate on the basis of a permit which was to impose the best available technology not entailing excessive costs. EU-wide emission limit values were to be elaborated.[7] This concept led to the elaboration of directives for large combustion installations[8] and incinerators.[9] However, the European Union went

---

[1] (1993) 3 *Bulletin of the European Communities*, para.1.5.2.
[2] Commission, proposal for a directive on air emissions from industrial installations [1983] OJ C139/5.
[3] Commission, proposal for a directive on large combustion plants [1984] OJ C49/1.
[4] Commission, proposal for a directive on air quality objectives for NOx [1983] OJ C258/3.
[5] See Ch.9, below.
[6] Directive 84/360 on the combating of air pollution from industrial plants [1984] OJ L188/20.
[7] Directive 84/360 [1984] OJ L188/20, art.8.
[8] Directive 88/609 on the limitation of emissions of certain pollutants into the air from large combustion plants [1988] OJ L336/1; this Directive has since been replaced by Dir.2001/80 [2001] OJ L309/1 and, in 2010, by Dir.2010/75 on industrial emissions [2010] OJ L334/17.
[9] Directive 89/369 on new installations for the incineration of municipal waste [1989] OJ L163/32; Dir.89/429 on the incineration of municipal waste from existing plants [1989] OJ L203/50; Dir.94/67

away from this concept and more or less implicitly—at least silently—took the decision that emission standards for industrial installations within the European Union should not be harmonised.[10] This policy found its expression in Directive 96/61—since then replaced by Directive 2008/1 and later on by Directive 2010/75[11]—which was based on the principle that the emission limits for an industrial installation were to be fixed on a case-by-case basis in the permit which were issued for the installation. This Directive which provided for the repeal of Directive 80/360 after a transition period, very largely affected air emissions. Three days after the adoption of Directive 96/61, a new framework Directive was adopted,[12] which established the legal frame for setting quality standards on air pollution and which was, via daughter directives, progressively put into operation.

8–02   Under the 6th Environmental Action Programme[13] the Commission submitted, in 2005, a thematic strategy on air pollution[14] which intended to provide for a long-term integrated air policy strategy.[15] The non-binding strategy established targets on the reduction of air pollution for sulphur dioxide (82 per cent reduction), nitrogen oxides (60 per cent), volatile organic compounds (51 per cent), ammonia (27 per cent) and fine particulate matters ($PM_{2.5}$—59 per cent) until 2020, compared to the year 2000. As the binding concentration limits in particular for fine particulate matters were not respected by the majority of Member States, a new Directive which replaced Directive 96/62, was adopted which also brought the different daughter directives back into one single legal text.[16]

Policies, strategies and measures concerning air pollution are strongly influenced by a number of basic factors which need to be borne in mind.

First, air emissions stem in particular from the combustion of fuels, and the energy policy within the European Union on the use of energy—nuclear energy, oil, gas, coal and lignite—varies considerably, depending also on the national availability of energy sources. Secondly, air emissions cannot be regarded separately from other environmental problems; while, for instance, nuclear energy does not emit significant quantities of air pollutants, it has numerous other environmental and other disadvantages, such as the technological risk, waste treatment and disposal problems, the location and decommissioning of installations, their vulnerability to terrorist attacks and their acceptance by the

---

on the incineration of hazardous waste [1994] OJ L365/34. All these Directives were since replaced by Dir.2000/76 on the incineration of waste [2000] OJ L332/91. In 2010, the provisions on waste incinerators were integrated into Dir.2010/75 [2010] OJ L334/17.

[10] See for a background to this shift in policy, A. Héritier, C. Knill and S. Mingers, *Ringing the Changes in Europe. Regulatory Competition and Redefinition of the State. Britain, France and Germany* (Berlin, New York, 1996).

[11] Directive 96/61 on integrated prevention and pollution control [1996] OJ 257/26; in 2008, this Directive was replaced by Dir.2008/1 [2008] OJ L24/8, and in 2010 by Dir.2010/75 [2010] OJ L334/17; see also para.4–40, above.

[12] Directive 96/62 on ambient air quality assessment and management [1996] OJ L296/55.

[13] Decision 1600/2002 laying down the 6th Community Environmental Action Programme [2002] OJ L242/1.

[14] Commission, Communication: Thematic strategy on air pollution, COM(2005) 446.

[15] See also Commission, The programme Clean Air for Europe (CAFÉ): a thematic strategy on air quality, COM(2001) 245.

[16] Directive 2008/50 on ambient air quality and cleaner air for Europe [2008] OJ L152/1. For more details see paras 8–04 et seq., below.

population. Also, nuclear energy is not economically competitive within the European Union—with the exception of France, where investments in the past have been heavily subventioned by state aid. Thirdly, air emission quantities largely depend on the level of economic development, which continues to vary considerably between Member States and makes common solutions difficult. Fourthly, and perhaps foremost, there seems to be no readiness in Western European society seriously to question present lifestyles, particularly private passenger and truck transport. The words used in the early 1990s by a President of the United States that the American way of life is not negotiable, appear also to be true for the European way of life—at least in the eyes of many citizens. Renewable energies have only recently become the subject of concentrated attention.[17] Since about the year 2000, the climate change and the awareness that fossil fuels constitute an exhaustible source of energy, led to a gradual strengthening of the policy on renewable energies, though its role in the overall concept of EU energy is still unsatisfactory.

At the international level, EU participation in the discussions on long-range transboundary air pollution has intensified, illustrating well the global nature of environmental (air pollution) problems. Furthermore, cooperation with the World Health Organisation (WHO)—mostly represented by its European Centre for Environment and Health—led to a situation where the European Union oriented its air quality standards on recommendations of the WHO.[18]

8–03

It is difficult to assess existing provisions, in particular the scientific, economic, mathematical, technical and political conditions of the different standards, the measuring mechanisms, the monitoring of the standards and of the measures which Member States, regions, local authorities and individual emitters are taking in pursuance of EU law, as these measures are highly complex, only perceptible to initiated experts and not sufficiently transparent. One practical consequence of this situation is that EU air pollution legislation is hardly enforceable: where a Member State is determined to reduce emissions, improve air quality and intensively work with clean-up programmes or reduction measures that are provided for in EU legislation, this legislation is a useful yardstick with which the different measures may be aligned, coordinated and structured. Where, in contrast, a Member State attaches less importance to air pollution or where its environmental policy ranks lower in the political priority, EU legislation will only with difficulties, if at all, be capable of leading to a continuous reduction of emissions and an improvement of air quality. This same problem with regard to the enforcement of quality standards had already been observed with regard to discharges into water, see Chapter 7, above.

In the last instance, air quality directives cannot really be enforced. It is true that the Court of Justice had paved the way for an enforcement of air quality directives by individual persons, by providing that whenever the exceeding of the limit values could endanger human health, the persons concerned must be in a position to rely on mandatory rules in order to be able to assert their rights.[19] However, the large discretion for administrations in the fixing of the number and

---

[17] Commission, Energy for the future: renewable sources of energy, Green Paper, COM(96) 576; White Paper for a Community strategy and action plan COM(97) 599.

[18] See in particular WHO, *Air Quality Guidelines for Europe*, 2nd edn (Copenhagen, 2000).

[19] Court of Justice *Commission v Germany* (C-361/88) [1991] E.C.R. I-2567; *Janecek* (C-237/07) [2008] E.C.R. I-6221.

location of measuring stations, of measuring methods, the frequency of measuring, the average values, etc, the publication of data only months or years later, leads de facto to the situation that EU air quality values constitute policy guidance standards rather than legal instruments. This explains the very low number of infringement cases under art.258 TFEU against Member States which are limited to cases of non-transposition of EU Directives or the absence of reporting,[20] but practically never deal with the lack of application in a specific case or in a specific agglomeration. Knowledge about the inter-relationship between air pollution and health—to humans and the environment—is not precise enough to allow the full assessment of these health effects and the transformation of such knowledge into legislative provisions. Generally, the European Environment Agency[21] gives a prudent but positive assessment of the measures taken on air pollution.[22] It sees the biggest ground for concern in the areas of the tropospheric ozone, particulate matters and acidification and signals that there is no EU legislation on the reduction of emissions of ammonia or particulate $PM_{2.5}$ matters.[23]

2.   AIR QUALITY VALUES

8–04   The basic EU instrument on air pollution is—next to Directive 2008/1 and now Directive 2010/75,[24] which only applies to some large industrial installations—Directive 2008/50.[25] This Directive deals with sulphur dioxide, nitrogen dioxide, benzene, carbon monoxide, lead, particulate matters (PM_{10}) and ($PM_{2.5}$) and tropospheric ozone.

Regarding its field of application, it constitutes a remarkable regress in environmental protection. Unlike previous directives, it no longer required that air quality standards shall have to be respected all over the territory of the Member States: "Member States shall ensure that throughout their zones and agglomerations, levels of sulphur dioxide, PM_{10}, lead and carbon monoxide do not exceed the limit values" (art.13). Zones and agglomerations had to be established by Member States, and it was in those zones and agglomerations that the air quality shall have to be assessed. A limit value was defined as a value that has to be attained within a given period and not to be exceeded thereafter.[26] However, the Directive provided for "margins of tolerance", within which the limit values may well be exceeded; furthermore, the definition of limit value

---

[20] The cases *Commission v Italy* (C-92/79) [1980] E.C.R. 1115, *Commission v Belgium* (C-186/91) [1993] E.C.R. I-851, *Commission v France* (C-320/99) [2000] E.C.R. I-10453, *Commission v Spain* (C-417/99) [2001] E.C.R. I-6015 concerned the non-transposition into national law; the cases *Commission v Germany* (C-58/89) [1991] E.C.R. I-2607, *Commission v Germany* (C-361/88) [1991] E.C.R. I-2567, *Commission v France* (C-13/90) [1991] E.C.R. I-4331, *Commission v France* (C-14/90) [1991] E.C.R. 4331, *Commission v France* (C-64/90) [1991] E.C.R. I-4335, concerned the transposition into national law by non-binding instruments.
[21] See Reg.1210/90 setting up the European Environment Agency [1990] OJ L120/1.
[22] European Environment Agency, *Environmental Signals 2001* (Copenhagen, 2002), pp.72 et seq.; EU emission inventory 1990–2008, Technical Report 7/2010 (Copenhagen, 2010).
[23] European Environment Agency, *Environmental Signals 2001* (Copenhagen, 2002), p.72.
[24] Directive 2008/1 [2008] OJ L24/8; Dir.2010/75 [2010] OJ L334/17.
[25] Directive 2008/50 [2008] OJ L152/1.
[26] Directive 2008/50 [2008] OJ L152/1, art.2.5.

itself provided that it may not be exceeded for more than a certain number of days per calendar year which means that it is not an absolute limit. Furthermore, when limit values were exceeded, Member States were obliged to draw up a clean-up plan which means that they may delay the respect of the limit values until the end of this—or even a second—plan. Finally, the locations where the Member States were requested to measure the concentration of pollutants, were fixed by the Member States themselves. The Directives established criteria; however, these criteria were very general and allow all sorts of measures which might significantly influence the measuring results.[27]

In appropriate cases alarm thresholds—these are values "beyond which there is a risk for human health from brief exposure and at which immediate steps shall be taken by Member States"—were to be fixed; where such values are exceeded, the population had to be alerted. No limit values were fixed for tropospheric ozone; for $PM_{2.5}$ the limit values applied only from 2015 onwards.[28]

The following limit values were established[29]:

8–05

Pollutant	Time	Limit value	Number of days per year where exceeding is allowed	Margin of tolerance
Sulphur dioxide	Hour	350 microgram/m³	24	150 microgram/m³
	Day	125 microgram/m³	3	
Nitrogen dioxide	Hour	200 microgram/m³	18	
	Year	40 microgram/m³		
Benzene	Year	5 microgram/m³		5 microgram/m³
Carbon monoxide		10 milligram/m³		60%
Lead	Year	0,5 microgram/m³		100%

[27] For example the sampling point "shall be between 1.5m (breathing zone) and 4m above the ground"—as if children could not be affected by air pollution (annex III); "traffic-oriented sampling probes shall be at least 25m from the edge of major junctions and no more than 10m from the kerbside" (annex III). In earlier EU legislation the requirement was that the measuring station should be placed where pollution was thought to be the worst.

[28] The reason given for this was that tropospheric ozone is not emitted, but is formed by reactions of different precursor substances, in particular under the influence of sunlight. And Member States found it impossible to respect limit values for $PM_{2.5}$ before that date.

[29] Directive 2008/50 [2008] OJ L152/1, annex XI. These limit values are in force since the beginning of 2010.

Particulate matters PM$_{10}$	Day	50 microgram/m^3	35	50%
	Year	40 microgram/m^3		20%

Member States were allowed to postpone the application of the limit values for benzene and nitrogen dioxide in a given zone or agglomeration by five years, provided they set up an air quality plan for those pollutants which had the objective to allow them to respect the limit values at a later stage. The same possibility exists for PM$_{10}$,[30] though the respect of the Directive's limit value had to be ensured by June 2011.[31] The limit value for PM$_{2.5}$ was fixed at 25 micrograms/m^3 as of 2015 and and 20 micrograms/m^3 as of 2020.

In the zones and agglomerations designated by them, Member States have to monitor ambient air quality. In particular, they have to establish measuring systems for air quality and to assess air quality. These systems vary according to the air pollution in question: in certain places, measurement from fixed stations is required; in other areas, where the limit values are not exceeded, modelling or indicative measurement are sufficient. Member States have then to establish a list of those zones and agglomerations where the limit values are exceeded. Such an exceeding is based on average concentrations, not on the fact that, for example, the limit values were exceeded in only one street. Member States have then to elaborate an air quality plan in order to keep the period of non-compliance as short as possible (art.23). These plans have to be sent to the Commission, by the latest two years after the discovery of the exceedings. The Commission is given no possibility to influence the content of the plan or monitoring progress in respecting the limit values. Its only way of action would be to start legal proceedings under art.258 TFEU—a very hypothetical option. It is true, though, that Member States have obligations to inform the Commission of details of their national compliance situation (art.27).

8–06   The difficulties of enforcing compliance with Directive 2008/50 became apparent in a case brought against the United Kingdom.[32] The United Kingdom had divided its territory under the Directive in 43 zones. In 2010, when the limit values for nitrogen dioxide (NO$_2$) were to be complied with, the United Kingdom found that these values were exceeded in 40 of the 43 zones. It elaborated clean-up plans for 24 zones, of which the Commission accepted nine, accepted three under conditions and objected to 16. Compliance for these zones were to be achieved by 2015. For 16 zones, the United Kingdom did not submit clean-up plans for approval to the Commission, because it was of the opinion that the

---

[30] Particulate Matter 10 (PM$_{10}$) is a particulate with a diameter of less than 10 micrometer.

[31] The limit value for PM$_{10}$ had already been fixed by Dir.1999/30 [1999] OJ L163/41; Member States were obliged to ensure that it was, as of January 2005, not exceeded during more than 35 days per calendar year. However, numerous cities had not taken measures to reach this result and were, since 2005, in open breach of EU law. This was the main reason for the EU to replace Dir.96/62 and its different daughter directives by Dir.2008/50—which delayed the requirement to respect the limit values until 2010/2011. See on this Commission, COM(2005) 446.

[32] Court of Justice, *ClientEarth v United Kingdom*(C-404/13) ECLI:EU:C:2013:2382.

deadline for compliance of art.22 of the Directive (five years) could not be reached anyway. The plans for theses 16 zones provided for compliance up until 2025.

The Court of Justice held that under art.23 of Directive 2008/50, the United Kingdom was obliged to comply with the NO_2-parameter "as soon as possible". It did not pronounce itself on the question, whether the deadline of 2025 complied with this requirement, but left this question to the national court. It did not either state that any non-compliance by 2015 constituted a breach of Directive 2008/50. This means that Member States have, de facto, a very large amount of discretion, whether and by when they comply with the Directive's limit values.

This case concerned one single parameter for one Member State. The Commission mentioned in 2013 that 17 procedures against Member States were pending in 2010 for non-compliance with the PM_{10} parameter.[33] However, the Court only gave judgments against three Member States, for exceeding the limit values for this parameter.[34] Until mid-2015, no other case was brought as regards this or any other parameter of Directive 2008/50 against any Member State.

At the same time, the Commission described the effects of air pollution as follows[35]:

8–07

"In 2010 [air pollution] caused over 400,000 premature deaths as well as substantial avoidable sickness and suffering including respiratory conditions (such as asthma) and exacerbated cardiovascular problems. The overall external costs of these impacts ranged from between €330–940 billion, including labour productivity losses and other indirect economic damages valued at €23 billion per year in 2010. Ecosystems are also suffering, with algal blooms, fish die-off and other ecosystem disruptions driven by nutrient nitrogen pollution ('eutrophication'). This problem is particularly acute in Europe's richest and most diverse natural zones, more than three-quarters of which are under threat."

The Commission declared in its new strategy of 2013 that compliance with Directive 2008/50 should be reached by 2020, and that by 2030 the premature deaths would be reduced by 40 per cent.[36] This means in clear terms that there will still be 240,000 premature deaths per year in 2030, a figure which is almost ten times higher than the number of premature deaths due to road accidents.

Directive 96/62 had set the framework for the elaboration of limit values for 13 explicitly enumerated pollutants. Eight of them had been covered by three daughter directives[37] and are now covered by Directive 2008/50. A fourth Directive covering the remaining pollutants from the list of Directive 96/62—cadmium, arsenic, nickel, mercury and polcyclic aromatic hydrocarbons (PAH)—should have been proposed at the end of 1999, but was only submitted in 2003 and adopted at the end of 2004.[38] The problem with these substances was

---

[33] Commission, A clean air programme for Europe, COM(2013) 718, p.2
[34] Court of Justice, *Commission v Slovenia* (C-365/10) ECLI:EU:C:2011:183; *Commission v Portugal* (C-34/11) ECLI:EI:C:2012:712; *Commission v Italy*(C-68/11) ECLI:EU:C:2012:815.
[35] Commission, COM(2013) 718, p.5.
[36] Commission, COM(2013) 718, p.5.
[37] Directive 2002/3 [2002] OJ L67/14; Dir.2000/69 [2000] OJ L313/12; Dir.2003/2 [2003] OJ L67/14.
[38] Directive 2004/107 [2005] OJ L23/3.

that Directive 96/62 required the fixing of binding limit-values and these substances are, at least as regards their compounds, known carcinogens. Industries which would be most affected by the provisions—oil refineries, cement producers, waste incinerators, chlor-alkali and glass producers, iron and steel processes, non-ferrous metal processes and combustion processes—argued that the economic costs for complying with limit-values were high, while the advantages for human health and the environment would be limited; it could not assume obligations beyond the non-binding provisions which are laid down in the different BREF-documents under Directive 2008/1.[39]

Directive 2004/107 therefore went away from the Council decision of 1996, only eight years after this decision had been laid down in Directive 96/62, to fix binding limit-values and limited itself to fix target values which were defined as "a concentration … to be attained where possible over a given period" (art.2(a)). The justification given in the Recital is in diplomatic language, yet clear: "With a view to cost-effective measures, ambient air concentrations of arsenic, cadmium, nickel and polycyclic aromatic hydrocarbons which would not pose a significant risk to human health, cannot be achieved in specific areas" (Recital 3). For mercury, not even a target value was fixed, with the argument that there would be a general strategy to reduce mercury in the environment; in the meantime, this strategy was published, however, without limiting industrial air emissions of mercury. Rightly so, this turn of policy approach with regard to heavy metals emissions was considered to be a "victory for industry".[40] Indeed, as the different substances are known as "human genotoxic carcinogens" (Dir.2004/107, Recital 3), their presence in the environment should be limited as far as possible. And as Directive 2008/1 only covers some industrial installations, a reference to the non-binding provisions of the BREF-documents is not likely to lead to significant emission reductions. A public discussion on this change of policy did not take place.

8–08   There are no other air quality values for pollutants that are fixed at EU level. Article 32 of Directive 2008/50 provided that the Commission shall review, by 2013, the situation of $PM_{2.5}$ and other pollutants and make appropriate proposals for legislation. The Commission complied with this request and proposed legislation for medium combustion plants and for national emission ceilings which also covered $PM_{2.5}$.[41]

3.   NATIONAL EMISSION CEILINGS

8–09   Also, Directive 2001/81 may be counted to belong to the area of quality standards.[42] The Council adopted it in 2001. The Directive had the objective to reduce acidification of the soil and to contribute to the reduction of levels of

---

[39] Directive 2008/1 [2008] OJ L24/8; see on this Directive in more detail Ch.4.

[40] See ENDS Daily, 20 December 2001, p.2; Environmental Issue Manager (Brussels) *Issue Tracker*, January 2003, p.9.

[41] Commission, COM(2013) 919 and 920. See also for the general strategy COM(2013) 917. As regards the emission ceilings for $PM_{2.5}$ see para 8–10 below.

[42] Directive 2001/81 on national emission ceilings for certain atmospheric pollutants [2001] OJ L309/22; see also European Environment Agency, NEC Directive, Status report 2014, Technical Report 217/2014 (Copenhagen, 2014).

tropospheric ozone. It fixed national emission ceilings for sulphur dioxide (SO_2), nitrogen oxide (NO_x), volatile organic compounds (VOC) and ammonia (NH_3). VOC is a precursor substance for tropospheric ozone. The other three pollutants are considered to be principally responsible for acidification and eutrophication which may cause damage to soils, aquatic and terrestrial ecosystems, and buildings and materials.

The Directive admitted that it is at present "technically" impossible to reach the guidance values which the WHO established for tropospheric ozone and acidification (Recital 7). Article 5 fixed as an objective to reduce, compared to 1990, the surface of excessive acidification by 50 per cent, reduce tropospheric ozone charges on human health by two-thirds and on vegetation by one-third. For each Member State, emission ceilings were fixed for each of the four pollutants which were to be reached by 2010 and were not be exceeded on any year after that date. For that purpose, Member States had to draw up programmes for the progressive reduction of national emissions and prepare national emission inventories. They had to report regularly to the Commission.

Already the title of the Directive which talked of national emission ceilings, pointed at the provenance of the Directive's concept from public international law. Indeed, the emission ceilings are very similar to those of a Protocol under the 1979 Convention on Long-Range Transboundary Air Pollution which the Member states signed in November 1999 and which was transposed into EU law by Directive 2001/81. How the emission ceilings for the different pollutants and for the different EU Member States were calculated, is not clear. While it is readily accepted that any reduction of the emission of pollutants into the air is useful, the chosen figures are somewhat arbitrary.

By 2010, the 28 EU Member States had almost all complied with the reduction of emissions.[43] Nine Member States exceeded their national ceilings for NO_x,[44] three exceeded the ceilings for ammonia (Finland, Spain and Denmark), and Luxembourg exceeded the ceiling for volatile organic compounds; the ceilings for SO_2 were respected by all.[45]

8–10

In 2013, the Commission proposed a new directive for national emission ceilings, concerning the pollutants of 2001 and $PM_{2.5}$.[46] The calculation of the ceiling for each Member State and each pollutant was again based on conclusions which had been adopted, in 2012, in the context of the Convention on the Long-Range Transboundary Air Pollution.[47] This Decision had established, for each Contracting Party, absolute emission data for the year 2005 and had then indicated by what percentage these quantities had to be reduced. The Commission proposal did not refer to the absolute values of 2005,[48] but only suggested the reduction of emissions by a certain percentage. The only source of information which is foreseen, are reports by Member States. Also, as some emissions are not

---

[43] European Environment Agency, NEC Directive Status report 2013 (Copenhagen, 2014).

[44] These Member States were Austria, Belgium, France, Germany, Ireland, Luxembourg, Malta, Slovenia and Spain.

[45] European Environment Agency, NEC Directive Status report 2013 (Copenhagen, 2014).

[46] Commission COM(2013) 920.

[47] Gothenburg Protocol, Executive Body, Decision 2012/2.

[48] It can only be supposed that the absolute figures are not taken up in the Commission proposal, because they conflict with the Commission's own data which it had assembled during the lifetime of Dir.2001/81.

included in the calculation and Member States have a considerable flexibility in the calculation of the emissions, all this makes the legislative proposal illegible, unenforceable and a sort of undesirable technocratic legislation.

To give an example: the proposal provides that the United Kingdom should reduce its emissions for SO_2 by 59 per cent, for NO_x by 55 per cent, for NH_3 by 8 per cent, for VOC by 32 per cent and for $PM_{2.5}$ by 30 per cent; the European Union's reductions should be –59 per cent for SO_2, –42 for NO_x, –6 per cent for NH_3, –28per cent for VOC and –22 per cent for $PM_{2.5}$. No explanation and no justification for these figures are offered and, as mentioned, these figures remain meaningless without the absolute figures of 2005. It can only be hoped that this form of legislation, which is anything but legislation which is "as open as possible and as closely as possible to the citizen" (art.1 TEU), is corrected during the legislative process.

8–11 National emission ceilings for sulphur dioxide and nitrogen oxides had already been fixed at EU level, for large combustion plants, by Directive 88/609.[49] In 2001, this Directive was replaced, with effect from the end of 2002, by Directive 2001/80.[50] This Directive introduced a number of measures concerning emissions of large combustion plants and overall national quantities which had to be reduced; leaving in part the option between the different approaches to Member States. For reasons of presentation, this Directive will be discussed in detail in para.8–23, below.

3. POLLUTION EMISSIONS FROM MOBILE SOURCES (PRODUCTS)

8–12 Pollution emission limit values from products were, historically, the first EU measures on air pollution. The purpose of these first provisions was, however, not to combat air pollution, but to ensure the free circulation of products.[51] The efforts undertaken by the European Union to reduce air emissions from products, in particular from means of transport, were not at all systematic. They concentrated on cars, since it became more and more obvious that individual passenger transport was the main generator of air emissions within the European Union. Measures to combat air emissions from trucks, railways, airplanes and ships were much less intense and less systematic. As regards the air polluting substances contained in fuels—e.g. lead in petrol and sulphur in diesel fuel—see para.6–13, above.

---

[49] Directive 88/609 [1988] OJ L336/1.

[50] Directive 2001/80 [2001] OJ L309/1.

[51] See Dir.70/220 on measures to be taken against air pollution by emissions from motor vehicles [1970] OJ L176/1, 2nd and 3rd Recital: "a regulation of 31 March 1969 on the composition of exhaust gases emitted from petrol engines of motor vehicles was published in France … those provisions are liable to hinder the establishment and proper functioning of the common market; … it is therefore necessary that all Member States adopt the same requirements…".

(a)   Air emission from cars

EU measures to reduce air emissions from cars started in 1970. These measures   **8–13**
concentrated on emission limit values, and, since the early 1980s, when the dying
forests signalled the need for more stringent measures, on the fuels used by cars.
Consequently, they were based on art.100, and since 1987 on art.95 EC (now
art.114 TFEU).

The European Union never considered to apply the principle of art.191(2)
TFEU and combat air pollution from cars at its source, e.g. by imposing the
construction of cars that do not exceed a maximum speed limit—for instance,
100km per hour—or which do not burn more than a certain amount of fuels per
100km[52]; the reason is probably that such considerations were considered to be
much too interventionist. It must be repeated that Directive 2009/125 on the
eco-design of energy-related products[53] would give the legal competence to the
European Union to impose such construction requirements; however, this
Directive explicitly excluded means of transport from its field of application.
Beginning in the early 1990s, directives also stated that progress in reducing air
emissions from cars was countered by the increase in the car fleet and the number
of kilometres driven by each individual car, so that the overall reduction of air
emissions was, at best, extremely small.

The European Union did, until now, not take measures to introduce taxes or
charges for cars according to their emissions into the environment; neither did it
take any measures for EU-wide tax incentives in order to promote the marketing
or use of less-polluting cars, as basic objections against EU tax measures made
such an approach impossible. A proposal from the Commission to fix the tax for
individual cars according to their CO_2-emissions, made in 2005, was not adopted
by the Council and was withdrawn in 2015.[54] Since the late 1980s, the European
Union has accepted that Member States can grant tax incentives for less-polluting
cars, albeit under very restrictive conditions[55] that made this instrument almost
worthless. Indeed, only temporary incentives were allowed, during the transition
period of the directive that reduced air emissions. Only incentives for new cars
were permitted; incentives for the retrofitting of existing cars were not. This, for

---

[52] See, however, European Parliament, Resolution of 10 April 1997 [1997] OJ C132/170, where the
Parliament requested that new cars do not consume more than 5 litres of petrol (4.5 litres of diesel)
per 100km as of 1 January 2005 and not more than 3 litres of petrol or diesel as of 1 January 2010.
The Commission concluded, in 1998, an agreement with the car industry on these issues, see below.
[53] Directive 2009/125 establishing a framework for the setting of eco-design requirements for energy
related products [2009] OJ L285/10.
[54] Commission, COM(2005) 261. Tax measures require unanimity in Council for their adoption
(art.113 and art.192(2) TFEU).
[55] See, e.g. Dir.94/12 relating to measures to be taken against air pollution by emissions from motor
vehicles and amending Dir.70/220 [1994] OJ L100/42, art.3, which repeated the standard formula for
such conditions for national tax incentives: "they shall apply to all new vehicles offered for sale on the
market of a Member State which comply in advance with the requirements of Directive 70/220, as
amended by this Directive; they shall be terminated with effect from the mandatory application of the
emission values laid down in Art.2(3) for new motor vehicles; for each type of motor vehicle, they
shall be for an amount lower than the additional cost of the technical solutions introduced to ensure
compliance with the values set and of their installation on the vehicle".

instance, made it impossible to give incentives for the retrofitting of existing cars with catalytic converters. It is interesting to see that the Commission concluded in 2000 that:

> "well-targeted, differentiated taxes are considered to be an effective tool to influence consumer behaviour, and can therefore confidently be expected to provide an effective means of accelerated improved performance in the transport sector, with a very low societal cost."[56]

8–14   This remark, it is true, was aimed at fuel charges. However, it is not clear why it would not also apply to emissions from cars or trucks.

If one considers that the lifetime of a car is at least 12 years and that standards that required the use of catalytic converters were only made mandatory for all new cars as of 1 January 1993, one can easily see that by the year 2005, when more or less all cars without catalytic converters have disappeared from the market, the resulting reduction in air emissions will have been eaten up by the traffic increase. The Commission predicted that by 2020 all emissions from road transport—except CO_2, the greenhouse gas—will have fallen to less than 20 per cent of their 1995 levels, despite the growth in transport; SO_2 emissions are predicted to fall to 10 per cent of their 1995 levels in 2005, NO_x emissions to fall to 30 per cent of their 1995 levels by 2010.[57]

Measures to reduce air emissions from cars have, since the early 1990s, been prepared by the Commission's so-called Auto/Oil Programme, which set up working groups where the European associations of the car and petrol industries were invited to "make available their considerable know-how and expertise".[58] Member States were kept informed of the discussions in informal meetings. Four specific meetings were organised to inform the "Members of the European Parliament"—thus not the Parliament itself—of the work carried out. Other interested groups were not consulted.[59] The Auto/Oil Programme tried to find combined solutions concerning the emission from cars, the quality and composition of fuels, and new emission control technologies, on a "cost-effective"[60] basis. Proposals for fixing emission limit values by the Commission were based on the results of this programme. Of course, these proposals can be—and were—criticised for not being based on an objective assessment, but rather on an assessment which conformed to the interests of these two industrial sectors, i.e. the car industry and the petrol industry. In any case, it seems unlikely that the Commission could develop policies and proposals which would be against the interests of these two industrial sectors. Also, the documents and data published do not really allow for a critical examination as to whether the suggested measures really constitute the best environmental protection potential or whether they are just a compromise between diverging interests.

---

[56] Commission, Review of the Auto-Oil II Programme, COM(2000) 626 of 5 October 2000, Pt 6.2.

[57] Commission, COM(2000) 626 of 5 October 2000, Pt 4.11.

[58] COM(96) 248, p.44; this remark referred to the Auto/Oil Programme which started in 1992 and had the task of developing an "objective assessment of the most cost-effective package of measures to reduce emissions ...".

[59] COM(96) 248, p.90.

[60] See the criticism of the European Parliament on the way in which this cost-effectiveness was calculated without taking into consideration social costs and environmental costs: Resolution of 18 February 1998 [1998] OJ C80/92.

Auto/Oil II started in 1997 and looked in particular at the development of the air quality measures to be adopted or implemented at EU level until 2010, also in so far as other sectors than the road transport sector were concerned. In contrast to Auto/Oil I, all interested stakeholders, including Member States, the European Parliament and non-governmental organisations, were invited to participate in the discussions.[61] The discussions of Auto/Oil II considerably influenced not only proposals and legislations in the transport sector, but generally all air pollution measures suggested by the Commission and adopted at EU level.   **8–15**

In 2006, the Commission reviewed the EU transport policy and concluded that "all transport modes must become more environmentally friendly, safe and energy efficient". It paid some attention to the negative environmental impact of cars and announced new measures for cars (Euro V) and trucks (Euro VI), but was mainly interested in increasing transport mobility—and thus quantity, and did not argue itself that the implementation of the different measures suggested would lead to a significant reduction of air pollution from motor vehicles.

In the early 1970s, different directives were adopted for petrol and diesel-driven cars. Later, this differentiation was abandoned, in the same way as was the differentiation between passenger cars, light and heavy commercial vehicles and trucks. Furthermore, recent directives have already announced the adoption of new provisions that are aimed at further strengthening the emission limit values and enter into details as to what such new proposals shall contain.[62] The numerous overlapping directives and proposals which use numerous acronyms, contain extensive technical details, measurements, control and test rules which all constantly change among themselves, as well as the lack of consolidating texts have led to a situation in which the legal provisions lack transparency and cannot really be checked by people other than specialist experts—which are in industry. This is strengthened by the fact that changes to previous provisions are normally signalled by expressions such as "40 per cent reduction", "70 per cent reduction", and so on; and it adds to confusion that such reductions are calculated by including, in addition, the reduction in the fuel composition or changes in test methods.

Directive 70/220 set, in 1970, limit values for carbon monoxide and unburned hydrocarbon emissions.[63] In 1977, limit values for nitrogen oxides were established.[64] The values for these three pollutants were progressively reduced by different directives.[65] In 1989, more stringent emission limit values for gaseous pollutants were introduced and progressively extended to all passenger cars. Emissions from diesel engines were fixed in 1972 and progressively reduced.[66] All emission limit values are the subject of an almost permanent review discussion.   **8–16**

---

[61] Commission, COM(2000) 626 of 5 October 2000.

[62] See, as an example, Dir.94/12 [1994] OJ L100/42, art.4.

[63] Directive 70/220 [1994] OJ L100/42.

[64] Directive 77/102 [1977] OJ L32/32.

[65] Directive 74/290 [1974] OJ L159/61; Dir.78/665 [1978] OJ L223/48; Dir.83/351 [1983] OJ L197/1; Dir.88/76 [1988] OJ L36/1; Dir.89/458 [1989] OJ L226/1; Dir.91/441 [1991] OJ L242/1; Dir.94/12 [1994] OJ L100/42.

[66] Directive 72/306 [1972] OJ L190/1; Dir.88/77 [1988] OJ L36/33; Dir.91/542 [1991] OJ L295/1.

The present emission limit values (mg/km) for passenger cars are as follows[67]:

Carbon monoxide (CO)		Hydrocarbons HC		NO$_x$		Particulates Pt	
Petrol	Diesel	Petrol	Diesel	Petrol	Diesel	Petrol	Diesel
1000	500	100	—	60	80	5	5

The biggest surprise in these values is the absence of an emission limit value for carbon dioxide (CO_2), the gas which is held to be primarily responsible for climate change and designated as such under the Kyoto Protocol on Climate Change.[68] In 1990 CO_2 emissions from passenger cars accounted for about 45 per cent of transport CO_2 emissions and about 12 per cent of total CO_2 emissions in the European Union; a 20 per cent increase was expected by 2000 and a 36 per cent increase by 2010.[69]

8–17　　In 1993, the Commission had announced a proposal for a Directive on an emission limit value for CO_2 for cars[70] and found support from the European Parliament.[71] This approach was heavily opposed by the car industry which found some support in Member States, in particular in France, Italy and Germany. In 1996, the Commission decided not to legislate, but to introduce financial incentives to lower fuel consumption, introduce a labelling scheme for fuel consumption of cars, conclude an environmental agreement with the car industry to reduce CO_2 emissions from cars and promote research and development[72]; at the same time, it started discussions with car manufacturers on an agreement. It is not clear what particular reasons have been pleaded for having an environmental agreement just for CO_2,[73] but not for the other above-mentioned pollutants.

In summer 1998, the Commission announced[74] that it was ready to accept the offer by ACEA (Association des Constructeurs Européens d'Automobiles), which groups together 11 European car manufacturers, to limit the CO_2 emissions for new cars which were brought into circulation in the EU from 2008 onwards to 140g per kilometre. This offer was different from what the Council had wished to see reached (120g per km by 2005 or, at the latest, by 2010). The agreement that was subsequently made consisted, in legal terms, of:

- a commitment by ACEA[75];

---

[67] Commission Reg.692/2008 [2008] OJ L199/1, annex XVII. These figures have remained unchanged since 2008. Since September 2014, Euro VI emission limit values apply to all newly admitted passenger cars. The only essential change is the reduction of permitted NOx emissions for diesel cars which were reduced from 180 to 80, see annex XVII, table 2.

[68] See para.9–01, below.

[69] See for the overall emission of CO_2 within the European Union, Written Question E-2572/96 (Amadeo) [1997] OJ C83/30.

[70] Commission, Legislative programme 1994, COM(93) 588, para.241.

[71] European Parliament Resolution of 27 October 1993 [1993] OJ C315/160.

[72] COM(95) 689; Commission Communication on transport and CO_2; COM(1998) 204.

[73] European Parliament Resolution of 19 February 1998 [1998] OJ C80/227, Pt 14.

[74] Commission, COM(1998) 495.

[75] Published as annex to Commission, COM(1998) 495.

- a recommendation by the European Commission, addressed to ACEA[76];
- an exchange of letters between the Commission and ACEA.

The commitment stated that as long as ACEA's promises were kept, ACEA assumed:

> "that this commitment provides complete and sufficient substitute for all new regulatory measures to limit fuel consumption or CO_2 emissions, and for any additional fiscal measures in pursuit of the CO_2 objectives of this commitment."

This expressed the expectation that the EU legislature—possibly also the national legislature—would not take regulatory measures to reduce CO_2 emissions from cars during the lifetime of the agreement. The commitment was, furthermore, based on several assumptions—amongst others, that non-ACEA car manufacturers would commit themselves to equivalent CO_2 reduction efforts. The agreement provided for a framework for a future monitoring procedure, which included the statement that the Commission's official reports on the monitoring results will not refer to individual companies' achievements, in order to avoid competition being distorted. The Commission entered into the agreement, once the Council had signalled its endorsement of the reduction targets and the European Parliament had reluctantly accepted the deal. The Committee of the Regions and the Economic and Social Committee had no say in the matter. Furthermore, the agreement was made with ACEA alone, not with the car manufacturers themselves. In the beginning, the agreement was made with ACEA which groups European and US car manufacturers. Later, similar agreements were concluded with the Japanese and Korean car manufacturers associations.[77]

8-18

The agreements referred to the EU market, not to cars which were marketed in other parts of the world, though such a restriction would normally also be the consequence of any regulatory measure.

The Commission published a number of progress reports on the implementation of the voluntary agreements. In its report for 2004, it quoted from a letter which it had received from ACEA and JAMA stating that these associations would not be able to reach the 2008 target by technical measures. In 2006, it became obvious that all three associations would not comply with their commitment by 2008. The Commission then made proposals for legislating which were adopted in 2009.[78] As of 2013, the average emissions per car fleet of a car producer was progressively limited to 130g per km, with considerable transition periods. This solution mainly favoured expensive cars with high CO_2 emissions. The rules applied only to new cars which were marketed within the European Union. Overall, the introduction of mandatory provisions was thus delayed by more than 15 years.

---

[76] Commission Rec.1999/125 on the reduction of CO_2 emissions from passenger cars [1999] OJ L40/49.

[77] Commission Rec.2000/303 on the reduction of CO_2 emissions from passenger cars (KAMA) [2000] OJ L100/55; Rec. 2000/304 on the reduction of CO_2 emissions from passenger cars (JAMA) [2000] OJ L100/57.

[78] Regulation 443/2009 [2009] OJ L140/1.

8–19   Regulation 443/2009 also stated: "From 2020 onwards, this Regulation sets a target of 95 g CO_2/km for the average emissions of the new car fleet" (art.1). However, in 2014, the following provision was inserted in Regulation 443/2009[79]: "(The Commission shall make a proposal) for the possible setting of a realistic and achievable target, based on a comprehensive impact assessment that will consider the continued competitiveness of the car industry and its dependent industries." This means that it is not yet clear which emission limit value will apply from 2020 onwards. Once more, the lobbying by the car industry was successful.

Regulation 510/2011 set limit values of 175 g/km as average value for the fleet of light duty vehicles and a conditional and thus not yet binding target of 147 g/km as of 2020; the Regulation again contained numerous derogations, "tricks" in the calculation method etc.[80] No CO_2 emission limits were fixed for heavy duty vehicles.[81] The Commission was only asked to "begin measuring fuel consumption and CO_2 emissions" from such vehicles.

(b)   Air emissions from airplanes, ships and machines

8–20   There are no EU emission limit values for ships and airplanes. Both sectors are, in part, regulated by global organisations (cartels), the International Maritime Organisation (IMO) and the International Civil Aviation Organisation (ICAO).

In 1998 the Commission submitted, for the first time, a proposal on the limitation of emissions from civil subsonic airplanes.[82] The proposal only concerned nitrogen oxides and did not contain an emission limit value, but only a formula for calculating such emissions. The proposal had been submitted because ICAO had not been able to agree on suggestions for reductions which had been submitted to ICAO bodies and discussed there. The EU proposal was based on the present art.100(2) TFEU, which is a surprising legal basis since all emission limit values for cars and commercial vehicles have been based on art.114 TFEU. When ICAO finally agreed new limit values which would apply to new engine designs after 2003, the Commission's proposal became obsolete and was no longer pursued.

Attempts by the EU to indirectly reduce the CO_2 emissions from airplanes by including them in the CO_2 emissions trading scheme of Directive 2003/87[83], were only partly successful: a directive which provided for such an inclusion as of 2012,[84] met with very strong resistance from third countries, including the United States, Japan, India, China and Russia. Though the Court of Justice considered the EU measures to be compatible with public international law,[85] the political pressure was so strong that the EU adopted Decision 377/2013[86] which "temporarily" suspended the application of the scheme to third countries, justifying this approach with ongoing discussions on CO_2 emission reductions at

---

[79] Regulation 443/2009 [2009] OJ L140/1, art.13(5), inserted by Reg.333/2014 [2014] OJ L103/15.
[80] Regulation 510/2011 [2011] OJ L145/1.
[81] Regulation 595/2009 on emissions from heavy duty vehicles (Euro VI) [2009] OJ L188/1.
[82] [1998] OJ C108/14.
[83] Directive 2003/87 [2003] OJ L275/32.
[84] Directive 2008/101 [2009] OJ L8, p.3
[85] Court of Justice, *Air Transport Association of America* (C-366/10) ECLI:EU:C:2011:864.
[86] Decision 377/2013 [2013] OJ L113/1.

international level. In 2014, a further Regulation exempted flights from and to airports outside the European Economic Area from the application of Directive 2003/87.[87] This exemption was limited to the end of 2016, but it is likely to be permanent.

There has been, to date, almost no EU provision to regulate air pollution emissions from ships. Internationally, the pollution from ships is discussed in the context of the Convention for the prevention of pollution from ships (MARPOL), to which the European Union is not a signatory. While some measures have been taken in that context, no measures have as yet been adopted at EU level. Directive 2005/33 limited the sulphur content of fuels used in marine shipping in the Baltic Sea and the North Sea.[88] Discussions on the introduction of environmentally differentiated shipping charges according to their emissions have been discussed internationally, but have not led to concrete action at EU level.

8–21

For internal navigation, Directive 2004/26 introduced emission limit values for inland waterways vessels, with regard to CO (5.0 g/kWh) HC and NO_x combined (7.5–11.0g/kWh) and particulates (0.4–05g/kWh).[89]

As regards machines, the European Union adopted, in 1997, for the first time, a Directive[90] which set air emission limit values for machines other than passenger and commercial vehicles, airplanes and ships; it thus concerned machinery such as compressors, forestry equipment, road-maintenance equipment, snow-plough equipment, aerial lifts, mobile cranes and ground supports in airports. The Directive was based on art.114 TFEU and concerned machinery which was type-approved after 1997; existing non-road mobile machinery was thus not affected. The emission limit values were introduced in two steps (1998 and 2000) and differentiated according to the power of the engine. In 2004, the Directive was amended; for the different machines, further differentiation was introduced.[91] The new emission values range from 3.5 to 5.5 g/kWh for CO, 4.0 to 7.5 g/kWh for HC and NO_x combined and 0.2 to 0.3g/kWh for particulates. Commission Regulations 2011/88 and 2012/46[92] brought in particular changes for test methods and other technical issues; Regulation 2012/46 also introduced a reporting obligation for CO_2 emissions, without, though, fixing limit values.

(c) Emissions of volatile organic compounds (VOCs)

Volatile organic compounds (VOCs) are generated from the handling of (motor) gasoline; this gasoline is stored before being distributed, which can take place by pipeline, road trucks, rail cars and by barge and ships. After that distribution, the gasoline is discharged to a storage tank. During all these stages of loading/ unloading, the gasoline generates VOCs. VOCs are among the precursors of photochemical oxidants such as tropospheric ozone which also is a potential greenhouse gas.[93] Some VOCs that are emitted are classified as toxic, teratogenic

8–22

---

[87] Regulation 421/2014 [2014] OJ L129/1.

[88] Directive 2005/33 [2005] OJ L191/59; see also para.6–13, above.

[89] Directive 2004/26 [2004] OJ L146/1.

[90] Directive 97/68 relating to measures against the emissions of gaseous and particulate pollutants from internal combustion engines to be installed in non-road mobile machinery [1998] OJ L59/1.

[91] Directive 2004/26 [2004] OJ L146/1.

[92] Commission, Reg.2011/88 [2011] OJ L305/1; Commission, Reg.2012/46 [2012] OJ L353/1.

[93] See paras 8–09 and 8–22, above.

or carcinogenic. The biggest emitting sectors are road transport, solvent use and the extraction and distribution of fossil fuels.

Directive 91/441 and other directives on motor vehicle emissions[94] had already introduced a number of measures to reduce VOC emissions from motor vehicles, the main source of such emissions, without fixing emission limit values. It is estimated that these measures will reduce VOC emissions from road transport by about one-third.

Council Directive 94/63[95] followed the same line; it dealt with the VOC emissions resulting from the storage of petrol and its distribution from terminals to service stations, and required Member States to make sure that the conditions laid down in the Directive and its annexes were complied with. The Directive was based on art.114 TFEU; it also applied to road trucks, which is the reason why it is mentioned in this chapter; yet it also applied to stationary sources and allowed Member States to fix more stringent provisions (arts 3(3) and 4(3)). The discussion of limiting VOC emissions from other stationary sources will be discussed at para.8–39, below. Contrary to what its title provided, this Directive did not contain any emission limit values, but rather laid down requirements for storage installations at terminals (stationary petrol tanks, annex I), for loading and unloading of mobile containers at terminals (annex II), for loading and storage installations at service stations and terminals, where the intermediate storage of vapour is carried out (annex III) and specifications for bottom-loading, vapour collection and overfill protection of European road tankers (annex IV). As mentioned, it was thus a measure that affected both mobile and stationary sources of VOC generation. Interestingly, the emission of VOCs from the charging of ships was only covered by a non-committing statement in a Recital.[96]

4. AIR EMISSIONS FROM INSTALLATIONS

(a) Framework provisions

8–23   EU law contains only very few provisions which relate to installations, since it is thought that products that circulate within the European Union should be exposed to uniform rules, but that installations do not circulate freely and therefore do not need uniform rules. This attitude was neither changed by the fact that products

---

[94] Directive 91/441 [1991] OJ L242/1; Dir.91/542 [1991] OJ L295/1; Dir.93/59 [1993] OJ L186/21; Dir.94/12 [1994] OJ L100/42.

[95] Directive 94/63 [1994] OJ L365/24.

[96] Directive 94/63 [1994] OJ L365/24, Recital 6: "On grounds of international standardisation and of safety during the loading of ships, standards must be drawn up at International Maritime Organisation level for vapour control and recovery systems to apply to both loading installations and ships, whereas the Community must therefore endeavour to ensure that the necessary provisions are introduced into the Marpol Convention during the current revision of Marpol due to be completed in 1996; whereas in the event that the Marpol Convention is not so revised, the Community, after discussion with its major trading partners, should propose appropriate measures to apply to ships and port installations servicing ships."

which leave installations compete with each other, nor by the knowledge that water discharges and air emissions[97] from installations circulate and pollute transnationally.

Following the discovery of dying forests in the early 1980s, the European Union discussed air pollution at a summit of Heads of State and governments in 1983. In 1984, it adopted a framework directive on air emissions from industrial installations,[98] which it based on arts 115 and 352 TFEU. The Directive introduced a general authorisation procedure for all installations which belonged to a positive list that was defined in an annex. The authorisation could only be given where:

> "all appropriate preventive measures against air pollution have been taken, including the application of the best available technology, provided that the application of such measures does not entail excessive costs"

and that the plant did not cause "significant air pollution" (art.4), in particular from a number of pollutants which were mentioned in an annex.[99] The Council committed itself to fix, "if necessary", emission limit values based on the best available technology not entailing excessive costs. For existing installations, "Member States shall implement policies and strategies, including appropriate measures, for the gradual adaptation" of these plants.

Directive 84/360 was transposed into national law by all Member States, but had a rather limited effect. The very loose drafting did not push for changes in the practice that had existed up to then. The "best available technology not entailing excessive costs" proved to be an empty formula that did not require measures to reduce air emissions. Efforts at EU level to elaborate—but not publish(!)—non-binding technical papers of what constituted, for a specific industrial sector, best available technology, had no visible effect on the permitted practice in Member States, particularly as the cost element remained decisive in each specific case.

Also, no measures were imposed, by virtue of Directive 84/ 360, on existing installations in order gradually to lead to air emission reductions. Since, on the one hand, Member States were allowed to take more stringent measures than those laid down in the Directive and, on the other hand, no action was taken against a Member State for lack of action, one here finds another example where the added value of EU legislation to environmental protection is small. Directive 84/360 ceased to exist in 2007, when Directive 96/61—replaced in 2008 by Directive 2008/1 which itself was later replaced by Directive 2010/75—became fully operational and also applied to existing installations.[100] It is significant also for the omission to enforce Directive 84/360 with regard to existing installations that the first ever judgment of the Court of Justice which stated that the Directive contained a legal obligation for Member States to progressively adapt existing

8–24

---

[97] Directive 2000/76 [2000] OJ L332/91 is the only Directive which also provided for provisions regarding the discharge of pollutants to waters, see art.8. When this Directive was, in 2010, integrated into Dir.2010/75 on industrial emissions, the emission limits were maintained.

[98] Directive 84/360 [1984] OJ L188/20.

[99] Directive 84/360 [1984] OJ L188/20, annex II: sulphur dioxide, oxides of nitrogen, carbon monoxide, organic compounds, heavy metals, dust, asbestos, glass and mineral fibres, chlorine, fluorine.

[100] Directive 96/61 [1996] OJ 257/26, art.20; Dir.2008/1 [2008] OJ L24/8.

installations to the requirements of the Directive, was given in July 2005,[101] 21 years after the adoption of the Directive and two years before it ceased to exist: as if the Commission could not have enforced art.13 of Directive 84/360 earlier!

(b) Combustion plants

8–25   Combustion plants with a capacity of more than 50 MW account for about 60 per cent of SO_2 emissions and 20 per cent of NO_x-emissions in the EC In 2001, Directive 2001/80[102] was adopted which replaced Directive 88/609[103] as of end 2002. However, the new Directive very largely repeated the text of the previous Directive. This repetition went so far as to provide for a derogation for Spain that was valid until 31 December 1999 (art.5(2)). Also, the emission limit values for new installations and the overall emission ceilings of SO_2 and NO_x for existing installations (annex I and II) were hardly amended or updated. Finally, Member States had to inform the Commission of their programmes to reduce emissions under art.3 at the latest on 31 December 1990—this provision was inserted into a Directive that was adopted on 23 October 2001! Directive 2001/80, taking over the previous provisions, provided for emission limit values for sulphur dioxide, nitrogen oxides and dust as regards new installations. For existing installations, the Directive introduced national emission ceilings for sulphur dioxides and nitrogen oxides. Calculated on the basis of emissions of the year 1980, Member States had to lower their total emissions in two (NO_x) or three (SO_2) stages until 2003. No update was made.

A new provision requested Member States to ensure a significant reduction of emissions until the end of 2007, by either requesting existing installations to respect the Directive's emission limits for new installations, or to make sure that existing large combustion installations participated in a national emission reduction plan which Member States "could" (not "had to") draw up in view of reducing emissions; thus, where a Member State decided not to draw up a national emission reduction plan, there was no obligation for existing installations![104]

Article 6 provided for an examination of possibilities to introduce combined heat-power equipment at the construction of new installations or a significant enlargement of existing installations. However, the taking of such measures was to depend on the "technical and economic feasibility" of providing such equipment—which obviously made this provision equivalent to a recommendation.

8–26   The Commission had to report, before the end of 2004, in particular on the necessity of taking further measures to reduce emissions, on emissions of heavy metals by large combustion installations, the cost-efficiency of further measures and the technical and economic feasibility of such measures. This provision—and

---

[101] Court of Justice, *Commission v Greece* (C-364/03) [2005] E.C.R. I-6159.

[102] Directive 2001/80 on the limitation of emissions of certain pollutants into the air from large combustion plants [2001] OJ L309/1.

[103] See in this regard Commission, Rec.2003/47 on the guidelines to assist a Member State in the preparation of a national emission reduction plan [2003] OJ L16/59.

[104] See however Commission, Evaluation of the Member States' emission inventories 2004–2006 for large combustion plants (2008). This report was made by a private company for the Commission; it indicated that 2,779 installations came under Dir.2001/80.

generally the limited review of Directive 88/609—found its explanation in the argument that operators of installations generally took the view that when they applied the best available technique, they contributed their share to emissions reduction and that a specific directive on large combustion installations had no right of existence any more. The Commission did not establish these reports,[105] but gave some vague assessments of the Directive in its proposal for the new Directive 2010/75.[106]

Directive 2001/80 was, as its predecessor Directive 88/609, only monitored with very great difficulties. Indeed, monitoring compliance with the overall reductions of pollutants' emissions was practically impossible, as the only information on actual emission quantities stemmed from Member States themselves and the emission quantities only referred to those existing plants that came under the Directive. And the share of existing plants that came under the Directive and other plants in the overall air pollution is not known.

Directive 2010/75 incorporated the provisions of Directive 2001/80; it maintained emission limit values for such plants for SO_2, NO_x, CO (carbon monoxide) and dust which were laid down in annex V.[107] Derogations are foreseen for plants which burn indigenous coal that contains too much sulphur (art.31), for plants which form part of a "transitional" (rather: derogatory) plan (art.22), plants which are intended to stop operations after a certain time (art.33), plants for isolated settlements (art.34) and district heating plants (art.35). New plants with more than 300 MW capacity are obliged to examine whether there is a possibility for the capture and underground storage of CO_2 (art.36).

In 2013, the Commission proposed a directive concerning the emissions of medium combustion plants which is at present under discussion.[108]

8–27

(c) Waste incineration installations

In 1989, the European Union adopted two Directives on municipal waste incineration plants. The Directives fixed general conditions for the authorisation and functioning of such incinerators, such as the minimum temperature (850°C for two seconds). Requirements for the design of installations were rather vague and largely corresponded to the requirements in Directive 88/609. In 1994, the European Union adopted a Directive on installations for the incineration of hazardous waste [109] which was based on art.192 TFEU and entered into effect in 1997. These three Directives were replaced by a new Directive of end 2000[110] which was based on art.192 TFEU and became effective, for new installations, end 2002, for existing installations end 2005. In 2010, this Directive was then incorporated into the new Directive on industrial emissions.[111]

The reason for this merger of the different texts was that the Directives on the incineration of municipal waste had to be updated anyway and that the environmental impairment through dioxins, heavy metals or other emissions or

8–28

---

[105] Commission, COM(2007) 843 and SEC(2007) 1679.
[106] Directive 2010/75 [2010] OJ L334/17, annex V.
[107] Directive 94/67 [1994] OJ L365/34.
[108] Commission, COM(2013) 919.
[109] Directive 2000/76 [2000] OJ L332/91 on the incineration of waste.
[110] Directive 2010/75 [2010] OJ L334/17.
[111] Directive 2010/75 [2010] OJ L334/17, annex VI.

discharges was the same, independently of which incineration source the pollutant came. Furthermore, it was considered that the far-spread public resistance against the waste incineration technology could best be overcome by strict standards, effective controls and transparency of permit and operation procedures.

Directive 2010/75 concerned, as its predecessor Directive 2000/76, almost all waste incineration installations. It excluded installations which exclusively burn vegetal waste, agricultural waste, radioactive waste, animal waste or waste on oil platforms are which incinerated there, finally installations for test or research purposes which burn less than 50 tonnes per year. The provisions of Directive 2010/75 also applied to installations, the principal objective of which is the production of goods or energy and which "use waste as a regular or additional fuel or in which waste is thermally treated for the purpose of disposal" (art.3 no.41) (co-incineration); to this category belong installations such as power plants, steel plants or cement kilns. The emission limit values which were fixed are less stringent for co-incineration installations[112]—as if the environmental impairment were less relevant in the case of co-incineration.

8–29   Installations need a permit for operation. Article 4 of Directive 2020/75 fixed the general conditions for such a permit. For example, the permit must indicate the type of (hazardous) waste which may be burnt, the sampling and measuring methods for air and water discharges or—for hazardous waste—the content of pollutants such as chlorides, PCP, PCB, fluorides, sulphur or heavy metals in the waste. A number of other measures have the objective to minimise environmental impairment. The minimum temperature, including in cases of co-incineration, is 850°Celsius, and, where hazardous waste is burned, 1,100°C (art.50). The installation must be equipped with an automatic system to stop the incineration process where this temperature is not reached, or where emission limit-values are exceeded, due to a disturbance. The following emission limit-values were fixed in annex VI (daily average):

Pollutant	Incineration	co-incineration	co-incineration in cement kilns
Dust	$10mg/m^3$	Part 4-formula	$30mg/m^3$
Gases	$10mg/m^3$	Part 4-formula	
HCl	$10mg/m^3$	Part 4-formula	$10mg/m^3$
HF	$1mg/m^3$	Part 4-formula	$1mg/m^3$
SO_2	$50mg/m^3$	Part 4-formula	
NO and NO_2	$200–400mg/m^3$	Part 4-formula	$500–800/m^3$
Cadmium and Tl	$0.05mg/m^3$		$0.05mg/m^3$
Mercury	$0.05 mg/m^3$		$0.05mg/m^3$
Dioxins/furans	$0.1ng/m^3$		$0.1ng/m^3$

However, large transition periods, derogation possibilities, exceptions for small installations and differentiations according to new or existing installations and, for cement kilns, according to the fuel used, were provided.

---

[112] [1998] OJ C372/11.

The Directive also fixed emission limit-values for discharges of waste water from the cleaning of waste gases into the water, in particular for heavy metals (annex VI, part 5). It detailed the measuring requirements and methods and imposed in particular an automatic, continuous measuring of emissions into the air and the water (annex VI, pt 6).

Overall, the requirements of the Directive which were almost entirely taken over from the previous Directive 2000/76, were rather strict and by far the most stringent requirements of any industrial installation that were laid down at EU level. The apprehension of the population against the pollution emissions from incinerators would therefore appear not to be completely justified—if the installation would permanently function according to the legal requirements. However, breakdowns or deficiencies in the operation, the burning of hazardous materials and other circumstances may easily lead to emissions which are toxic or dangerous. This also applies to co-incinerators, though there is less public concern. For this and other reasons, co-incineration and combined heat-power generation by incinerators are the techniques which are being used more and more, and attempts are being made to find new names for the installations, in order to avoid the negative image of "waste incinerators".

8–30

(d)   Volatile organic compounds (VOCs) from stationary sources

The Commission had planned, in 1993/1994, to submit a proposal for a directive on VOC emissions resulting from refuelling operations at service stations. Since it was not able to submit such a proposal, seven Member States—most of them with a more active environmental policy—adopted national measures.[113] In 1999, the Council adopted Directive 1999/13 on emissions of VOCs from solvent-using industries,[114] which was a follow-up to Directive 94/63.[115] In 2010, the Directive was integrated in the new Directive on industrial emissions.

8–31

As in Directive 1999/13, Directive 2010/75 referred to installations and activities using organic solvents; thus, for instance, coating processes, coil coating, dry cleaning, printing, surface cleaning, manufacturing of pharmaceutical products, fat extraction, rubber conversion, or wood and plastic lamination are covered. For the different activities, thresholds and emission limit values were set, based on the solvent consumption, the emission limit (mg of organic carbon per cubic metre) and the diffuse/total emission limit, expressed as a percentage of solvents input (annex VII, part 2). For vehicle coating installations, no emission limit values were fixed; instead, a formula was to be used by such installations (annex VII, pt 3).

Instead of applying the emission limit values fixed by the Directive, an installation could also recur to a "reduction scheme specially designed for his installation", provided that comparable results were achieved (annex VII, pt 5). When an individual operator was able to demonstrate that the respect of the emission limit values was not "technically and economically feasible", Member

---

[113] Denmark, Germany, Italy, Luxembourg, the Netherlands, Austria and Sweden.
[114] Directive 1999/13 on the limitation of emissions of volatile organic compounds due to the use of organic solvents in certain activities and installations [1999] OJ L85/1; proposal [1997] OJ C99/32.
[115] Directive 94/63 [1994] OJ L365/24. See, para.8–21, above; as mentioned, that Directive also partly covered stationary sources.

States were entitled to grant a derogation from the limit values, "provided that significant risks to human health or the environment are not to be expected" and the operator could demonstrate that he applied the best available technique.[116]

5. NOISE AND ELECTROMAGNETIC WAVES

(a) General aspects

8–32   Data on noise levels within the European Union are limited and fragmented. The Commission estimated in 1996 that almost 80 million people in the European Union "suffer from noise levels that scientists and health experts consider to be unacceptable" (above 65dB(A)) and that an additional 170 million citizens are living in areas where the noise levels are such as to cause serious annoyance during the daytime (55–65dB(A)).[117] The European Environment Agency estimated for the year 2000 that about 50 million people were exposed to traffic noise levels above 65 Ldn dB[118] and some 120 million to traffic noise level above 55 Ldn dB. Traffic noise is the main source of outdoor noise, followed by neighbourhood and aircraft noise.[119] In 2014, the Agency indicated that the number of people exposed to more than 55 Ldn dB was 125 million; it mentioned 10,000 premature deaths due to noise and reported on other damaging factors of noise.[120]

An EU strategy to reduce noise levels within the European Union was announced about 30 years ago, in the context of the different environmental action programmes.[121] In 1996, the Commission published a Green Paper, "Future noise policy", where it identified noise as one of the principal local environmental problems.[122]

In the follow-up to that Green Paper, the European Union adopted in 2002 a Directive on environmental noise.[123] The Directive was based on art.192 TFEU and became effective in mid-2004. It intended to avoid, prevent or reduce environmental noise; such noise was defined as:

> "unwanted or harmful outdoor sound created by human activities, including noise emitted by means of transport, road traffic, rail traffic, air traffic and from sites of industrial activity ..." (art.3(a)).

---

[116] Directive 2010/75 [2010] OJ L334/17, art.59(2).
[117] Commission, Green Paper on future noise policy, COM(96) 540, pp.1a and 3.
[118] Ldn, a day-night level, is a descriptor of noise level based on the energy equivalent noise levels (Leq) over the whole day with a penalty of 10 dB(A) for night-time noise (22.00–07.00 hours).
[119] European Environment Agency, TERM 2000, *Are We Moving in the Right Direction?* (Copenhagen, 2000), p.32.
[120] European Environment Agency, Noise in Europe 2014, EEA Report 10/2014 (Copenhagen, 2014). See also the data assembled in Commission COM(2011) 321.
[121] See 2nd Environmental Action Programme [1977] OJ C139/1, Pts 67 et seq.; 4th Environmental Action Programme [1987] OJ C328/5, Pt 4.5.
[122] Commission, COM(96) 540; see also European Parliament Resolution of 10 June 1997 [1997] OJ C200/ 28.
[123] Directive 2002/49 relating to the assessment and management of environmental noise [2002] OJ L189/12.

The Directive applied to environmental noise to which humans are exposed, in particular in built-up areas, public parks or other quiet areas in agglomerations, in the open country, near schools, hospitals or other noise-sensitive buildings and areas. Noise which is caused by the exposed person himself, noise from domestic activities, created by neighbours, at the workplace or inside means of transport or in military areas was not covered.

8–33

Before 2007 Member States had to draw up strategic noise maps,[124] showing the noise situation in the preceding calendar year. These maps had to be made available to the Commission and the public and be updated at least every five years. They referred to:

- agglomerations with more than 250,000 inhabitants;
- major roads which have more than six million passages per year;
- major railways which have more than 60,000 train passages per year;
- major civil airports which have more than 50,000 take-offs or landing per year.

By 2008, Member States had then to draw up, make publicly available and regularly update action plans to manage noise issues, if necessary. The measures taken were at the discretion of Member States (art.8(1)). By 2012 the maps and plans must also cover agglomerations with more than 100,000 inhabitants, roads with 3 million passages and railways with more than 30,000 passages.

The Directive provided for extensive reporting to and by the Commission,[125] for technical provisions concerning the measuring and assessing of noise, for minimum requirements for strategic noise planning and action plans as well as for the data which are to be sent to the Commission. However, the Commission did not and does not seriously monitor the operation of Directive 2002/49, by publishing, for example, the noise levels found, comparing the action plans, share best practices, and push for measures that reduce the noise levels.[126] According to art.11, the Commission should have reported, by July 2009, on the implementation of Directive 2002/49. This report finally appeared in June 2011.[127] It identified a considerable amount of shortcomings in implementation, which were also due to vague and unclear formulations in the Directive. The Commission saw, however, no reason to propose an amendment of the Directive or take actions against Member States, but reflected on guidance documents.

8–34

EU measures to reduce noise levels until now concerned noise emissions of certain products. The main objective of these directives consists in assuring their free circulation within the European Union and to make sure that this circulation

---

[124] Directive 2002/49 [2002] OJ L189/12, art.3: a strategic noise map is a map designed for the global assessment of noise exposure in a given area due to different noise sources or for overall predictions for such an area.

[125] European Environment Agency, Noise in Europe 2014, EEA Report 10/2014 (Copenhagen, 2014), p.13, reported that only 44% of the reporting obligations had been complied with.

[126] See, e.g. the Report from the European Environment Agency: towards a resource-efficient transport system, TERM 2009, Technical Report 2/2010 (Copenhagen, 2010), where the Agency reported (p.20) that 164 agglomerations were obliged to report on their noise levels; 102 had reported on road noise, 93 on railway noise, 76 on air noise and 94 on industry noise. 82,576 reports were expected on major roads, but only 21,310 were delivered. 12,315 reports should have been made on major railways; 5,310 were delivered. Of 78 airports, 66 reported.

[127] Commission COM(2011) 321.

is not hampered by different noise standard levels at national level. For this reason, the directives set noise emission levels only for those products that are implicated in intra-EU trade; by contrast, Member States may set independent noise standards for products intended exclusively for the domestic market.[128] They may also provide for specific standards for the use of the products in sensitive areas.

All noise levels fixed in the specific directives are based on the work of international standardisation organisations. They fix noise levels for products that are put on the market for the first time, but contain no provisions on noise emissions throughout the lifetime of a product.

(b) Transport

8–35   Motor vehicle noise emissions have been regulated since 1970, when noise emission limit values were introduced.[129] This Directive 70/157 was based on art.115 TFEU. Later amendments were introduced, mainly when technical progress had already led to a practical reduction of noise levels[130]; since 1987, such amendments have been based on art.114 TFEU. The noise limits for cars were gradually made stricter.[131]

In 2014, a new Regulation was adopted which repealed Directive 70/157.[132] It provided for new noise levels which were progressively to be applied from 2016, 2022 and 2026 onwards. For passenger cars, the ordinary levels were 72, 70 and 68 respectively; however, the more powerful a passenger car became, the higher were the permitted noise levels; thus a passenger car with an engine power between 150 and 250kw only had to comply with the levels of 78, 77 and 76dB respectively. The same system was applied for vehicles (N group) used for the carriage of goods: the permitted levels ranged from 72, 71, 69 to 82, 81 and 79dB. In view of the fact that in the affluent societies of Europe more and more consumers buy big passenger cars, there are doubts whether these levels will lead to an overall decrease of noise from cars.[133]

For two- and three-wheelers, emission limit values have existed since a Directive of 1978,[134] which was amended several times and provided for a reduction of around 3dB(A). Again, the limit values apply only to new motocycles.

---

[128] As regards noise emissions from cars, this so-called "optional harmonisation approach" was abandoned by Dir.92/97 [1992] OJ L337/1, which introduced the total harmonisation approach: all vehicles which are put into circulation within the European Union must comply with the Directive's requirements.

[129] Directive 70/157 [1970] OJ L42/16.

[130] See, for instance, Dir.77/212 [1977] OJ L66/33, 2nd Recital: "whereas for the protection of the general public from noise nuisance, suitable measures are required to reduce the noise level of motor vehicles; whereas such a reduction has been made possible by the technical progress in motor vehicle construction"; similar observations are made in Dir.81/334 [1981] OJ L131/6, 1st Recital; Dir.84/372 [1984] OJ L196/47, 1st Recital; Dir.84/424 [1984] OJ L238/31, 2nd Recital.

[131] They were fixed at 82dB in 1972, 80dB in 1982, 77dB in 1988/90 and 74dB in 1995/96, see Commission COM(96) 540.

[132] Regulation 540/2014 on the sound level of motor vehicles and of replacement silencing systems [2014] OJ L158/131.

[133] See in this sense already Commission SEC(2011) 1505 in the impact assessment for its Regulation proposal.

[134] Directive 78/1015 [1978] OJ L349/21.

A Directive concerning the admissible noise levels from new tyres was adopted in 2001,[135] but replaced in 2009 by a Regulation.[136] The permitted rolling noise level was fixed between 70 and 75dB (annex II).

8–36

Aircraft noise has, since 1979, been regulated by a number of directives,[137] which were based on art.100 TFEU and which applied, at EU level, to standards set by the International Civil Aviation Organisation (ICAO); the ICAO levels depend on the aircraft weight and number of engines. The EU directives did not fix emission limit values, but referred to the provisions laid down by the ICAO. Directive 92/14 provided for a ban, as of 1995, of civil subsonic airplanes which did not comply with the ICAO "chapter 3" requirements, or with the "chapter 2" requirements, but were not more than 25 years old.[138] A number of airplanes from airline companies from third-world countries were exempted from these provisions, because European airlines had sold these planes to the third world countries prior to 1995. A number of other derogations were also foreseen.

In 1998, the Commission proposed a ban on registration of airplanes which had been modified in order to comply with the "chapter 3" requirements, the so-called "hush-kitted" aircraft.[139] As this requirement hit, in particular, older airplanes that were used in the United States or by US companies, there were excited discussions as to whether this requirement de facto discriminated against the United States. Under the political pressure from that country, which threatened retaliation measures and also argued that some hush-kitted aircraft were less noisy than modern aircraft (Airbus), the Council Regulation that finally adopted the proposal,[140] postponed the entry into effect of the measure so that from April 2002 onwards, hush-kitted aircraft were to be prohibited at EU airports, unless they were operated at EU airports before May 2000.

The terrorist attacks on US cities on 11 September 2001, were used by the United States discreetly to suggest again a withdrawal of Regulation 925/1999. This time, the European Union gave in: in a record time of four months, a new Directive, based on art.100(2) TFEU, was prepared; it was adopted in March 2002 and repealed Regulation 925/1999.[141] In its place, the European Union took over the concept of the United States: noise-induced restriction for airplanes had to be airport-specific and had to be limited to the necessary environmental objective which had to be established for each airport (art.4). Hush-kitted airplanes—which were not named as such, but called "marginally compliant aircraft"—received protection in the form of a phased restriction (art.6), hush-kitted airplanes registered in developing countries (sic!) which had used European airports before, received a derogation for 10 years (art.7). Urban airports—annex I listed them as being Berlin-Tempelhof, Stockholm-Bromma, London City and Belfast City—were allowed to adopt more stringent provisions with regard to hush-kitted airplanes.

8–37

---

[135] Directive 2001/43 [2001] OJ L211/25; legally, this Directive was an amendment to Dir.92/23 [1992] OJ L129/95.

[136] Regulation 661/2009 [2009] OJ L 200/1.

[137] Directive 80/51 [1980] OJ L18/26; Dir.89/629 [1989] OJ L363/27.

[138] Directive 92/14 [1992] OJ L76/21, amended by Dir.98/20 [1998] OJ L107/4.

[139] [1998] OJ C329/98.

[140] Regulation 925/1999 [1999] OJ L115/1.

[141] Directive 2002/30 [2002] OJ L85/40.

Instead of creating uniform conditions for airplane noise within the European Union which would be normal under a uniform ("common") transport policy, this approach imposed the burden on each airport to impose noise restrictions. In view of competition problems—aircraft companies which are confronted with the possibility of such restrictions are likely to threaten to use the next airport, where no such restrictions exist[142]—noise rules for individual airports are not very likely. Measures on noise restrictions are therefore likely to follow the example of night-flight restrictions which also can, in theory, be introduced by each airport, but which are not introduced—for competition reasons.[143]

Quite rightly, therefore, the airplane operators considered the Directive first of all to constitute a "protection against the use of operating restrictions",[144] while the Commission itself was satisfied at "how well the objectives of the directive have been achieved".[145] Nevertheless, in 2011 it suggested a new legislative act which was adopted in 2014 and repealed Directive 2002/30.[146] This new Regulation, based on art.100(2) TFEU, harmonised and strengthened the conditions for the individual airports to introduce operating restrictions for noise reasons. Any such decision had to be preceded by a noise assessment and an assessment of the cost-effectiveness of the measure. Three months before its adoption, it had to be notified to the Commission, to the other Member States and to "interested parties", accompanied by a written report which justified the intended measure (art.8). A restriction decision had to be open to appeal, independent of existing judicial possibilities. The Regulation provided for some exceptions for airplanes from developing countries in order to avoid "undue economic hardship", and let existing restrictions continue.

8–38 This Regulation will make the taking of restriction measures by local authorities, such as night flight restrictions, even more difficult than until now.

An EU White Paper on transport policy of 1992 announced EU measures to fix acceptable noise levels in the vicinity of airports.[147] This announcement remained without any follow-up.

No EU provisions exist for railways. A proposal for a directive, submitted in 1983, was withdrawn by the Commission in 1993. The introduction of high-speed trains in the European Union, also promoted by the rules on trans-European networks (arts 170–172 TFEU) since the Maastricht Treaty of 1993, did not lead to a change in this situation. A Commission report of 2008[148] identified some problems with railway noise, but did not lead to any concrete proposals.

---

[142] See also Written question E-1021/02 (Hortefeux) [2002] OJ C277/E/132; a good example is the case of a DHL company which had its EU headquarters at Zaventem airport (Brussels/Belgium). Planes from overseas landed at night, the freight was charged on other planes and transported to different European countries. Following extended complaints from citizens over too much noise at night, the Belgian authorities negotiated with DHL on noise reduction measures. These negotiations remained unsuccessful and DHL displaced its EU headquarters to Leipzig/Germany—with a loss of some 20,000 jobs in Brussels.

[143] Commission, White Paper on a Community strategy on sustainable mobility COM(92) 494.

[144] Commission, COM(2008) 66, p.8.

[145] Commission, COM(2008) 66, p.3.

[146] Regulation 598/2014 [2014] OJ L173/65.

[147] Commission, White Paper on a Community strategy on sustainable mobility COM(92) 494.

[148] Commission, Rail noise abatement measures addressing the existing fleet COM(2008) 432.

(c) Construction machines

At the end of 2000, the European Union adopted a Directive on the noise levels **8–39**
of outdoor machinery, construction plant, garden equipment and equipment used
for specific vehicles.[149] The Directive which was based on art.114 TFEU,
replaced a number of previous Directives. It applied to new machines and
equipment and intended, first of all, to ensure the free circulation of these
machines within the EU. Member States may not prevent the placing on the
market of machines that comply with the requirements of the Directive, but are of
course free to determine sensitive areas where the equipment may not be used or
where it may be used only during certain hours. For a number of machines and
equipment, noise emission limit-values were fixed (art.12) which vary between
96dB(A) and 109dB(A); new values apply since 2006 which range from 84dB(A)
to 106dB(A).[150] Where an EU noise emission limit value was laid down, this
must be labelled on the machine; where no level was fixed, the machine only has
to be labelled with its noise level (art.13) The Directive also determined
measuring standards. There was no requirement to maintain the noise level for
new machines during the total service life of the machine or for some years at
least.

After the adoption of the Directive, it turned out that some manufacturers had
difficulty in complying with the more stringent values; derogations were
introduced, as "the intention was never to restrict the placing on the market of use
… of equipment solely based on technical feasibility".[151] In other words, the limit
values were not meant to protect the environment.

New household equipment was the subject of another framework Directive,
which left Member States the freedom to fix emission limit values, but fixed a
frame for such requirements.[152] No specific EU measures have subsequently been
taken. Thus, Directive 96/594 was repealed; Member States were allowed to use
the provisions of that Directive, until new measures were taken at EU level. The
energy labels fixed for certain household appliances provided for an indication of
the noise level. Whether this approach will be maintained under the new
Directive 2010/30,[153] is as yet uncertain.

The European Union has not so far fixed quality objectives for noise emissions **8–40**
in sensitive areas such as, for instance, urban centres, residential areas, near
airports, hospitals or schools.

Overall, observation of the noise levels within the European Union is highly
inadequate and the EU measures protecting against excessive noise levels also
seem inadequate. This protection, by fixing quality standards, tends to be left to
Member States. Directive 2002/49 on environmental noise did not, in any way,
significantly change the situation, all the more as there is hardly an attempt to
enforce it.

---

[149] Directive 2000/14 relating to the noise emission in the environment by equipment for use outdoors [2000] OJ L162/1.
[150] Directive 2005/88 [2005] OJ L344/46.
[151] Directive 2005/88 [2005] OJ L344/46, Recital 2.
[152] Directive 86/594 [1986] OJ L344/24.
[153] Directive 2010/30 on the indication by labelling and standard product information of energy and other resources by energy related products [2010] OJ L153/1.

(d)   Electromagnetic waves

8–41   There are no EU provisions on electromagnetic waves from electrical power lines and other sources which are thought, sometimes, to cause problems to the health of people living next to such power lines. The Commission stated that there was no "convincing scientific evidence" of electromagnetic fields causing cancer.[154]

Directive 2011/92 on the environment impact assessment of certain projects requires an environment impact assessment for electrical power lines of more than 15km in length; however, the competent authorities remain free to decide on such projects, whatever the outcome of the assessment.[155]

In 1998, the Commission proposed a Council recommendation, based on art.168 TFEU, on "the limitation of exposure of the general public to electromagnetic fields",[156] where essentially Member States are invited to take action in order to limit exposures to electromagnetic fields. Electrical power lines are not specifically addressed. The Council adopted this recommendation in 1999.[157] Requests by the European Parliament to update this recommendation and to adopt other measures in order to reduce the risk from electromagnetic fields,[158] remained without an echo. The Council and the Commission continue to argue that "there is currently no well-established scientific evidence of a causal relationship"[159] between such waves and human illness.

---

[154] Written Questions E-1387/97 (Baldi) [1997] OJ C373/115; E-4190/97 (Caccavale) [1998] OJ C196/96; E-1788/98 (Sierra Gonzalez et al.) [1999] OJ C50/93.

[155] See generally, paras 4–09 et seq., above.

[156] Commission, COM(1998) 268.

[157] Recommendation 1999/519 [1999] OJ L199/59.

[158] European Parliament, Resolution of 2 April 2009 on health concerns assessed with electromagnetic fields [2010] OJ C137E/38.

[159] Directive 2013/35 on the minimum health and safety requirements regarding the exposure of workers to the risks arising from physical agents (electromagnetic fields) [2013] OJ L179/1, Recital 7.

CHAPTER 9

Climate Change and Ozone Depletion

1. GENERAL REMARKS

Since the Lisbon Treaty came into force on 1 December 2009, climate change issues are mentioned in the Treaties: art.191 TFEU fixes as one of the objectives of EU environment policy "combating climate change". This insertion is not particularly convincing, as climate change policy is a horizontal policy which requires numerous EU policies to re-orient themselves in view of this objective; this refers in particular to energy policy, but also to transport, internal market, commercial, development, agricultural and competition policy. Thus, it would have been wiser to insert the fight against climate change at the beginning of the FEU Treaty, for example in art.11.

Action regarding climate change attempts to reduce anthropogenic interference with the climate in order to prevent a global temperature increase and greenhouse gas concentrations in the atmosphere that are significantly higher than pre-industrialised levels.[1] The appearance of climate change issues as a topic of EU environmental policy is recent. The 4th EU Environment Action Programme, which covered the period 1987–1992,[2] mentioned the "greenhouse effect" of human activities and climate change only marginally[3] and announced that the EU research programme would cover, among others, "climatology and natural hazards, addressing long-term problems, such as potential climate changes due to an increase of the CO_2 concentrations in the atmosphere".[4] In 1989, the Commission submitted a first communication to the Council on climate

---

[1] See the definition of climate change in art.1(2) of the UN Framework Convention on Climate Change of 9 May 1992, signed in New York: "Climate change means a change of climate which is attributed directly or indirectly to human activity that alters the composition of the global atmosphere and which is in addition to natural climate variability observed over comparable time periods."

[2] See 4th Environment Action Programme 1987–1992 [1987] OJ C328/5.

[3] See 4th Environment Action Programme 1987–1992 [1987] OJ C328/5, Pt 2.3.20: "Looking further ahead into the future it is clear that difficult problems could arise from the use of fossil fuels if the build-up of atmospheric carbon dioxide levels and the 'Greenhouse effect' are shown (as certain scientists fear) to have serious impacts on climate and agricultural productivity worldwide. In case further scientific research should confirm the likelihood of such impacts, the Community should already be thinking about possible responses and alternative energy strategies. The Commission will continue its studies in this context."

See also Pt 7.2.3: "Tropical forests ... have a profound influence on climate and on global natural cycles. Because tropical forests benefit people in so many ways, the alarming rate of forest destruction is a matter of grave concern."

[4] See 4th Environment Action Programme 1987–1992 [1987] OJ C328/5, Pt 6.3.

change and its impact.[5] The Council was quick to react: in 1990, it committed itself in a non-binding resolution to stabilise CO_2 emissions by the year 2000 at their 1990 level.[6]

In the 5th Environment Action Programme (1993–2000), climate change issues played a considerably greater role: the programme dedicated a whole section to climate change. It identified carbon dioxide (CO_2), chlorofluorocarbon (CFCs) nitrous oxide (N_2O) and methane (CH_4) as the main agents for climate change[7] and tried to fix objectives:

1. "no exceeding of natural absorbing capacity of planet earth";
2. "no emissions of ozone layer depleting substances"—and targets up to the year 2000 and announced a number of actions to be undertaken.

9–02   In 1994 the European Union adhered to the UN Climate Change Convention[8] and has since pursued an active policy to address the issues of climate change.

Climate change is not a subject which is included in the list of policies and activities which are mentioned in arts 3 and 4 TFEU. The legal basis for measures addressing climate change issues is, depending on the nature of the measure, arts 43 (agriculture), 91 or 100 (transport), 113 (taxation), 114 (internal market), 207 (trade), 194 (energy) or 192 (environment) TFEU. In the absence of a specific legal basis in the past, energy-related measures, therefore, were normally based on arts 192 or 352 TFEU. In particular, art.192 TFEU was of increasing importance in the area of energy policy measures. For example, the above-mentioned Decision 94/69 to adhere to the Convention on Climate Change was based on art.130s EC Treaty, the predecessor of the present art.192 TFEU. Furthermore, the Decision to adhere to the Kyoto Protocol[9] and different Decisions on energy saving,[10] and alternative energies,[11] the Decision on a monitoring mechanism of greenhouse gas-emissions[12] and the first Directive on the energy performance of buildings[13] were all based on art.192(1) TFEU. Politically and legally the competence of the European Union to deal with climate change issues and to adopt EU-wide measures was not seriously disputed, it being understood that this competence was shared between the European Union and the Member States. It is to be expected that in future the energy-related measures on energy saving and energy efficiency will be based on art.194 rather than on art.192 TFEU, though the two provisions are not entirely congruent.

---

[5] Commission, The Greenhouse Effect and the Community, COM(89) 656.

[6] (1990) *Bulletin of the European Communities*, October 1990, no.1.3.77.

[7] Commission, Towards Sustainability. A European Community programme of policy and action in relation to the environment and sustainable development [1993] OJ C138/5, Pt 5.1.

[8] Decision 94/69 [1994] OJ L33/11; the Convention itself is published at p.13.

[9] Decision 2002/358 concerning the approval, on behalf of the European Community, of the Kyoto Protocol to the United Nations Framework Convention on Climate Change and the joint fulfilment of commitments thereunder [2002] OJ L130/1.

[10] Decision 91/565 [1991] OJ L307/34; Dec.96/737 [1996] OJ L335/50; Dec.647/2000 [2000] OJ L79/6.

[11] Decision 93/500 [1993] OJ L235/41; Dec.98/352 [1998] OJ L159/53; Dec.646/2000 [2000] OJ L79/1.

[12] Decision 99/296 amending Dec.93/389 [1993] OJ L167/31 (for a monitoring mechanism of Community CO_2 and other greenhouse gases [1999] OJ L117/35).

[13] Directive 2002/91 on the energy performance of buildings [2003] OJ L1/65; in 2010, this Directive was replaced by Dir.2010/31 on the energy performance of buildings [2010] OJ L153/13.

In 1991, the Commission adopted a Communication on measures to combat global warming[14] which suggested, essentially, three types of measures: energy conservation and improved energy technology, monitoring mechanisms for emissions and fiscal measures. These measures were, in later years, prolonged and adapted and, as regards the first group of measures, clarified to include the reduction of greenhouse gas emissions. Several conferences of Heads of State and Governments and environmental and energy Councils dealt with climate change strategies. Following the signature of the Kyoto Protocol in 1997, where finally the obligations of the contracting parties were clarified, the Commission submitted, in 2000, a new draft for an EU strategy.[15] The European Climate Change Programme's (ECCP) objective was to identify and develop all those elements "that are necessary for the implementation of the Kyoto Protocol". This requires a comment on the objectives of a climate change strategy. The Commission stated that it followed a double concept: on the one hand, strengthening the EU policies and measures regarding climate change, on the other hand developing an emission trading scheme within the European Union.

The Council discussed the Communication at several occasions and also adopted several resolutions concerning climate change policies. However, the Council was cautious in assessing in detail the Commission's programme and limited itself instead to request the Commission to submit, as soon as possible, concrete proposals in order to reduce greenhouse gas emissions.[16] The European Parliament regretted that the Communication did not contain a precise action plan with a time plan, but rather a list of potential or desirable activities.[17] The Commission did not see reasons to change its attitude. It realised that the other institutions had not really disapproved its approach and continued its policy, being aware that there was no clear action programme for climate change. The subsequent discussions showed that all discussions continued to concentrate on the Commission's approach.

9–03

The 6th Environment Action Programme, adopted in 2002, stated that EU climate change policy should try to align to the "long term objective of 2°Celsius over pre-industrialised levels and a CO_2 concentration below 550 ppm".[18] In 2007, the European Council declared that global temperature should only rise by maximal 2°Celsius and committed the European Union to reduce its greenhouse gas emissions by at least 20 per cent below 1990 levels by 2020, and by 30 per cent, provided that other developed countries committed themselves to comparable emission reductions and economically more advanced developing

---

[14] Commission, COM(91) 249.

[15] Commission, Communication on EU policies and measures to reduce greenhouse gas emissions: towards a European Climate Change Programme (ECCP), COM(2000) 88.

[16] See in particular Resolution of 8 March 2001 and 8 June 2001.

[17] European Parliament Resolution of 26 October 2000 [2000] OJ C197/397.

[18] Decision 1600/2002 laying down the 6th Community Environment Action Programme [2002] OJ L242/1, art.2(2).

countries contributed adequately according to their responsibilities and respective capacities.[19] This commitment was inserted into a Decision of 2009 which was based on art.192(1) TFEU.[20]

However, at a conference in Copenhagen in December 2009, global negotiations on a follow-up agreement on the Kyoto Protocol failed, and neither industrialised countries nor developing countries made formal commitments as regards the reduction of greenhouse gas emissions for the time after 2012. Subsequently, the EU institutions did not increase the reduction commitment to 30 per cent, but decided to leave it with 20 per cent. No further progress was reached for a new global agreement in subsequent international discussions, though several countries made unilateral promises to reduce their greenhouse gas emissions. At a meeting in Doha (2012) the EU committed itself to reduce its greenhouse gas emissions until 2020 by 20 per cent, compared to 1990. Anticipating an important international meeting in Paris at the end of 2015, the EU adopted the objectives to reduce, by 2030, its greenhouse gas emissions by 40 per cent compared to 1990, to ensure a share of renewable energies in the overall consumption of energy by 27 per cent and to improve its energy efficiency also by 27 per cent.[21]

2.   THE KYOTO PROTOCOL

9–04   The objectives of the Climate Change Convention of the United Nations were[22]:

> "to achieve ... stabilization of greenhouse gas concentrations in the atmosphere at a level that would prevent dangerous anthropogenic interference with the climate system."

The European Union's Decision on the 6th Environment Action Programme[23] repeated this objective and then continued[24]:

> "Thus a long term objective of a maximum global temperature increase of 2°Celsius over pre-industrial levels and a CO_2 concentration below 550 ppm shall guide the Programme. In the longer term this is likely to require a global reduction in emissions of greenhouse gases by 70% as compared to 1990 as identified by the Intergovernmental Panel on Climate Change (IPCC)."

Thus, while it is clear that "dangerous anthropogenic interference" with the climate system is to be avoided, it is not completely clear what is to be done to achieve this goal. Almost all depends on scientific data and assessment. In 1999, the Commission was of the opinion that CO_2 emissions had to fall "by at least

---

[19] European Council, meeting of 8–9 March 2007, President's conclusions, Doc.7224/07 Rev.1 of 2 May 2007.
[20] Decision 406/2009 on the efforts of Member States to reduce their greenhouse gas emissions to meet the Community's greenhouse gas emission reduction commitments up to 2020 [2009] OJ L140/136.
[21] European Council, minutes of the meeting of 23–24 October 2014, document EUCO 169/14.
[22] United Nations Framework Convention on Climate Change of 9 May 1992, art.1.
[23] Decision 1600/2002 [2002] OJ L242/1.
[24] Decision 1600/2002 [2002] OJ L242/1, art.2(2).

35% by 2010, if long-term temperature increases are to be limited to 1.58 by 2100".[25] Fourteen months later, it was of the opinion that:

> "a global reduction of 20–40% (depending on actual rates of economic growth and thus greenhouse gas emissions as well as the success of measures taken to combat climate change) over 1990–2020 will need to be aimed at"

and that "global emissions of greenhouse gases need to be reduced by approximately 70% over 1990 levels in the longer term".[26] As mentioned, the Council cautiously took up the second figure only.

The implementation of the Kyoto Protocol is seen, under this perspective, as an objective for the shorter term. In 1997, this Kyoto Protocol, a protocol under the Climate Change Convention, was concluded.[27] It covered six greenhouse gases, carbon dioxide (CO_2), methane (CH_4), nitrous oxide (N_2O), hydrofluoro-carbons (HFCs), perfluorocarbons (PFCs) and sulphur hexafluoride (SF_6). The Contracting Parties listed in an annex to the Protocol—all industrialised countries—committed themselves to reduce the emissions of these six gases[28] "in the commitment period 2008 to 2012" (art.3(1)), compared with 1990, to a percentage that was laid down in an annex. For the European Union which was expressly mentioned in the annex, and its—by then—15 Member States, this figure was fixed at 92 per cent so that the European Union had to reach a reduction of greenhouse gases by 8 per cent. As the European Union decided to approve of the Kyoto Protocol and adopted Decision 2002/358 in this regard; there was thus a legal obligation to reduce greenhouse gas emissions within the European Commission by 8 per cent by 2012 at the latest.

However, the Kyoto Protocol contained another provision. According to its art.25, it entered into force once 55 Parties to the Climate Change Convention "incorporating Parties included in Annex I which accounted in total for at least 55 percent of the total carbon dioxide emissions for 1990 of the Parties included in Annex I" had agreed to it. The United States signed the Protocol under the Clinton administration, but recalled this signature under the Bush administration and declared that they would not ratify the Protocol. As the United States was the biggest generator of greenhouse gas emissions worldwide, the complicated calculation method under the Protocol led to the necessity that most of the other industrialised countries that are listed in annex I had to adhere to the Protocol, before this could enter into effect. This led to a lot of horse-trading, in particular also with Japan and Russia. Finally, Russia adhered to the Protocol at the end of 2004, so that it entered into effect on 16 February 2005, more than seven years after its adoption.

9–05

---

[25] Commission, Europe's environment: what directions for the future? The global assessment of the European Community action programme of policy and action in relation to the environment and sustainable development COM(1999) 543, Pt 3.1.

[26] Commission, Communication on the sixth environmental action programme of the European Community—Environment 2010: our future, our choice, COM(2001) 31, Pt 3.2.

[27] The Protocol is published at [2002] OJ L130/4.

[28] The different gases have a different global warming potential (GWP). This potential is calculated on the basis of CO_2, the most spread greenhouse gas. The global warming potential for CO_2 is 1, for methane 24.5, for nitrous oxide 320, for HFC between 97 and 12.000, for PFC 5.700 to 11.900 and for SF6 22.200, see Reg.842/2006 [2006] OJ L161/1, annex I. There are some scientific uncertainties on these figures.

The European Union's strategy, prior to 2005, consisted of deploying enough international activity in order to make the Kyoto Protocol become effective. Worldwide, there did not appear to be other countries to be prepared to play a leading role in the attempt to promote the Kyoto Protocol, except the UN Secretariat; the role of that Secretariat is, however, hardly able to take on such a function, as it lacks the most elementary financial and human resources to do so. Similarly, the European Union is hardly equipped to be the driving force for the promotion of the Kyoto Protocol either. In its external relations with other countries, trade questions are largely predominant. Its climate change department lacks the human resources to play an active role worldwide. And many questions to make the Kyoto Protocol operational—measuring methods, frequencies and stations, legislative and administrative infrastructural measures, identifying sources, introducing technologies, etc—required a considerable know-how on technical and scientific details as well as financial means to ensure smooth transition periods, allow the taking into consideration of local specificities or sectoral problems and the approval of policy-makers, parliaments and public opinions in the different countries. The few persons working on climate change issues within the Commission's climate change department were hardly able to assume such work for the whole of the European Union, though they had very great human, financial and administrative support from EU Member States; they were not equipped to be in the driving seat worldwide, all the more as—mainly due to the "mixed agreement" character of the Climate Change Convention and the Kyoto Protocol—Member States appeared, at the international level, autonomously, but do not rally behind the EU institutions or the Commission to speak and act with one voice internationally.[29]

9–06   Within the European Union, the Commission tried, prior to the negotiations which led to the 1997 signing of the Kyoto Protocol, and in particular after that signature, to reach an EU consensus on the strategy to follow.[30] This was only in part successful, as Member States did not wish to see a complete and coherent EU climate change policy. Therefore, Member States agreed among themselves—without a corresponding Commission proposal—how they would organise themselves with regard to the commitment under the Kyoto Protocol. Based on existing emissions, economic development and technical possibilities, they politically agreed to a burden-sharing, which allowed some Member States to increase their greenhouse gas emissions while others had to reduce them. This burden-sharing was, in 2002, made legally binding[31] and provided for the following percentages which were to be respected by 2012 (1990=100):

Belgium	92.5	Luxembourg	72
Denmark	79	Netherlands	94

---

[29] A confirmation of this point might be seen in the fact that for the global climate change negotiations in Copenhagen, December 2009, the EU Commission did not even ask for a negotiation mandate, which had the consequence that the United Kingdom, France, Germany and the other EU Member States all spoke for themselves and the EU as an organisation did not play any significant role during the negotiations. This situation also existed in subsequent international meetings.

[30] Commission, Climate Change—towards a European Union post-Kyoto strategy, COM(98) 353; see also the preceding Commission communication—Climate Change—the EU approach for Kyoto, COM(97) 481.

[31] See Dec.2002/358 [2002] OJ L130/1, annex II.

Germany	79	Austria	87
Greece	125	Portugal	127
Spain	115	Finland	100
France	100	Sweden	104
Ireland	113	UK	87.5
Italy	93.5		

Decision 2002/358 was based on art.192(1) TFEU. A number of Member States had favoured the use of art.192(2) TFEU which would have provided for unanimity; the reason was not that they opposed the Decision, but that they wanted to keep a veto right for future decisions on climate change. However, as the Commission had threatened to have the question of the correct legal basis clarified by the Court of Justice, and there was a strong political interest for the European Union to show at the Johannesburg World Summit which took place in September 2002, that it had complied with its commitments under the Kyoto Protocol and was able to take the global lead in climate change matters, art.192(1) was finally accepted as the appropriate legal basis.

In 2009, a new burden sharing was agreed, for the period 2013–2020 and for the 27 Member States.[32] The Decision was again based on art.192(1) TFEU. The Decision requested each Member State to reduce its greenhouse gas emissions in a linear manner by a percentage fixed in an annex, but put as the reference year no longer 1990, but 2005. Where the annual emissions exceeded the required emissions, corrective measures should apply (art.7) which consisted in increased reduction quantities for the following year, multiplied by an abatement factor of 1.08, the requirement to develop a corrective action plan and the temporary suspension of the possibility to transfer part of the emission allocations to another Member State. In contrast, the Decision neither mentioned what would happen when a Member State was continuously in delay with reducing its emissions, nor what would happen if a Member State did not reach the required reduction by 2020. In both cases, the only consequence would be an infringement procedure under art.258 TFEU which is, though, not very effective legally and hardly imaginable politically.

The Decision concerned emissions from fuel combustion, fugitive missions from fuels, industrial processes, solvent and other product use, agriculture and waste, but excluded emissions from installations that were covered by Directive 2003/87 on emission trading (art.1 and annex 1).[33] Whether the 2005 emission data for these different sectors are really known, is very questionable.

9–07

The reduction quota were fixed, according to Recitals 8 and 9, on the principle of solidarity between Member States, the objective to reach a fair distribution between the Member States and the gross domestic product of each Member State. However, the use of the year 2005 as a baseline was arbitrary. This Decision favoured those countries which deployed less efforts between 1990 and 2005 to reduce their emissions, such as Spain, Portugal, Ireland, Italy or Greece, as is shown by the following table:

---

[32] See Dec.406/2009 [2009] OJ L140/136.
[33] Directive 2003/87 establishing a scheme for greenhouse gas emission allowance trading within the Community [2003] OJ L275/32.

Table: Member States emissions since 1990 and reductions/increases by 2020[34]:

Member State	Quantities emitted in 1990 in Tg[35]	Quantities emitted in 2005 in Tg	Quantities to be emitted in 2020 in Tg	Reduction/ increase quantities according to Dec.406/2009 (%)	Reduction/ increase by 2020 compared to 1990 (%)
Belgium	143	142	120.7	−15	−15
Bulgaria	118	71	85.2	+20	−27
Czech R.	195	146	159.1	+9	−24
Denmark	69	63	50.4	−20	−27
Germany	1215	969	833.3	−14	−32
Estonia	42	20	22.2	+11	−47
Ireland	55	70	56.0	−20	+1
Greece	106	132	126.7	−4	+16
Spain	288	441	396.9	−10	+37
France	563	554	479.4	−14	−15
Italy	516	574	499.4	−13	−3
Cyprus	5	10	9.5	−5	+90
Latvia	27	11	12.9	+17	−51
Lithuania	49	23	27.0	+15	−49
Luxembg.	13	13	10.4	−20	−20
Hungary	99	80	88.0	+10	−10
Malta	2	3	3.3	+10	+65
Netherlds	212	212	178.1	−16	−16
Austria	79	93	78.1	−16	−1

[34] For the quantities emitted, the figures were taken which the EU officially sent to the United Nations and which had been approved by all Member States, see European Environment Agency, Annual European Community Greenhouse Gas Inventory Report 1990–2007 and Inventory Report 2009. Technical Report 4/2009, Copenhagen 2009, tables ES 3 and ES 7.
[35] One teragram (Tg) corresponds to one million tonnes.

Poland	459	387	390.9	+1	−15
Portugal	59	89	97.9	+1	+66
Romania	243	149	177.3	+19	−31
Slovenia	19	20	20.8	+4	+10
Slovakia	73	49	55.2	+13	−14
Finland	71	69	58.0	−16	−19
Sweden	72	67	55.6	−17	−24
UK	771	653	548.5	−16	−29
EU-27	5564	5111	4088.8	20	−26

If one compares the quantities in this table with the commitments laid down in Decision 2002/358, quoted above, it becomes evident that the reduction efforts by (the 15 "old") Member States between 1990 and 2005 were rather limited. In 2014, the Commission found that the effective reduction of greenhouse gases in 2012 was 18 per cent (compared to 1990).[36]

The emission picture is completely different when the emissions per capita are considered, an approach which the European Union has not yet taken; globally, though, such an approach will ultimately be the only equitable approach to reach solutions, with transfer rights and other in-built flexibility mechanisms.

9–08

Emission of greenhouse gases per capita (in kg)[37]:

Member State	Emissions 1990 per capita	Emissions 2005 per capita	Emissions 2020 per capita (according to Dec.406/2009)
Belgium	13.690	13.540	11.574
Bulgaria	15.204	9.148	10.977
Czech R.	19.079	14.285	15.570
Denmark	12.751	11.642	9.310
Germany	14.727	11.745	10.101
Estonia	31.169	14.842	16.470

---

[36] Commission COM(2014) 15.

[37] Own calculation. The data from the previous table were taken and divided by the population of each Member State. The population figures stem from Eurostat, "Total population in 2005", http://epp.eurostat.ec.europa.eu/cache/ITY_OFFPUB/CH_02_2010/EN/CH_02_2010-EN.PDF [Accessed 30 September 2010]. The population of 2005 was also used for 1990 and 2020.

Ireland	13.385	17.035	13.628
Greece	9.564	11.910	11.369
Spain	6.674	10.247	9.222
France	8.969	8.825	7.637
Italy	8.826	9.818	8.541
Cyprus	6.674	13.348	12.680
Latvia	11.706	4.749	5.580
Lithu-ania	14.305	6.715	7.867
Lux-embg.	28.186	28.186	22.548
Hun-gary	9.804	7.922	8.714
Malta	4.967	7.450	8.195
Nether-lds	13.001	13.001	10.921
Austria	9.633	9.633	9.525
Poland	12.024	10.138	10.239
Portugal	5.603	8.453	9.297
Roma-nia	11.220	6.880	8.186
Slove-nia	9.511	10.012	10.411
Slova-kia	13.557	9.100	10.245
Finland	13.558	13.176	11.068
Sweden	7.990	7.435	6.171
UK	13.383	13.092	10.473
EU-27	11.328	10.406	8.324

Luxembourg, Estonia and the Czech Republic were predicted to be, in 2020, the biggest emittors, Latvia, Sweden, and France the countries with the lowest per capita emission.

It appears that the EU as a whole complied with its commitment under the Kyoto Protocol: while the EU indicates a figure (for EU-28 of −19.8 per cent in 2012, compared to 1990, the European Environment Agency indicates a reduction, for EU-15 of −11.8%.[38]

In 2012, an international Agreement was signed in Doha, according to which some industrialised countries made commitments to further reduce their greenhouse gas emissions until 2020. The European Union accepted a reduction of 20 per cent, compared to 1990 (base-year) levels. It signed the Agreement in early 2015.[39]

9–09

3.   EMISSION TRADING WITH GREENHOUSE GASES

In March 2000, the Commission adopted a Green Paper on greenhouse gas emissions trading[40] which was followed one year later by a proposal for a Directive establishing a scheme for greenhouse gas emission allowance trading within the European Union. Without significant amendments, the proposal was adopted in 2003 as Directive 2003/87.[41] The Directive which, in the beginning, only covered carbon dioxide (CO_2) gases, established a legal framework for an emissions trading scheme which was launched from 2005 onwards. The scheme was limited to installations which were mentioned in an annex I and which concern, essentially, installations covered by Directive 2008/1,[42] i.e. iron and steel furnaces; glass manufacturing installations; oil refineries; coke ovens; smelters and cement kilns; pulp and paper mills of a particular size. Installations which came under Directive 2003/87 had to receive a permit for the emissions of greenhouse gases. Overall, some 45 per cent of all greenhouse gas emissions were covered by the Directive.

9–10

In 2009, the Directive was revised.[43] Flights which arrive at or depart from an EU airport were included and the number of installations covered was increased. For specific types of installations, gases other than CO_2 were also included. The proposal on including airplanes met strong objections from non-EU airlines and their host countries (United States, China, Russia, Japan, Brazil, India, Mexico and others). These countries threatened legal measures and economic sanctions. In view of these objections, the EU retracted. It used the ongoing negotiations within the International Civil Aviation Organisation (ICAO) to suspend the application of its provisions to flights which started from or landed on airports outside the European Economic Area.[44] The suspension was limited until 2016, but it is very likely that it will continue, even if ICAO does not reach an agreement

---

[38] See the references in para.9–24, below.

[39] Decision 2015/146 [2015] OJ L26/1.

[40] Commission, Green Paper on greenhouse gas emissions trading within the European Union, COM(2000) 87.

[41] Directive 2003/87 [2003] OJ L275/32.

[42] Directive 2008/1 on integrated pollution prevention and control [2008] OJ L24/8; this Directive codified the earlier Dir.96/61 [1996] OJ L257/26. In 2010, it was replaced by Dir.2010/75 on industrial emissions [2010] OJ L334/17.

[43] Directive 2009/29 amending Dir.2993/87 so as to improve and extend the greenhouse gas emission allowance trading scheme of the Community, [2009] OJ L140/63.

[44] See Dec.377/2013 [2013] OJ L 113/1, Reg.421/2014 [2014] OJ L129/1.

Applications for the permit had to contain specific information on the installation, in particular the materials the use of which was likely to lead to greenhouse gas emissions, the sources of emissions from the installation and the measures planned to monitor emissions (art.3). Member States were obliged to draw up a national plan which indicated the total quantity of allowances that were intended to be allocated (art.9). These plans had to be published and notified to the Commission. The Commission could reject the plan, if it was incompatible with the Directive. However, it is the Member States which determined the quantity of allocations and the calculation method, not the Commission.[45]

9–11   At least 95 per cent of the allowances for installations had to be attributed free of charge for the period 2005 to 2007 (art.10). Each Member State had to decide on the total quantity of allowances it would allocate for the first three-year period of the national plan (2005–2007), and then for subsequent plan periods. The amendment of 2009 provided that the allowance would have to be, as of 2013, auctioned and no longer be issued free of cost, as the free allocation had, in the past, led to rather generous attributions of allowances by some Member States. The auctioning is likely to increase the price of allowances which might make it more interesting to invest in cleaner technologies rather than buy emission allowances.

Allowances are transferable between persons within the European Union without restrictions. Every year, the operator of an installation must surrender a number of allowances that is equal to the total emissions from that installation; these allowances will then be cancelled (art.12). The Directive also provided for sanctions in cases where the operators of installations did not correctly report on emissions or emitted more gases than allowed (arts 15 and 16). The 2009 amendment of the Directive provided that the total quantity of emission allowances be reduced, as of 2013, by 1.74 per cent per year, in order to reduce the excessive amount of emission allowances which led to too low prices for them. As this reduction appeared still to be insufficient, the Commission proposed in 2014 to take from the market 12 per cent of the allowances which had been on the market two years ago and to place them into a stability reserve.[46] By mid-2015, no decision had yet been taken on that proposal.

As Directive 96/61 required installations to conform, as regards emissions, to the best available technology, and as the purchase of pollution emission allowances would enable an installation to emit more pollutants than admissible under the "best available technology", Directive 2008/1 was amended (art.26). This amendment leads to the result that an installation which purchased emission allowances would no longer be obliged to comply with the best available techniques, as regards greenhouse gas emissions.

9–12   The proposal for a directive had raised considerable concern: the legal competence of the European Union to legislate in this area and the political opportunity to introduce the proposal were questioned. This criticism overlooked that the Kyoto Protocol had, at the request of the United States, introduced the possibility for international emission trading. While no contracting party was

---

[45] See General Court, *Poland v Commission* (T-183/07) [2009] E.C.R. II-3395; the appeal was rejected (C-504/09P), ECLI:EU:C:2012:178; *Estonia v Commission* (T-263/07) [2009] E.C.R. II-3463; the appeal was rejected (C-505/09P) ECLI:EU:C:2012:179.

[46] Commission COM(2014) 20.

obliged, under the Protocol, to participate in such a system, it was thus clear that a global emission trading scheme could be introduced at international level. Then it is difficult to imagine that the European Union should not be entitled to set up such a system of its own.

The Kyoto Protocol had not only introduced the emission trading system, but also provided for two other instruments, the Joint Implementation and the Clean Development Mechanism. Both these instruments concern specific projects. Joint implementation projects may be undertaken in developed countries or in countries with economies in transition. For a specific project, two countries may agree to a joint emission target. Special mechanisms ensure that the joint implementation does not lead to a double counting of the emission reductions. This method allowed an investment, e.g. by Denmark, in a clean technology project in Russia or in Ukraine, which would be capable of being realised with less investment costs than in Denmark. Care will have to be taken to avoid double counting of the reduction.

The Clean Development Mechanism is permitted in developing countries which were not subjected to targeted reductions of emissions under the Kyoto Protocol. It also concerned specific projects. An investment by a developed country in a developing country would be counted for the emissions in the developed country. In this way, an investment in a developing country could be realised at a lower cost than in the developed country, and would give the developing country the advantage of modern, clean investment, while the developed country would incur less cost than it would have with an investment at home. At the same time, the global quantities of greenhouse gases would be reduced.

In 2004, the European Union adopted Directive 2004/101 which amended   9–13
Directive 2003/87 and established "a scheme for greenhouse gas emission allowance trading within the Community, in respect of the Kyoto Protocol's project mechanisms".[47] This Directive, based on art.192(1) TFEU, enabled operators in the European Union to use the mechanisms of joint implementation and clean development mechanisms. The Commission had proposed that a maximum level of 6 per cent of the total emission allowances which had been issued could be used for Joint Implementation investments[48]; however, the Council did not accept this limitation, in order to avoid too heavy a burden for the installations.

These Joint Implementation and Clean Development Mechanisms may not concern nuclear installations, land use and land use change and forestry; these restrictions were already found in the Kyoto-Protocol. The Commission had originally also considered exempting installations for the production of hydro-electric power, but had abandoned this idea in view of the strong resistance from interested groups.

The Directive tried to strike a balance between environmental and economic considerations. Indeed, it might be tempting for Member States to fulfil their obligations to reduce greenhouse gas emissions by ensuring non-expensive investments in other countries or in technologies that have, in turn, considerable environmental disadvantages.

---

[47] Directive 2004/101 [2004] OJ L338/18.
[48] Commission proposal for a directive, COM(2003) 403, new art.11(a)(2).

9–14   Directives 2003/87 and 2004/101 concentrated the attention on the economic instruments in the area of climate change. However, it needs to be underlined that the two Directives do not as such lead to a reduction of greenhouse gases; they only allow cost-effective investments. There is still a dispute whether the two Directives which require high administrative costs for calculation, registration, transparency, reporting obligations, etc were actually successful in reducing the emissions.[49] It has to be admitted, though, that they constituted a way to obtain the political consensus of Member States in Council, to jointly commit to the reduction of greenhouse gas emissions. It is more than doubtful whether an obligation to reduce CO_2-emissions in the more classical way—emission limit values, bans etc—would have been able to overcome the objections from political and economic operators.

4.   ENERGY EFFICIENCY

9–15   In order to promote better energy conservation and use, the European Union adopted Directive 93/76 which was based on arts 175 and 308 EC (now arts 192 and 352 TFEU) and had as its objective to improve energy efficiency in housing, cars and industrial installations and to promote public investment schemes.[50] It requested Member States to draw up and implement programmes for: the energy efficiency of buildings; the billing of heating; air-conditioning and hot water costs on the basis of annual consumption; thermal insulation of new buildings; and regular inspections of boilers and energy audits of undertakings with high energy consumption. Details for the drawing-up of such programmes were left entirely to Member States.

Though it was clear from the beginning that the loose drafting of the Directive would not make it very efficient, it took nine years before the Council agreed the next measure, a Directive on the energy performance of buildings.[51] The Directive was based on art.192(1) TFEU and became operational at the beginning of 2006; its effects will only gradually be felt, as not too many new buildings are constructed. Member States had to apply a methodology of calculating the energy performance of buildings, according to criteria laid down in the Directive. Member States had then to set minimum energy performance requirements. New buildings would have to comply with these requirements; existing buildings with a used floor area of over 1,000m² had to upgrade their energy performance, should they undergo major renovation and this was "technically, functionally and economically feasible" (art.5). Where a building was constructed, sold or rented out, an energy performance certificate was to be made available to the interested person. Boilers fired by non-renewable liquid or solid fuel, and older heating installations with boilers had to be inspected at regular intervals, in order to reduce energy consumption and limit CO_2 emissions; inspections also had to be provided for air-conditioning systems.

---

[49] See G. Winter, "The Climate is no Commodity; Taking Stock of the Emissions Trading Scheme" (2010) *Journal of Environmental Law* 1.

[50] Directive 93/76 to limit carbon dioxide emissions by improving energy efficiency (SAVE) [1993] OJ L237/28.

[51] Directive 2002/91 on the energy performance of buildings [2003] OJ L1/65.

In 2010, this Directive was replaced by a new Directive.[52] The new Directive was based on the energy provision of art.194(2) TFEU; in order to overcome the fact that in the energy chapter, a provision which corresponds to art.193 TFEU and allows Member States to maintain or introduce more stringent national measures, the Directive itself contained such a provision (art.1(3)). As Directive 2002/91, the new Directive applied to new and existing buildings which underwent major renovation; though the limitation of 1000m^2 was deleted, the Directive continued not to be applicable to all existing buildings. Furthermore, the Directive introduced a common method for calculating the energy performance of buildings and asked Member States to set minimum requirements for the energy performance of buildings and building elements (such as apartments). These measures were also to include products and appliances—heating, air-conditioning, hot water generation, lighting, etc which were installed in buildings; for these, technical requirements were to be laid down by Member States.

By 2020, all new buildings and by 2018 all new buildings occupied and owned by public authorities will have to be nearly zero-energy buildings; a nearly zero-energy building was defined as a building that has a very high energy performance, as determined in accordance with annex I to the Directive. The nearly zero or very low amount of energy required should be covered to a very significant extent by energy from renewable sources, including energy from renewable sources produced on-site or nearby.[53] Member States were asked to draw up national plans to increase the number of nearly zero-energy buildings.

9–16

A system of certification of the energy performance of buildings was to be elaborated by Member States which had to include the energy performance and reference values, in order to allow a comparison of the certificates. The energy performance certificate is to be handed over to a buyer or tenant of a building or building unit. Heating systems, boilers and air-conditioning systems in buildings were to be regularly inspected.

In 2012, the EU adopted a general directive on energy efficiency, based on art.194(2) TFEU.[54] The Directive explicitly allowed Member States to adopt more stringent measures. It fixed an overall (non-binding) objective of saving, by 2020, 20 per cent of the Union's primary energy consumption, "compared to projections".[55] Member States were asked to fix an indicative national energy efficiency target, taking into account the EU energy and climate change policy and other measures at EU or national level to promote energy efficiency.

Furthermore, the Member States were requested to:

9–17

- establish a long-term strategy for mobilising investment in the renovation of the national stock of residential and commercial public or private buildings (art.4); this requirement was due to the fact that some 42 per cent of the energy consumption in the European Union was done in buildings;
- make an inventory of central government building (art.5(5));

---

[52] Directive 2010/31 on the energy performance of buildings [2010] OJ L153, p.13.
[53] Directive 2010/31, art. 2 no.2. Annex I specifies how the energy performance shall be calculated.
[54] Directive 2012/27 on energy efficiency [2012] OJ L315/1.
[55] Directive 2012/27 [2012] OJ L315/1, Recital 2.

- ensure that 3 per cent of heated and/or cooled buildings owned and occupied by central government is renovated each year to meet minimum energy performance standards (art.5);
- ensure that central governments purchase only products with a high energy-efficiency performance (art.6),
- set up an energy-efficiency obligation scheme which ensures that energy distributors and/or retailers reach "a cumulative end-use energy savings target"—to be fixed by the Member State on the basis of some provisions in the Directive (art.7);
- ensure the availability of independent energy audits (art.8); small and medium-sized enterprises (SME) and private households were to be persuaded of the benefits of such audits; for non-SME companies, the energy audit was compulsory (art.8(4));
- ensure that final consumers for electricity, natural gas, district heating, district cooling and domestic hot water are provided with individual meters that accurately reflect the actual energy consumption (art.9); this requirement is, however, nuanced by the proviso that the obligation exists "in so far as it is technically possible, financially reasonable and proportionate", which transforms the requirement de facto into a recommendation;
- assess the potential of cogeneration and efficient district heating and cooling (art.14)—in the hope that Member States will then take the appropriate measures;
- ensure that energy regulators pay sufficient attention to energy efficiency issues (art.15).

Member States were encouraged to set up an Energy Efficiency National Fund to support national energy efficiency initiatives (art.20).

The Directive established a good framework for those Member States that have the political will to promote energy efficiency. Where this is not the case, the enforcement of the Directive will be rather difficult, as most of the provisions mentioned above contain derogations or possibilities to exempt certain activities or other nuances. The reaching of the 20 per cent is thus much more a political wish than a commitment that can be enforced—and measured.

9–18   Since the early 1990s, several EU decisions have aimed at the demonstration and dissemination of cleaner and more efficient energy techniques, or for the promotion of alternative energies. However, the financial means which were made available at EU level were remarkably insufficient.[56]

Since 2006, financial resources were made available, for renewables, energy efficiency and the promotion of energy in transport, within a framework programme "Intelligent Energy—Europe".[57] The amount made available for

---

[56] Decision 91/565 [1993] OJ L307/34 (12 Member States, five years, €35 million); Dec.96/737 [1996] OJ L335/50 (25 countries, five years, €45 million); Dec.647/2000 [2000] OJ L79/6 (26 countries, five years, €66 million); Dec.93/500 [1993] OJ L 235/1 (12 Member States, five years, €40 million); Dec.98/352 [1998] OJ L159/53 (26 countries, two years, €22 million); Dec.646/2000 [2000] OJ L79/1 (26 countries, five years, €77 million).

[57] Decision 1639/2006 establishing a competitiveness and innovation framework programme (2007–2013) [2006] OJ L310/15.

energy was estimated at €724 million. As non-EU states also participate in the programme—overall some 35 states—this amounts to a sum of about €3 million per state and year.

5. RENEWABLE SOURCES OF ENERGY

In 1997, the Commission adopted a White Paper on renewable sources of energy[58] which suggested, among other things, to increase the percentage of renewable energies from 6 to 12 per cent by 2010. This political intention required a whole series of measures, such as price differentiation between conventional and renewable energy sources, labelling, research and development measures and financial assistance. Most of these measures would have to be taken at the level of Member States.

    9–19

As the Council and the European Parliament[59] requested the Commission to make concrete proposals, the Commission submitted, in 2000, a proposal for a Directive on the promotion of electricity from renewable sources of energy, which the Council adopted in 2001.[60] The Directive was based on art.192(1) TFEU and became operational at the end 2003. It provided that Member States should encourage greater consumption of energy from renewable energy sources and fixed, for that purpose, national indicative targets. The Member States had to publish every two years a report on progress to reach these targets, and report whether these national targets are consistent with the

> "global indicative target of 12 per cent of gross national energy consumption by 2010 and in particular with the 22.1 per cent indicative share of electricity produced from renewable energy sources in total Community energy consumption by 2010 (art.3(4))."

Member States were allowed to give financial support to producers of electricity in order to achieve the objectives of the Directive.

Electricity from renewable sources was not required to be labelled. However, a guarantee of origin of electricity had to be issued "in response to a request" (art.5). Member States also had to ensure that operators of transmission and distribution (grid) systems guarantee the transmission and distribution of electricity produced from renewable energy sources (art.7).

In 2003, Directive 2003/30 on the promotion of the use of biofuels for transport was adopted, based on art.175(1) EC Treaty.[61] It concerned liquid or

---

[58] Commission, Energy for the future: renewable sources of energy, Green Paper, COM(96) 576; White Paper, COM(1997) 599).

[59] Council Resolution of 8 June 1998 [1998] OJ C198/1; Resolution of European Parliament [1998] OJ C210/215.

[60] Directive 2001/77 on the promotion of electricity produced from renewable energy sources in the internal electricity market [2001] OJ L283/33.

[61] Directive 2003/30 on the promotion of the use of biofuels or other renewable fuels [2003] OJ 123/42.

gaseous fuels for transport that were produced from biomass.[62] The Directive set an indicative target for Member States which had to reach a 2 per cent share in total sales of petrol and diesel fuels by December 2005, and 5.75 per cent by December 2010; these targets were not reached. Member States were obliged to report annually on total sales of transport fuel and the share of biofuels, as well as on measures taken to boost production of biofuels. The environmental problems of biofuels—extensive land use, use of pesticides and other chemicals, monocultures, problems of biodiversity—were not addressed by the Directive.

9–20   Both Directives 2001/77 and 2003/30 were amended and progressively repealed by a Directive on the promotion of the use of energy from renewable sources which was adopted in 2009.[63] The Directive was based on art.192(1) TFEU, with the exception of arts 17–19 which deal with biofuels and for which art.114 TFEU was fixed as a basis. It set mandatory national targets for the overall share of energy from renewable sources in gross final consumption of energy, and also for the share of energy from renewable sources in transport. Energy from renewable sources was defined as "energy from renewable non-fossil sources, namely wind, solar, aerothermal, geothermal, hydrothermal and ocean energy, hydropower, biomass, landfill gas, sewage treatment plant gas and biogases" (art.2(a)); the definition of biomass was slightly changed with regard to the earlier legislation.[64] The national targets together had to reach "a target of at least a 20% share of energy from renewable sources in the Community's gross final consumption of energy in 2020" (art.3). This target was rather ambitious, as in 2005 only Denmark, Estonia, Latvia, Austria, Portugal, Romania, Slovenia, Finland and Sweden had a part of renewables in the overall consumption of fuels of more than 15 per cent.[65]

Furthermore, "each Member State shall ensure that the share of energy from renewable sources in all forms of transport in 2020 is at least 10% of the final consumption of energy in transport" (art.3(4)). The different targets for Member States as regards gross final consumption of energy were laid down in annex I. The repartition was made, as explained in Recital 15, according to the different points of departure for Member States, their past efforts, their gross domestic product, and fairness and adequacy of the allocation; the final result remained relatively arbitrary.

Member States were obliged to draw up national renewable energy action plans (art.4) which had to contain an annual "indicative trajectory" which had to be followed. Where the trajectory was not respected within two years, an amendment of the action plan was required. Other provisions of the Directive dealt with the calculation of the share of energy from renewables, the cooperation

---

[62] As regards the definition of biomass, see Dir.2001/77 [2001] OJ L283/33, art.2(a): "biomass shall mean the biodegradable fraction of products, waste and residues from agriculture (including vegetal and animal substances), forestry and related industries, as well as the biodegradable fraction of industrial and municipal waste".

[63] Directive 2009/28 on the promotion of the use of energy from renewable sources [2009] OJ L140/16.

[64] "Biomass means the biodegradable fraction of products, waste and residues from biological origin from agriculture (including vegetal and animal substances), forestry and related industries including fisheries and aquaculture, as well as the biodegradable fraction of industrial and municipal waste" (art.2(e)); see also fn.59, above.

[65] See Dir.2009/28, annex I. The share of Germany was 5.8%, Spain 8.7%, France 10.3%, Italy 5.2%, Poland 7.2% and United Kingdom 1.3%.

between Member States and with third countries, access to and operation of the grids, and reporting requirements. The choice of means was left almost entirely to the Member States. The Directive also addressed, in detail, the problems of biofuels and fixed sustainability criteria for their use (arts 17–19), which were, though, rather vague and did not appear to solve the environmental problems which are caused by an extensive use of land for the purpose of biofuels production. The Directive did not provide for any sanctions for the case of non-compliance, leaving this entirely to the—in this regard rather unsatisfactory—procedure under art.258 TFEU.

The Commission report on compliance[66] which reported on data until 2010, indicated that Member States had difficulties in reaching the objectives. This was true, according to the Commission, for wind and biomass energy, whereas the photovoltaic sector developed positively. Also, the use of biofuels in transport would require a supplementary measure in order to reach the 10 per cent target by 2020. About one-third of all biofuels used in the European Union were imported, with Argentina, Indonesia, Brazil and the United States being the biggest exporters. The share of renewables in the overall energy consumption of the European Union was 12.7 per cent in 2010, that in the transport sector 4.7 per cent.

9–21

Member States were allowed and even encouraged to give state aid in order to support renewable energy measures. The Court of Justice held in 2001 that it was possible to restrict such measures to the national production of renewables[67]; it did not see reasons, in 2014, to change its mind, despite the progress in setting up an EU-wide internal energy market.[68]

6.   LIMITING EMISSIONS OF GREENHOUSE GASES

Until now, the Union was very reserved as regards the limitation of the emission of greenhouse gases, or the ban or restriction to use certain gases. In the area of installations, the European Union left, under Directive 2010/75, the decision to limit or prohibit the emission of greenhouse gases to the national permitting authorities. For products, the most important limitations of emissions concerned the car sector. After the failure of the voluntary agreement with the car industry to limit CO_2 emissions—see para.8–17, above—the Union adopted provisions on CO_2 emissions by passenger cars in 2009 which will progressively become

9–22

---

[66] Commission COM(2013) 175 and SWD(2013) 102.
[67] Court of Justice *PreussenElektra* (C-379/98) ECLI:EU:C:2001:160.
[68] Court of Justice, *Aaland Vindkraft* (C-573/12) ECLI:EU:C:2014:2037; *Essent* (joined cases C-204/12 to C-208/12) ECLI:EU:C:2014:2192.

applicable as of 2013,[69] and for light commercial vehicles.[70] No such limits exist, until now, for trucks, though an emission limit for methane was introduced in 2009.[71]

Regulation 517/2014, based on arts 192 TFEU, limited the use of fluorinated greenhouse gases in appliances.[72] It provides a 79 per cent reduction of such gases until 2030. Directive 2006/40, based on art.114 TFEU, progressively prohibited the use of certain greenhouse gases in air-conditioning systems of cars.[73]

In order to get rid of CO_2, the European Union furthermore adopted Directive 2009/31 on the geological storage of CO_2.[74] This Directive which was based on art.192(1) and entered into effect in mid-2011, attempted to set a legal framework in order to allow the underground storage of CO_2, though the technique of such underground storage is not yet certain; with regard to climate change, the Directive itself called it "bridging technology", as it meant to give more time to greenhouse gas emitting installations which could, instead of reducing their emissions, put these emissions underground. Member States were given the freedom to allow or prohibit underground storage of CO_2 in parts of their territory. Each storage site needed a specific permit, for which an environmental impact assessment had to be made. The storage sites have to be inspected regularly; should leaks appear, an action plan has to be put into action which should provide for the necessary steps to stop the leak.

9–23   After the closure of the site, the operator shall normally remain responsible for the necessary post-closure measures for 20 years. Afterwards, the state shall be responsible for the post-closure care. CO_2 which is stored underground shall not be considered waste; however, the CO_2 which is leaking from the storage site has probably to be regarded as waste.

By 2013, all Member States had transposed the Directive into national law. Several Member States made use of the opportunity under art.4 to prohibit altogether (Finland, Luxembourg, Belgium (Brussels Region), Austria, Estonia, Ireland, Latvia, Slovenia and Sweden); or restrict (Czech Republic, Germany) the storage of CO_2.[75] The Commission admitted that carbon capture and storage in the EU had "not yet taken off",[76] the main reason being the high costs for this technique, while the costs for CO_2 emission trading allowances were very low. The Commission indicated that the available space for storing CO_2 within the

---

[69] Regulation 443/2009 setting a performance standard for new passenger cars as part of the Community's integrated approach to reduce CO_2 emissions from light duty vehicles [2009] OJ L140/1.

[70] Regulation 510/2011 setting environmental performance standards for new light commercial vehicles [2011] OJ L145/1.

[71] Regulation 595/2009 on type-approval of motor vehicles and engines with respect to emissions from heavy duty vehicles (Euro VI) an on access to vehicle repair and maintenance information [2009] OJ L188/1.

[72] Regulation 517/2014 on fluorinated greenhouses gases [2014] OJ L150/195; this Regulation replaced Reg.842/2006 [2006] OJ L161/1, which had been based on arts 192 and 114 TFEU.

[73] Directive 2006/40 relating to emissions from air-condition systems in motor vehicles [2006] OJ L161/12. This Directive became effective after the adoption of Commission Reg.706/2007 laying down the requirements for a harmonised test to discover leakages [2007] OJ L161/33.

[74] Directive 2009/31 on the geological storage of carbon dioxide [2009] OJ L140/114.

[75] Commission, Report on the implementation of Directive 2009/31, COM(2014) 99.

[76] Commission, Communication on the future of carbon capture and storage in Europe, COM(2013) 180.

European Union was estimated at about 300 Giga tons (117 Gigatonnes under conservative estimations). As the European Union emitted about 2.2 Gigatonnes of CO_2 per year, the storage room would be sufficient for several decades.

7. MONITORING MECHANISMS; RESULTS

The European Union adopted a Decision to monitor all anthropogenic greenhouse gas emissions and to have Member State reporting on such emissions.[77] The Commission regularly reported under this Decision, evaluating the national programmes to limit greenhouse gas emissions and the progress to reach the targets committed under the Kyoto Protocol and other Union commitments.

9–24

It follows from the latest Report, which covered the period up to 2012,[78] that greenhouse gas emissions within the European Union decreased between 1990 and 2012 by 19.2 per cent for EU-28. The Commission projected that EU-28 will, by 2020, decrease its greenhouse gas emissions by 21.0 per cent, compared to 1990. This achievement was reached despite the growth of the gross domestic product (GDP) by 45 per cent between1990 and 2012.

The official figures, conveyed to the UN Secretariat of the Climate Convention, correspond to the figure of –19.2 per cent between 1990 and 2012; if emissions/removals from land use, land-use change and forestry are included, this figure is –21 per cent. The decreases are for CO_2 16.2 per cent; CH_4 33.8 per cent; NO_2 36.8 per cent; and HFC, PFC and for SF_6 an increase of 58.1 per cent.[79]

The global figures are less positive: the overall global CO_2 emissions between 1990 and 2012 increased from 22.7 billion tonnes to 34.5 billion tonnes, thus by more than 50 per cent.[80]

9–25

8. FISCAL MEASURES

In 1992, the Commission proposed a Directive for a tax on fossil fuels, the tax level to be to 50 per cent of the energy content and to 50 per cent of the carbon content of the energy product; the amount suggested was up to $10 per barrel of

9–26

---

[77] Decision 525/2013 on a mechanism for monitoring and reporting greenhouse gas emissions and for reporting other information at national and Union level related to climate change [2013] OJ L165/13; this Decision replaced Dec.280/2004 [2004] OJ L 49/1.

[78] Commission, Report on progress towards achieving the Kyoto and EU 2020 objectives, COM(2014) 689. See, however, European Environment Agency, Progress Report towards 2008–2012 Kyoto targets in Europe, Technical Report 18/2014 (Copenhagen, 2014), which reported (p.9): "EU-15 total GHG emissions were 11.8% below base-year emissions (on average, during the 2008–2012 period)". The discrepancy between the two figures just clarifies that the monitoring and reporting mechanism remains largely incomprehensible for the general public. The Agency also reported that between 30 and 50% of the reduction may be attributable to the economic crisis in Europe.

[79] United Nations, National greenhouse gas inventory data for the period 1990–2012, document FCCC/SBI/2014/20 of 17 November 2014.

[80] Netherlands Environmental Assessment Agency, Trends in global CO_2 emissions, 2013 Report (The Hague, 2013).

oil.[81] The proposal was based on arts 113 and 192 TFEU and thus needed the unanimity of the Council. The proposal indicated that it would only become applicable if other OECD states also introduced a similar tax or took equivalent measures (art.1(2)). This made the proposal unrealistic, as neither the United States, Japan nor Australia, the countries in question at that time, ever considered introducing an energy tax.

Since the negotiations in the Council showed that it was impossible to reach unanimity—in particular the United Kingdom and Spain were opposed to tax measures being adopted at EU level—the Commission amended its proposal.[82] Under the new proposal, Member States remained free whether or not to introduce, a carbon/energy tax. If they did so, they were to comply with the structural requirements fixed in the proposal. However, this amended proposal did not find approval in the Council and is now to be considered as obsolete.

In 2003, the Council adopted, on the basis of art.113 TFEU, Directive 2003/96 on the taxation of energy products and electricity which introduces minimum tax rates on all energy products,[83] including coal, natural gas and electricity, as well as motor and heating fuels. National tax rates are harmonised in three stages of two years' interval each. Energy intensive industries and agricultural, horticultural and forestry sectors may be exempted from the tax, if they enter into national environmental agreements, participate in emission trading schemes or otherwise contribute to reduce energy consumption. Member States were allowed to introduce reduced tax rates for bio-fuels and electricity which was produced from alternative energies. Where bio-fuels are used for local public passenger transport, the excise duty could be waived altogether.

9–27   In 2005, the Commission made a proposal for a Directive on the taxation of passenger cars according to their CO_2 emissions.[84] This proposal was thought to bridge the gap between the car industry's commitment to reduce the CO_2 emissions of cars to 140g per km by 2008 and the political objective of the Council to reach car emissions of 120g per km by 2010. However, it met with strong objections in Council and, of course, from the car industry. The main reason for the Member States' objection is that Member States do not want to adopt EU-wide taxes and prefer to have this residue of national sovereignty remain in their hands. As at end of 2014 the proposal had still not been adopted, the Commission withdrew it.[85]

9. GENERAL OBSERVATIONS

9–28   Overall, the European Union has initiated a very considerable number of measures in order to reduce emissions from point sources, promote changes in the use of fuels, incite professionals and citizens to change their behaviour or their lifestyle in order to reach the objectives of the Kyoto Protocol. Not all of these measures which also concern measures in the area of agriculture, fisheries,

---

[81] [1992] OJ C314/11.

[82] Commission, COM(95) 172.

[83] Directive 2003/96 restructuring the Community framework for the taxation of energy products and electricity [2003] OJ L283/51.

[84] Commission, proposal for a directive on passenger-related taxes, COM(2005) 261.

[85] [2015] OJ C80/17.

energy, transport, development policy, industrial policy and competition were mentioned here. The European Union did reach the targets of the Kyoto Protocol and reduce its greenhouse gas emissions by 2012 by 8 per cent compared to 1990; also, the further commitment to reduce the greenhouse gas emissions by 20 per cent by 2020, is very likely to be reached. The problem of the EU climate change policy lies first in the fixing and complying with targets for 2020 and 2050 which do not only require, within the European Union, "measures as usual" to reduce emissions, but rather the putting into effect of efficient climate-change policies in the different sectors of energy, transport, agriculture, industry, etc. The present measures give the impression that the attitude of "business as usual" continues in large parts of EU and national policies. The 20 per cent target for 2020 is hardly ambitious, and scientists appear to be more and more in agreement that from the point of view of climate change, it is not sufficiently ambitious. The political concessions which are constantly made for nuclear energy, coal-fired installations, petrol and gas only slow down the necessary reconversion of the EU economy and society to a carbon-free status. Member States which are, at present, heavily dependent on coal—Poland and some other Eastern European countries—quite seriously oppose measures which would lead to its reduced role as an energy source.

The second problem is the global dimension of climate change. No successful global climate change policy can be made without the participation of the United States; this country is too big, too influential and too often imitated by other countries in order to be left aside. And it will not be possible to ask countries such as China or India to reduce their greenhouse gas emissions, without the United States doing the same.

The European Union is not a global power and does not have the weight to lead the world towards a successful climate change policy. Its attempts to influence the climate change negotiations worldwide, were rather harshly brushed aside at the global summit in Copenhagen 2009, by the United States and China, but also by Brazil, Australia, Canada, India and other countries. The inability to speak with one voice, paired with the ambition of the bigger Member States—Germany, United Kingdom, France in particular—to speak for themselves and the lack of a strategy to advance the global discussions were the main reasons for this result. Initiatives such as the making of a new EU Treaty along the model of the Euratom Treaty, but for renewable energies, or a concrete suggestion to conclude an international climate change agreement with the some 80 states of the Cotonou Agreement and test the cooperation between developed and developing countries in this format, remained reflections by academics; no visionary or strategic initiative came from the European Union, though everybody in the European Union knows that the fight against climate change will never be won by measures within the European Union alone.

A new global summit is to take place in Paris at the end of 2015. It is likely to lead to some self-commitments by the majority of States to reduce their greenhouse gas emissions in a more or less distant future (2030, 2025)—without control and without sanctions. The target of not exceeding a 2° increase in temperature is likely to be repeated, but the measures adopted are not likely to match this target. It is thus more likely that temperature increase of three, four or even more degrees by the end of the century will be reached. **9–29**

10.   OZONE DEPLETION

9–30   The depletion of the ozone layer was discovered at the end of the 1970s and was relatively quickly attributed to a number of chlorine and bromine compounds which were of human origin. These substances are mainly used as coolant, aerosol gas, cleaning agents and fire extinguishers.

At the international level, ozone-depleting substances are regulated by the Montreal Protocol on some 200 substances that deplete the ozone layer, which was concluded in 1987 and to which the European Union adhered[86] and which is regularly updated. Regulation 1005/2009 which replaced earlier regulations[87] transposed the provisions of the Protocol into EU law, though it went further than the Protocol. The Regulation was based on art.192 TFEU, though art.114 would have been the more correct legal basis, as the Regulation deals with product-related standards.

The Regulation banned the production, placing on the market and use of CFCs, other fully halogenated CFCs, halons, carbon tetrachlorides, 1,1,1-trichloroethanes, and hydrobromofluorocarbons. The production, placing on the market and use of methyl bromides was progressively phased out by 2004. The production of hydrochlorofluorocarbons (HCFCs) had to be progessively stopped by 2025. From 2008 onwards, the production was limited to 35 per cent of the production of 1997; from 2014 onwards this quantity is 20 per cent, and from 2020 15 per cent of that of 1997 (art.3(3)). The placing on the market or use of such substances is, since 2009, prohibited (art.4 (3.h)). The reason for this long transition period is that a number of producers had developed these substances as a substitute for CFCs and were not prepared to write off their investments; and they found support in this attitude from their national governments. The Regulation limited the use of HCFCs in a number of substances such as aerosols, sprays, cooling systems, air-conditioning, but provided for extensive derogations. Quantities which a producer does not use, may be traded within the contracting parties to the Montreal Protocol.

9–31   The European Union reserved the option of allowing the production of banned or restricted substances for essential use, where no substitutes or recycled substances were available. Detailed rules dealt with the import and export of ozone-depleting substances from and to third countries. The export of such substances to countries which did not adhere to the Montreal Protocol was prohibited, and even of substances other than HCFCs to all countries (art.11). The Commission issues licences for imports of ozone-depleting substances from third countries, where this is still legal; import of such substances from countries which are not party to the Montreal Protocol is forbidden (art.8). Undertakings are obliged to inform the Commission in detail on production, processing, recycling, uses and other data on ozone-depleting substances. The Commission may ask national authorities to make investigations as regards these substances. The Regulation also dealt with the recycling of ozone-depleting substances, the

---

[86] Decision 88/540 (1988) OJ L297/8. The Montreal Protocol was elaborated in the context of the Vienna Convention of 1985 on the protection of the ozone layer. The EU also adhered to the Vienna Convention by Dec.88/540.

[87] Regulation 1005/2009 on substances that deplete the ozone layer [2009] OJ L286/1.

monitoring, Member States' information obligations, controls and sanctions, which must be "effective, proportional and deterrent" (art.21).

Between 2006 and 2012 the production of substances which are covered by the Montreal Protocol in the European Union decreased from some 259 million metric tonnes to 171 million metric tonnes, their import from 185 million to 8.8 million metric tonnes.[88] Though the Montreal Protocol provided for less strict production and trade provisions for developing countries than for industrialised countries, it was considered that the ozone layer may recover around 2050, if the present measures continue to be applied.[89]

---

[88] European Environment Agency, Ozone depleting substances 2012, Technical Report 13/2013 (Copenhagen, 2013).
[89] European Environment Agency, Environment in the European Union at the turn of the century (Copenhagen, 1999), p.99.

CHAPTER 10

Waste

1. WASTE MANAGEMENT POLICY AND LAW

Waste management issues played a role in EU environmental policies from its very beginnings. The Commission's communication of 1972 mentioned the necessity of preventing waste generation and to promote waste recovery.[1] The 1st Environment Action Programme discussed the question of what action on waste management could usefully be tackled at EU level and announced the harmonisation of legislations.[2] The 2nd Action Programme declared that a comprehensive waste management policy was necessary, which should include measures for prevention, reclamation and disposal of waste.[3] The 3rd Action Programme repeated the intentions of the Second Programme in similar form and announced promotional measures for waste prevention and recovery.[4]

10–01

The EU dimension of waste management problems fully came into the open when the incident of the Seveso barrels occurred in 1982. Forty-one barrels containing highly toxic waste, which stemmed from a major industrial accident in Seveso in 1976, were shipped, with the consent of Italian public authorities, but in contradiction to the provisions of Directive 78/319,[5] from Italy, and disappeared. Many EU Member States were afraid that the waste might have secretly been brought to their territory.[6] The European Parliament set up, for the first time, an inquiry committee and, in its final conclusions, criticised the Commission for not having properly exercised its role as guardian of the Treaty and ensured the application of existing EU rules on waste management. It expressly asked for the elaboration of a consistent and coherent EU waste policy.[7]

The 4th Environment Action Programme confirmed the previous policy objectives and underlined, in particular, the importance of promoting clean technologies and recycling of waste; it also announced a specific communication on a waste management strategy.[8]

---

[1] [1972] OJ C52/1, p.12.
[2] 1st Environment Action Programme (1973–1977) [1973] OJ C112/1, Ch.7, s.1.
[3] 2nd Environment Action Programme (1977–1982) [1977] OJ C139/1, paras 174–201.
[4] 3rd Environment Action Programme (1983–1986) [1983] OJ C46/1, para.29.
[5] Directive 78/319 on toxic and dangerous waste [1978] OJ L84/43.
[6] The wastes were later found back on a non-authorised storage site in France, transported to Switzerland and, it was reported, incinerated there.
[7] European Parliament Resolution of 8 June 1983 [1983] OJ C184/50; Resolution of 16 March 1984 [1984] OJ C104/147; Resolution of 11 April 1984 [1984] OJ C127/67. See also Economic and Social Committee [1984] OJ C206/62.
[8] 4th Environment Action Programme (1987–1992) [1987] OJ C328/1, para.5.3.

10–02   This strategy communication was finally made in 1989.[9] It essentially fixed five strategic guidelines:

1. the prevention of waste generation;
2. the promotion of recycling and reuse;
3. the optimisation of final disposal;
4. the transport of waste;
5. remedial action.

In concluding chapters, the Commission stated the objective that "as far as possible waste is disposed of in the nearest suitable centres", but that the situation was "different with waste to be recycled". Furthermore, it confirmed that "waste arising within the Community which cannot be recycled should be treated within the Community where possible and exported only in exceptional circumstances". These statements constituted the basis of the proximity and self-sufficiency principles, which are now laid down in art.16 of waste Directive 2008/98.[10]

The 5th Environment Action Programme referred back to the 1989 strategy[11]; it repeated its guiding principles and announced rather ambitious waste management targets for the year 2000.[12] These targets were made somewhat less ambitious by the 1996 review of the waste management strategy of 1989,[13] which confirmed the hierarchy of principles while stating that, within the recovery principle:

> "where environmentally sound, preference should in general be given to the recovery of material over energy recovery operations. This reflects the greater effect on the prevention of waste produced by material recovery rather than by energy recovery."[14]

10–03   The 6th Environmental Action Programme linked waste management to the sustainable use of natural resources. It proposed a significant reduction in the quantity of waste going to disposal and the volume of hazardous waste that was

---

[9] Commission, A Community strategy for waste management SEC(89) 934.

[10] Directive 2009/98 on waste [2008] OJ L312/3; this Directive had replaced Dir.75/442 [1975] OJ L194/23, amended by Dir.91/156 [1991] OJ L78/32 and codified under the number 2006/12 [2006] OJ 114/9. Article 16 reads: "Member States shall take appropriate measures ... to establish an integrated and adequate network of waste disposal installations and of installations for the recovery of mixed municipal waste collected from private households. This network shall be designed to enable the Community as a whole to become self-sufficient in waste disposal as well as in the recovery of waste ... and to enable Member States to move towards that aim individually ... The network shall enable waste to be disposed of or waste to ... be recovered in one of the nearest appropriate installations ..."

[11] 5th Environment Action Programme [1993] OJ C138/5, para.5.4.

[12] Amongst others, a stabilisation of quantities of waste generated at 300kg per capita and year; a recycling/reuse rate of paper, glass and plastics of at least 50 per cent; markets for recycled materials; reliable EU data on waste generated, collected and disposed; a functioning system of liability for hazardous waste; and an inventory of risks for hazardous waste.

[13] Commission, COM(96) 399.

[14] See also Council Resolution of 24 February 1997 [1997] OJ C76/1; European Parliament Resolution of 14 November 1996 [1996] OJ C362/241; Economic and Social Committee [1997] OJ C89/2; Committee of the Regions [1997] OJ C116/74.

produced (art.8), and suggested the development of quantitative and qualitative reduction targets of all relevant wastes.[15]

The 7th Environmental Action Programme sent out four key objectives to be reached by 2020[16]:

- waste should be considered and treated as a resource; this would "open up new markets, create new jobs, and reduce dependence on imports of raw materials, while having lower impacts on the environment". This objective was repeated and strengthened in a further Commission communication with the title: "Towards a circular economy. A zero waste programme for Europe"[17]; under this strategy, waste would no more be landfilled— "wasted"—but through recycling and recovery re-introduced into the economic circle;
- absolute waste generation and waste generated per capita are in decline;
- landfilling is limited to non-recyclable and non-recoverable waste;
- energy recovery is limited to non-recyclable waste.

Specific actions were not announced in this action programme.

The different policy statements at EU level have, to date, left open three basic policy decisions which very considerably influence waste management policy and legislation at EU level.

Waste policy and product policy. Waste prevention was and continues to be the first and most important objective in EU waste management policy, confirmed by all statements and repeated in the waste framework Directive 2008/98.[18]   10–04

Preventing the generation of waste, however, means that a product policy is followed which is more than a curing of symptoms. While it seems neither desirable nor realistic to suggest that the basis of the consumer society should be changed because of waste considerations, a very useful step would be systematically to reduce the presence of dangerous substances in products, wherever alternatives are available.[19] No such systematic attempts exist at EU level at present.[20] Since waste management is an end-of-the-pipe technique, its conception and implementation must necessarily be influenced by actions or omissions that are taken "upstream". And as long as there is no product policy, the concept of waste prevention remains a sort of wishful thinking.

---

[15] Decision 1600/2002 laying down the 6th Environment Action Programme [2002] OJ L242/1.
[16] Decision 1386/2013 on a General Union Environment Action Programme to 2020 "Living well, within the limits of our planet" [2013] OJ L354/171, paras 39, 40 and 43.
[17] Commission, COM(2014) 398.
[18] See Council Resolution of 24 February 1997 [1997] OJ C76/1, paras 16 and 17: "waste prevention should be first priority for all rational waste policy, in relation to minimising waste production and the hazardous properties of waste; ... efforts made in this respect need to be increased, inter alia, by improving the environmental dimension of technical standards, by reducing the presence of dangerous substances where less dangerous alternatives are available ...." Dir.2008/98 [2008] OJ L312/3, art.4: "The following waste hierarchy shall apply as a priority order in waste prevention and management legislation and policy: (a) prevention; (b) preparing for re-use; (c) recycling; (d) other recovery, e.g. energy recovery; and (e) disposal".
[19] See also para.6–04, above.
[20] See paras 6–01 et seq., above.

Waste as a renewable source of energy. EU declarations since 1996 proclaim that, in principle, material recycling of waste should have priority over waste incineration with energy recovery.[21] This priority was also established in several EU Directives, including, as mentioned, in Directive 2008/98.[22] In practice, however, the European Union frequently takes measures to promote waste incineration (with energy recovery) rather than waste recycling. This manifests itself in several areas: as regards energy policy, waste is considered a source of energy which is sometimes available at a low price and used as a substitute for fossil fuels. An example is Directive 2010/75 which exempts certain installations that burn waste altogether from their field of application, and which provides extensive provisions on co-incineration—which is no more than the incineration of waste in production installations.[23]

10–05 In its policy on renewable sources of energy, the Commission went so far as to consider the incineration of municipal waste as a renewable source of energy.[24] The Council and Parliament were more restricted; they declared "biomass" a source of renewable energies which they defined as follows[25]:

> "the biodegradable fraction of products, waste and residues from biological origin of agriculture (including vegetal and animal substance), forestry and related industries including fisheries and aquaculture as well as the biodegradable fraction of industrial and municipal waste."

As, however, the notion of "biodegradable" is nowhere defined in EU law and as there is not either any obligation to separate biodegradable from non-biodegradable fractions of waste, one might well imagine how precise this definition is in practice and how easy it is to incinerate industrial waste under this formula. Generally, agricultural policy is interested in seeing agricultural waste—called "biomass"—recognised as a renewable source of energy, which allows the granting of tax relief or state aid for the generation of biofuels and at the same time see the considerable quantities of agricultural waste reduced by incineration. Furthermore, EU research policy has a tendency to promote high-technology and large-scale projects such as the incineration of (hazardous) waste rather than the small-scale technology of separation, sorting, material recycling or composting of waste.

The instruments to increase recycling and recovery, are numeric targets. However such targets, are neither enforceable nor enforced. In practice, they

---

[21] See para.10–03, above. See also Council Resolution of 24 February 1997 [1997] OJ C76/1, which is, to say the least, ambiguous: "[The Council] recognises, as regards recovery operations, that the choice of option in any particular case must have regard to environmental and economic effects, but considers that at present, and until scientific and technological progress is made and life-cycle analyses are further developed, reuse and material recovery should be considered preferable where and insofar as they are the best environmental option." See also the waste hierarchy in art.4 of Dir 2008/98, quoted in fn.18, above.

[22] Directive 94/62 on packaging and packaging waste [1994] OJ L365/10; Dir.2008/98 [2008] OJ L312/3, art.4.

[23] Directive 2010/75 on industrial emissions [2010] OJ L334/17.

[24] [2001] OJ C153/81.

[25] Directive 2009/28 on the promotion of the use of energy from renewable sources [2009] OJ L140/1, art.2(e); it is to be noted that Dir.2010/75 [2010] OJ L334/17, art.2 no.31, did not include waste of animal origin in the definition of "biomass".

constitute policy orientations; their achievement depends on the policy which the different Member States develop and pursue.

EU responsibilities and Member States' responsibilities. A consistent EU   **10–06**
waste management policy has also not been developed, because it is not clear to what extent waste management strategies, policies and measures are to be established at EU or at national level. Member States generally prefer to keep responsibility for management options, including questions on investments into cleaner technologies, clean-up and others, at national level, also, because the waste management infrastructure—waste collection and treatment, recycling and recovery installations, the transporting of waste, etc—is set up and monitored by them, not by the European Union.

The Court of Justice decided, in 1992, that waste materials are, in the EU terminology, products, though of a specific nature, to which the present art.34 TFEU applied.[26] This judgment ended a long controversy as to whether waste issues came under the provisions of the free circulation of goods, the freedom to provide services or whether they were not covered by the EU Treaties at all. However, the discussion continued at all levels as to what extent the specific nature of waste justified a limitation of the provisions of arts 34 et seq. TFEU, in other words, to what extent Member States were entitled to set national standards for waste. While EU waste legislation between 1975 and 1987 was based on arts 115 and 352 TFEU,[27] the Commission, since 1987, based all its proposals for waste legislation on art.115 TFEU. Only when the Court of Justice declared, in 1993, that Directive 91/156, which amended Directive 75/442 on waste, was rightly based on art.192 TFEU,[28] did this Treaty provision prevail and did the Commission recur to that article. Subsequently, most waste measures were based on that provision, except two product-related waste Directives.[29] It is obvious, though, that art.192 TFEU leaves Member States with greater discretion for national measures, since art.114 TFEU primarily aims at establishing the internal market which requires uniform rules, while art.192 TFEU primarily aims at protecting the environment; under art.114, national measures are systematically controlled and eventually "authorised", if they comply with the conditions laid down in that article, while art.192 does not contain conditions, etc. This leads, in practice, to measures which are adopted on the basis of art.192 TFEU at a relatively low common denominator, since Member States that wish to see higher provisions adopted can easily be referred to the provision of art.193 TFEU.

To give some examples of political divergence within the European Union: a number of local authorities have set up installations for the incineration or the landfill of waste; this leads to a clear interest to see the waste which was

---

[26] *Commission v Belgium* (C-2/90) [1992] E.C.R. I-4431: "waste has a special characteristic. The accumulation of waste, even before it becomes a health hazard, constitutes a threat to the environment, because of the limited capacity of each region or locality for receiving it."
[27] An exception was Dir.85/339 on liquid beverage containers [1985] OJ L176/18, which was adopted on the basis of art.352 TFEU alone.
[28] *Commission v Council* (C-155/91) [1993] E.C.R. I-939.
[29] Directive 91/157 on batteries [1991] OJ L78/38; Dir.91/157 was replaced, in 2006, by Dir.2006/66 on batteries and accumulators and waste batteries and waste accumulators [2006] OJ L266/1. This Directive was based on arts 114 and 192 TFEU; Dir.94/62 [1994] OJ L365/10.

generated at local level also treated or landfilled in these installations, in order to use the available capacities, but restricts the shipment of waste within the European Union.[30]

10–07   The preference for material recycling over incineration with energy recovery, which was laid down in the EU strategy, was also discussed in Germany and the United Kingdom, but was, in these two Member States, finally not laid down in the relevant political and legal documents. Scandinavian Member States, the Netherlands, France and others, strongly promote the incineration of at least municipal waste.[31] The general scarcity of sites for landfills favours waste incineration, unless a very active waste prevention, reuse and recycling policy is pursued; this again presupposes a product policy, which predominantly comes into the realm of EU policy.[32]

Other uncertain aspects concern the question, whether waste management measures are to be taken at EU or at national level, the treatment and disposal of radioactive waste, the shipment of waste to third countries, the clean-up of contaminated land and old landfills, provisions on liability and monitoring measures. And it is significant that almost all measures which the Commission suggests in order to establish a circular economy[33] are recommendations, suggestions, invitations etc.

2.   WASTE INSTALLATIONS

(a)   Siting

10–08   There are no EU provisions on the location of waste treatment or disposal installations. The Directive on industrial emissions[34] which incorporated an earlier Directive on the incineration of waste[35] is silent on the question of siting. The proposal for a directive on the landfill of waste stipulated that landfills had to be placed at a distance of 0.5km from residential areas, waterways, water bodies, etc in the case of municipal landfills and 2km from residential areas in the case of hazardous landfills.[36] The Directive, adopted in 1999, deleted any precise minimum distance requirement and limited itself to requiring that the landfill does not pose a serious environmental risk.[37] Finally, no specific provisions exist for the location of installations for radioactive waste.

EU restrictions for the location of a waste installation flow from arts 4(4) of Directive 2009/147[38] and 6(2) of Directive 92/43,[39] where such installations could constitute a significant disturbance of the habitats or of the species

---

[30] This was the underlying situation in Court of Justice, *Dusseldorp* (C-203/96) [1998] E.C.R. I-4075.

[31] See, next to the Dutch situation which was described in *Dusseldorp* (C-203/96) [1998] E.C.R. I-4075 the German situation, underlying *Daimler-Chrysler* (C-324/99) [2001] E.C.R. I-9897.

[32] See on the EU product policy, para.6–01, above.

[33] Commission, COM(2014) 398.

[34] Directive 2010/75 [2010] OJ L334/17.

[35] Directive 2010/75 [2010] OJ L334/17.

[36] [1997] OJ C156/19, annex I, para.1(1.1.a).

[37] Directive 1999/31 on landfills [1999] OJ 182/1, annex I, para.1(1.1.a).

[38] Directive 2009/147 on the conservation of wild birds [2010] OJ L286/36.

[39] Directive 92/43 on the conservation of natural habitats and of wild fauna and flora [1992] OJ L206/7.

protected in them. Furthermore, a site may—at least de facto—not be chosen where the operation of the installation would, despite precautionary measures that are eventually taken, lead to a breach of the requirements of art.13 of Directive 2008/98.[40] In extreme cases, the siting of an installation may injure human rights,[41] which the EU institutions and national courts must also safeguard.

Before they are authorised, hazardous waste disposal installations must be the subject of an environmental impact assessment; the same requirement applies to incineration installations for the recovery or the disposal of non-hazardous waste that have a capacity of more than 100 tonnes per day.[42] For other waste installations, Member States must either examine case by case whether an environmental impact is necessary, or fix thresholds beyond which such an assessment is necessary.[43]

(b) The choice of a type of waste installation

The choice of the waste installation—landfill, composting plant, recycling plant, incineration plant with or without energy recovery—is at the complete discretion of Member States. It is true that art.4 of Directive 2008/98 provides for a waste "hierarchy".[44] However, this hierarchy is, legally speaking, a recommendation ("encourage"); indeed, para.2 of art.4 asks Member States to consider, when deciding on a measure, the economic viability and several other aspects. The provision, seen in its general context, does not appear to oblige, for example, the United Kingdom, to abandon its landfills—where about 80 per cent of all waste is presently disposed of—and turn to recovery, recycling or waste prevention measures. This is a policy orientation, but it is unthinkable to bring the United Kingdom to the Court of Justice for not respecting its obligations out of Directive 2008/98, art.4. Indeed, endless legal disputes could take place on the question whether a Member State really has done enough as regards waste prevention. If waste prevention were a legal obligation, the Commission would be obliged, under art.17 TEU, to take legal action against Member States which did not do enough for waste prevention; the same would apply where a Member State favoured landfills over incineration of waste. In reality, such an action has never been taken or even considered by the Commission.

10–09

---

[40] Directive 2008/98 [2008] OJ L312/3, art.13: "Member States shall take the necessary measures to ensure that waste management is carried out without endangering human health, without harming the environment and, in particular: (a) without risk to water, air, soil and plants and animals; (b) without causing a nuisance through noise or odours; and (c) without adversely affecting the countryside or places of special interest."

[41] See European Court on Human Rights, *Lopez Ostra v Spain*, judgment of 9 December 1994 (41/1993/436/515), where an installation had been built at a distance of 12 metres from a private home.

[42] Directive 2011/92 on environmental impact assessment [2012] OJ L26/1. The Court of Justice, *Commission v Italy* (C-486/04) [2006] E.C.R. I-11025, clarified that an environmental impact assessment is also required for waste recovery installations of a specific size.

[43] As regards Dir.2011/92, see also para.4–30, above.

[44] Directive 2008/98 [2008] OJ L312/3, art.4 (fn.18, above).

(c) Permits

10–10 The permitting of waste treatment and disposal plants is, in general, subject to provisions of national legislations. For some[45] installations, Directive 2010/75[46] and its preceding directives required a permit since 1999; the Directives required the permit to provide for the use of the best available technique and the setting of specific conditions and, in particular, emission limit values for pollutants.[47]

While there are no specific provisions on facilities for the treatment, and in particular the incineration, of nuclear waste, specific requirements apply to (non-nuclear) waste incineration installations, which are laid down in Directive 2010/75.[48] The Directive sets emission limits for certain heavy metals and other pollutants, including emissions of dioxins and furans.[49] It also provides for detailed conditions on the operation of the incinerators, such as minimum temperature of the burner and measures for cases of operation disturbance.

Directive 2010/75 replaced earlier Directives on the incineration of municipal waste, because from the point of view of the environment it was considered to be irrelevant whether the dangerous emissions stem from one or the other type of incinerator.

10–11 Directive 2010/75 does not apply to animal waste. Animal waste is regulated under Regulation 1069/2009,[50] as specific provisions had become necessary when the "mad cow disease" broke out in the 1990s.[51] The Regulation, based on the public health provision of art.168(4) TFEU,[52] laid down detailed provisions on the conditions under which animals and material that come under Regulation 1069/2009, may be incinerated. According to Directive 2008/98, products and by-products which come under Regulation 1069/2009 are treated as waste when they are incinerated, co-incinerated, landfilled or which go to a biogas or composting plant;[53] it follows from this, that Directive 2010/75 which applies to waste incinerators,[54] and Directive 1999/31 on landfills[55] apply.

---

[45] Essentially, installations for the recovery or disposal of hazardous waste with a capacity exceeding 10 tonnes per day, municipal waste incinerators with a capacity of more than 3 tonnes per hour, installations for disposal of non-hazardous waste (biological and chemical process) with a capacity of more than 50 tonnes per day, landfills with a capacity of more than 25,000 tonnes or receiving more than 10 tonnes per day.
[46] Directive 96/61 [1996] OJ L257/26. In 2008, this Directive was replaced by Dir.2008/1 [2008] OJ L24/8, and in 2010, its provisions were incorporated into Dir.2010/75 [2010] OJ L334/17. See also para.4–40, above.
[47] Directive 96/61 became applicable to existing installations from 2007 onwards. See also para.4–44, above.
[48] Directive 2010/75 [2010] OJ L334/17.
[49] See in more detail, paras 8–28 et seq., above.
[50] Regulation 1069/2009 laying down health rules as regards animal by-products and derived products not intended for human consumption [2009] OJ L300/1; this Regulation replaced Reg.1774/2002 [2002] OJ L273/1. See also para.10–54, below.
[51] Until then, Dir.90/667 was applicable, concerning laying down the veterinary rules for the disposal of animal waste, for its placing on the market and for the prevention of pathogens in feedstuffs of animal or fish origin [1990] OJ L363/51.
[52] Regulation 1069/2009 erroneously refers to art.152(4) TFEU which does not exist.
[53] Directive 2008/98 [2008] OJ L312/3, art.2(2)(b).
[54] Directive 2010/75 [2010] OJ L334/17.
[55] Directive 1999/31 on the landfill of waste [1999] OJ L182/1.

Installations that use waste as regular or additional fuel (waste co-incineration plants)—at present, in particular, power plants, cement kilns and steel plants—are regulated by the provisions of Directive 2010/75 on incinerators (arts 42 et seq.). Where the main purpose of an installation is the thermal treatment of waste, the specific provisions of Directive 2010/75 apply which differentiate between incineration and co-incineration plants.

(d) Landfills

As regards landfills, the Commission submitted a proposal for a Directive in 1991.[56] In 1996, the European Parliament rejected the Council's common position on the proposal[57] with the argument that it contained too many derogations. The Commission then submitted a new proposal which the Council adopted in 1999.[58] The Directive has the same field of application as the present Directive 2008/98; thus, in law, it also applies to radioactive waste landfills, for which at present no specific EU provisions exist;[59] in practice, though, Directive 1999/31 is ignored with regard to radioactive waste landfills. For high-level radioactive waste and spent fuels which are to be disposed of, no disposal facility exists at present in the European Union.[60]

10–12

> "Finland and France are the only Member States where the disposal capacities will be available for the [high-level and spent fuels] waste which is going to arise in the next two decades. Germany will only cover the needs for disposal from 2040, and Sweden from 2070. The disposal capacities are insufficient to cover the radioactive waste in the coming decades in the rest of the Member States with present or past programmes of nuclear power generation."[61]

Directive 1999/31 applies to all authorised or non-authorised landfills that are in operation; where existing landfills did not comply with its requirements, they had to be adapted by 2009 at the latest or had to be closed. In principle, any storage of waste on land or into land—thus also under ground—is considered a landfill. However, temporary storage prior to disposal operations that does not exceed one year, or three years prior to treatment operations, is excluded from the definition of landfill. The Directive introduced three classes of landfills: for hazardous waste, for non-hazardous waste and for inert waste. It laid down detailed provisions for the permitting of landfills and the conditions accompanying a permit, and in particular for water control and leachate management, the protection of soil and water, gas control, stability and barriers to free access, and the closure of landfills. Criteria and procedures for the acceptance of waste at landfills were laid down in 2002.[62]

---

[56] [1991] OJ C190/1.

[57] [1996] OJ C59/1.

[58] Directive 1999/31 [1999] OJ L182/1.

[59] See on the shipment of radioactive waste, para.10–43, below.

[60] Commission, 7th situation report, Radioactive waste and spent fuels management in the EU, SEC(2011) 1007, p.9.

[61] Commission, 7th situation report, Radioactive waste and spent fuels management in the EU, SEC(2011) 1007, p.22

[62] Decision 2003/33 [2003] OJ L11/27.

Neither Directive 2008/98 nor Directive 1999/31 deal in detail with unauthorised landfills. The Court of Justice clarified in a number of judgments that Member States do not only have the obligation, flowing out of Article 36 of Directive 2008/98 to prohibit the unauthorised landfilling,[63] but that they also must clean up unauthorised landfills.[64] This raises the important question of differentiating between such clean-up operations and the cleaning of contaminated sites which are not covered by EU law. As EU law prohibited since 1977, when Directive 74/442[65] became applicable, the unauthorised dumping of waste, it must be concluded that the legal clean-up obligation under EU waste law exists since that time; for Member States which joined the EU after 1977, the borderline date is that of their accession to the European Union. Contaminated sites are then sites which already existed in 1977 or at the moment of the accession. No publicly accessible inventory exists for them.

(e) Decommissioning of installations

10–13　There are no specific EU provisions on the decommissioning of waste installations or, indeed, other industrial installations such as, for instance, nuclear power plants. The demolition of buildings, structures or installations leads to the generation of (movable) waste, for which the general provisions apply. Where such installations contain asbestos, art.7 of Directive 87/217[66] applies, which requires that the release of asbestos fibres does not cause "significant asbestos pollution"—whatever that means. For the rest, the general provision of art.13 of Directive 2008/98[67] also applies to decommissioning of installations.

The decommissioning of offshore oil platforms was the subject of a decision under the OSPAR Convention, taken in 1998,[68] which provided for a prohibition of putting such installations into the sea or maintaining them there after use; the decision allowed contracting parties to grant, under certain conditions, a derogation. The Commission proposed that the European Union approve this decision.[69] However, the proposal was not discussed in detail by the Council and has become obsolete in the meantime.

There are no EU-wide rules on the decommissioning of nuclear installations. The Commission estimated the costs for decommissioning of about 15 per cent of the investment cost for the installation.[70] The EU structural funds do not co-finance the decommissioning of nuclear installations[71]—which did not

---

[63] Directive 2008/98 [2008] OJ L312/3, art.36: "Member States shall take the necessary measures to prohibit the abandonment, dumping or uncontrolled management of waste."

[64] Court of Justice, *Commission v Italy* (C-196/13) ECLI:EU:C:2014:2407; *Commission v Greece* (C-378/13) ECLI:EU:C:2013:2405; see also *Commission v Italy*(C-137/07) ECLI:EU:C:2007:250.

[65] Directive 75/442 [1975] OJ L194/23.

[66] Directive 87/217 on the prevention and reduction of environmental pollution by asbestos [1987] OJ L85/40.

[67] See Dir.2008/98 [2008] OJ L312/3, art.13.

[68] OSPAR Dec.98/3 on the disposal of disused offshore installations [1998] OJ C158/11. As regards OSPAR in general, see para.7–34, above.

[69] [1999] OJ C158/10.

[70] Commission, Nuclear Safety in the European Union, COM(2002) 605, p.3.

[71] Regulation 1300/2013 on the Cohesion Fund [2013] OJ L347/281, art.2; Reg.1301/2013 on the Regional Funds [2013] OJ L347/289.

prevent the EU from providing €154 million in its 2014 budget for the decommissioning of nuclear installations.[72]

(f) Contaminated land

The Directive on landfills does not deal with issues of contaminated land, such as closed landfills, unauthorised discharges, abandoned military or industrial sites and so on. No EU inventory of such contaminated land sites exists,[73] but the majority of Member States set up national inventories.[74] Thus, in Germany, the number of suspected contaminated sites registered is about 190,000; this figure does not include military sites and sites for the production of armaments. The total number is thought to be well over 240,000. Austria has a list of 2,584 and Finland of 10,400 contaminated sites. In the United Kingdom, estimates go from 50,000 to 100,000,[75] while France sometimes quotes a figure of about 1,000 contaminated sites.[76] Based on Member States' data and estimations, the European Environment Agency estimated the number of contaminated sites in 25 Member States to be of "more than two million sites".[77] No official work is done at EU level concerning the identification of sites, classification, prioritisation and so on. However, in the context of its research policy, the Commission set up, in 1996, a "Concerted action on risk assessment for contaminated sites" (CARACAS) and two other similar networks, NICOLE (1996) and CLARINET (1998).

In its proposal for a directive establishing a framework for the protection of soil of 2006, the Commission suggested the elaboration of an EU inventory of contaminated sites[78] and estimated that about 3.5 million sites in the European Union were potentially contaminated. The proposal was rejected by a blocking minority in Council[79]; in 2014, the Commission withdrew it. The cleaning up of contaminated sites thus remains the responsibility of Member States.

10–14

---

[72] EU budget for 2014 [2014] OJ L51/1, p.II/1197.

[73] See also para.10–12 above.

[74] European Environment Agency, Progress in management of contaminated sites (CSI015/CSI003)—Assessment published in May 2014 (Copenhagen, 2014). According to that report, only Poland, Slovenia, Portugal and the United Kingdom had no inventory. In Belgium, Germany, Italy, Greece and Sweden, the inventories existed at regional level.

[75] National Westminster Bank, *Contaminated Land: Counting the Cost of Our Past* (London, 1992), p.3.

[76] See, for instance, *Le Monde*, 7 April 1998, p.10: "Le gouvernement relance l'inventaire des sites pollués … la France compte officiellement 896 lieux contaminés. En réalité, il en existe 200,000 à 300,000, de nature et d'impact différents."

[77] European Environment Agency, *The European Environment. State and Outlook 2005* (Copenhagen, 2005), p.171. In its 2014 publication on Progress … (fn.74, above), which covered 39 European countries, the Agency estimated this figure to be 2.5 million.

[78] Commission, COM(2006) 232.

[79] See paras 5–06 et seq., above.

(g) Port reception facilities

10–15   In 2000, the European Union adopted a Directive on port reception facilities for ship-generated waste and cargo residues[80]; the Directive was based on art.100(2) TFEU and became operational at the end of 2002.[81] EU Member States were required to ensure that there are facilities in ports for the reception of waste from ships; for that purpose, each port was obliged to establish a waste reception and management plan. All ships that use a port of a Member State shall deliver all ship-generated waste to a port reception facility. In order to avoid the waste being discharged into the sea, the Directive provided that ships have to pay a fee for the port reception facilities, "irrespective of actual use of the facilities" (art.8). This might start competition among the ports as to the amount of the fee. By 2005, the Commission should have reported on the national fee systems and their impact and proposed appropriate amendments, but, by mid-2015, has not yet done so. There were no specifications set for the reception facilities. However, Member States have to update the waste management plan for each individual port at regular intervals.

3.   WASTE MATERIALS

(a)   Framework provisions

10–16   Eurostat, the Statistical Office of the European Union, publishes data on waste generation and treatment on the basis of Regulation 2150/2002 on waste statistics.[82] According to these data which are based on information from Member States, the European Union had generated, in 2010, 2,506 million tonnes of waste; 101.4 million tonnes was hazardous waste.[83] The evolution of municipal waste generation per capita (kg) was as follows[84]:

Member State	1995	2013	Change in %
Belgium	455	439	–4
Bulgaria	594	432	–38
Czech Republic	302	307	+2
Denmark	521	747	+43

[80] Directive 2000/59 on port reception facilities for ship-generated waste and cargo residues [2000] OJ L332/81.
[81] The Court of Justice found that Spain, Italy, Greece, France and Finland had not complied with their obligations in time, see *Commission v Spain* (C-480/07) ECLI:EU:C:2008:715; *Commission v Italy* (C-368/07) ECLI:EU:C:2008:523; *Commission v Greece* (C-81/07) ECLI:EU:C:2008:172; *Commission v France* (C-106/07) ECLI:EU:C:2007:766; *Commission v Finland* (C-523/06) ECLI:EU:C:2007:584.
[82] Regulation 2150/2002 on waste statistics [2002] OJ L332/1.
[83] Eurostat, *Waste statistics, Statistics explained* (Luxembourg, 2014).
[84] Eurostat, Municipal waste statistics (kg per capita) *http://ec.europa.eu/eurostat/web/products-datasets/-/tsdpc240* [Accessed 30 September 2015]

Germany	523	517	−1
Estonia	371	293	−21
Ireland	512	586	+14
Greece	392	506	+51
Spain	510	449	−12
France	475	530	+12
Croatia		404	
Italy	454	491	+8
Cyprus	595	624	+5
Latvia	254	312	+18
Lithuania	426	433	+2
Luxembourg	587	653	+11
Hungary	460	378	−18
Malta	395	570	+44
Netherlands	539	526	−2
Austria	437	578	+32
Poland	285	297	+4
Portugal	352	440	+25
Romania	342	272	−20
Slovenia	596	414	−31
Slovakia	295	304	+3
Finland	413	493	+19
Sweden	386	458	+19
United Kingdom	498	482	−3
EU 27	473	481	+2

The relatively slight increase (EU +2%) in 18 years is also due to the economic crises, as the EU figures for 1999 (511 kg), 2003 (514 kg), 2007 (524 kg) and 2010 (504 kg) demonstrate.[85]

---

[85] Eurostat, Municipal waste statistics (kg per capita) *http://ec.europa.eu/eurostat/web/products-datasets/-/tsdpc240* [Accessed 30 September 2015]

Recycling operations increased, between 2004 and 2010, from 41 per cent of the waste to 49 per cent, whereas disposal of waste decreased from 54 per cent to 45.4 per cent. Incineration increased from 4.9 per cent to 5.6 per cent.[86]

10–17   As regards radioactive waste, the Commission generally differentiates between low-, medium- and high-level waste.[87] About 545,000 m³ of radioactive waste were thought, in 2007, to be produced annually within the European Union (EU-25), out of which 4,100m³ was high-level waste; to these have to be added 44,600 TE(tonnes equivalent) of spent nuclear fuels.[88] Considerable quantities of radioactive waste, including all high-level waste and spent fuels for disposal, are placed in what is called "interim storage", sometimes for years or decades, as no final landfill site for high-level radioactive waste has as yet been decided upon within the European Union.

The basic legal instrument for waste materials is Directive 2008/98, which constituted a fundamental review of Directive 75/442, its review in 1991, and its codification in 2006. Directive 2009/98 is the framework instrument for waste legislation at EU level.[89] The Directive defined waste, established a hierarchy for waste management (prevention—recovery—safe disposal) and basic requirements for all waste management activities, introduced a licensing requirement for all persons who are active in waste treatment, disposal and management operations, and requested that Member States draw up waste management and waste prevention plans and regularly report on the Directive's transposition and implementation.

The Directive, which was based on art.192 TFEU, no longer aimed, as its predecessor, at obtaining an alignment of waste management policies and provisions within the European Union. Member States were keen to maintain their different national approaches to waste management, whether these were successful or less successful.

10–18   Waste management policy within the European Union—at EU level and within Member States—was and is still heavily influenced by the attempts, in particular from economic operators, to deregulate waste policy and submit waste production, treatment, trade and disposal to a minimum of rules only. This goes in part hand in hand with efforts from administrations, not to introduce an EU-wide waste management system, but to leave it to Member States—or regions or local authorities—to decide to what extent they want to allow wastes being traded, treated and disposed of. These policy and/or interest-driven concepts appear mainly in the discussions on the definition of waste on the one hand, and on the treatment of waste, the export-import restrictions and the shipment of waste on the other hand.[90]

In 1975, an EU definition on waste had been established.[91] However, this definition referred back to the different national law of Member States and was

---

[86] Eurostat, Waste Statistics. Data from July 2013 to July 2014, *http://ec.europa.eu/eurostat/en/web/products-press-releases/-/8-26032015-AP* [Accessed 30 September 2015]

[87] Low, medium and high refer to the concentration of radio-nucleides in the radioactive waste and hence to the intensity of the emitted radiation.

[88] Commission, SEC(2011) 1007.

[89] Directive 2008/98 on waste [2008] OJ L312/3.

[90] See, for this last point, paras 10–35 et seq., below.

[91] Directive 75/442 [1975] OJ L194/23, art.1 (a): "'waste' means any substance or object which the holder disposes of or is required to dispose of pursuant to the provisions of national law in force".

therefore considered not to be precise enough. Thus, in 1991, and in conformity with parallel definitions within the OECD and the Basel Convention on the Transboundary Shipment of Hazardous Waste to which the European Union adhered,[92] it was replaced by a new definition in Directive 75/442 which declared waste any substance or object in the categories set out in an annex I which the holder discards or intends or is required to discard.[93] Directive 2008/98 maintained that definition, but deleted the reference to Annex I, so that the definition now runs: "Waste shall mean any substance or object which the holder discards or intends or is required to discard."[94]

The definition was and continues to be used in numerous other EU waste legislation.[95] Directive 2006/12, art.1 had requested the Commission to draw up "a list of wastes belonging to the categories listed in annex I". This list had been established in 1994.[96] In 2000, it was completely revised and merged with the EU list on hazardous waste which had been drawn up under Directive 91/689, and updated in 2014.[97] Article 7 of Directive 2008/98 referred to that list, though it conceded large discretion to Member States, such as the possibility to consider some hazardous wastes as non-hazardous, or to consider that materials which were on that list, were in fact not waste. At present, the list contains some 650 entries.

The field of application of Directive 2008/98 is very broad, though there are the following exclusions foreseen[98]:   **10–19**

- gaseous effluents emitted into the atmosphere; such emissions are excluded, obviously for the reason that air pollution provisions would apply;
- land (in situ), including unexcavated contaminated soil and buildings permanently connected with land[99];
- uncontaminated soil and other material excavated in the course of construction activities;
- radioactive waste[100];
- decommissioned explosives[101];

---

[92] Decision 93/98 [1993] OJ L39/1.

[93] Directive 2006/12 [2006] OJ 114/9, art.1(a). Annex I contained a list of 16 categories of materials which were to be considered waste. The last category referred to "any materials, substances or products which are not contained in the above categories". This meant that the categories did not define "waste" but referred back to the general definition.

[94] Directive 2008/98 [2008] OJ L312/3, art.3 no.1.

[95] See, e.g. Dir.91/689 on hazardous waste [1991] OJ L377/20; Reg.259/93 on the shipment of waste [1993] OJ L30/1; Dir.94/62 on packaging and packaging waste [1994] OJ L365/10 etc.

[96] Commission Dec.94/3 [1994] OJ L5/15.

[97] Commission Dec.2000/532 [2000] OJ L226/3; Commission Dec.2014/955 [2014] OJ L370/44.

[98] See for details Dir.2008/98 [2008] OJ L312/3, art.2.

[99] With this exclusion, a judgment by the Court of Justice, *Van de Walle* (C-1/03) [2004] E.C.R. I-7613, was reversed which had declared that the definition of waste also included unexcavated contaminated soil, as well as parts of buildings that were connected with land.

[100] See on radioactive waste, Dir.2011/70 [2011] OJ L199/48 and para.10–30, below. The main difference to general waste legislation is at present that nuclear waste which is recoverable or recyclable is not classified as "waste", but as "product".

[101] Why decommissioned explosives are excluded from the scope of the Directive is not clear. No explanation is offered in the Recitals.

- faecal matter and non-hazardous agricultural or forestry materials used in farming, forestry or the production of energy through non dangerous processes.

The large exclusion of agricultural and forestry waste can only be explained by successful lobbying from those sectors. In particular, it is not clear why faecal matter should not be considered "waste". Should they be seen as products?[102] As with nuclear waste, the exclusion is not rational, but the outcome of the EU bargaining process.

Furthermore, some waste materials are excluded "to the extent that they are covered by other Community legislation".[103] This wording solved a problem of the previous Directive 2006/12, where the word "Community" was lacking. The Court of Justice had then decided that "other legislation" could also apply to national legislation.[104] The new wording makes this interpretation impossible.

10–20   It is obvious that the definition of waste is a legal creation and therefore exposed to criticism; as does any definition, it contains an arbitrary element. Whether a corporal object is called a good, product, substance, residue, pollutant, discharge (of pollutants), emission or waste, is a question of legal agreement. From the point of view of environmental protection, the name which is given to a specific object is not very relevant; what matters is the contamination or pollution which that object causes or risks causing.

The criticisms against the—unanimously agreed—definition of waste stem in particular from concepts that look at the difference between product and waste from an economic perspective: under this concept, "waste" should not be applied to objects that have an economic value and could thus be recycled or recovered; to such materials, product legislation should apply in full. It is no surprise that such concepts are in particular defended by economic vested interest groups. The main weakness of this concept is that every object has an economic value somewhere in the world.[105] If one were following this argument, there would be no waste from precious metals, from steel, copper, iron, etc as all these materials have an economic value and can be recycled or reused. The contradiction goes even further, as the incineration of material is generally, and rightly so, considered to be a recovery operation, where the energetic part of the material is used, for heating purposes, to generate energy etc. As such incineration with energy recovery gives economic advantages—the use of ordinary fuel is not necessary—all materials that burn and generate heat[106] would have to be considered "products" and not "wastes".

It is not to be examined whether such a definition of "waste" could be viable. It is, in any case, not the definition of EU legislation, and in particular not that of Directive 2008/98. Legally, there can be no doubt that the EU concept of waste

---

[102] See also Court of Justice, *Vera pig farm* (C-416/02) ECLI:EU:C:2005:511.

[103] See for details Dir.2008/98 [2008] OJ L312/3, art.2(2).

[104] Court of Justice, *Avesta Polarit Chrome Oy* (C-114/01) [2003] E.C.R. I-8725; see also the very critical comment L. Krämer, *Environmental Liability* (2003), p.231.

[105] The notion "economic value" cannot be limited to national frontiers, as economic questions per se are independent of administrative-political considerations and notions: international trade may take place in objects which have no value for one person, but a high value for another one. For example, in South Asia even parts of plastic bags are collected from landfills and sold.

[106] Technically, the generation of heat is feasible with a calorific value of 5,000–6,000kj.

also includes recoverable or recyclable material. The enumeration of recovery operations in annex II to Directive 2008/98 on waste—not on products!—would not make sense, if material that is destined for a recovery operation was not covered by that Directive.

Germany had adopted, in 1986, legislation that declared in essence that recoverable items were not waste but secondary raw materials. It was only after the Court of Justice stated, nine years later, that this provision was incompatible with EU law,[107] that Germany changed its legislation; the Court expressly found that the definition of waste under Directive 91/156[108]—which corresponds to the present definition of Directive 2008/98—would not allow recoverable waste to be excluded from the waste definition. A similar provision to the German one was then, in 1996, introduced by Italy, which led to the same verdict by the Court of Justice.[109] Despite that, Italian legislative efforts to exempt certain materials from the application of waste legislation continue.[110]

10–21

Since this way of proceeding is not really promising, discussions subsequently concentrated on the concept of "discard" which is not defined in EU law. All products become waste, which normally occurs at the end of their useful lifetime. This question has nothing to do with the economic value that the item eventually still has: where a new television set is, after two months' use, thrown away or dumped on the street, it is discarded, even if somebody passes by, takes the television and uses it for several years. Horse manure might be an excellent fertiliser for the garden: it remains true that where it is left on the road, it constitutes—a real production residue—waste.

Since recovery (recycling) is considered a waste management activity, it is logical that an item can be discarded, even where it is collected or transported with a view to being recycled or recovered. This is, *de lege lata* and *de lege ferenda*, heavily argued about, in particular where residues of production are at stake.[111] Admittedly, the borderline between residues of production, which the European Union considers waste, and the generation of two products, is not always easy to make. Thus, where steel is cut to make the body of a car, gold is worked on to make a golden ring or wood is cut, the residues—steel scrap, gold dust and wood chips—are discarded and thus constitute waste. Where chemical substances are processed to produce two chemical preparations, one of these cannot be considered the residue of the other; normally, thus, they are both products. As with all borderline cases, the final decision is to be made on a case-by-case basis.

In the end, the Court of Justice will be the final arbiter, and has started, in a number of judgments, to be so.[112] It does not seem to have found the right balance in all cases. Thus, in case C-416/02 it stated that pig manure which can

10–22

[107] *Commission v Germany* (C-422/92) [1995] E.C.R. I-1097.

[108] Directive 91/156 [1991] OJ L78/32.

[109] *Tombesi* (C-304/94) [1997] E.C.R. I-3561.

[110] See, e.g. the facts of *Niselli* (C-457/02) [2004] E.C.R. I-10853; *Commission v Italy* (C-103/02) [2004] E.C.R. I-9127.

[111] A good example is the Resolution on (steel) scrap, adopted by the Consultative Committee of CECA on 10 October 1997 [1997] OJ C356/8.

[112] *Vessoso and Zanetti* (joined cases C-206 and 207/88) [1990] E.C.R. I-1461; *Zanetti* [1990] (C-359/88) E.C.R. I-1509; *Commission v Germany* (C-422/92) [1995] E.C.R. I-1097; *Tombesi* (C-304/94) [1997] E.C.R. I-3561; *Inter-Environnement Wallonie* (C-129/96) [1997] E.C.R. I-7411; *Beside* (C-192/96) [1998] E.C.R. I-4029; *Dusseldorp* (C- 203/96) [1998] E.C.R. I-4075.

be brought out on farmland was not waste, but a product.[113] This contradicts the Court's earlier judgments according to which a subsequent use of a material cannot be decisive for the question, whether it has to be classified as product or as waste. And, transferred to industrial production, it means that production residues which *can* be used in production, would constitute products.

Directive 2008/98 tried to answer these questions politically, by introducing the concept of "by-product" into EU waste legislation. Article 5(1) reads as follows:

> "A substance or object, resulting from a production process, the primary aim of which is not the production of that item, may be regarded as not being waste referred to in point 19 of Article 3 but as being a by-product, if the following conditions are met: a) further use of that substance or object is certain b) the substance or object can be used directly without any further processing other than normal industrial practice c) the substance or object is produced as an integral part of the production process; and d) further use is lawful, i.e. the substance or the object fulfils all relevant product, environment and health protection requirements for the respective use and will not lead to overall adverse environmental or human health impacts."

Decisions on whether these conditions are fulfilled will be taken by the comitology procedure at EU level (art.5(2)). Until mid-2015, the EU did not take any such decision.

10–23   In my opinion, this provision will lead to the consequence that precious metal residues, metal residues in general, and numerous other production residues will, in time, no longer be considered waste but by-products to which product legislation applies. The "normal industrial practice" which is not further specified, will lead to more pressure from economic operators to have production residues excluded from waste legislation. The notion of "overall adverse impacts" is not really a limitation to the decision-making under this provision. And the (welcome) political side-effect is that the amount of waste will decrease.

Directive 2008/98 introduced another way of limiting the application of waste law. Article 6(1) of that Directive reads:

> "Certain specific waste shall cease to be waste … when it has undergone a recovery, including recycling, operation and complies with specific criteria to be developed in accordance with the following conditions: a) the substance or object is commonly used for specific purposes; b) a market or demand exists for such substance or object; c) the substance or object fulfils the technical requirement for the specific purposes and meets the existing legislation and standards applicable to products; and d) the use of the substance or object will not lead to overall adverse environmental or human health exposure."

Decisions under this provision are again taken by comitology procedure at EU level. However, in the absence of such decisions, Member States may take decisions at national level; they then have to notify the Commission and other Member States under Directive 98/34[114] of their draft decision.

---

[113] Court of Justice, *Vera pig farm* (C-416/02) [2005] E.C.R. I-7369.
[114] Directive 98/34 [1998] OJ L204/37.

The Commission adopted provisions on the question of when scrap metal,[115] copper scrap[116] and glass cullets[117] cease to be waste. It failed, at least until mid-2015, to adopt provisions on when recovered paper ceased to be waste.[118] The reason was, in simplified terms, that the Commission wished to see waste paper already lose its status as waste, when it is, according to CEN-standard EN 643, sorted into different categories, according to its humidity, contamination, quality etc. The European Parliament, though, objected to that proposal, as it considered that the sorting of waste did not yet end its waste characteristics.

The differentiation is relevant, in particular as regards the shipment— shipment of products which is largely unregulated, or shipment of waste where strict provisions apply—and the export of such materials. Until now, a material was classified as waste, until the recycling or recovery process had been finished—thus, for example, the sorted used paper had been transformed into new paper, so that the transport of used paper was a transport of waste. The Commission proposal, influenced by strong lobbying from vested interests, tried to change this borderline.   **10–24**

Directive 2008/98 introduced the concept of extended producer responsibility (art.8) and repeated the polluter-pays principle (art.14). The concept of extended producer responsibility, originally developed by Scandinavian countries, is based on the understanding that the responsibility of the producer does not end with the manufacturing of the product. When the product is on the market, he has labelling, information guarantee, eventually warning and take-back obligations. And when his product ends its useful lifetime and becomes waste, he has responsibilities as to the collection and treatment of this waste, since he also had the profit from it. With this reasoning, producers and their associations (including importers) can be made responsible for organising and financing take-back systems, collect waste from consumers and users and ensure that such waste is properly recycled, recovered and/or disposed of.

EU law already provided for such concepts in Directives 2000/53 on end-of-life vehicles[119] and 2012/19 on waste from electrical and electronic products.[120] Directive 2008/98 only gave a framework to the concept, and left it to Member States as to what extent they want to recur to this concept.

As regards the polluter-pays principle, the Directive, repeating the previously applicable EU law, imposed the application of this principle in national waste legislation. This has far-reaching consequences for national legislation. Thus, the Court of Justice had held that a petroleum company could be held liable for damage caused by petrol that had spread into the environment following a ship accident, though the company had excluded all such liability by way of contracts with the shipowner.[121] In another case, the Court held that municipalities in the Member States were not entitled to charge the cost for collecting waste according   **10–25**

---

[115] Commission, Reg.333/2011 [2011] OJ L94/2.

[116] Commission, Reg.715/2013 [2013] OJ L 201/14.

[117] Commission, Reg.1179/2012 [2012] OJ L337/31.

[118] See Commission proposal, COM(2013) 502.

[119] Directive 2000/53 on end-of life vehicles [2000] OJ L269/34.

[120] Directive 2012/19 on waste electrical and electronic equipment (WEEE) [2012] OJ L192/38.

[121] Court of Justice, *Commune de Mesquer* (C-188/07) [2008] E.C.R. I-4501.

to the size of the ground from which the waste was taken; rather, the actual quantities of waste which were collected had to form the basis of charging the cost.[122]

The main instrument of the Directive is the waste management plan which Member States shall have to establish and regularly update (art.28). The Directive gave a number of indications as to the content of such plans. The plans shall have to be sent to the Commission which does not have, though, any obligation to assess, compare or otherwise evaluate the plans. This is consistent with past experience. Indeed, Member States were, since 1977, obliged to elaborate and monitor waste management plans and to inform the Commission thereof. However, the Commission has never made any evaluation of those plans or drawn attention to omissions, inconsistencies or failures. Directive 2008/98 now "invites" the European Environment Agency to annually review progress in the completion and implementation of the national waste management plans (art.30(2)). This is an elegant way of complying with art.17 TEU and ensuring that EU law is applied by Member States!

(b) Hazardous waste

10–26 Council Directive 78/319 on toxic and dangerous waste[123] was substituted, in 1991, by Directive 91/689.[124] This Directive defined hazardous waste, introduced a licensing requirement for installations which process hazardous waste, and requested management plans for hazardous waste to be drawn up and regular information on installations which handled hazardous waste. Member States had to report regularly on the implementation of the Directive. Directive 2008/98 repealed this Directive and incorporated some provisions on hazardous waste into its own provisions.

As with the notion of "waste", difficulties appeared as regards the concept of "dangerous waste". The Directive of 1978 gave a definition of dangerous waste[125] that was soon considered to be too vague. For that reason, it was replaced, in Directive 91/689,[126] by a "listing approach": hazardous was a waste which was listed in an EU positive list.[127] Directive 2008/98 changed this approach again and considered waste as "hazardous" "which display one or more of the hazardous properties listed in Annex III" (art.3 no.2). This Annex lists in

---

[122] Court of Justice, *Futura* (C-254/08) ECLI:EU:C:2009:149.

[123] Directive 78/319 on toxic and dangerous waste [1978] OJ L84/43.

[124] Directive 91/689 on hazardous waste [1991] OJ L377/20.

[125] Directive 78/319 on toxic and dangerous waste [1978] OJ L84/43, art.1(b): "'toxic and dangerous waste' means any waste containing or contaminated by the substances or materials listed in the Annex to this Directive of such a nature, in such quantities or in such concentrations as to constitute a risk to health or the environment".

[126] Directive 91/689 on hazardous waste [1991] OJ L377/20; the word "hazardous" was presumably preferred to "dangerous", because the Basel Convention on the shipment of waste used this terminology; in substance, there is no difference between "hazardous" and "dangerous".

[127] Directive 91/689 on hazardous waste [1991] OJ L377/20, art.1(4): "... 'hazardous waste' means: wastes featuring on a list drawn up ... on the basis of Annexes I and II to this Directive ... These wastes must have one or more of the properties listed in Annex III. The list shall take into account the origin and composition of the waste and, where necessary, limit values of concentration ...; any other waste which is considered by a Member State to display any of the properties listed in Annex III. Such cases shall be notified to the Commission and reviewed ... with a view to adaptation of the list."

general terms 15 hazard categories.[128] As regards the precise decision, whether one of the hazard categories applies to a specific waste, the test methods and possible limit values, the annex to Directive 2008/98 referred to two EU Directives on chemical substances and preparations,[129] without considering that these Directives had, at the time of application, already been replaced by Regulation 1907/2006.[130] In order to reach a somehow uniform understanding of what constitutes hazardous waste, art.7 of Directive 2008/98 determined that the "list of waste shall be binding as regards determination of the waste which is to be considered to be hazardous waste".[131] Member States may, though, in specific cases consider non-hazardous waste as hazardous, or hazardous waste as non-hazardous; in both cases, they have to inform the Commission, so that the waste list may be updated.[132] They may also "consider waste as non-hazardous waste in accordance with the list of waste referred to in paragraph 1 (of Article 7)".[133] Normally, the principle has been maintained that waste is hazardous when it is marked as hazardous in the EU list on waste.

The main problems linked to the EU definition of hazardous waste are that Member States use, in their national legislation, different terminology, such as "special waste", "chemical waste", "specially controlled waste" and so on. These different definitions made it possible to establish national waste lists that are different from the EU list. To complicate things further, the Basel Convention on the shipment of hazardous waste and the OECD have established hazardous waste lists, which are different from the EU list, a legal situation that generates difficulties, inconsistencies, grey markets and illegal practices.

Directive 2008/98 only contained few provisions on hazardous waste. The **10–27** general provision of art.13 that waste shall be treated without harming human health or the environment, also applied to hazardous waste. Article 18 stated that hazardous waste shall not be mixed with other hazardous or non-hazardous waste or materials and neither may it be be diluted. However, this provision does not apply to operators which have a licence, where the mixing or dilution corresponds to the best available technique or where the provisions of art.13 are respected[134]; furthermore, the provision does not apply to hazardous household waste.

---

[128] See, e.g. Dir.2009/98: "H7: Carcinogenic: substances and preparations which, if they are inhaled or ingested, or if they penetrate the skin, may induce cancer or increase its incidence"; "H8: Corrosive: substances and preparations which may destroy living tissue on contact", "H14: Ecotoxic: waste which presents or may present immediate or delayed risk for one or more sectors of the environment".

[129] Directive 67/548 [1967] OJ 196/1; Dir.1999/45 [1999] OJ L200/1. It had already been mentioned in Ch.6 that Dir.67/548 only provided for test methods on the effect of chemical substances on humans and the aquatic environment, but not on other parts of the environment, such as plants and animals.

[130] Regulation 1907/2006 [2006] OJ L396/1.

[131] As to the waste list, see Dec.2014/955 [2014] OJ L370/44.

[132] See Court of Justice, *Commission v Austria* (C-194/01) [2004] E.C.R. I-4579, where the Court stated that Member States were not obliged to transpose the waste lists word by word into their national legal system. The consequence of that judgment is that the notions of waste and of hazardous waste will continue to vary from one Member State to the other. While thus between Stockholm and Madrid, everybody has the same notion of what is a car, there are differences with regard to waste.

[133] See for details Dir.2008/98 [2008] OJ L312/3, art.7.

[134] See the wording of art.13 (fn.40, above).

In 2011, the EU adopted, for the first time, a directive on spent fuel and radioactive waste,[135] based on arts 31 and 32 Euratom Treaty. The Directive became applicable in August 2013; the Commission had to start proceedings under art.258 TFEU against Belgium, Germany, Spain, France, Cyprus, Italy, Croatia, Latvia, Lithuania, Austria, Poland, Romania and Sweden, because those Member States had not transposed the Directive in time into their national law.[136]

"Spent fuel" is considered either to be a usable resource or—when no further use is foreseen—a radioactive waste (art.2.10 and Recital 20). This definition means that recoverable radioactive waste is not considered to be waste, but to be a product.

The Directive aims at protection workers, the general public and future generations (art.1); the environment, fauna and flora are not mentioned. The Directive does not apply to authorised releases (art.3), which means that discharges of radioactive waste into waters would neither fall under Directive 2008/98 nor under this Directive 2011/70. In substance, the Directive essentially requests Member States to draw up and monitor management programmes for radioactive waste; it does not contain a fraction of the details which are laid down in Directive 1999/31 on landfills; and no word is spent on whether radioactive waste may be disposed on ordinary or hazardous waste-landfills. The proposition in the proposal that Member States draw up a safety plan for radioactive waste, was not retained in the Directive.

10–28 The Directive does not contain any quality requirement as to the treatment or disposal of radioactive waste. In recital 16, it mentions the existence of international safety principles which were set up by the International Agency for Nuclear Energy. However, neither are these principles laid down as such in the Directive nor are Member States requested to respect them.

In view of the very poor content of this Directive, Recital 24 almost sounds cynical. It reads:

> "It should be an ethical obligation of each Member State to avoid any undue burden on future generations in respect of spent fuels and radioactive waste, including any radioactive waste expected from decommissioning of existing nuclear installations. Through the implementation of the Directive, Member States will have demonstrated that they have taken reasonable steps to ensure that that obligation is met."

(c) Waste prevention

10–29 Directive 2008/98 fixed as the first priority for waste legislation and waste management the prevention of waste generation (art.4). The aim was "breaking the link between economic growth and the environmental impacts associated with the generation of waste" (art.29). It obliged Member States to set up waste prevention programmes (art.29) and offered, in annex IV, a list of 16 measures that could form part of such programmes. The programmes shall be regularly updated.

---

[135] Directive 2011/70/Euratom establishing a Community framework for the responsible and safe management of spent fuels and radioactive waste [2011] OJ L199/48.
[136] Written Question E-001376/14 (Van Brempt) [2014] OJ C331/51.

A closer look at the measures which were favoured by annex IV shows their vague and general character of mainly promotional character.[137] Nowhere were Member States obliged to take binding measures to reduce waste generation. The basic error of the Directive's provisions on waste prevention was that it does not recognise that in order to prevent waste generation there must be a product policy, because before a material becomes waste, it was a product; a product policy which aims at the prevention of waste generation will have to address cleaner technologies, eco-design of products and improve the eco-efficiency of production and consumption patterns.

However, there is a basic decision by the European Union not to pursue an active, integrated product policy, and to limit itself, in the context of its product policy, to non-binding measures. However, such non-binding measures will not reduce the generation of waste. Neither does the Commission consider developing a tax on waste generating products (packaging, PVC, etc) and it is not in any way concerned about waste generation in private households (food, appliances, chemicals, etc).

The result of the past policy is that waste quantities have constantly risen in the European Union, hand in hand with economic growth. No significant change of this evolution is visible[138] and it must be expected that Directive 2008/98 will not change the trends. The waste quantities might be reduced, though, because of the above-mentioned changes on "by-products" and on end-of waste decisions.   **10–30**

(d) Waste recovery

Waste recovery includes reuse, material recycling and incineration with energy recovery. Directive 2008/98 defined re-use as "an operation by which products or components that are not waste are used again for the same purpose for which they were conceived".[139] However, a material may also be reused, where it had been discarded: a piece of furniture has been placed on the roadside to be taken away by the waste collection services—its taking up by a person and its continued use constitutes a recovery operation. However, where an object is re-used without having been discarded—a friend, visiting a home, discovers a pair of shoes in a corner which are disused, takes them and wears them—the object has never become waste; so no waste recovery operation is involved. The repair of a dress, or the reuse of packaging, such as empty bottles, normally comes into the second category, so the classification of reusable packaging as products by Directive 94/62[140] is correct.[141]   **10–31**

---

[137] See,e.g. annex IV, no.1: "The use of planning measures, or other economic instruments promoting the effective use of resources"; no.4: "the promotion of eco-design"; no.9: "the use of voluntary agreements, consumer/producer panels or sectoral negotiations, in order that the relevant businesses or industry sectors set their own waste prevention plans or objectives or correct wasteful products or packaging"; no.13: "the promotion of creditable eco-labels".

[138] See para.10–16, above.

[139] Directive 2008/98 [2008] OJ L312/3, art.3 no.10.

[140] See Dir.94/62 on packaging and packaging waste [1994] OJ L365/10, art.1(5)–(9) where a reusable packaging is not considered to be waste.

[141] See for the notion of re-use also Court of Justice, *Oliehandel* (C-307/00 to 311/00) [2003] E.C.R. I-1821.

In 2005, the Commission presented a thematic strategy for the recycling of waste.[142] The Commission suggested to create a "European Recycling Society", but has not proposed concrete measures.

Directive 2009/98 enumerated in annex II a non-exhaustive list of recovery operations. It suggested practical measures to be taken by Member States, in order to promote reuse, recycling and recovery. Where "technically, environmentally and economically practicable, waste should be collected separately" (art.10)—which was not more than a recommendation.

10–32   With regard to paper, metal, glass and plastic from households and equivalent waste streams, the Directive prescribed separate collections by 2015; a recycling target of 50 per cent by weight was to be reached. For non-hazardous construction and demolition waste, the recycling target, to be reached by 2020, is 70 per cent (art.11). Details for the calculation methods were set out by the Commission.[143] This approach will most likely lead to the abandoning of separate collection and recovery targets for packaging waste under Directive 94/62, as it does not make sense to provide, for example, for targets for paper from packaging waste and from other origins.

In 2014, the Commission proposed to set higher targets.[144] However, the new Juncker Commission withdrew this proposal early 2015, arguing that it was not ambitious enough. A new proposal is announced for the end of 2015.

In the past, the greatest discussions were provoked by the classification as recovery operation the "use principally as a fuel or other means to generate energy". Indeed, several Member States had, in their national legislation, established calorific values below which a waste could not be considered to come under this process. While it might be necessary to specify under which circumstances a waste principally serves as a fuel, it was obviously not legal to set these conditions at national level.

10–33   In a judgment of 2003, the Court of Justice clearly rejected, under Directive 2006/12, the possibility of using the calorific value of waste as a criterion for differentiating between recovery (recycling) and disposal operations.[145] The Court also clarified that the shipment of municipal waste to a waste incinerator could not *normally*—whatever that means—be regarded as a shipment for recovery, even if the incinerator uses the energy from the incineration in part or in full.[146] The Court was of the opinion that, in such a case, the waste was not substituting a fuel; rather, the objective of the incineration was the thermal treatment of waste, and not the making of products or the production of energy. These judgments played a considerable part in the discussion on the review of the waste Directive (see para.10–24, above), as there were strong forces which would like to see all waste incinerators which burn waste and use the energy to be classified as recovery installations; this would facilitate waste shipments and increase the profitableness of such incinerators. Environmental groups, in contrast, pleaded for a classification of such installations as disposal installations, as they prefer the composting, recycling and reuse of materials. Directive 2008/98 now introduced a complicated formula in annex IV, according to which

---

[142] Commission, Thematic Strategy on the prevention and recycling of waste, COM(2005) 666.

[143] Commission, Dec.2011/753 [2011] OJ L310/11.

[144] Commission, COM(2014) 397; see also SWD(2014) 207.

[145] Court of Justice, *Commission v Germany* (C-228/00) [2003] E.C.R. I-1439.

[146] Court of Justice, *Commission v Luxembourg* (C-458/00) [2003] E.C.R. I-1553.

an incinerator which incinerates municipal waste shall be considered a recovery installation when it reaches a certain energy efficiency value.[147]

To date, the European Union has not fixed provisions on the quality of recycling: where 10kg of materials out of 1,000 tonnes of waste are extracted and recycled, it is obviously not possible to consider the whole process—shipment, storage, extraction—a recycling operation. EU specifications are urgently required. The formula of annex IV applies only to waste incineration, not to material recycling operations.

Since Directive 2008/98 was based on art.192 TFEU, Member States are entitled, under art.193 to identify recovery operations other than those listed in annex II. They are then obliged to notify the Commission. This leads to a decision by way of a committee procedure under Directive 2008/98 to adapt annex II to the new situation (art.38).

(e) Disposal of waste

Directive 2008/98 limited itself to the statement that waste should be disposed of without harming human health or the environment; at the same time, it prohibited the abandonment or dumping of waste (art.36). It also contained in annex I a list of operations that are classified as disposal operations.[148] The legal status of this list is the same as the list in annex II for recovery operations, so the reader can be referred to the remarks above, para.10–29. The specific disposal operations are not frequently contested. Germany considered the placing of waste into old mines and other underground cavities as recovery operations, since this disposal would prevent the cavities from caving in.[149] This interpretation contradicted several operations in annex IIA of Directive 75/442.[150] When the Court of Justice established some conditions under which underground storage of waste could be considered to be a recovery operation,[151] Germany introduced legislation to better delimitate underground disposal and recovery operations. Under Directive 2008/98, "backfilling"—the filling of caves, mines etc with waste—is not classified as a material recovery.[152]

At present, EU law contains only a few limitations on the landfill of waste. Directive 1999/31 on landfills[153] banned the landfilling of liquid waste, explosive, corrosive, oxidising, flammable waste, infectious hospital waste and of whole and shredded used tyres; furthermore, the landfilling of biodegradable municipal waste will have to be considerably reduced. Apart from that, Directive

10–34

---

[147] See also the further considerations for interpreting the formula in annex IV, laid down in art.38 of Dir.2008/98.

[148] It should be noted that Dir.75/442 originally also included recovery and recycling operations in the word "disposal". The differentiation between the two notions was introduced into EU law by Dir.91/156 in 1991.

[149] Between 1994 and 2001, between 1.5 and 2 million tons of waste were placed in old mines in Germany.

[150] Directive 75/442 [1975] OJ L194/23, annex IIA, D1: "Tipping above or underground (e.g. landfill, etc.)"; D3: "Deep injection (e.g. injection of pumpable discards into wells, salt domes or naturally occurring repositories, etc.)"; D12: "Permanent storage (e.g. emplacement of containers in a mine, etc.)".

[151] Court of Justice, *Abfall Service Austria* (C-6/00) [2002] E.C.R. I-1961.

[152] See Dir.2008/98 [2008] OJ L312/3, art.11

[153] Directive 1999/31 [1999] OJ L182/1.

2008/98 prohibited the uncontrolled management of waste. Thus, there is no ban on, for instance, shipping the waste into the outer space, burying BSE-infected cattle, or providing for seabed insertions of waste. There are also no restrictions in EU law as regards the incineration of waste; thus, it is unclear why annex I states that incineration of waste at sea is prohibited under EU law. No such provision exists; only the incineration without a permit is prohibited.

(f) Shipment of waste

10–35 Directive 78/319[154] had laid down some general requirements on the shipment of waste. Subsequent to discussions which took place within the framework of the OECD and which also concerned the shipment of waste between the United States and the European Union, the Commission proposed, in the early 1980s, an EU directive on the shipment of waste.[155] This proposal, for the first time, introduced into waste law a differentiation between shipments in the European Union that crossed the frontier of a Member State and other shipments, a clear departure from the concept of the single EU market and of the common transport policy, as laid down in art.3(f), 70 and 94 EC Treaty in its version applicable at that time. The Council adopted the proposal in 1984,[156] and it was then, in 1986, amended in order to also cover the shipment of hazardous waste to third countries.[157]

Directive 84/631 introduced a system of prior informed consent for shipments of hazardous waste: the holder of waste had to notify the competent authority of the Member State where he wanted to ship the waste, and to use a standardised consignment note in which he had to specify details of the waste, its destination and details of the shipment. The authority had to acknowledge receipt of the notification before the shipment could be effected.

The adoption of the 1989 Basel Convention on shipments of hazardous waste[158] followed a number of serious incidents concerning illegal shipments from industrialised to developing countries; this Convention and OECD measures on waste shipments adopted in reaction to that Convention led the European Union completely to review its provisions and to adopt, in 1993, a Regulation that was based on art.192 TFEU and concerned all waste shipments.[159] An important amendment in 1997 largely stopped the export of hazardous waste to third countries. A major change of legislation took place in 2006, when Reg.1013/2006 on the shipment of waste was adopted.[160]

---

[154] Directive 78/319 [1978] OJ L84/43.

[155] [1983] OJ C53/3.

[156] Directive 84/631 on the supervision and control within the European Community of the tranfrontier shipment of hazardous waste [1984] OJ L326/31; see also below regarding the question of environmental liability for damage caused by (the shipment of) waste.

[157] Directive 86/279 [1986] OJ L181/13.

[158] Basel Convention on the control of transboundary movements of hazardous wastes and their disposal, 1989; the EU adhered to the Convention by Dec.93/98 [1993] OJ L39/1.

[159] Regulation 259/93 on the supervision and control of shipments within, into and out of the European Community [1993] OJ L30/1; amended (export ban) by Reg.120/97 [1997] OJ L22/14.

[160] Regulation 1013/2006 on shipments of waste [2006] OJ L190/1; by Reg.660/2014 [2014] OJ L 29/33 the Regulation was amended, in particular in order to strengthen the inspection obligations of Member States.

In 2013, the European Union adopted a regulation to promote the sound   **10–36**
elimination of end-of-life ships.[161] The underlying problem of ships was that, at
the end of their useful lifetime, they were sailed to South Asia and were there sold
in order to be dismantled in ship recycling facilities in Bangladesh, Pakistan,
India and China. The dismantling and recycling conditions in these countries (and
to a lesser extent China) are, under social and environmental perspectives,
appalling. The dismantling takes place in the open air with little or no protection
for workers and almost no care for the environment.

End-of-life ships are, legally, waste, and as they contain normally hazardous
liquids (oil) and frequently asbestos or other hazardous substances, they are
hazardous waste, the export of which for disposal or for recycling is, under EU
law, prohibited. This prohibition is based on a corresponding provision of the
Basel Convention to which the European Union adhered. In order to bypass this
legislation, ships are sailing to South Asia with cargo, i.e. as "products", and the
dismantling/recycling decision is only taken in South Asia.

Regulation 1257/2013, anticipating a rather soft international convention
(Hong Kong Convention) which has not yet entered into force, provides for a
number of measures in order to stop the present form of ship recycling. Among
other things, an inventory of recycling facilities is to be set up which will list only
those facilities which comply with minimum social and environmental standards.
In order to bypass the provisions of Regulation 1013/2006, Regulation 1257/2013
declared that Regulation 1013/2013 did not apply to ships which came under
Regulation 1257/2013 (art.27). In my opinion, this is not in compliance with the
obligations which the European Union has accepted under the Basel Convention
which considers ships as hazardous waste, unless they are cleaned from all
hazardous substances, and which prohibits the export of hazardous waste. It is
true that this export ban has, internationally, not yet entered into force; however,
under the Vienna Convention on the Law of Treaties 1969, the European Union is
bound by the export ban, as it has adhered to it.

(i) Waste shipments to and from third countries

The first distinction to be made is between hazardous and non-hazardous waste.   **10–37**
This distinction does not follow the lines of Directive 2008/98 and the lists on
waste and on hazardous waste that had been adopted at EU level.[162] Rather, due
to historical reasons, the Council decided to largely follow a listing system which
had been developed by the OECD. Therefore, the question whether a waste is
hazardous or not is decided by the lists in the annexes to Regulation 1013/2006
(see art.36 of that Regulation). In this way, EU law in practice has a list of
hazardous wastes[163] and another list for the shipment of hazardous waste though
this is no longer called "hazardous waste list"; this is a model of non-
transparency.

---

[161] Regulation 1257/2013 on ship recycling [2013] OJ L330/1.
[162] See para 10–18, above.
[163] Decision 2000/532 as amended by Commission Dec.2014/955 [2014] OJ L370/44.

A second distinction is made by the Regulation between whether the shipment is made for disposal or for recovery purposes; for these, the definitions in Directive 2008/98 apply.[164]

Imports of waste for disposal of any kind into the European Union are prohibited, with the exception of imports from countries that are parties to the Basel Convention or where specific import agreements have been made either by the European Union or by Member States (art.41). The import of waste for recovery is prohibited, but such waste may be imported from countries which apply the OECD decision on waste shipment and from other countries with which specific agreements have been made.[165]

10–38 Exports for recovery of wastes which are not hazardous—these are now listed in annexes III and IIIA, though for the time being, these annexes are empty—are the subject of a complicated procedure (art.37). The Commission has to ask each third country, for all types of non-hazardous waste, whether it was ready to accept such waste, and, if yes, which kind of control procedure it wished to see applied. As there are more than 180 countries which had to be addressed, and as some of these countries did not answer at all, gave incomplete answers or subsequently changed their position, the different provisions which are now adopted by the Commission, have constantly to be changed and adapted.[166]

The delay was also due to the fact that the Commission had based its proposal on the trade provision of art.207 TFEU[167] and had proposed that those third countries that had indicated that they did not wish to receive waste, should nevertheless be able to obtain such waste, though under the control procedure which applied to hazardous wastes; the Commission had argued that some of these countries "may not be fully aware of the significance of their decision for those parts of their industrial sector which can use 'green' list waste for transformation and further processing".[168] This question is now regulated by art.37(2) of Regulation 1013/2006: where a third country does not answer a request, it has to be informed of the intended shipment which may then only go through where a written agreement by the third country is given.

All exports of *hazardous* waste for disposal are prohibited, except to EFTA countries which are also party to the Basel Convention. Furthermore, the European Union decided in January 1997[169] that as of 1 January 1998 all shipments for recovery to third countries were also prohibited, with the exception of industrialised countries.[170] This measure was a follow-up to a decision of 1995 under the Basel Convention to ban the shipment of waste for recovery to non-industrialised third countries.[171]

---

[164] See paras 10–31 et seq., above.
[165] See for details Reg.1013/2006 [2006] OJ L190/1, arts 43 et seq.
[166] See Commission, Regs 801/2007 [2007] OJ L179/6; 1418/2007 [2007] OJ L316/6.
[167] In *Commission v European Parliament and Council*(C-411/06) [2009] E.C.R. I-7585, the Court of Justice clarified that the present arrt.192 and not the present art.207 TFEU was the correct legal basis for Reg.1013/2006.
[168] Commission, COM(94) 678, para.11.
[169] Regulation120/97 [1997] OJ L 22/14.
[170] Formally, the exception was made for countries which apply the OECD decision of 30 March 1993 on the shipment of waste for recovery.
[171] See Dec.97/640 adhering to this Basel Convention Decision [1997] OJ L272/45.

As regards the waste that comes under this export ban, Regulation 1013/2006   **10–39**
established its own lists of wastes (annex V), even though the management of
these lists and their daily use are bound to create ongoing problems for export
controls, customs officers, etc.

(ii)   Shipments between Member States

Non-hazardous wastes that are destined for recovery may freely circulate   **10–40**
between Member States; their shipment need not be notified. Regulation
1013/2006 expressed this principle by referring to wastes which do not come
under specific annexes. Regulation 1013/2006 allowed a Member State to take
the necessary measures to prevent movement of wastes that were not in
accordance with its waste management plans,[172] a provision that has until now
not been frequently used.

Shipments of waste for disposal were subject to the principles of proximity
and self-sufficiency,[173] principles that, normally, only applied to waste disposal,
not to waste recovery shipments. However, Directive 2008/98 added to this the
recovery of municipal waste. This means in practice that municipalities could
prohibit the shipment of municipal waste to other places, where they wanted to
incinerate such waste themselves,[174] a provision which had been favoured in
particular by Germany, as German municipalities have large over-capacities.
Directive 2008/98 also allowed Member States to object to shipments for
recovery which went to waste incinerators, "where it is established that such
shipments would result in national waste having to be disposed of or waste
having to be treated in a way that is not consistent with their waste management
plan".[175] Member States may prohibit generally or partially or object systematically to waste shipments for disposal; furthermore, they may also object to
individual shipments.[176]

Subject to the changes which Directive 2008/98 introduced, shipments of
hazardous waste for recovery may not be objected to systematically. Rather, the
grounds for objection are laid down in art.12 of Regulation 1013/2006 and may
also not be extended by a Member State that invokes its right, under art.193
TFEU, to set more stringent requirements.[177] Again, the details of the intended

---

[172] Regulation 1013/2006 [2006] OJ L190/1, art.12(1)(k).

[173] See on the distinction between shipments for disposal and shipments for recovery, Court of Justice *Ragn-Sell* (C-292/12) ECLI:EU:C:2013:820.

[174] Directive 2008/98 [2008] OJ L312/3, art.16: "1. Member States shall ... establish an integrated and adequate network of waste disposal installations and of installations for the recovery of mixed municipal waste collected from private households ... 2. The network must be designed to enable the Community as a whole to become self-sufficient in waste disposal as well as in the recovery of waste referred to in paragraph 1, and the Member States to move towards that aim individually ... 3. The network shall enable waste to be disposed of or waste referred to in paragraph 1 to be recovered in one of the nearest appropriate installations."

[175] Directive 2008/98 [2008] OJ L312/3, art.16(1).

[176] Regulation1013/2006 [2006] OJ L190/1, art.4(3).

[177] See, however, also Court of Justice, *Dusseldorp* (C-203/96) [1998] E.C.R. I-4075. The Court did not allow the Netherlands to recur to art.176 EC Treaty (now art.193 TFEU), because the objections which were allowed under Reg.259/93, were not applicable to the case.

shipment must be notified to the competent authorities, which may, in the case of dangerous waste, give tacit consent, but must agree in writing to the shipment of hazardous waste.

10–41   Overall, these provisions are rather sophisticated and bureaucratic; the number of possibilities for Member States to object to a shipment for recovery has even increased from five to 11 causes. The provisions must be understood as a reaction to several abuses of previous provisions, in particular those under Directive 84/631, but also reflect the will of Member States, *not* to have an internal EU market for shipments of waste, as well as of some Member States (Germany, Netherlands, Denmark) to allow local monopolies for municipal waste treatment. This is not quite understandable, as the bureaucratic provisions introduced by Regulation 1013/2006 are strict enough to prevent abuses.

(iii)   Shipments within Member States

10–42   Shipments of waste within Member States are barely regulated at all. Regulation 1013/2006 stated in art.1(5) that only art.33 applies to such shipments. This provision only required Member States to set up a monitoring and control system which is coherent with EU law. There was no change with regard to the previous legislation.

Information on the implementation and practical application of the Regulation is vague; in particular, there is a lack of precise data on shipments between Member States and on exports and imports. The Commission reported in 2006, 2009 and 2012 on shipments of waste,[178] the last report covering the years 2007 to 2009; 2009 is thus the last year on which information is available. Transparency is further made more difficult, as different terms are used for hazardous waste,[179] and as "exports" and "imports" sometimes refer to movements out of an EU Member State and sometimes only to movements outside the European Union. The Commission reported 400 illegal shipments in 2009, half of them between EU Member States; however, it considered the real number to be considerably higher, referring to a working group of IMPEL—see on this para.2–15, above—which had reported that one out of five waste shipments in the European Union did not comply with the requirements of Regulation 1013/2006.[180]

(iv)   Shipment of radioactive waste

10–43   Directive 2011/70/Euratom on spent fuels and radioactive waste allows the shipment of radioactive waste to another Member State, when there is an agreement between the two Member States for such a shipment.[181] Exports to non-EU countries are allowed, based on an agreement with the third country and on the condition that the third country ensures a high level of safety in general

---

[178] Commission, SEC(2006) 1053; SEC(2009) 811 and COM(2012) 448 and SWD(2012) 244,

[179] See on that para.10–27, above.

[180] Commission, COM(2012) 448, p.9.

[181] Directive 2011/70/Euratom [2011] OJ L199/48.

and with regard to the specific disposal facility, where the waste is to be disposed (art.4). In a report of 2013, the Commission declared itself unable to control compliance with that provision.[182]

Directive 2006/117 which replaced Directive 92/3, is based on arts 31 and 32 of the Euratom Treaty; it only deals with the shipment of radioactive waste and spent fuels which are to be disposed[183]; it was largely inspired by Directive 84/631 on the shipment of waste which had, however, been replaced in the meantime by Regulation 1013/2006. Consequently, radioactive shipments are dealt with by way of a directive, whereas shipments of non-hazardous and hazardous waste are the subject of a regulation; normally, one would expect the more stringent form of the regulation to apply to materials which present the higher risk.

Radioactive waste is defined as "any material which contains or is contaminated by radio-nucleides and for which no use is foreseen", a definition which implies that recyclable or recoverable radioactive waste is—for shipment purposes—not waste. In that, the definition is not in line with that of Directive 2008/98.

Shipments between Member States require the agreement of the authorities of the country of dispatch and of destination; normally, the absence of an answer within two months is considered to show tacit consent to the shipment. Exports of radioactive waste require the authorisation of the authorities of the dispatching country, which have to make contact with the country of destination. No export is allowed to countries of the Cotonou Convention, to Antarctica and to countries that are not able properly to manage radioactive waste; the assessment is made by the authorities of the exporting Member State. The Directive does not contain any provision concerning the possibility of Member States adopting a partial or total ban on the import of nuclear waste, though some Member States have banned the import of nuclear waste unilaterally.

10–44

Overall, Directive 2006/117 is considerably less stringent than Regulation 1013/2006. Also, conditions for authorising an export to third countries are less stringent than those for a shipment between Member States. Finally, as with hazardous waste, an export ban on radioactive waste to other than OECD countries is not foreseen.

4. SPECIFIC WASTE STREAMS

The European Union has regulated a number of waste streams. The purpose of the provisions is to promote waste recycling and recovery, safe disposal of waste and to ensure that different national provisions on waste management do not unnecessarily affect the integrated rules on the free circulation of goods. A useful

10–45

---

[182] Commission, Report on the implementation by the Member States of Council Directive 2006/117/Euratom on the supervision and control of the shipments of radioactive waste and spent fuels, COM(2013) 240, p.10.
[183] Directive 2006/117 on the supervision and control of the shipments of radioactive waste and spent fuel [2006] OJ L337/1; Dir.92/3 [1992] OJ L35/24.

assessment of five waste stream directives—on packaging, end-of-life vehicles, batteries, sewage sludge and PCB/PCT—was made by the Commission in 2014.[184]

(a) Packaging

10–46   Packaging waste is thought to constitute up to 40 per cent of municipal waste; in 2011, there were some 80 million tonnes of packaging waste on the EU market.[185] As early as the first environmental action programme it was announced that packaging issues would be looked at more closely; however, the Commission's initiative met with considerable hostility from economic operators, which were of the opinion that it would be better for the European Union to abstain from this area. The Directive, which the European Union finally adopted in 1985, was based on art.352 TFEU and was limited to liquid beverage containers.[186] It asked Member States to set up programmes for reducing the volume of liquid beverage containers. These programmes could even be implemented by voluntary agreements, which showed the Directive's limited objective.

Implementation of this Directive had only very limited success.[187] A number of Member States had adopted national measures on regulating packaging; attempts to have these measures declared void by the Court of Justice failed.[188] Since Germany, having been urged to do so by the Commission, introduced far-reaching measures on packaging, the Commission proposed a general Directive on packaging waste, which was adopted in 1994.[189] The Directive, based on art.114 TFEU, tried to lay down uniform provisions on the free circulation of packaging as well as on the protection of the environment. It asked Member States to promote prevention, reuse and recycling of packaging, to set up collection systems for packaging waste, and established binding recovery and recycling targets for the different packaging materials.[190] Furthermore, the Directive asked for standards for packaging, limited the content of heavy metals, and requested Member States to draw up management plans for packaging and to report regularly on the implementation measures.

Most Member States were late in transposing the Directive. As the recycling and recovery targets were fixed relatively low, a number of Member States made

---

[184] Commission, SWD(2014) 209.

[185] Commission, SWD(2014) 209, p.49.

[186] Directive 85/339 on containers of liquids for human consumption [1985] OJ L176/18.

[187] In 1990, five Member States had not yet transposed the Directive: see Commission, 8th report on monitoring application of Community law (1990) [1991] OJ C338/1, p.160. The Court of Justice gave judgments in the following cases: *Commission v Luxembourg* (C-252/89) [1991] E.C.R. I-3973; *Commission v Spain* (C-192/90) [1991] E.C.R. I-5933; *Commission v France* (C-255/93) [1994] E.C.R. I-4949.

[188] *Commission v Denmark* (C-302/86) [1988] E.C.R. 4607, where a deposit and return system for packaging was attacked; and *Enichem v Cinisello Balsamo* (C-380/87) [1989] E.C.R. 2491, where tax measures on non-biodegradable plastic packaging were in question.

[189] Directive 94/62 on packaging and packaging waste [1994] OJ L365/10.

[190] Directive 94/62, art.6, provided that, by the year 2001, between 50 and 65 per cent of packaging waste had to be recovered and 25–45 per cent were recycled; the minimum percentage for each packaging material was 15 per cent. Less stringent requirements were fixed for Greece, Ireland and Portugal.

use of the possibility under art.6(6) to get higher targets approved by the Commission. For the rest, the integration of the environmental and internal market requirements was only partly successful: imprecise drafting[191] and a loose reference to standards,[192] which did not fulfil the commitments of the Directive, placed the responsibility of achieving the Directive's objective on reducing quantities and promoting reuse and recycling of packaging back on to Member States which were not too keen to get into a battle with the packaging industry and the retailers. While the Directive allowed (national) environmental measures—for example to restrict the use of PVC packaging, impose returnable bottles, tax packaging and other measures—it did not impose them. This favoured divergency among Member States, not harmonisation.

In two cases which dealt with the German system on packaging, the Court recognised that Germany was entitled to introduce a mandatory system for deposit and return, in order to promote the use of returnable bottles.[193]   **10–47**

The target dates for recovery and recycling under art.6 applied until 2001. Targets for the period 2001–2006 were fixed by an amendment to Directive 94/62 in 2004[194] and extended until 2008.[195] Once more, the targets were fixed at a relatively low level. Consequently, the 2008 recycling targets were achieved[196] by all Member States; the recovery targets of 2008 were achieved by all Member States, except Cyprus, Latvia, Malta, Poland and Romania, several Member States largely overachieving them.[197] The prevention of packaging waste generation (art.4) had limited results which were mainly due to the reduction of weight in packaging; the "essential requirements" laid down in Article 9 and annex II, were too vaguely formulated to have any significant preventive influence.

No further amendment of the targets of Directive 94/62 was decided since 2008. This can only be explained by the fact that Directive 2008/98 now introduced recycling targets for paper, metal, plastic and glass, whether they

---

[191] See, e.g. art.5: "Member States may encourage reuse systems of packaging, which can be reused in an environmentally sound manner, in conformity with the Treaty"; the relationship to the recycling targets of art.6 is not clear. Another example is art.6 itself, which sets targets but does not establish measuring methods. Under certain conditions, Member States may even fix more stringent targets than those of art.6: see art.6(6) and Commission Dec.1998/3940, [1999] OJ L14/25.

[192] Under art.9, Member States shall admit only such packaging on their markets that comply with all essential requirements of annex II. Annex II provides that packaging shall be designed, produced and commercialised in a way as to minimise its environmental impact when it is disposed of. Furthermore, packaging shall be so manufactured that the presence of noxious substances is minimised with regard to their presence in emissions, ash or leachate when packaging is incinerated or landfilled. This might easily lead to national measures as regards metal cans, aerosols, non-biodegradable or PVC-containing packs, etc with endless debates about whether such measures are permissible.

[193] Court of Justice, *Radlberger* (C-309/02) [2004] E.C.R. I-11763; *Commission v Germany* (C-463/01) [2004] E.C.R. I-11705.

[194] Directive 2004/12 [2004] OJ L47/26.

[195] These targets for 2008 are (art.6): a minimum of 60 per cent of packaging material to be recovered; between 55 and 80 per cent of packaging material to be recycled; recycling targets for glass and paper and cardboard: 60 per cent each; recycling target for metals: 50 per cent; recycling target for plastics 22.5 per cent; recycling target for wood: 15 per cent.

[196] The Commission itself, though, puts some caution on this statement, as apparently, a number of Member States consider that the quantities which are collected "for recycling", are also actually recycled—which is not the case, Commission. SWD(2014) 209, p.52.

[197] Commission, SWD(2014) 209, p.17.

come from packaging or from other sources.[198] No legal objection could be raised against this more general approach—if it were not that of producer responsibility. Indeed, until now, packaging producers and importers paid for the collection and recovery of packaging waste. They will not pay for the collection of other than packaging materials, and controversies may be expected who shall bear the cost of the system for the separate collection of materials, which the correct percentage of packaging is, whether the collection shall be made by municipalities or by private business, who should bear the eventual economic loss or take the possible economic benefits, etc.

10–48   In 2014, the Commission proposed new recycling targets for packaging,[199] without explaining how the different targets in Directives 2008/98 and 94/62 would be reconciled with regard to the payment for the separate collection systems. This proposal was repealed, though, in early 2015.

(b)   Batteries

10–49   A second Directive, based on art.114 TFEU, regulated batteries and accumula-tors.[200] The Directive limited the content of some heavy metals—mercury, cadmium and lead—in some batteries. These batteries also had to carry a mark—a crossed-out dustbin[201]—indicating that they should not be thrown out with ordinary household waste; Member States had to organise a separate collection system for the batteries under the Directive. After an amendment of 1998, the use of batteries that contain mercury was almost completely forbidden.[202]

As the Directive only referred to some batteries, Member States had difficulties in getting it off the ground, to elaborate plans and to set up effective collection systems.[203] A revision was made in 2006, when Directive 2006/66 was adopted and Directive 91/157 repealed.[204]

The new Directive declared that its primary objective was to minimise the negative impact of batteries on the environment, but that it also wanted to ensure the smooth functioning of the internal market. Therefore, it was based on art.192(1) TFEU and, in relation to arts 4 (prohibition to place certain batteries and accumulators on the market), 6 (batteries which comply with the requirements of the Directive, may circulate freely) and 21 (labelling require-ments) on art.114 TFEU. It applied to all batteries, except to batteries for security

---

[198] See para.10–29, above.
[199] Commission, COM(2014) 397.
[200] Directive 91/157 on batteries and accumulators containing certain dangerous substances [1991] OJ L78/38.
[201] Introduced by Dir.93/86 [1993] OJ L264/51.
[202] Directive 98/101 [1999] OJ L1/1.
[203] *Commission v Italy* (C-303/95) [1996] E.C.R. I-3859; *Commission v Belgium* (C-218 to 222/86) [1996] E.C.R. I-6817; *Commission v France* (C-282 and 283/96) [1997] E.C.R. I-2929; *Commission v Germany* (C-236/96) [1997] E.C.R. I-6397; *Commission v Spain* (C-298/97) [1998] E.C.R. I-3801; *Commission v Belgium* (C-347/97) [1999] E.C.R. I-309; *Commission v France* (C-178/98) [1999] E.C.R. I-4853; *Commission v Greece* (C-215/98) [1999] E.C.R. I-4913; *Commission v Italy* (C-143/02) ECLI:EU:C:2003:179.
[204] Directive 2006/66 on batteries and accumulators and waste batteries and accumulators [2006] OJ L266/1. Directive 2013/56 [2013] OJ L329/5, amended Dir.2006/66, restricting in particular further the presence of cadmium and mercury.

and military purposes and batteries that are sent into space (art.2). Batteries with more than 0.0005 per cent of mercury by weight and portable batteries with more than 0.002 per cent of cadmium may not be placed on the market; an exception applied to button cells with a mercury content up to 2 per cent by weight.

Member States had to set up appropriate collection schemes for portable batteries, but could request producers to do so. Producers and persons acting on their behalf have to bear the costs of the collection schemes (art.16). Such systems may not charge end-users. Article 10 fixed binding collection targets for batteries—25 per cent by 2012 and 45 per cent by 2016—though an export outside the collection Member State or even outside the European Union was allowed and counts for the target, "if there is sound evidence that the recycling operation took place under conditions equivalent to requirements of this Directive" (art.15). The disposal of batteries in landfills and the incineration of industrial batteries was prohibited (art.14). 10–50

The Commission assessment of Directive 2006/66 stated that the 2012 collection targets were "almost" achieved, and that Belgium, Luxembourg, Austria, Germany, the Netherlands France and Sweden had already reached the 2016 targets in 2012.[205] Considerable problems exist as regards the collection of small portable batteries. The ecodesign requirements of the Directive are too vague and would need improvement. The Commission took no measures to ensure compliance with the Directive.

(c) Used oils

Directive 75/439, the very first environmental directive,[206] which was based on arts 115 and 352 TFEU, provided for the safe collection, treatment, storage and disposal of waste oils. Member States had to give priority to the recycling (regeneration) of waste oils, "where technical, economic and organisational constraints so allow". The discharge of waste oils into waters and drainage systems was prohibited. Activities concerning the collection, treatment and disposal of waste were to be licensed. Waste oils may not contain more than 50 parts per million of PCB/PCT. 10–51

Member States all transposed the Directive into national law, though sometimes with a considerable delay.[207] Its application only had limited success: the recycling clause did not fulfil expectation; most waste oils were incinerated; recycling remained a subordinate activity.

A Court judgment of 1999[208] clarified that Member States were obliged to give to the regeneration of used oils priority over incineration. As a consequence,

---

[205] Commission, SWD(2014) 209, p.29.
[206] Directive 75/439 on the disposal of waste oils [1975] OJ L194/23.
[207] See *Commission v Italy* (C-21/79) [1980] E.C.R. 1; *Commission v Italy* (C-30 to 34/81) [1981] E.C.R. 3379; *Commission v Belgium* (C-70/81) [1982] E.C.R. 175; *Inter-Huile* (C-172/82) [1983] E.C.R. 555; *Rhone Alpes Huiles* (C-295/82) [1984] E.C.R. 575; *Commission v France* (C-173/83) [1985] E.C.R. 491; *Procureur de la République v Assoc. de Défense de Bruleurs de Huiles Usagées* (C-240/83) [1985] E.C.R. 531; *Commission v Belgium* (C-162/89) [1990] E.C.R. 2391; *Commission v Italy* (C-366/89) [1993] E.C.R. I-4201; *Vanacker and Lesage* (C-37/92) [1993] E.C.R. I-4947.
[208] Court of Justice, *Commission v Germany* (C-102/97) [1999] E.C.R. I-5051. Germany was found to have breached EU law, because it had not given priority to the recycling of used oils. Later on, similar judgments were given in *Commission v Sweden* (C-201/03) ECLI:EU:C:2004:198;

the Commission introduced procedures under art.258 TFEU against all Member States except Italy and France. However, this only increased Member States' objections which had even introduced reduced tax rates for using waste oils as fuels. In particular, the cement industry was keen to use waste oils as fuels. In view of that, the Commission, basing itself on contested studies, announced that the preference of material recycling was not cost-effective. Despite protests, it proposed, when presenting the proposal to review Directive 2006/12, to repeal Directive 75/439 which was successful: Directive 2008/98 repealed Directive 75/439.[209]

(d) PCB/PCT

10–52   Directive 76/403[210] contained provisions to promote the recycling and control the disposal of PCB/PCT, a persistent organic pollutant that is carcinogenic and mutagenic. As recycling turned out to be impossible, the Directive was replaced in 1996 and, after eight years of negotiations, by Directive 96/59,[211] which provided for the decontamination and disposal of all products containing PCB/PCT. This equipment must be inventoried, labelled and reported. Member States were obliged to set up, by September 1999, disposal plans and ensure that PCB/PCT was removed from the environment by 2010 at the latest.

"The 31 December 2010 deadline for the complete decontamination or disposal has not been met by most Member States to a large extent. Conclusive inventories of PCB equipment are missing."[212] The Commission admitted that no recent and sufficient data on the Directive's application were available, but that it had not done anything to change this situation; in particular, it had not started proceedings under art.258 TFEU.[213] This Directive is thus another demonstration of the need to monitor compliance, as otherwise even legally binding obligations are ignored by Member States, with no pressure from the public, from NGOs or other interests.

(e) Sewage sludge

10–53   Directive 86/278, based on the present arts 115 and 352 TFEU, deals with the use of sewage sludge in agriculture.[214] The Directive fixed maximum limit values for concentrations of heavy metals in the sludge and in soil and defines conditions for the use of sewage sludge. Sludge and the soil on which it is used must be regularly analysed in order to make sure that the heavy metal concentrations are not exceeded. Member States were expressly allowed to set more stringent requirements. Presumably, in view of that, the values fixed by the Directive were

---

Commission v United Kingdom (C-424/02) ECLI:EU:C:2004:452; *Commission v Portugal* (C-92/03) [2005] E.C.R. I-867; *Commission v Austria* (C-531/03) [2005] E.C.R. I-837.

[209] See Dir.2008/98 [2008] OJ L312/3, art.41.

[210] Directive 76/403 on the disposal of PCB/PCT [1976] OJ L108/41.

[211] Directive 96/59 on the disposal of PCB/PCT [1996] OJ L243/31.

[212] Commission, SWD(2014) 209, p.13.

[213] Commission, SWD(2014) 209, pp.32 and 69.

[214] Directive 86/278 on the protection of the environment, and in particular of the soil, when sewage sludge is used in agriculture [1986] OJ L181/6.

not too severe. Several Member States adopted more stringent requirements at a national level "often way above" the limit values of the Directive.[215]

The use of sewage sludge in agriculture, which contains heavy metals and other hazardous substances, has met increasing objections from farmers and the food industry who are afraid of food contamination. Several Member States prohibited the spreading of sludge altogether. The Commission did not comment on whether such a ban is compatible with EU law. In my opinion, such a ban is allowed under art.12 of the Directive and art.193 TFEU. The free circulation of sludge—arts 34–36 TFEU—cannot be invoked, as the trade in sludge is not prohibited and no discrimination of producers or traders is visible. It is not the case that such a ban would be considered disproportionate, as it must be left to each Member state to decide how far it wants to go in the preventive protection of its soil—which is a non-renewable source.

A review of Directive 86/278, required under the 6th Environment Action Programme,[216] and favoured by most Member States, has never been proposed, and appears to have been abandoned. This Directive is another example of legislation which was not monitored by the Commission. The Commission admitted that the values fixed are clearly outdated, that new contaminants and substances appeared in sludge, that it never made a risk assessment as regards the (short- and long-term) risk of sludge for soil and food, that it never took any proceedings against Member States under art.258 TFEU, and that, "in its present form, the Directive is clearly outdated".[217]

(f) Animal waste

Directive 90/667 laid down hygienic provisions for the disposal and processing of animal waste.[218] The Directive was an early EU reaction to BSE ("mad cow disease"); it introduced "high-risk" and "low-risk" animal waste and stated that high-risk waste had to be adequately incinerated or buried in order to prevent environmental impairment. The Directive was mainly targeted at ensuring disposal of BSE waste without causing problems for humans or the environment.   **10–54**

After the full outbreak of the mad-cow disease and some other EU-wide scandals linked to animal feed and animal waste, Directive 90/667 was replaced by Regulation 1774/2002 which was based on art.168 TFEU; this Regulation was in turn replaced by Regulation 1069/2009 which applies at present.[219] Regulation 1069/2009 avoided almost entirely the word "waste", though many of the material regulated would come under the definition of "waste" of Directive 2008/98; the Regulation preferred the word "animal by-product".[220] The material was divided into three categories:

---

[215] Commission, SWD(2014) 209, p.33; see e.g. Court of Justice, *Commission v Belgium* (C-260/93) [1994] E.C.R. I-1611.

[216] Decision 1600/2002 [2002] OJ L242/1, art.8(2.iv).

[217] Commission SWD(2014) 209, p.34.

[218] Directive 90/667 [1990] OJ L363/51.

[219] Regulation 1774/2002 [2002] OJ L273/1; Reg.1069/2009 [2009] OJ L300/1.

[220] Regulation 1069/2009 1069/2009, art.3.1: "'animal by-products' means entire bodies or parts of animals, products of animal origin or other products obtained from animals, which are not intended for human consumption, including oocytes, embryos and semen".

- category 1 was mainly high-risk material which was suspected or proven to be infected with diseases communicable to humans or animals;
- category 2 included material which did not belong to the other two categories, and which appeared to present a certain risk; and
- category 3 concerned material which did not present risks.

Material from categories 1 and 2 may only be shipped to another Member State with the agreement of the latter (art.48). Reasons for refusing such an agreement were not given and were not laid down in the Regulation. The disposal of category 1 material was differentiated according to the risk that was linked to it; some parts could only be incinerated, other parts could also be landfilled or processed. Similar, but less strict, conditions applied to material from category 2, whereas for material from category 3, art.13 of Directive 2008/98 applied; this meant that it must be treated or disposed of without risk to humans or the environment.

10–55   The Regulation further contained relatively summary provisions on the approval of intermediary plants, storage plants, processing, oleochemical, biogas and composting plants and in particular rather detailed provisions for EU controls in Member States, inspections, on-the-spot checks and audits. Its relationship to Directive 2008/98 is not quite clear. Though, in theory, the scope of application of both texts is clearly defined, in practice the Commission hardly deals with questions of animal waste under Directive 2008/98, but considers that all animal waste is excluded from the provisions of Directive 2008/98.

(g)   End-of-life vehicles

10–56   A Directive of 2000 deals with end-of-life vehicles[221] of which about 15 million per year are generated within the European Union. The Directive was based on art.192 TFEU and became effective in April 2002. It contained a number of provisions to prevent waste generation from cars, by imposing restrictions on the manufacturing of new cars. Cars which were marketed after July 2003 were not allowed to contain lead, cadmium, mercury or hexavalent chromium (art.4); a derogation clause in annex II which was regularly updated, allowed some exceptions. With the much more industry-friendly approach by the Barroso Commission, this clause was used, after 2003, to cut back the original limitations and to accommodate car manufacturers with many more exceptions—though the purpose of the clause was originally to further reduce the number of exceptions.

Furthermore, the Directive contained recovery and recycling targets for cars which were gradually to be reached by 2015.[222]

Member States had to establish take-back schemes for end-of-life vehicles which had to allow the last user to give back the car without having to pay costs (art.5(4)). A car could only be deregistered—in particular with the fiscal authorities—where its user presented a certificate of dismantling which was remitted to the user by one of the dismantling bodies. These provisions tried to

---

[221] Directive 2000/53 on end-of-life vehicles [2000] OJ L269/34.
[222] Re-use and recovery of 95 per cent of the car weight, reuse and recycling of at least 85 per cent. There were intermediate targets for 2006.

establish the principle of producer responsibility which make the producer also responsible for his products once they reached the end of their service life and become waste.

The Directive contributed to considerably reduce the presence of heavy metals in cars. The intermediate targets for 2006 were reached by most Member States in 2011,[223] some[224] reaching even the 2015 targets at that time.

10–57

Problems exist, because the distinction between a used car and an end-of-life vehicle is not sharply enough defined. This allows in particular the illegal export of end-of-life vehicles as used cars or their treatment by illegal operators: in 2008, 4.1 million cars thus disappeared.[225]

(h) Waste electrical and electronic equipment

Directive 2012/19 on waste electrical and electronic equipment (WEEE), which replaced Directive 2002/96, followed in its structure the model of Directive 2000/53.[226] It was based on art.192 TFEU and is intended to cover electrical and electronic waste, of which was 8.3 million tonnes were produced in 2005, with an estimated 12 million tons in 2020. The Directive contained a positive list of the categories of equipment which was covered.[227]

10–58

WEEE is to be collected separately; since the end of 2006, a separate collection rate of at least 4kg on average per inhabitant/per year is to be reached; this obligation is replaced, as of 2016, by an average collection of the products put on the market (45 per cent in 2016, 65 per cent in 2019) (art.7). Collection facilities had to be set up which enable final holders and distributors to return WEEE free of cost. Normally, distributors which supply new equipment shall be obliged to take back the old equipment free of charge from private users or owners. Collected WEEE shall be brought to authorised treatment facilities; the disposal of collected WEE is prohibited (art.6).

Collected WEEE shall be treated, recycled or recovered, according to best available techniques. The above-mentioned collection targets of art.7 may be lower for all Member States—except Estonia and Cyprus—which joined the Union since 2004. The Directive tries to ensure that the collection from private households is free of charge (art.5). For the rest, detailed provisions deal with the responsibility of producers to finance collection systems. Producers are also required to respect the recovery targets fixed in annex V (art.11). These targets are different for different product groups and become stricter over time: they range from 50 to 75 per cent for recycling in 2015 to 55 to 80 per cent as of 2018, and from 70 to 80 per cent of recovery in 2015 to 75 to 85 per cent as of 2018.

---

[223] Commission SWD(2014) 209, p.24. The re-use and recycling targets were not reached by Estonia, France and Hungary.

[224] Commission SWD(2014) 209, p.24. These Member States were Belgium, Bulgaria, Germany, Denmark, Latvia, Malta, Poland and Slovakia.

[225] Commission SWD(2014) 209, p.26.

[226] Directive 2012/19 on waste electrical and electronic equipment [2012] OJ L192/38; this Directive replaced Dir.2002/96 [2003] OJ L37/24.

[227] Large and small household appliances, IT and telecommunications equipment, consumer equipment, lighting equipment, electrical and electronic tools, toys, leisure and sports equipment, medical devices, monitoring and control instruments and automatic dispensers.

10–59   In order to inform consumers and users, electrical and electronic equipment had to be marked with a crossed-out wheeled bin (art.15).[228] The Directive contained a considerable number of other information obligations for producers and distributors, as well as reporting obligations for Member States and the Commission. As the Directive covered new ground, adaptation of its provisions by Parliament and Council was foreseen, in particular as regards the quantified targets.

A particular concern which the Directive tried to address was the large amount of electrical and electronic waste which was exported from the Union under the qualification of "product". Annex VI requires detailed evidence from an exporter that he actually exports products and not waste material: in particular, the responsible person shall submit the contract and the invoice which states, among other things, that the equipment is functional. He must submit evidence of "evaluating or testing ... on each item" of the consignment which proves its functionality, and must submit a declaration that "none of the equipment" constitutes waste. Where these conditions are not fulfilled, the consignment shall be considered an illegal shipment of waste.

The Directive did not contain provisions on the ban of hazardous substances in electrical and electronic equipment. In contrast to Directive 2000/53 on end-of-life vehicles which included such provisions, the Council and the European Parliament accepted the Commission's proposal that such restrictions should be enshrined in a separate directive which was adopted at the same time as the WEEE Directive.[229] The reason for this procedure was that this separation allowed Directive 2002/95 to be based on art.114 TFEU. As a consequence, no Member State was allowed to maintain or introduce further bans or restrictions of dangerous substances in electrical and electronic equipment than those laid down in Directive 2011/65, except under the very strict conditions of art.114(4) and (5) TFEU. As with Directive 2000/53, the exception clause in Directive 2011/65 for certain uses of heavy metals was used, since 2004, to considerably increase the number of exceptions.

10–60   Member States had some difficulties in setting up the collection, dismantling and recycling systems at local and regional level, as this required close cooperation with industry, for which both sides were not always well prepared.

(i) Mining waste

10–61   In 2006, the European Union adopted Directive 2006/21 on mining waste.[230] This Directive was a consequence of the accidents of Aznalcollar in Spain and Baia Mare in Romania. When investigating these accidents, the Commission found that mining activities were largely exempted from existing EU environmental legislation and that the provisions of Directive 1999/31 on landfills did not always comply with practices in the mining industry.

---

[228] See para.6–54, above; that symbol is also used for batteries which must be collected separately, see para.10–49, above.

[229] Directive 2011/65 [2011] OJ L174/88; this Directive replaced Dir.2002/95 [2003] OJ L37/19. It was amended by Commission delegated Dir.2015/863 [2015] OJ L137/10 which prohibited the use of four phthalates in electrical and electronic equipment (DEHP, BBP, DBP and DIBP).

[230] Directive 2006/121 on the management of waste from the extracting industries [2006] OJ L102/15.

The Directive tried to lay down basic provisions for the storage and treatment of mining waste, the prevention of accidents, the permitting of mining activities and for reducing the strict standards for landfills under Directive 1999/31 by accommodating the mining industry.

(j) Other waste streams

Besides these measures, to which asbestos waste questions should be added,[231] **10–62** other waste streams are being examined by the European Union; the 6th Environment Action Programme mentioned explicitly construction and demolition waste, and biodegradable waste.[232] While construction and demolition waste is not likely to be subjected to EU provisions in the near future—Directive 2008/98 provided for a recycling target of 70 per cent by 2020—a proposal for biodegradable waste,[233] which includes provisions on the composting of waste, has for a number of years been requested by Member States, economic operators and the European Parliament. As the Commission opposes a new directive, Directive 2008/98 only contained some general observations on bio-waste; the Commission was again invited to assess the situation and, if it considered it appropriate, come up with a proposal (art.22).

It is unlikely that the Commission will propose, in the years to come, new legislation for specific waste streams.

A Council Recommendation from 1981 on waste paper tried to promote the recycling of waste paper,[234] but remained largely unacknowledged. Its impact on economic or administrative practices was insignificant.

---

[231] See para.4–50, above.

[232] Decision 1600/2002 [2002] OJ L242/1, art.8(2.iv).

[233] Directive 2008/98 [2008] OJ L312/3 now defines bio-waste as follows (art.3 no.4): "biodegradable garden and park waste, food and kitchen waste from households, restaurants, caterers and retail premises and comparable waste from food processing plants".

[234] [1981] OJ L355/56.

CHAPTER 11

Legal Aspects of Integrating Environmental Requirements

1. GENERAL REMARKS

Article 11 TFEU requires that environmental protection requirements are incorporated into other EU policies.[1] This message has been part of the EC Treaty since 1987, when for the first time provisions on environmental protection were incorporated into the Treaty. Indeed, it was clear by then, and it is now even more evident than ever, that the relatively few environmental regulations and directives which the European Union has adopted since 1975 will neither, in themselves, reach a high level of environmental protection nor protect, preserve and improve the quality of the environment or avoid its deterioration. The use of chemicals, the growth of transport and the use of fossil or nuclear fuels continues and even increases. Directives on car emissions will help little in making transport sustainable, since besides the emissions the cars themselves are also the problem. Without specific environmental provisions the environment would probably be in a much worse state; however, this does not necessarily mean that quality of life, in urban centres or elsewhere, has improved, that the progressive disappearance of fauna and flora species has stopped or that climate change problems, tropical forest decline or other environmental problems generally have become insignificant.

11–01

The concept of sustainable development, now also used in art.3(3) and (5) and Recitals 9 TEU and 11 TFEU, tries to assemble all the opposing interests between environmental protection and economic progress into one formula, in order to find a political compromise to which everybody can agree. This attempt is doomed to fail, because the concept of sustainable development is void of sense and is given a political content according to the political actor who uses it.[2]

The integration requirement of art.11 TFEU is nevertheless the most important of the provisions which govern environmental policy,[3] since it constitutes the bridge between environmental policy and all the other policies at EU level. Any effort to describe the achievements of the integration of environmental requirements into the other EU policies would also have to address the EU policies in general, not only the legal aspects of integration. Since this book does

---

[1] Article 11 TFEU: "Environmental protection requirements must be integrated into the definition and implementation of Union policies and activities, in particular with a view to promoting sustainable development."

[2] See paras 1–14 et seq., above.

[3] See for this and the other requirements, paras 1–28 et seq., above.

not try to examine policies themselves, but to describe legal measures, its presentation of the other policies will necessarily remain limited and even rudimentary. Some indication as to the necessity of an approach to integration which combines political, legal, economic and strategic action might appear from the list of criteria which the European Environment Agency established for assessing the integration of environmental actions into sectoral policies[4]:

1.   Is there qualitative identification of all environmental costs/benefits?
2.   Is there quantification of environmental costs/benefits?
3.   Are all external costs internalised into market prices (part of the polluter-pays principle)?
4.   Are economic instruments designed to achieve behaviour change rather than just revenue raising?
5.   Are environmentally damaging subsidies being withdrawn?
6.   Is there an environmental impact assessment of projects before implementation?
7.   Is there strategic environmental impact assessment of policies, plans and programmes at different spatial levels?
8.   Is environmental procurement a cornerstone of purchasing strategy?
9.   Are there environmental management measures within the sector and monitoring of their implementation?
10. Have eco-efficiency targets and indicators been developed and used to monitor progress?

11–02   Legal (binding or not binding) or political instruments for the application of these criteria have, up to now, not been developed at EU level, with the exception of a Directive on strategic environmental assessment of plans and programmes.[5] Thus, the list is an accumulation of wishful thinking: neither energy nor transport policy, neither fishery nor agricultural policy ever tried to consciously follow the ten points. For all policies, though, it should be clear that the integration of environmental issues must be conceived of as a process which might take decades to achieve and does not depend on one or the other legal or political measure which is adopted; examples would be changes in transport policy, the renouncing of nuclear energy or the transition to environmentally friendly agriculture, where organic farming would be the rule, not the exception.

The Commission tried, in 1993, to organise its internal administration in such a way so as to allow it better to take into consideration environmental requirements[6]; these administrative measures were reviewed in 1997.[7] However, it is significant that it was not really attempted to give these decisions the widest publicity possible; in this way, any serious control of their implementation by the other institutions, the media or the public was lacking.

The Commission measures provided mainly for the following actions[8]:

---

[4] European Environment Agency, *Europe's Environment, the Second Assessment* (Aarhus, 1998), Ch.14.

[5] Directive 2001/42 [2001] OJ L197/30; see also para.4–33, above.

[6] Commission, SEC(93) 785.

[7] Commission, Press Release IP/97/636 of 11 July 1997; the Commission's (1997) *Bulletin on European Union*, no.7/8 is silent on this issue.

[8] Written Question E-0649/97 (Diez de Rivera Icaza) [1997] OJ C367/33.

- All Commission proposals are assessed on their environmental effects. Where such effects are likely to occur, an environmental impact assessment is to be made.
- Proposals for new legal measures should, in the explanatory memorandum, describe and explain environmental effects and environmental costs and benefits.
- The Commission work programme identifies with a green asterisk those proposals that will have significant environmental effects.
- In all relevant Commission departments, contact persons for the integration of environmental requirements were designated.
- An environmental network of director generals is set up, which is chaired by the director general for the environment and where the director generals of the most important departments are represented. The emphasis is laid on the total coordination of environmental questions and the interdependency between environmental policy and other political measures.
- A specific unit is created inside the environmental directorate-general, which is directly placed under the responsibility of the director general and which is charged with the implementation of the environmental action programmes and the integration of environmental requirements into other political measures.
- The Commission's annual report is partly modified; it now contains, for key political areas, an indication of which environmental considerations were taken into account.
- The Commission took a number of measures for its recycling, waste management and purchase policy ("green accounting"). A strategy paper was adopted in December 1995, which set a framework for these activities.
- Progress in better integrating environmental requirements into other policies are regularly assessed. The reviewed version of the 5th Environment Action Programme contains detailed information on the integration of environmental requirements into other EU measures.

The overall effect of these measures on the orientation of the Commission's 11–03 policy was insignificant. No environmental impact assessment was made for any new Commission proposal. In particular, the administrative (re-)structuring measures were bluntly rejected by the administration itself. The greater accentuation of environmental requirements, for example in the Commission's regional policy at the end of the 1990s, was less attributable to the above-mentioned measures than to the more environmentally oriented approach by the Commissioner in charge of regional policy.

The Commission did not ensure the implementation of these measures, but tried, since 2003, to make a new start for integration, by providing for an impact assessment for its major legislative proposals and important communications which defined future policies.[9] Under this policy, all such proposals shall be examined as regards their economic, social and environmental impact; furthermore, intensive consultations with stakeholders—government experts, trade and industry, environmental and consumer protection services—were to

---

[9] See most recently Commission, Impact assessment guidelines, 15 January 2009, SEC(2009) 92; see also more closely para.4–36, above.

take place. This policy led to the elaboration of lengthy documents which accompany legislative and other major proposals. However, generally these impact assessments are written when the political decision to propose legislation is already taken; they thus serve as a supplementary explanation of the measure which was proposed, not as an objective assessment.[10] Furthermore, the more important a measure politically is, the less precise is the assessment. For example, whether the mandatory introduction of filters for diesel cars will be proposed in order to reduce the emission of particulates, is not made subject to an environmental impact assessment, but depends on the question, whether the Commission is able to persuade the car industry and the car-producing Member States that such a measure should be taken. Once the decision is taken, an impact assessment will announce the environmental and human health-benefits of that measure.

11–04   Economists have, until now, not managed to convincingly assess in economic terms—and this is almost the only argument that counts at EU level—the advantages or disadvantages of a specific measure for the environment. The diminution of bird species in Europe or the damage made to soil every day—soil erosion, sealing, pollution, compaction and the other elements are mentioned in para.5–09, above—the particulates in the air which are supposed to cause some 400,000 deaths per year in the European Union and an unknown number of sick persons—nobody ever has calculated the impact. In contrast, when the cost for industry is in question, each environmental measure leads to an outcry that it would cause the loss of jobs and of competitivity, economic advantages for China and higher prices, and very precise figures are given to prove how dangerous this or that environmental proposal would be for industry. This is the reason, why so many environmental proposals are watered down and watered down even before the Commission presents them as official proposals. And this is the reason why, in practice, the Commission's idea of "better regulation" turns against the environmental policy and the concrete measures envisaged under this policy.

Until now, the impact assessment initiative of 2003 did not significantly contribute to the integration of environmental requirements into other sectors of EU policy. Reversely, it certainly has contributed to slowing down or blocking environmental initiatives for reasons of industry or trade interests. This might in part be due not to the instrument of impact assessment itself, but to the fact that, since the beginning of the twenty-first century, the Commission is more prepared to follow ideas of new liberalism. The Commission seems to see the European Union more as an inter-state cooperation body than a Union, and its own role more as a Secretary than a policy institution. What is lacking in the system, despite many good words in the Lisbon Treaty on European Union, is openness, transparency and accountability which will allow the policy-makers to balance the arguments fairly. Secondly, of course, there is a lack of a reliable method of measuring the impacts of a given measure on the environment, but also on society as a whole. This deficiency cannot be overcome for the time being: how can an environment impact on future generations be measured? The Commission could, of course, make ex-post evaluations of EU environmental measures, in order to learn its lessons, but it does not systematically do so. At the end of the day, it

---

[10] See generally L. Krämer, "Impact Assessment and Environmental Costs in EU Legislation" [2014] *Journal of European Environmental and Planning Law* 201.

remains that at the decision-making table—of the Commission, of the European Union—the environment is poorly represented, as it neither votes nor has a voice.

The creation of a directorate-general for climate change issues, in 2010, and the transfer of responsibilities such as biotechnology or animal testing, to other administrations within the Commission, rather contributed to further marginalising the environmental issues, administratively, but also politically. More and more the needs of environmental protection are comparable to the role which religion issues play in general policy: nobody openly contests their importance, but in the daily work, the requirements are all too often set aside.

The 5th Environmental Action Programme (1993) had singled out five areas of activity as target sectors where particular efforts were to be made in order to integrate environmental requirements in those policies, namely the manufacturing industry, energy, transport, agriculture and tourism.[11] For three of these sectors—the manufacturing industry, energy and tourism—the European Union did not, in 1993, even have an express competence for action. **11–05**

The "particular efforts" turned out to be purely on paper. Neither was there any infrastructure set-up—such as a network inside the Commission, regular joint meetings between environmental bodies and the specific ministers of Member States, Council meetings, public conferences, discussions, etc—nor were there any concrete joint actions launched. The reason for this failure was that the action programme had been elaborated by the Environmental Commissioner and had later been discussed by the environmental working group and the environmental ministers in Council—but agricultural, transport and energy administrations and policy-makers had not been associated with the work ("integrated"); they had other objectives and priorities and did not pay attention to the words in the action programme.

The negotiations and the signing of the Amsterdam Treaty in 1997 led to the transfer of the provision in environmental integration into other EU policies from art.174 to art.6 EC Treaty.[12] As a follow-up, the Luxembourg Council of Heads of State and Governments discussed in December 1997 how this new art.6 could be made operational, and charged the Commission to report on a possible strategy. The Commission prepared a report on the question[13] which the Heads of State and Governments discussed at their meeting in Cardiff in June 1998. That meeting invited the transport, energy and agriculture Councils to elaborate strategies for integrating environmental requirements into their sectors and to report on it. In December 1998, the internal market, industry and development Councils were asked to also elaborate a strategy. And in June 1999, the fisheries, economic and general affairs Councils were invited to develop a strategy.

Different integration papers were submitted by the Commission[14] and "approved" by the different Council configurations. However, these "approvals" were not made in a formalised way; the same is true for the discussions by the **11–06**

---

[11] 5th Environment Action Programme [1993] OJ C138/1, pp.28 et seq.

[12] See also para.1–28, above.

[13] Commission, Partnership for integration—a strategy for integrating environment into EU policies, COM(98) 333.

[14] See Commission, COM(98) 716 and COM(99) 640 (transport); COM(98) 571 (energy); COM(99) 22 and COM(2000) 20 (agriculture); COM(1999) 263 (internal market); COM(1999) 36 and COM(2000) 264 (development); COM(2001) 143 (fishery); COM(2000) 576 (economic questions); and SEC(2002) 271 (external affairs).

Heads of State and Governments. They constituted thus at best a sort of political commitment for the different Councils; and also the Commission felt not in any way legally—probably not either politically, as differences in the opinions were covered by diplomatic language—bound by the Councils' resolutions or other statements.[15] While the process of developing and discussing "strategies" was never formally brought to a halt, it progressively turned more in political declamation than leading to a work programme with objectives, priorities and timetables. Following a Commission Communication in 2004,[16] the Cardiff process is dead. The only thing that is annoying is that art.11 TFEU continues to exist and requests to integrate environmental requirements into the other policies.

This integration process crossed with the "sustainability process" which was started in Lisbon 2000 and promised to make the European Union the most performing economy worldwide in ten years, ensuring at the same time high social protection. During the Swedish Presidency, the Heads of State and Governments added an environmental dimension to the Lisbon process for employment, economic reform and social progress.[17] The fixing of a target date led to the attempt to develop measurement instruments, in order to assess progress towards 2010; this created the efforts to develop indicators. As the environment did not really have environmental performance indicators, their number remained limited; in particular, these indicators were neither really representative nor were they "filled" with reliable national or regional data.[18] Measuring integration of environmental requirements into other policies thus remains an adventure and, in practice, is largely ignored or selective: environmental arguments are being used, when it suits, to support other arguments.

In 2010, the Commission adopted its strategy paper for 2020 "smart, sustainable and inclusive growth".[19] Environmental concerns were reduced to climate change and energy issues; the accent was, as in 2000, on growth and jobs, and the Juncker Commission, in office since end of 2014, has not given the slightest sign of being willing to change this priority.

11–07 The conclusion of this short description of past and present efforts is that any political and administrative effort to give life to art.11 TFEU at EU level has been abandoned or, in a number of policy areas—consumer protection, competition policy, development policy—even not seriously started. There are some tendencies in "greening" the policy in the area of fishery, agriculture, and, in

---

[15] It should be remembered that in 1999 the Commission resigned and was replaced; the European Parliament changed its political majority after general elections; in a number of Member States, governments changed.

[16] Commission, Integrating environmental considerations into other policy areas—a stocktaking of the Cardiff process, COM(2004) 394.

[17] Lisbon Statement: "The Union is to become the most competitive and dynamic knowledge-based economy in the world, capable of sustainable economic growth with more and better jobs and greater social cohesion". The European Council in Stockholm 2001 added to that: "the European Union sustainable development strategy should complete and build on the Lisbon statement by including an environmental dimension".

[18] See more closely paras 1–14 et seq., above. There is up to now (mid-2015) no general provision on environmental indicators and their representativity in EU policy and law.

[19] Commission, COM(2010) 2020: Europe 2020; smart, sustainable and inclusive growth. Smart growth was described as "developing an economy based on knowledge and innovation", sustainable growth as "promoting a more resource efficient, greener and more competitive economy", and inclusive growth as "fostering a high-employed economy delivering social and territorial cohesion".

particular due to the climate change discussions, also on energy. However, these efforts are due to external pressure: the European Union had to react to the problem that fish had disappeared because of overfishing; that the Common Agricultural Policy had become too expensive and too restrictive to imports; and that climate change raised the necessity to take energy-related measures at EU level, though there was no explicit legal competence to do so. The Lisbon Treaty created an EU competence for energy issues and made agricultural and—to a large extent—fisheries policies areas of shared competence. As regards the integration of environmental requirements, this constitutional change is not likely to improve the present situation.

The integration of environmental requirements into other policies, a legal requirement under art.11 TFEU, will start to become a reality once the Court of Justice annuls an EU regulation or directive, because it did not respect art.11. Whether the Court will ever give such a judgment, is, of course, unknown. Until that time, art.11 will remain a nice objective that is not taken seriously by the EU institutions and administrations.

2. AGRICULTURAL POLICY

Since December 2009, when the Lisbon Treaty on European Union entered into **11–08** effect, agricultural policy is of shared competence between the Union and the Member States; until then, it had been a common policy, i.e. the Union had exclusive competence. Agricultural policy is based on arts 38–44 TFEU. Agricultural policy pursues the objectives of art.39,[20] which may, in general terms or in concrete measures, conflict with the environmental objectives of art.191 TFEU.

The Commission's progress reports of 1999 and 2000, on integrating environmental requirements into the agricultural sector, mentioned above, remained relatively general, but recognised that the agricultural policy had not changed much. The European Environment Agency identified the agriculture/ forestry sector as a principal contributor to the environmental problems of climate change, chemicals, soil, waste, acidification, biodiversity, inland waters and marine and coastal zones.[21] The Agency gave this resumé[22]:

> "Overall, fertiliser and pesticide use in Europe has decreased since the late 1980s, owing to improved application methods in the West and reduced agricultural output and incomes in Eastern Europe. The number of cattle and pigs has fallen in Europe as a whole, although animal manure remains a pollution problem in north-western Europe and is causing increasing problems in southern Europe. Water use for irrigation has increased, causing wetland loss and supply shortages in some areas. Soil compaction and other forms of soil degradation caused by agricultural practices

---

[20] Article 39(1) TFEU: "The objectives of the common agricultural policy shall be: (a) to increase agricultural productivity by promoting technical progress and by ensuring the rational development of agricultural production and the optimum utilisation of the factors of production, in particular labour; (b) thus to ensure a fair standard of living for the agricultural community, in particular by increasing the individual earnings of persons engaged in agriculture; (c) to stabilise markets; (d) to assure the availability of supplies; (e) to ensure that supplies reach consumers at reasonable prices".

[21] European Environment Agency, *Europe's Environment, the Second Assessment* (1998), Ch.14.1.

[22] European Environment Agency, *Europe's Environment, the Second Assessment* (1998), Ch.14.2.

(for example desertification and salinisation) are still widespread, especially in southern Europe and in the Newly Independent States.

Habitats and species are under increasing threat from intensive agriculture in all parts of Europe, but particularly in the European Union due to current Common Agricultural Policy priorities that continue to place emphasis on increasing yields. In parts of Central and Eastern Europe, there has been an increase in chemical-free food production, for economic reasons."

In 2001, the Agency reported that agricultural negative impact on land use, water use, river water quality, eutrophication and biodiversity was still significant, impacts on water use and biodiversity even increasing.[23] In 2002, it mentioned that nutrient surplusses on agricultural land remained a serious problem, causing nitrate pollution of groundwaters and eutrophication of aquatic ecosystems, furthermore, that specialising farming practices—practices which has been pushed by the common agricultural policy—had a negative impact on biodiversity. The 2005 Report did not address agricultural impacts as such; it reported that the water pollution through nitrates has been reduced between 1990 and 2000, with large regional differences, though.[24] In its 2007 report, the Agency identified soil erosion, greenhouse gas and ammoniac emissions, the increase of irrigable areas within the European Union (12 per cent between 1990 and 2000), the threat of diffuse pollution to ground and surface water, the continued decline of biodiversity loss as of particular concern and made the general observation: "Most environmental objectives and targets are not concrete enough to assess, whether they are realised."[25]

11–09 The 2015 Synthesis Report of the European Environment Agency[26] does not contain a specific section on agriculture. However, the different subtitles in Chapter 3 are relevant enough—though, of course, not all trends are attributable to the agricultural sector alone:

- Biodiversity decline and ecosystem degradation reduce resilience.
- Land-use change and intensification threaten soil ecosystem services and drive biodiversity loss.
- Europe is far from meeting water policy objectives and having healthy aquatic ecosystems.
- Water quality has improved, but the nutrient load of water bodies remains a problem.
- Despite cuts in air emissions, ecosystems still suffer from euthrophication, acidification and ozone.
- Marine and coastal biodiversity is declining, jeopardising increasingly needed ecosystem services.
- The impacts of climate change on ecosystems and society call for adaptation measures.

[23] European Environment Agency, *Environmental Signals 2001* (Copenhagen, 2001), p.49.
[24] European Environment Agency, *Environmental Signals 2002* (Copenhagen, 2002), p.44; *The European Environment, State and Outlook 2005* (Copenhagen, 2005), p.352.
[25] European Environment Agency, Integration of environment into EU agricultural policy—the IRENA indicator-based assessment report, EEA Report 2/2006 (Copenhagen, 2007).
[26] European Environment Agency, *The European Environment—state and outlook 2015*, Synthesis Report (Luxembourg, 2015).

- Integrated management of natural capital can increase environmental, economic and social resilience.

The objectives of agricultural policy, laid down in art.39 TFEU, have not changed since the beginning of the European Union (1958). Environmental considerations came only very slowly into perspective. A 1985 Green Paper devoted, for the first time, a special section on the environmental effects of agriculture.[27] In 1988 a Communication on "agriculture and the environment" followed, which was based on the assumption that the Common Agricultural Policy was already under pressure anyway and did not need supplementary pressure from the environmental side.[28] The general problems of agricultural policy led in 1992 to a substantial reform of the Common Agricultural Policy. Although environmental improvement was not among the main objectives of this reform, increased efforts were taken subsequently to ensure income to farmers by progressively considering them to be nature conservationists, with access to environmental money. In pursuance of this policy, measures were gradually introduced to grant financial aid for environmental services provided by agriculture, such as the production of energy, forest-fire prevention, water protection, stabilisation of carbon dioxide and other greenhouse gas emissions, recycling of organic waste, nature conservation and biodiversity management, tourism and recreation, soil conservation, landscape management, the setting aside of land and less intensive production methods or forestation. The principal objective remained, however, financial aid to farmers.

Since 1986, the European Union provided for means to protect forests against air pollution, by collecting reliable data and giving financial support for forest conservation measures. These provisions were reviewed in 2003, together with a more systematic strategy on forest management which takes environmental concerns into consideration,[29] but repealed in 2007.[30] A Regulation of 1991 established and defined rules on organic agriculture and the labelling of products thereof; in 1999, it was enlarged to include animal production,[31] and, in 2007, replaced by the actually applicable Regulation.[32] Organic farming has been on the increase since the early 1990s. It counts for about 5.4 per cent of total agricultural land in the European Union, but continues to be low in the 13 new Member States; Sweden, Italy, Austria, Finland and Denmark having more than 5 per cent, Malta, Bulgaria, Cyprus, Poland and Romania having no or almost no organic farm activity.[33] Overall, though, the Commission is not too favourable towards organic farming as it competes with traditional agriculture.

---

[27] Commission, Perspectives for the common agricultural policy, COM(85) 333.

[28] Commission, COM(88) 338.

[29] Regulation 3529/86 [1986] OJ L326/5; Reg.2152/2003 concerning monitoring of forests and environmental interactions in the Community (Forest Focus) [2003] OJ L324/1; see also para.5–04, above.

[30] Regulation 614/2007 (LIFE+) (2007) OJ L149/1.

[31] Regulation 1804/99 [1999] OJ L222/1.

[32] Regulation 2092/91 [1991] OJ L198/1; this Regulation was replaced by Reg.834/2007 [2007] OJ L189/1.

[33] European Environment Agency, *The European Environment, State and Outlook 2005* (Copenhagen, 2005), pp.356 et seq.

11–10   Regulation 2080/92 introduced a system of financial aid for afforestation.[34] Another Regulation of 1992 on agricultural production methods compatible with the requirements of environmental protection and the maintenance of the countryside[35] introduced a system of financial aid which aimed at the reduction of pollution caused by agriculture and at the promotion of farmers as nature conservationists and protectors of the landscape. The Regulation's role became increasingly important for the efforts to integrate environmental requirements into agriculture; in 1998, aid distributed by them covered about 15 per cent of all farmers and 20 per cent of EU farmland, though the number of contracts and the surface covered do not yet mean much with regard to the quality of these agri-environmental measures. This system was progressively extended as a second pillar of the EU agricultural policy: while the first pillar provided for direct payments to farmers and subsidies for agricultural products which were paid completely from the EU budget, this second pillar promoted a policy of rural development which included the promotion of agricultural and forestry competitiveness, the protection of the environment, and the improvement of quality of life in rural areas. The measures under the second pillar were in part financed by the Member States.

The European Union did not consider re-orienting its common agricultural policy for the years to come, but remained in the classical scenario.[36] Rather, following the traditional orientations of the agricultural policy, earlier provisions were replaced by Regulation 1305/2013 which grouped the different financial support schemes for rural development.[37] Agri-environment support could be given to contribute to a "more territorially and environmentally balanced, climate friendly and resilient" agricultural sector. Articles 15–39 and annex II of the Regulation specified the conditions and amounts which may be granted for organic farming (€450 to 900 per hectare and year) farming in mountain areas, in other handicapped areas (€25 to 450 per hectare), for farming activities in Natura 2000 areas, areas which are important under the Water Framework Directive 2000/60 (€50 to 500 per hectare and year), payments for voluntary animal welfare commitments (€500) and payments for afforestation measures (up to €200 per hectare). Farmers had to commit themselves for at least five years. The support was to be calculated on the basis of income forgone, additional costs resulting from the commitment given and the need to provide an incentive— which again gives a lot of latitude. The maximum amounts are €700 per hectare. New provisions of 2009 provide for state aid (or EU funding) for farmers who commit themselves to measures on climate change, renewable energies, water and biodiversity.[38]

Support for forestry "shall contribute to the maintenance and development of the economic, ecological and social functions of forests in rural areas". It could be given among others, to the investment to improve and rationalise the

---

[34] Regulation 2080/92 [1992] OJ L215/96.

[35] Regulation 2078/92 [1978] OJ L215/85.

[36] Commission, The CAP towards 2020. Meeting the food, natural resources and territorial challenges of the future, COM(2010) 672.

[37] Regulation 1305/2013 on support for rural development by the European Agricultural Fund for Rural Development (EAFRD) [2013] OJ L347/487. This Regulation replaced Reg.1698/2005 [2005] OJ L277/1.

[38] Regulation 74/2009 [2009] OJ L30/100.

harvesting, processing and marketing of forestry products, to the promotion of new outlets for the use and marketing of forestry products, the establishment of associations of forestry holders, etc. The amounts varied between €725 per hectare for farmers or associations thereof and €185 for any other private law person. These provisions sometimes make it difficult to see the environmental dimension of such measures.

EU measures that directly affect agriculture mainly stem from environmental **11–11** policy, such as the protection of waters against nitrates from agricultural sources,[39] the use of sewage sludge in agriculture[40] or the environmental impact assessment of agricultural projects.[41] The overall results of these measures are not yet impressive.

In 2001, the Commission announced an action plan for biodiversity in agriculture[42] which tried to give priority to:

- the conservation of genetic variety;
- the protection of wild fauna and flora; and
- to life support systems.

No concrete measures accompanied this action plan. It is therefore not surprising that a significant impact of this plan could not be found.[43] The nitrate reduction policy, centred around Directive 91/676, may not give results for some time, if at all. The same must be said of the thematic strategy on the sustainable use of pesticides, submitted in 2005, which led to the adoption of Directive 2009/128 aimed at the establishment of national action plans to promote the sustainable use of pesticides.[44] It can thus be fairly stated that changes as regards the impact of agriculture on the environment are likely not to be forced by the EU institutions, and will occur more by progressive changes in agricultural practice (globalisation, trend towards agro-industry) than by a policy to integrate environmental requirements into the agricultural policy.

Article 39 TFEU provides that agricultural products shall reach consumers at **11–12** reasonable prices. This could, in theory, also include the environmental costs which are caused by the production and distribution of agricultural products. However, agricultural prices, which are presently fixed by the EU institutions, do not reflect environmental costs at all. For a number of years, political pressure tried to align these prices with global prices for agricultural products; however, it is implicitly accepted that a price system for agricultural products could not simultaneously reflect environmental costs and align with world market prices. Hence, the more the polluter-pays principle is applied in agriculture, the greater will be the need to avoid competition with agricultural products from the world market, since products from many regions in the world—quite apart from labour costs—do not take environmental concerns into account. As regards the political

---

[39] Directive 91/676 [1991] OJ L375/1; see para.7–19, above.
[40] Directive 86/278 [1986] OJ L181/6; see para.10–53, above.
[41] Directive 2011/92 [2012] OJ L26/1; see para.4–30, above.
[42] Commission, COM(2001) 162, vol.III.
[43] European Environment Agency, *10 Messages for 2010 Agricultural Ecosystems* (Copenhagen, 2010).
[44] Directive 2009/128 establishing a framework for Community action to achieve sustainable use of pesticides [2009] OJ L309/71.

strategy, therefore, the European Union should reflect whether there is not a need to export environmental (and social) standards of the agricultural sector, instead of having the global discussion almost exclusively centred on the import of agricultural products into the European Union and on the price barriers which the European Union erected. Not much of such a policy is visible at present.

While it was mentioned in para.11–08, above, that the objectives of agricultural policy (art.39 TFEU) have not changed since 1958, the instruments progressively changed. A reform of 1992 started to move away from the policy of price and production support towards direct income aid for farmers and rural development matters. This was intensified by measures decided in 2003 which aimed at decoupling direct payments to farmers from production and to make them more conditional on agricultural and environmental practice. However, changes take time. "At present, agricultural support, even the direct payments, is still, in its major parts, tied to the level of (past) agricultural production than the reward of specific environmental services by farmers".[45] Subventioning agricultural products from organic farming to a level that they are not more expensive than products which come from traditional farming has not yet become a policy objective in agriculture. Also, the major recommendations which the European Consultative Forum made in 1998 to reach sustainable agriculture within the European Union were not taken over by the EU institutions.[46] The Court of auditors of the European Union, in a report of the year 2000, was of the opinion that the European Union had not yet reached significant progress in greening agriculture,[47] though the above-mentioned efforts in making the farmer the steward of the environment and pay him for that still continue and are even intensified. This situation was not significantly changed until 2015. The Commission action plan for organic farming concentrated on awareness-raising and information, but did not foresee financial support.[48]

3. FISHERIES POLICY

11–13 Under the Lisbon Treaty, the competence on fisheries is shared between the Union and the Member States (art.4(2.d) TFEU), except as regards the "conservation of marine biological resources under the Common Fisheries Policy" (art.3(1.e) TFEU), for which there is an exclusive EU competence. The basic Regulation concerning the Common Fisheries Policy dated from 2002; it replaced an earlier Regulation of 1992 and required that this Policy should take account of its implications for the marine environment.[49] In 2013, it was replaced by a new framework regulation.[50]

---

[45] European Environment Agency, *Environmental Signals 2002* (Copenhagen, 2002), p.52.

[46] European Consultative Forum on the environment and sustainable development: towards sustainable agriculture in Europe (Luxembourg, 1998).

[47] Court of Auditors, Special Report 14/2000 on the Greening of the CAP, together with the answers by the Commission [2000] OJ C353/1.

[48] Commission, Action plan for the future of organic production in the European Union, COM(2014) 179. Organic farming had a market share of 5.4 per cent (p.2).

[49] Regulation 2371/2002 on the conservation and sustainable exploitation of fishing resources under common fisheries policy [2002] OJ L358/99, replacing Reg.3760/92 [1992] OJ L389/1.

[50] Regulation 1380/2013 on the Common Fisheries Policy [2013] OJ L354/22.

The Commission indicated as the main problems of fishery the overexploitation, the pressure on non-target organisms and on the physical environment, the excessive capacity of the European fleet, the negative impact of aquaculture, in particular as regards water quality, dissemination of diseases and parasites and the introduction of alien species and unsatisfactory implementation of EU measures.[51] It pleaded for an ecosystem-based approach to fisheries management and suggested a series of measures to come closer to this. These objectives are less to be reached by legislative than by political decisions; and those policy decisions are therefore not described here.

Concrete EU measures for protecting fish and other marine resources are rare. Provisions on the mesh size, the nets to be used, the minimum size of fish which may be landed—all have some influence on the catches, though these measures are normally not taken in order to protect the marine environment or the fish. The European Union decided an almost complete ban on the use of drift-nets, exempting, though, the Baltic Sea, due to the representation of interests[52] which became fully effective in January 2002; in the Baltic Sea, the ban was only applied as of 2008. Measures under Directive 92/43 to protect natural habitats,[53] the different measures on water policy and management[54] and the integrated management of coastal zones[55] also have considerable influence on fisheries. As regards controls, the Council adopted a Regulation to establish a control system applicable to the Common Fisheries Policy.[56] Satellite surveillance was made compulsory, and from 1 January 2000 onwards all EU fishing vessels and those of third countries operating in EU waters with a length of over 20m had to be equipped with a Vessel Monitoring System which enabled them to be tracked and monitored.

Regulation 2371/2002 had tried to reduce the overfishing of stocks and the overcapacity of the EU fishing fleet. The measures were not really successful. Multi-annual management plans for 17 stocks were introduced. However, in 2011, the Commission reported[57] that 60 per cent of the fish were fished beyond sustainable maximum yield.[58] The main reason for this was, as the Commission reported, that the Council did not follow the scientific advice which based itself on maximum sustainable yield: "on average, Council exceeded advice by 45%, with peaks as high as 50% (2005) and 51% (2008)".[59]   **11–14**

Attempts to influence aquaculture are mainly channelled through giving financial support to installations that decrease their environmental impact. The

---

[51] Commission, COM(2009) 163 and COM(2011) 417.

[52] Regulation 1239/98 laying down certain technical measures for the conservation of fishery resources [1998] OJ L171/4.

[53] Directive 92/43 [1992] OJ L206/7; see also para.5–13, above.

[54] See Ch.7 of this book.

[55] Recommendation 2002/413 concerning the implementation of Integrated Coastal Zone Management in Europe [2002] OJ L148/24.

[56] Regulation 2846/98 [1998] OJ L358/5.

[57] Commission, COM(2011) 418.

[58] "Sustainable maximum yield" was defined by the Commission, COM(2011) 418, as "the highest catch that can be safely taken year after year and which maintains the fish population size at maximum productivity". Regulation 1380/2013 [2013] OJ L354/22, art.4(1) no.7 defined it as "the highest equilibrium yield that can be continuously taken on average from a stock under existing average environmental conditions without significantly affecting the reproduction process".

[59] Commission, COM(2011) 418, p.2.

2008 directive on the marine environment[60] is not likely to have any influence on the Common Fisheries Policy; as it was mentioned above, para.7–34, it proposed first of all to continue the monitoring of the European waters by the same (Convention) structures that exist at present. Also, it mainly dealt with water issues, but not with the fauna and flora of the marine environment. In 2006, the Commission stated[61]:

> "Whereas some stocks, like herring and mackerel, are exploited in levels approaching sustainability, catches of many bottom-living European fish stock have declined dramatically in recent decades. There has simply been too much fishing in relation to the productive potential of the stocks."

As regards the European fishing fleet, the Commission itself admitted that it was too big for the limited quantities of fish that were available, conceding thereby that practically nothing had changed in this regard over the last 10 years, despite all the words on sustainability in Regulation 2371/2002.

11–15   As the fishing associations loudly invoke the social problem linked to the decline of employment in the fisheries sector, and as a number of Southern European States—France, Spain, Italy, Portugal and Greece in particular—back this concern, any drastic change in the EU fisheries policy will be difficult to bring about.

Regulation 1380/2013 repeated much of the environmental language of Regulation 2371/2002 and introduced a number of new provisions, such as the obligation to land all catches (art.15) or the certain regionalisation of the Fisheries Policy (art.17). It did not follow the idea that the policy decision on allowable catches, which is taken every year, should be bound by the scientific advice on this matter.[62] Overall, it remains to be seen whether the Council and the Member States are prepared to actually apply the new Regulation according to its letter and to its spirit. It must also be stated that the over-dimensioned EU fishing fleet is already by now—and will continue to do so in the future—fishing in third countries' waters, on the bases of so-called partnership agreements with third countries.[63] Overfishing is thus by now a global and no longer just an EU problem.

Changes with regard to the Fishery Policy are therefore likely to come from inside: when there is no longer enough fish to catch, more care might be taken of the marine environment.

---

[60] See Dir.2008/56 establishing a framework for Community Action in the field of marine environment policy (Marine Strategy Framework Directive) [2008] OJ L164/19.

[61] Commission, Implementing sustainability in EU fisheries through maximum sustainable yield, COM(2006) 360.

[62] A first Regulation adopted under the system of Reg.1380/2013 shows that the Council continues to deviate from the opinion of its scientific adviser, the International Council for the Exploration of the Seas (ICES); see on the one hand Commission, COM(2014) 552 with the ICES proposals, on the other hand Council Reg.1221/2014 [2014] OJ L330/16.

[63] In mid-2015, there existed about 20 such agreements with third countries, see e.g. the agreements with Guinea [2009] OJ L156/35, Madagascar [2014] OJ L365/6; Seychelles [2015] OJ L40/1, Senegal [2015] OJ L65/1.

4.   TRANSPORT POLICY

With the Lisbon Treaty, the EU Transport Policy (arts 90–100 TFEU) became a   **11–16**
policy sector of shared competence (art.4(2.g) TFEU), while it had been, until the
end of 2009, a sector of exclusive EU competence. However, this construction by
the EC Treaty had never been realised; national transport policies continued to
exist and were in large areas much more relevant than EU transport policy. The
EU transport policy was for a long time targeted towards realising the four Treaty
freedoms for goods and services, capital and labour. The introduction of an
environmental chapter into the Treaty in 1987 has not yet fundamentally changed
this situation.

Transport policy contributes to the environmental problems linked with
climate change, acidification, tropospheric ozone, biodiversity, urban environment and technological and natural hazards, furthermore to land use, noise, waste
generation and marine pollution. Subsequent to the different environmental
action programmes, which mentioned the problems of the environment, the
Commission first issued a Green Book in 1992 on environmental problems linked
to transport,[64] which was quite quickly followed by a White Paper.[65] The White
Paper denounced the increase of environmental constraints over the last 20 years
and proclaimed that the consideration of environmental aspects was an integral
part of a common transport policy. In order to reduce the environmental impact of
transport, the White Paper pleaded for the adoption of strict standards for exhaust
emissions, energy consumption and noise emissions, as well as standards on
technical controls for cars, the establishing of noise level limits around airports,
and environmental impact assessments for infrastructure plans and projects,
including cost-benefit analyses. It pleaded for the promotion of public transport,
bicycles and electric cars, the reduction of private car use and the reduction of
land use for transport infrastructure projects.

Sustainable transport was defined by the Council as:

> "a transport system that:
>   allows the basic access and development needs of individuals, companies and
> societies to be met safely and in a manner consistent with human and ecosystem
> health, and promotes equity within and between successive generations;
>   is affordable, operates fairly and efficiently, offers choice of transport mode, and
> supports a competitive economy, as well as a balanced regional development;
>   limits emissions and waste within the planet's ability to absorb them, and uses
> non-renewable resources at or below the rates of development of renewable
> substitutes while minimising the impact on the use of land and the generation of
> noise." (Council, Resolution of 4–5 April 2001.)

This definition at least mentions the environment in substance, though in a   **11–17**
vague form. And it seems significant that the environmental concerns are
mentioned last in the list of objectives; this ignores the fact that the competitive
economy and balanced regional development cannot be ensured without
appropriate environmental protection, whereas the environment can well continue
to exist without competitive economy and balanced regional development.

---

[64] Commission, Green Book on the impact of transport on the environment, COM(92) 46.
[65] Commission, White Paper on a Community strategy on sustainable mobility, COM(92) 494.

Finally, the objective of promoting public means of transport, so dear to environmental policy, is apparently not an objective of transport policy. And the importance of such a definition should not be overestimated: where it is not followed by practical steps to put it into reality, it remains an empty shell.

Already in 1993, the 5th Environmental Action Programme which was entitled "Towards sustainability" had stated that:

> "because of the projected increases in the volume of cars used, the mileages driven and increases of road freight traffic, the transport ... will offset any potential reduction attributable to the introduction of new emission standards."

Its suggestions were to:

> "reduce operational pollution, limit the infrastructural development of land use, reduce traffic and congestion and prevent or reduce risks inherent in the transport of dangerous goods and wastes."

11–18   It suggested, in particular, road taxes, road pricing, regulation and fiscal incentives for fuels and vehicles and a change in user behaviour.[66] In 1995, the Commission adopted an action programme on transport 1995–2000[67] and a Green Paper on fair and efficient prices in the transport sector.[68] In 1998, the Commission adopted communications on sustainable transport, transport and CO_2 and the environment and heavy goods vehicles[69]; 1999 followed with a communication on air transport and the environment,[70] in 2001 a White Paper,[71] in 2006, 2008 and 2009 other communications, and in 2011 another White Paper.[72]

The White Paper of 2011 suggested three environmentally relevant objectives for 2050: (1) halve the conventionally fuelled cars in urban transport by 2030 and phase them out by 2050; (2) reduce greenhouse gas emissions from transport by 60 per cent by 2050 (compared to 1990); (3) fully apply the "user pays" and the "polluter pays" principle in transport. However, concrete measures on how to achieve these objectives were not given.

Overall, there was thus an impressive number of opinions, statements, resolutions and other political measures on the environmental impact of transport that have been adopted by the different EU institutions.

11–19   Legally, the most important measures are the efforts to limit the pollution emissions by cars and lorries.[73] The present concept is to reduce greenhouse gas

---

[66] 5th Environment Action Programme [1993] OJ C138/5, para.4.3.
[67] Commission, COM(95) 302.
[68] Commission, COM(95) 691.
[69] Commission, COM(98) 716; transport and carbon dioxide, COM(98) 204; Environment and heavy goods vehicles, COM(98) 444.
[70] Commission, Air transport and environment COM(99) 640.
[71] Commission, White Paper—European transport policy for 2010: time to decide COM(2001) 370.
[72] Commission, COM(2006) 314; (2008) 433; (2009) 279. White Paper: Roadmap to a Single European Transport Area. Towards a competitive and resource-efficient transports system, COM(2011) 144.
[73] See Ch.8 of this book.

emissions from transport by 2050 by 60 per cent (40 per cent from aviation and 40 per cent from maritime bunker fuels).[74]

The European Union only recently managed to introduce economic instruments, such as fees for the use of motorways.[75] EU rules on fees for the use of roads or airports, incentives for the use of less-polluting vehicles, fiscal advantages for public transport, or even simply the comprehensive promotion of electric cars do not exist.[76] Also, the recurrence to eco-points, used in the agreement with Austria on the Alpine transit,[77] has never been used as a model for measures within the European Union. There seems to be only very limited political determination, at EU level and at the level of Member States, to introduce the necessary changes in the form of a coherent strategy and legally binding acts. Only a minority of Member States pursue a national transport policy that integrates environmental requirements. Attempts to increase car production and to create a more efficient transport infrastructure—motorways, roads, railway lines, ports, airports and so on—are at the centre of transport policy practically everywhere; the necessity of creating this corresponding infrastructure reduces the efficiency of environmental measures.

A good example of non-integration is the European Union's 7th Environmental Action Programme.[78] It suggests enhancing the sustainability of the Union's cities and indicates that this would need "innovative approaches for urban public transport and mobility" (section 95). However, it does not cover the problems which are caused by urban transport, such as noise, air pollution where the EU limit values are regularly exceeded in large parts of the European Union, traffic congestion, land use in cities etc. "Sustainability" is the magic word which covers everything and means nothing.

All policy statements and other measures have not changed the trends. The European Environment Agency stated in 2001 that overall trends for transport policy were negative, in particular the decoupling of transport growth from economic growth, the management of demand for travel, the progress towards more environmentally friendly modes and the improvement of fuel efficiency; only trends in the reduction of resources and outputs that damage the environment, as well as efficient pricing had not worsened.[79] In the same year, a special indicator report from the European Environment Agency[80] indicated that out of 34 trend indicators for transport 19 were negative,[81] 12 were stable[82] and only two[83] were positive. The trend indicators for 2012 showed a slight

11–20

---

[74] Commission COM(2011) 144, p.5

[75] Directive 1999/62 on the charging of heavy goods vehicles for the use of certain infrastructures [1999] OJ L187/42 which replaced Dir.93/89 [1993] OJ L316/19, which had been annulled by the Court of Justice: *Parliament v Council* (C-21/94) [1995] E.C.R. I-1827, only fixes the frame for charges.

[76] See European Parliament Resolution of 22 January 1993 [1993] OJ C42/256.

[77] See Reg.3637/92 [1992] OJ L373/1; Dec.92/577 [1992] OJ L373/4.

[78] Decision 1386/2013 [2013] OJ L354/71, annex.

[79] European Environment Agency, *Europe's Environment, the Second Assessment* (1998), p.30.

[80] European Environment Agency, *TERM 2001—Indicators Tracking Transport and Environment Integration in the European Union* (Copenhagen, 2001). European Environment Agency, Towards a resource-efficient transport system, TERM 2009, Technical Report 2/2010 (Copenhagen, 2010).

[81] These mainly refer to improving shares of rail and public transport.

[82] Mainly for same emissions and the development of strategies.

[83] Investments in infrastructure and volatile organic compound emissions.

improvement in the energy performance, but the Agency was uncertain to what extent this was due to the economic crisis. The greenhouse gas emissions were, in 2012, 20.5 per cent higher than in 1990, and the share of renewables in transport was 5.1 per cent.[84]

The Commission's Communications of 2006, 2008 and 2009 paid some lip-service to the environment, but then discussed in great detail, what measures could be taken to have more roads, more traffic and more mobility. The shift from road to rail ("Modal shift") was not mentioned as a target any more. In 1996, the Commission concluded that transport in the European Union was not sustainable.[85] In 2011, the conclusions, drawn by the Commission itself were still the same.[86] In this way, transport policy is a good example of (not) integrating environmental requirements in other policies: the analysis of what could and should be done is made; however, the concrete actions bluntly ignore the environmental requirements. No serious will exists at EU level to elaborate and implement an environmentally sound transport policy.

5. ENERGY POLICY

11–21   As already mentioned, EU energy policy operated until the entry into force of the Lisbon Treaty (December 2009), without an express legal basis in the Treaty. Article 3 EC Treaty only allowed the taking of (some) "measures" in the area of energy. The lack of an express Treaty competence on energy did not prevent arts 154–156 EC Treaty (now arts 170–172 TFEU) from providing for the creation, under the EC Treaty, of trans-European networks, amongst other things, in the area of energy infrastructure.

According to the new art.194 TFEU, EU energy policy has the following main objectives:

1.   ensure the functioning of the internal energy market;
2.   ensure the security of energy supply;
3.   promote energy efficiency and energy saving;
4.   promote the development of new and renewable forms of energy; and
5.   promote the interconnection of energy networks.

Article 194 TFEU explicitly stated that these objectives shall be pursued while taking into consideration the protection of the environment. Thus, the environment has at least been identified as one of the elements which influence EU energy policy measures, which is not the case in any other EU policy.

11–22   Within the framework of these objectives, the Commission identified, already in 1997, three vital points on which EU energy measures must act: reduce dependence on supplies from energy sources outside the European Union, ensure more competitive prices for energy products and make energy markets more

---

[84] European Environment Agency, Focusing on environmental pressures from long-distant transport, TERM 2014, transport indicators tracking progress towards environmental targets in Europe, EEA Report 7/2014 (Copenhagen, 2014), p.7.
[85] Commission, Progress report on the implementation of the European Community programme on policy and action in relation to the environment and sustainable development, COM(96) 624, p.32.
[86] Commission, COM(2011) 144, p.2: "The transport system is not sustainable".

compatible with environmental objectives.[87] One reason for the slow progress in reaching these objectives is that Member States rely heavily on national sources of energy—oil in the United Kingdom, gas in the Netherlands, nuclear energy in France and Belgium, coal in Germany and Poland, for example—and wish to keep national responsibility for energy policy measures, including the responsibility to determine the price of energy.

The EC Treaty, the Coal and Steel Treaty and the Euratom Treaty all provided for energy measures. The Euratom Treaty was conceived in order to promote the peaceful use of nuclear energy, but very largely lost its political raison d'être when in the 1960s France refused to integrate nuclear policy into the EU mechanisms and Germany also went its own way. The Treaty of Lisbon did not include the Euratom Treaty and its provisions; the Euratom Treaty is thus a Treaty that stands on its own—an odd construction, as the main institutions (Commission, Council, European Parliament) are identical under the Treaty on European Union and the Euratom Treaty, and the different policies are, of course, closely interlinked. The construction finds its explanation in the different nuclear energy policies pursued by the Member States and by the determination of the "nuclear countries" (France and the United Kingdom in particular) not to suffer any interference from the Union on their national policies and measures.

At present, about half of the 28 EU Member States do not have nuclear energy production on their territory, mainly for environmental reasons. Sweden, Germany and Belgium have taken a political decision to phase out nuclear energy, though national policy changes might reverse these decisions. As the nuclear energy industry is extremely influential—backed also by the French and British governments—EU decisions on nuclear matters, including those relating to climate,[88] frequently took nuclear energy and its continuity for granted. Nobody dared even raising at EU level the environmental impact of nuclear installations, the risk of accidents or terrorist attacks, nuclear wastes, decommissioning of nuclear installations and the overall energy balance of nuclear energy. As regards energy decisions which were based on the Euratom Treaty, in particular on arts 30, 31, 34 and 37, they did not discuss the impact of nuclear energy on the environment in any significant way; they mainly considered effects of nuclear energy on human health, but not on fauna and flora or other environmental assets, and even there the approach is not consistent.[89] The nuclear industry, supported largely by governments, treats nuclear matters as a closed shop and has succeeded in having adopted only minimum provisions at EU level.[90] The dilemma that art.192 TFEU allows restrictions on nuclear energy activities for environmental reasons, but that the Euratom Treaty provisions are

---

[87] Commission, COM(97) 167.

[88] For climate change issues, see also paras 9–01 et seq., above.

[89] See, e.g. Commission Opinion [1997] OJ C291/5 on the discharge of radioactive substances from Sellafield (UK). The Opinion, based on art.37 of the Euratom Treaty, did not discuss at all the impact of such discharges on the Irish Sea, on the UK environment, or on marine fauna and flora. When the Commission examined the effects of French nuclear tests in Mururoa, it looked at their effects on people in other states (the Pitcairn Islands, United Kingdom), but neither on French citizens in Mururoa nor on the environment.

[90] See para.4–47, above on nuclear installations and on the prevention of nuclear accidents, paras 10–13 and 10–43, above on nuclear waste and para.7–13, above on radioactive substances in water.

interpreted as being *leges speciales* to the TFEU provisions and aim at the promotion of nuclear activities, is largely ignored by the EU institutions—and the public.

11–23   The Treaty on Coal and Steel entered into effect in 1952 and ended in 2002. Its functions were taken over by the European Union. It mainly provided for measures on coal, though measures on lignite could also be taken under certain conditions. The function of coal as the main energy resource in the European Union—which had taken over from wood in the nineteenth century—had already, at the end of the 1950s, been replaced by oil. The serious adaptation problems caused by this change continue to exist and have contributed to reducing the discussions on environmental problems linked to coal.

All energy resources with the exception of nuclear energy are thus subject to the provisions of the EU Treaties. Energy use contributes significantly to climate change and air pollution, acidification, tropospheric ozone creation, waste generation, soil degradation, marine and coastal zone problems and technological hazards issues, furthermore and use by installations and networks, water pollution and light pollution. As some of these environmental problems do not occur with the use of nuclear energy, the ongoing discussion on climate change leads to certain attempts to promote nuclear energy, although this energy is economically not competitive—except in France, where it has been subventioned for decades—and neither the problems of disposal of nuclear waste nor of decommissioning of nuclear installations have been solved. Furthermore, the population in the EU continues, in its majority, to be opposed to nuclear technology, which leads to nuclear decision-making bodies acting in a very closed-shop manner: openness, transparency, accountability and public participation are notions that cannot be attributed to the nuclear sector. EU measures on the safety of nuclear installations, nuclear waste and the shipment of nuclear waste are completely insufficient and not comparable to the measures which were adopted for non-nuclear installations and waste.[91]

As regards environmental-related energy measures, most provisions were based, in the past, on arts 192 or 352 TFEU. Article 192(2) TFEU expressly maintained a veto right for Member States in important energy matters, by providing for unanimous decisions in such cases.[92] Since the end of the 1980s, a number of political, not legally binding statements were made on the relationship between energy and the environment,[93] including the statement to stabilise carbon dioxide emissions by the year 2000 at the level of 1990, in order to combat the greenhouse effect.[94]

11–24   Of the different actions taken in pursuance of the energy policy, measures on energy saving, energy taxes and on renewable energies are—next to the measures

---

[91] See Dir.2009/71/Euratom on nuclear safety of nuclear installation [2009] OJ L172/18; Dir.2011/70/Euratom on spent fuels and radioactive waste [2011] OJ L199/48; Dir.2006/117 on the shipment of radioactive waste [2006] OJ L337/1.

[92] Article 192(2) TFEU: "[The Council shall unanimously adopt] ... measures significantly affecting a Member State's choice between different energy sources and the general structure of its energy supply." See also para.2–89, above.

[93] Commission, COM(88) 174; Energy and the environment COM(89) 369.

[94] Commission, (1990) 10 *E.C. Bulletin*, para.1.3.77; this commitment was made in a form of Council conclusions, i.e. in a political and unpublished form.

to combat climate change[95]—of particular interest here. The following measures on energy saving and on renewable energies were adopted: Directive 93/76 (SAVE I), which aimed at an improvement of energy efficiency in housing, cars and industrial companies[96]; Decision 91/565, which provided for financial assistance for energy saving measures[97]; Decision 93/500 (ALTENER), which promoted, particularly through financial incentives, renewable sources of energy[98]; and Decision 96/737 (SAVE II) which granted further financial assistance for energy-saving measures.[99] Generally, the amount of financial assistance that was made available by these measures was modest.[100] The discussion on climate change progressively led to the promotion of bio-fuels as a source of energy and, more generally, to the promotion of renewable energy sources.[101] The European Union succeeded in fixing binding targets for the share of renewable energies in the total energy consumption. However, the attempt to fix binding targets on energy efficiency failed, as the Member States claimed that this was a question of national competence (subsidiarity). In 2012, a Directive on energy efficiency was adopted which fixed an indicative target of 20 per cent increase in energy efficiency—without giving a base year of comparison.[102]

As regards taxes, the Commission proposed, in 1992, a tax on carbon dioxide emissions and energy.[103] The proposal was intended, in particular, to combat the greenhouse effect. It provided for an exception of renewable energies[104] and stated that:

"in order to safeguard the competitiveness of Community industry, the tax arrangements cannot be applied in the Member States until such time as other member countries of the OECD have brought in a similar tax or measures having an equivalent financial impact."

This announcement condemned the proposal, since Japan and the United States, in particular, clearly indicated that they had no intention of introducing a similar tax. The amended proposal,[105] which is in the meantime obsolete, provided for some conditions for the introduction of the tax, but left it entirely to the discretion of Member States whether they wished to introduce an emission/energy tax. Such a tax has been introduced by Scandinavian states and

---

[95] See Ch.9, above.

[96] Directive 93/76 [1993] OJ L237/28; see also the Commission's proposal COM(92) 182, which had proposed going considerably further.

[97] Decision 91/565 [1991] OJ L307/34.

[98] Decision 93/500 [1993] OJ L235/14.

[99] Decision 96/737 [1996] OJ L335/50.

[100] €45 million for four years for SAVE II (fn.91, above), €22 million for ALTENER II for two years (fn.90, above).

[101] Directive 2009/28 on the promotion of the use of energy from renewable sources [2009] OJ L140/16.

[102] Directive 2012/27 on energy efficiency [2012] OJ L315/1.

[103] [1992] OJ C196/1; see also para.9–22, above.

[104] Renewable energies were not defined; the proposal provided for exemptions for fuel wood and wood charcoal, products resulting from the distillation or processing of wood, and, furthermore, any product of agricultural or vegetable origin and crude or esterified vegetable oils. Compare that to the definition of renewable energies in Dir.2009/28 [2009] OJ L140/16, art.2(a): "energy from renewable non-fossil sources, namely wind, solar, aerothermal, geothermal, hydrothermal and ocean energy, hydropower, biomass, landfill gas, sewage treatment plant gas and biogas".

[105] Commission, COM(95) 172.

the Netherlands; several states have signalled that they would be ready to increase the tax, but abstained from it in order not to expose their industry to competitive disadvantages in comparison with other EU Member States. The considerations at EU level about energy tax measures continue, though, alimented by efforts to promote measures against climate change, to promote renewable sources of energy and to help farmers to become bio-fuel/energy producers (and to be paid for that).

In 2003, the Council adopted a Directive on the taxation of energy products.[106] This Directive repealed earlier Directives; it imposed minimum tax rates on all energy products. Energy-intensive industries and the agricultural, horticultural, piscicultural and forestry sectors could request to be exempted from the tax, provided they entered into national environmental agreements, participated in emission trading schemes or in equivalent agreements. The minimum levels of taxation, as of 2010, were fixed as follows (in €):

for industry and commerce use		heating fuels and electricity	
Petrol (1000l)	421		
Unleaded petrol	359	(heavy fuel oil)15	
Diesel	330	21	21
Kerosene	330	21	0
LPG (1000kg)	125	41	0
Natural gas	2.6/gigajoule	0.3 gigajoule	0.3 gigajoule
Electricity	1,0/MKwh		

11–25   As can be seen, this table does not show much of the favouring of renewable energy or the promotion of biofuels. The subvention of diesel fuel in comparison to petrol cannot really be explained with environmental considerations. Also, Member States remained free to impose unleaded petrol or not. And as its predecessors, Directive 2003/96 contained numerous transition periods, derogations and exceptions.

The Council also agreed to promote the use of bio-fuels for transport and invited Member States to fix non-binding targets at national level, in order to reach a (non-binding) target of 5.75 per cent of fuels for transport stemming from bio-fuels by 2010.[107] Though these targets were not respected, in 2009 a binding target was fixed, according to which the share of bio-fuels in transport should reach, by 2020, 10 per cent.[108]

Renewable energies—in particular wood, solar, water, geothermal and wind energy—played, until very recently, a modest role at EU level. This sector

---

[106] Directive 2003/96 restructuring the Community framework for the taxation of energy products and electricity [2003] OJ L283/51.
[107] Directive 2003/30 on the promotion of the use of biofuels or other renewable fuels for transport [2003] OJ L123/42.
[108] Directive 2009/28 [2009] OJ L140/16.

accounted for 1.6 per cent of energy supply in 1973 and 1.5 per cent in 1989.[109] Its share has risen since, in particular due to the intense discussions on climate change. In 1996, the Commission adopted a Green Book and, subsequently, in 1997, a White Paper on renewable energies, where it announced its objective to reach a market share of 12 per cent by the year 2010 and 22 per cent of electricity produced by renewable energies (both figures for EU-15).[110]

Directive 2009/28 fixed, for 2020, a binding target of 20 per cent share of renewable energy in the total energy consumption, 10 per cent of bio-fuels in transport.[111] To what extent these targets will be reached, remains to be seen. At present, the traditional energy sources, in particular coal, oil and nuclear energy, continue to prevail and to absorb most of the state aid and EU funding. Member States appear prepared to have the EU energy policy move them towards renewable energies, at a pace which is not too quick. However, the policies on traditional energy sources remain very largely determined by national decisions.   **11–26**

The trends in energy policy are not positive. The European Union did not manage to decouple economic growth and energy consumption. Energy prices generally remained low or even fell, offering little incentive to reduce energy consumption. And the use of renewable energies did not progress as had been hoped.[112]

In early 2015, the Juncker Commission adopted a new strategy paper for an energy union[113] which fixed five objectives; energy security, an integrated energy market, energy efficiency, decarbonising the economy and research, innovation and competitiveness. The sections on energy efficiency and decarbonisation only took over the existing objectives which were mentioned above, but did not come up with new elements. Other environmental requirements of an energy policy, land use, infrastructure, nuclear concerns, etc were not discussed at all.

The European Parliament has for a number of years been asking for more measures to promote renewable energies,[114] amongst others to consider the conclusion of a new EU Treaty along the model of the Euratom Treaty, but dealing with policies and measures on renewable energies; to consider spending as much money for the promotion of renewable energies as was spent for research on nuclear fusion (€840 million per year). To date, such ideas have not found an echo among EU institutions or among Member States.   **11–27**

---

[109] Commission, "Energies for the future: renewable sources of energy": Green Paper, COM(96) 576; White Paper, COM(97) 599.

[110] Commission, Green Paper, COM(96) 576.

[111] Directive 2009/28 [2009] OJ L140/16.

[112] European Environment Agency, *Europe's Environment, the Second Assessment* (1998), p.34.

[113] Commission, A framework strategy for a resilient energy Union with a forward-looking climate change policy, COM(2015) 80.

[114] Resolution of 19 January 1993 [1993] OJ C42/31; Resolution of 28 May 1993 [1993] OJ C176/216; Resolution of 4 July 1996 [1996] OJ C211/27; Resolution of 14 November 1996 [1996] OJ C362/279; Resolution of 15 May 1997 [1997] OJ C167/60.

6. TRADE POLICY

11–28   EU trade policy is mainly based on arts 206 et seq. TFEU, which give exclusive competence to the European Union in matters of commercial policy. The Council and Member States interpret these provisions narrowly and accept the European Union's exclusive competence only where no other matters than commercial issues are discussed which deal with products. This considerably limits the area of exclusive EU competence, because most international agreements also concern other issues of foreign economic policy, such as economic cooperation, investments, financial and technical assistance, and exchange of advisers or experts; according to the Council, agreements that include such aspects do not come under arts 206–207 TFEU. This matter is highly controversial. With regard to a free trade agreement that the European Union negotiated with Singapore, the Commission announced that it would ask the Court of Justice for an opinion under art.218(11) TFEU, whether this agreement comes under the exclusive competence of the European Union or is a mixed agreement. Such an opinion will have strong impacts on other trade agreements, in particular with Canada and the United States.

EU decisions to adhere to international environmental conventions which contain trade elements are normally based on art.192, not art.207 TFEU. Examples are decisions to adhere to the Montreal Protocol on ozone-depleting substances[115] or to the Basel Convention on the shipment of hazardous waste[116]; also Decision 2015/451 to adhere to the CITES Convention on trade in endangered species of fauna and flora was based on art.192.[117] This last Decision was adopted, after an amendment of 1983 to the CITES Convention which allowed the adhering of the European Union had entered into force in 2013. Following a judgment of the Court of Justice, the adhesion to the Rotterdam Convention on the export and import of dangerous chemicals was based on arts 207 and 192 TFEU jointly.[118]

EU environmental measures are affected more and more by the globalisation of economies. In 1994, a new World Trade Organisation (WTO) was set up, which replaced the General Agreement on Tariffs and Trade (GATT) and has the objective of promoting international trade.[119] The WTO took over the GATT rules, which had been drafted in 1947 and did not expressly address environmental issues; it follows the primary objective of promoting free international trade; environmental measures are mainly seen and treated as being barriers to trade. In a half-hearted attempt to discuss ways for reconciling trade and environmental issues, the WTO set up a Committee on Trade and Environment, which should discuss environmental and trade aspects, though it did not have any power to set up rules or provide for concrete proposals; this Committee has not managed to play any significant role in WTO policy. The WTO statutes also provided for a dispute settlement system to solve conflicts

---

[115] Decision 88/540 [1988] OJ L297/8.
[116] Decision 93/98 [1993] OJ L39/1.
[117] Decision 2015/451 [2015] OJ L 75/1.
[118] Court of Justice, *Commission v Council* (C-178/03) [2006] E.C.R. I-107; see on the double legal basis paras 2–70 et seq., above.
[119] The European Union adhered to the WTO by Dec.94/800 [1994] OJ L336/1.

between, amongst others, environment and trade; decisions by the WTO in this area are binding upon the contracting parties and financial sanctions are foreseen in the case of non-compliance.

As in the case of the relationship between the European Union and its Member States,[120] the questions concerning whether the EU environmental measures affect the rules of free international trade have to differentiate between situations where no international environmental measures have been taken, and those cases where international conventions on the protection of the environment exist.

11–29

Where no international environmental agreements exist, an EU measure which endeavours to protect the environment is, in principle, compatible with GATT/WTO rules, if it does not constitute a means of arbitrary or unjustifiable discrimination and where it is "necessary", amongst other things, "to protect human, animal or plant life or health" (GATT Agreement, art.XX(b)) or relating "to the conservation of exhaustible natural resources" (art.XX(g)). Different GATT/WTO panels used the word "necessary" in art.XX to introduce a proportionality test into measures by contracting parties. This thus makes the WTO provisions similar to those of art.36 TFEU—except that the European Court of Justice's interpretation of art.34 TFEU, which also allows legitimate national environmental protection measures to restrict trade, has, as yet, no counterpart in the WTO provisions.

Of particular concern is the discussion as to whether WTO rules allow contracting parties to take trade-restricting environmental measures which protect the environment outside their own jurisdiction. Such measures may either concern the environment in other contracting states such as tropical rainforests or endangered species (tigers, elephants) or the so-called "global commons" that do not belong to the jurisdiction of anybody, such as the high sea, its resources and its fauna, the climate, the ozone layer and so on.

In 1991 and 1994, two different GATT panels considered US restrictions on imports of tuna fish caught with so-called purse-seine nets, which also trapped and killed large numbers of dolphins. The United States had prohibited the use of those nets and had, furthermore, banned the import of tuna that was caught with capturing methods which did not correspond to the US legislation. The first panel denied that the measures were compatible with art.XX(b), since they had extraterritorial effects[121]; the second panel expressly stated that GATT also allowed extra-territorial measures,[122] but was of the opinion that the measures were disproportionate. Neither finding has been approved by the relevant WTO/GATT Council and have therefore remained unofficial.

11–30

Until now, EU environmental measures have not yet been examined under WTO procedures; the international debate is rather politicised and might well lead, within a short time, to such an examination. Possible measures that might come under such examination are: the EU provisions on eco-labelling,[123] which

---

[120] See paras 3–03 et seq., above.

[121] "The record indicates that the concerns of the drafters of Article XX (b) focused on the use of sanitary measures to safeguard life or health of humans, animals or plants within the jurisdiction of the importing country."

[122] "The panel further observes that, under general international law, states are not in principle barred from regulating the conduct of their nationals with respect to persons, animals, plants and natural resources outside of their territory. ..."

[123] Regulation 66/2010 [2010] OJ L27/1; see para.6–42, above.

developing countries, in particular, consider to constitute trade barriers; the import restrictions on fur of animals caught with leghold traps[124]; and also packaging, labelling and recycling, the ban of certain substances, products or production methods and eco-taxes.

In 2006, a WTO panel decided in a dispute between United States, Canada and Argentina against the European Union.[125] The dispute concerned the question, whether the de facto moratorium on the authorisation for the placing on the market of new genetically modified products—see on that para.6–38, above—constituted an unjustified barrier to international trade. The panel held that the moratorium constituted a "measure" and that it could not be justified. To the extent that it continued to exist, the European Union was asked to take measures in order to restore free trade; the EU argued that it had already amended its legislation by adopting Directive 2001/18 and Regulation 1829/2003[126] and ended its moratorium.

11–31   It may be doubtful, whether this dispute really concerned an environmental matter. However, the case shows the potentially large impact which the WTO rules—including those on dispute settlement—may have on the EU policy.

In 2009, the European Union adopted a regulation that banned the trade in seal products.[127] Canada and Norway brought this case before the WTO, arguing that this was an unjustified barrier to free trade. However, the WTO accepted that the EU measure was justified on grounds of public morals (art.20 GATT-Agreement) and only requested some minor corrections,[128] which the Commission proposed to the Council.[129]

This WTO decision clarifies that animal welfare considerations may justify the restrictions of international trade. The basic justification of this is that life, health and natural resources—which are a short formula equivalent to the environment—are not available in unlimited quantities and cannot really be regarded to constitute trade barriers. Where measures are taken to protect the environment, which are neither discriminating nor disproportionate, such measures are also allowed, under WTO rules, to restrict international trade; and the differentiation between production and production standards cannot really lead to different results in this regard. It seems clear to me that, for instance, the US measures in the above-mentioned tuna–dolphin case contained an element of protectionism (discrimination).

11–32   The problem with weighing the interests between trade and environment at international level lies in the fact that trade and economic interests prevail quantitatively and qualitatively in international discussions, particularly in developing countries.[130] There is hence all the more need for tribunals or dispute-settlement bodies where environmental considerations are given the same

---

[124] Regulation 3254/91 [1991] OJ L308/1; see para.5–38, above.

[125] WTO, DS 291 USA against European Union, Panel Report of 29 September 2006.

[126] Directive 2001/18 on the deliberate release into the environment of genetically modified organisms [2001] OJ L106/1; Reg.1829/2003 on genetically modified food and feed [2003] OJ L268/1. See, however, now Dir.2015/412 on the restriction of cultivating GMO-plants within the European Union [2015] OJ L68/1.

[127] Regulation 1007/2009 [2009] OJ L286/36.

[128] WTO Docs WT/DS400 and 401/AB/R of 29 April 2014, see also para.5–37, above.

[129] Commission, COM(2015) 45.

[130] This is a matter of human behaviour which goes beyond environmental issues: "Ventre affamé n'a pas d'oreille" (J. de la Fontaine); "Erst kommt das Fressen und dann die Moral" (B. Brecht).

amount of attention as trade matters—which does not seem to be the case at present. Indeed, if one looks at the different reactions of GATT and WTO panels, where environmental and/or health matters were discussed, environmental matters do not have the same weight as economic or trade matters. In international discussions, outside concrete cases, even the European Union has a tendency to let trade interests prevail over environmental interests, for instance by arguing that measures to protect the environment outside the jurisdiction of the acting state should only be allowed where they are in conformity with internationally agreed measures.[131] The necessity of avoiding, on the one hand, protectionist measures that take the formal appearance of environmental protection (green protectionism) and, on the other hand, of allowing legitimate environmental protection measures, is likely to find some compromise solutions only gradually; it is not surprising that legal writers look particularly to regional solutions, such as the European Union or the North America Free Trade Area (NAFTA), in order to find solutions for the problems of integrating environmental requirements into international trade rules. Article 114(7) TFEU shows a possible future solution: much of the pressure on dolphins, sea turtles and other environmental assets would be avoided if the world community were willing and able to adopt worldwide measures to ensure adequate protection of dolphins, turtles or of marine mammals in general.

Also, where environmental measures have been taken at international level, their compatibility with WTO/GATT rules may nevertheless be contested. In particular, there is considerable discussion as to whether the three above-mentioned conventions on trade in endangered species, in ozone-depleting substances and in hazardous waste are in conflict with the general WTO rules. The panel on the GMO-standstill in the European Union which gave its report in September 2006, touched on these questions, in a more general form, though. It held that the rules of WTO prevailed over other conventions, at least as long as not all WTO Member States had adhered to the other conventions. This opinion appears to be in conflict with rules of public international law (the Vienna Convention) and can be better explained by motivations to let trade rules prevail than by an attempt to balance diverging interests. The legal question as to which international agreement should prevail—the WTO agreement or the specific environmental convention—will have to be decided politically. Under the existing rules of international law, it is not possible to solve this question. Since all three environmental conventions have been elaborated under the auspices of the United Nations, it appears to be only consequent to assume that measures which are adopted by states or by the European Union, and which are in compliance with these international conventions, cannot be tackled under WTO rules. The fact that such trade restriction measures are also to be applied against states which have not ratified these specialised conventions, is not decisive.

The Montreal Protocol, the Basel Convention and the CITES Convention all allow the contracting parties to adopt more stringent provisions than those of the conventions in order to protect the environment[132]; and the European Union has,

---

[131] Commission, COM(96) 54; see also the reproach by the European Parliament, Resolution of 24 May 1996 [1996] OJ C166/260.

[132] Basel Convention on the control of transboundary movement of hazardous wastes and their disposal (1993) OJ L39/3, art.3(11); CITES Convention [1982] OJ L384/1, art.XIV. The Montreal Protocol is formally a Protocol of the Vienna Convention on the protection of the ozone layer; the

in the different areas coming under those three conventions, made use of this possibility. The question then is whether such additional domestic measures that are taken at EU or at national level are also compatible with WTO rules. The problem has not yet been discussed in detail in legal literature. My own opinion is that such measures are also compatible with WTO rules, since they rest on an explicit authorisation of the conventions, which expresses the wish to improve environmental protection as far as possible. It is self-evident, though, that here, again, a careful examination has to take place in order to avoid such measures being discriminating or disproportionate.

11–33   Perhaps in order to compensate for the fact that it is not able to play a prominent role in international discussions within the United Nations—on climate change, migration issues etc—the European Union has strongly promoted, during the last decade, bilateral trade agreements with other countries. A free trade agreement with South Korea entered into force in 2011.[133] Negotiations on an agreement with Singapore and with Canada (Comprehensive Economic and Trade Agreement, CETA) were completed and negotiations with the United States on a Transatlantic Trade and Investment Partnership (TTIP) Agreement are ongoing since 2013. The negotiations take place in secret; the European Parliament and the public only become aware of the detailed content of the Agreement when the negotiations end. With regard to the TTIP, this led to a public outcry, forcing the Commission into publishing a number of preparatory documents—though not the results of negotiations, the concessions made and the compromises agreed.

While the Korean free trade agreement is more or less a classical agreement, dealing with trade issues, the Canadian and US agreements go much further, also touching on environmental issues. Thus, a dispute settlement procedure under CETA and TTIP provides—this is the state of discussions in mid-2015—that investors may, before an arbitration tribunal, claim compensation from the European Union or EU Member States, when measures impaired their investments.[134] Such a provision does not appear to be compatible with arts 268 and 340 TFEU which gives exclusive competence to the EU Court of justice to decide on extra-contractual damages against the European Union. What worries further is that the arbitrators are not necessarily independent, that the procedure is largely confidential and that their interpretation of EU law might differ from that of the Court of Justice. The most disturbing factor, though, is that there is no objective necessity to recur to arbitration, when damages are claimed against the European Union and EU Member States, as the court systems in Europe function.

For the environment, the setting up of a regulatory committee, foreseen in TTIP and, less precisely established, in CETA, is also dangerous. This committee

---

European Union became a party to that Convention and the Montreal Protocol in 1988 (Dec.88/540 [1988] OJ L297/8); art.2 of that Convention allows additional domestic measures.

[133] Decision 2011/269 on the signature and provisional application of the Free Trade Agreement between the European Union and its Member States and South Korea [2011] OJ L127, p.1; the Agreement is published on p.6.

[134] There are worrying cases of such claims pending at present. After the Fukushima nuclear accident, Germany decided to step out of nuclear power. In 2012, the Swedish company Vattenfall brought a case to an arbitration tribunal, claiming €700 million compensation. In 2011, the Regional Government of Quebec decided to restrict fracking in the region. The company Lone Pine Resources then filed a claim of CA $250 million for damages caused by that regional legislation.

intends to discuss any regulatory project which one side—thus the European Union, its Member States, the United States and its states—intend to adopt and which might impair the free trade between the two regions. One might easily imagine how measures on the restriction of chemicals, the cultivation of GMOs, or on emission limit values, once they are based on the precautionary principle, meet objections from the US side, as the precautionary principle is not recognised there. The preventive effect of interventions from the regulatory committee will most likely affect in particular measures on the protection of health, the environment, consumers and workers.

A member of the European Commission indicated in 2013 that TTIP would establish a big transatlantic internal market. The problem is that the European Union does not only have to realise an internal market, but also to achieve a high level of environmental protection within the European Union, see art.3 TEU, arts 11, 114 and 192 TFEU. Such an obligation lacks entirely in the "transatlantic internal market" which will thus lead to negative integration—all environmental, health and social measures are perceived as barriers to free trade which should be avoided as far as possible. "Between the strong and the weak, the legislation makes free and the freedom suppresses", indicated the French philosopher La Rochefoucauld in the 17th century.   **11–34**

The discussions on international trade and the environment are considerably affected by political events at international level, in particular by the Iraq war of 2003. Before and after these events, in particular the United States—in this often followed by Australia, New Zealand, Japan, Canada, Mexico and South Korea—showed, at international level and in conferences, negotiations or meetings under existing conventions, a very limited interest in environmental protection and acted as the principal proponent of free trade; this attitude might be favoured by the fact that there is no environmental ministry in the US government which leads to the result that international discussions, unless they are purely technical, are led by either the Department of Commerce or the Department of State. Discussions on finding the appropriate balance between trade and environmental interests will not become easier by the Iraq events which have at least clarified to everyone that, internationally, the rule of law is not the guiding rule for negotiations: power, political pressure and the promotion of interests are the important, if not determining, factors. This makes any speculation about the evolution of international environmental law and its relationship to trade law almost impossible.

7.   TOURISM AND THE ENVIRONMENT

The Lisbon Treaty enabled the European Union to carry out actions "to support, coordinate or supplement" the actions of the Member States in the area of tourism (art.6(d) TFEU). Article 195 TFEU specified this possibility, excluding though "any harmonisation of the laws and regulations of Member States".   **11–35**

Tourism contributes in particular to land, energy and water use, waste generation and, via travelling, to air pollution and climate change. It is developing into the largest service industry in the European Union. Particular areas of attention are coastal zones, the Mediterranean and the Alps.

While the integration of environmental requirements into tourism was considered, under the 5th Environmental Action Programme, one of five priority policy areas, this approach changed rather rapidly. The 6th Environmental Action Programme mentions tourism in half a phrase[135] and also the European Environment Agency stopped mentioning tourism as a separate sector of its report on environmental trends.[136] Thus, environmental measures on tourism became, within 10 years, a negative priority for the European Union.

11–36   Legal matters on tourism are affected by the lack of an explicit competence on tourism. Hence, objectives of tourism policy are not fixed at EU level—except for the statement that tourism should be or become sustainable. And no legal instruments have until now been adopted or proposed to promote this vague idea. The integration of environmental requirements into tourist policy measures remains thus incoherent, largely based on financial assistance to pilot or demonstration projects.

The idea of eco-labels for restaurants, beaches,[137] villages or other holiday resorts has not led to any EU-wide initiative, though eco-labelling for accommodation has significantly increased in the European Union over the last 20 years. In 2003, the European Union adopted rules for attributing the EU eco-label to accommodations and fixed conditions for that; this was followed by an eco-label for camping sites.[138] Both provisions put the emphasis on water and energy saving. To what extent hotels and camping sites apply for the eco-label is not yet clear.

There are no attempts until now to address the problems of tourism in coastal zones or in mountainous areas. The European Union adhered to the Convention on the Alps,[139] and its Protocols on mountain farming, tourism, and soil conservation, but not to its Protocols on landscape management, mountain forestry, and transport; and as, anyway, the application of international conventions is not monitored by the European Union as long as there are no internal EU measures, this accession has not changed the situation. It rather appears that the same experience which economic and tourist development has caused to the Alpine environment, is being repeated in other mountainous regions, such as the Pyrenees, the Carpates, etc. It is therefore no surprise that all indicators for tourism which the European Environment Agency has established—modal split in tourism transport, environmental costs as part of tourist pricing, carrying capacity of destinations, reduction of energy use—are negative; only the above-mentioned evolution in eco-labelling is seen as stable.[140]

11–37   In 2014, the Commission proposed a recommendation[141] containing quality principles of tourism which should be followed by tourist operators. The proposal

---

[135] Decision 1600/2002 [2002] OJ L242/1, art.6(2.e): (Priority actions should be) "promoting the integration of conservation and restoration of the landscape values into other policies including tourism, taking into account relevant international instruments".

[136] European Environment Agency, *Europe's Environment, the Second Assessment* (Aarhus, 1998), p.30.

[137] See in this regard the blue-flag system, para.7–14, above.

[138] Decision 2003/287 (tourist accommodation services) [2003] OJ L102/82; Dec.2005/338 (campsite services) [2005] OJ L108/67.

[139] Decision 96/191 [1996] OJ L61/31.

[140] European Environment Agency, *Europe's Environment, the Second Assessment* (Aarhus, 1998), p.24.

[141] Commission, European tourism quality principles, COM(2014) 85.

suggested good staff training, the adoption of a policy aimed at consumer satisfaction, providing for cleaning and maintenance planning, and ensuring that information for tourists is correct, clear and accessible; all this aims more at tourist protection than at environmental protection.

CHAPTER 12

Implementation

1. OBLIGATIONS OF MEMBER STATES TO APPLY EU LAW

(a) Treaty provisions

The Lisbon Treaties do not contain environmental provisions which Member States would have to transpose into, or to apply in, their national legal order. Article 4(3) TEU states that Member States shall assist the Union in carrying out its tasks and facilitate achieving its tasks.[1] However, this does not mean that they would have to place in their national legislation the objective of attaining a high level of environmental protection or the aim that environmental requirements are incorporated into the other policies pursued at national level. In contrast, art.4(3) TEU requires Member States to abstain from any measures at national level, which would make it more difficult or impossible for the European Union to move towards a high level of environmental protection or to make the different EU policies "greener", i.e. environmentally more friendly.

    12–01

The environmental provisions of the Treaties are not formulated in such a way that they are self-executing or, in EU terminology, directly applicable. While art.34 TFEU prohibits creating or maintaining barriers to trade within the European Union, art.101 TFEU prohibits trade-distorting agreement between undertakings, art.102 prohibits abuses of dominant positions and art.107 TFEU state aids, no corresponding provision exists in environmental law, for instance forbidding environmental pollution. National enforcement bodies or courts do not therefore have to align Member States' laws to instructions that come from EU primary law.

(b) Secondary legislation

The situation is completely different as regards secondary EU environmental law. Under art.192(4) TFEU, it is, in principle, the Member States that have to implement the different measures which have been adopted in pursuance of EU environmental policy. This provision is somewhat superfluous, since in other EU

    12–02

---

[1] Article 4(3) TEU: "Pursuant to the principle of sincere cooperation, the Union and the Member States shall, in full mutual respect, assist each other in carrying out tasks which flow from this Treaty. The Member States shall take any appropriate measure, general or particular, to ensure fulfilment of the obligations arising out of the Treaties or resulting from the acts of the institutions of the Union. The Member States shall facilitate the achievement of the Union's tasks and refrain from any measure which could jeopardise the attainment of the Union's objective."

policies, too, where no such provision exists, the implementation of measures is an obligation for Member States which follows from art.4(3) TEU. EU directives and decisions address Member States; EU regulations apply in all Member States without even any transposing act (art.288 TFEU). In no situation is there any decision by a national Parliament or regulating body required or admitted to accept or not to accept EU secondary law provisions. This then is the fundamental difference that distinguishes EU environmental law from public international law, which requires, in order to become valid, an express act by the national legislative body.

Regulations are directly applied in each Member State (art.288(2) TFEU); and while environmental regulations frequently contain specific provisions that require Member States to take action—such as the appointing of responsible authorities, the publication of reports or even the taking of executive provisions—their general attribute of being directly applicable remains unchanged; the specific provision then has the characteristics of a directive and needs to be implemented, unless it is, in substance, a recommendation. Similar observations apply to decisions, which normally deal with a specific, concrete situation; where a specific provision in a decision is, in substance, that of a directive, it would require implementation as if it were a directive.[2]

"A directive shall be binding, as to the result to be achieved, upon each Member State to which it is addressed, but shall leave to the national authorities the choice of form and methods" (art.288(3) TFEU). As EU legislation must be applied by Member States—this follows from arts 4 and 17 TEU[3]—Member States have two main obligations as regards EU environmental directives: they must incorporate the provisions of the directive into their national law and they must ensure that these provisions are actually complied with.

(i) Transposition

12–03   Practically all[4] environmental directives contain a provision that requests Member States to transpose the directive's provisions into national law.[5] Generally, such a transposition into national law has to be done by an express

---

[2] See, more generally, paras 2–34 et seq., above.

[3] Article 17 TEU: "The Commission ... shall ensure the application of the Treaties, and of measures adopted by the institutions pursuant to them. It shall oversee the application of Union law under the control of the Court of Justice of the European Union."

[4] The exceptions are Dir.76/464 on pollution caused by certain dangerous substances discharged into the aquatic environment of the Community [1976] OJ L129/23, where this clause was probably forgotten; Dir.91/692 on standardising and rationalising reports on the implementation of certain directives relating to the environment [1991] OJ L377/48; and Dir.2015/12 on the cultivation of genetically modified organisms [2015] OJ L68/1.

[5] See, e.g. art.23 of Dir.92/43 on the conservation of natural habitats and of wild fauna and flora [1992] OJ L206/7:

"1. Member States shall bring into force the laws, regulations and administrative provisions necessary to comply with this Directive within two years of its notification. They shall forthwith inform the Commission thereof.

2. When Member States adopt such measures, they shall contain a reference to this Directive or be accompanied by such reference on the occasion of their official publication. The methods of making such a reference shall be laid down by the Member States.

3. Member States shall communicate to the Commission the main provisions of national law which they adopt in the field covered by this Directive."

binding legislative or regulatory provision, "in order to secure full implementation of directives in law and not only in facts".[6] The Court of Justice has, on numerous occasions, rejected Member States' attempts to transpose the requirements of an environmental directive into national law by means of a multi-annual plan, an administrative circular or a similar instrument.[7] Its main argument was the absence of legal certainty for individual persons and undertakings that was created by such a transposition, as it was not clear which rights and obligations followed out of an EU directive.[8] Since the Court of Justice is of the opinion that directives which fix quality standards also give certain legal rights to individuals, most of the provisions of a directive will have to be transposed into national law by a binding provision. This applies even to the establishment of the requirement to set up clean-up programmes or waste management programmes; indeed, such programmes also contain information for individuals about future objectives, about measures taken and envisaged and so on.

Exceptions apply only to those provisions which provide for obligations of the Council, the Commission or other institutions, and, in addition, to provisions which exclusively concern the Member States' relations to the EU administration and ask them, for instance, to send a report regularly to the Commission. Even in such cases, though, the limits to Member States' obligations are not altogether clear: the Court of Justice held that a provision that requires regional or local authorities in border regions to consult with authorities from the adjacent Member State, had to be transposed into national law.[9] The same applied to a provision where a Member State was allowed to grant a derogation under a directive, but had to inform the Commission thereof; where that Member State delegated the right to grant derogations to regional or local authorities, it had to ensure expressly that it was informed of the granting of derogations in order to be able to comply with its own requirements towards the Commission.[10] In the same way, it could also be argued that a Member State's implementation report to the Commission, where the Member State reports how a piece of EU legislation was transposed into the national legal order and how it was applied in practice, ensures transparency of implementation and compliance, allows individuals to take action themselves or otherwise orient their behaviour, and that it therefore has an external effect which requires its transposition into legally binding national legislation.

---

[6] *Commission v Germany* (C-131/88) [1991] E.C.R. I-825 at [8].

[7] *Commission v Netherlands* (C-96/81) [1982] E.C.R. 1791; *Commission v Germany* (C-131/88) [1991] E.C.R. I-825; *Commission v Germany* (C-361/88) [1991] E.C.R. I-2567; *Commission v France* (C-13/90) [1991] E.C.R. I-4327; *Commission v Germany* (C-58/89) [1991] E.C.R. 4983; *Commission v Germany* (C-262/95) [1996] E.C.R. I-5729.

[8] See, e.g. *Commission v Germany* (C-131/88) [1991] E.C.R. I-825 at [6]: "The transposition of a directive into domestic law does not necessarily require that its provisions be incorporated formally and verbatim in express, specific legislation; a general legal context may, depending on the content of the directive, be adequate for the purpose provided that it does indeed guarantee the full application of the directive in a sufficiently clear and precise manner so that, where the directive is intended to create rights for individuals, the persons concerned can ascertain the full extent of their rights and where appropriate, rely on them before the national courts."

[9] *Commission v Belgium* (C-186/91) [1993] E.C.R. I-851.

[10] *Commission v Germany* (C-237/90) [1992] E.C.R. I-5973.

The necessity of transposing definitions in an EU directive into national law probably depends on the subject-matter that is regulated: the more directly individual rights and obligations might be affected by a definition, the greater the need to transpose a directive's definition into national law. Good examples are the definitions of "waste" and "hazardous waste" under Directive 2008/98[11]: Member States' legislation often does not use the words "hazardous waste", but "specific waste", "waste which is to be controlled", "chemical waste", "industrial waste" and other definitions. These linguistic differentiations have consequences as regards monitoring, surveillance, statistics, customs and police controls and other administrative matters, which impinge in turn on private agents, individuals or administrations. For this reason the Commission has adopted the position that the definitions for waste and for hazardous waste had to be transposed literally into national laws. The Court of Justice required a transposition of a definition at least in those cases, where an omission to transpose created doubts as to the meaning of provisions.[12]

12–04 The transposition of an environmental directive, which contains mandatory requirements, cannot be made by non-binding national measures, in particular by administrative provisions, since:

> "mere administrative practices, which by their nature may be changed at will by the authorities, cannot be regarded as constituting proper compliance with the obligation on Member States to which a directive is addressed (*Commission v Italy* (C-429/85) [1988] E.C.R. 843; *Commission v Netherlands* (C-339/87) [1990] E.C.R. I-851)."

For this reason, implementation of an environmental directive through an environmental voluntary agreement is not possible, unless an EU directive expressly so provides[13]; such a possibility was foreseen, for the first time, by some provisions of some waste directives.[14] As environmental agreements only apply to contracting bodies, the equality of citizens with regard to rights or obligations that a directive grants is not ensured. Transposition of a directive by environmental agreements that are not generally binding is therefore not possible.

A transposition is also necessary in those cases where the Member State in fact already complies with the requirements of a directive. The legal certainty that economic operators and individuals are entitled to expect would be completely undermined if the local, regional or national administration could argue that the

---

[11] Directive 2009/98 on waste [2009] OJ L312/3.

[12] Court of Justice, *Commission v France* (C-443/08) [2009] E.C.R.I-79; *Commission v Luxembourg* (C-32/05) [2006] E.C.R. I-4323; *Commission v Belgium* (C-120/09) [2009] E.C.R. I-223.

[13] In the same sense, Commission Rec.96/733 concerning environmental agreements implementing Community directives [1996] OJ C333/59.

[14] Directive 2000/53 on end-of-life vehicles [2000] OJ L269/34; Dir.2002/96 on waste electrical and electronic equipment [2003] OJ L37/24; Dir.2006/66 on batteries and accumulators [2006] OJ L266/1. Directive 85/339 on liquid beverage containers [1985] OJ L176/18, which is often quoted as allowing implementation of directives by environmental agreements, is not relevant: indeed, the Directive required Member States to set up packaging reduction programmes and then allowed the implementation of such programmes by non-binding measures; the Directive has in the meantime been repealed.

factual situation corresponds to the requirements of the directive and places the burden of proof that this is not the case on the person arguing that transposition is necessary.[15]

No obligation to transpose the requirements of a directive exists where it is physically impossible that the problem dealt with by the directive could ever occur in a Member State. Thus, Luxembourg or Austria would not be obliged to transpose requirements of a directive on coastal waters or (sea) port reception facilities.[16] In contrast, these Member States would normally be obliged to transpose the directive on (the sea discharge of) waste from the titanium dioxide industry,[17] even if they had no such industry on their territory, as this situation could change and, furthermore, titanium dioxide waste from other Member States might be transported to states that do not have such an industry.[18] **12–05**

The transposition measures must cover the whole of the territory of a Member State. This observation sounds more trivial than it is. Indeed, in many Member States responsibility for environmental issues lies at least partly with regional authorities; this is the case for Austria, Belgium, Germany, Italy and Spain. But in other Member States, too, environmental legislation is partially split; thus, environmental regulations in the United Kingdom are partly taken in or for Wales, Scotland, Northern Ireland or Gibraltar, and in Finland, the Aaland Islands have a specific legislative status. Finally, waste management plans in Sweden and the United Kingdom are traditionally set up at local level.

From the point of view of the European Union, it is not relevant whether a provision of EU law is transposed by one single act at national level or by a number of regional regulations, as long as the transposition measures cover the whole of the territory.

It is much more difficult to comply with the second substantive requirement for the transposition measure; that is, that the EU environmental requirement is correctly transposed. First, a Member State may not rely on the wording in which a specific directive is drafted in the Member State's language—all EU languages have the same legal value (art.55 TEU) and that wording may differ from one language to the other. For that reason, the true sense of a provision has to be discovered, which may well vary between specific linguistic versions.[19] Secondly, it has already been mentioned in para.3–01, above, that EU law is autonomous and has to be interpreted without recurring to identical or similar notions that exist in national law. Thus, the same word might be used in EU environmental law and in national law and yet the two meanings are quite **12–06**

---

[15] *Commission v Netherlands* (C-339/87) [1990] E.C.R. I-851.

[16] See, e.g. Dir.2008/56 establishing a framework for Community action in the field of marine environmental policy (Marine Strategy Framework Directive) [2008] OJ L164/19, art.26(7) which provides that Member States without marine waters are only obliged to comply with art.6 (regional cooperation) and art.7 (designation of competent authorities).

[17] Directive 78/176 [1978] OJ L54/19.

[18] See in this sense also Court of Justice, *Commission v Portugal* (C-435/99) [2000] E.C.R. I-11179. In practice, the Commission has accepted that Member States that do not have a titanium dioxide industry formally commit themselves to transposing the Directive as soon as such an industry is established on their territory or where waste from such industry is shipped into their country; for the reasons mentioned, this practice is not in compliance with EU law.

[19] Court of Justice, *Spain v Council* (C-36/98) [2001] E.C.R. I-779; *Kraaijeveld* (C-72/95) [1996] E.C.R. I-5403; the last case concerned the interpretation of Dir.85/337 on environment impact assessment.

different: this potential conflict is increased by the fact that EU law prevails over national law. However, since EU law stems from a source of law other than national law, it might carry different concepts, theories or structures that do not fit into the national legal or administrative infrastructure. An example is art.9(2) of the Directive on the conservation of wild birds,[20] which provided that local nature protection authorities may give derogations from trading, hunting and other bans under the Directive, after having examined the local situation; however, such local nature protection authorities do not exist in Ireland.

Another complication is that EU environmental law provisions normally come up against a structured and elaborate system of national rules that have been built up over years or decades, and into which the provisions then have to be integrated. The EU provision is then perceived—and all too often also treated—as an immigrant, if not as an intruder.[21]

Where the EU environmental law provision sets numerical values such as emission limit values, quality standards or targets, national legislation will have to adopt these numerical values. Economic operators and individuals must have the opportunity to find in the national statute books what these numerical values are.[22] The same applies to bans on substances or products. For other provisions, it is normally difficult to establish fixed rules, since it follows from art.288 TFEU that a word-by-word transmission of the EU provision is not required.

12–07   A correct transposition also requires the establishing of sanctions for non-compliance with the EU provisions.[23] It is true that EU directives do not contain more than very general provisions on sanctions for non-compliance, and regulations, too, remain very general. The reason for this is that sanctions are in many countries understood as criminal or quasi-criminal sanctions and that the European Union has, until now, abstained from providing for criminal sanctions in cases, where the provisions of a directive or regulation are not respected; even where administrative sanctions could be used, there is considerable self-restraint used by the European Union when addressing the details of sanctions. This also applies to environmental regulations, though it follows from art.261 TFEU that regulations could contain penal sanctions.[24] The Court of Justice interpreted art.4(3) TEU to mean that national sanctions for non-compliance with EU law must be equivalent to sanctions for breach of equivalent national law provisions; furthermore, that they must be effective and proportionate and dissuasive.[25] This or a similar formula is used in numerous EU environmental directives or regulations. The transposition of this formula in the different legal orders of Member States has, until now, not been the subject of any serious control.

---

[20] Directive 2009/147 on the conservation of wild birds [2010] OJ L20/7.

[21] Commission, European governance—a White Paper, COM(2001) 428, [2001] OJ C287/1, p.21: "the feeling persists that Community rules are 'foreign laws'".

[22] See *Commission v Germany* (C-361/88) [1991] E.C.R. I-2567: "It is clear that legal certainty also requires the specific transposal of individual limit-values, maximum permissible concentrations and emission values into national legislation. A general reference to Community legislation is not permitted."

[23] *Commission v Greece* (C-68/88) [1989] E.C.R. 2965.

[24] Article 261 TFEU: "Regulations ... may give the Court of Justice of the European Union unlimited jurisdiction with regard to the penalties provided for in such regulations."

[25] *Commission v Greece* (C-68/88) [1989] E.C.R. 2965.

(ii)   Application

Finally, Member States are under an obligation to ensure the practical application   **12–08**
of EU environmental law. The transposition itself is only a formal legal act,
whereas the protection of the environment begins when emissions are reduced,
substances no longer put on the market or (the equivalent) into the environment,
habitats protected, and so on. The practical application of environmental
provisions is the most serious problem that national, EU and international
environmental law faces. Even a piece of national legislation that copies a
directive word for word will remain a mere piece of paper unless it is applied.

Some unique features which seriously affect the full application of EU
environmental law in practice must be remembered. Since environmental
provisions try to protect the general interest of the European Union, they differ
markedly from agricultural, transport or industry legislation, which primarily
affects specific vested interests. Where vested interests are in question, law
making and law enforcement take place, in Western Europe, in constant
public—and sometimes not so public—discussions with the representatives of
those vested interests; this discussion also continues within the various
administrations, parliaments and decision-making bodies. Vested interest groups
are also used to ensure the transmission of knowledge on the specific legislation
and in this way contribute either to ensuring compliance with the legal rule or
bringing about concerted action against that rule, often even preventing its
generation. This lobbying function of vested interest groups has become an
integrated factor of decision-making at EU level and at the level of Member
States.

The general interest "environment" has no vested interest defender. Environmental organisations in Western Europe, though they are committed to promote
the general interest "environment", are structurally and financially too weak to
defend environmental interests effectively over a long period of time. While there
is consensus that the environment needs adequate protection and that economic
development should be "sustainable", the implementation of concrete, legally
binding measures proves difficult wherever other, diverging interests appear. The
environment, without a voice and without strong lobby groups, loses out in
almost every specific conflict of interests. Since, furthermore, local, regional and
national administrations in the 28 Member States are not all convinced to the
same extent that EU environmental standards are to be enforced, complied with
and applied in practice, practical application of EU environmental provisions,
which are thought to be more or less uniform varies very considerably within the
European Union.

General features also contribute to this situation. In a number of Member   **12–09**
States, particularly in the south and in the Member States which adhered since
2004, environmental problems are perceived to be the problems of affluent
society; hence there is an attitude among economic operators, and also among
administrations, that economic progress is of primary necessity and that
environmental concerns should be tackled once the economic level of richer
Member States has been reached. To this has to be added the different
enforcement culture which exists in the European Union, traditional weaknesses
of central government in some Member States, the lack of national environmental

infrastructures such as adequate administrations at local, regional and national level, and a lack of environmental information and education, of general awareness, of environmental research bodies, laboratories and test or monitoring or enforcement bodies. And for a number of years, neo-liberal thinking in the Anglo-Saxon world has concentrated on economic growth, shareholder value and other ideologies which consider the environment to be a sort of *quantité négligeable*.

2. MONITORING TRANSPOSITION AND APPLICATION

(a) Implementation reports

12-10   Almost all EU environmental directives have contained, since the mid-1970s, a provision asking Member States to report on the implementation of the directive. Typically, such reports had to be made every three years.[26] The Commission was charged with producing, on the basis of these national reports, an EU report on the implementation of the directive in question; the normal period for these reports was, similarly, every three years.

This system did not lead to the desired result, since neither the Member States' implementation reports nor the Commission's comprehensive reports were drawn up regularly; Member States' reports were not even regularly made public by the Member States or the Commission. Only for the Bathing Water Directive[27] were regular reports published; however, these dealt with the state of quality of bathing water rather than the implementation of the Directive. Also, monitoring of a number of parameters was omitted and the data transmitted from the Member States were, until recently, not comparable.

In order to improve the reporting system, in 1991 the Council adopted a Directive that restructured the reporting requirements.[28] This Directive introduced the requirement for Member States to report, every three years, on the implementation of the different directives in a given sector (for instance, water, air or waste). The reports were to be based on questionnaires which were set up by committee procedure at EU level, in order to allow the national reports to address the same issues. The reporting period was three years.

12-11   The Directive has not significantly improved the situation. The reports on water, waste and chemicals were published after considerable delay; a report on air pollution is still not published. And those directives that have been adopted since 1991 have only partly aligned their reporting requirements to Directive 91/692. Where Member States submit reports to the Commission, these reports, together with the national implementing legislation which is at the Commission's disposal anyway, allow a relatively clear picture to be gained on the transposition of a directive into national law. However, such reports normally do not contain information on difficulties of practical application or cases of non-compliance,

---

[26] See, however, Dir.2006/7 on the quality of bathing water [2006] OJ L64/37, where art.13 provided for annual reports by Member States and by the Commission.

[27] Directive 76/160 [1976] OJ L31/1. This Directive is now replaced by Dir.2006/7 [2006] OJ L64/37.

[28] Directive 91/692 [1991] OJ L377/48.

lacunae and omissions on the side of local, regional or national administrations, inspections, sanctions, or on specific interpretations of individual provisions. They report on measures taken and legislation adopted, not on results achieved and the state of the environment.

Commission implementation reports are, overall, very disappointing, apart from the reports on the quality of bathing waters, which continue to be published annually. Directive 91/692 did not lead to a systematic attempt to improve implementation reporting, despite other announcements.[29] Generally, the Commission's different reports on the implementation of the environmental directives have, in the past, been marked by the fact that the information contained therein came almost exclusively from the (central) administration of Member States. For that reason, the EU reports, like the national reports, give a relatively reliable picture on the legal and administrative parts of implementing EU directives—for those Member States that did report. However, less information will be found on, for example, monitoring frequency and intensity, practical non-compliance, gaps and omissions of the administrations and results achieved. In order to address this problem, part of reporting on the implementation of EU environmental directives was delegated to the European Environment Agency, without the completeness and quality of the reports significantly improving. Also, a review of the environmental reporting provisions were announced several years ago, but has not yet led to concrete proposals.

The Commission has, it is true, conducted some studies of its own on the practical implementation of environmental directives in the Member States, although inevitably only a limited number of these studies have been undertaken. Their value is limited, though, by the fact that it has proved extremely difficult to gain access to the data held by the national, regional or local authorities on the practical application—and non-application; no administration would be easily persuaded to release data showing that a directive is not properly monitored or applied in practice, whether the failure is found in the frequency and results of inspections, the attitude of economic operators that were controlled, the pollution levels recorded or the respect of the conditions laid down in the permits that the administrations have granted. And the Commission does not even make such transposition studies publicly available, but keeps them confidential—for no legitimate reason; this increases administrative secrecy and makes research into effects of EU environmental legislation significantly more difficult.

(b) The Commission's monitoring function

The Commission has to ensure that EU environmental law is applied (art.17 TEU). This provision is the nucleus which has allowed the Commission to develop, over the years, a system of monitoring transposition, application and enforcement, which goes far beyond anything that is known in the relations

12–12

---

[29] Commission, Implementing Community environmental law, COM(96) 500, para.58: "Through the most effective use of the Reporting Directive, and close co-operation with the European Environmental Agency, the Commission will ensure that the best possible information is available on the effectiveness of Community environmental measures and can be used in the formulation of its policies on environmental measures. The Commission will launch and co-ordinate case studies to evaluate the transposition, application and enforcement of selected provisions of Community environmental law."

between states. It is this monitoring task of the Commission that has caused the Commission to be called the "guardian of the Treaty".

It should, however, not be forgotten that it is Member States which have, according to arts 4 TEU and 192(4) TFEU, the obligation to ensure the implementation of EU environmental law; this then means that Member States have to ensure that EU environmental law is applied. The establishment and functioning of the European Union is also the task of Member States and it is they which have to ensure that "their" constitution—the Lisbon Treaties—including its environmental provisions, is properly applied.[30]

The Commission's task is to ensure that all EU primary and secondary environmental law is applied in particular regulations, directives and decisions. As regards international conventions, it has already been stated that the Commission does not monitor their application within the European Union, not even in cases where the European Union adhered to them. This self-restraint has never been justified or reasoned in public. It is legally unjustifiable. Indeed, where the European Union adheres to an international environmental convention, the convention becomes part of EU law (art.216(2) TFEU). The Commission then has to ensure its application, as art.17 TEU does not differentiate between different parts of EU law. By adhering to a convention, the European Union makes the commitment that it will ensure compliance with provisions of this convention throughout the territory of the European Union. This obligation rests with the European Union as such and pertains to the whole EU territory, even where a specific Member State has not ratified the international convention in question. Once the European Union has adhered to the international convention, Member States are obliged, under art.4 TEU, to take the necessary steps in order to allow the European Union to respect its international commitments. This legal obligation was confirmed in substance by the Court of Justice in a case against France which had not ratified an international agreement. But the European Union had, and the Court found that France was obliged to respect the requirements of the international agreement.[31]

12–13   In reality, it is clear that the Commission has a particular responsibility of ensuring application of EU environmental law, because the European Union is the source of these legal provisions. The Commission does not have any structures to monitor application of environmental legal provisions; this is ensured, rather, by the general Commission administration. In particular, the Commission does not have any inspection bodies to examine whether and to what extent EU environmental law is actually complied with.[32] Discussions on green inspectors have been emotionalised as being an intrusion on national sovereignty and, furthermore, as being incompatible with the subsidiarity principle. This criticism omits to mention that there are Commission inspectors in the areas of

[30] Commission, Implementing Community environmental law, COM(96) 500, para.25: "The Commission simply cannot monitor the thousands of individual decisions taken each year ... in the different parts and levels of authority within the Member States. The daily application and enforcement ... must be fully ensured by the authorities in the Member States. ..."
[31] Court of Justice, *Etangs de Berre* (C-213/03) [2004] E.C.R. I-7357; *Commission v France* (C-239/03) [2004] E.C.R. I-9325.
[32] Recommendation 2001/331 [2001] OJ L118/41 recommends Member States to provide for inspectors in environmental matters; a corresponding recommendation for the EU institutions does not exist.

competition, veterinary, customs, regional and fishery policy, without questions of interference or subsidiarity ever having been raised. The Commission is very cautious in considering the setting up of EU inspectors.[33] The Council and Member States are clearly opposed to EU environmental inspectors.[34] The option of making fact-finding site visits, which is available to the Commission,[35] is hardly ever used as the Member States do not like such visits and the Commission concurs.

Since 1983 the Commission has published annual reports on monitoring the application of EU law,[36] which include a chapter on environmental legislation; attempts in 1991/1992 to produce a specific environmental report met the resistance of the Commission administration and failed. The reports publish some general data and trends on the application of EU environmental law, but do not provide complete transparency, do not establish data which are comparable over the years, and are not always completely reliable[37]; since about 2001, they have become more and more general and vague and principally report on cases which have been brought to the Court of Justice or where a reasoned opinion had been issued, without giving details and without explaining where the application of a specific directive stands with regard to a specific Member State. The reports are therefore of a rather limited informative value.

(c) Monitoring by other bodies

The European Parliament does not fulfil any significant function in the monitoring of EU environmental legislation. Members of the Parliament pose, it is true, a great number of written or oral questions, which include issues of application of environmental legislation; however, these initiatives remain non-systematic. Since the year 2000, the European Parliament occasionally organised debates in its Environmental Committee, where the Commission has to give an account of its monitoring of the application of environmental provisions. These debates did not lead to any organisational consequences.

12–14

Where the European Parliament receives a petition from a citizen within the European Union, it does not—contrary to the practice in most Member States—itself investigate the facts which underlie the petition, but leaves the investigation to the Commission to clarify the facts, for which the national administration is the principal interlocutor. This is a dubious practice, because the Commission is, and has been for some time, rather selective in its handling of cases, and petitions sometimes also complain on the Commission's passivity.

---

[33] Commission, Implementing Community environmental law, COM(96) 500, para.9: "Further consideration would be given as to whether there might be a need for a limited Community body with auditing competencies."

[34] Council Resolution of 7 October 1997 [1997] OJ C321/1.

[35] See an example of such site visits in *Commission v Greece* (C-103/00) [2002] E.C.R. I-1147.

[36] See 24th report on monitoring application of Community law (2006), COM(2007) 398; 25th report (2007), COM(2008) 777; 26th report (2008), COM(2009) 675 [1997] OJ C332/1; 27th report (2009), COM(2010) 538.

[37] See H. Somsen, "Current issues of implementation, compliance and enforcement of EC environmental law: a critical analysis", in L. Krämer (ed.), *Recht und Um-Welt, Essays in Honour of Prof. Dr. Gerd Winter* (Groningen: Europa Law Publishing, 2003), p.415.

The European Environment Agency, which was set up in 1990,[38] does not have any role in monitoring the application of EU environmental law. When the Agency was set up, the European Parliament had vehemently requested such a monitoring role, following, in that, the example of the US Environmental Protection Agency. However, it could not persuade the Council, which only conceded that in art.20 of Regulation 1210/90 a clause should be inserted according to which the Council would check "at the latest within two years", whether the Agency should be allocated tasks in the monitoring of the application of EU environmental law. When the Commission submitted the corresponding proposal in 1997, it did not suggest giving monitoring tasks to the Agency[39]; the European Parliament had forgotten its previous insistence and the Council did not take this issue up either.[40]

12–15   The EU Ombudsman, set up under art.228 TFEU, has the task of controlling complaints of maladministration in the activities of the EU institutions or bodies. This might include maladministration in the treatment of citizen complaints in environmental matters or general omissions in the monitoring of application of environmental legislation. His office has a staff of some 70 persons. His control activities occasionally deal with environmental issues, but try to avoid becoming a complaint instance against decisions taken by the Commission.[41]

The Commission announced, in the 5th Environment Action Programme, that it would set up an implementation network which would aim "primarily at exchange of information and experience and at the development of common approaches at practical level, under the supervision of the Commission".[42] However, at that time Member States had already started to set up themselves an informal implementation network. As they vigorously opposed any mechanism at EU level that would give the Commission more options to monitor application of environmental provisions, they accepted the Commission as a member of that network, but kept its informal nature, and, since 1993, have called it the "European Union Network for the Implementation and Enforcement of Environmental Law" (IMPEL).[43] At present, the network consists of representatives of the enforcement and monitoring bodies of Member States and Commission representatives; however, since a number of Member States do not have such specific enforcement and monitoring bodies, officials from central or regional administrations take part in the network. IMPEL mainly deals with exchange of experience on practical application and enforcement issues, exchange of staff, and the elaboration of guidelines for different aspects of application. IMPEL is financed jointly by Member States and the Commission. Its impact on the actual application of environmental directives is very limited, since it concentrates on horizontal questions. In 2008, its structure was turned into that of a (private) association—which reveals all the more that its objective is not the monitoring of compliance of Member States with EU law.

---

[38] Regulation 1210/90 [1990] OJ L120/1; see also para.2–15, above.
[39] [1997] OJ C255/9, amended [1998] OJ C123/6.
[40] Regulation 933/1999 [1999] OJ L117/1 amending Reg.1210/90 [1990] OJ L120/1.
[41] See European Ombudsman, Annual Report 1996 [1997] OJ C272/1.
[42] Commission, 5th Environment Action Programme [1993] OJ C138/5, Ch.9.
[43] Commission, Implementing Community environmental law, COM(96) 500, paras 54 et seq.

(d) Citizen complaints

As the Commission does not have any inspectors, controllers or decentralised   **12–16**
administrations which would inform it on the application of EU environmental
law within the whole of the European Union, its main source of information on
possible omissions in the application of EU environmental provision is the
information that comes from outside the administrations, in particular from
citizens.

The Commission instituted, in the late 1960s, a complaint system for citizens,
in order to obtain information on non-technical barriers to the free circulation of
goods. The Commission offered to intervene with Member States' administration
in order to eliminate border controls and other barriers. Since the mid-1980s, the
system has developed considerably as regards environmental complaints. The
fact that individuals were able to register a complaint with the Commission
stimulated EU-wide awareness of the environment, demonstrated to the citizen
that the Commission was also accessible to the man in the street and made it clear
to the individual that he had some responsibility for his environment, that he
could become active in contributing to the preservation and protection of the
environment and that environmental impairment should not be taken as an Act of
God, against which nothing can be done. This was particularly important for
southern European Member States.

Environmental complaints to the Commission came—and come—from
individuals, environmental or professional organisations, national, regional or
European deputies, local administrations, political parties, ambassadors and
occasionally even from environment ministers of Member States.[44]

The Commission considered as a complaint any written statement that invokes   **12–17**
the breach of EU (environmental) law and asked the Commission to intervene to
repair this breach. The formal requirements for such a complaint are very low; the
reason for this lies in the fact that the Commission has, under art.17 TFEU, the
possibility of starting, even without having received a complaint, an inquiry into
possible breaches of EU law by a Member State. Procedurally, such an official
inquiry is treated in exactly the same way as a complaint. To facilitate the
introduction of complaints, the Commission had even drawn up and published a
form.[45]

The complaint is registered in a central Commission register. The Commission
stated in 2002 that "all complaints received are registered, without any selection".
The registration had as a consequence that the complainant was kept informed as
to the evolution of the complaint and that only the Commission as an
institution—not an individual official—could decide on the final outcome of it.

The Commission tries to obtain as much factual information from the
complainant as possible, which often overburdens the person who has introduced
the complaint. For the rest of the facts, the Commission seeks to obtain factual
and legal information from the (central) administration of the Member State
against which the complaint is directed. In rare cases, expert advice is taken.

---

[44] The number of complaints went from 10 in 1982 to 697 in 2002. Since then, the number of
complaints has reduced, partly because the Commission no longer registers all complaints it receives,
it has voiced its reluctance to instruct individual cases and has tried to reach arrangements with
Member States on breaches of EU environmental law.

[45] [1989] OJ C26/1; reviewed [1999] OJ C119/5.

Hearings or witnesses' testimony are never taken in environmental cases. Also, inspections in Member States do not take place; in very rare cases, visits to the affected sites in the form of fact-finding missions have been organised, but not more frequently than once per year.

12–18 In the 1980s, the Commission committed itself—both on the complaint form and in different declarations towards the public—to instruct each complaint; in 1999, it indicated that its administrations would decide according to the internal rules and priorities whether they would examine a complaint or not.[46] And in 2002, the Commission further reduced its commitment to examine each complaint. Under the Barroso Presidency, the Commission set up a pilot scheme: when a complaint is received, it is registered in a special register.[47] Then, the Commission addresses the Member State in question to find out what the problem is and how it could be solved. The difference to the complaint system is that the Commission administration cooperates behind closed doors with the national administration in order to arrange things; as this is outside any public participation and no information is released, very often the national administration—which frequently is at the origin of the problem by granting permits, remaining passive or disregarding environmental law—gets away with its practice. Also, this practice led during recent years to a refusal to register complaints where Commission officials felt that no breach of Community law was likely, or to similar abuses, which was a clear contradiction to the Commission's own commitment to register all complaints.[48]

Anyway, no sanction exists against an omission to instruct properly, except for disciplinary measures and, eventually, the intervention of the European Ombudsman. The complainant has no direct rights as regards the omission to examine a complaint or to treat it by way of the arrangement (pilot) procedure. Overall, this change in administrative practice by the Commission led, within five years, to the reduction in the number of instructed cases, for example against Spain from some 480 to 30—though no change in the Spanish environmental policy or practice occurred.

The Commission refused all requests to lay down, in a legal instrument, the procedures for examining potential breaches of EU environmental law. Such a legal instrument exists in competition law, where complaints by private persons or associations or media reports are taken by the Commission as valuable sources of information for examining potential breaches.[49] The difference of treatment between competition and environmental law is flagrant and has no justification.[50]

12–19 At the end of the instruction period of a petition, a complaint, or an own-initiative investigation, which shall not, according to the Commission's internal instructions, extend beyond one year, the Commission can decide either to file the case or to open formal proceedings, under art.258 TFEU, against a

---

[46] See the different versions of the complaint forms [1989] OJ C26/1; reviewed [1999] OJ C119/5.
[47] Commission, A Europe of results—applying Community law, COM(2007) 502.
[48] See the Commission's own evaluations which are, of course, positive, COM(2010) 70 and COM(2011) 930.
[49] Commission, Reg.774/2004 relating to the conduct of proceedings by the Commission pursuant to arts 81 and 82 EC Treaty [2004] OJ L123/48.
[50] See also L. Krämer, "The Environmental Complaint in EU Law" [2009] *Journal of European Environmental and Planning Law* 13.

Member State.[51] Upon intervention of the European Ombudsman, the Commission changed its rules in 1997; before it decides to file a complaint, the complainant is heard and has the right to present observations.[52] This procedural guarantee, however, does not give any right to a complainant as regards the final decision which the Commission takes; neither can he oppose the filing of the complaint nor can he oblige the Commission to start legal proceedings under art.258 TFEU against a Member State. The complainant also does not have a right to ensure the Commission makes adequate use of its discretion or, in other words, to see that the Commission's decision is not grossly arbitrary, for instance with regard to previous Commission decisions.

The Court of Justice, obviously motivated by political, not legal considerations, has rejected all attempts to oblige the Commission to start proceedings under art.258 TFEU or not to close a file.[53] The Court argued that the decision under art.258 is not a decision which can be tackled under art.263 TFEU since it forms an accessory part of a subsequent Court procedure.[54] Furthermore, a complainant is not in the position of a person entitled to take action before the European courts under art.263(4)) TFEU, since a decision under art.258 would not be addressed to the complainant. Finally, the Commission has a margin of discretion which cannot be questioned by individual complainants.[55] In particular, the latter argument could hardly be called convincing, if one reads art.258 TFEU ("the Commission ... shall deliver ...", in contrast to the fact that it "may" bring a case before the Court of Justice).

Practice has shown that an environmental case, a complaint or a petition has a greater chance of leading to a positive result when the conflict between the environmental interests and the diverging economic interests is discussed in public. The mobilisation of public opinion constitutes an important element of ensuring the taking into consideration of environmental interests and demonstrates at the same time the—at least partly—political character of the complaint procedure; this political character also appears through the lack of control of the Commission's decisions, which facilitates policy interventions in the decision-making procedure.

Complaints procedures in environmental matters normally take a considerable **12–20** time. Their lack of transparency, the obvious reluctance of the Commission to examine complaints and the—overall—limited results, in particular as regards large infrastructural projects, have not led to a situation where the Commission is perceived as a true complaint institution. This is strengthened by the fact that the Commission has tried, since about 2001, to do everything it can to discourage complaints.[56]

---

[51] See para.12–24, below.

[52] Commission, 15th report on monitoring application of environmental law (1997) [1998] OJ C250/1, p.10.

[53] See Court of Justice, *Star Fruit Company* (C-247/87) [1989] E.C.R. I-291; *Asia Motors* (C-72/90) [1990] E.C.R. I-2181; *Sateba v Commission* (C-422/97) [1998] E.C.R. I-4913.

[54] General Court, *Dumez v Commission* (T-126/95) [1995] E.C.R. II-2863.

[55] *Star Fruit* (C-247/87) [1989] E.C.R. I-291 and *Asia Motor France v Commission* (C-29/92) [1992] E.C.R. I-3935.

[56] See for details, L. Krämer, (fn.50, above).

(e) Direct effect of environmental provisions

12–21   In an effort to make EU provisions fully operational for the individual citizen, the Court of Justice had, by the early years of the European Union, already developed the doctrine of direct effect. It started with judgments which stated that provisions of the EC Treaty also had direct effects in favour of citizens, who were entitled to invoke these provisions before the courts. Later the Court extended this doctrine to provisions of directives which could also, under certain conditions, be invoked by citizens before national courts.[57] This constituted a deviation from the provision of art.288 TFEU, which states that regulations, but not directives, are directly applicable and that directives must be transposed into national law in order to have legal effect. The Court justified this decision by the fact that a Member State should not be entitled to take advantage of the fact that a directive was not or was not correctly or completely transposed into national law. For that reason this doctrine was only applied in favour of individuals, but never—for instance in criminal cases—against individual persons.[58] Furthermore, the Court did not apply this doctrine in cases where two individuals were in dispute.[59] This demonstrates that the direct effect of a directive is construed, by the Court, as a sanction against the deviating Member State.

The following conditions must be fulfilled for a provision of a directive to be directly applicable:

- the period for transposing a directive into national law has expired;
- a Member State has not, or has not correctly, transposed the provisions of a directive;
- the provision of a directive is unconditional, i.e. the provision "is not subject, in its implementation or effects, to the taking of any measure either by the institutions of the Community or by the Member States"[60];
- the provision is sufficiently precise to be relied on by an individual and applied by the court; this is the case "where the obligation which it imposes is set out in unequivocal terms"[61]; and
- the provision explicitly or implicitly confers rights to an individual as against a Member State. In this regard the Court of Justice held on several occasions that where a provision dealt with the relations between

---

[57] See, e.g. *Comitato di Difesa della Cava* (C-236/92) [1994] E.C.R. I-483: "The Court has consistently held that wherever the provisions of a directive appear, as far as their subject-matter is concerned, to be unconditional and sufficiently precise, those provisions may be relied upon by an individual against the State where the State fails to implement the directive in national law by the period prescribed or where it fails to implement the directive correctly."

[58] See, e.g. Court of Justice, *Arcaro* (C-168/95) [1996] E.C.R. I-4705: "a directive may not by itself create obligations for an individual and … a provision of a directive may not therefore be relied upon as such against such a person … a directive cannot, of itself and independently of a national law adopted by a Member State for its implementation, have the effect of determining or aggravating the liability in criminal law of persons who act in contravention of the provisions of that directive".

[59] Court of Justice, *Dori* (C-91/92) [1994] E.C.R. I-3325: "The effect of extending that case-law [on direct effects] to the sphere of relations between individuals would be to recognise a power in the Community to enact obligations for individuals with immediate effect, whereas it has competence to do so only where it is empowered to adopt regulations".

[60] Court of Justice, C-236/92 [1994] E.C.R. I-483.

[61] Court of Justice, C-236/92 [1994] E.C.R. I-483.

administrations, it did not give rights to individuals.[62] I have defended the argument that, for the test as to whether a provision of EU law grants rights to an individual, the provision has to be constructed in such a way as if it were contained in a regulation; then it would have to be checked as to whether in such a case the provision would confer an improved position, a legal advantage. It has to be admitted, though, that the question of whether a provision confers a "right" to a person is extremely difficult to answer.

As the Court of Justice constructs the direct effect as a sanction against a Member State which has not, or has not correctly, transposed a directive, it is only logical that it does not apply the doctrine of direct effect in favour of the state, for instance in a criminal procedure against a polluter, or in relations between a citizen and a polluting installation. These limitations and the general difficulties with the interpretation of when a provision has direct effect make this doctrine of rather restricted use.

The Court of Justice refused to give direct effect to art.9(3) of the Aarhus **12–22** Convention[63] which had been ratified by the EU and was thus part of EU law.[64] It argued that it followed from the words "if any" that art.9(3) required the taking of implementing measures by the Contracting Parties; thus it was not unconditional. In its reasoning, the Court did not (wish to) consider that the words "if any" do not *require* the taking of implementing measures, but only *allow* the taking of such measures. No Contracting Party of the Aarhus Convention is obliged, under art.9(3) to lay down (restrictive) criteria regarding access to justice in environmental matters. This might lead to an *actio popularis* situation in environmental matters. However, such an approach exists at present in Portuguese environmental law. It shows that the Court's reasoning is not legal, but political.

This position of the Court of Justice is all the more regrettable as the Court also refused to apply its concept of *effet utile* (useful effect) to art.9(3) of the Aarhus Convention, concerning access to the EU courts: in case C-240/09 the Court stated (emphasis added)[65]:

> "it must be observed that these provisions [Article 9(3) of the Aarhus Convention], although drafted in broad terms, are intended to ensure effective environmental protection ... if the effective protection of EU environmental law is not to be undermined, it is inconceivable that Article 9(3) of the Aarhus Convention be interpreted in such a way as to make it in practice impossible or excessively difficult to exercise rights conferred by EU law. It follows that ... it is for the national court, in order to ensure effective juridical protection in the fields covered by EU environmental law, to interpret the national law in a way which, *to the fullest extent possible*, is consistent with the objective laid down in Article 9(3) of the Aarhus Convention."

---

[62] *Cinisello Balsamo* (C-380/87) [1989] E.C.R. 2491 and *Security International v Signalson* (C-194/94) [1996] E.C.R. I-2201.

[63] Aarhus Convention, art.9(3): " ... each Party shall ensure that, where they meet the criteria, if any, laid down in its national law, members of the public have access to administrative or judicial procedures to challenge acts and omissions by private parties and public authorities which contravene provisions of its national law relating to the environment."

[64] Court of Justice, *Lesoochranárske zoskupenie* (C-240/09) [2011] E.C.R. I-1255; confirmed in *European Parliament and Council v Milieudefensie* (C-401/12P) ECLI:EU:C:2015:4.

[65] *Lesoochranárske zoskupenie* (C-240/09) [2011] E.C.R. I-1255 at [46]–[50].

12–23   The refusal to apply the same principle to ensure "to the fullest extent possible" access to the EU courts and without giving the slightest explication for this omission, demonstrates the double measure which the Court of Justice applies to access to the national courts and access to the EU courts.

3.   SANCTIONS FOR NON-APPLICATION

(a)   Action under art.258 TFEU

12–24   By far the most important instrument at the Commission's disposal when fulfilling its obligation under art.17 TEU is art.258 TFEU.[66] This provision provides for a three-stage procedure[67]:

1.   formal notice of breach of obligations to the Member State;
2.   issue of a Reasoned Opinion; and
3.   application to the Court of Justice.

Steps (1) and (2) together constitute the prejudicial procedure, which has the objective of enabling the Member State to comply with its obligations under EU law or to present its arguments to the Commission on why there is no breach of EU law. For this reason the Commission, which alone may initiate the procedure under art.258, is obliged to specify clearly the object on which it considers the Member State's breach to have occurred (object of litigation).[68]

The formal notice to a Member State that is considered to be in breach of its obligation does not require a specific form. In practice, however, notice is always given in the form of a letter. The decision to send such a letter is taken by the Commission after detailed preparation of the Commission services. The formal letter is agreed word by word at administrative, legal and political level, before it is formally notified to the Member State. This careful preparation is also due to the view held by the Court of Justice that the Commission's letter defines the object of litigation for any subsequent Court proceedings.[69] Thus, the Commission cannot, in any subsequent part of the procedure under art.258 TFEU, include any additional point of complaint against a Member State, since the Member State would not have had "the opportunity to present its observations" on such points. Since, however, the factual side of the case is normally not completely clarified, changes in the legal assessment are, of course, possible.

---

[66] See wording of art.258 TFEU: "If the Commission considers that a Member State has failed to fulfil an obligation under the Treaties, it shall deliver a reasoned opinion on the matter, after giving the State concerned the opportunity to submit its observations. If the State concerned does not comply with the opinion within the period laid down by the Commission, the latter may bring the matter before the Court of Justice of the European Union."

[67] The procedural provisions regarding art.258 are not codified, in contrast to the competition provisions of art.108 TFEU, see Commission Reg.774/2004 [2004] OJ L123/48. The Commission stated in Written Question E-2496/98 (Watson) [1999] OJ C142/18 that the provisions regarding art.258 had been published in the introduction to the Commission's 10th report on monitoring application of Community law (1992) [1993] OJ C233/1, and that later amendments were published in the successive annual reports. This is simply not correct.

[68] *Commission v Spain* (C-266/94) [1995] E.C.R. I-1975.

[69] *Commission v United Kingdom* (C-337/89) [1992] E.C.R. I-6103.

Normally, the Member State has two months to reply to the Commission's Letter of Formal Notice. However, since, on average, the Commission discusses and decides on cases under art.258 only once every six months, the time available to Member States for a reply is almost always much longer.

Where the Commission is not satisfied with the Member State's answer, it may decide to issue a Reasoned Opinion. The Reasoned Opinion is produced in the same form as the letter of formal notice. The facts of the dispute are supposed to have been clarified during the procedure preceding the decision to issue a Reasoned Opinion. The Reasoned Opinion gives a detailed and comprehensive description of the case as it presents itself in the opinion of the Commission, indicates the legal opinion and describes, in particular, in detail how EU environmental law has been breached. Should proceedings subsequently be initiated with the Court of Justice, the facts no longer need to be clarified and the dispute can normally be confined to legal issues. On average, the time-span between the dispatch of the letter of formal notice and the judgment of the Court of Justice was between: **12–25**

- 1992 and 1994: 57 months;
- 1995 and 1997: 47 months;
- 1998 and 1999: 68 months;
- 2000 and 2001: 59 months;
- 2002 and 2003: 45 months;
- 2004 and 2005: 47 months; and
- 2006 and 2007: 47 months.[70]

This time-span does not appear to have been shortened since then.

The Commission occasionally publishes a press release on those disputes which it considers politically or environmentally important. The impact of such press releases is sometimes considerable, depending on the sensitivity of the media to the issue. However, the Commission does not make public either the Letter of Formal Notice or the Reasoned Opinion. This practice, for which no explanation can be found in art.258 TFEU, is justified with the argument that the confidentiality of the relations between Member States and the Commission would otherwise be disturbed and a smooth solution to the problem made more difficult. This attitude seems to be neither in the interest of the environment nor of the citizen and it is not conducive to an open society; finally, it is not compatible with Reg.1049/2001 on access to documents held by EU institutions.[71]

The Commission has a large discretion to apply to the Court of Justice and, in practice, less than 10 per cent of cases where the procedure under art.258 was initiated are actually submitted to the Court of Justice. There is no delay required in submitting the application to the Court, or need the Commission, to demonstrate a specific legal interest in order to obtain a judgment. The

---

[70] The procedure before the Court (under art.258 TFEU) takes between 18 and 20 months; the remainder is due to the pre-litigation phase between the Commission and the Member State. See L. Krämer, "Environmental Judgments by the Court of Justice and their Duration" in [2008] *Journal for European Environmental and Planning Law* 263.

[71] See L. Krämer, Access to Letters of Formal Notice and Reasoned Opinions in Environmental Matters [2003] *Journal for European Environmental and Energy Law* 197.

Commission has concentrated over the past ten years on cases where there has been a lack of or bad transposition of EU legislation into national law; cases where the existing law is badly applied are exceptional.[72]

12–26 The Court's decision under art.258 TFEU states that there is a breach of EU environmental law, unless the application is dismissed. The Court neither annuls the national measures that caused the breach of EU law nor does it pronounce on the measures that have to be taken; it is up to the Member State to comply with the judgment and take the necessary measures.

Between 1976 and 2015, the Court of Justice decided about 700 environmental cases under art.258; the average time-span, including the prejudicial procedure, has been, almost four years.

The Lisbon Treaties introduced art.260(3) TFEU, according to which the Commission may, in a procedure under art.258 TFEU, ask the Court to fix a lump sum or a penalty payment against a Member State "which has failed to fulfil its obligation to notify measures transposing a directive adopted under a legislative procedure"; the Court may not go beyond the Commission's proposal, in deference to art.260(2) TFEU. In environmental measures, art.260(3) TFEU has not yet been applied by the Court.

12–27 It is arguable whether this provision also applies where a Member State has not transposed specific provisions of a directive, or where these provisions were incorrectly transposed. The Court of Justice has not yet decided on this issue. The Commission held that it was entitled to bring such cases to the Court under art.260(3) TFEU[73] and started several procedures against Member States in this sense.[74] My own opinion is that art.260(3) TFEU aims at an accelerated compliance of a Member State with EU law. When questions have to be discussed such as whether definitions need to be transposed into national law and whether national provisions in their context completely transpose an EU provision, this might lead to long and protracted discussions. Such procedures are better placed under art.258 than under art.260(3) TFEU. Also, the borderline between arts 258 and 260(3) TFEU becomes very difficult to determine.

(b) Action under art.259 TFEU

12–28 Article 259 TFEU allows Member States to take judicial action against another Member State which has not fulfilled its environmental obligations under the EU Treaties. However, no such case has ever been brought before the Court in environmental matters. Member States instead rely on the Commission to take action.

---

[72] The main reason is probably that in cases of bad application the factual side of the case needs to be clarified often enough before the Court of Justice which is burdensome and time-consuming. I cannot prove, but would not exclude, that the Court itself signalled to the Commission not to submit cases of bad application. The task of the Court is indeed much easier when it has to compare whether national legislation complies with EU law.

[73] Commission, SEC(2010) 1371.

[74] *Commission v Austria* (C-663/13), pending; *Commission v Ireland* (C-236/14) pending; the two cases concern the non-transposition of definitions and some provisions of Dir.2009/98 on renewable sources of energy [2009] OJ L140/16. *Commission v Belgium* (C-302/14) pending; *Commission v Finland* (C-329/14) pending; these two cases concern the failure to transpose several provisions of Dir.2010/31 on the energy performance of buildings [2010] OJ L153/13.

(c)   Action under art.260 TFEU

Where a Member State does not comply with a judgment by the Court, the **12–29** Commission may, under art.260 TFEU, start a new procedure. The justification for that is probably the continued non-compliance with EU law and, at the same time, the contempt of the Court that is enshrined in the non-execution of the judgment. Since the entry into force of the Lisbon Treaty, the procedure is no longer the same as under art.258 TFEU. Indeed, the Commission only has to send out a Letter of Formal Notice; if it is not satisfied with the Member State's answer or if the Member State does not answer, the Commission may go directly to the Court of Justice, without sending out a Reasoned Opinion (art.260(2) TFEU). It then shall specify the amount of the lump sum or[75] of a penalty payment to be paid by the Member State concerned. The Court may then impose a lump sum or a penalty payment.

The Commission issued a number of communications regarding the methods for calculating the penalty payments.[76] For each case, a basic amount of (currently) €650 is fixed. This figure is multiplied with a figure between 1 and 3 according to the duration of the infringement, and another figure between 1 and 20 according to the seriousness of the infringement. This sum is then multiplied with a co-efficient which the Commission determines according to the ability of the Member State to pay the penalty and which is calculated according to its net domestic product and the weight of its votes in Council.[77]

Until mid-2015, the Court of Justice delivered a number of judgments under art.260 in environmental cases:

Case	Member State	Reason for the penalty	Amount of the penalty
C-387/97[78]	Greece	unauthorised landfill in the river valley of Kouroupitos (Crete)	€20,000 per day
C-278/01[79]	Spain	bad quality of inland bathing waters	€624,150 per year and per 1% of not complying waters

---

[75] The word "or" was interpreted by the Court, in *Commission v France* (C-304/02) [2005] E.C.R. I-6263, as allowing to impose a lump sum *and* a penalty payment. Since then, this became the general practice of the Commission and the Court.

[76] Commission, [1996] OJ C242/6; [1997] OJ C63/2; SEC(2005) 1658; SEC(2010) 923; C(2012)6106; C(2013)8101.

[77] This present co-efficient varies between 0.35 for Malta and 21.29 for Germany.

[78] Court of Justice, *Commission v Greece* (C-387/97) ECLI:EU:C:2000:356; first judgment C-45/91, ECLI:EU:C:1992:164.

[79] Court of Justice, *Commission v Spain* (C-278/01) ECLI:EU:C:2003:635; first judgment C-92/96, ECLI:EU:C:1998:53.

C-121/07[80]	France	incorrect transposition of Dir.2001/18 on genetically modified organisms	lump sum of €10 million
C-304/02[81]	France	no control of compliance with fisheries restriction measures	lump sum of €20 million euro; €57.6 million for every six months of non-compliance
C-279/11[82]	Ireland	incorrect transposition of Dir.85/337 on environmental impact assessment	lump sum of €1.5 million
C-374/11[83]	Ireland	Dir.75/442 domestic waste waters may not go to septic tanks	€12,000 per day of non-compliance
C-533/11[84]	Belgium	incorrect transposition of Dir.91/271 on urban waste water in five municipalities	lump sum of €10 million euro; €859,404 for every six months of non-compliance
C-576/11[85]	Luxembourg	bad application of Dir.91/271 on two plants	lump sum of €2 million; €2,800 per day of non-compliance

[80] Court of Justice, *Commission v France* (C-121/07) ECLI:EU:C:2008:695; first judgment C-419/03, ECLI:EU:C:2004:467.
[81] Court of Justice, *Commission v France* (C-304/02) [2005] E.C.R. I–6263; first judgment C-64/88, ECLI:EU:C:1991:240.
[82] Court of Justice, *Commission v Ireland* (C-279/11) ECLI:EU:C:2012:834; first judgment C-66/06, ECLI:EU:C:2008:637.
[83] Court of Justice, *Commission v Ireland* (C-374/11) ECLI:EU:C:2012:827; first judgment C-188/08, ECLI:EU:C:2009:670.
[84] Court of Justice, *Commission v Belgium* (C-533/11) ECLI:EU:C:2013:659; first judgment C-27/03, ECLI:EU:C2004:418.
[85] Court of Justice, *Commission v Luxembourg* (C-576/11) ECLI:EU:C:2013:773; first judgment C-452/05, ECLI:EU:C:2006:737.

C-196/13[86]	Italy	unauthorised landfills	lump sum of €40 million; €42,800,000 penalty, minus €400,000 per closed and cleaned landfill
C-378/13[87]	Greece	unauthorised landfills	lump sum of €10 million; €14,520,000 penalty, minus €40,000/80,000 per closed and cleaned landfill
C-243/13[88]	Sweden	updating permits under Dir.2008/1 one installation in default	lump sum of €2 million; €4,000 per day of non-compliance

In its judgments, the Court approved the general method of calculation of the Commission, but underlined that it alone had the right to finally fix the penalty amounts to be paid. It may reduce or increase the financial penalty with regard to the Commission proposal or not fix a penalty at all. Its calculation is not specified in detail, but much more general than that of the Commission.

12–30

In case C-387/97 (*Kouropitos*), Greece paid €4.5 million. Then it had fenced the case and operated an interim landfill. The Commission closed the file. Later, the Court confirmed in cases C-196/13 against Italy and C-378/13 against Greece that EU waste law not only required the closing of a landfill, but that also the waste had to be removed. In case C-278/01, Spain was ordered to pay some €624,000 per year and for each percent of inland bathing waters that did not comply with the requirements of EU law.[89] Later, the Commission filed the case, in an obviously erroneous interpretation of the judgment.[90]

---

[86] Court of Justice, *Commission v Italy* (C-196/13) ECLI:EU:C:2014:2407; first judgment C-135/05, ECLI:EU:C:2007:250.

[87] Court of Justice, *Commission v Greece* (C-378/13) ECLI:EU:C:2014:2405; first judgment C-502/03, ECLI:EU:C:2005:592.

[88] Court of Justice, *Commission v Sweden* (C-243/13) ECLI:EU:C:2014:2413; first judgment C-607/10, ECLI:EU:C:2012:192.

[89] Court of Justice, *Commission v Spain* (C-278/01) ECLI:EU:C:2003:635.

[90] Directive 76/160 on bathing water required that 95 per cent of all samples taken from bathing waters had to conform to the EU requirements. The Commission found that 94.7 per cent of Spanish bathing waters complied with EU requirements and filed the case, because the 0.3 per cent were not relevant. It confounded the overall quality of the Spanish bathing waters with the compliance of the individual water.

(d) State liability

12–31 According to the Court of Justice, a Member State may also be liable for damages towards private individuals because it has breached EU law by failing to transpose an EU Directive into national law.[91] The Court laid down a number of conditions for such a liability: there must be a serious breach of EU obligations; the EU Directive must confer rights to individual persons; the content of these rights is identifiable by reference to the Directive; and there exists a causal link between the Member State's obligations and the damage suffered by the person affected. Fault or negligence on the part of the Member State is, however, not required. Until now, this theory has not been applied to environmental cases, though there might be some potential for such cases, all the more so since the theory also applies to cases where a directive has not correctly or completely been transposed. As the Court also considered that individuals also acquire rights from quality objectives,[92] the construction of such damages could, in future, be considerable.

(e) Financial sanctions

12–32 Financial sanctions for breach of EU environmental law exist in theory. Indeed, the different regulations for the EU Structural Funds and the Cohesion Fund provide that measures which are financed or co-financed by the European Union must comply with the European Union; the formula that they had to comply with in EU environmental law was deleted in 2006.[93] Thus, according to this provision, measures could not be financed with EU funds if they failed to comply with all the provisions of EU environmental law. As a consequence, each measure which was undertaken in a Member State without respect of EU environmental law—an example would be the construction of a motorway without an environmental impact assessment—could, in the past, lead to a refusal of financial assistance or to the recuperation of the sums paid.[94] Subsequent to an obiter dictum by the General Court,[95] the Commission considered the procedures under art.258 TFEU and under the provisions of the different funds that deal with the recovery of the financial assistance as independent from each other. Thus, the start of a procedure under art.258 or even a judgment by the Court of Justice did not automatically lead to the Commission recovering the sums paid; rather, the Commission reserved the right to examine, in each individual case, what steps were to be taken. This evolution ended in 2006, when the new Regulations on the

---

[91] Court of Justice, *Francovich v Italy* (C-6 and 9/90) [1991] E.C.R. I-5357; *Factortame* (C-48/93) [1996] E.C.R. I-1029.

[92] *Commission v Germany* (C-361/88) [1991] E.C.R. I-2567; *Commission v Germany* (C-131/88) [1991] E.C.R. I-825.

[93] See, e.g. Reg.2081/93 [1993] OJ L193/5, art.7 and Reg.1164/94 on the Cohesion Fund [1994] OJ L130/1, art.8. The new formula of art.6 of Reg.1303/2013 on the Structural Funds [2013] OJ L347/320 reads: "Operations supported by the European Structural and Investment Funds shall comply with applicable Union law and the national law relating to its application."

[94] Regulation 2081/93 [1993] OJ L193/5, art.24; Reg.1164/94 [1994] OJ L130/1, annex II, art.H; see also Commission, 15th report on monitoring application of environmental law (1997) [1998] OJ C250/1, p.76.

[95] *An Taisce/WWF v Commission* (T-461/93) [1994] E.C.R. II-733.

Structural Funds and the Cohesion Fund provided that non-compliance with EU law did not normally entitle the Commission to retain funds.[96]

When Germany delayed, in the 1990s, the designation of natural habitats under Directive 92/43,[97] the Commissioners for Regional Policy and Environment wrote, in June 1999, a letter to announce that financial means under the structural funds would not be able to be attributed to Germany, as the sums might serve to realise projects which would be realised within future habitats. This letter considerably accelerated the designation procedure in Germany.[98]

Since the Commission's decision to recover or not to recover its financial assistance cannot be attacked by any third person, and since the Commission does not publish details of cases where EU environmental law was not respected, nor any information as to how often it has suspended, refused or recovered financial assistance,[99] the main value of the provisions is likely to lie in a preventive effect: where a Member State is asked, prior to the financing of a project, whether it has complied with all EU environmental law provisions, this might lead to a more careful consideration of such provisions. From media reports, it is known that the Commission, in the past, has sometimes refused financial assistance or at least threatened to do so; however, no quantification can be given. I know of no case, and no publicly available document records any case, where financial assistance was ever definitely refused in an environmental case.

Article 16 of the Directive on greenhouse gas emission trading[100] provides for penalties against companies. The provision reads: **12–33**

> "Member States shall ensure that any operator who does not surrender sufficient allowances by 30 April of each year to cover its emissions during the preceding year shall be held liable for the payment of an excess emission penalty. This excess emission penalty shall be EUR 100 for each tonne of carbon dioxide equivalent."

This provision may lead to quite important penalties and thus ensure compliance by operators.[101] Its importance, however, lies in its precedence for other EU legislation: nothing would oppose provisions in a directive which stipulates that Member States must ensure that operators of industrial installations which, for example, emit too many emissions into the air or the water, which do not respect accident prevention measures or which do not comply with the best available practice, pay a penalty for such non-compliance. Until now, the

---

[96] Regulation 1083/2006 laying down general provisions on the European Regional Development Fund, the European Social Fund and the Cohesion Fund [2006] OJ L210/25, arts.99 et seq.

[97] Directive 92/43 [1992] OJ L206/7.

[98] The letter is mentioned in European Parliament, Resolution of 16 March 2000 [2000] OJ C337/333.

[99] The Commission's 14th and 15th reports on monitoring application of Community law (1996 and 1997) [1997] OJ C332/1, p.70 and [1998] OJ C250/1, p.76 contained for the first time a chapter on monitoring compliance under the Structural Funds. These chapters were virtually identical, though they concerned two different years, and remained very abstract. For 1996, the Commission stated that EU environmental law was not respected in 23 cases, for 1997 in 25 cases. There is neither an indication on the different cases nor is there any information on whether financial assistance was suspended, refused or recovered. The Commission's 18th (COM(2001) 309), 19th (COM(2002) 324), 23rd (COM(2006) 416) and later reports no longer gave a number.

[100] Directive 2003/87 establishing a scheme for greenhouse gas emission allowances within the Community [2003] OJ L275/32.

[101] See *Billerud* (C-203/12) ECLI:EU:C:2013:664.

European Union has not made use of this possibility. However, such provisions would considerably increase the effectiveness of EU law, because they would give to national supervising authorities an instrument to enforce compliance. As long as EU law does not foresee that such financial sanctions are criminal sanctions, there is no any risk of subsidiarity problems.

(f) Criminal sanctions

12–34   In 2001, the Commission made a proposal for a directive to protect the environment through criminal law[102] for a number of specific bans and prohibitions which had already been laid down in EU legislation. Member States were to provide criminal sanctions for cases of intentional or grossly negligent breach of the relevant requirements. These cases concerned, for instance, the unauthorised disposal of waste, the deliberate discharge of solid or liquid waste into waters, illegal trade in endangered species or ozone-depleting substances. Member States were to decide themselves on the kind of criminal sanctions which they wanted to introduce.

The proposal was based on art.192 TFEU. While the European Parliament approved of it, the Council was of the opinion that the EC Treaty did not allow for criminal sanctions and refused to discuss the proposal. Instead, the Council adopted, under art.35 of the Treaty on European Union, a framework decision on criminal sanctions in environmental cases.[103] The main difference between the two provisions was that there was no EU competence for monitoring application of decisions under the third pillar of the Treaty on European Union, as a provision that corresponds to art.258 TFEU lacked in the other Treaty. The framework decision is thus best compared with an international convention. The Court of Justice declared in 2005 that the Treaty on European Union applied only where no EU provisions applied. Therefore, it declared the Council's framework decision void, because legislation on criminal sanctions in the environmental sector could be based on art.192 TFEU.[104] In a later decision, the Court declared that while the European Union had the competence to deal with criminal matters, the type and level of the criminal penalties was the competence of the Member States.[105] On this basis, Directive 2008/99 was adopted which requires a number of actions which the Member States must provide for criminal sanctions, when they were unlawful and committed intentionally or with at least serious negligence.[106] Such actions concern the emission or discharge of polluting substances which cause or are likely to cause harm to humans or damage to the environment; waste treatment or disposal which causes or is likely to cause harm to humans or damage to the environment; the shipment of waste in non-negligible quantities; the operation of a plant which causes or could cause harm to humans

---

[102] [2001] OJ C180/238.

[103] Decision 2003/80 [2003] OJ L29/35.

[104] Court of Justice, *Commission v Council* (C-176/03) [2005] E.C.R. I-7879.

[105] Court of Justice, *Commission v European Parliament and Council* (C-440/05) [2007] E.C.R. I-9097. It is to be noted that the Court did not explain, with one single word, *why* the type and level of sanctions was the exclusive competence of the Member States.

[106] Directive 2008/99 on the protection of the environment through criminal law [2008] OJ L328/28.

or damage to the environment; the damaging of fauna or flora; the deterioration of a protected habitat; trade in endangered species; and trade in ozone-depleting substances.

As the Member States fix the type of sanctions and their level, the Directive is not likely to change the status quo or to have a significant impact on the protection of the environment.

Environmental crime is a considerable growth industry, within Europe and **12–35** worldwide. The most important areas are illegal trade in endangered species, in ozone-depleting substances, illegal logging and trade in tropical timber and other wood, dumping of and trade in waste and, finally, illegal fishing. No concrete measures have yet been taken by the European Union to combat organised environmental crime. Article 83 TFEU allows the European Union to adopt directives in areas of particularly serious crime with a cross-border dimension, and enumerates the areas to which this provision applies. The environment does not figure in this list, though the Council may unanimously decide to add other areas to the list.

(g) Interim measures

Article 279 TFEU provides that the Court of Justice may prescribe any necessary **12–36** interim measure in cases before it. This provision does not state whether the Commission may also take interim measures as soon as it discovers a breach of EU law. However, it is now generally accepted that the Commission has no such powers and that the decision on interim measures can only be taken by the Court of Justice. The Commission may appeal to the Court to prescribe such measures, but this can only take place where a case is pending before the Court or where it is submitted to the Court together with the request for the interim measure. The Commission has then to demonstrate the urgency and necessity of the measure, in particular if there is a risk of a serious and irreversible damage that might otherwise occur.

Attempts by the Commission to stop the construction of a dyke that would have destroyed a bird habitat were rejected, since the Commission was not able to show the urgency of such a measure.[107] An attempt by an environmental organisation to stop the construction of a tourist information centre in a natural habitat was rejected, because a national court had already stopped the project.[108] The attempt to stop, by way of interim measures, the French nuclear tests in Mururoa in 1995, was rejected as inadmissible, since the private applicants were not directly and individually concerned and thus had no standing.[109] Recently, though, the Court stopped by an interim decision the application of a regional legislation on bird hunting in Italy and Malta and the construction of a motorway in Poland which would have destroyed a Natura 2000 area.[110]

---

[107] *Commission v Germany* (C-57/89R) [1989] E.C.R. 2849.

[108] *An Taisce v Commission* (C-407/92R), Decision of 6 July 1993.

[109] General Court, *Danielsson v Commission* (T-219/95R) [1995] E.C.R. II-3051.

[110] Court of Justice, *Commission v Italy* (C-503/06R) [2006] E.C.R. I-141; *Commission v Poland* (C-193/07R) ECLI:EU:C:2007:218; *Commission v Malta* (C-76/06R) [2008] E.C.R. I-64.

Generally, it can be said that it will hardly ever be possible to demonstrate the urgency and necessity of interim measures under art.258 TFEU, since the pre-Court stage, during which no interim measures are possible, takes almost three years.[111]

(h)   Action by individuals

12–37   EU environmental law does not provide for any active role for citizens or their organisations to ensure full application of EU environmental law. The role of monitoring application is given to the Commission, though it is obvious that the Commission is not the owner or the unique stakeholder of the environment; however, in that respect EU environmental law is basically no different from law in most Member States and, indeed, most other industrialised countries. It seems that it is almost only the United States that ensures that there is the possibility for its citizens and private organisations actively to monitor application of environmental law. Within the European Union, the idea of having private citizens actively pursuing general interest matters such as the application of environmental law and, thereby, the protection of the environment, is not strongly developed. Member States in the tradition of Roman law resist it, as the concept of an "open society" and the activation of citizens as law enforcers has no tradition in law. In Scandinavian Member States, a concept of the modern welfare state seems to lead to the conclusion that it is best for public authorities to ensure the application of environmental law.[112] The complaint procedure, described in paras 12–16 et seq., above, does not enable citizens actively to pursue any lack of compliance with EU law.

Actions against Member States can only be taken by the Commission; its decision to act or not to act under art.258 TFEU cannot be challenged by citizens. Where the Commission itself causes environmental impairment, there is hardly any possibility for a citizen to take action against the Commission, since that citizen is not directly and individually concerned. The jurisprudence by the Court of Justice, which grants citizens some "rights" under EU environmental directives, has had no influence whatsoever on individuals' and their organisations' right of standing under EU law.

In 1998, the European Union and all Member States signed the Aarhus Convention on "access to information, public participation in decision-making and access to justice in environmental matters", which had been elaborated under the auspices of the United Nations. This Convention, which is entered into force in 2001, was ratified by the European Union[113]; it provides for access to justice[114] for "members of the public concerned (a) having a sufficient interest or, alternatively (b) maintaining impairment of a right, where the administrative procedural law of a Party requires this as a precondition". This provision includes environmental organisations. In implementing the provisions of the Aarhus

---

[111] See para.12–25, above.

[112] See Court of Justice, *Djurgaarden* (C-263/08), ECLI:EU:C:2009:631; Sweden, one of the most advanced countries in environmental protection, had granted access to justice only to environmental organisations with more than 2,000 members.

[113] Decision 2005/370 [2005] OJ L124/1.

[114] In the wording of art.9(2) of the Convention, this means "access to a review procedure before a court of law and/or another independent and impartial body established by law".

Convention, the Commission proposed, in 2003, a directive to give environmental organisations a right of standing in national courts.[115] Member States considered, however, that access to justice was their exclusive competence and did not adopt the proposal. In 2014, the Commission withdrew its proposal.

In order to avoid being accused of measuring with two measures, the Commission also made a proposal for a regulation to improve access to the European Courts by the environmental organisations. The proposal was adopted in 2006, as Regulation 1367/2006.[116] It did not amend the present provisions of arts 263 and 265 TFEU. Thus, the access to the European Courts has not been improved which is incompatible with the requirements of the Aarhus Convention.

12–38

In a judgment of 2011, the Court declared art.9(3) of the Aarhus Convention[117] to be, together with the Aarhus Convention itself, part of EU law. It held, however, that art.9(3) did not have direct effect, because that provision granted access to the courts only once the conditions which were laid down by Member States were complied with. The Court encouraged the national courts to interpret art.9(3) broadly and do the utmost in order to ensure, in environmental matters, large access by private persons or environmental organisations to the national court.[118] The judgment did not explain why a Member State should be allowed to invoke its own omission to lay down conditions on access to justice in order to maintain the national status quo and not fully apply art.9(3).

In March 2011, the Compliance Committee of the Aarhus Convention held that the restrictive practice by the EU Court of Justice to practically bar any access of environmental organisations to the EU Court, was incompatible with the provisions of the Aarhus Convention.[119] The Compliance Committee rejected in particular the argument raised by the European Union that the possibility to address a national court which could then introduce, under art.267 TFEU, a preliminary procedure before the Court of Justice, was sufficient to satisfy the requirements of the Aarhus Convention.

The extent to which an individual can address national courts and claim a breach of EU law is governed by national law; no general EU provisions exist. At present, there has been no attempt to improve the possibilities for individuals actively to ensure the application of EU environmental law. A Commission communication of 1996 is silent in that respect[120]; the Council's resolution on that communication is no more explicit.[121]

12–39

---

[115] Commission, COM(2003) 624; see also paras 4–17 et seq., above.

[116] Regulation 1367/2006 on the application of the provisions of the Aarhus convention on access to information, public participation in decision-making and access to justice in environmental matters to Community institutions and bodies, [2006] OJ L264/13; see also paras 4–06 et seq., above.

[117] Aarhus Convention [2005] OJ L124/3, art.9(3): "In addition and without prejudice to the review procedures referred to in paragraphs 1 and 2 above, each Party shall ensure that, where they meet the criteria, if any, laid down in its national law, members of the public have access to administrative or judicial procedures to challenge acts and omissions by private persons and public authorities which contravene provisions of its national law relating to the environment."

[118] Court of Justice, *Lesoochranárske zoskupenie VLK* (C-240/09) ECLI:EU:C:2011:125.

[119] Aarhus Convention Compliance Committee, Findings and recommendations of the Compliance Committee with regard to communication ACCC/C/2008/32 concerning compliance by the European Union of 14 April 2011.

[120] Commission, Implementing Community environmental law, COM(96) 500 of 22 October 1996. The communication mainly addresses measures at national level and considers, at EU level, better information, cooperation and consultation.

[121] Council Resolution of 7 October 1997 [1997] OJ C321/1.

Where a national court is seized with a litigation that involves EU environmental law, it has the possibility to submit to the EU Court of Justice a preliminary question on the validity or the interpretation of EU law; when the judgment of the national court "against whose decisions there is no remedy under national law", that court is obliged to submit preliminary questions to the Court of Justice, when these questions are relevant in the case before it.[122] For an individual person or an environmental NGO, this provision is of limited value: the decision, whether to submit a preliminary question to the Court of Justice, depends on the national court. The national court also formulates the question. As, on average, preliminary cases before the Court of Justice take about 16 months, many national courts omit putting such questions, for fear of delaying the litigation.

Overall, the provision of the Aarhus Convention that private persons and environmental organisations should have the right to bring before EU courts actions against acts and omissions of the EU public authorities, remains very largely dead letter. Neither art.263(3) TFEU nor the procedures under art.267 TFEU offer an access to courts that corresponds to the requirement of art.9(3) of the Aarhus Convention. It was thus quite correct that the Aarhus Convention Compliance Committee found that access to EU justice, as it is organised at present, is not in compliance with the Convention.[123]

12–40 To what extent the monitoring of application of EU environmental law should be ensured by the EU staff or should be, at least to some extent, externalised, is a question of legal and institutional policy. It is obvious that Member States—and even less actual or potential polluters—do not like to be checked as to their environmental performance. The administrations, the governments and the EU institutions prefer maintaining the quasi-monopoly of the EU institutions and of national administrations to bring public and private polluters before the courts. Whether the environment can indefinitely survive the present monitoring practice, which is all too often influenced by political or administrative intervention or private lobbying, is not a question to be dealt with here.

---

[122] See art.267 TFEU: "The Court of Justice of the European Union shall have jurisdiction to give preliminary rulings concerning: (a) the interpretation of the Treaties; (b) the validity and interpretation of acts of the institutions, bodies, offices or agencies of the Union. Where such a question is raised before any court or tribunal of a Member State, that court or tribunal may, if it considers that a decision on the question is necessary to enable it to give judgment, request the Court to give a ruling thereon. Where such a question is raised in a case pending before a court or a tribunal of a Member State against whose decisions there is no judicial remedy under national law, that court or tribunal shall bring the matter before the Court."

[123] Aarhus Convention Compliance Committee (fn. 119, above).

CHAPTER 13

EC Environmental Law and Policy

1. INTRODUCTION

EU environmental policy orientations were first formulated in 1971/1972 and progressively expanded since. They were anchored in the EC Treaty in 1987 by the Single European Act and further fine-tuned by the Treaty amendments of 1993 (Maastricht Treaty), 1999 (Amsterdam Treaty) and 2001 (Nice Treaty). In December 2009, the Lisbon Treaties on European Union entered into effect, after long negotiations on what constitutional basis the Union should rest. This last event only demonstrated that the European Union does not enjoy the prerogatives of a state; in particular, it may act only where it has been expressly so authorised by the Lisbon Treaties. Any comparison with domestic environmental law in the Member States, of which there have been 28 since 1 July 2013, or with the United States is therefore necessarily misleading.

This becomes obvious in the area of environmental law and policy which is part of European law and policy. It is difficult to determine what the European interest in environmental protection is, how far it goes in specific cases and which measures should be taken at which level in order to protect the environment in Europe. There are no European radio or television stations, no European press and, more generally, no European public opinion which would discuss the general environmental interest of the European Union, and not just the French, German, UK or Spanish interest in the European Union. Lawyers very largely continue to perceive and discuss European environmental law from a national law perspective. One might find some consolation in the remark from Arthur Toynbee that the wheels of a car turn around themselves, and yet move the car ahead; however, when the car is called "European Union" which shall achieve an ever closing union among the peoples of Europe, there is some need to discuss the car's equipment, driving instruments and, most of all, the direction which it shall take and is actually taking.

Law alone cannot answer these questions. Making environmental legislation for some 500 million people in the European Union is possible. However, in view of the diversity of culture and education in the different parts of the European Union, the difference of climate, geography and other environmental conditions, the difference of economic and social development and of policies within the 28 Member States and their regions, such European environmental legislation must necessarily be general in character and leave many details to the local, regional and national level.

Also, law as a tool to protect the environment has its inherent limitations. The European Union might adopt thousands more directives or regulations to protect

13–01

13–02

the environment: if the mentality of humans to impair the environment is not reduced, if the ecological footprint of everyone and of the European society is not reduced, all this environmental legislation constitutes food for lawyers, but does not change the societal reality which is marked by the simple fact that the European environment—and more so, the global environment—is sick and becomes slowly, but continuously worse, not better.

There is a consensus, expressed in several Council political statements, declarations and resolutions that the present life-style within the European Union is not sustainable.[1] This consensus, though, did not yet lead to significant steps in order to revert the situation—and there are many reasons for this, among them considerations of competitiveness, economic growth, welfare and human greed. No politician at European level or within the 28 Member States has ever dared declaring, as the then President of the United States declared for his country, that "the European life-style is not negotiable", meaning that significant changes in life-style are not acceptable. Yet, in practice, the European Union does not behave differently from the United States, though there are differences, as Europe has another history and culture, is less wealthy and has less geographical space. Also, the emphasis which the European Union puts on economic growth and the neglect of non-economic values—social, environment and culture—progressively flattens such differences and makes one forget that one cannot live on bread alone. Policies may influence and change trends, but then political leaders need vision, strategic thinking, leadership capacity and credibility. These are qualities which are rare—everywhere in the world, including in Europe.

2. PRIMARY LAW

13–03   The structure of the EU Treaties still reflects the preponderance of economic interests over environmental (and social) interests. The EU Treaties deal in detail with internal trade, the four freedoms, transport, agriculture etc. After some antecedents, the integration provision of art.11 was inserted, in 1999, into the Union Treaty to ensure that the three environmental provisions of arts 191 to 193 TFEU influence all other EU policies and progressively "green" them. This concept was to be completed by the overall objective of the European Union to reach a sustainable development (arts 3 TEU and 11 TFEU) and to aim at a high level of environmental protection (arts 2 TEU, 114 and 191 TFEU).

However, this concept was and is based on the *political* decision to aim for integrating environmental requirements into other policies, to aim for a high level of protection and for a sustainable development. The legal provisions as such are not sufficient. And as the Court of Justice never decided that art.11 TFEU constituted a *legal* requirement, that a specific measure was not of *high* level of environmental protection or what the precise content of sustainable development was in a given context, the concept of the EU Treaties remains unfulfilled.

---

[1] See, e.g. 5th Environment Action Programme [1993] OJ C38/1, recitals: "The Council and the Representatives of Member States, meeting in Council, agree that many current forms of activity and development are not environmentally sustainable … agree that the achievement of sustainable development calls for significant changes in current patterns of development, production, consumption and behaviour."

The weight of environmental law is different, if one compares it, for example, with the economic provision of art.34 TFEU which stipulates that there should be no quantitative restrictions on the free circulation of goods or measures having equivalent effect. This provision was not only interpreted by the Commission—and confirmed by the Court of Justice—as prohibiting trade restrictions, it was also interpreted as giving individual persons and companies the right to invoke this clause in courts and have all measures which contradicted it declared void. The interpretation of art.34 TFEU was thus not left to the Commission or to the public authorities alone, but could also be, and was in fact, influenced by citizens.

There is no provision in arts 191 to 193 TFEU which prohibits environmental **13–04** pollution or impairment. Formulating such a provision would not be too difficult, as the sole prohibition is not less precise than the original wording of art.34 TFEU. Indeed, the Avosetta Group, a group of European environmental lawyers, suggested a formula to be inserted into the Treaty: "Subject to imperative reasons of overriding public interests, significantly impairing the environment or human health shall be prohibited". However, inserting such a provision into the Treaty would have meant that citizens could tackle provisions or practices which contradicted this rule in courts—which would have broken the monopoly of the administration to decide, by action or by inaction, what is good for the environment, what a high level of protection is and to what extent measures in other policy areas contradicted the environmental requirements. The Avosetta formula has therefore no chance of ever being included in any future Treaty.

The other big lacuna in the present Treaty provisions, from the point of view of environmental protection, concerns nuclear energy. Article 11 TFEU applies to the EU Treaties as such, not to the Euratom Treaty. It would have been easy to insert a provision similar to art.11 into the Euratom Treaty. But this has not been done. And it is disappointing to see that nuclear energy policy which has the biggest negative environmental potential of all industrial activities, due to the longevity of radiation, risk of accidents, terrorist attacks, waste issues, etc, is not even contained by any environmental provision, while at the same time the European taxpayer—who has, in about half of the Member States, expressly rejected nuclear energy—pays huge amounts for nuclear research and infrastructure, nuclear installations, their decommissioning and their waste.

Is there a lack of a provision on an individual right to a clean environment in the European Treaties? Human rights generally are formulated in the Charter on Fundamental Rights which has, under art.6 TEU, "the same legal value as the Treaties"; the environmental provision there resembles art.11 TFEU.[2] This could therefore plead in favour of an explicit human right to a clean environment. However, experience in Member States shows that not much is won with the insertion of such a human right into the constitution (or, for the European Union, into the Lisbon Treaties), as almost all depends on the concrete, political organisation of protecting the environment—such as the environmental infrastructure and administration, the policy rank of environmental issues, the

---

[2] Charter on Fundamental Rights [2000] OJ C364/1, art.37: "A high level of environmental protection and the improvement of the quality of the environment must be integrated into the policies of the Union and ensured in accordance with the principles of sustainable development."

determination of local, regional and national administrations to take effective action in favour of the environment, education of the population—including courts, media, academics, etc.

13–05   Member States which have an individual right to a clean environment in their constitution do not fare environmentally better than those Member States where the protection of the environment is "only" a constitutional policy orientation provision (*Staatszielbestimmung*). And the EU Treaties do already include, in arts 3 TEU, 11, 114 and 191 to 193 TFEU, such policy orientation provisions. What would be necessary, though, is a change in the above-mentioned situation that under the EU Treaties—including its art.263(4) TFEU on access to the European Courts—the Commission's and Member States' administrations have the de facto monopoly of enforcing the environmental provisions, including those of the EU Treaties themselves. In this regard, an individual right to a clean environment would be of use.

The environmental principles of art.191(2) TFEU—the principles of precaution and prevention, the principle that environmental damage should be tackled at the source and the polluter-pays principle—helped to justify specific legal measures, but were not interpreted as to require a specific solution to a problem or to prohibit this or that measure. To have such an effect, their precise content and their borders are too vague. These principles could be completed by others, such as the substitution principles, though this would raise the same problems: the question when a dangerous chemical substance should be replaced by another, less harmful substance can only be decided in view of the characteristics of both substances, their use, the availability of substitution substances, cost elements and even legal considerations. Where the use of a substituting substance would make the EU producers dependent on a third country patent holder, the policy decision on that substance will not remain uninfluenced. This proves that the insertion into the Treaties of, for example, a substitution principle would not change much of the present situation.

Overall, the constitutional frame for the protection of the environment at EU level is satisfying. Some fine-tuning might be necessary or desirable in this or that provision; standing for citizens or environmental organisations could be introduced via secondary legislation. However, the Treaty enables the EU institutions and the EU Member States to lead an active, coherent and consistent environmental policy of and within the European Union—if the political will to do so exists.

3.   LAW-MAKING AND THE QUALITY OF EC LAW

(a)   On law-making

13–06   When EU environmental law appeared in the statute books in the mid-1970s, it met, at national level, largely virgin ground. Few environmental provisions existed at that time and the progressive development of EU environmental legislation led several Member States—Greece, Ireland, Spain, Portugal,

Luxembourg, Italy, in part also the United Kingdom, France and Belgium—to take over that legislation rather than develop national rules on the basis of a national environmental policy.

Today, national environmental law consists in many Member States in southern Europe, as well as in all 13 Member States, which adhered to the Union since 2004, of more or less 100 per cent of the transposition and incorporation of EU environmental law. And for most of the other Member States, this figure varies between 65 and 80 per cent. In theory, the conditions are very favourable for an intensive consensus-building at European level on the orientation of legislation, its degree of detail, on issues to address and on instruments to develop. To this has to be added the overall umbrella provision of art.193 TFEU which allows Member States to maintain or introduce more stringent national provisions. EU environmental law thus has the potential to be the foundation on which, according to the ecological, social and economic conditions in the different parts of the European Union, national or regional supplementary environmental provisions are allowed to be built.

Practice, though, developed differently. As the national administration and policy had the de facto monopoly to protect or not to protect the environment, legislation that was made at EU level was frequently perceived as interfering with this monopoly. And while at the political level Member States regularly agreed, in EU Environment Action Programmes, to objectives, principles and priorities of EU legislative activity, at the administrative level this was not always followed—though it has to be admitted that the two levels cannot always easily be distinguished. As the devil of environmental protection is in the detail and not in great principles such as "sustainable development", "best technique" or "the polluter shall pay", the making of environmental EU legislation gave ample opportunity to protect the national administrations' monopoly. The absence of environmental provisions at national level did not therefore mean that a Member State would be in favour of seeing such provisions imported from the European Union. In concrete terms, this reluctance manifested itself in various forms, such as the stopping of new legislative initiatives,[3] the changes of approaches to tackle environmental pollution,[4] the watering down of proposals[5] and the establishment of provisions which could alone be monitored and controlled by the national administration[6]; of course, the EU administration was not neutral in this effort, but often contributed to it, also according to the national provenance of the different EU officials. The efforts had the (welcome) side-effect that the administrations' monopoly was also affirmed with regard to national environmental organisations, citizen groups and public opinion bodies.

---

[3] Examples are the proposals for directives on the dumping of waste at sea, on a permit requirement for all industrial installations, on provisions on airport noise or on access to justice.

[4] Examples are the shift from emission limit values to quality standards in air and water legislation, the substitution of provisions for certain industrial sectors by non-binding BREF documents or on the producer responsibility in waste management legislation.

[5] Examples are Dir.98/83 on drinking water [1998] OJ L330/32; Dir.2004/35 on the administrative obligation to clean up orphan damage [2004] OJ L143/56; and Dir.2004/107 on the omission to fix quality standards for heavy metals in air [2005] OJ L23/3.

[6] Examples are Dir.2000/60 on water framework [2000] OJ L327/1; Dir.2006/7 on the quality of bathing water [2006] OJ L64/37; Reg.1013/2006 on the shipment of waste [2006] OJ L190/1; and Dir.2004/35 on environmental liability [2004] OJ L143/56.

13–07   The problem with this approach was that the individual national administration which pleaded for a reduced EU environmental legislation, had its own national situation in mind; for example, it did not wish to see the European Union interfere—this was frequently the attitude prevailing in the United Kingdom; or it wished to ensure its regional power—this was the prevailing motivation of the German Länder—or it was of the opinion that its own national environmental provisions were better anyway than those which could be generated at EU level; this last attitude was frequently found in the Netherlands. Neither national administration paid much attention to the fact that the alternative to EU environmental provisions was not that there would be national provisions in what is now 28 Member States. Rather, the alternative was that some Member States would have national legislation on a specific item, but the large majority would not. This lack of European perspective of national decision-takers has dominated the law-making process at European level for decades, though it has never been openly discussed.

Despite this reluctance, EU environmental law achieved a number of quite remarkable results, in quantity and also in quality. The following list of ten pieces of EU environmental law which would, without the EU legislation, not have been subject of national environmental legislation in the vast majority of—old and new—Member States, serves to illustrate this point; it could easily be prolonged: environment impact assessment, participation in decision-making, accident prevention, integrated pollution prevention and control, drinking water, waste incinerators, end-of-life vehicles, packaging and packaging waste, habitat protection and bird protection.

The Commission's administration was and is not strong enough to ensure the adoption of environmental legislation at a high level against or without the support of national administrations. Its allies are not numerous: public opinion, the best ally of the environment, hardly exists at EU level; environmental scientists are almost not organised at EU level; the European Parliament re-acts, but hardly ever has the historic memory or the scientific support which would enable it to play an active role in environmental law-making; and European environmental organisations lack human and financial resources.

(b)   The quality of EU environmental law

13–08   These imperfections of the law-making process affect the quality of environmental legislation. EU environmental law was developed ad hoc, without strategic thinking how to organise a specific sector (water, air, waste). Amendments were also made on an ad hoc basis, often as a follow-up to accidents or incidents. Where framework legislation was created, its basic orientations were questioned and changed after few years, discrediting the nature of a framework legislation; examples are Directives 76/464 on water discharges,[7] 84/360 on industrial air pollution[8] or 96/62 on air quality standards.[9] More recent framework legislation—for fresh water (Directive 2000/60[10]), marine waters (Directive

---

[7] Directive 76/464 [1976] OJ L129/23.
[8] Directive 84/360 [1984] OJ L188/20.
[9] Directive 96/62 [1996] OJ L296/55.
[10] Directive 2000/60 [2000] OJ L327/1.

2008/56[11]), pesticide use (Directive 2009/128[12]) or flooding (Directive 2007/60[13])—are so vague and general in their content that their added value to the protection of the environment appears questionable. Indeed, where a Member State has the will to protect the environment in one of the areas mentioned, it may find useful orientation and support in such framework legislation; however, where this political will does not exist, the improved environmental protection will hardly ever be achieved, as the framework legislation mainly works with analysis, planning and reporting as EU instruments.

The codification of environmental legislation into one or several basic texts has never been seriously considered at European level. After the Commission's somehow populist announcement in 2001, to reduce the volume of EU legislation by 25 per cent, efforts were undertaken to incorporate all amendments of a directive or a regulation into one single text, without touching the substance, though. In this way, overlapping, contradictions and inconsistencies between different environmental pieces of legislation are not reduced, though this form of law-making also sails under the name of "codification".[14] In some Member States, the putting together of environmental provisions into one legal act or code has been successfully brought to an end. For a foreseeable time, such initiatives will not take place at European level.

Also, at EU level, there is no instrument to measure the quality of environmental legislation. The only reasonable yardstick is whether the legislation has led to an improved permanent protection or not. On that, it is undoubtedly true that EU environmental legislation has contributed to the adoption of environmental legislation in all 28 Member States. Subsequently, this led to the installation of environmental ministries, the creation of environmental structures—local and regional administrations, environmental groups, environmental education, discussion of environmental issues in the media, creation of specialised institutes, laboratories and others—and to the discussion of environmental issues in national policies. However, this alone does not yet protect the environment. To illustrate this point, an example of a decision by the Court of Justice may be quoted. A citizen had applied to the Court because his private property had been inserted into the EU-wide list of habitats of European importance under Directive 92/43 and he was of the opinion that this Commission decision was wrong. The Court rejected his application as inadmissible[15] because he was not directly affected by the Commission decision. The Court held that the selection of habitats in a national list and the subsequent decision and publication of a European list were all preparatory acts which did not affect the private property. This means that the existence of Directive 92/43 since 1992 has not, with regard to habitats, led to concrete protection; rather, this protection of the environment with regard to specific habitats will only begin once conservation measures have been taken.

---

[11] Directive 2008/56 [2008] OJ L164/19.

[12] Directive 2009/128 [2009] OJ L309/71.

[13] Directive 2007/60 [2007] OJ L284/27.

[14] Examples are Dir.2010/75 on industrial emissions [2010] OJ L334/17; Dir.2008/50 on ambient air quality and cleaner air for Europe [2008] OJ L152/1.

[15] Court of Justice, *Sahlstedt a.o. v Commission* (C-362/06P) [2009] E.C.R. I-2903; General Court, *Sahlstedt a.o. v Commission* (T-150/05) [2006] E.C.R. II-1851.

13–09   The biggest merit of EU environmental legislation is that it exists, and that this existence compelled all Member States to have equivalent provisions in their national statute books. On this set of rules, environmental policy can build where the political will exists.

Also, EU environmental law has not prevented Member States from maintaining or introducing into national legislation more stringent provisions. And no area is visible where a Member State was prevented from protecting its national environment because of the existence of EU environmental legislation. One might think of the area of biotechnology as an exception: it is well known that countries such as Austria or Denmark would prefer not to have genetically modified seeds on their land, or fruit, vegetables or meat in their shops which contains GMOs. However, it was explained in Chapter 6, above, that the European Union—deliberately—placed legislation on GMOs on the product-related art.114 TFEU, not on the environmental-related art.192 TFEU. Member States agreed to that on several occasions. Then they have difficulties in arguing that they can no longer protect their environment in the way which they think best.

In 2015, the Juncker Commission suggested that Member States should, when transposing EU legislation into national law, not go beyond the provisions that had been adopted at EU level (gold-plating).[16] As regards EU environmental law, this proposal is in contradiction to art.193 TFEU which expressly provides for such a possibility. Politically, the Communication and in particular the proposal to stop gold-plating, reveals the Commission's intentions: any legislation is perceived, in the Communication, as a burden (for business) and should, whenever possible, not go beyond what the Commission—and later the European Parliament and the Council—considered as adequate.

13–10   The proposal also fundamentally misunderstands the concept of environmental protection within the EU: the underlying concept of arts 191–193 TFEU is not the harmonisation of (national) legislation; rather, the basic concept is to reach a high level of environmental protection. And this might *require* differentiation of environmental protection measures, according to the geography, the climate (wind, sunshine, tides and other factors), the constitutional and political structures in a Member State, citizens' awareness of the necessity and the need to protect the environment etc. The proposal would be a little bit less disturbing if the Commission were indeed, in its legislative proposals on the protection of the environment, aiming at a high level of protection; then, stricter measures at the level of Member States would be less necessary. However, unfortunately, a high level of environmental protection is not an objective which the Commission normally has in mind. Rather, it has a tendency of declaring *any* proposal which it makes to aim at such a high level—which is, of course, simply incorrect.

EU environmental legislation often lacks the necessary precision and details. Definitions of "renewable energy" which includes the "biodegradable fraction of industrial and municipal waste",[17] of "good environmental status" in Directive 2000/60, Directive 2008/56 on marine waters—where the marine environment is

---

[16] Commission, Better regulation for better results—an EU agenda, COM(2015) 215, paras 8 and 9; see also the Commission proposal for a new interinstitutional agreeement on better regulation, COM(2015) 216, para.31.

[17] Directive 2009/28 [2009] OJ L140/16.

practically reduced to the quality of *waters*—and of "participation" are loosely drafted and invite different interpretations or abuses. Environmental "plans" and "programmes", "best available technique", reports and monitoring obligations are not defined with the necessary rigidity. More examples could be given. The often-heard argument that in an enlarged European Union of 28 Member States this flexibility is inevitable, is simply misleading: between Stockholm and Sofia, Lisbon and Riga, everybody knows what a car is and understands the term in the same sense. Yet, there is no uniform definition of hazardous waste.[18] In contrast, the Directive on three-wheel cars has 454 pages in the EU Official Journal,[19] and the number of large, very detailed CEN and CENELEC standards is beyond 15,000, and rising. This demonstrates that a European Union needs EU (uniform) definitions. Vague definitions in EU environmental law appear to be due more to the influence of British administrative law; they make law monitoring and application difficult, if not impossible. Article 193 TFEU which allows Member States to better protect their environment, is not an excuse for not precisely defining what the EU legislation is about.

The greatest problem as regards the quality of environmental law are those pieces of EU environmental legislation which are, de facto, unenforceable. The issue will be discussed in more detail in paras 13–17 (Application of environmental law) and paras 13–36 (EU environmental law and Member States), though it also affects the quality of law. It had been argued in Chapters 7 (water) and 8 (air) that EU quality standards are practically unenforceable against Member States. As the Commission has, in any case, the obligation to ensure that environmental law is not only transposed into national law, but also "applied" (art.17 TEU), it should think twice before it suggests the setting of quality standards at EU level. And if it does propose them, its proposals should contain provisions which repair this enforcement problem. This has never been done in the past. The consequence is that quality standards are not enforced in the European Union. And it should be remembered that nothing discredits the legislation in a society more than its non-application.

(c) Better regulation

For about 20 years, starting with the Edinburgh summit of the Heads of State and Governments 1991, there have been efforts to deregulate environmental provisions that had been adopted at EU level. In order to hide their objective, these efforts sail under the flag of "better regulation". While there were some efforts in the mid-1990s and by the Prodi Commission (1999–2004) in this regard,[20] the Barroso Commission (since 2004) has made the subject of better regulation one of its central topics,[21] and the Juncker Commission follows this line.[22] It believes that deregulating the environment and other areas will create employment, make the European economy more competitive and will, overall, strengthen the European Union, internally and globally (Lisbon process).

13–11

---

[18] Directive 2008/98 [2008] OJ L312/3.
[19] Directive 97/24 [1997] OJ L226/1.
[20] See Commission, European Governance—a White Paper [2001] OJ C287/1.
[21] Commission, Communication: Better regulation for growth and jobs, COM(2005) 97.
[22] Commission, COM(2015) 215.

This neo-liberal policy orientation, which I consider wrong, will not be discussed here. The Commission received part of an answer of the European citizens in the form of the negative referendum on the European Constitution in France and the Netherlands in 2004, in the continuously reduced number of voters in European elections and in the increase of anti-EU political parties and movements in the Member States. What is to be mentioned here is what the Commission itself declared, in 2001, when it presented its political environmental programme for the next 10 years[23]:

> "Despite improvements on some fronts, we continue to face a number of persistent problems. Of particular concern are climate change, the loss of biodiversity and natural habitats, soil loss and degradation, increased waste volumes, the build up of chemicals in the environment, noise and certain air and water pollutants. We also face a number of emerging issues such as pollutants that affect the functioning of our hormone systems. Forecasts suggest that with current policies and socio-economic trends, many of the pressures that give rise to these problems, such as transport, energy use, tourist activities, land-take for infra-structure etc. will worsen over the coming decade."

If this description is correct—and there is no serious environmental analysis which ever contradicted it—then there is some need for the Juncker Commission to explain to the European citizen, in detail, how these trends can be reversed by the deregulation policy which it pursues.

13–12   There are several such basic contradictions. For example, under the "Better regulation" policy, the Commission announced that it would try to promote the use of voluntary agreements with industry, including in the sector of environmental policy. In contrast, the 6th Environment Action Programme declared quite unambiguously that "legislation remains central to meeting environmental challenges".[24] No attempt was made to clarify this difference in approach. In 2001, the Commission announced that it would promote tripartite contracts between European regions, the Member State concerned and the European Union, in order to promote environment protection[25]; there was no follow-up, but no explanation either. "Governance", a central topic of the Prodi Commission, has disappeared from the policy agenda of the Barroso and the Juncker Commissions. The Cardiff process, initiated by the European Council and which should also influence law-making and the quality of legislation, has been buried in silence, without any explanation to the European citizen.

All this leads to a credibility gap: how can the European citizen believe what the European institutions declare, if this is no longer true a short time afterwards? The Commission is not a government which might change policies after elections that brought new political forces to power. Rather, the Commission has to act in

---

[23] Commission, COM(2001) 31, p.10.
[24] See Dec.1600/2002 [2002] OJ L242/1, Recital 12. This statement constituted an answer to the Commission's proposal for the 6th Environmental Action Programme, COM(2001) 31, where the Commission stated: "In some cases, non-regulatory methods will be the most appropriate and flexible means of addressing environmental issues. The Commission is currently examining new methods of governance, including alternatives to traditional regulation such as voluntary commitments and agreements, which could improve the ability of enterprise to innovate and change."
[25] Commission, COM(2005) 97.

the common European interest (art.17 TEU) and it is difficult to understand why and how this interest changes within a short time.

4. THE DIFFERENT ENVIRONMENTAL SECTORS

A look at the different sectors of EU environmental law has to start with the 7th Environment Action Programme itself. This was adopted in the form of an EU decision[26] and is thus legally binding. The programme contains a number of binding commitments to reach specific results in different sectors[27]; furthermore, it contains a number of instructions to the EU institutions and, in particular, to the Commission to tackle this or that aspect of environmental policy.[28] If the fact that the 7th Programme was adopted by way of a decision had any sense, then the Commission is obliged to follow the mandates and instructions which the programme contains, and this for the lifetime of the Programme—or at least until the Programme had been amended. It makes no sense to elaborate a programme, to proceed to extensive consultations with all stakeholders, to discuss it at European level for more than two years, have it adopted by way of co-decision under active cooperation of the Commission, and then ignore its content.

Other environmental *programmes* announced in a less binding form—as communications, thematic strategies, green papers, white papers, strategies or framework legislation—suffer a similar destiny. They are often ignored by the administrative structures in the Commission, Parliament and Council which are affected by them and thus are not much more than an accumulation of good words. One principal reason for this is that the environmental programmes are elaborated by the environmental structure.[29] And while they are formally adopted by the Commission as a whole, the industry, agricultural, transport or energy departments, hardly having participated in their elaboration, do not feel committed to follow the programmes' objectives, principles and priorities, as they have, in their respective sector, to pursue their own objectives, principles and priorities. This pattern continues in the European Parliament and the Council. In other words: the integrative part of the EU institutions to make one coherent policy, is limited. The different parts of EU policy—transport, industry, agriculture, consumer, environment, etc—are horizontally little integrated, but work vertically and rather autonomously.

13–13

---

[26] Decision 1386/2013 [2013] OJ L354/171.

[27] See Dec.1386/2013 [2013] OJ L354/171, annex, para 28: "the 7th EAP shall *ensure* that by 2020..." (emphasis added). The same wording is used in paras 43, 54, 65, 73, 84, 89, 95 and 106.

[28] See Dec.1386/2013 [2013] OJ L354/171, annex: the paras quoted in fn.27 above contain 60 such instructions. As examples are quoted: "increasing efforts to reduce soil erosion and increase soil organic matter, to remediate contaminated sites and to enhance the integration of land use aspects into coordinated decision-making involving all relevant levels of government, supported by the adoption of targets on soil and on land as a resource, and land planning objectives" (para.28 VI); "developing measurement and benchmarking methodologies by 2015 for resource efficiency of land, carbon, water and material use and assessing the appropriateness of the inclusion of a lead indicator and target in the European Semester" (para.43 IV).

[29] Environmental structure is understood as being the environmental directorate general within the Commission, the environmental committee in the European Parliament and the environmental working group as well as the environmental ministers in the Council. Similar structures exist for agriculture, energy, etc.

As regards the *horizontal legislation* which tries to follow the principles of an open society and give citizens more access to environmental information and more participation rights in decision-making, it is clear that the EU institutions do *not* try to be as open, transparent and accountable as possible. There are different cultures in the European Union in this regard, and the German, French and British culture which is far away from the openness of the Scandinavian culture, largely dominates the EU institutions and makes the phrase of art.1 of the Treaty on European Union, that decisions are to be taken as openly and as closely to the citizen as possible, rather theoretical for the time being. At the level of Member States, the spirit of openness and participation which underlies the Aarhus Convention, influences the daily practice in Scandinavian Member States and in the Netherlands. Elsewhere, much change in mentality of the administration is still needed, before openness, transparency and accountability will be the leitmotif of daily work.

13–14 Looking at *industrial installations*, it is understandable that the European Union did not establish conditions for the emissions of all industrial installations; and it is a policy choice to opt for the best-technique approach, in order not to have to establish the limitations for the different groups of installations and the pollutants by way of EU legislation. However, whether there should not be a general provision which covers *all* industrial installations—80 per cent are small- and medium-sized companies—and requires a permit for their emissions into the environment, is arguable. Also, general requirements with regard to greenhouse gas emissions, resource management and waste handling could be imagined. On this, the European Union relies on the Member States and this aspect will be discussed below.

There is no comprehensive legislation on *biodiversity*. The two Directives on birds (2009/147) and fauna, flora, habitats (92/43) are clearly not sufficient to protect EU nature. Directive 92/43 applies only to species and to habitats under threat. If it is correct that nature slowly retreats from the European continent, a more general legislation which also impacts on transport policy, agricultural policy, energy policy, the trans-European networks, etc would be needed. Such legislation could also usefully include considerations on wild animal welfare; indeed, animal welfare is one marked feature of differentiation of European values with regard to other parts of the world.

The absence of an environmentally oriented *product* policy was discussed in Chapter 6, above. Climate change considerations generated the adoption of a directive on the eco-design of energy-related products[30]; it would have been even more logical to extend the field of application of this Directive to all products, as it is a framework directive anyway. This would have been all the more consistent, as the product safety legislation does not deal with environmental concerns.

13–15 In the *water* sector, the European Union has largely given up its attempts to get a fixed set of minimum standards; it left the determination of "good environmental status" to the different river basin management bodies and, for marine waters, to the European regional conventions. Also, the other EU directives in the water sector show this retreat from integrated standards.

Air pollution provisions from transport appear to be dictated more by the car industry than by environmental or human health concerns. The growing car fleet

---

[30] Directive 2009/125 [2009] OJ L285/10.

eats up reduction efforts made by the legislation, and the car industry's wish for planning security makes it impossible to quickly introduce technical innovations such as the particulate filter for diesel cars. Emissions of point sources such as installations diminished, though the overall air pollution, including its effects on soils, forests and human health is still worrying. The figure launched by the Commission itself, that more than 400,000 people die prematurely every year in the European Union due to air pollution, should lead to an outcry; instead, the reaction of the EU institutions is more or less a shrugging of shoulders.

As regards *noise*, a first directive of 2002 is not properly monitored by the Commission, and thus proves largely inefficient.[31] The European Union is deficient in establishing noise reduction standards from transport vehicles (motorcycles, cars, trucks, airplanes). Here, legislation follows the technical evolution rather than driving innovation by legal standards that would have to be reached within a certain period. Compliance with standards throughout the lifetime of the product, and not only at the time when it is first placed on the market, is another issue which needs to be addressed. Furthermore, noise around airports (night flight ban, noise levels) would urgently require an EU-wide solution; letting the individual airport find solutions, is just inappropriate, since the airports in the European Union are in strong competition with each other. As mentioned in Chapter 8, the European Union took the opposite view.

Climate change issues have not yet led to a fundamental rethinking of energy **13–16** policy issues at EU level. The targets of the Kyoto Protocol were respected with existing measures including some supplementary measures on energy saving and the promotion of alternative energies. The major problems, however, lie beyond the Kyoto date of 2012, and the measures to address emission of greenhouse gases by the year 2020 and beyond would need to be fully complied with and strictly monitored. Here, the lack of political leadership of the European Union is particularly felt. In view of this passivity, time works for the return of nuclear energy and the continuation of coal and lignite.

In the *waste* sector, the announcement of moving the European Union towards a recycling society has not been followed by concrete action. Waste goes on the cheapest treatment or disposal path, and the EU instruments have not yet reoriented the majority of waste streams to economically more useful paths. Resource management, prevention of waste generation, recycling, the departure of the highly unpopular incineration of waste—all this would require an integrated and coherent product policy for which not even the preliminary reflections have started at EU level. Attempts in 2014 to increase the recovery and recycling targets were stopped by the Juncker Commission in 2015, as it did not fit into the priorities for jobs and growth. Confronted with protests from public opinion and Member States, the Commission made a U-turn and declared that the proposal was withdrawn because it was not ambitious enough.

---

[31] Directive 2002/49 [2002] OJ L189/12.

5. THE CREDIBILITY OF THE PROCESS TO MONITOR APPLICATION

(a) The monitoring policy

13–17   It follows from arts 5 TEU and 192(2) TFEU that Member States have to implement EU environmental law—which means its transposition into national law, its application and enforcement. This is often forgotten. Member States frequently implement and apply EU environmental law not because they perceive the need to ensure an adequate protection of the environment but because the Commission threatens legal action under art.258 TFEU. This is particularly true of Member States which derive their national environmental legislation entirely from EU environmental law, as the national environmental structure is normally not too well developed and not too influential in the political power game.

The Commission started to shift its monitoring policy and intends to concentrate on the *transposition* of environmental directives, much less on its actual *application*. It has not managed in the past to ensure a transformation in time by the majority of Member States and the problem of incorrect and/or incomplete transposition continues to exist. With regard to the incorrect transposition, the Commission treats Member States differently, due to unsystematically addressing problems and resource problems.

The Commission's policy of reducing or abandoning of monitoring the effective application of EU environmental legislation by Member States has some advantage, but also a number of strong disadvantages. This policy saves resources, avoids disputes and litigation with Member States on individual cases and allows the Commission to better concentrate on transposition questions.

13–18   A great legal disadvantage lies in the fact that art.17 TEU is unambiguous: it requires the Commission to ensure that EU environmental law is not only transposed, but actually applied. The Commission is thus not entitled to ignore how the law is applied in practice.

The second disadvantage is perhaps even greater. As Member States have successfully prevented any green police, inspectors and other similar enforcement mechanisms in the area of the environment, the principal source of information for the Commission is the citizen complaint. Such a complaint demonstrates the citizens' interest in environmental as well as in European issues. Where this interest is frustrated, because the Commission does not examine the complaint or arranges fake solutions with the Member State in question, the citizen might rightly ask, why *he* should bother about the European Union. He then must perceive the European Union as a Union for big interests, but not for the man in the street. And where he gets the feeling that the EU environmental law is something for the statute books, but can be breached in practice, without consequences, he will not bother about the environment either. The European Union has considerable difficulties in explaining to European citizens why they should vote in European elections, what concrete advantage there is for the individual citizen in its daily life to belong to the European Union and what all these costly institutions in Bruxelles and other places stand for. Environment protection is popular with citizens all over Europe, and in particular with the younger generation. In this area, the Commission could improve its image and show that it is down to earth, close to the citizen, not just committed to the free trade and other policy areas—which means little to the citizen in the street. The Commission's present approach to environmental issues contributes to alienate the young from the EU concept—probably the most disastrous long-term effect of the present policy.

(b) Administrative secrecy

Closely linked to these general considerations is the Commission's policy of **13–19** considering that the whole implementation and enforcement policy, in particular the Letters of Formal Notice and Reasoned Opinions in the environmental sector which are addressed to Member States, are not accessible to citizens. The reason given is that the confidentiality between the Commission and Member States would otherwise be disturbed. The underlying assumption is that the protection or lack of protection of the environment at national level is a matter between the Commission and the Member State in question—as if the Commission or the Member State or its administration were the owner of the environment. As the Commission decisions are the result of a long and detailed internal process, where all administrative, legal, technical and political arguments are weighed, this secrecy is neither comprehensible nor justified. And it is a poor consolation that the Court of Justice implicitly approved the Commission's practice in a number of judgments.

In policy terms, two observations need to be made. First, Member States with an "open society" approach to administrative secrecy—the Netherlands, Sweden, Denmark, possibly also Austria and Finland—do make the Letters of Formal Notice and Reasoned Opinions available to the public, apparently without any negative consequence. Secondly, in other areas such as industrial, internal market, pharmaceutical, insurance or competition policy, or transport and energy policy, Letters of Formal Notice and Reasoned Opinions are systematically available to the interested trade and industry associations. There is not even a discussion on the necessity to keep the Commission's opinion confidential. This shows that, overall, the system works with two measures: letters which are of interest to citizens are kept secret, while letters which are of interest to vested interest groups are accessible.[32] It is difficult to see how this policy increases the credibility of the European Union in the eyes of the citizen in the street.

(i) Environmental inspectors

It was mentioned that Member States did not accept the idea of environmental **13–20** inspectors which do not exist, at present, at EU level. Little public discussion has taken place on this during the last 15 years, though there is a need to explain: when a company makes an illegal merger with a company in another Member State, and the Commission hears of it, the Commission may inspect the site, hear

---

[32] As long ago as 1985, E. Rehbinder formulated—in a more general context—on access to the EU decision-making process: "Outside access to this process is generally limited to well organised industry groups" (E. Rehbinder and R.Stewart, *Environmental Protection Policy* (Berlin-New York, 1985), p.334). This remark remains valid, also with regard to the decision-making process under art.258 TFEU.

witnesses, seize documents and pronounce, at the end of the day, fines against the company, against which the company may appeal to the General Court, and then appeal to the Court of Justice. And when the same company exports hazardous waste, in breach of its EU obligations, and the Commission hears of that, the Commission may send a Letter of Formal Notice to the Member State in question; it has, as a source of information, the Member State's answer. At the end of the procedure, the Commission may bring the *Member State*—not the company—to the Court of Justice, because the company has acted illegally. The judgment states the facts, but does not pronounce a fine.

This comparison of the procedure shows the doublespeak. Where the company wishes to increase its profits by concluding a merger, it may be fined; but where it wishes to increase its profits by exporting hazardous waste instead of having it treated properly, there is no sanction. This difference of treatment cannot be explained to either a citizen in the street or a law student. It just shows that environmental interests are ranking lower. Why can the Commission, in the first example, send inspectors to examine the facts, but not in the second? Why are veterinary inspectors sent to 140 countries worldwide in order to check sanitary conditions of slaughterhouses, why are fishing boats equipped with a satellite system and have, furthermore, their landings inspected? The measuring with two different measures as regards inspections is obvious.

The Commission's own monitoring policy is in need of being controlled. According to the jurisprudence of the European Courts, the Commission's decision to open or not open proceedings under art.258 TFEU, cannot be controlled in court.[33] All the more would it be necessary to have the Commission's practice audited, in order to see where it is inconsistent, contradictory, where it favours some or disadvantages other Member States or industrial sectors, where the Commission omits to take obvious cases to court which even under its own criteria would be priority cases, etc. This has never happened until now. As a very first step, environmental organisations should systematically bring such cases of differentiated treatment of Member States—on air pollution in urban agglomerations, on waste treatment, on noise levels, on water management etc—before the European Ombudsman.

(ii) International conventions

13–21   It is the monitoring policy of the Commission—nowhere laid down in writing, it is true—not to monitor the transposition and application by Member States of international environmental conventions to which the EU has adhered. An exception is made in cases where the international convention had been transposed into EU law by an environmental regulation or, less frequently, a directive; however, the Commission then monitors the transposition and application of this EU legislation, not of the international convention itself.

Again, this policy is in breach of the Commission's legal obligation under art.17 TFEU: as the international convention becomes, by the adherence of the European Union, part of EU law (art.216(2) TFEU), the Commission has the legal obligation to ensure its application. Article 17 TEU does not differentiate

---

[33] General Court, *Dumez v Commission* (T-126/95) [1995] E.C.R. II-2863.

between the different instruments of EU law. The Court Justice's confirmation of this legal situation[34] has not yet led to any change in the Commission's practice.

(c) Credibility

With the enlargement of the European Union to 28 Member States, environmental law-making has undoubtedly become more difficult. All the more would it be important to ensure that the existing legislation is actually applied. Numerous Council and European Parliament resolutions call on the Commission to ensure a full and complete application of existing environmental rules. And there are also a number of self-commitments by the Commission in this regard: in 2005, the Barroso Commission declared: **13–22**

> "The Union should deliver in terms of implementation and reach out to every European. First, the Union must work well, and be seen to work well ... Failure to apply European legislation on the ground damages the effectiveness of Union policy and undermines the trust on which the Union depends ... Prompt and adequate transposition and vigorous pursuit of infringements are critical to the credibility of European legislation and the effectiveness of policies."

This statement is contradicted by the practice of the Commission to drastically reduce the monitoring of effective application of environmental legislation in specific cases.

6. INSTITUTIONS

(a) Commission

The Commission's mission to act in the common European interest, its monopoly of making legislative proposals and the fact that it is the only institution whose members are permanently present at the seat of the European Union (Bruxelles) gives it a very powerful position to steer environmental protection policy in the European Union. The Commission has enough financial means to launch studies and research on environmental questions. And it has at its side the European Environmental Agency which supplies the necessary data.   **13–23**

The Commission is not surrounded with environmental advisers. It has not set up a scientific, academic, technical, ecological or socio-economic group of advisers which could advise—in particular on its own initiatives—on medium- and long-term trends in environmental issues, comment on actual problems from a point of view away from vested interests or highlight specific developments that are likely to affect the environment. A forum on environment and sustainable development which was to advise the Environmental Commissioner, was quickly dissolved and replaced by an industry dominated round table group which advised the President of the Commission.[35] Environmental groups are not

---

[34] Court of Justice, *Commission v France* (C-239/03) [2004] E.C.R. I-9325; *Pêcheurs des Etangs de Berre* (C-213/03) [2004] E.C.R. I-7357.

[35] Commission, Dec.93/91 [1993] OJ L328/33 (establishment of the committee); Dec.2001/704 [2001] OJ L120/1 (dissolution).

convened in a consultative group either. This structure is different from structures in agriculture, industry, transport or energy, where the Commission, often together with the Council, sets up formal or informal consultative or advisory groups which discuss sector-related policies *trends* and evolutions.

A politician who is all of a sudden oppointed as an Environmental Commissioner or at the top of the administration, is bound to listen to someone as he simply cannot know all environmental intricacies[36]; he will thus turn either to persons from his home country or to networks which stem from his former activity—whatever that was. The result is less strategic thinking and less long-term reflection; also, the relay between top politicians is not ensured, when changes at the political level or top management occur, a new network has to be formed.

13–24   The only "advisory" group which the Environmental Commissioner meets regularly is the Environmental Policy Review Group, which groups the top officials of central environmental administration of Member States. The group is informal and its agenda, minutes and the results of its meetings are not accessible to the public. Whether the group, from its composition, is willing and capable to give the best advice for the *European* environment, may be doubtful; it may be assumed that the interests of Member States are at least not forgotten.

As regards the staff level of the Commission, the policy, introduced during the last 15 years, to see every official move jobs after three to five years, increases mobility, but produces officials who think more of their career, do not really become experts in their area and are thus not always able to argue with Member States' officials or vested group representatives. This makes the European civil service too easily prone to adopt solutions which satisfy the interlocutors, without necessarily satisfying the needs of the environment.

Within the Commission, the integration of administrations which would be required by the integration requirement of art.11 TFEU, is not a success. Administrations normally work vertically, i.e. with their administrative hierarchy, the respective Parliamentary committee and the Council working group. There are no institutional or otherwise regular meetings between the environmental department and other departments within the Commission. One of the reasons for this situation is the fact that in such a meeting, when it is multilateral, the environmental official would regularly be confronted with a majority of officials who represent growth and economy-interested departments (industry, transport, agriculture, fishery, regional policy, competition, fiscal matters, etc) and could hardly hope to see his point of view prevail. And there are not enough human resources for regular bilateral meetings. This pattern is found at all levels of the hierarchy, Commissioner, director-general, director, head of unit or desk officer. As there is enough work anyway, in all departments, the temptation is great not to discuss environmental issues horizontally, except in cases of necessity.

13–25   This incapacity of the Commission to discuss environmental issues in an integrated way, is felt particularly strongly at sensitive points of policy. Examples are the problems of climate change on transport, which would, of course, require

---

[36] A good example is Karmenu Vella, since end of 2014 the member of the EU Commission in charge of the environment. He had studied architecture and opened a private office on architecture. He served in the tourism, bank and financial business sector and was minister for public works, industries, tourism and finance in Malta. He appears to never have had any political or social connection with the environmental sector.

regular, intense discussions among the administrations of transport, but also of agriculture, energy, industry, trade, regional policy, foreign relations and the environment with a view to conceive a strategy. The 6th Environment Action Programme had developed some considerations in this regard and measures to adopt, however, without significant input from other vertical structures than the environment; these considerations and the measures proposed have very largely been ignored since 2002 and were not taken up by the 7th Action Programme. Another example is the question of environment and development policy, where the departments of development policy, economic, industry, trade, agriculture, fisheries, consumer protection, social affairs would need to develop an integrated strategy on the European Union's policy with regard to the environment and development. This has not been done; therefore, the conclusion of the Court of Auditors of mid-June 2006—20 years after the insertion of the requirement to integrate environmental requirements into the other EU policies!—was quite blunt: "the environment has yet to be effectively mainstreamed into the Commission's development cooperation".[37] Similar descriptions could be made on agricultural policy, product policy, energy policy and other policy sectors.

As regards the outside contacts, in 2001 the Commission placed its work under the principles of openness, participation and accountability, also effectiveness and coherence.[38] The question of openness and transparency was already raised and will be further discussed below at paras 13–31 et seq., in the section on citizens and the EU environmental law and policy. As regards accountability the Commission does not really explain why it takes certain measures or does not take certain measures. Some examples, taken at random, might explain the point:

- Almost all environmental directives require the elaboration, by Member States, of implementation reports and the elaboration, by the Commission, of EU-wide reports. The Commission complies with this obligation in about one case out of two and normally with a considerable delay which diminishes the value of its reports. The Commission does not explain its delays, change its approach or otherwise try to improve the situation. Member States reports are normally not even made accessible, although with the internet such access would be easy.

- The implementation reports themselves report normally on legislative measures that have been taken by Member States, but almost never on results. However, from the point of view of the environment, it is the result that matters. There is almost no attempt from the side of the Commission to explain what the state of the environment is before and after the EU and national implementation measures were taken. The reader of the reports thus learns about the legislation, while it may be assumed that he is interested in the protection of the environment; these two things are different.

- The Commission's practice, mentioned in para.13–21, above, is of not monitoring the application of international conventions.

---

[37] Court of Auditors, Special Report 6/2006 concerning the environmental aspects of the commission's development cooperation [2006] OJ C235/1, no.84.
[38] Commission, COM(2005) 97, p.7.

- The Marine Strategy Framework Directive does not deal with the marine environment, but only with marine waters which have to reach a good environmental status by 2021.[39] There is no explanation given why the Directive does not address issues of fauna and flora, air emissions from ships, noise, waste dumping and other aspects.

- The 6th Environment Action Programme requested the elaboration of a directive on biodegradable waste, which means essentially one on compost.[40] For once, there was a consensus among the majority of Member States, the European Parliament's environmental committee, and environment and industry organisations that EU-wide standards on compost and, more generally, on biodegradable waste are highly desirable; in particular also for countries in Southern and Central and Eastern Europe, where the soil is in need of nutrients.

- The Commission might have good reasons not to make such a proposal. The presentation of a proposal for a directive on the protection of soil would have been a good opportunity to explain its attitude. However, the Commission never explained if and why it considered such a proposal to be inadequate. Directive 2009/98 on waste charged the Commission again to examine the situation and, eventually, come up with a proposal—without any follow-up or any explanation from the Commission as to why it remained inactive.

The list could be prolonged. The impression is that of an administration which knows best what is good for the environment and does not consider it necessary to give account of its acts and omissions.

13–26 The Commission's credibility problem was illustrated at paras 13–17 et seq., above, in the area of monitoring the application of environmental law. This problem is not limited to application issues. Another example is that of the treating of sustainability issues. The question of whether there has not been given an erroneous interpretation to the notion of sustainability development itself, shall not be treated here again. But it is difficult to understand why the Commission adopts a strategy on sustainable development and establishes guiding principles for it,[41] when in the daily practice it only takes one part of that strategy, the part on economic growth (Lisbon agenda) and promotes it. This is an inconsistency which signals to the public that the strategy on sustainable development is pure rhetoric.

A similar rhetoric is found in the Commission's approach to transport problems. The different strategy papers duly mention that transport also causes environmental concerns and is not sustainable—and then move on to greater mobility, more traffic infrastructure and more aviation. There is simply no serious attempt to integrate environmental requirements into the elaboration and implementation of transport policy.

These examples could be multiplied for other sectoral policies.

---

[39] Directive 2008/56 [2008] OJ L164/19.
[40] Decision 1600/2002 [2002] OJ L242/1, art.8.
[41] Council, Strategy on sustainable development, doc.10917/06 of 26 June 2006.

(i) European Parliament

The European Parliament has, in particular through its active environmental   **13–27**
committee, constantly tried to strengthen legislative proposals on environmental
issues which the Commission had submitted. This was and is more difficult,
when the majority in Parliament is conservative, as conservative parties are
traditionally less committed to environmental questions. Yet, overall, the
European Parliament proved to side rather with the environment than with vested
interests.

Parliament's problems are structural. The deputies do not stay permanently in
Bruxelles, but share their time between their constituency, Bruxelles, where the
Parliamentary committees work, and Strasbourg, where Parliamentary plenary
meetings are held. This leads to the result that contact between Parliamentarians
and the Commission or the Council are rather more rare than frequent.

The political parties in Parliament are not organised in the same way as at
national level. They do not work on the same files as the Commission
administration or, indeed, the national administrations in the capitals which then,
later, meet in the Council working groups. Parliament's scientific and
documentary service cannot rebalance this deficit. The result is that the
Commission normally knows the environmental file better than the Parliament,
and that Parliament has to react to the Commission's initiatives, but cannot be
pro-active. This institutional deficit of the Parliament is particularly obvious in
the conciliation discussions under art.294 TFEU, where the deputies are
confronted with the combined experts' know-how of all capitals who know the
specific file, often for many years. Their opinions therefore regularly prevail.

The Parliament does not systematically control the implementation and   **13–28**
application of the environmental legislation which it has co-decided. It cannot be
argued that this is not Parliament's task, because the Parliament as co-legislator
must be interested to know whether the European environmental legislation
effectively works, and if not for what reasons it does not work. Also, the
Parliament has to control the Commission's activity; this requires an active,
systematic look at application questions. In this regard the democratic system of
checks and balances does not work properly.

In its contacts with the public, Parliament is the most open European
institution. Its members, due to a lack of detailed knowledge of the complex
subjects which the Commission environmental legislative proposals have to deal
with, normally recur to interest groups to receive briefings. The European
environmental groups frequently find interlocutors in members of the environmental committee—and so do other interest groups with members of Parliament
which are closer to their interests. Systematic consultations in the form of
hearings could make the consultation process more transparent, but are
exceptional.

As, in general, the European Parliament is not yet a fully fledged Parliament
comparable to national parliaments, its role in environmental law-making and in
controlling the "government"—if one may so call the Council and the
Commission together—is not really efficient.

(b)   Council

13–29   The Council's environmental activity is very largely determined by the Commission's legislative proposals. These are discussed in working groups where environmental attachés of the Permanent Representations of Member States and experts from central national administrations meet, together with Commission officials who defend the proposal. Strategic discussions do not normally take place in these working groups which limit themselves to finding concrete solutions on the basis of instructions from the capitals. The working groups do not have outside contacts; whether individual members have, depends on their personal decisions.

Strategic discussions may take place on the occasion of discussion on action programmes, under "other business" matters at formal Council meetings, or when the environmental ministers meet at the two annual informal Council meetings, for which the Presidency prepares a topic for discussion. As these informal ministerial meetings do not vote, adopt resolutions or other documents, their capacity of committing all members for the future, and thus their influence on long-term environmental policy is limited.

The Council Presidency regularly holds contacts with the Commission on matters that concern the organisation of the work. These contacts also include more general reflections on the different files, though they do not enter into the political area. As the Presidency changes every six months, no long-term or more general discussions occur. Contacts with the European Parliament are much less frequent.

13–30   Outside opinions regarding the Council work reach the Council via the capitals, not directly. This again is cause and effect at the same time for the lack of forming a European public opinion.

If one looks at the institutions, the main charge to develop strategic environmental thinking, long-term orientations and to steer the European environmental policy lies with the Commission which itself is not sufficiently equipped for such a think-tank task and, furthermore, does itself not feel bound by strategies such as action programmes. During the last ten or so years, the Commission more and more considered the protection of the environment as only being a question of climate change and a carbon-free economy and more or less ignored the other parts of the environment.

7.   CITIZENS AND EU ENVIRONMENTAL LAW AND POLICY

13–31   EU environmental law and policy is popular with European citizens. Eurobarometer's regular surveys on the opinion of European citizens' thinking on EU issues show that over the last two decades a high percentage—80 per cent and more—of citizens rank environmental issues as very important and among the three to five top priorities for the European Union. This result is not surprising, if one remembers that for many people in the Member States environmental legislation and the accompanying policy originates at EU level. The citizens in the street wish to see more EU legislation and better protection of the environment, for which they also feel responsible. As the European Union has the objective to be a Union at the service of its citizens and not just a free trade area, one would expect that it should try to bring citizens closer to the making and implementing of EU environmental law and policy.

It had already been mentioned that the Commission has not organised an environmental consultative committee or forum which it could consult. Communication activities by the Commission or by the different Commission offices in Member States are not targeted to inform or consult citizens on environmental matters, to make the administrative and political machinery of the EU institutions more transparent and more comprehensible. The communication activity of the Commission in environmental matters is not impressive, and where the language is not diplomatic, it is unfortunately often closer to marketing or publicity concerns than to neutral information. The Commission environmental reports and communications do not appear to reach the citizen in the street, for reasons of language, too complex contents, and the fact that they are not disclosed; also, very often the problem is not presented and options for solutions discussed, but a specific solution as the right one is pushed ahead. Environmental information and education of citizens might not be the primary task of the Commission, but networking and more concerns for the receiver of the information, including the young receiver, might be worthwhile. And it is little consolation, that the European Parliament and the Council do not fare better in this area.

Access of citizens to environmental information remains difficult, even in times of the internet. It was already mentioned that the EU institutions are not yet prepared for openness and transparency. Too much information is declared sensitive even after the relevant decision has been taken. The Commission shows a considerable sensitivity towards the interests of some Member States and of economic groups to keep studies, surveys, findings and other issues confidential. Key examples are information on nuclear issues and on genetically modified organisms. Risk assessments, cost-benefit analyses, impact assessments, planning instruments, but also reports on meetings between members of the Commission and vested interest groups, communications on files etc—the list is long, where a normal citizen has difficulties in obtaining access to documents. Regulation 1367/2006, which transposes the Aarhus Convention into EU law and applies to the EU institution,[42] did not really lead to significant changes. And it is telling that the Regulation excludes banking activities from its field of application, in order to exempt the European Investment Bank—a derogation which is not foreseen under the Aarhus Convention.

Where the Commission receives a complaint from a citizen that access to environmental information was refused in a Member State, it refers that citizen to the national court. This is another way of disappointing citizens; indeed, art.17 TEU constitutes an own obligation for the Commission to ensure that the law is applied; the general reference to a national court is not a way to comply with this obligation. Other factual difficulties in obtaining access to environmental information—unreasonably high costs, long delays for answers or no answer at all, systematic refusals to grant access, etc—are not examined by the Commission, as it wishes to have as little to do with practical questions of

13–32

---

[42] Regulation 1367/2006 [2006] OJ L264/13.

applying EU environmental law (see para.13–17, above). For the citizen, the Commission is perceived as the guardian of EU law; if then the same Commission does not take up issues of practical application, disappointment is inevitable.

Not much needs to be said about citizen participation in environmental decision-making at EU and national level. The Commission appears to understand consultations as being synonymous with participation—which it is not. Internet consultations are not an equivalent to citizens' participation either. What is lacking in particular is the laying of accounts: the Commission does not explain why the opinions and comments from environmental groups or persons were not taken over or why it preferred a more economic—to a more environment—oriented approach.

As regards citizens' participation in the decision-making process at national level, the corresponding legislation is still too recent to be capable of being assessed. At present, the positive elements for citizens that there is such legislation at all, certainly prevail. Generally, the participation of citizens in the decision-making process on environmental issues is disappointing; the Aarhus Convention has not changed much in this regard, whether there are questions on trans-European networks for transport or energy, infrastructure projects, or nuclear energy—the larger a project is, the less the concerned population appears to be able to effectively participate in the decision-making process.

13–33 Giving citizens and/or environmental organisations the opportunity to have environmental acts or omissions controlled by courts was one of the objectives of the Aarhus Convention to which the European Union has adhered. However, the Council was of the opinion that the present provisions of art.263(4) TFEU were compatible with the letter and the spirit of that Convention and that no change was necessary with regard to access to the European Courts. Even if this were legally correct—in my opinion, the Aarhus Convention does require a change of the present state of affairs[43]—the political aspect remains: access to the European Courts in environmental matters is de facto impossible for individuals and for environmental organisations. A softening of this de facto monopoly of the Commission—more than 80 per cent of all environmental cases are brought by the Commission—would also be of particular political importance, as it would also eventually hold EU institutions environmentally responsible.

A proposal for a directive to improve access to national courts was likewise not accepted by the Council which invoked subsidiarity reasons. This means that Member States will decide on improved access to justice in environmental matters and all indicators point into the direction that the status quo will largely remain. Thus, for example, a company which is of the opinion that an environmental legislation of a Member State—including legislation which is based on EU law—impedes the placing on the market of its products, may go to court and challenge that legislation by virtue of art.34 TFEU. However, an environmental organisation which is of the opinion that legislation allows too much emissions into the air or the water, cannot appeal to a court.

---

[43] See now, in the same sense, Aarhus Convention Compliance Committee, Draft findings and recommendations with regard to Communication ACCC/C/2008/32 concerning compliance by the European Union, April 2011.

The recent example of air pollution by particle matters is a good illustration of this argument. The relevant national and EU legislation is not respected in a number of urban agglomerations. The Court of Justice had declared, in 1991, that air quality standards also protect human health and must allow citizens to claim their respect in court. This line of judgments was repeated in 2007.[44] However, the legislation continues to not be respected and no application of environmental groups has, until now, led to the result that even the breach of EU law is acknowledged.[45]

Lawyers will explain the difference between the rights of a company and of an environmental organisation in cases like this. Politically, this is more difficult. And it adds to the disappointment which European citizens must feel, that the European Union amended the existing legislation to give Member States further delays in respecting their obligations which existed since 1999.[46]

13–34

As a way of assisting citizens in contributing to protect the environment, the Commission had instituted the complaint procedure, being however careful of formalising the procedural rules in any legal act. While at the end of the 1980s the Commission promised to examine each complaint as to its merits,[47] it went away from this commitment and now only promises to register each complaint; but it reserves the right to treat or not to treat complaints as to its own priorities; and what is more, the registration takes place in a so-called pilot-register and is submitted to a non-public arrangement procedure between the Member State in question and the Commission. Instead of a formal instruction, the Commission thus looks for arranging things, though it is in most cases the public authority itself which is disregarding EU environmental law.[48] Apart from the fact that there are, in the meantime, clear signs that environmental complaints are not being registered at all, this change of procedure—decided without any participation by the public—leads to the fact that individual desk officers decide on how to proceed with complaints. Seen from the point of view of the citizen, who sits in Crete, Madeira, Cork or Tampere, the message which is sent from the Commission when his complaint is not examined, is clear:

> "It may be that the specific project on which you complain, is breaching EU environmental law. However, your Member State has correctly transposed the relevant EU legislation into national law. Therefore, we decided not to look into your specific case."

If one compares this with the Commission's message of early 2005, mentioned in para.13–22, above, the discrepancy becomes obvious. And it also becomes obvious why the frustration about the EU institutions is growing at local level, not diminishing.

Instead of taking complaints on individual cases as a sampling way which allows it to get an impression, how EU law works in practice, the Commission sees individual complaints as an undesirable practice which should best be

13–35

---

[44] Court of Justice, *Janecek* (C-237/07) [2008] E.C.R. I-6221.
[45] See also the saddening development in the air pollution case concerning the United Kingdom, *ClientEarth* (C-404/13) ECLI:EU:C:2014:2382.
[46] Directive 2008/50 [2008] OJ L152/1.
[47] See the text which accompanied the complaint form issued by the Commission [1989] OJ C26/1.
[48] Commission, COM(2002) 725.

abandoned. And the remark has to be made that neither in competition matters nor in internal market affairs, would such handling of complaints be made.

In conclusion, it may fairly be stated that EU institutions deploy very limited efforts to bring the European Union in environmental matters closer to the citizen. Citizens are rather asked to take the initiative themselves—ask for access to information, file complaints—and see their initiatives often come to nothing.

8. MEMBER STATES AND EU ENVIRONMENTAL LAW AND POLICY

13–36   The EU Treaties' concept of distributing responsibilities between the European Union and Member States is quite clear: there is shared responsibility for the European environment. Member States have the responsibility to protect the environment; and certain measures are to be taken at EU level (art.5 TEU).

The political reality is somehow different. Member States rely heavily on the European Union for environmental measures. It was already mentioned that for more than half of the Member States, "environmental law" is more or less equivalent to "EU-derived environmental law". This means that where the European Union does not take legislative measures, in the majority of the Member States no legislative action will be taken either. This contradicts the objective of the European Union to ensure an economic, but also social and environmental playing field which is more or less at the same level—and this aspect is frequently overlooked by countries with a strong, though not necessarily pro-environmental national policy, such as the Netherlands, the United Kingdom, Germany and the German Länder, or France.

The result of this repartition of responsibilities and political practice is that EU environmental policy is squeezed between two different orientations. On the one hand, Member States insist on the application of arts 5 TEU and 193 TFEU, with the consequence that the European Union should only regulate where this is absolutely necessary, and should take a low common denominator in order to leave Member States the option to maintain or introduce more stringent provisions. On the other hand, Member States do not themselves develop national measures to protect, preserve and improve the quality of the environment. Countries such as the United Kingdom, Germany or Austria have even taken, in one or the other form, the decision not to adopt national environmental legislation which goes beyond the relevant EU measure (gold-plating), frustrating thus the concept of arts 5 TEU and 193 TFEU.

13–37   There are numerous examples of this. The most obvious is the absence of environmental action programmes in Member States. The EU action programmes concern the EU level; the attempt of the 5th Environment Action Programme, also to address targets and measures to be taken at national level,[49] was a complete failure. However, protecting the European environment is, under the Treaties, also the task of Member States. From the point of view of the environment, it is not relevant whether it is protected through a local, national or

---

[49] 5th Environment Action Programme [1993] OJ C38/1.

EU measure, as long as it is protected. This simple truth is often forgotten in Member States who just rely on the European Union to provide for the necessary protection.

Other examples range from environmental liability via soil protection, permits for small and medium-sized companies, environmental impact assessments for smaller infrastructure projects, marine water and groundwater protection, to contaminated site provisions, access to justice in environmental matters, coastal zone protection, fights against soil erosion or pollution emission registers. For most of these areas there is some legislation in some Member States; however, the overall perspective for the territory of the European Union, seen from the bird's eye view, is an unsatisfactory degree of protecting the environment. This reflects the different role which the protection of the environment plays in the political hierarchy of the Member States. While it ranks high in some, it ranks very low in others, especially in those where the environmental legislation is more or less completely EU-derived.

The high degree of environmental protection at which the Treaty aims, is normally ignored during the EU law-making procedure. The same applies to the principle that environmental damage should be rectified at source, that the polluter should pay or that environmental requirements should be integrated into the legislation of other policy areas. These principles of the EU Treaties are perceived as EU principles; but when Member States discuss in Council on a Commission proposal, they do not look at the European Union's (environmental) interest, but at their own (environmental, economic and social) interest. And this conflict of interest cannot easily be solved, as on the one hand, the Commission itself which should have defined the EU environmental interest, might have failed in that, due to pressure from vested interest groups or internal differences of opinion on the right approach; on the other hand, the Commission representative, confronted with representatives of 28 Member States, would have to be a superman to impose his point of view.

The Council environment working group does not normally wait for the European Parliament's opinion on a Commission proposal before discussing it. Rather, discussions in the working group run parallel with Parliament's discussion. It is normal that the working group reaches a political compromise on a Council position with regard to a proposal before the Parliamentary opinion is delivered. This practice increases the Council's dominance in the legislative process, though it contradicts the objective of art.294 TFEU. **13–38**

The monitoring of adopted EU environmental law varies considerably from one Member State to another. Again, this reflects the different degree of environmental awareness in Member States, though there is a second element. Member States' administrations perceive EU environmental law sometimes as imported law, as immigrant law, which stems from an outside source and which is different from national law.[50] Such an attitude can be found, for example, in Germany, France or Italy. More generally, EU law is monitored because the Commission asks for such a monitoring, not because it corresponds to its own conviction. Inevitably, the concept of imported law has practical consequences as regards the frequency and intensity of monitoring, sanctions for breaches, etc.

---

[50] Commission, European Governance—a White Paper [2001] OJ C287/1, p.21: "At the same time, the feeling persists that Community rules are foreign laws".

The national implementation reports which Member States send to the Commission report, as mentioned, on measures taken, not on results achieved. They practically never deal with lacunae, omissions, breaches of provisions, with sanctions pronounced, etc. The implementation reports thus do not give an idea of an EU directive's effectiveness.

13–39   The enforcement of EU environmental law is entirely in the hands of Member States and practically no information is made public on that, not even in the previously mentioned implementation reports. The Commission does not monitor enforcement practices, and with all necessary caution it might be stated that the intensity of enforcement, in particular as regards pollution emissions, permit controls, water and soil contamination, and planning-related measures such as impact assessments or participation provisions varies considerably from one Member State to another. And the Commission hardly ever monitors the application of regulations; these are directly applicable and, thus, Member States often do not feel obliged to monitor the application themselves.

It is difficult to identify different groups among Member States with regard to monitoring deficiencies. Some Member States make it a point of national honour to transpose EU environmental legislation in time. For others, delayed transposition is the rule. Some Member States consider that the provisions of EU law, once they are in the national statute books, have to be enforced; this includes the United Kingdom, the Scandinavian states and the Netherlands. Others do not see a problem in having contradictions between the law in the statute books and the law as it is applied; this attitude is not limited to environmental law.

It is too early to finally rank the 13 Member States which joined the European Union since 2004 into one of these categories. Generally, however, it can be said that under the former Communist system, the state that produced the environmental legislation and the state-owned companies were the biggest polluters of all. This created a certain cynicism in citizens: why should legislation be respected if it is broken in particular by those who made it? This cynicism continues to exist and will be difficult to overcome. It adds to the point which is also true for the 15 "old" Member States, that the placing of environmental legislation into the statute books is easy, but that the real problems appear when these environmental provisions are to be applied. Application of environmental law remains, also in the new Member States, the biggest of all legal—and political—problems.

9.   THE EUROPEAN UNION AS A GLOBAL ENVIRONMENTAL PLAYER

13–40   The European Union does not play an active role at global level when it comes to the elaboration of environmental standards. The jealousy of Member States to appear themselves at the international scene and to be seen as a sovereign state is too big. Own initiatives from the European Union would probably have to be classified as part of a foreign (environmental) policy and share all the difficulties of an EU foreign policy. The participation in international discussions on new environmental conventions is based, according to the treaties (art.218 TFEU), on a Council mandate. In practice, Member States are reluctant to give such a mandate, as then the Commission would normally represent the European Union and this would restrict Member States' negotiation opportunities. It is therefore almost normal that in such international negotiations the Commission is present without a mandate, discusses and negotiates together with Member States and tries to coordinate Member States' positions in order to make the European Union speak, as far as possible, with one voice or at least take similar positions.

All this does not facilitate the role of the European Union as such, but has to be accepted as part of international diplomacy. More relevant is the aspect that the United States, for more than 25 years, has proven to be incapable or unwilling to assume international leadership in environmental matters. As the European Union, for the reasons sketched out above, is not in a position to assume leadership functions, global environmental issues are at present not properly dealt with. Examples are issues of environmental crime (trade in timber, waste, exotic species, fish, etc), the provisions of biodiversity, the Convention on hazardous waste, the Arctic Area, the environmental behaviour of multinational companies, chemicals, access to water resources, soil erosion, desertification, the construction of dams and many others.

The global discussions on climate change, where the European Union played a very active role and did assume global leadership, are not proof to the contrary. In that case, the European Union grew into a leading role due to a change in the US attitude towards climate change. However, the European Union—neither the Commission nor the Commission jointly with Member States—is not equipped to assume a permanent global leadership function in climate change. Fossil fuel energy responsibilities are too dispersed within the European Union, human resources too small, the scientific and technical data on the situation worldwide are too scattered, diplomatic services of the European Union itself do not yet exist, the financial tools which such a leadership role requires, are not available, etc.

In international negotiations which would require an integrated approach by **13–41** the European Union, such as combining agricultural with environmental questions, the European Union negotiates under trade-agricultural perspectives alone, as it has not implemented art.11 TFEU. Thus, for example, the proposal to open up EU agricultural markets on the condition that the environmental and health standards of the European Union (pesticide residues, sanitary conditions etc) are taken over internationally, has apparently not even crossed the mind of the EU negotiators. The lack of integrating environmental requirements into the EU development policy[51] also makes the EU position in this area difficult in international forums. Generally, the European Union is much more interested to promote exports of European products and services than to have an international policy which effectively integrates environmental considerations.

The implementation of international environmental conventions within the European Union has already been mentioned. Though, overall, the European Union's monitoring process regarding the application of law is quite impressive and could serve as a model for many a regional organisation—Mercosur, Nafta, the Asean Group, etc—the European Union behaves internationally as the

---

[51] See Court of Auditors, Special Report 6/2006 concerning the environmental aspects of the commission's development cooperation [2006] OJ C235/1, no.84

Member States with regard to the Commission: reports are sent late, they report on measures, not on results, they try to give a positive image of the European Union and to hide imperfections.

At present, the European Union has neither the internal structures nor resources to assume a role as global environmental player. This certainly also has consequences for the present state of the global environment—which is not good, if one thinks of climate change, poverty, biodiversity, chemicals, water problems, etc.

10. PERSPECTIVES

13–42   As the environment has no voice, there is a tendency for declaring that things are slowly getting better. The statement of the European Environment Agency of 2001 that the state of the European environment shows some progress but offers a poor picture overall,[52] turned into the following statement in 2015[53]:

> "Europe's natural capital is not yet being protected, conserved and enhanced in line with the ambition of the 7th Environment Action Programme approach. Reduced pollution has significantly improved the quality of Europe's air and water. But loss of soil functions, land degradation and climate change remain major concerns, threatening the flow of environmental goods and services that underpin Europe's economic output and well-being.
>
> A high proportion of protected species (60%) and habitats (77%) are considered to be in unfavourable conservation status, and Europe is not on track to meet its overall target of halting biodiversity loss by 2020, even though some more specific targets are met. Looking ahead, climate change impacts are projected to intensify and the underlying drivers of biodiversity loss are expected to persist.
>
> ... European greenhouse gas emissions have decreased by 19% since 1990 despite a 45% increase in economic output. Other environmental pressures have also decoupled in absolute terms from economic growth. Fossil fuel use has declined, as have emissions of some pollutants from transport and industry. More recently, the EU's total resource use has declined by 19% since 2007, less waste is being generated and recycling rates have improved in almost every country.
>
> ... [T]he level of ambition of existing environmental policies may be inadequate to achieve Europe's long-term environmental goals. For example, projected greenhouse gas emission reductions are currently insufficient to bring the EU onto a pathway towards its 2050 target of reducing emissions by 80–95%.
>
> ... [T]here have been marked improvements in the quality of drinking water and bathing water in recent decades and some hazardous pollutants have been reduced. However, despite some improvements in air quality, air and noise pollution continue to cause serious health impacts, particularly in urban areas. In 2011, about 430,000 premature deaths in the EU were attributed to fine particulates (PM 2.5). Exposure to environmental noise is estimated to contribute to at least 10,000 premature deaths due to coronary heart disease and strokes each year. And growing use of chemicals, particularly in consumer products, has been associated with an observed increase of endocrine diseases and disorders in humans.

---

[52] European Environment Agency, *Environment in the European Union at the Turn of the Century* (Luxembourg, 1999).

[53] European Environment Agency, *The European Environment—state and outlook 2015* (Copenhagen, 2015), pp.11–13.

The outlook for environmental health risks in coming decades is uncertain, but raises concern in some areas. Projected improvements in air quality, for example, are not expected to be sufficient to prevent continuing harm to health and the environment, while health impacts resulting from climate change are expected to worsen."

The state of the EU environment is not satisfactory, the biggest challenges being climate change, the conservation of nature and biodiversity, the omnipresence of chemicals and the problems of urban agglomerations. And the expectancy that there will be 9 billion people on earth by 2030 who all need food, shelter, water, energy and a job, draws the attention to the fact that the EU problems are even small compared to the global challenges which lie ahead, that they are in part already the problems of today and require credible leadership now.

The EU structures to adequately deal with the global and regional challenges could be improved. Active citizen involvement is indispensable, if ever the environmental policy is to produce results. And the European Union will never be able to play an active and positive role on the evolution of the global environment, unless it gets its own house in order.

Environmental legislation is not everything, but is a very important factor to **13–43** distribute justice in society, to determine rights and obligations and to balance diverging interests. Western society has not found any other means to achieve these results than legislation, and I doubt that in modern society with the important role of economics other means can fulfil the same function. "Between the strong and the weak, it is the law which makes free and the freedom which oppresses": these words of La Rochefoucauld of the seventeenth century remain valid today and should warn against the hope that economic instruments can ensure justice in the society.

The European Union will need, for a foreseeable time, environmental legislation and its effective application. More and more, this will also become relevant at the global level. It is hoped that decision-makers at all levels are aware of this and will find the vision, the strategy, the will and the capacity to develop legal instruments which effectively protect, preserve and improve the quality of the environment, nationally, Europe-wide and globally. The environment can survive without humans, but humans cannot survive without the environment.

INDEX

This index has been prepared using Sweet and Maxwell's Legal Taxonomy. Main index entries conform to keywords provided by the Legal Taxonomy except where references to specific documents or non-standard terms (denoted by quotation marks) have been included. These keywords provide a means of identifying similar concepts in other Sweet and Maxwell publications and online services to which keywords from the Legal Taxonomy have been applied. Readers may find some minor differences between terms used in the text and those which appear in the index. Suggestions to *sweetandmaxwell.taxonomy@thomson.com*.

All references are to paragraph number

Aarhus Convention
    access to environmental information,
        4–04—4–08
    access to justice, 4–16—4–21
    action by individuals, and, 12–37—12–38
    Environment Agency, and, 2–15
    generally, 12–37—12–38
    participation in decision-making, 4–09—4–15
    right to clean environment, 4–03
Access to information
    horizontal measures, and
        European level, 4–06—4–08
        national level, 4–04—4–05
Access to justice
    horizontal measures, and
        European level, 4–19—4–21
        national level, 4–16—4–18
Accident prevention
    horizontal measures, and, 4–54—4–56
Acid rain
    air pollution, and, 8–01
Aeroplanes
    air pollution, and, 8–20
    composition and marketing of products, and,
        6–21
Aerosols
    national legislation, and, 3–39
    ozone depletion, and, 9–30
    packaging, and, 6–20
    technical standards, and, 6–63
Agricultural policy
    see also **Common agricultural policy**
    biodiversity legislation, and, 13–16
    biomass, and, 1–29
    Commission, and
        administrative structures, 2–04
        generally, 13–24
    EU decision-making, and, 2–95—2–96

    forestry, and, 5–05
    generally, 11–08—11–12
    national legislation, and, 3–29
    organic farming, and, 6–49
    planning and land use, and, 4–29
    waste, and, 10–04—10–05
Air pollution
    aeroplanes, from, 8–20
    cars, from, 8–13—8–19
    combustion plants, 8–25—8–27
    emission ceilings, 8–09—8–11
    energy policy, and, 8–02
    EU law, 8–01—8–03
    EU policy, 8–01
    industrial installations, from
        framework provisions, 8–23—8–24
        introduction, 8–01
        large combustion plants, 8–25—8–27
        VOCs, 8–31
        waste incineration plants, 8–28—8–30
    limit values, 8–05
    machines, from, 8–21
    mobile sources, from
        aeroplanes, 8–20
        cars, 8–13—8–19
        introduction, 8–12
        machines, 8–21
        ships, 8–20—8–21
        VOCs, 8–22
    national emission ceilings, 8–09—8–11
    quality measures
        generally, 8–04—8–08
        introduction, 8–03
    ships, from, 8–20—8–21
    stationary sources, from
        framework provisions, 8–23—8–24
        introduction, 8–01
        large combustion plants, 8–25—8–27